CREATIVE WRITING:

THE KELLY MANUAL OF STYLE!

2014

THE KEY TO SUCCESS

THE COMPLETE GUIDE TO CREATIVE WRITING

**STRAIGHT TALK AND STRAIGHT ANSWERS &
HOW TO WRITE YOUR BEST SELLING BOOK AND MOVIE SCRIPT**

KELLY CHANCE BECKMAN

INTRODUCTION:

THIS IS NOT THE USUAL *'HOW TO WRITE CREATIVELY BOOK.'* THIS BOOK IS ABOUT WHY WE WRITE AND WHY WE CONTRIBUTE OUR TIME, LIVES AND SOULS TO WRITING. THIS BOOK EXPLAINS HOW TO WRITE LIKE A GRAND MASTER AND HOW TO WRITE A BEST SELLING BOOK.

IT IS IMPORTANT THAT YOU MUST FIRST BE A STORYTELLER THEN A WRITER. THE CREATIVE JUICES HAVE TO FLOW FIRST. CAN YOU FIRST TELL YOUR STORY OUTLOUD BEFORE YOU WRITE? **THEN WE WRITE A #1-STORYTELLER'S SYNOPSIS: A PARAGRAPH.** *CHAPTER 7* **EXPLAINS THE THREE KINDS OF SYNOPSIS AND GIVES SEVERAL EXAMPLES.**

THEN, WE WRITE TO OUR READER, HE IS THE ONE WHO LISTENS; HE IS OUR AUDIENCE! HE SUPPORTS OUR WRITING LIFE. HE IS ALSO OUR BENEFACTOR; HE BUYS OUR BOOKS!

THEN, WE **WRITE #3 A CHAPTER BY CHAPTER SYNOPSIS TO CAPTURE ALL OF OUR BESTSELLER**.

WE DISCUSS CREATIVE WRITING FROM THE TOP DOWN: THE THEORIES, THE ESSENTIALS, BASIC STRUCTURES AND ALL THE GRAMMATICAL UPDATES. WE DISCUSS SENTENCE AND PARAGRAPH STRUCTURE SO IMPORTANT TO GREAT WRITING. NOVEL WRITING IS NOT ENGLISH 101.

NOW WE GET TO THE MEAT AND POTATOES OF WRITING: HOW TO STORY-TELL, HOW TO WRITE WITH PASSION AND CONVICTION. MORE IMPORTANTLY, HOW TO WRITE WITH **ILLUMINATION** FOR THE READER. OUR #3 CHAPTER BY CHAPTER SYNOPSIS IS OUR GUIDE. (CH 7).

WE CHANGED SOME OF THE TRADITIONAL STRUCTURES TO IMPROVE YOUR GRASP OF THE SUBJECT AND TO PROVIDE NEW METHODS TO IMPROVE YOUR CHARACTERS, PLOTS, CLIMAXES AND WORD CHOICE. **YOUR NEW STYLE WILL BE THE RESULT.**

THEN, WE GUIDE YOU HOW TO WRITE A BOOK –THE PROCESS- STRUCTURE AND THE MANY DO'S AND DON'TS. THEN GUIDE YOU THROUGH THE BUSINESS OF BOOKS THAT TURNS THAT GREAT MANUSCRIPT UPSIDE DOWN.THE BOOK BECOMES OUR MAGIC CARPET RIDE. IT TAKES US TO PLACES WE'VE NEVER BEEN AND EXPERIENCES WE ONLY DREAM ABOUT. IT IS OUR TICKET TO ADVENTURE AND TO THE UNIVERSE.

THE 'KELLY STYLE' TAKES YOU STEP BY STEP, CHAPTER BY CHAPTER TO A NEW STYLE OF WRITING FROM YAWN TO GREATNESS!

DO YOU WANT TO BE A GREAT WRITER? READ ON:

WHY BUY THIS BOOK?

FIRST, THIS BOOK IS DIFFERENT FROM OTHERS ON CREATIVE WRITING. **HERE IS THE PROOF**:

KELLY STYLE IS DIFFERENT!

WE HAVE TO FIRST OPEN UP YOUR CREATIVE SIDE; THEN SHOW YOU HOW TO USE THE MANY TOOLS OF WRITING. THE DIFFERENCE IS PLAIN WRITING AND GREAT WRITING! **YOUR FINAL BOOK EVOLVES THRU THREE LEVELS OF SYNOPSES: STORY TELLING, DETAILED & CHAPTER BY CHAPTER (A VERY ROUGH STRUCTURE)TO BOOK DRAFT, TO MANUSCRIPT TO FINAL MANUSCRIPT.**

STORYTELLING:THE KELLY STYLE IS FIRST **STORYTELLING**, A PROCESS OF FINDING THE KERNEL OF YOUR STORY (IDEA) AND THE MAIN CHARACTERS AND THE PLOT=THE EVENTS ON WHICH YOUR STORY IS APPEALING. **STORYTELLING** CAPTURES THE IDEA(S), ABOUT A PARAGRAPH IN LENGTH, WHEN WRITTEN.

IDEAS: IF YOU DO NOT HAVE A STORY IDEA- GO TO CH 5.0.2.2. FOR OUR UNIVERSAL THEME-IDEA GROUPS AND MOVIE TITLES CH 41.0.0.1. TO FIND THE UNDERLYING IDEAS ABOUT WHICH YOU WANT TO WRITE.

YOUR STYLE: YOUR STYLE IS DEVELOPED USING EXPERIENCE AND CREATIVITY; NOT FOLLOWING THE TREADED PATH OF OTHERS. YOUR WRITING IS ENHANCED WITH NEW WRITING TOOLS: IDEAS LISTS, SOURCE LISTS, CHAPTER TOPICS, STORYTELLER'S SYNOPSIS, DETAILED SYNOPSIS, CHAPTER BY CHAPTER SYNOPSIS COUPLED WITH CHAPTER TOPICS, WE ADD TIMELINES ,THEMES, ADD DETAILS TO THE CHARACTERS AND FINALLY OUR FIRST **ROUGH DRAFT IS BORN 30 TO 100 PAGES.**

WE CONTINUE WRITING BUILDING CHAPTERS & TOPICS AND CHARACTERS AND PLOTS. THEN, WE PROVIDE THE OTHER TOOLS OF THE WRITING CRAFT: GUIDED STEP BY STEP PROCESSES WITH YOUR PROGRESS MEASURED . WE PROGRESS INTO MANY EDITING AND DRAFT REVISIONS. A DRAFT=½ BOOK LENGTH.

THEN, WE RELEARN THE BASIC TOOLS OF SENTENCE AND PARAGRAPH STRUCTURE.TO THESE WE ADD FIGURES OF SPEECH, SCENES, SETTINGS, DIALOGUE, PLOTS AND DRAMATIZATION . OUR HERO AND VILLAIN, BRING ALL OF THIS TO LIFE. AT THIS POINT, WE HAVE COMPLETED A **BOOK DRAFT**- ¾ BOOK LENGTH. WE WRITE, EDIT & REVISE MORE.

NOW WE TRANSFORM THE ORDINARY INTO GREATNESS. HARD WORK AND HUNDREDS OF EXAMPLES FROM THE MASTERS SHOW US HOW. WE READ ALOUD. OUR STORY BEGINS TO TAKE ON A NEW DIMENSION OF SOUND AND PICTURESQUE WORDS. WE POLISH IT AND SOON IT IS READY TO BE BORN, AS A **MANUSCRIPT**. WE CONTINUE WRITING .

THE KEY TO THE KELLY STYLE IS TO TRANSFORM YOUR WRITING STYLE INTO A DARING, CREATIVE AND SUCCESSFUL BOOK. **A BOOK OF MAGIC AND IMAGINATION THAT READERS WILL NOT PUT DOWN.**

MY ADVICE IS:
1. **WRITE BECAUSE THE FIRE BURNS WITHIN YOU AND NOTHING CAN PUT IT OUT!**

2. **WRITE WITH PASSION FOR YOUR READER…HE IS THE ULTIMATE CRITIC.**

SYNOPSES DEFINED:

IMPORTANT: DO NOT USE AN OUTLINE OR BIBLIOGRAPHY!!!!!!
1. STORYTELLING: A VERBAL PARAGRAPH OR TWO:
THE WRITER BEGINS TELLING HIS STORY **OUTLOUD**. HE DIVES IN AND TELLS THE STORY OUTLOUD TO HIS INVISIBLE AUDIENCE. YES, IT HAS NO FORMAL ORGANIZATION AND IT MAY STUMBLE. HE SEEKS THE **UNIVERSAL THEME**, THE MAIN IDEA AND ANSWERS WHY THE READER WANTS TO HEAR HIS STORY. **ITS SIMPLE!** WE CAPTURE THAT GREAT IDEA, **THAT KERNEL,** THAT OUR BOOK IS ABOUT IN **THREE SYNOPSES:**

2. SECONDLY, **THE DETAILED SYNOPSIS,** WHICH IS A SHORT SUMMARY OR A COUPLE OF PAGES MAX. ABOUT A FICTION GENRE-THEME AND STORYLINE. WE DEFINE THE FIRST KEY ELEMENT OR 'KERNEL,' **THE IDEA**, THE ESSENTIAL PART, OR OUR FRUIT SEED, ON WHICH OUR BOOK TAKES LIFE.

3. THIRD, WE WRITE OUR **#3-CHAPTER BY CHAPTER SYNOPSIS**, A LIST OF CHAPTER TOPICS WHICH GO INTO THAT CHAPTER. WE BRING OUR IDEA GROUPS AND CHARACTERS INTO A WHAT HAPPENS NEXT FORMAT: A ROUGH DRAFT OF CHAPTERS.

IT IS COMPLETE FRAMEWORK ON WHICH TO HANG CHARACTERS, PLOTS, THEMES, TIMELINES, CLIMAXES AND STORY. A WRITER FORMS A BOOK STRUCTURE WITH THE SIX W'S, SOME CLIMAXES, SOME THEMES, PLACES AND WHEN IN TIME IT HAPPENS. THEN, WE HAVE SEVERAL BOOK DRAFTS, TO WHICH WE POLISH OUR STORY UNTIL **A BOOK DRAFT, FROM WHICH A MANUSCRIPT EVOLVES**.

THE READER'S EXPECTATIONS:
THE READER HAS SOME EXPECTATIONS AS TO YOUR BOOK'S PLOT-DRAMATIZATION AND LOVES IT WHEN YOUR CHARACTERS COME ALIVE. THEY LOVE YOU WHEN YOU TEASE THEM, MAKE THEM LAUGH AND MAKE THEM CRY. SO YOUR UNIVERSAL AND SUPPORTING THEMES MUST FIT, TEASE AND THEN SURPRISE THEM. ALL YOUR HARD WORK WITH YOUR STORYTELLER'S SYNOPSIS, ARE AIMED TO GET THE RIGHT COMBINATION OF WORDS DOWN, '*CHOICE WORDS.*' **CHOICE AND ILLUMINATED WORDS CONNECT THE READER TO OUR STORY AND TO US, THE WRITER.** THE READER BECOMES PART OF OUR STORY. IT IS HE WHO IS THE HERO OR VILLAIN!

IT IS WHY HE BUYS OUR BOOK.

WHY BOOKS?

BOOKS…WHERE CREATION AND IMAGINATION BEGINS!
BOOKS HOLD THE WORLD'S STORIES - FROM THE EARLIEST
KNOWN STORIES, MYTHS AND LEGENDS UP TO TODAY'S FICTION.

OUR IMAGINATION FREES US TO TRAVEL TO NEW WORLDS, TO
RE-CREATE OUR LIVES IN NEW CHARACTERS, PLACES AND
ADVENTURES. WE BEGIN A JOURNEY TO OTHER WORLDS, THRU
TIME AND BECOME OUR DESIRES. A HERO, A VILLAIN, A PIRATE,
A SEA CAPTAIN, A SECRET AGENT, A WOMAN PRESIDENT, A
LEADER OF A COUNTRY, OR A COWBOY. WE CAN BECOME
ANYONE OR ANYTHING OUR IMAGINATION CAN DREAM OF.

THE WRITER'S JOB IN CREATING THESE BOOKS IS TO GET THE
READER TO FEEL HE IS PART OF THAT STORY. THE READER WILL
ACT OUT OUR GREAT CHARACTERS, IN PLACES AND IN EVENTS
WE DRAMATIZE. HE WILL SPEAK GREAT WORDS AND
ILLUMINATE DIALOGUE. HIS SOUNDS AND SENSES WILL TINGLE
AND TITILLATE. TRUTH, TIME AND HISTORY WILL HOLD NO
BOUNDS FOR HIM.

OUR BOOKS WILL TRANSFORM WRITERS FROM THE EARLIEST
SCRIBES, TO MONKS PRODUCING 'ILLUMINATED' WORKS, TO
WRITERS, AUTHORS AND ON TO **GRAND MASTER WRITERS**
CAPTURING UNIVERSAL THOUGHTS. WE WILL JOIN THESE
HEADY VOICES.

BOOKS WILL SATISFY OUR DREAMS, DESIRES AND PLEASE OUR
SOULS. WE WILL ESCAPE THE DAILY GRIND AND TROUBLES. OUR
MINDS WILL GROW, LEARN AND ADAPT TO NEW THINKING AND
METHODS.

BOOKS AND WRITERS WILL ALLOW US TO READ, TO LISTEN AND
SPEAK SMALL AND GREAT WORDS. WORDS FULL OF SOUNDS,
PICTURES AND ADVENTURE. WORDS THAT HELP OR HURT.
WORDS THAT RAISE US UP, WORDS SO POWERFUL; SURELY A
WRITER'S GOD GIVEN TALENT.

KCB.

CONTENTS

IV. MARKETING YOUR BEST SELLER

MASTER INDEX LISTINGS:-312

THE NEW KELLY STYLE FEATURES:

NEW QUALITY & PROGRESS CHECK LISTS

HOW TO USE THIS BOOK:

HERE IS SOME KEY FEATURES TO HELP THE WRITER LEARN THE
CREATIVE PROCESS:

PARAGRAPH NUMBERS:
ARE **SEQUENCE NUMBERED IN 4 DIGIT CODES** TO HELP TRANSITION
FROM ONE AREA TO ANOTHER.

CHAPTER REFERRALS ARE [BRACKETED] FOR EASE OF FINDING.

CHAPTER TOPICS:
A SUBJECT LISTING' AT THE TOP OF EACH CHAPTER.

CAPITAL LETTERS : ARE USED AS THIS IS A TEXTBOOK.
ALSO, LARGE FONT, BOLD, UNDERLINES AND ITALICS ARE USED TO
VARY THE IMPORTANT FROM THE MINOR TOPICS.INDEX 7-PAGE 325.

CLASS LESSONS -BOXED ITEMS:
ARE PROVIDED TO INCREASE THE WRITING EXPERIENCE AND INSIGHT.

CREATIVITY TASKS:
ARE ADDED TO INCREASE YOUR CREATIVITY AND TO CHANGE YOUR
WRITING STYLE.

EXAMPLES:
HUNDREDS ARE GIVEN TO LEARN NEW STYLES & TO USE WHEN
WRITING.

PROGRESS MEASUREMENT:
YOUR PROGRESS ALONG THE PATH TO CREATIVE WRITING SHOWS
RESULTS AS: "I CAN DO THIS' OR AS WRITING GOALS ARE MET.
COMPLETION OF THESE STEPS WILL INCREASE YOUR CONFIDENCE AND
RECORD IMPROVEMENTS.

CHECK LISTS: A GUIDE:
CHECK LISTS ARE PROVIDED FOR THE NOVICE WRITER TO VERIFY KEY
ELEMENTS ARE PRESENT IN THEIR WRITING. THESE GUIDE THE WRITER
WHEN YOUR WRITING STALLS OR IS INCOMPLETE OR STYLE IS MISSING.

SUBJECT LISTS:
REFER TO THE INDICES AND SUBJECT LIST AT THE REAR OF THE BOOK:
BOTH WILL HELP YOU FIND YOUR 'SEARCH' TOPIC.

USE CHS 31 & 36 **TO COMPARE AND CONTRAST YOUR PRESENT WORK
AND SEE WHAT IS MISSING.**

*DO: = NEW WRITER: DO THESE TASKS:
WHEN YOU SEE THIS, SYMBOL: DO= DO WRITE
THESE TASKS TO LEARN TO WRITE CREATIVELY.

THE KELLY STYLE PROCESS:

IS EXPLAINED IN CH 4 WHICH DETAILS THE STEPS FROM BEGINNING WRITING TO THE FINAL PUBLISHING OF YOUR BOOK.

*DO USE THIS BOOK AS A TOOL.

1.WHEN READING THIS BOOK, USE IT AS A TOOL AN OBJECT FOR NOTING KEY AREAS OF YOUR INTEREST.
PLEASE 'USE' A BRIGHT HIGHLIGHTER AND 'WRITE' SHORT NOTES 'WRITE' KEY WORDS IN THE MARGINS WITH COLORED INK. 'ADD' STICKY NOTES TO FLAG SPECIAL ATTENTION AREAS.

2. *'USE A SHORT NOTE METHOD' TO IDENTIFY YOUR NEEDS AND WEAK POINTS: PLOTS, CLIMAXES, WORD CHOICE, ORGANIZATION ON THE BLANK PAGES AT REAR OF THE BOOK.*

3. *DO 'MARK-UP' THE SUBJECT INDEX AT THE BACK OF THE BOOK.*

4. *HAVING TROUBLE WITH ONE ITEM IN YOUR WRITING: REVIEW THAT CHAPTER, COMPARE YOUR DRAFT, DO THE CLASS EXERCISES AND* __WRITE ALL THREE SYNOPSES.__*[DO NOT SKIP THIS STEP].*

5. *WRITER'S BLOCK: [CH 35].*

6. *NEED HELP!---SEE THE INDICES AT THE BACK OF THE BOOK FOR FINDING HELP, DEFINITIONS, TOPICS, WEB RESOURCES AND SUBJECT LISTS. [CHS 35-39].*

7. *FICTION IS DIFFERENT FROM OTHER WRITING:-
DO NOT USE AN OUTLINE OR A BIBLIOGRAPHY. USE BETTER TOOLS: LIKE 3 SYNOPSES, IDEA LISTS, SOURCE LISTS, CHECK LISTS, AND HOW TO'S ARE PROVIDED. USE THE 'OUR PROGRESS' MEASUREMENTS AT EACH STEP.*

8. **DO COMPARE AND CONTRAST YOUR FINAL MANUSCRIPT WITH [CH 36.]. COMPLETE YOUR UNIVERSAL THEMES AND SUPPORTING THEMES. [CH 11]. EDIT AND IMPROVE IT UNTIL YOU SAY IT IS READY.*

9. *USE CHS 36-39-52 FOR A THOROUGH REVIEW OF YOUR FINAL MANUSCRIPT. __DO NOT SKIP THIS STEP.__*

10. *NOW COMPARE IT TO THE MARKETPLACE. CHECK THE TITLE AND COVER ART. THE REAR COVER IS YOUR MARKETING MESSAGE FOR YOUR BOOK.. PUT ANY REVIEWS INSIDE THE BACK COVER. [CHS 52-53].*

11. *FOLLOW THE STEPS TO ORGANIZING, PUBLISHING AND MARKETING YOUR BOOK. [CHS 29-38-39-49-52-54].*

12. *LAST, WRITE LIKE THE GREAT MASTERS, [CH 28.].TELL YOUR STORY OUTLOUD FROM BEGINNING TO END. WRITE IT IN YOUR NEW STYLE FOR THE READER! WAIT, THEN REVIEW IT ONE MORE TIME. THEN SEND IT! OUR BABY IS BORN! WE HAVE JOINED THE RANKS OF THE WRITER.*
__13.__ SEE THE TABLE OF CONTENTS ON PAGES 7-8.

WHY THE KELLY STYLE WORKS?
1. WE BEGIN WITH TELLING OUR STORY.
VERBALLY, WE CAPTURE THE "IDEA" OF OUR BOOK. WE ANSWER BASIC
QUESTIONS LIKE WHY IS OUR READER INTERESTED AND WHY IT IS
IMPORTANT TO HIM?

[OUR PROGRESS: *WHEN WE DON'T HAVE THAT GREAT IDEA WE TAP OUR
"IDEA LIST." AND THEN WE HAVE A STORY TO TELL. WE CHOOSE A POINT OF
VIEW---HOW IS THE STORY TOLD, BY WHOM OR WHAT METHOD?]*

2. WE WRITE THREE SYNOPSES: *[CH 6]*
A. WE START WITH A **SHORT STORYTELLER'S SYNOPSIS** [A PARAGRAPH
OR TWO] TO CAPTURE THE IMPORTANT IDEA-THE 'KERNEL', OUR MAIN
CHARACTER, VILLAIN, GENRE AND UNIVERSAL THEME. OUR CHARACTER
HAS A CONFLICT...THE RESOLUTION IS PART OF OUR STORY. THIS IS OUR
STORYLINE, WITH WHICH WE TELL FRIENDS AND FAMILY OUR BOOK IS
ABOUT.

B. FROM THIS WE ORALLY TELL OUR STORY, THIS WILL BECOME OUR
STORYTELLER'S VERSION, THEN WE ADD PIECES OF DESCRIPTIVE
INFORMATION. THEN **STEP 2**, WE EDIT AND WRITE A **DETAILED
SYNOPSIS**, WE FLESH IT OUT WITH MAIN CHARACTERS, PLOTS,
DESCRIPTIONS & SOUNDS, A BEGINNING AND MAYBE AN ENDING. [CH 8].

C. **THE CHAPTER BY CHAPTER SYNOPSIS.** *[CH 9].*
WE BEGIN TO ADD CHARACTERS, PLACES, THEMES, PLOTS AND SUBJECTS
FROM OUR RESEARCH INTO **A SHORT LIST OF TOPICS** AT THE
BEGINNING OF EACH CHAPTER. WE FIND A COMMON THREAD AND THAT
BECOMES OUR THEME OF THAT CHAPTER.

SYNOPSES –THREE TYPES: *[REFER CHAPTER 7].*
WE REVIEW AND ADD TO ALL OF THE THREE TYPES BEFORE WRITING
OUR ROUGH DRAFT. EACH GIVES US AN AMAZING TOOL AND FORMAT TO
FOLLOW. *ALL THREE MERGE TO BECOME THE BACKBONE OF OUR
BOOK.*

[*OUR PROGRESS:* *WE HAVE A 'SHORT SYNOPSIS' (A PARAGRAPH) , THEN A
STORYTELLER'S(SEVERAL PAGES), AND 'CHAPTER BY CHAPTER SYNOPSIS'
OF A FEW PAGES.] .[CHS 7 TO 9]. THESE THREE EVOLVE INTO A BOOK.*

3. WE FORM A BOOK'S STORY STRUCTURE:*[CH 10].*
WE START DEVELOPING MAIN CHARACTERS, SETTINGS, THEMES,
LANGUAGE, AND TIME FRAMES. WE FORM A STORY PLOT ON WHICH
THEY INTER-REACT. WE ADD DETAILS TO A CHARACTER LIST [CH20]AND
ADD TO OUR IDEAS LIST.[CH 5.]

[*OUR PROGRESS:* *WE HAVE SOME BASICS DOWN AND OUR BOOK HAS A
ROUGH ROADMAP. WE CONTINUE TO FLESH IT OUT. OUR CHAPTER BY
CHAPTER SYNOPSIS GROWS INTO A ROUGH DRAFT. ALSO, WE HAVE A
DETAILED CHARACTER LIST [CH 20] AND BEGIN TO PLACE "TOPICS INTO
CHAPTER TO CHAPTER FORMATS."].WE CONTINUE TO ADD, EDIT AND
POLISH IT.*

4. ORGANIZATION: [CH 29]

CREATIVE WRITING—THE KELLY MANUAL OF STYLE

WE ORGANIZE FOR EACH SINGLE BOOK, SAVE OUR BOOK MASTERS [ON COMPUTER], OUR COMPUTER FOLDERS AND PAPER VERSIONS OF OUR DRAFTS, RESEARCH, AND SOURCE LISTS.

5. RESEARCH & INVESTIGATION: [CH 34].
WE MUST RESEARCH PLACES, STREET NAMES, MOUNTAIN RANGES, CITIES, METHODS OF TRAVEL, DRESS, LANGUAGE OR A HUNDRED DETAILS WE WISH TO USE IN OUR BOOK. WE BEGIN BY ORGANIZING OUR RESEARCH. RESEARCH EVOLVES BY FINDING THE SUBJECT MATTER. THUS, A SUBJECT LISTING.

[OUR PROGRESS: WE BEGIN A SOURCE LIST BY SUBJECT, BUILDING ONE ON A COMPUTER IS A SIMPLE TASK IN WORD OR EXCEL FORMAT. WE NUMBER THEM 1 TO 100]. [CH 34]

6. CHAPTERS AND TITLES:
WE BEGIN TO WRITE THE OPENING SENTENCE, FOLLOWED BY SUPPORTING INFORMATION, FOLLOWED BY THE IMPORTANT CLOSING SENTENCE. DON'T WORRY WE ONLY HAVE THE BEGINNINGS OF A DRAFT SO FAR. WE ADD SOME OF OUR FIGURES OF SPEECH, COMPARE-CONTRAST, SITUATIONS AND PROGRESSIVE HAPPENINGS, LIKE CLIMAXES, MINI-PLOTS, IDEAS AND THE CHARACTER THOUGHTS IN ITALICS TO MOVE THE STORY ALONG OUR ROADMAP. WE MIGHT EVEN SELECT A DRAFT CHAPTER TITLE. **DON'T DO ANY EDITING AT THIS POINT.**

[OUR PROGRESS: CHAPTER TOPICS ARE DEFINED, CHARACTERS ARE FLESHED OUT IN MORE DETAIL, INTRODUCTION OF CHARACTER TO READER AND WHAT IS THE PREDICAMENT? (SOME OF OUR PLOT). WE FLESH OUT THE SIX W'S IN EACH CHAPTER].

7. TIMELINE: [CH 26]
THE PURPOSE OF A TIMELINE IS TO KEEP YOUR STORY MOVING AND NOT ALLOWING AN OPEN-ENDED SCENE TO JUST FADE. FOR EXAMPLE, TIMING IS CRITICAL IF YOUR DOING A MURDER MYSTERY OR COURT TRIAL. THE EVENTS SHOULD PROGRESS ALONG WITH AN ORDERLY SEQUENCE OF EVENTS. THE TIMING IMPACTS THE CHARACTERS, PLOT, SCENE, SETTINGS AND CLIMAXES. LETS SAY A MAIN CHARACTER MEETS HIS ADVERSARY... WHAT HAPPENS FIRST? SECOND? IS THERE A CHASE? ARE BULLETS FIRED? HOW DOES THE DIALOGUE HAPPEN BETWEEN THEM? IS THERE A CLIMATIC EVENT OR IS PART OF THE PLOT REVEALED? NOR DO WE WANT TO LEAVE A CHARACTER DANGLING WITH NO ENDING OR CLOSURE. DID THEY ALL DIE AT THE END?

[OUR PROGRESS: WE HANDLE TIME AS IN CALENDAR AND DAYLIGHT, BUT TIMING IS ALSO A SEQUENCE OF EVENTS. DO DRAW A LINE WHERE EVENTS, CHARACTERS, CLUES, OR CLIMAXES ARE INDICATED BY USING THE CHAPTER TOPICS AT THE BEGINNING OF EACH CHAPTER. THE MORE CRITICAL THE EVENT OR CLIMAX THE MORE A TIMELINE WILL HELP MANAGE THE SEQUENCE AND THE RESULT. [CH 29.].

8. STYLE: [CH 38]
WE DEVELOP A STYLE AS WE WRITE AND GAIN EXPERIENCE. STYLE IS THE COMBINATION OF LANGUAGE, THE SPECIFIC WORD CHOICE, THE CHARACTERS THEMSELVES AND THEIR CONTRIBUTION TO THE STORY.

CREATIVE WRITING—THE KELLY MANUAL OF STYLE

STYLE IS ALSO THE OPENING SENTENCE STRUCTURE, THE MIDDLE SUPPORTING AND THE ENDING SENTENCE OR GIFT WRAPPING. **STYLE** IS HOW WE HANDLE THE SETTING, THE SCENE AND THE VARIOUS PLOTS AND CLIMAXES. THE CHARACTERS MUST REACT TO THE SITUATION AND CLIMATIC EVENT. WE CREATED THEM AND THE STORY AS IF IT WAS REAL. WE USE THE 7 WRITER'S TOOLS.

[OUR PROGRESS: WE LEARN A NEW STYLE ALONG THE WAY, WHILE LEARNING TO WRITE. A STYLE ALMOST FITS THE BOOK AND WILL VARY FROM THE VARIOUS FICTION TYPES AS A WESTERN NOVEL WILL BE DIFFERENT TO A HISTORICAL PIECE. WE LEARN THE IMPORTANCE OF THE FIRST SENTENCE AND THE VERY FIRST SENTENCE BEGINNING OUR NOVEL... VERY CRITICAL PIECES OF WRITING. WE SET THE HOOKS FOR THE READER TO WANT TO READ ON AND ON, PAGE BY PAGE, AND CHAPTER BY CHAPTER ; UNTIL HE GETS IT!]

9. THE FINISH: THE DRAFT: THE EDIT:
THE FINISH IS NOT THE FINISH! YES, WE HAVE CLIMAXES, THE STORY RESOLVES ONE WAY OR THE OTHER, OR THE CHARACTER GOES ON TO THE NEXT BOOK OR DIES. THE WRITER HAS ONLY COMPLETED THE DRAFT VERSION. [REFER CHS 30-31-32-36.]

[OUR PROGRESS: WE MUST EDIT THIS DRAFT VERSION TO CATCH FLAWS, TO CORRECT SPELLING, PUNCTUATION AND A LONG LIST OF CHECK LISTS. WE DO THIS OVER AND OVER AND RE-WRITE EACH TIME AS NECESSARY. WE FIX CHAPTER TITLES TO MATCH THE FINAL STORY. WE READ IT OUTLOUD. WE USE PROOFREADERS MARKS. NOW WE POLISH IT WITH BETTER WORDS, CLARITY AND UNDERSTANDING. WE PUT ON OUR READER'S HAT AND READ IT. DO I GET IT? IS THE STORY BELIEVABLE? COULD IT BE BETTER? ONLY WE CAN SAY WHEN IT IS READY. IT'S LIKE WE ILLUMINATE THE WORK...IT ALMOST GLOWS WITH COMPLETION.]
LAST, WE A DO A FINAL REVIEW. [CH 36].

10. THE BUSINESS OF BOOKS: [CH39].
IN OUR SPARE TIME, WE LEARNED HOW TO SET UP OUR WRITING SPACE, OUR COMPUTER AND HOW TO ORGANIZE AND WRITE A BOOK. WE COMPLETED A "ALMOST FINAL BOOK-A DRAFT." THEN WE EDIT & POLISH IT ONCE MORE READY FOR THE PUBLISHER. NOW WE ARE READY TO PREPARE FOR THE COMPARATIVE WORLD OF BOOKS, PUBLISHING, BOOK SELLING AND MARKETING. WE COMPARE OUR BOOK TITLE AND STORY TO OTHERS IN THE MARKETPLACE.

WE DESIGN OR SELECT ART WORK FOR A FRONT COVER AND WRITE THE COPY FOR THE REAR. HOPEFULLY VERY COMPATIBLE WITH OUR STORY. WE GO TO SEVERAL BOOK SELLERS AND REVIEW WHAT WE SEE. HOW DOES OUR BOOK AND ITS COVER STAND UP? COMPARE THE TITLES SITTING THERE ...DOES OUR HAVE PUNCH? IS IT TOO LONG OR SHORT? DID A BEST SELLER USURP OUR TITLE? BACK TO THE DRAWING BOARD FOR A NEW TITLE OR COVER ART. [CH 53].

OUR PROGRESS:
WE LEARN A LOT ABOUT BOOK SELLING AND MARKETING. WE SELECT A PRINT ON DEMAND (POD) PUBLISHER OR WRITE QUERY LETTERS TO PUBLISHING HOUSES. WE USE THE TIME TO COMPLETE OUR NOVEL. WE FILE THOSE SOURCE DOCUMENTS AND DRAFTS INTO OUR CARDBOARD BOX. WE MAKE BACK UP DISCS AND COPY OUR FILES FOR POSTERITY AND PLACE IN A SAFE SPACE. WE USE A REPUTABLE POD PUBLISHER LIKE LULU AND

*UPLOAD OUR BOOK AND WRITE COPY FOR THE HOOK---BUY THIS BOOK BECAUSE! RESULT: NOW I HAVE A PUBLISHER AND A WEB SITE TO SELL BOOKS AND A "STOREFRONT" OR WE WAIT FOR THE **PUBLISHING HOUSE** TO REPLY TO OUR **QUERY LETTER** AND WAIT AND WAIT!*
THE END? NO! WE BEGIN OUR NEXT BOOK.] [CH 27-39].{BRIDGES?}
OR WE BEGIN SCREENWRITING OUR BOOK. [CH 40].

SECTION III-**THE KELLY CREATIVE PROCESS**:

CHAPTER ONE:
CH 1.0.0.0. WHAT IS WRITING?-GENRE'?
INTRODUCTION:
LET US TALK ABOUT WRITING IN GENERAL, THE WRITER'S AND EDITOR'S ROLES AND WHAT WE KNOW ABOUT WRITING FICTION.

DESCRIBE WRITING... WHAT IS IT EXACTLY?
THEN, THINK ABOUT THE TYPES OF WRITING, DIVISIONS, THEMES AND GENRE'[1.4.2.0.]. MOST IMPORTANTLY, WE LEARN THE 5 TYPES OF FICTION AND WHICH ONE ARE WE GOING TO WRITE ABOUT IN OUR BOOK?

WE LEARN ABOUT THE **BOOK CLASSIFICATION SYSTEM** AND **GENRE'**. WHERE DOES OUR BOOK FIT? WHERE DO FIND OUR BOOK IN THE LIBRARY AND AT THE BOOKSELLERS? WE SELECT A TYPE AND WRITE IN OUR STORYTELLER'S SYNOPSIS. [CH 16.3.0.0.].

CH 1.0.0.1. CHAPTER TOPICS:
IN THE BEGINNING: OUR GOALS:
1. WE DEFINE OURSELVES AS THE BEGINNING WRITER
2. WE SELF EVALUATE OUR SKILLS AND WHAT WE WANT TO IMPROVE.
3. WE DEFINE WHAT IS WRITING?
4. WE DO STORYTELLING.
5. WE DEFINE CREATIVITY.
6. WE MAKE IDEA GROUPS AND 2 IDEA LISTS.
7. WE LEARN ABOUT ALL TYPES OF WRITING.
8. WE FIND OUR BOOK CLASSIFICATION.
9. WE FIND OUR MAJOR AND MINOR GENRE'?
10. WE LEARN 5 TYPES OF FICTION.
11. WE LEARN THE ACT OF WRITING.
12. WE EDIT OUR BOOK DRAFT.
13. WE DO OUR BOOK PLAN.
14. WE DO WRITE THREE KINDS OF SYNOPSES.
15. WE USE 7 KEY WRITING TOOLS.
16. WE COMPARE OUR MANUSCRIPT TO THE MASTERS.

1.0.0.2. THE BEGINNING WRITER:
1. IF YOU HAVE WRITTEN A LETTER, A JOURNAL , SHORT STORY OR NOVEL YOU ARE A **BEGINNING WRITER**.
IF YOU PUBLISHED, YOU ARE AN AUTHOR. IF YOU PUBLISHED 10 OR MORE BOOKS OR ARTICLES, YOU MIGHT BE A MASTER WRITER! MASTER WRITERS ARE SELECTED ON AWARDS AND

CREATIVE WRITING—THE KELLY MANUAL OF STYLE

MERITS AS STYLE OR CHARACTERS OR NUMBER OF BEST
SELLERS, USUALLY BY A LITERARY GROUP. [CH 61.]. MASTER WRITERS
BECOME: GRAND MASTER WRITERS.

2. DO YOU WANT TO IMPROVE YOUR 'WRITING' OR CREATE YOUR
   MASTERPIECE?
3. **DO YOU UNDERSTAND WRITING IS A COMPLEX PROCESS
   AND EVEN FRUSTRATING AND A VERY TIME CONSUMING PROCESS?**

4. ARE YOU WILLING TO LEARN NEW METHODS AND DEVOTE THE TIME
   TO IMPROVE? ARE YOU WILLING TO   ABSORB AND USE NEW
   TECHNIQUES? CAN YOU EDIT THEM?
5. WILL YOU READ ALL TYPES OF LITERATURE AND DEFINE
   SOME INTO GENRE'S? [CH 1.0.0.0.]
6. ARE YOU COMPUTER LITERATE? CAN YOU USE THE
   INTERNET? CAN YOU DO A 'COPY AND PASTE?'
7. CAN YOU USE 'WORD SOFTWARE' TO BEGIN YOUR
   WRITING?
8. DO YOU UNDERSTAND THE DIFFERENCES BETWEEN THESE <u>THREE</u>:
   HIGH SCHOOL ENGLISH 101 OR A COLLEGE LITERATURE
   PAPER AND CREATIVE WRITING?
9. ARE YOU READY TO BEGIN A JOURNEY THAT WILL TRAVEL FROM
   WRITER TO AUTHOR TO A MASTER WRITER AND HIGHER?

10. **CAN WE STORYTELL?** CAN WE BLEND OUR READING,
    WRITING AND CREATIVITY INTO A STORY? CAN WE
    GROUP A SERIES OF IDEAS INTO A THEME? CAN WE
    WRITE A SHORT PARAGRAPH EXPLAINING WHAT OUR
    STORY IS ABOUT?

IF WE CAN DO THE TEN THINGS LISTED ABOVE, WE ARE READY TO BEGIN
THINKING AND DOING WHAT A WRITER DOES. ONLY THIS TIME WE WILL
BE AT A HIGHER LEVEL.

BEFORE WE TURN OFF THE COMPUTER AND TURN OUT THE LIGHT; WE
WILL DISCOVER THE WRITER'S UNIVERSE AND OUR PURPOSE IN LIFE.
THEN, WE WILL LEARN WHY WRITING IS FULFILLING TO US.

IN ALL WALKS OF LIFE AND STAGES OF WRITING, WE BEGIN BY WRITING.
THE LAYING DOWN OF WORDS ON PAPER OR ON THE COMPUTER SCREEN.
ONLY THEN, **WE LEARN WRITING IS SO MUCH MORE!**

CLASS LESSON:
1.1.0.1. LET'S DISCUSS WRITING AND CREATIVITY AND HOW ARE THEY
CONNECTED?
1.1.0.2. **CREATIVITY:** HOW DO WE GET IT-USE IT AND MELD IT WITH OUR
WRITING?

- DISCUSS HANDS-ON WAYS TO INFUSE YOUR LIFE WITH
  CREATIVITY, LIKE IMPROVING YOUR WRITING SPACE, DOING
  RESEARCH, OBSERVATION, AND READING THE MASTERS.

- SUGGEST WAYS TO CHANGE YOUR MENTAL OUTLOOK, AT
  MUCH LESS THAN A SHRINK WOULD CHARGE.

- DISCUSS CHANGING OUR FOCUS ON CREATIVITY FOR THE SAKE
  OF CREATIVITY, AND FOR THE SAKE OF A BETTER, MORE
  INSPIRED LIFE.

- DEVELOP AN IDEAS LIST: EXAMPLES: REFER CH 5.0.2.2 AND CH 41. USE PROMPTS OR IDEAS THAT CHALLENGE US TO WRITE MORE.

- DRAW ON EVERYTHING AROUND US: PEOPLE-PLACES-RESEARCH-ODD FACTS-HISTORY-ETC.

1.1.0. 0. DESCRIBE WRITING:
A. WRITING IS LIKE DRIVING A CAR AT NIGHT!
THERE IS ONLY SO FAR YOU CAN SEE AHEAD.

TRY TO LET YOUR STORY DEVELOP AS THE FLOW COMES TO YOU…JUST GET IT DOWN. FORGET STRUCTURE, PUNCTUATION, OUTLINES, ETC. SIT WITH YOUR PAD OR LAPTOP, OR PC AND JUST WRITE…DON'T THINK WHAT YOU ARE WRITING IS GOOD OR BAD…THAT'S WHY YOU EDIT SO MUCH. YOU CAN THROW IT OUT LATER, OR REUSE IT LATER, OR MOVE IT ANYWHERE IN BOOK OR FROM ONE CHAPTER TO ANOTHER…..A GREAT FEATURE OF COPY AND PASTE.

WRITING IS GETTING THE BASIC IDEAS DOWN ON PAPER, FIRST.

B. WRITING IS OUR ELOQUENT VOICE.

C. WRITING IS STORYTELLING ON PAPER.

D. WRITING IS CREATING FINE ART.

E. WRITING IS OUR IMAGINATION GONE WILD.

F. WRITING IS A LOVE LETTER.

G. WRITING IS SOMETHING MEANINGFUL!

H. WRITING IS EMOTIONAL.

I. WRITING IS MANY TYPES AND STYLES.

J. WRITING IS A DEMANDING MISTRESS!

K. WRITING IS   ? (ADD YOUR OWN HERE).

1.2.0.0. WRITING TYPES:
BUSINESS WRITING: 'BIZ/TECH'
BUSINESS WRITING IS ANY KIND OF WRITING ASSIGNMENT YOU TAKE ON FOR A BUSINESS. THIS CAN MEAN WRITING FOR THE INTERNAL PLAYERS OF THE BUSINESS ITSELF: .E.G.
A NEWSLETTER FOR A COMPANY'S EMPLOYEES, OR WRITING FOR THE BOTTOM LINE OF THE BUSINESS, SUCH AS WRITING MARKETING BROCHURES OR POWERPOINT PRESENTATIONS. FOR MORE INFORMATION ON BUSINESS WRITING, BE SURE TO **WEB SEARCH**: *BLOGGING, COPYWRITING, TECHNICAL WRITING AND WEB CONTENT WRITING* AND *SEARCH ENGINE OPTIMIZATION*.

CREATIVE WRITING—THE KELLY MANUAL OF STYLE

BLOGGING: BLOGGING IS THE ACT OF UPDATING WEB CONTENT IN A DATE-ORDERED POSTING. IT DIFFERS FROM SIMPLE WEB WRITING IN TONE, FORMALITY, AND FEATURES SUCH AS COMMUNITY-BUILDING AND COMMENTS. COMPANIES OR INDIVIDUALS MAY HIRE FREELANCE BLOGGERS TO MAINTAIN THEIR BLOG AND FACILITATE SOCIAL, COMMUNITY BUILDING, IN ADDITION TO DIRECTLY OR INDIRECTLY PROMOTING A PRODUCT, PERSON OR SERVICE

CONTENT WRITING: CONTENT WRITING IS WRITING SPECIFICALLY FOR THE INTERNET. CONTENT WRITING DIFFERS FROM BLOGGING BECAUSE IT IS OFTEN MORE STATIC AND FORMAL, ALTHOUGH BLOG POSTS ARE OFTEN REFERRED TO AS 'CONTENT' TOO.

COPYWRITING: COPYWRITING IS WRITING FOR PROMOTION OR MARKETING PURPOSES. IT IS WRITING TO SELL SOMETHING INCLUDING INDIRECT SALES. WRITING PRESS KITS, WHITE PAPERS AND INFORMATIONAL BROCHURES. IN GENERAL, COPYWRITING AIMS FOR A PURCHASE FROM THE READER.

CRITICAL WRITING: CRITICAL WRITING IS WRITING IN REVIEW MODE. IT IS WRITING TO ANALYZE OR INTERPRET SOMETHING. EXAMPLES INCLUDE BOOK REVIEWS, MOVIE REVIEWS AND PRODUCT REVIEWS.

COMPARATIVE WRITING:
DO ANALYZE THE GRAND MASTERS OF WRITING AND CURRENT AUTHORS, INCLUDING YOURSELF. [CH. 28].

ESSAY/NON-FICTION WRITING:
ESSAYS ARE WRITING ABOUT EXPERIENCES-THOUGHTS-INTERESTING OR IMPORTANT THINGS ABOUT OR FOR YOU. ESSAYS USED IN HIGH SCHOOL ENGLISH OR COLLEGE ENGLISH, USE A FORMAT OF INTRODUCTION, BODY AND CONCLUSION.

BACK THEN , THEY STARTED WITH AN OUTLINE AS A FRAMEWORK. I PREFER TO WORK WITH A LIST OF IDEAS AND THEN GROUP THEM. THEN BEGIN WITH MY INTRODUCTION…EXPLAINING WHY THIS IS IMPORTANT TO READER. I ANSWER THE SIX W'S AND DO THE BRIDGE [CH 26]. FOR THE CONCLUSION.

THIS GENRE CAN INCLUDE MEMOIRS AND ANECDOTES, OR IT CAN BE EDUCATIONAL OR PERSUASIVE IN ITS AIM. IT SHOULD BE LONG ENOUGH TO COVER THE SUBJECT AND ILLUSTRATE IT AND CONCLUDE THE RESULT OR SIGNIFICANCE. WE ANSWER THE QUESTIONS…WAS IT INTERESTING AND WHAT DID THE READER LEARN?

FICTION WRITING:
OBVIOUSLY A VERY BROAD CATEGORY, AND LIKELY TO BE ANYWHERE IN LENGTH FROM A PARAGRAPH ALL THE WAY UP TO AN ENTIRE SERIES OF BOOKS, FICTION WRITING IS STORY TELLING AND BOOK WRITING. FICTION WRITERS MAY OVERLAP INTO *NON-FICTION WRITING, POETRY, HISTORY AND/OR GHOSTWRITING.* **THERE ARE 5 TYPES OF FICTION GENRE'**.[REFER CH 1.0.4.2.1.]

CREATIVE WRITING—THE KELLY MANUAL OF STYLE

GHOST WRITING: GHOSTWRITING IS WRITING ANY AND ALL OF THE OTHER GENRES <u>ON BEHALF OF SOMEONE</u> ELSE, USING THEIR NAME, AND ALLOWING THEM THE CREDIT FOR THE PIECE.

JOURNALISTIC WRITING-AP STYLE:
THIS IS WRITING IN 'AP PYRAMID STYLE' FOR MAGAZINES AND NEWSPAPERS. JOURNALISTIC WRITERS MAY PRODUCE MAGAZINE CONTENT ON JUST ABOUT ANYTHING, NEWSPAPER COLUMNS, FEATURE STORIES.

JOURNALS:
WRITING A JOURNAL IS ABOUT WRITING YOUR THOUGHTS, A SLICE OF LIFE OR AN EXPERIENCE. IT IS ABOUT PRIVACY (MAYBE SOMETHING YOU DON'T WANT TO SHARE BUT WRITING IT DOWN MAKES YOU FEEL BETTER AND CLARIFIES THE SITUATION. IT IS A GOOD WAY TO PUT PAST EVENTS OR DISTURBING EVENTS IN PERSPECTIVE. YOU CAN GO ON BE BETTER PREPARED FOR YOUR FUTURE).

WRITING A JOURNAL IS ABOUT MY WORLD AND HOW I SEE IT AND HOW IT IMPACTS MY LIFE. THE EVENTS COULD BE EMOTIONAL LIKE A DEATH IN THE FAMILY, A CAR CRASH OR UPLIFTING LIKE A NEW BABY. **WRITE IT FOR YOURSELF.**
IF YOU WISH TO SHARE IT, IT SHOULD TAKE THE FORM OF A SHORT STORY OR ESSAY WITH THE FORM OF INTRODUCTION, BODY AND CONCLUSION.

POETRY WRITING:
WRITING CREATIVE VERSE. THOSE WHO WRITE POETRY MAY ALSO OVERLAP INTO OTHER "CREATIVE" GENRES. RHYME AND METER AND LINKING THOUGHTS TOGETHER. NEWER VERSIONS VARY.
DO WRITE THE SOUND WORDS: REPETITIVE SOUNDS AND MUSICAL PAUSES INTO OUR BOOKS. THINK SOUNDS FROM WORDS: BANG, BOOM, BURP, SCREECH, RAT-TAT-TAT...ETC. [SEE CHAPTER 19 TO USE SOUND WORDS IN OUR WRITING].

SCRIPT WRITING: [CH 40].
WRITING SCRIPTS FOR SPOKEN WORD PERFORMANCE OR RECORDING.

TECHNICAL WRITING: WRITING TO TECHNICAL STANDARDS OR AS INSTRUCTIONS OR TO CONVEY INFORMATION IN A SPECIALIZED FIELD. TECH WRITERS ARE LIKELY TO PRODUCE WHITE PAPERS, INSTRUCTION MANUALS, HOW TO ASSEMBLE INSTRUCTIONS, OR SIMILAR DOCUMENTATION. <u>SUPPORTIVE SOFTWARE</u> IS USED AS VISIO DIAGRAMS, WORD ART, PHOTO INSERTION AND SPREADSHEET OR CHART FORMATS.VISIO DIAGRAMS OR BUSINESS PROCESS DOCUMENTATION ARE PART OF THIS TO STANDARDIZED EACH SPECIFIC STRUCTURE AND FORMAT" IS THE KEY TO TECHNICAL WRITING.

WEB WRITING: SIMILAR TO CONTENT WRITING, BUT MAY ALSO INCLUDE WRITING FOR EZINES, ONLINE COLUMNS OR SPECIFICALLY FOR SEARCH ENGINE OPTIMIZATION. MAY SHARES SOME TRAITS WITH *BUSINESS WRITING, BLOGGING, CONTENT WRITING AND COPYWRITING.*

CREATIVE WRITING—THE KELLY MANUAL OF STYLE

WEB CONTENT COMES IN MANY FORMS, SUCH AS ARTICLES, COLUMNS, HOW-TO STEPS, OUTLINES, OR LISTS. CONTENT CAN BE PART OF A WEBSITE, SUCH AS WHEN A BUSINESS OFFERS ARTICLES OR POINTERS ABOUT ITS FIELD AS A PORTION OF THE SITE. OR, THE ENTIRE WEBSITE CAN BE CONTENT-BASED, SUCH AS SITES LIKE EHOW.COM OR WIKIPEDIA, IN WHICH THE CONTENT ITSELF IS THE FINAL GOAL OF THE SITE.

1.0.3.1. WEB COPYWRITING. [INDEX 3].
DEFINITION: THIS IS JUST A FANCY NAME FOR WRITING OF TEXT ESPECIALLY FOR A WEB PAGE SITE. WEB COPYWRITING IS SIMILAR TO WRITING CONTENT FOR ANY OTHER TYPE OF PUBLICATION. HOWEVER, REALLY GOOD WEB WRITING CAN HAVE AN ENORMOUS EFFECT ON SEARCH ENGINE POSITIONING (HOW YOUR SITE FALLS IN THE RANKINGS), SO IT SHOULD BE A PROMINENT PART OF YOUR OVERALL SEARCH ENGINE OPTIMIZATION (SEO) PLAN. WRITING FOR A NEW WEB PAGE SITE REQUIRES, STRUCTURE, LAYOUT AND CONCISE WORDING.

1.4.0.0. BOOK CLASSIFICATION SYSTEM:
12 CATEGORIES- 4 BOOK DIVISIONS – 2 FICTION DIVISIONS-
5 FICTION GENRE.

OUR GOAL:
WE ARE GOING TO SELECT OUR CLASSIFICATION FOR OUR PARTICULAR BOOK AND WRITE IT ON OUR STORYTELLER'S SYNOPSIS FORMAT EACH TIME. OUR FINISHED BOOK WILL BE CLASSIFIED BY THIS BOOK CLASS. SYSTEM.

1.4.1. 0. LITERARY CATEGORIES: 12 CATEGORIES
A-Z LITERATURE & AUTHORS
GENRES, THEMES & TOPICS
GLOSSARY OF LITERARY TERMS
LITERARY CALENDAR
LITERARY HISTORY
LITERATURE AND BOOK BASICS
PERIODS & MOVEMENTS
QUIZZES AND TESTS
QUOTES, SAYINGS & LINES
READ AND STUDY BOOKS
STUDY GUIDES
WORLD LITERATURE

DO SELECT ONE LITERARY CATEGORY: 'GENRES, THEMES AND TOPICS, '
AND WRITE IT ON THE TOP OF YOUR STORYTELLER'S OR CHAPTER SYNOPSIS.

1.4.2.0. FOUR BOOK DIVISIONS: *SELECT ONE:*
1. *BOOK DIVISION FOR BOTH FICTION AND NON-FICTION WRITERS.*
2. **THE JOURNALISM DIVISION,: MAGAZINE AND NEWSPAPER.**
3. **THE BIZ-TECH DIVISION, FOR BUSINESS AND TECHNOLOGY WRITERS.**
4. **PROSE AND POETRY-FREE VERSE -HAIKU.**

DO SELECT ONE: **'BOOK DIVISION.'** *THIS GOES INTO OUR STORYTELLER'S SYNOPSIS.. [EXAMPLE: CH 7]*

1.4.3. 0. MAJOR GENRE': BOOKS

ACTION & ADVENTURE
AUTOBIOGRAPHY-MEMOIR
BOOKS-BANNED
BIOGRAPHY
CAPTIVITY NARRATIVES
CHILDREN'S BOOKS
COOKBOOKS
CRIME /DECECTIVE-ACTUAL
DRAMA / PLAYS
ESSAY
FAMILY SAGAS
FICTION
FOLKLORE –LEGENDS-MYTHS- MYTHOLOGY-FAIRY TALES
GHOST STORY
HUMOR
INSPIRATIONAL
JUVENILE CLASSICS
MAGIC REALISM
NATURE
NONFICTION
POETRY
READS-MUST-LIST TO DO
REALISM
REFERENCE
RHETORIC
ROMANCE
SCIENCE-SPACE
SPY-SECRET AGENT
STORYTELLING
TECHNICAL
TECHNOLOGY
TEEN
TRAVEL
WRITING-CREATIVE-HOW TO
WRITING-TECHNICAL-TECHNICAL-BLOGS-BIZ-RESEARCH

***WRITER: DO SELECT ONE** MAJOR GENRE' , **FICTION**, AND WRITE IT ON YOUR STORYTELLER'S SYNOPSIS AND THE FICTION DIVISION BELOW.*

1.4.4.0. BOOK DIVISIONS- 5 FICTION DIVISIONS:
= FICTION & NON-FICTION.

1.4.5 .0. FICTION-GENRE'-5 TYPES:

1. LITERARY & GENERAL FICTION

2. HISTORICAL FICTION

3. MYSTERY-SUSPENSE & THRILLER

4. SCIENCE FICTION & FANTASY

5. SHORT FICTION & PULP

CREATIVE WRITING—THE KELLY MANUAL OF STYLE

DO SELECT ONE: FICTION GENRE' AND WRITE IT ON YOUR STORYTELLER'S SYNOPSIS. THIS MATCHES TO YOUR BOOK TYPE.

1.4.6.0. MAJOR AND MINOR GENRE' DEFINED:
NOW WE SELECT OUR MAJOR AND MINOR GENRE AND WHY IS IT IMPORTANT TO OUR BOOK AND ITS STYLE OF WRITING WITHIN.

A TRUE COMPARISON OF OUR WORK TO ANOTHER SHOULD BE BASED ON LIKE PROPERTIES. GENRE' DEFINES THESE AS RECURRING PATTERNS, COMPONENTS CALLED CATEGORIES, THUS A GENRE' CLASSIFICATION SYSTEM.

1.4.7. 0. A BROAD GENRE' DEFINITION:
THE WORD _GENRE'_ IS MOST OFTEN USED TO CLASSIFY VARIOUS MEDIA AND FORMATS BASED ON RECURRING PATTERNS AND COMPONENTS. HOWEVER, WITHIN BROAD GENRES, SUCH AS 'FICTION' YOU WILL FIND MANY SUB-GENRES.

A GENRE IS A CATEGORY OF LITERATURE, WITH A DISTINCTIVE STYLE. GENRE IS ALSO USED TO CATEGORIZE BOOKS AND ARRANGE THEM IN BOOKSTORES, SO IT'S USEFUL TO SEE WHERE YOUR WORK FITS.

1.4.8. 0. EXAMPLE: A LIBRARY FILES FICTION BOOKS AWAY IN THE "FICTION" SECTION BY THE LAST NAME OF THE AUTHOR.

1.5.0. 0. YOUR COMPETITION-A COMPARISON:
CHECK OUT YOUR COMPETITION IN YOUR CLASSIFICATION, VISIT THE LIBRARY AND YOUR LOCAL BOOK SELLER. [CH 52-53].

1.6.0. 0. THE ACT OF WRITING:
THERE IS A WHOLE LIST OF TERMINOLOGY AND NARRATIVE DESCRIPTIONS-PLOTS-SUB PLOTS-POINTS OF VIEW- SETTINGS-ELEMENTS OF STYLE- FIGURES OF SPEECH-LITERARY TECHNIQUES---SIMILAR TO SOME OF THE ABOVE. JUST BEGIN WRITING, FORGET COMMA USE, CAPITALS, PERIODS, ETC. JUST BEGIN TO WRITE IT ---WRITE IT BETTER--- EMBELLISH IT--- WRITE A PARAGRAPH---THEN ADD A FIRST SENTENCE WHICH GRABS THE READER. WRITE IT AGAIN, OR CHANGE IT AT ANYTIME. FOLLOW THE THEME THROUGHOUT THE PARAGRAPH THEN END IT WITH A SIMILAR BUT CONCLUSIVE STATEMENT.
IT'S LIKE GIFT WRAPPING YOUR PARAGRAPH!

1.6.1. 0. AFTER THE MANUSCRIPT IS FINISHED?
EXAMPLE, I GET WITHDRAWAL AFTER WRITING A BOOK FOR A YEAR: I'M READY FOR MY NEXT ONE OR GEE! I WORKED SO HARD ON IT, THAT I'M GONNA MISS WORKING ON IT!
THE CHINESE HAVE A SAYING: _"THAT IT IS GOOD TO LEAVE THE PAST BEHIND SO THE FUTURE CAN BEGIN!"_

I USE A LITTLE SAYING TO REMIND ME OF MY DUTY TO FINISH IT PROPERLY OR TO WAIT. NOPE...CREATIVE WRITING IS NOT IT!
CLASS: LET'S SEE IF YOU CAN FIGURE IT OUT?

1.6.2.0. NOW WE CAN ANSWER THE QUESTION: WRITING IS?: IS IT?
THE JOY OF WRITING?
WORLD HISTORY?
MY ROMANCE OF THE CENTURY?
WHY JOHNNY FLUNKED COLLEGE AND WENT TO WAR?
WHY I STARTED WORLD WAR III?
HOW TO COOK CHINESE?
AH! HA!
STORY TELLING 101
HOW TO MAKE A MILLION IN REAL ESTATE?
HOW TO FIND SUCCESS, LOVE AND HAPPINESS?
HOW TO WRITE A BEST SELLER BOOK.

1.6.3 .0. CLASS: WRITING IS? WHAT WOULD BE YOUR CLOSING SENTENCE?

THE REAL ANSWER TO WRITING IS?
...IT IS ____AH! HA!

1.6.4.0. CLASS: WRITE: WHAT IS DIFFERENCE BETWEEN WRITING AND STORYTELLING?
OR WHICH CAME FIRST, "THE CHICKEN OR EGG?"

WHITEBOARD: WRITE DOWN THEIR ANSWERS. -THREE COLUMNS: WRITING -STORYTELLING-OTHER:

STORYTELLING IS VERBAL. SAYING IT OUTLOUD.
COULD A STORY BE A PLAY? A MOVIE? YES, BUT ITS AUDIENCE & THE POINT OF VIEW AND STRUCTURE ARE DIFFERENT. [REFER CH 6 FOR STORYTELLING].

WRITING IS WRITTEN. A BOOK , A JOURNAL, A POEM, , A NOVEL, SHORT STORY, A PLAY ON PAPER OR ELECTRONIC FORM. IN ITS SIMPLE FORM: IT IS WRITTEN DOWN.

**IN WRITING, ARE WE MISSING ANOTHER MEDIA:
GRAPHIC...PICTURES. A MOVIE, A MAP, A PAINTING. ARE THEY
WRITING? STORYTELLING? IF NOT...WHY?**

1.6.5. 0. CLASS ?:
WHAT IS MORE IMPORTANT? THE STORY, THE WRITER, OR THE READER?
*THE READER.---- *DO DISCUSS THE DIFFERENCES:*

1.6.6.0. CLASS: NOW HOW MUCH DOES IT COST? $100 OR $10,000
MONEY, CLASS TIME, WRITING PROJECTS, EDITING REWRITE?
HOMEWORK, GIVE UP SOCIAL TIME? TAKE TIME AWAY FROM OTHERS,
WORK, SLEEP. *THE COST IS MORE THAN MONETARY. DISCUSS OTHERS?*

1.6.7. 0. SATISFACTION OR WHAT DO WE GET OUT OF OUR HARD WORK?...OUR BOOK?

ANS? *SATISFACTION OF GIVING…A PARTNERSHIP OF GIVING SMILES OR HAPPINESS TO ANOTHER AND RECEIVING SATISFACTION? TELLING A STORY FOR SATISFACTION, FOR PLEASURE OF IT, FOR THE POETRY OF IT?* DISCUSS: HOW DO WE MEASURE? IS IT HEAVEN? SMILES? MONETARY REWARD? SUCCESS?
ANS: ANSWERS DO VARY BUT ALL OF THEM ARE CORRECT.

1.6.8.0. CLASS ?: FAVORITE AUTHOR?
ANS: WHY? WHAT DO YOU GET FROM HIS WRITING? IS HE/SHE A GOOD WRITER? WHAT MAKES A GOOD WRITER A GOOD STORYTELLER?

1.7.0.0. OUR BOOK PLAN:
CONSIDER WRITING THESE ELEMENTS:
PARAGRAPH TOPICS: *PLOT-DRAFT-REVISIONS-FEEDBACK-WAITING FOR MATURITY-[SEE CH 10-BOOK PLAN-STORY STRUCTURE]*

1.7.0.1. GIVE SOME THOUGHT TO PLOT: [SEE CH 21 PLOT]
WRITING A NOVEL CAN BE A HUGE UNDERTAKING, UNORGANIZED AND COMPLEX TASK. YOU MIGHT SAY HUNDREDS OF TASKS, WHICH NEED YOUR ATTENTION.

BEGIN WITH A SHORT SYNOPSIS. A CONDENSED VERSION OF YOUR STORY. THINK ABOUT SIX W'S: WHO WHAT WHY, WHEN, WHERE AND **WOW!** ANSWER ALL OF THESE AND YET TELL THE STORY IN BRIEF. NO MORE THAN TWO PAGES.

THREE KINDS OF SYNOPSES:

1. SHORT STORYTELLER'S SYNOPSIS.
2. DETAILED SYNOPSIS
3. CHAPTER BY CHAPTER SYNOPSIS.

OTHERS WORK WITH INDEX CARDS, PUTTING A DIFFERENT SCENE ON EACH ONE. STILL OTHERS HAVE A CONFLICT AND A GENERAL IDEA OF CLIMAX OR ENDING FOR THE BOOK; THUS, WHERE THEY PLAN TO END UP AND THEN DIVE IN. PLOT, MAIN CHARACTERS AND KEY EVENTS SHOULD COME OUT OF THE SHORT STORYTELLER'S SYNOPSIS.

1.7.0.2. GET A FIRST DRAFT DOWN.
FOCUS ON GETTING THE STORY DOWN ON PAPER.
GRAB THE KEY ELEMENTS AND WRITE IT DOWN. START AT THE BEGINNING OF STORY. THIS MIGHT BE A SHORT STORY IN LENGTH. AT THIS POINT YOU ARE GRABBING ALL THE IDEA GROUPS AND BEGINNING TO WRITE A BOOK **DRAFT.** *THIS WILL NOT LOOK LIKE A BOOK AT THIS POINT!*

1.7.0.3. BE PREPARED TO REVISE. [CH 30].
WRITING A NOVEL INVOLVES A LARGE AMOUNT OF WORK BETWEEN FIRST DRAFT AND PUBLISHED BOOK. THE FIRST DRAFT WILL BE BAD, DISORGANIZED AND CONFUSING. ENTIRE CHAPTERS WILL DRAG AND SEEM UNCONNECTED. SENTENCES WILL BE POOR: TOO SHORT, TOO LONG, WRONG VERB TENSES, HANGING PARTICIPLES, POOR WORD

CHOICES, AND BAD PUNCTUATION. IF IDEAS DON'T CONNECT. **IT IS OKAY!** REMEMBER YOU ARE WRITING A DRAFT, OVER AND OVER, MANY TIMES BEFORE IT GETS INTO SHAPE AS A BOOK.

1.7.0.4. DO NOT SOLICIT FEEDBACK AT THIS POINT.

STOP AND SEE WHAT YOU COULD DO TO MAKE IT BETTER. DON'T JUST HOPE THE READER WON'T NOTICE. IF YOU WANT YOUR BOOK TO BE GOOD, REVISE WITH YOUR MOST INTELLIGENT, MOST THOUGHTFUL READER IN MIND. DO NOT ASK FRIENDS OR WIVES TO REVIEW AT THIS TIME...PRESENT THEM ONLY WITH THE FINISHED MANUSCRIPT. YOU WILL GET DISCOURAGED. **REMEMBER A BOOK IS NOT READY UNTIL YOU SAY IT IS READY! BESIDES YOU HAVE MANY 'TO DO STEPS' TO GO THROUGH YET.**

1.7.0.5. PUT IT ASIDE.

IF YOU FIND YOURSELF BANGING UP AGAINST THE SAME PROBLEMS OR WALL WITH EVERY DRAFT, IT MAY BE TIME TO WORK ON SOMETHING ELSE FOR A WHILE OR ? [CH 35- SOLVING WRITER'S PROBLEMS].

REVIEW THE '**TO DO STEPS**,' DID YOU GATHER ALL OF THE IDEAS INTO GROUPS? REVIEW **THE PLOT**...WAS IT COMPLETE? WAS IT WORTHWHILE...DO YOU FORGET ANY ELEMENT OF IT? WAS IT SUPPORTED BY NEW EVENTS, ACTIONS AND CHARACTERS? FIRST, FIX ANY FLAWS TO YOUR PLOT. [CH 21]. **YOUR PLOT IS THE FRAMEWORK** ON WHICH WE HANG THE REST OF THE STORY ELEMENTS.

DID YOU WRITE THAT **SYNOPSIS** AND FULLY DEVELOP IT BEFORE WRITING THE DRAFT? DID WE FULLY **COMPLETE OUR 'MASTER IDEA LIST' AND IDEA GROUPING AND WRITE ONE AGAIN FOR JUST OUR LATEST PROJECT BOOK? -"OUR DETAILED BOOK IDEA LIST."**

YEP, THERE ARE TWO IDEA LISTS!!!! [SEE CH 5]

IF YOU FIND YOURSELF LOSING YOUR WAY, GO BACK TO THE BOOK PLAN. DID YOU WRITE ONE? THEN, BEGIN AGAIN WITH THE FUN PARTS OF WRITING. WRITE SOME BASIC PAGES THAT BELONG TO YOUR BOOKS ORGANIZATION: [SYNOPSIS: OUR INTRODUCTION], TITLE PAGES, SUBJECT INDICES, TABLE OF CONTENTS, GLOSSARY, ETC.

CREATE SOMETHING NEW; READ FOR FUN. WITH EACH NEW PROJECT YOU TAKE ON AND BOOK YOU READ, YOU'LL LEARN NEW LESSONS. WHEN YOU COME BACK TO YOUR NOVEL -- AND YOU WILL COME BACK TO IT -- YOU'LL SEE IT WITH MORE EXPERIENCED EYES.

1.8.0.0. OUR PROGRESS:

1. WE LEARN WRITING IS?

2. WE LEARNED THE VARIOUS FORMS OF WRITING.

3. WE LEARNED ABOUT WRITING FROM A TOP DOWN APPROACH.

4. WE LEARNED ABOUT 12 LITERARY DIVISIONS, GENRE' AND 2 FICTION'S GENRE'.

5. WE LEARNED THE 4 BOOK DIVISIONS AND 2 FICTION DIVISIONS.

6. WE LEARNED THE 5 FICTION GENRE' AND TYPES.

7. *DO:WE CLASSIFIED OUR ROUGH DRAFT.

CHAPTER 2
2.0.0.0. THE KELLY PROCESS-OVERVIEW
CHAPTER TOPICS: MASTER TO DO LIST-THE KELLY PROCESS EXPLAINED-
ESSENTIALS YOU WILL LEARN- BASIC STEPS TO WRITING.

2.0.0.0. INTRODUCTION:
WRITING A BOOK IS A LONG AND COMPLEX PROCESS.
 WE BEGIN BY **DOING SIMPLE TASKS IN THEIR ORDER** TO FORM A BOOK
DRAFT.

 HERE IS AN OVERVIEW OF THE STEPS NEEDED TO BE FINISHED AS WE
PROGRESS TO A FINISHED MANUSCRIPT. EACH STEP BELOW HAS A
CHAPTER REFERENCE TO ALLOW YOU TO FIND THE SPECIFICS FOR EACH
TASK.

2.0.1.0. STEP BY STEP: *'THE KELLY PROCESS:'*
YOUR ORGANIZATION & CREATIVITY BEGINS HERE:
I. *DO WRITE THESE FIRST: 3 SYNOPSES:
1. WRITE DOWN A SHORT VERSION(1) OF YOUR STORY, A PARAGRAPH
   OR TWO. THIS IS OUR STORY SUMMARY. [CH 6].
2. NOW SAY IT **OUT LOUD**. REVISE THE PARAGRAPHS. THUS, TO TELL A
   FRIEND WHAT YOUR BOOK IS ABOUT.
3. WRITE A LONGER VERSION WITH A MAIN CHARACTER AND
   VILLLAN AND THE PREDICAMENT. **STORYTELLER'S VERSION** [CH 7].
4. WRITE IT AGAIN (3) WITH THE IDEA KERNAL, THE BASIC PLOT, TIME
   PERIOD, UNIVERSAL THEME AND CHAPTER TOPICS.[CH 8].
5. WRITE THE GENRE. IF FICTION DO THIS:

6. **THROW AWAY THE OUTLINE.**
7. GET A STURDY CARDBOARD BOX-FOR SYNOPSES, PAPER COPIES OF
   MASTERS, DRAFTS, NOTES, MANUSCRIPTS
8. START A MASTER BOOK TITLE LIST. [CH 52-53].
9. START A MASTER CHARACTER LIST. [CH 20].
10. START A MASTER IDEAS LIST [CH 5] GENERAL TOPICS, THEN DO ONE
    SPECIFIC FOR YOUR NEW BOOK.
11. START A MASTER SOURCE LIST NOT A BIBLIOGRAPHY. THIS IS YOUR
    RESOURCE LIST AND ONE FOR FUTURE RESEARCH.[CH 34].
12. CARRY A NOTEBOOK FOR WRITING DOWN AN IDEA, DIALOGUE OR
    CHANGES AS YOU ARE AWAY FROM YOUR SPACE. ANOTHER AT
    BEDSIDE. [CH 5].
13. ORGANIZE YOUR WORK SPACE -GET ALL YOUR TOOLS, BOOKS,
    REFERENCE MATERIALS ORGANIZED FOR A QUICK FIND.[CH37].
14. BUY THE LARGEST DICTIONARY YOU CAN AFFORD.
15. START A 'TO DO' LIST IN WORD. e.g. WRITE THE 'INTRO
    PAGES' TO YOUR BOOK, TITLE, COPYRIGHT, ETC.
16. FIND A DIFFERENT **EDIT SPACE**, USE THE PROOFREADER MARKS.CH 32
17. **COMPUTER**: SET UP A MASTER AND ARCHIVES FOLDERS IN
    COMPUTER-[CH33].
18. BEGIN A TABLE OF CONTENTS FOR YOUR NEW BOOK.
19. ORGANIZE YOUR MASTER DRAFT OF CHAPTERS.[CH 29-36].
20. WRITE WITHOUT INHIBITION. IT'S A DRAFT.[CH 4].

21. EDIT AND PROOF READ-CHART. [CH 11].
22. KELLY STYLE: ADD THE CREATIVE STUFF! [CH 4].
23. RE-WRITE, RE-EDIT, RE-PROOF. MANY TIMES! [CH 39].
24. DO COMPARE YOUR WRITING & EDITING CHECK LISTS-REWRITE.
25. ADD YOUR NEW STYLE ELEMENTS
26. COMPARE MANUSCRIPT TO GRANDMASTER'S CHECK LIST-REWRITE.
    [CH 28].
27. ILLUMINATE IT. ---AND POLISH IT! READ ALOUD FOR WORD
    FLOW AND SOUNDS. [CH 19].
28. WRITING & EDITING CHECK LISTS REVIEWED. [CH 31].
29. FIX ANY AND ALL ERRORS OR CHANGES AS FOUND.
    DO STEPS IN CH 36-FINAL MANUSCRIPT REVIEW.
29. TYPE CHANGES. PRINT OUT.
30. DO <u>FINAL REVIEW</u> OF HARD COPY. [CH 36].
    ENTER CHANGES AND REVIEW COMPUTER VERSION.
31. <u>DO MARKETING PLAN AND RESEARCH IT. [CH 54].</u>
32. PREPARE TO PUBLISH- FOLLOW BOOK SET UP
    PROCEDURE. <u>ALLOW TIME</u> TO DO IT CORRECTLY.
33. REVIEW PAGE PLACEMENT AND BLANK PAGE (NO
    HEADERS, FOOTERS OR PAGE NUMBERS) AT END.[CH13].
34. REVIEW TABLE OF CONTENTS TITLES MATCH? PAGE
    NUMBERS MATCH? [CH 13].
35. COMPLETED COMPUTER MASTER DRAFT READY?
    [REFER **CH 38** ON PUBLISHING FOR DETAILED INSTRUCTIONS.]
36. FOLLOW UPLOADING INSTRUCTIONS FOR COPY.[CH49].
    (CONVERT WORD TO PDF IF REQUIRED BY THE PUBLISHER.)
37. UPLOAD **FRONT COVER**. [CH 49] .[JPG-PNG FILES ONLY]
    CHECK PIXEL SIZE. PRINT IT BEFOREHAND, NOT BLURRY?
38. ENTER **SPINE TEXT**: TITLE & AUTHOR'S NAME, COLOR
    AND SIZE.
39. ENTER **BACK COVER** PICTURE OR TEXT, MARKETING
    INFO, ISBN # AND LEAVE ROOM FOR PUBLISHER'S LOGO
    AND BAR CODE.
40. **REVIEW COMPLETE COVER** FOR ACCURACY, SPACES,
    VERB TENSE, PUNCTUATION, TITLE SIZES, AND ETC.
41. **UPLOADING:**
    UPLOAD TO YOUR "<u>MASTER BOOK TITLE AND DATE</u>"
    [CH 49] PROJECT FILE INTO THE PUBLISHER'S PAGE.

THIS PROCESS WILL GIVE AN ACKNOWLEDGEMENT BACK TO YOU THAT
THE BOOK IS RECEIVED/UPLOADED SATISFACTORILY. CHECK YOUR
LULU STOREFRONT FOR ITS VIEW. IF ANY ERRORS, CORRECT THESE
BEFORE FINAL APPROVAL. ONCE, THIS IS DONE CHANGES WILL COST
YOU MONEY AND DELAY YOUR BOOK. **DO NOT RUSH THIS PROCEDURE.**

43. *<u>DO</u>: **ORDER ONE PROOF COPY OF YOUR BOOK**. [CH 49].
REVIEW AND GIVE IT FINAL APPROVAL. **IT IS YOUR LAST CHANCE** TO
CORRECT ANY ERRORS. DOUBLE CHECK ISBN # INSIDE COPYRIGHT PAGE
#2, AND ON REAR COVER. ALSO, REAR BARCODE SHOULD APPEAR ON
PROOF COPY WITH ISBN # ABOVE IT.

44. **IF SOMETHING IS WRONG**: [CH 30].
    CORRECT YOUR MASTER FILE, OR COVER OR CHANGE SOMETHING
    THAT NEEDS FIXING AND RE-UPLOAD IT AGAIN. THIS IS THE
    "BIRTHING OF YOUR BOOK"….MAKE SURE IT IS CORRECT.]

45. **SUMMARY:** AT THIS POINT YOUR BOOK IS COMPLETE, SUBMITTED, FINAL 'PROOF COPY' REVIEWED AND ABSOLUTE FINAL APPROVAL IS GIVEN. **DO:** ORDER **2 COPIES FOR COPYRIGHT PURPOSES AND ONE FOR YOURSELF.**

46. MARKETING STEPS: [CH 54].
AT THIS POINT BEGIN DOING THE **MARKETING STEPS** [CH 54] AND UPDATE YOUR WEB PAGE, LULU STORE FRONT AND WRITER'S PROFILES ON SEVERAL SITES. DO LIST YOUR BOOK, ITS ISBN NUMBER AND A SMALLER PIXEL SIZE PHOTO OF COVER. USE THE 'ADD GOOGLE SEARCH FEATURE' FROM LULU PUBLISHING OR YOUR PRINT-ON-DEMAND PUBLISHER. AFTER THE COMPLETE BOOK IS UPLOADED, THIS 'ADD GOOGLE SEARCH' ITEM WILL APPEAR ON YOUR LULU PROJECT PAGE. DO SELECT IT.

47. COPYRIGHT: [REFER TO CH 45].
AT THIS POINT, SEND OFF 2 COPIES TO COPYRIGHT OFFICE, ALONG WITH THE CORRECT FORM AND FEES. [INDEX 3].

48. PREPARE A PRESS RELEASE. [CH 54].

49. FOLLOW THE MARKETING PLAN, MEASURE ITS SUCCESS, RE-VAMP, CONTINUE. [CH 54].

50. WHEN ALL OF THE MARKETING IS COMPLETE. BEGIN YOUR NEXT BOOK. **IT IS EASIER THE SECOND TIME!**

48. CLASS ROOM LESSONS:
THE CLASSROOM LESSONS ARE ONLY AS EXAMPLES TO TEACH US HOW TO IMPROVE OUR WRITING OR TO THINK OUT OF THE BOX WITH OUR WRITING. INCLUDED ARE LESSON PLANS, CLASS EXERCISES AND HOMEWORK: WITHIN EACH CHAPTER, THERE ARE CLASSROOM LESSONS, EXERCISES AND QUIZZES TO HELP THE WRITER UNDERSTAND THE IN-DEPTH PROBLEMS AND SITUATIONS ENCOUNTERED WHILE WRITING. THIS SHOULD HELP A WRITER EVEN A PROFESSIONAL WRITER TO KEEP HONING HIS/HER SKILLS.

EXERCISES: SOME EXERCISES ARE VERBAL, SOME ARE NOTES FOR THE BLACKBOARD. SOME ARE NOT TRADITIONAL IN STYLE OR FORMAT, SOME ARE 'IN AND OUT OF THE BOX' THINKING.

THE IDEA IS TO THINK, SMELL AND LIVE WRITING. WRITERS SHOULD NOT BE RESTRICTED BY SMALL TYPE AND BLACK AND WHITE PAGES. WE SHOULD INCLUDE OUR FREEDOMS TO USE MULTI-TEMPLATES, FONTS, COLORS, BORDERS AND NON-STANDARD WRITING STYLES.

CREATIVITY IS ONE OF OUR MAIN STRENGTHS. WE LIVE IN A WORLD OF SMALL TYPE, SAYING "DO NOT SHOUT" WITH CAPS. BULL HOCKEY! ORIGINAL PRINTINGS WERE ALL IN CAPITAL LETTERS. GRAB ANY AND ALL METHODS TO COMMUNICATE.

EXPERIENCE TEACHES US THAT WE LIVE IN A MULTI-DIMENSIONAL WORLD OF COLOR, SOUND AND THE SENSES; SO WHY DO WE WRITE IN ONE DIMENSION?

> **THIS BOOK USES ALL OF THE TYPE STYLES TO HELP YOU**
> **UNDERSTAND WHAT GOES TOGETHER AND WHAT IS IMPORTANT.**
>
> FONT CODES: TIMES NEW ROMAN-CAPITALS-TEXT BOOK
> FONT SIZE: 8 REGURLAR PARAGRAPHS
> FONT SIZE:14-16 CHAPTER TITLES.
> FONT: **BOLD FONT** AND <u>UNDERLINES</u>: IMPORTANT!
> FONT: *ITALICS: NEXT IN IMPORTANCE.*
> *'TERMS.'—SINGLE QUOTE MARKS.*
> "DIRECT QUOTES" –USE DOUBLE QUOTE MARKS
> CROSS-REFERENCES-BRACKETS: [CH].
> BOX OUTLINES: IMPORTANT GROUPINGS
> COLOR BLUE: CHAPTER TITLES & CLASS LESSONS

2.0.3.0. <u>WRITING</u>:
<u>6 W'S-WHO WHAT-WHY-WHEN-WHERE-WOW!</u>
DRAFTS-EDITING-REWRITES-STEP BY STEP PROCESS.

2.0.4.0. <u>ESSENTIALS YOU WILL LEARN:</u>
BASIC WRITING ESSENTIALS
BOOT CAMP BASICS-SENTENCES STRUCTURES
BASIC INDICES FOR REFERENCE
BOOK IDEAS
BOOKS-ORGANIZATION
BOOKS-DRAFTS
BRIDGES
CHARACTERS
CRITICISM-REJECTIONS
DIALOGUE
DRAMATIZATION
EDITORS & EDITING
INDICES-REFERENCE
GENRE'S
GETTING PUBLISHED
GLOSSARY
GRAMMAR
IDEA GROUPINGS
LANGUAGE
MANUSCRIPTS
MARKETING
MOVIE TITLES
PLOT
POINT OF VIEW
RESOURCES & WEB SOURCES
SETTINGS
SOURCE LIST
STACKING
STRUCTURE
SYNOPSES
SUBMISSIONS
THEORY-LITERARY
VILLAINS
WRITE FICTION
WRITE NON-FICTION

CREATIVE WRITING—THE KELLY MANUAL OF STYLE

WRITE RESEARCH
WRITERS-MASTERS
WRITERS ON WRITING
WRITING IN GENRE'S
WRITING EXERCISES
WRITING PROCESS
WRITING RESEARCH SOURCE LISTS
WRITING A BEST SELLER
**IF YOU ARE GOING TO WRITE, YOU MIGHT AS WELL BE THE BEST
WRITER YOU CAN BE. IMPROVING YOUR WRITING IS SOMETHING
YOU CAN DO YOUR ENTIRE LIFETIME.**

2.0. 4.1.-CLASS LESSON:
WRITE ONE TITLE, ONE SENTENCE ABOUT WHICH TYPE OF WRITING WE LIKE.
WRITE A PARAGRAPH ABOUT THIS IN DETAIL. WRITE THE CLOSER SENTENCE.

2.0.5.0. ---10 BASIC STEPS TO BEGINNING OUR WRITING:
WHITEBOARD: WRITE: DO THE WRITE THING!

2.0.5.1. WRITE: DO THE 'WRITE' THING!
PRACTICE: EVERY WORKING WRITER WILL TELL YOU THAT TO GET
BETTER AT WRITING, YOU JUST HAVE TO WRITE.

WRITE AS MUCH AND OFTEN AS YOU CAN: WRITE STORIES POEMS,
WRITING EXERCISES, ESSAYS, GRANTS, HISTORY, JOURNALISM, LETTERS,
MANUSCRIPTS, NEWS STORIES, PLAYS, POEMS, PROCEDURES, SHORT
STORIES, SPEECHES, RESUMES, TECHNICAL WRITING, INDICES,
RESEARCH, NEWS COPY, ADVERTISING, EDITORIALS,
... AD INFINITIUM!

***DO:THE W-4 RULE: WRITE—WRITE EVERYTHING-
WRITE WELL-WRITE WITH IMAGINATION!**

2.0.5.2. READING: TWO TYPES:
1. NEXT IN IMPORTANCE TO WRITING IS READING.
READ YOUR OWN MATERIAL **OUTLOUD.**
DID ITS SOUNDS FLOW SMOOTHLY? DID THE WORD CHOICE HELP ITS
UNDERSTANDING? MARK IT WITH CHECK MARK IF OKAY, OR MARK IT
"ADD" OR WRITE OUT A COMMENT IN THE RIGHT HAND MARGIN.

2.0.5.3. READING YOURS & OTHER AUTHORS:
READING OTHER AUTHORS ESPECIALLY THE "MASTERS" HAVE A
UNIQUE READING AND WRITING STYLE.
[SEE CH 28] WHICH DISSECTS KEY ATTRIBUTES OF THE MASTER WRITER?
CH 39 PUTS THESE ATTRIBUTES INTO ACTION FOR YOUR BESTSELLER.

THE IMPORTANCE OF READING IS HOW DID THESE WRITERS DO THEIR
WRITING? NOW READ IT ALOUD. DID SENTENCES AND PARAGRAPHS LINK
TOGETHER? DID THE THOUGHTS CONNECT? DID YOU UNDERSTAND
WHAT THE WRITER SAID? READING ALOUD LETS YOU HEAR AND FEEL
HIS WORDS. DID THE CHOICE OF WORDS FLOW MUSICALLY, STRONG,
WEAK, OR ERRATICALLY? DID THE VOWELS AND CONSONANTS REPEAT
FOR EFFECT?

CREATIVE WRITING—THE KELLY MANUAL OF STYLE

WHAT MECHANICS OR FIGURES OF SPEECH DID THE WRITER USE? DID
THEY HOLD YOUR ATTENTION? WHAT WAS NOTICEABLE: WORDS,
ACCENTS, DESCRIPTION, MOOD, TONE OR ATMOSPHERE? DID THE SCENE
AND DIALOGUE MATCH?

CHARACTERS: [CH 20].
HOW DID THEY MAKE THEIR CHARACTERS COME ALIVE WITH DIALOGUE,
SCENE AND DRAMATIZATION? DID THE CHARACTERS SEEM REAL, HAVE
A SENSE OF BELIEVABILITY, OR WAS THEIR ACTIONS OR REACTIONS
FITTING TO THE SCENE?

NOW, RE-WRITE YOUR DRAFT. WAS YOURS ANY BETTER? DIFFERENT?
THIS IS YOUR STYLE STARTING TO DEVELOP.

2.0.5.4. NOTHING IS OFF LIMITS TO YOUR WRITING:
OBSERVE PEOPLE AND PLACES. THEY REACT DIFFERENTLY IN A PARK,
OR DARK ALLEY, ON A TRAIN, OR CLIMBING A MOUNTAIN. HOW ABOUT
YOUR DAILY ROUTINE? WOULD YOU BE ABLE TO WRITE IT WITH
DETAIL?

OBSERVATION:
PAY ATTENTION TO THE THINGS AROUND YOU. OBSERVE THE WAY
THINGS LOOK, AND HOW THEIR APPEARANCE CAN CHANGE IN
DIFFERENT LIGHT. OBSERVE THE SOUNDS AND SMELLS AND FLAVORS
AROUND YOU. BE AWARE OF HOW MOOD CAN AFFECT WHICH DETAILS
YOU NOTICE. DO YOUR WRITING WITH ALL FIVE SENSES AND YOUR
INTELLECT AND IMAGINATION!

2.0.5.5. EXPERIENCE:
THINGS ARE EASIER TO WRITE ABOUT IF YOU HAVE EXPERIENCED THEM
OR CAN WRITE ABOUT THEM WITH EXPERIENCE. RESEARCHING PLACES,
BUILDINGS, AND MAPS ETC. IS WAY OF ADDING A NEW DIMENSION TO
YOUR PLOT OR SCENE/EVENT OR CHARACTER.

EXAMPLE:
IF YOUR CHARACTER IS RUNNING THROUGH A CAIRO MUSEUM AT
MIDNIGHT, WHAT WOULD HE SEE OR ENCOUNTER? THE USUAL MUMMY
CASES, GLASS DISPLAYS, LIGHT, DARK SPACES, SOUNDS, DARK GREEN
STATUES, TURN CORNERS, CLIMB WIDE STAIRS, PEER THROUGH
WINDOWS IN DAY OR NIGHT, OR CLIMB/DESCEND MULTIPLE FLOORS?
WOULD HE ESCAPE THROUGH A DOOR, A WINDOW, OR JUMP FROM A
BALCONY? ANSWER TO YOURSELF: THE 6 W'S: WHY WAS HE
THERE…SEARCHING FOR CLUES, MEETING WITH SOMEONE? DID IT ADD
TO THE PLOT OR WAS IT SOME SMALL ADVENTURE? KEEP IT RELEVANT.

IN MY EXAMPLE IT WAS LATE AT NIGHT, MEETING AN OLD FRIEND FOR
SECRET INFORMATION. HE WAS LATER IN THE CHAPTER KILLED IN THE
MUSEUM BESIDE THE DARK GREEN DIORITE STATUE OF RE' AND IN MY
ARMS. [THE MAIN CHARACTER'S SENSES AND EMOTIONS ARE
DRAMATIZED] AS THE BAD GUYS WERE CHARGING UP THE BROAD
STAIRS FIRING BULLETS BY THE BUCKET; THEN, HE ESCAPES INTO THE
NIGHT BY JUMPING FROM A SECOND STORY BALCONY. STILL, HE IS NOT
SAFE! HE HEADS TOWARDS HIS DESTINATION WITH THE CODEX HIDDEN
IN HIS BLACK ROBE. HIS HORSE IS…

2.0.5.5.1. HERE IS THE IDEA GROUP USED: HIS REASON FOR MEETING AT MUSEUM, TIME OF NIGHT, WHAT INFORMATION DOES THE **CODEX** PROVIDE, [ITS IMPLIED IMPORTANCE], WHY IS IT IMPORTANT, WHO ARE THE BAD GUYS AND THE DESCRIPTIONS. THE **DIALOGUE** SHOULD EXPLAIN THE EVENT (SCENE) AND ITS AFTERMATH (EMOTIONS AND FINAL DETERMINATION-MINI-CLIMAX?). HIS SUPPORTING CHARACTER WAS ALSO THERE. HIS HORSE'S RUNNING RHYTHM…HIS HEAD PUSHING INTO THE WIND, HIS HOOFS, HIS BREATHING, HIS TAIL, THE CHARACTER'S FACE, TEARS, MOTION AND HIS ROBE FLYING LIKE A
….

NOW, **WORD CHOICE AND DESCRIPTIONS** SHOULD EXPLAIN THE ACTION, THE DRAMA OF THE EVENT, THE EMOTIONS AND THE IMPACT OF THE TWO KEY EVENTS (THE KILLING AND BAD GUYS WANTING HIM DEAD). THEN, THE SLIGHTLY MINOR EVENT OF THE MUSEUM'S ROLE AS THE SCENE. (THE STATUE WAS PART OF THE CLUES USED TO SOLVE THE MYSTERY). WILL HE RETURN TO THE MUSEUM? DO SOMETHING IMPORTANT WITH THE CODEX? AND HOW WILL THIS SUPPORT THE PLOT OR THE FUTURE CLIMAX? (OUR **STORYTELLER'S SYNOPSIS** HAS THE PLOT AND CLIMAXES FIGURED OUT---WE ARE ADDING THE <u>DESCRIPTIVE</u> AND <u>SUPPORTING</u> INFORMATION AS WE WRITE.
THE FINAL CLIMAX OR TWIST OR EVEN CHARACTER MAY CHANGE IT ALL!

*DO: **DISSECT THAT CHAPTER:** YOU WOULD FIND ALL OF THE IDEA GROUPS, DESCRIPTIONS, ACTION, PLOT THEME, DRAMATIZATION AND DIALOGUE TO PROMOTE THE CONTINUATION OF THE STORY; THUS, **STORYTELLING** FIRST, THEN WRITING!

IS OUR STORYTELLING AND THE WRITING OF IT MISSING SOMETHING? WAS IT PICTURESQUE? WERE WE VAGUE? DID THE READER GET IT? … DO A COMPUTER 'SAVE' AND ADD THOSE THOUGHTS NOW AND ADD MORE DETAIL LATER.

2.0.5.6. RESEARCH: [REFER CH 34]
WRITING WHAT YOU KNOW IS GOOD ADVICE.
WRITE USING ANY METHOD OR WRITING DEVICE…LETTERS, NEWS PAPER HEADLINES, POEMS, MUSIC <u>WITHIN</u> YOUR WRITING…USE ANY DEVICE TO HELP YOUR PLOT AND CHARACTER; THUS HELP YOUR **STORYTELLING** BE BELIEVABLE TO YOUR READER.

RESEARCH IS ANOTHER; BUT DON'T JUST RESEARCH THE NEXT THING YOU WANT TO WRITE ABOUT--RESEARCH ANYTHING THAT INTERESTS YOU. YOU NEVER KNOW WHERE YOU MIGHT FIND THAT TRULY GREAT STORY IDEA. BUILD UPON THAT **'IDEA LISTING'** AND **IDEA GROUPS** WITHIN. **[REFER CH 5.0.0.0.]**

2.0.5.7. VOCABULARY-GLOSSARIES:
EXPAND YOUR WRITING SKILLS BY EXPANDING YOUR VOCABULARY. BECOME COMFORTABLE WITH YOUR VOCABULARY; BUT DON'T NEGLECT ORDINARY WORDS. BUILD UPON THESE. DON'T BE AFRAID TO USE TERMS AND FOREIGN LANGUAGE PHRASES. HOWEVER, EXPLAIN TERMS IN BRACKETS, OR EXPLANATORY SENTENCES. IF A HEAVY USE OF TERMS IS USED, PROVIDE A GLOSSARY INDEX IN THE REAR OF THE BOOK.

(YES, EVEN IN FICTION). *EXAMPLE:* ABBREVIATIONS, MILITARY TERMS, CHINESE OR OTHER LANGUAGES, TECHNOLOGY TERMS, GEOGRAPHICAL TERMS AND SCIENCE TERMS. USE THE APPROPRIATE SYNONYM OR ANTONYM WHEN CHOOSING WORDS FOR YOUR CHARACTER; MAKE IT APPLICABLE.

- ***DO: SEE WRITING–EDITING-PUBLISHER GLOSSARIES IN THE INDICES AT THE REAR OF THE BOOK.***

NOTE: THE ABBREVIATED CHARACTER LIST IS ALWAYS IN THE BOOK FRONT. YOU MAY INCLUDE A MORE DETAILED INDEX IN THE REAR.

2.0.5.9. DO PLAY TO DEVELOP A CREATIVE SIDE: [CH 3]

WRITE SOME THINGS FOR FUN THAT AREN'T MEANT FOR AN AUDIENCE. TRY OUT ALL THOSE NEW WORDS YOU'VE BEEN LEARNING, SEE HOW FAR YOU CAN TWIST GRAMMAR WITHOUT MANGLING IT BEYOND RECOGNITION, OR DEFINITELY TRY OUT A NEW FIGURE OF SPEECH. EXPERIMENT WITH DIALOGUE AND DRAMATIZATION, THESE ARE KEY TO THE CREATIVE PIECES YOU NEED. ADD A NEW FORMAT TO YOUR PRESENT WRITING: ADD A LETTER, A NEWS HEADLINE, AND A POEM OR ADD A MYSTERY ELEMENT, A CLUE OR PERSON. ***TRY SHOWING NOT TELLING.***

TRY A NEW FORM OF **POETRY** (EVER WRITTEN A SESTINA?) OR MAKE UP YOU OWN. ADD A *GROUPING OF WORDS THAT REPEAT A SOUND* OR VOWEL TO ADD MORE INTERESTING DESCRIPTIONS TO PLACES AND BUILDINGS WHILE WRITING FICTION..

'PLAY' IS WHEN DISCOVERIES AND IMPROVEMENTS ARE MADE. COLLECT OR WRITE EXAMPLES OF AN ITEM YOU WOULD LIKE TO LEARN OR ADD TO YOUR WRITING.

2.0.5.10 READ ALOUD: [STORYTELLING] [SEE CH 6].

A REALLY GOOD WAY TO FIGURE OUT HOW THE WORDS ARE FLOWING IS TO READ SOMETHING OUTLOUD. MOST 'OUTLOUD' READERS READ TO THEMSELVES IN THEIR 'EDIT SPACE' OR WHEN '**RE-WRITES**' ARE BEING DONE ON THEIR COMPUTER.

USE OF SOUND IN YOUR WRITING [CH 19].

WE TALK ABOUT THE **"SOUND"** OF WORDS ON A PAGE. IF YOU STUMBLE OVER THE WORDS WHEN READING OUT
LOUD, YOUR READERS WILL PROBABLY STUMBLE TOO. PLUS, YOU'LL NOTICE THINGS LIKE '**ALLITERATION**'
WHICH ARE REPETITIVE CONSONANT SOUNDS THAT YOU MIGHT MISS OTHERWISE? '**ASSONANCE**' IS THE REPETITIVE SOUNDS OF INTERNAL VOWELS OF NEIGHBORING WORDS. OR FIGURES OF SPEECH AS **PARALANGUAGE**: WHICH USES PITCH, HUSKINESS, LOUDNESS ASSOCIATED WITH MOOD, TEMPER, ACTION, ATTITUDE AND PERSONALITY. **USE THESE SOUND WORDS WHEN WRITING FICTION.**

DO INCLUDE POETIC VERSE AND REPETITIVE WORDS. THE **POETIC PRINCIPLE** ALLOWS YOU TO TIE SOUNDS WITH THOUGHTS AND MEANINGS, WITH EMPHASIS ON SOUNDS,
LEARN TO USE **FIGURES OF SPEECH** AND ADD DEPTH TO YOUR WRITING. SEE CH 23- FIGURES OF SPEECH.

2.0.5.11. *DO: EDIT/ REWRITE-OVER & OVER**. [SEE CH 31].
THE TRUE ART IS IN THE **EDITING**.
 CREATE AND USE AN '**EDITING CHECK LIST.**' USE ONLY ONE OR TWO OF
THESE FOR EACH EDITING TIME PERIOD. YOU WILL EDIT MULTIPLE TIMES
SO DON'T SWEAT PERFECTION OR TRY TO PERFORM MULTI-TASKING ALL
AT ONCE. EXPERIENCE TEACHES US TO FIRST BE CONCERNED WITH
SPEECH, SOUNDS, POINT OF VIEW AND VERB TENSE. BE CAREFUL OF 'IS'
AND 'WAS'-PRESENT AND PAST TENSE. ON FIRST DRAFTS, CHECK FOR
'IDEA GROUPS' ---WAS ALL OF THEM INCLUDED. TRY TO CAPTURE ALL
THE CHAPTER 'IDEAS' IN YOUR OPENING, CLOSING AND SUPPORTING
PARAGRAPHS.

2.0.6.0. THE BASICS:
DON'T GET TOO CRITICAL AT THIS POINT OR WORRY IT'S NOT PERFECT;
JUST GET THE BASICS DOWN IN WRITING. YOUR BOOK IS STILL A <u>DRAFT
VERSION</u>.

**THE CREATIVE PROCESS IS EVOLUTIONARY. IT MAY TAKE 30
EDITS AND RE-WRITES TO GET YOUR BOOK READY FOR THE
PUBLISHER.**

2.0.7.0. INSPIRATIONAL IDEAS:[CH 5]
WITH EACH READING THEN EDITING AND RE-WRITE WE MAKE IT MORE
COMPLETE. INCLUDE THOSE 'INTUITIVE' IDEAS WE RECEIVE AS WE
PERFORM THESE TASKS. ACCEPT THEM AS NATURAL TO THE CREATIVE
PROCESS. WHILE A FIRST DRAFT MAY HAVE GREAT ENERGY, ACTION OR
EMOTION; IT WILL ALSO HAVE LOTS OF MISTAKES: BAD WORD CHOICES,
TYPOS, GRAMMATICAL ERRORS AND WRONG VERB TENSES THAT NEED
FIXING. EDITING IS MORE THAN THAT!

EXAMPLES: PERHAPS YOU USED THE SAME PHRASE TOO OFTEN OR
YOUR WORDING GIVES TOO MUCH AWAY OR A POOR CHOICE OF WORDS
DEFLECTS THE THOUGHT PROCESS. PERHAPS, WE SPOIL THE SUSPENSE
OR IT ISN'T CLEAR ENOUGH. SOMETIMES THE CORE OF A STORY IS GOOD;
BUT THE ENTIRE STRUCTURE NEEDS TO BE REDONE. ALL OF US WRITERS
DO NEED TO ADD BETTER FIGURES OF SPEECH, DIALOGUE, SCENES,
SETTINGS AND DRAMATIZATION TO OUR PARAGRAPHS. ONLY THEN,
WILL OUR CHAPTERS TAKE ON A WHOLE NEW MEANING FOR THE
READER. IT'S LIKE MUDDY WATER IN THE BEGINNING AND LATER
EVOLVING INTO A FINE CHAMPAGNE WINE WITH BUBBLES TO TICKLE
OUR READER'S MIND.

2.0.8.0. 'KELLY STYLE' IS ABOUT LEARNING SO MANY LITERARY AND
GRAMMATICAL THINGS AND YET MOST IMPORTANTLY GIVE OUR
WRITING "LIFE." YES, THAT "CREATIVE PROCESS" THAT IS SO ELUSIVE TO
MANY WRITERS AND PUBLISHERS. WRITING <u>IS</u> AN EVOLUTIONARY AND
YET, A VERY CREATIVE ART FORM!

YOU ARE NOW ON A PATH TO GREAT WRITING!
THE JOURNEY BEGINS! [CH 3].

2.0.9.0. CLASSROOM LESSON 4:
WHAT IS CREATIVE WRITING TO ME?
WHAT WRITING SKILLS DO I NEED TO IMPROVE UPON?

HAVE I DONE THESE 10 THINGS WHEN WRITING?
HAVE I READ OUT-LOUD MY WORK?
DO MY SENTENCE STRUCTURES OR PARAGRAPHS NEED WORK?
DO THEY ILLUMINATE THE READER?
IS MY WRITING FUN?
DO YOU HAVE AND USE AN IDEA LIST?
HAVE YOU TRIED OTHER TYPES OF WRITING?
STYLES? COLORS? FORMATS? IDEAS?

2.0.9.1. COMPLETE THIS: WRITING IS THE 3-W'S?

2.0.10.0. WRITING IS THE 3 WHAT'S:

I WRITE WHAT I LIKE,
WRITE WHAT I KNOW AND
WRITE WHAT MY READER WANTS TO KNOW.

IMPORTANT:

*DO: COMPLETE THE STORYTELLER, THE DETAILED AND CHAPTER BY CHAPTER SYNOPSIS BEFORE WRITING YOUR BOOK.

THIS KEEPS YOUR FOCUS AND ALLOWS THE CREATIVE PROCESS TO KICK IN.

2.1.0.0. OUR PROGRESS:
1. WE LEARNED THAT 'TO DO PLAN' HELP US ORGANIZE ALL THE TASKS .
[CH 2.]

2. THE KELLY PROCESS IS EXPLAINED. [PAGE 11.]

3. WE REVIEWED THE KEY ELEMENTS TO WRITING AND-ESSENTIALS YOU
*   WILL LEARN AS WE PROGRESS.[CH 2.0.4.0.]*

4. THE 10 BASIC STEPS TO WRITING ARE EXPLAINED[CH 2.0.5.0.]

5. WE COMPLETED THE WRITING TASKS.[CH 2.1.0.0.]

BOOK TITLE?
IF YOU HAVE A TITLE AT THIS POINT, TRY RESEARCHING IT ON THE
INTERNET, WHILE TITLES ARE NOT COPYRIGHTED, YOU MAY WANT TO
CHANGE IT OR WAIT UNTIL THE BOOK DRAFT IS COMPLETE. REVIEW
CHAPTERS 53 AND 54. YOU MANY ALSO ADD A SECOND TAG LINE
TO FURTHER DEFINE YOUR TITLE.
e.g. I CHANGED THIS BOOK TITLE TO INCLUDE YEAR AND A NEW LOGO.
e.g. PAPER SOLDIERS HAD A LOT OF USE, SO I DEFINED IT WITH
    "THE WAR WRITERS."
THUS, 'PAPER SOLDIERS-THE WAR WRITERS.'

CHAPTER 3
3.0.0.0. THE CREATIVE PROCESS:
CHAPTER TOPICS: *POP QUIZ-WRITING VERSUS STORYTELLING-COST OF WRITING-YOU THE WRITER- THE READER- YOUR FAVORITE AUTHOR..*

3.0.2.0. LET'S EXPLORE CREATIVITY:
CREATIVITY IS A NEBULOUS AREA. IT ALMOST BLENDS WITH STYLE. CREATIVITY IS THE ORIGINAL THOUGHT COMING TO MIND, OR FROM OUR IDEA LISTS OR "OUT OF THE BLUE."

CREATIVITY MARRIES WITH THE GRAND MASTER'S STYLE [CH 28] TO PROVIDE A UNIQUE AND CREATIVE WRITING STYLE. CREATIVITY IS THE KERNEL OF OUR STORY AND ITS PATH TO CONCLUSION. WE ALL HAVE IT. WE JUST NEED TO DEVELOP IT FURTHER.

3.0.0.0. WHITEBOARD: THE NAME OF THIS CLASS IS?
WHITEBOARD: WRITE WELL? COMMUNICATE WELL?

3.0.2.1. ORIGINAL THOUGHTS:
I OFTEN WONDER WHERE THE ORIGINAL THOUGHTS COME FROM?
MY OVERWORKED MIND?
THE SUB-CONSCIOUS?
FROM EXPERIENCING LIFE?
FROM OTHER IDEAS?
FROM CONVERSATIONS?
FROM OBSERVATIONS?
FROM "DIVINE THOUGHTS"
FROM OTHER AUTHORS AND BOOKS?
FROM MOVIES?
FROM ENVIRONMENT?
FROM OTHER PEOPLE?
FROM TRAVEL?
FROM RESEARCH?
FROM ANALYSIS?
FROM OUT OF THE BLUE?
FROM LISTS?
FROM IDEA GROUPS?
FROM STORIES I HEARD?
FROM SCHOOLS?
FROM TEACHERS?

YOUR ANSWER?_____?
MY ANSWER: ALL OF THESE AND MORE.

I LEARNED, EXPERIENCED LIFE AND TRAVELLED ENOUGH TO RECOGNIZE AN IDEA, ALTHOUGH ORIGINALLY MINE OR NOT.

I HAD TO PRACTICE WRITING THEM DOWN ON SLIPS OF PAPER, IN MY COMPUTER, IN JOURNALS AND ON NAPKINS.
I LEARNED THAT MY MIND , THOUGH TRYING TO CONTAIN THOUSANDS OF PIECES OF INFORMATION WAS OVERTAXED AND OFTEN I FORGOT **THE INSPIRATION OR KERNEL OF THE IDEA**.

IT WAS LIKE TRYING TO REMEMBER DREAMS!

SO NOW I WRITE IT DOWN, WHEN FLASHES OF SOMETHING HIT ME. THE KEY IS TO RECOGNIZE IT AND WRITE IT DOWN.

FOR EXAMPLE, I AM DOING RESEARCH…DIGGING IN INDICES, LIBRARY LISTS, TABLE OF CONTENTS, SUBJECT INDEXES, OR BOOK TITLES OR ON THE INTERNET. ANOTHER SUBJECT COMES TO MIND…I WRITE IT DOWN, EVEN THOUGH IT WAS NOT RELATED.

OVER TIME, YOU WILL GATHER MORE OF THESE "IDEAS," "FACTS," "INSPIRATIONS" "LISTS" AND OTHER ONE WORD OR TWO WORD CLUES… ALL OF THESE:

DO: WRITE THESE ON YOUR IDEAS LISTS.

OVER TIME, YOUR IDEA LISTS WILL GROW.
WHAT IS A COUPLE HUNDRED OF "IDEAS" WHEN THERE IS SEVERAL MILLION SUBJECTS OR TOPICS OUT THERE.
DO KEEP ADDING THEM OVER TIME AND KEEP THEM UPDATED.

3.0.2.2. HOW I ORGANIZE IT: [CH 33].
1. MS WORD SOFTWARE HELPS ME CATEGORIZE MY "IDEAS LIST" BY SUBJECT OR MAIN CATEGORIES. I PERSONALIZE IT AND ALPHABETIZE IT .

2. DO: CREATE A RESEARCH LIST. [CH 34].
USE YOUR RESEARCH TO DESCRIBE AND ILLUMINATE YOUR PARAGRAPHS. KEEP IT RELATED NOT JUST FILLER WORDS.

3. DO: CREAT A NEW SOURCE LIST: [CH 34].
ALL OF THIS IS WHY I HAD TO CREATE A NEW TYPE OF SOURCE LIST. THE OLD" STYLE BIBLIOGRAPHY" AND SUBJECT LIST DID NOT WORK.

4. IDEAS-SUMMARY: [REFER TO BOOKS: CH 5- OR MOVIES: CH 41 .
I LIKE TO THINK IDEAS ARE A CHAIN OF INFORMATION, THE WRITER MUST DEVELOP AND USE IN HIS WRITING. THE CREATIVITY PART IS CONNECTING IT TO OUR WRITING. WE EMPLOY THEM IN OUR SENTENCES, FIGURES OF SPEECH AND IN THE LANDSCAPE OF PLOTS AND EVENTS. DOING THAT IS OUR CREATIVITY!
3.3.0.0. OUR PROGRESS:
1. WE LEARNED TO USE OTHER SOURCES- INTERNET SEARCHES-AN IDEAS LIST- OBSERVATIONS-LIFE'S EXPERIENCES. [CH 34].

2. WE DO RESEARCH TOPICS AND PLACES FOR OUR BOOK..[CH34].

3. WE CREATED NEW LISTS TO HELP WITH CREATIVITY. [CHS 5-41].

4. WE BEGIN TO WRITE A SOURCE LIST. [CH 34]

CHAPTER 4

4.0.0.0. THE NEW KELLY WRITING STYLE:

THE WRITING PROCESS CONSISTS OF SO MANY STEPS, TERMS, WHAT IS ALLOWED BY THE THEORISTS...THE AP, CHICAGO, THE MLA RULES, OR ORGANIZATIONAL REQUIREMENTS AND FINALLY WHAT THE EDITOR AND PUBLISHER WANTS. CONFUSING...?

(PAUSE)   AH! HA!

THEN MARKETING HAS ANOTHER SET OF RULES.

THE WRITING PROCESS IS ONLY ABOUT THE WRITER CONNECTING TO THE READER WITH HIS STORYTELLING.

THAT IS THE "AH! HA!" YOU SEEK. IT IS THE HOLY GRAIL FOR WRITING!

4.0.1.0. THE WRITING PROCESS BEGINS:

4.0.0.1. *DO : WRITE A STORYTELLER'S SYNOPSIS; [CHAPTER 7]. *
CAN YOU TELL SOMEONE WHAT IT IS ABOUT? STORY-TELL IT OUT-LOUD! NOW WRITE IT AS YOU TOLD IT.

4.0.0.2.* DO START A DETAILED SYNOPSIS [CH 8]. AND A
         CHAPTER BY CHAPTER TOPIC SYNOPSIS [CH 9].*

4.0.0.3. TO CAPTURE THE **KERNEL** OF THE YOUR BOOK IDEA, THE TITLE
         OR THE SCENE OR DIALOGUE WE WANT. WE WILL IMPROVE
         ON ALL OF THESE AS WE GO ALONG. KEEP IT SIMPLE!
         START WITH THE OPENING SENTENCE-VERY IMPORTANT
         TO A STORY'S TONE.

4.0.0.3. USE THE CREATIVE POWERS YOU HAVE TO SUPPLEMENT THIS.
KEEP IN MIND YOUR WRITING IS A ROUGH DRAFT, SO IT IS NOT PERFECT AT THIS STAGE.

4.0.0.4. *DO: WRITE THE TITLE PAGE, A DRAFT AND YOUR NAME AS
AUTHOR. (SMILE!). NO! NOT AN AUTHOR YET!

40.0.5. *DO: SET UP YOUR PAGE AS A BOOK IN WORD, USE THE CORRECT
MARGINS FOR A 6X9 NOVEL. REFER TO SET UP INSTRUCTIONS IN PUBLISHING FORMATS. [CH 13].

4.0.0.6. *DO: CREATE A SOURCE LIST: [REFER CH 34].

DO COLLECT REFERENCE DATA ON THE PLACE, PERSONS, OR FACTS LIKE DATES OR HISTORY, START THE SOURCE DATA LIST # PROCESS.

NOTE: THIS IS NOT A BIBLIOGRAPHY FORMAT.

EXAMPLE: A BIBLIOGRAPHY FORMAT IS NOT A WORKABLE FORMAT IN FICTION TO LOCATE INFORMATION **QUICKLY**. GRAB A BOOK AND TRY TO FIND A SUBJECT OR PIECE OF DATA QUICKLY.

USING OUR SOURCE LIST WE HAVE ADDED A KEY WORD OR SEVERAL KEY WORDS TO FIND WHAT THE ARTICLE OR BOOK IS ABOUT. THUS

CREATIVE WRITING—THE KELLY MANUAL OF STYLE

CREATING A GROUPING. THE SOURCE MATERIAL IS THUS GROUPED BY NUMBERING IT 1 TO 100.

FOR FICTION, THIS IS AN EXPEDIENT METHOD.
OF COURSE YOU COULD CREATE A SPREADSHEET WITH KEY WORDS AND DO A "SEARCH" FUNCTION TO LOCATE THE KEY WORD.

4.0.1.7. **DO NOT WRITE AN OUTLINE. **
CREATIVITY IS STIFLED BY TRYING TO MAKE IT FIT A HIGH SCHOOL FRAMEWORK. OUTLINES DO WORK FOR HIGHLY STRUCTURED WORKS LIKE A TECHNICAL WORK.

FOR FICTION, AN OUTLINE IS REPLACED BY A SYNOPSIS. YOU ARE TRYING TO GUIDE YOUR WORK ON SEVERAL LEVELS AT ONCE. CHARACTER, SCENE, DIALOGUE, PLOT, CLIMAXES AND CONTINUITY BETWEEN CHAPTERS. A SYNOPSIS ALLOW YOU TO CHANGE THE DIRECTION FOR PLOT TWISTS AND YOUR NEW STYLE.

FOLLOWING AN OUTLINE, MIGHT MAKE YOUR WRITING A COOKIE CUTTER AFFAIR; THUS, LIKE EVERYONE ELSE'S.

---

*DO A COMPARE WITH AN OUTLINE VERSUS A SYNOPSIS:

4.0.1.7.1. HERE IS THE TEST FOR AN OUTLINE: COMPARE THE OUTLINE TO THE STORYTELLER'S SYNOPSIS. DID YOU GET ALL OF THE ELEMENTS NEEDED FOR YOUR BOOK IN THE OUTLINE? ARE YOUR OUTLINE STORIES CREATIVE? HOW DID DIALOGUE, PLOTS, CLIMAXES FARE? DID YOU GET THE SIX W'S?

NOW, GO TO CHAPTER 7 AND WRITE A STORYTELLER'S SYNOPSIS.

HOW DID YOUR RESULT WORK OUT? DID THE SYNOPSIS GIVE YOU THE CREATIVITY YOU WERE MISSING?

TRY TO CAPTURE IN WORDS AND PICTURE WORDS THE STORY. THEY CAN ALWAYS BE EDITED OR COPY PASTED. EDIT LATER. GET A FIRST DRAFT WRITTEN DOWN.

THEN **TRY WRITING YOUR THREE SYNOPSES** AND UPDATING THEM AS YOU GO ALONG. IF YOU ARE STUCK OR YOUR WRITING GETS LOST, GO BACK TO THE SYNOPSES TO SEE WHERE IT WENT OFF TRACK.

DOUBLE CHECK YOUR **TIMELINE**…DOES IT MATCH YOUR SYNOPSIS? THESE WERE NOT SUGGESTED AS A WRITER'S WORK EXERCISE BUT RATHER AS GUIDES TO KEEP YOUR BOOK MOVING AHEAD. DOES YOUR READER SENSE YOUR LOSS? YOUR WRITING SKILLS AND CREATIVITY COME TO A CROSS ROADS HERE. WHEN CHAPTERS SEEM TO END ABRUPTLY, WE CLOSE THE BOOK, RATHER THAN PROVIDE A CONTINUATION TO THE READER. **WE NEED A BRIDGE OVER THESE STOPS OR GAPS IN YOUR WRITING.** PERHAPS A RETURN TO THE PLOT LINE OR TIMELINE WILL GIVE YOU A CLUE WHAT IS WRONG. *TIME FOR THINKING IS PARAMOUNT AT THIS POINT AS THIS MIGHT CHANGE THE TONE OR DIRECTION WHERE OUR STORY IS HEADED. MMMMM!* THINK ABOUT THE READER…IS HIS EXPECTATIONS DIFFERENT OR CAN WE GIVE

HIM AN ALTERNATIVE? EDITING THE LAST BIT? CHANGE DAY TO NIGHT OR SCENE? TAKE A PLANE INSTEAD OF A TRAIN? ADD A CHARACTER? OR INTRODUCE A DIFFERENT CIRCUMSTANCE OR EVENT?

4.0.1.8. *** DO:** **SET UP THE BASICS**: A COPYRIGHT PAGE, A TABLE OF CONTENTS, THINK ABOUT CHAPTER TITLES, MAKE A LIST. A DEDICATION PAGE ETC. PUT IN ORDER IN YOUR DRAFT COMPUTER FILE. [REVIEW CH 13].

4.0.1.9. **ROUGH DRAFT:** [CH 29-30].
YOU DON'T HAVE A BOOK YET, JUST A ROUGH DRAFT… SO KEEP WRITING. LATER THIS WILL BECOME A MANUSCRIPT .

4.0.1.10. **DEVELOP A CHARACTER LIST:** [CH 20] AND EMBELLISH IT. THINK ABOUT THE TWO SUPPORTING CHARACTERS FOR EACH MAIN CHARACTER. ADD THEM TO LIST. WHAT DOES THE READER SEE IN THE CHARACTER? CHARACTER TRAITS, FEELINGS, IS HE THE GOOD GUY OR THE VILLAIN?

4.0.1.11. **THINK ABOUT THE PLOT,** [CH 21] THE 6 W'S… WRITE THEM DOWN. THINK ABOUT THE GENRE…IS IT FICTION, A MYSTERY, AND A THRILLER, SCI-FI OR HISTORICAL.

4.0.1.12. IF YOU KNOW THE STORYLINE OR BEGINNING, MIDDLE OR END, EMBELLISH THE SUMMARY SYNOPSIS BY DOING A 'SAVE AS" COPY FOR THE 'STORYTELLER'S SYNOPSIS COPY.]

[REFER CH 12] ADD THIS AND DATES TO SYNOPSIS… A PERIOD IN TIME. IF TIME HAS A BEARING ON THE PLOT, WRITE OUT A TIMELINE. [CH 26].

4.0.1.13. **PLACE AND SCENE:** [CH 25] WHERE DID THIS *MAJOR EVENT* HAPPEN? CAN YOU DESCRIBE IT IN DETAIL… STREET NAMES, COBBLESTONE, ARCHITECTURE OR FASCINATING FACTS. EMBELLISH IT. MAYBE DO RESEARCH OR REVIEW TRAVEL GUIDES AND MAPS AND INCREASED READING TO KNOW THE FACTS IF THEY APPLY TO YOUR STORY OR SCENE.

4.0.1.14. BASIC ELEMENTS:
DRAW FROM THESE SUPPORTING BASIC ELEMENTS TO WRITE FROM. ASK YOURSELF, WHAT DOES THE READER SEE OF MY CHARACTER, THE PLACE, THE SCENE (EVENTS) CONFLICT AND DIALOGUE?

4.0.1.15. **THINK ABOUT GENRE** *[SEE CH 1.0.4.0.0. ON GENRE']*. IS IT FICTION AND A MURDER MYSTERY? IS IT A CHILDREN'S BOOK? A ROMANCE? THESE REQUIRE ADDITIONAL ELEMENTS TO THE BASIC BOOK.

4.0.1.16. THINK 4 DIMENSIONALLY:
SPACE-TIME-PAST-NOW-FUTURE-COLORS-SENSES-EMOTIONS- THINK LARGER THAN THE ONE DIMENSIONAL WORDS. CHARGE UP! SLAY THE ONE WORD DRAGON!

CREATIVE WRITING—THE KELLY MANUAL OF STYLE

4.0.1.17. COLOR?
DOES A PICTURE STIMULATE THE PROCESS?
EXAMPLE:WILL COLOR WORDS ADD TO THE DIMENSION OF THE OBJECT
WORDS? E.G. USE WORD 'BLOOD.' NOW USE THE PHRASE: "COPPER
SMELLING, DARK CRIMSON ESCAPING BLOOD?"

A HIGH LEVEL COLOR WOULD BE "LIFE POURED UPON THE SIDEWALK.
A DEEPER LEVEL COLOR WOULD BE: 'BILLIE JOE'S LIFE POURED UPON
THE SIDEWALKIN CRIMSON COLOR.

4.0.1.18. SYMBOLS?
MURDER WEAPON? CODE WORDS, HIDDEN SECRETS FROM READER, FIVE
SENSES, GEOGRAPHY? BANK HEIST? TREASURE MAP? WHAT THOUGHTS
DO WE WANT CHARACTER OR READER TO THINK?

DID THE READER FEEL THE BANG? - BANG? AS HIS YOUNG LIFE SEEPED
INTO THE NIGHT DESERT SAND!

HIS PAIN AND CONFLICT FINALIZED IN A MOMENT OR TWO OF SHOCK
AND THE FINAL RELEASE.   {CONTINUE WITH YOUR NEXT SENTENCE}.

4.0.1.19. WHAT TRAGEDY WILL TEST THE MAIN CHARACTER?
[CH 20-21] WILL THEY DIE, LIVE HAPPILY? BE CHANGED? DEATH-
SORROW-LOVE-FAILURE? USE COMEDY AND TRAGEDY AS POWERFUL
COMPARISONS. CONTRAST YOUR CHARACTER AND VILLIAN.

4.0.1.20. WHAT ROLE WILL SUPPORTING CHARACTER PROVIDE TO MAIN CHARACTER? BEST FRIEND, LOVE INTEREST? FAMILY?
AUTHORITY FIGURES? THE POLICE? THE GOVERNMENT? SPIES? THIEVES?
VICTIM? WHAT SORT ARE THEY? [CH 20].

4.0.1.21. WHAT MAKES MY BOOK UNIQUE?
THE STORY? NEW FACTS? TWISTS? WHY DOES MY READER WANT TO
READ THIS? DOES OPENING PAGE IN BOOK WANT HIM TO READ MORE?
COMPELLING STORY? LANGUAGE? PLACES? DIALOGUE? THE ENDING? IS
IT SATISFYING OR A CLIFF HANGER? IS IT MARKETABLE?

4.0.1.22. ORGANIZATION: [CH29-33].
PREPARE MY WORKSPACE, MY TOOLS, MY COMPUTER, MY FILES, ETC.
THEN, PREPARE MY NECESSITIES: OFFICE SUPPLIES, EQUIPMENT, COPIES,
BOOK SHELVES, CARDBOARD BOX. A DIFFERENT PLACE TO EDIT.
PREPARE MY COMPUTER ORGANIZATION: MASTER BOOKS, TITLE FILES,
MY IDEA FILE, FILES OR EACH CHARACTER, TABLE OF CONTENTS ETC.
[CH 33].

4.0.1. 23. WRITE, WRITE, WRITE. [CH 4].
DON'T SWEAT THE SMALL STUFF, JUST WRITE IT, EITHER LONG HAND OR
BY COMPUTER. TYPE IT INTO THE BOOK FORMAT. DO NOT EDIT.

4.0.1.24. EDIT-EDIT-PROOFREAD! [CH 31-36].
(SEE CHAPTER 11 ON EDITING AND PROOF SYMBOLS)
ONLY, REPEAT ONLY WHEN YOU HAVE WRITTEN THE DRAFT, BEGIN
PUNCTUATION, CHOSE WORDS CAREFULLY, AND ADD TO IT.

4.0. 1.25.0. **DO NOT DELETE ANYTHING, YET. CAREFULLY CHOSEN PROSE MAY BE USED ELSE WHERE OR EXPOUNDED UPON. MOVE IT TO BOTTOM OF CHAPTER OR CREATE A PAGE CALLED "OVERFLOW." MARK WITH A "D" = DELETE SYMBOL, A CURSIVE "E."=EDIT .

4.0.1.26.DO: WRITE THE CHAPTER BY CHAPTER   TOPICS:

IF YOU GET OFF TOPIC IN CHAPTER: **WRITE TOPICS** AT THE TOP OF EACH CHAPTER, THUS HELPING TO ORGANIZE WHAT THE CHAPTER SHOULD CONTAIN. [CH 9].

4.0.1. 27. MOVE FORWARD IN THE PROCESS, FROM WRITING TO EDITING, TO DIALOGUE IMPROVEMENT, SPELLING WORD CHOICE . DO THIS OVER AND OVER UNTIL YOU CAN READ IT OUTLOUD.

4.0.1. 28. COMPLETE EACH CHAPTER.
DO THEY FLOW TOGETHER? DO PARAGRAPHS FLOW TOGETHER; THUS THE CONTINUITY OF THE STORY MOVES ALONG.

4.0.1.29. FINISH FIRST BOOK ROUGH DRAFT. [CH 31].
DOES IT "SOUND" COMPLETE?
WHAT IS MISSING? IS IT PREDICTABLE? CHANGE IT.
EDIT IT. MOVE IT, ADD MORE OR EDIT OUT WHAT DOESN'T MAKE SENSE.
DOES THE BASICS APPEAR COMPLETE?
WHAT WILL MAKE IT BETTER? IS ANYTHING MISSING?

4.0.1.30 DOES THE READER GET IT?
THE AH HA! DOES HE EMPATHIZE? FEEL THE EMOTIONS WITHIN THE BOOK? DOES PARTS OF IT MAKE HIM THE OBSERVER OR THE PARTICIPANT? DO THE ACTION SCENES MAKE HIM TENSE, PROUD, OR HATE? TAKE ACTION, ACT OUT? RELATE? AGAIN DIFFERENT EMOTIONS AND SENSES ON EDGE?

A GREAT BOOK DRAWS THE READER INTO THE STORY!

4.0.1.31. DO ALL THE LITERARY PARTS FIT TOGETHER?
[CH 15-19].
DO OUR SIMILES, METAPHORS MAKE SENSE? DO WE ENLIGHTEN? DO WE MAKE HIM THINK DIFFERENTLY? DO OUR PLACES AND EVENTS CAUSE HIM TO THINK DIFFERENTLY OR JUST INFORM HIM? DO ANY OF THE THEORIES LESSONS LEARNED HELP OUR FIT? DOES OUR PLOT, VOICE, POINT OF VIEW AND MOSTLY DIALOGUE CREATE THE MASTER PIECE WE WANT.

I F NOT, CHANGE IT, WRITE NEW, AND WRITE MORE!
CHALLENGE OURSELVES TO WRITE BETTER, MORE IN DEPTH AND WITH CONVICTION. [SEE CH 30 FOR 7 WRITING TOOLS].

4.0.1.32. LAST, WRITE WITH PASSION.
WRITE WITH A GOOD UNDERSTANDING OF OUR CHARACTER, OUR READER AND LASTLY OUR EDITOR AND PUBLISHER. FOLLOW THE LESSONS AND EXAMPLES FOR IMPROVEMENT. READ THE GREAT MASTER WRITERS... WHAT MADE THEM GREAT?

4.0.1.33
BECOME THE MASTER WRITER:
YOU WILL FIND A GREAT STORYTELLER, A WORTH WHILE PLOT; BUT ALWAYS GREAT DIALOGUE, WORDS, ACTIONS, EVENTS AND MEMORABLE CHARACTERS BRING THESE BOOKS TO LIFE. <u>AS ALWAYS, THE READER HAS THE LAST LAUGH!</u>

WE WRITE, WRITE, SEARCHING FOR THAT BETTER METHOD, THAT GREATER WORD, THE BETTER SCENE, THAT IS WHY WE WRITE; WE EARN IT!

4.0.1.34.

IMPORTANT!
WRITE BECAUSE WE HAVE A NEED TO WRITE WITH FIRE AND PASSION AND CANNOT BE CONSUMED BY FAILURE OR REJECTION. WE ARE CREATING…CREATING ART.
WHEN, WE REACH THIS POINT WE ARE A <u>'WRITER.'</u>

NOW, LET'S PRACTICE ON BECOMING
"A GREAT WRITER!"   TOGETHER, LET'S FIND OUT HOW!
THEN, WE WILL PUBLISH! TAKE THAT TO THE BANK!

<u>IN THE BEGINNING, THERE WERE JUST WORDS. NOW THE UNIVERSE AWAITS! LET'S START THERE…AT THE EDGE!</u>

4.2.0.0. OUR PROGRESS:
1. WE LEARNED THE KELLY PROCESS AND HOW TO USE IT TO IMPROVE OUR WRITING.

2. WE ANALYZE WHY OUR BOOK IS UNIQUE.

3. WE DISCARDED THE OUTLINE IN FAVOR OF THE SYNOPSIS.

CHAPTER 5

5.0.0.0. BOOK IDEAS LISTINGS:

CHAPTER TOPICS:
IDEAS-WHERE DO THEY COME FROM- BOOK IDEA GROUPINGS [CH 5]-MOVIE IDEAS LIST-[CH41].

ONE IDEA LEADS TO ANOTHER!

5.0.1.0. BOOK IDEA LISTINGS: DO CREATE TWO KINDS:

DON'T FORGET THE IDEAS PAGE... YOU KNOW THOSE LITTLE BRAINSTORMS WHEN YOUR NOT WRITING... THE PHRASES, THE IMAGES, THE CHAPTER NAMES, NEW CHARACTERS, PLOTS, CLUES, DREAMS, WHEN YOUR DRIVING, SLEEPING, ETC. **ADD THOSE HINTS OR INSPIRATIONS OR SENSORY ITEMS. TRUST THEM! THEY BECOME PART OF THAT INTUITIVE CREATIVE SIDE WE ARE LOOKING FOR**

5.0.2.0. TWO KINDS OF IDEA LISTS:

1. *DO:* CREATE ONE MASTER LIST FOR MANY BOOK POSSIBILITIES [MASTER BOOK TITLES & IDEAS LIST-COMBINE WITH THE MOVIES LIST-CH 41]. ADD YOUR OWN INSPIRATIONS, FLASHES-DREAMS-CATCHY WORDS. **LOOK BEHIND THE TITLES FOR THE IDEA AND THEME**.

2. *DO:* CREATE FOR THE **ONE SPECIFIC BOOK IDEA LIST** YOU ARE NOW WRITING ABOUT. [YOUR TITLE-IDEA GROUPS-CHAPTER TITLES]. THESE BECOME YOUR CHAPTER TOPICS [CH 9].

* DO: = FOR WRITER DO THESE TASKS.

√**5.0.2.1. MASTER BOOK IDEAS LIST.** √ **CHECK LIST:**
NOTE THE VARIOUS IDEA GROUPINGS: *EXAMPLE: MY LIST: "WHAT I MIGHT WRITE ABOUT!" BRAINSTORMING & NONSENSE:*

5.0.2.2. IDEAS LIST/THEMES/BOOK TITLES/KEY WORDS: EXAMPLES:

[MOVIES TITLES & IDEAS-CH 41].
[THEMES & SUPPORTING THEMES- REFER CH 11]
NOTE: BELOW ARE SOME IDEA GROUPINGS AS YOU MIGHT USE IN A BOOK'S KERNEL: 'CAPTURE THE IDEA.'

THESE IDEA GROUPING INCLUDE A UNIVERSAL THEME AND SUPPORTING IDEA GROUPS: THEME IS WAR: AFRICA-SLAVERY-CHILD SLAVERY-SEX TRADE-CUTTING OFF HANDS-SMUGGLING-TRIBAL WAR-PLACES-DICTATORS-GANGS-WEAPONS-ETC.

THE KERNAL : THEME= 'WAR' IN AFRICA OVER CHILD SLAVERY .

THEME: WHITE GIRLS TAKEN FOR SEX TRADE:
IDEA GROUPS: CHAPTER TOPICS
STOLEN CHILDREN-LIVES-BEATINGS-SEX-AGE-MASTERS-WHO-WHERE-HOW-TRAITS-LACK OF LAWS-INVESTIGATIONS-RESULTS.

CREATIVE WRITING—THE KELLY MANUAL OF STYLE

> FOR EXAMPLE: TAKE ANY TITLE BOOK-MOVIE OR IDEA, TRY TO
> LOOK BEHIND THE TITLE FOR THE IDEA, USE THE UNIVERSAL THEME
> AND THE KERNEL FOR YOUR BOOK.

BOOK TITLES-IDEAS-THEMES-CHAPTER TITLES- A BILLION SUBJECTS:
30 SECONDS TO MIDNIGHT
A BRIGHT SHINING LIE-(VIETNAM)-
A NOBLE AND SAVAGE HEART (KELLY BECKMAN)
A PROMISE
A SECRET GIFT--TED GUP-2011
 A SLIGHT CASE OF HERO
A THOUSAND BLACKBIRDS
A VOICE IN THE WIND
A WEEK IN WINTER-MAEVE BINCHY-2014
ACT OF TREASON (FLYNN-2007)
ADULTERY (NAT HAWTHORNE)
ADVERSITY
AFFAIRS OF THE HEART (KELLY BECKMAN-2011)
AFRICA
AFRICAN NATIONS
AGONY AND ECSTASY(THE CREATORS)
ALL THAT GLITTERS
AMERICA [THEME]-PEOPLE-STRUGGLE-LIVES-CRIME-LOVE-HONOR- ETC]
AMERICAN DREAM
AMERICAN WAR HERO
AN AMERICAN TRAGEDY (THEO DREISER)
AN INFINITE SPACE IN TIME
AND NOW MY LOVE
AND THE MOUNTAINS ECHOED-KHALED HOSEINI-2013
ANOTHER LIFETIME, ANOTHER DREAM
ARCHAEOLOGICAL FIND
ARMY [THEME= WAR-PEACE-WHERE-WHO-WHAY-SUSPENSE-LIFE-DEATH]
ASIA [PLACE]
ASK AVERYANYTHING-MARO ELIOT-AMAZON
ASSASSINS
AUGGIE AND BANGER-BECKMAN-(2011)-LULU PRESS
AUTOBIO. OF MARK TWAIN-MARK TWAIN-2011
BIOLOGICAL WEAPONS
BIRD OF PARADISE
BLACK ROSE-NORA ROBERTS-2014
BLOND BOMBSHELL
BLONDES AND OTHER DANGEROUS WOMEN (KELLY BECKMAN-2010)
BLOOD STONE
BONE BY BONE-(PETER MATTHIESSEN)-1999
BOOK OF HEROES
BOOMERANG
BOY MEETS GIRL. GETS MARRIED. BOY DIES.
BOY SOLDIER-RITTER-2004
BOY SOLDIERS OF THE GREAT WAR-2006
BRANDED: TRAITOR
BULLET BY BULLET-(KELLY BECKMAN)
BULLETS, BUGLES AND CANNONFIRE(KELLY BECKMAN-2011)
CALL TO TREASON-(TOM CLANCY)-2004
CHARLIE CHAN-(YUNTE HUANG)-2011
CHILD ABUSE-[THEME]
CHILDREN OF PARADISE (FRED D'AGUIAR)
CHINA FROG

CREATIVE WRITING—THE KELLY MANUAL OF STYLE

CHINESE AMERICAN: AMT TAN, MAXINE HONG KINGSTON,
CITIZEN PANIC
CIVIL DISOBEDIENCE (THOREAU)-[THEME]
CLAN RIVALRY
CLEAR WATER, -------
COCKROACHES-(JO NESBO)-2014
COCOA PLANTATIONS
COLD HEART
COLLECTIVE MASS DELUSION [THEME]-
COMMAND AUTHORITY-TOM CLANCY-2014
CONGRESS
CONSCIENCE [THEME]-
CONSPIRACIES GALORE
CONSPIRACY THEORY
CONSTELLATION DRAGON
COUNTRIES-PLACES-LOCATIONS
CORAL BEACH ROAD
CREATIVE WRITING-3RD PRINTING-BECKMAN-2014
CRIME [THEME]-
CROSS AND CRESCENT
CRUSADE TO THE PYRAMID OF LIGHT
CURSE OF THE RED DIAMOND
CUSTOMS-[THEMES=MAYAN-CHILEAN-AFRICAN-MIDDLE EAST,ETC]
DANCE OF THE DRAGON
DANGER CLOSE-(BOYKIN)-2010
DANGER-CLOSE UP
DARK LIES THE ISLAND-(KEVIN BARRY)-2013
DEAD END
DEAD LETTERS
DEADLINE-(SANDRA BROWN)-2014
DEATH (POE) (FAULKNER)
DEATH OF A HERO
DEEDS & WILLS
DEMOCRACY ON THE MARCH IN MIDDLE EAST
DESERT WIND
DESIRE UNDER THE SUN
DESPERATE LAND-(KELLY BECKMAN)
DESTINY (DICKINSON)
DETECTIVE STORIES-[CRIME THEME]-
DIAMONDS AND DRAGONS-CHILDREN'S BK
DIAMONDS, DRAGONS, AND DANGEROUS WOMEN
DISAPPEAR LIKE SHADOWS IN LIGHT
DIVORCE
DIXIE HIGHWAY [PLACE]-
DOCTOR SLEEP-(STEPHEN KING)-2014
DRAGON STAR (many authors)
DRAGON PRINCE
DRAGON'S CLAW
DREAMS IN PARIS
DREAMS, DRUMBEATS AND SUPERHEROES
DRIVING ME CRAZY
DRUGS
EMERALD ____
ENDLESS SUMMER
ESPIONAGE-STOLEN CODES[THEME SPYING]
EYE OF RE
EYE OF THE SUN

CREATIVE WRITING—THE KELLY MANUAL OF STYLE

FIRST LOVE-(JAMES PATTERSON)-2014
FLAMINGO BEACH
FLAMINGO ROAD
FLASHBACK
FOLLOW ME
FOLLOW THE SUN
FORBIDDEN BEACH
FORBIDDEN PARADISE
FOREVER DIAMONDS
FOREVER IS FOR... [THEME =TIME].
FORTUNES OF LOVE AND WAR
FROG LEGS
FROGS, PHARAOHS, AND
FROM EARTH TO ETERNITY
FROM HERE TO ETERNITY BEACH
FROM WAR TO ETERNITY
GENIUS
GENTLE KINGS, CRUSADER KNIGHTS AND DRAGON PRINCES
GERM WARFARE[THEME=WAR].
GHOSTS
GIVE ME TREASON OR GIVE ME-(KELLY BECKMAN)
GORE (EDGAR ALLEN POE)
GOTHIC (JOYCE CAROL OATES)
GOVERNMENT
GOVERNMENT SECRET PAPERS
GREAT GAME OF KINGS(KELLY BECKMAN)
GREAT GATSBY-(F. SCOTT FITZGERALD
GREED
GROTESQUE (FLANNERY O'CONNOR)
GROWING OLD
GUERRILAS
HALL OF HEROES-(KELLY BECKMAN)
HAPPINESS-GRACE & KELLY BECKMAN-2011
HEART OF SAND
HERO FOUND-THE GRTST POW ESCAPE-VIETNAM-2010
HERO! TRAITOR! SPY!-(KELLY BECKMAN)
HEROES OR TRAITORS-GEARY?-2003
HEROES PREFER REDHEADS-(KELLY BECKMAN)
HEROES, VILLIANS AND TRAITORS-(KELLY BECKMAN)
HIGH TIDE
HIGHLY UNLIKELY SCENARIO, A (RACHEL CANTOR)
HIJACKING
HISTORY
HONG KONG ISLAND
HONOR & SIN (FAULKNER-THE SOUND & FURY)-MACBETH
HOSTAGE-DON BROWN-2005
HOW THE LIGHT GETS IN-(LOUISE PENNY)
HUMBLE HEROES IN WW2-2007
HUMOR (MARK TWAIN)(JAMES THURBER)(DOROTHY PARKER)
HUMORISTS: (ROBERT BENCHLEY, WILL ROGER),
HURRICANE ISLAND
I AM ABRHAM(LINCOLN)-JEROME CHARYN-2014
IN A COLD HEART
IN COLOR DYING
INFERNO-(DAN BROWN)-2013
IN HARM'S WAY-2010
IN PARADISE-[FLORIDA]- (PETER MATTHIESSEN)-2014

INSURGENT-(VERONICA ROTH)-2013
IN THE BEGINNING THERE WAS ONE MAN AND ONE DEED!
IN THE COMPANY OF GODS
IN THE LAND OF MAKE BELIEVE
IN THE LAND OF SUMMER [PLACE]
IN THE LAND OF SUNSHINE
IRELAND [PLACE]
ISLAND IN THE SUN-(J.D. SALINGER-KEN SLAWENSKI)-2011.
JEALOUSY
JEWISH----
JUST 5 MINUTES MORE-(KELLY BECKMAN)
JUST ANOTHER HERO-(DYER)-2010 [THEME=HERO]
KILLER-JON KELLERMAN-2014
KILLING MR WATSON-(PETER MATTHIESSEN)1990
KING OF COURTS
KNIGHTS OF THE RED DIAMOND
LANDSCAPE (STEINBECK)
LAST CAR OVER THE SAGAMORE BRIDGE-(PETER ORNER)
LAST EXIT TO PARADISE
LAST WAR IN PARADISE-(KELLY BECKMAN)
LAW (GRISHOM)
LIFE [THEME]
LIFE AFTER LIFE-(KATE-ATKINSON)-2013
LITTLE BIT OF HEAVEN, A
LONE SURVIVOR-(MARCUS LUTREL)L-2014
LORDS OF LIGHT
LOST MAN'S RIVER-(PETER MATTHIESSEN)-1997
LOVE {THEME}
LOVE GIVEN, LOVE TAKEN
LOVE IS A BULLET THRU THE HEART-(KELLY BECKMAN)
LOVER-TRAITOR-HERO-SPY
MAGIC
MALAAY PIRATES
ME BEFORE YOU-( )-AMAZON
MEDIA IN TERROR-MUHAMMED ADEEL JAVAID
MEDITATION-GRACE & KELLY BECKMAN-2011
MEN GET IT-WOMEN DON'T.
MEXICAN DRUG TRADE
MIDDLE EAST [PLACE]
MIDNIGHT HERO-[THEME=HERO]
MISS KAY'S DUCK COMMANDER KITCHEN-(KAY ROBERTSON)-2014
MONK SEE! MONK DO!
MONUMENT MEN –NON-FICTION-(ROBT EDSEL-BRET WITTER)
MOONLIGHTBAY
MORALITY (MARY GORDON)[THEME]
MURDER (IN COLD BLOOD-TRUMAN CAPOTE)
MURDER-MAYHEM AND MYSTERY
MY FORBIDDEN PARADISE
MY LIFE AS A DOG
MY LIFE AS AN ANGEL
MY MOTHER KILLED CHRIST-( )-AMAZON
MY OWN PRIVATE WAR [THEME=WAR]
MYSTERIOUS HERO
MYSTERIOUS STRANGER (MARK TWAIN)
NATIONAL GEOGRAPHIC
NATIVE AMERICAN: N.SCOTT MOMADAY, LESLIE MARMON
NEVER-NEVER LAND

NEW SPECIES FOUND
NIGHT OF THE TEARDROP-(KELLY BECKMAN)
NIGHTMARE [THEMES-MENTAL HEALTH-VISIONS-SCARY]
NINE INCHES-TOM PERROTTA)-2013
NINTH DRAGON
NO DREAMY NO STORY-[PLACE AUSTRALIA].
NO MATTER WHAT
ONE HUNDRED APOCALYPSES AND OTHER-(LUCY CORIN)
NO WHERE ELSE ON EARTH
NUCLEAR
OBAMA'S WARS- (BOB WOODWARD).-2011
OF ALL THE SUNRISES IN TIME
OF DREAMS AND DRAGONS
OH!
OLD LETTERS
OLD MAN AND THE SEA-(HEMMINGWAY)[THEME MAN VS SEA]
OLD MAN WALKING IN THE RAIN-CHILDREN'S RHYMEE
ONE DAY AFTER FOREVER
ONE MORE THING-B.J. NOVAK-2014
OPIUM TRADE
ORPHAN TRAIN-CHRINSTINA BAKE-2014
OUR SOLDIER BOYS-MANVILLE-2010
PARADISE ISLAND
PARADISE LOST
PARTS OF BIBLE FOUND
PASSENGER AIRLINER SHOT DOWN.[THEME=WAR=TERRORISM]
PEACE-[THEME] (GHANDI-CONTRAST WAR-
PIRATES OF MY HEART
PIRATES-(MANY)
POEMS-(MANY)
POISONING OF THE POTOMAC RIVER
POLICE STORIES [THEME=CRIME-VICTIMS-]
POVERTY [THEME] (FAULKNER)
PRACTICAL PALEO-(DIANE SANFLIPPO)-2013
PRINCE OF DRAGONS
PRISONER
PRIVATE-L.A.-(JAMES PATTERSON)-2014
PROMISE OF SUNSHINE
PROMISES FROM HEAVEN
PYRAMIDS
QUALITIES THAT MAKE PEOPLE FREE AND NATIONS GREAT
QUEEN MOTHER
QUEEN OF DIAMONDS
QUEST FOR THE RED DIAMOND
RABBIT REDUX-(VIETNAM WAR)-
RED CROSS, RED HEART
RED FISH, BLUE FISH, BLACK DEATH
RED HEART-RED EARTH (KELLY BECKMAN)-1999
RED LIPSTICK
REDHEADS, BAD AND BEAUTIFUL (BECKMAN-2010)
REDHEADS, THE MOST DANGEROUS OF ALL-(KELLY BECKMAN)-2011
REFUGEES **[THEME-WAR]**-REVOLUTION-
REGIONAL EXPERIENCES (NICK. SPARKS, FAULKNER)
RELIGION HYPOCRISY (SINCLAIR: ELMER GANTRY)
REVOLUTIONARY *–[THEME=WAR].*
RIDE THE WHIRLWIND
RIGHT BETEEN THE EYES-(KELLY BECKMAN-2007)

RISING SUN AND FALLING NIGHT-(KELLY BECKMAN)
RIVERBOAT- (MARK TWAIN)
ROAD TO ETERNITY
ROBBER BARONS
ROBOTIC WARRIORS
ROYAL BLOOD
RUSSIA [THEME-WAR-REVOLUTION-PLACE-CITIZENS]
SAINTS, NOR KINGS NOR KNIGHTS
SALINGER- (DAVID SHIELDS)
SANCTUARY (FAULKNER)
SANDS OF TIME
SATELLITES
SAVAGES ON THE SHORE
SCANDAL
SCIENCE MAGAZINE
SECRET WARS [THEME-WAR-SECRET-WHO-PLACE-]
SECRETS AND LIES-(TRUMAN CAPOTE)
SECRETS OF RED BEACH
SECRETS OF THE SUN TEMPLE-(LOTS)
SEMINOLE
SHADOW COUNTRY (PETER MATTHIESSEN)-892 PAGES-2007
SHADOWS IN LIGHT
SHADOWS IN THE SAND
*SHOOT THE HERO!-(*SILKO, LOUISE ERDICH, SHERMAN ALEXIE)
SILENT BEACH, THE
        SILKO, LOUISE ERDICH, SHERMAN ALEXIE,
SINS
SINS OF MY FATHER
SLAVE CHILD-[THEME=SLAVERY]- (STOWE)
SOLDIER BOYS-HUGHES?-2003-GERMAN
SOLDIER BOYS-(MC CAULEY)-
SOLDIER OF FORTUNE
SOUL AND FURY (FAULKNER)
SPACE
SPIES, THIEVES AND OTHER FRIENDS (KELLY BECKMAN-2003)
SPIRITUAL PATHWAY-GRACE & KELLY BECKMAN-2011
SPYING-AMERICAN STYLE
STAR OF RED MAGNIFICENCE
STILL LIFE WIH BREAD CRUMBS-ANNA QUINDLEN-2014
STOLEN NUCLEAR MATERIAL
STONE OF DESTINY
STORY-DREAMS ALIVE
STORYTELLER (BERNARD MALAMUD, MARK TWAIN,
STRUGGLE [THEME]
STRUGGLE TO SURVIVE (THEO DREISER)
SUGAR BEACH
SUMMER SOLSTICE
SUMMER'S PROMISE
SUN RISING
SUNCATCHER
SUPER HAWKS-NEWS TRIBUNE-2014
SURRENDER
SYCAMORE ROW-(JOHN GRISHAM)-2014
TALL TALES (MARK TWAIN)
TEMPLARS-KNIGHTS
TENTH OF DECEMBER-(GEORGE SAUNDERS)-2013
TERIBLE SWIFT SWORD

CREATIVE WRITING—THE KELLY MANUAL OF STYLE

TERROR-(STEVEN KING)
THE ALPS
THE BATTLE OF GODS AND MEN
THE BOOMERS- KELLY BECKMAN-2007)
THE BOY & THE SENSCHAL
THE BLUSH-POEM(KELLY BECKMAN-2011)
THE CHINESE LANTERN
THE CHOSEN ONE
THE COLOR MASTER-(AIMEE BENDER)-2013
THE COUNTERFEIT AGENT-(ALEX BERENSON)-2014
THE DEPRESSION (STEINBECK-GRAPES OF WRATH)* [THEME=TRAGEDY-
                    DEPRESSION-POVERTY]*

THE DESERT WIND
THE ENEMY WITHIN
THE FINKLER QUESTION-HOWARD JACOBSON-2011
THE FRENCH SECRET RECIPE
THE GOLDEN DRAGON-OPIUM
THE GOLDEN OBELISK
THE GOLDFINCH-(DONNA TARTT)-2014
THE GOOD MAN/THE BAD MAN [THEME]
THE GRUNT
HERO [THEME]-
THE HALL OF HEROES-(KELLY BECKMAN)
THE HERO AND OUTLAW-2001
THE HERO MUST DIE-(KELLY BECKMAN)
THE HEROES-ABERCROMBIE-2011
THE HIGH AND MIGHTY
THE HUSBAND'S SECRET-(LIANE MORIARTY)-2013
THE INVENTION OF WINGS-SUE MONK KIDD-2014
THE IRISH PRINCE-(KELLY BECKMAN)
THE LAST HERO
THE LAST HERO-2007
THE LAST HEROES-GRIFFIN-2008
THE LONGEST RIDE-(NICHOLAS SPARKS)-2014
THE LONGEST WAR
THE LOVE AFFAIRS OF NATHANIEL P-(ADELLE WALDMAN)-2013
THE LOWLAND-(JHUMPA LAHIRI-
THE MAN IN THE MIRROR
THE MARTIAN-ANDY WEIR-2014
THE MONUMENTS MEN-ROBERT M EDSEL-2014
THE NOTEBOOK-(NICHOLAS SPARKS)-
THE OCEAN AT THE END OF THE LANE-(NEIL GAIMAN)-2013
THE PASSION IN POETRY-(KENVER REGIS)-AMAZON
THE PENDULUM SWINGS
THE PHARAOH'S TREASURE
THE PROMISE
THE QUIET HERO
THE ROAD FROM GAP CREEK-(ROBERT MORGAN)-2013
THE SELL OUT OF AMERICA
THE SEX TRADE IN AMERICA
THE SHADOW
THE SILENT SPEAK VOLUMES
THE SILVER STAR-(JEANNETTE WALLS)-2013
THE SIXTH EXTINCTION (ELIXZ. KOLBERT)
THE SPACE BETWEEN US- (   )-AMAZON
THE SPY BIZ

CREATIVE WRITING—THE KELLY MANUAL OF STYLE

THE TRAITOR'S WIFE-(ALLISON PATAKI)-2014
THE UNSUNG HERO
THE WARRIOR
THE WEIRDNESS (JEREMY BUSHNELL)
THE WORLD KEEPS SPINNING
THE YELLOW PARAKEET MURDER
THIEF OF HEARTS
THUNDER IN THE BAY
THUNDER ON RED BEACH
TIDEWATER TANGO-KELLY BECKMAN-2014
TIME OF EVERLASTING LIFE
TIME TRAVELER
TIN SOLDIER
TRAGEDY [THEME]
TRAITOR: BOOMERS –(KELLY BECKMAN-2007)
TRANSALANTIC-(COLUM MCCANN)-2013
TRAVEL
TREASON- NEVIN-2002
TREASON-DESCRIPTION SEARCH-MANY
TREASON-DON BROWN-2005
TREASURE OF THE SUN PYRAMID
TREASURE ON THE BEACH
TROUBLE IN PARADISE BEACH
U.S. INTELLIGENCE WAR **[THEME**-SPYING-FOES- ETC]
UNDERGROUND NEWSPAPER: (NORMAN MAILER-
UNDERGROUND NEWSPAPERS
VIETNAM WAR: RABBIT REDUX, A BRIGHT SHINING LIE,
WAGE SLAVERY
WALKING POINT (WAR)
WALL STREET SECRETS
WAR-[THEME]ACTS OF-LIFE-DEATH-HERO-TRAGEDY-
WAR CORRESPONENT-(KELLY BECKMAN)
WAR HERO
WAR IN PARADISE
WAR IN THE HEART
WAR IS FOREVER FOR
WAR MAKES US INTO DIFFERENT PEOPLE
WAR OF SUPEROWERS
WAR OF WORDS
WAR OR PEACE
WARRIOR FOR THE GODS
WARRIOR PHARAOHS
WE CANNOT AFFORD WAR ANYMORE-(KELLY BECKMAN-2007)
WEALTH (F. SCOTT FITZGERALD-GREAT GATSBY)
WHALING (HERMAN MELVILLE)
WHAT IS FOREVER FOR-(KELLY BECKMAN)
WHITE DRAGON
WHITE FEATHER
WINTER'S TALE-(MARK HELPRIN)-2014
WITCHES
WIZARDS
WOMEN-GET IT, MEN DON'T
WONDER-(R.J.PALACIO)-2013
YANKEE DOODLE HERO
YOU KNOW WHEN THE MEN ARE GONE-SIOBHAN FALLON-2011
CANADA: (STEPHAN LEACOCK, ALFRED PURDY, MAVIS GALLANT,
    MARGARET LAWRENCE, ALICE MUNRO, MICHAEL ONDAATJE)

5.0.2.2. EXAMPLES: FROM NEWSPAPER HEADLINES VIA NET:
TIP: ADD A NEWSPAPER STORY TO YOUR FICTION BOOK
DO SAVE CLIPPINGS INTO THAT ALPHABETICAL SUBJECT FILE BOX OR
FILE CABINET. ADD THESE TO YOUR IDEAS LIST.

5.0.2.3. MOVIE TITLE IDEAS: COMPARED TO BOOKS:
REFER TO [CH 41] FOR MOVIE TITLES.
1. MOVIES HAVE A SIMPLE TITLE- THO CATCHY!
2. MOVIES HAVE A BOOK SYNOPSIS BUILT IN,
3. ALONG WITH GREAT DIALOGUE, MATCHING SCENES ,
4. HIDDEN LIGHTING, HIDDEN BACK STORY AND PLOT.
5. VISUAL RATHER THAN ALL WORDS. (WE USE PICTURESQUE WORDS),
6. BRIDGES ARE A LITTLE VAGUE & GENERALLY SCENE TO SCENE.
7. A NARRATOR TELLS THE STORY, WITH THE STORY AND CHARACTERS
   TAKING OVER.
8. THE UNIVERSAL THEME IS THERE BUT SIMPLIFIED.
9. THE SUPPORTING THEME IS PARAMOUNT AND AMPLIFIED.
10. THE VISUAL DRAMA IS SHORTER AND SIMPLER. (PICTURE OF A 1000
    WORDS).
11. GREAT MOVIES COME FROM GREAT BOOKS AND GREAT SCREEN
    PLAYS. THUS, STRONG CHARACTERS, STRONG PLOTS AND DRAMA.
12. DRAMA IS KING! IN ACTION MOVIES, ACTION LIFTS UP THE DRAMA.

5.0.2.4. MAINTAIN A "CONTROVERSY LIST ON OUR IDEAS LIST.
U.S. APPROVES ATOM BOMB FOR INDIA—WHY?
ARIZONA WRITES IMMIGRATION LAWS -TERRORISTS-GENOCIDE
(DARFUR)- HIJACKING- ROBOTIC WARRIORS- REFUGEES
YOUR SUBJECT OF INTEREST HERE

5.3.0.0. DETAILED IDEA LIST & IDEA GROUPINGS FOR ONE BOOK:
MAINTAIN A "MASTER IDEA LIST" IN WORD FORMAT AND DO: (RIGHT
MOUSE CLICK) A "SEND "SHORTCUT TO DESKTOP" TO KEEP IT HANDY.

5.3.1.0. BOOK IDEAS:
SELECT A NEW AND TIMELY SUBJECT AND ONE NOT WRITTEN A LOT
ABOUT, RESEARCH BOOK SITES, SUBJECTS, OTHER MEDIA, AND THE
INTERNET BOOK SELLERS.

5.3.2.0. REVIEW SUBJECT INDICES OF SOURCE BOOKS.
CAPTURE AN IDEA TOPIC AND RESEARCH IT IN OTHER SOURCES.

5.5.0.0. IDEA GROUPINGS:
5.5.1.0. ONE BOOK IDEA GROUPINGS: [EXAMPLE: CH 5.4.1.0.]
WE HAVE CHOSEN A STORY WITH UNIVERSAL AND SPECIFIC THEME
ELEMENTS. WE HAVE CHOSEN A LIMITED NUMBER OF CHARACTERS AND
NOW WE BEGIN TO ASSEMBLE THE FIRST TO LAST SEQUENCE OF EVENTS
WE BEGIN TO 'PUT IN ORDER' THOSE GROUPS INTO CHAPTERS GROUPS.

5.5.3.0.

IMPORTANT:
• DO: PLACE THESE IDEA GROUPS INTO THE CHAPTER TOPICS AT THE TOP OF EACH CHAPTEROF YOUR DRAFT.

5.6.0.0. OUR PROGRESS: *WE HAVE CREATED **TWO IDEAS LISTS**:*

1. MASTER IDEAS/SUBJECTS/TITLES LIST. THIS WILL GROW AS WE WRITE-EDIT-RESEARCH ETC. AS LONG AS WE WRITE.

2. A NEW LIST FOR A SINGLE BOOK AS WE GRASP AN BOOK IDEA. WE BEGIN TO ASSEMBLE THE EVENTS, CHARACTER-EVENTS ETC.

3. NOTICE THIS ONE IS ABOUT TOPICS WITHIN EACH CHAPTER AND WE THINK ABOUT AND WRITE THE OPENING SENTENCES FOR EACH CHAPTER. [REFER TO CH 14 -OPENING SENTENCES].

4. WE LEARNED SOME BASICS ABOUT CHAPTER GROUPINGS AND A SEQUENCE OF EVENTS. FROM THESE, WE WILL GIVE A CHAPTER TITLE, WRITE AND OPENING SENTENCE FOR EACH AND

CHAPTER 6
6.0.0.0. STORYTELLING:
THE BEGINNING OF THE CREATIVE PROCESS:

SKILL TOPICS:
STORYTELLER-WRITER-RESEARCHER-EDITOR-CRITIC-ORGANIZER- -PROJECT MANAGER- PUBLISHER-MARKETER-AD MAN-WEB SEARCHER-REVISIONIST.
THE 6 W'S -A WRITER'S PROFILE?-A PERFECTIONIST?
THE DEADLINE-INSIGHT-UNIQUE ADVICE-COMMITMENT-INVOLVEMENT-RESPONSIBLE FOR CONTENT
IS IT PLEASANT- EASY TO READ-READER IS SMART
ILLUSTRATE-INDEX-MAPS-REFERENCES-SUB HEADINGS
CROSS-REFERENCES-MULTI-MEDIA
PACK FULL OF INFORMATION-CHALLENGE THE READER WITH THEORIES-IS IT DIFFERENT THEN THE PACK?-NEW TOPIC?-DYNAMIC-ACTION PACKED?

CHAPTER TOPICS:
GREAT READER-WRITER?
IS IT WRITING, STORYTELLING OR AH! HA!
HOW TO WRITE, EDIT AND ENJOY THE PROCESS OF WRITING OR COVER TO COVER & UNDERCOVER
OR GETTING PAID BY THE WORD
OR GEE! I JUST WANTED TO WRITE IT DOWN!
OR SAVE THE WORLD, WRITE IT, AND SAVE IT FOR POSTERITY
DO USE A SOURCE NUMBER, NOT A FOOTNOTE. (FICTION).

A STORYTELLER'S SYNOPSIS: 1 OR 2 PARAGRAPHS ONLY.
TO CREATE A SYNOPSIS (A PARAGRAPH OR TWO) WRITE DOWN YOUR BOOK KERNEL IDEA, THE MAIN CHARACTER AND THE PLOT AND ANY MAJOR CLIMAX. ***DO:** NOW WRITE IT IN **PARAGRAPH FORM**. ADD WHAT THE STORY IS ABOUT, ADD THE KERNEL IDEA ,A MAIN CHARACTER AND NARRATOR.

6.0.1.0. A GREAT WRITER MUST BE A GREAT READER FIRST!
I BEGAN WRITING WITH THE REALIZATION, AFTER HAVING READ THOUSANDS OF BOOKS AND ARTICLES, THAT I COULD DO IT BETTER, BE CLEARER, AND MORE DESCRIPTIVE. MY WRITING HAD TO CONVEY AN EXPRESSED IDEA WITH ACCURACY AND BREVITY. MY AUDIENCE WAS BOTH MY READER AND LISTENER OF AN IDEA. THOUGHTS BECAME TOOLS OF MY TRADE NOT JUST WORDS. MASTERING THE READING SKILLS LED TO BETTERING WRITING SKILLS.

6.0.2. 0. A GREAT EDITOR CREATES A GREAT WRITER!
 A WRITER IS HIS WORSE CRITIC WHEN IT COMES TO PROOFING AND EDITING UNCLEAR WORDS OR PHRASES OR WHEN CHECKING PERSON-TENSE OR GRAMMAR. AS I MASTERED THE TECHNICAL SKILLS OF TIME LINES, PLANNING AND SEQUENCE OF EVENTS I ASSIMILATED ALL OF THESE INTO THE EDITING PROCESS AND IMPROVED THE WRITING. TRANSLATION OF WORDS INTO COMMUNICATION, SOMETHING THE READER COULD UNDERSTAND AND APPRECIATE. HE APPRECIATES MY CLARITY, MY BREVITY, WHEN CONVEYING AN IDEA. THE PROCESS

CREATIVE WRITING—THE KELLY MANUAL OF STYLE

SHOULD BE LOGICAL, ORDERLY AND PRESENTED IN A MANNER THE EDITOR/READER CAN UNDERSTAND.

WRITING WAS MORE THAN BEING CREATIVE AND EDITING IT OVER AND OVER, UNTIL IT WAS CLEAR AND CORRECT. IT WAS THE SOLE PURPOSE BEHIND MY COMMUNICATING OF THE ORIGINAL IDEA.

IT WAS ALSO ATTITUDE! IT WAS WORK AND FUN AT THE SAME TIME! SURE WRITING IS WHAT I DO. BUT MORE THAN THAT, IT IS WHAT I ENJOY AND IT MOTIVATES ME.

CLASS DISCUSSION :WHAT KIND OF WRITING ARE YOU INTERESTED IN?

6.2.6.0. SUMMARY: THE WRITER IS STORYTELLER FIRST?
CLASS: LECTURE & DISCUSSION:
- A STORYTELLER:
- A PRODUCT OF HIS EXPERIENCE?
- A RESEARCHER
- AN OBSERVER
- COMMUNICATOR
- A LISTENER
- POSSESSES SOME TALENT

6.2.7.0. IS STORYTELLER DIFFERENT?
-STYLE
-CHOICE OF WORDS
-IMAGERY
-CHARACTER DEVELOPMENT

6.2.8. 0. CLASS: WHAT MAKES A STORYTELLER IN YOUR EYES?
-TALENT TO INVOLVE ME (THE READER) IN THE STORY.
-READER INTEREST IN STORY
-READER INTEREST IN TITLE.
-   INFORMS ME ABOUT SUBJECTS I FIND INTERESTING.

6.2.9.0. "YOU MUST BE THE READER, THE WRITER, THE EDITOR AND THE PUBLISHER……. ALL JUST TO BE THE "WRITER!"

6.2.10. 0. A TOUGH ACT!
ACT ONE: FIRST TELL YOUR STORY,
ACT TWO: THEN WRITE:
TO YOUR READER, THEN THINK ABOUT YOUR STORY AND BEGIN BY TELLING IT TO YOURSELF. NOT WRITING. FIRST TELL YOUR STORY OUTLOUD TO YOURSELF. THEN WRITE AS YOU TOLD IT. WRITING IS THE SECOND ACT, NOT VICE VERSA.

AH! HA!   THE BIGGEST LESSON OF ALL: YOU ARE A STORY TELLER FIRST (VERBAL STORY)AND A WRITER SECOND, (WRITTEN STORY).

6.2.11.0. HOW TO WRITE, EDIT AND KEEP YOUR SANITY!
PUT THE JOY BACK IN YOUR WRITING AND REMOVE THE STRUCTURE, THE JUDGMENT CALLS OF GOOD OR BAD, THE NEED TO EDIT RIGHT AFTER, THE DECISION TO QUIT TOO SOON.

> **WRITING IS SIMPLE: WRITE WHAT YOU KNOW TO SOMEONE YOU DON'T ---YOUR READER.**

6.3.0.0. BASICS: HOW DO WE DO THIS?

> **6.3.1.1. CLASS: BEGIN BY WRITING THE 6W'S:** [CH 9.0.0.0.].
> THE WHO, WHAT, WHY, WHEN, & WHERE. (NOW, THERE ARE 6= "WOW")
>
> 6.3.1.2. WRITE THEM DOWN IN RANDOM ORDER,
>
> 6.3.1.3. PICK THE MOST INTERESTING ONE OF THE GROUP
>
> 6.3.1.4. WRITE A PARAGRAPH WITH SIMPLE SENTENCES OF THIS MOST INTERESTING ONE OF THE GROUP.

6.3.1.5. * DO: WRITE A COMPLETE PARAGRAPH: [CH 7].
WRITE YOUR STORY INCLUDING ALL PARTS OF THE PARAGRAPH CONSTRUCTION. THE FIRST SENTENCE---INTRIGUING, TEASE YOUR READER INTO WANTING MORE. GIVE HIM THE MEAT OF THE PARAGRAPH, THEN THE SIZZLE---THE CLOSING SENTENCE AND LEAD OFF INTO THE NEXT.

6.3.1.6. SEE PARAGRAPH CONSTRUCTION IN [CH 8].

6.3.1.7. COMMON THREAD-YOUR THEMES:
FIGURE OUT THE COMMON TREAD THAT CONNECTS THESE **CHAPTER TOPICS** TOGETHER. THEY CONNECT SOMEHOW…PLACE, OR TIME, OR THEY KNOW THE SAME PEOPLE, OR ARE THEY ARE OPPOSITES, OR MORTAL ENEMIES, OR LOVERS, OR EVEN RANDOM…CHANCE ENCOUNTER. I LIKE RANDOM…IT'S PART OF THE MYSTERY OF YOUR STORY. **THIS COMMON THREAD BECOMES YOUR THEME.**

6.3.1.8. NOW, THINK STORYTELLING: NOT WRITING:
WHAT YOU ARE REALLY TRYING TO DO IS TELL A STORY AND AFTERWARDS JUST WRITE IT DOWN.

6.3.1.9. THEN, EMBELLISH YOUR MAIN CHARACTER:
NEXT, THINK WHO IS THE MAIN CHARACTER?
CAN YOU DESCRIBE HIM IN ALL DIMENSIONS?
HEIGHT, WEIGHT, COLOR OF HAIR, PROTESTANT OR CATHOLIC, A PRIEST, A SOLDIER, A TEENAGER, AN OLD MAN, A WOMAN, BEAUTIFUL, UGLY, SCARED, HOBBIES, CHILDREN, SECRETS, SINS, FAMILY, TIME PERIOD…WESTERN, MODERN CITY, COUNTRY TOWN, FOREIGN LAND, FOREIGN CITY, WHAT IS HIS HEART LIKE, HIS SOUL, HIS MIND, HOW HE TREATS OTHERS, IS HE LIKE OTHER FARMERS, COWBOYS OR PIRATES OR STARS? WHAT IS LIKABLE, DISLIKEABLE, HIS MOODS, HIS FEARS, HIS PASSIONS. HIS FRIENDS, HIS GIRLFRIENDS, WIVES, EX-WIVES.

CREATIVE WRITING—THE KELLY MANUAL OF STYLE

CONTINUE THIS THOUGHT PROCESS. ILLUMINATE YOUR CHARACTERS AND COMPLETE YOUR CHARACTER LIST & DESCRIPTIONS. [REFER TO CH 20].

NOW YOU COULD WRITE SEVERAL PAGES ABOUT JUST YOUR MAIN CHARACTER, NOW YOU UNDERSTAND HIM OR HER A LITTLE.

6.3.1.10. WHAT IS YOUR CHARACTER'S WORLD LIKE:
WHERE DOES HE LIVE, WORK, OR FLEE FROM? IS IT A PERIOD OF TIME? A PLACE? A SECRET, WHICH KEEPS HIM THERE? A WOMAN? A VILLAIN, A GOOD GUY TO CONTRAST HIM AGAINST? SECRETS AND MYSTERIOUS PARTS ARE GOOD...BUILD ON THEM.

6.2.3.1.11. RANDOM IDEAS, RANDOM THOUGHTS, WHAT IS RANDOM? FREEDOM?
THUS NOT IN A SPECIFIC ORDER. IS IT CHAOS OR DISORGANIZATION?

WHY RANDOM? ...GENERALLY I FIND MY WRITING IS ABOUT RANDOM THINGS AND BEGIN WITH THE FIRST SENTENCE OR PARAGRAPH ...SOMETIMES IT STAYS THERE WHERE I WROTE IT, SOMETIMES I MOVE IT TO ANOTHER CHAPTER, ANOTHER BOOK, SOMETIMES IT GETS EDITED OUT. YOU AS THE WRITER HAVE THE FREEDOM TO MOVE IT OR CHANGE IT, DISCARD, AND REWRITE, ETC.

6.3.1.12. HOW I DESCRIBE WRITING & THE RULES AND EXAMPLES:
A. WRITING IS LIKE DRIVING A CAR AT NIGHT!
THERE IS ONLY SO FAR YOU CAN SEE AHEAD.
TRY TO LET THE STORY DEVELOP AS THE FLOW COMES TO YOU...JUST GET IT DOWN. *DO: **WRITE THE WORDS DOWN AS THEY COME TO YOU.**

B. SPACE & TIME: TIP:
CHOOSE A SPACE AND TIME? BE COMFORTABLE, WHERE YOU WRITE IS AS IMPORTANT AS WHAT YOU WRITE! DO YOU CARRY A JOURNAL? DO YOU CARRY YOUR BOOK? YOUR CHAPTERS AS YOU FINISH THEM? WRITE OFTEN, YOU WILL GET BETTER AS YOU WRITE MORE AND POLISH IT, EDIT IT DISCARD IT. YOU LEARN AND GROW. WATER YOUR GARDEN, DO YOU RESEARCH, AND WRITE WITHOUT JUDGING YOURSELF. CHOOSE A COMFORTABLE TIME TO WRITE...EARLY MORNING, LATE EVENING, SATURDAY MORNING, WHEN SPOUSE IS TRAVELING, OR BEFORE WORK.

C. YOUR BOOK IS YOUR CANVAS, YOUR WORDS ARE YOUR COLORS, USE A BIG BRUSH!
THINK ABOUT WRITING LIKE A GREAT CANVAS AND YOU ARE ABOUT TO PAINT A PICTURE WITH WORDS AND TELL A STORY. REFLECT ON THAT PICTURE---DID YOU DESCRIBE IT FULLU? THE NICE PART IS YOU CAN CHANGE WORDS, THE PARAGRAPH, THE CHAPTER, MOVE IT, DELETE IT OR ADD TO IT, RIGHT UP UNTIL YOU SAY IT IS FINISHED.

D. WRITING IS EMOTIONAL-USE IT!
....HAPPINESS, SAD, BIRTHS AND DEATHS DO OCCUR.
THEN IT'S HAPPINESS AND SADNESS ALL ROLLED INTO ONE:

CREATIVE WRITING—THE KELLY MANUAL OF STYLE

EXAMPLE, I GET WITHDRAWAL AFTER WRITING A BOOK FOR A YEAR: I'M READY FOR MY NEXT ONE OR GEE! I WORKED SO HARD ON IT, THAT I'M GONNA MISS WORKING ON IT!

THE CHINESE HAVE A SAYING: "THAT IT IS GOOD TO LEAVE THE PAST BEHIND SO THE FUTURE CAN BEGIN!"
I USE A LITTLE SAYING TO REMIND ME OF MY DUTY TO FINISH IT PROPERLY OR TO WAIT UNTIL I SENSE IT IS COMPLETE. DO WRITE ONE FOR YOURSELF.

E. BE THE BOSS: CONTROL THE TIME WHEN:
"IT AIN'T OVER UNTIL I SAY IT'S OVER! OR WE WON'T PUBLISH UNTIL' IT'S TIME! OR THANK GOD, I FINALLY FINISHED THAT ONE!" OR "ONE FINAL EDIT!" OR THE NEXT ONE WILL BE BETTER AND IT WILL BE A _____!

F. REMEMBER THERE ARE NO HARD OR FAST RULES:
SOME BOOKS COME EASY AND FINISH EASY---SOME REQUIRE WORK ALL THE WAY THROUGH. SO BE PATIENT…WORK EVERY CHANCE YOU GET AND DON'T LOSE HEART!

CLASS?
WHAT IS MORE IMPORTANT? THE STORY, THE WRITER, OR THE READER?
ANS 3. KNOW YOUR READER: YOUR AUDIENCE
THE READER, THE AUDIENCE---HOW CAN I SATISFY HIS QUEST FOR KNOWLEDGE, HIS QUESTIONS DEMANDING ANSWERS, HIS INTEREST IN MY STORY?

WHO IS THE READER….ALL AGES? , A MAN, A WOMAN, OR A GROUP OF PEOPLE:
HE, SHE OR THEY ARE YOUR AUDIENCE: WHAT INTERESTING FACT OR SITUATION HAPPENED THEY MIGHT WANT TO KNOW ABOUT?

ANS: ? ARE YOU THE WRITER AND THE STORY TELLER?
ARE YOU TELLING THE STORY (FIRST PERSON- I AM TELLING THE STORY)…OR IS YOUR CHARACTER (SECOND PERSON), OR THRU A JOURNAL, NARRATOR (THIRD PERSON) , A BEST FRIEND, ONE OF THE CHARACTERS? A FAMILY MEMBER? THRU MANY PEOPLE OR PLACES OR EVENTS? (ANS: YES TO ALL). [PERSON: REFER CH 24].[VOICE-CH 6].

CLASS ?: IS THE "PERSON" YOU
USE TELLING THE STORY AN IMPORTANT SELECTION? EXPLAIN!

G. *DO YOUR OWN EDITING OF PLOT-CHARACTER-FLOW- AND MOSTLY THE PARAGRAPHS: THIS IS CALLED OVER AND OVER AND OVER AGAIN!
- SOME WILL NEVER SEE DAYLIGHT ON THEIR OWN, BUT SEVERAL PARAGRAPHS HAVE BEEN.
-MINE WAS SOMEONE READING OVER MY SHOULDER WHILE I WROTE…TYPOS AND ALL… A GUESS?
- YEP… A TYPO OR FORGOT_____, OR DIDN'T CAPITALIZE, ETC.
        THAT WHY YOU DO YOUR OWN EDITING. OVER AND OVER AND OVER AGAIN!

CREATIVE WRITING—THE KELLY MANUAL OF STYLE

- USE SOME STANDARD CODES SO YOU DON'T SPEND A LOT OF TIME
WRITING THEM OUT EACH TIME. EXAMPLE: SP= SPACE, M=MOVE,
R=REVISE/REWRITE, PU=PUNCTUATION, CIRCLE IT, 'X' IT OUT, ETC.
[SEE **CH 32** FOR COMPLETE PROOFREADING CODES].

H . *DO: READ IT OUTLOUD:
 - TRY READING ALOUD TO SEE IF IT FLOWS SMOOTH. IF YOU CAN'T
READ IT SMOOTHLY…IT IS PROBABLY NOT SMOOTH. SOMETIMES ROUGH
IS OKAY, TOO. DEPENDING ON WHAT YOUR WRITING…IS YOUR
CHARACTER A "ROUGH AROUND THE EDGES" PERSON…IT'S OKAY.

I. LAST OF ALL, KEEP WRITING OFTEN:
IF YOU LOSE INTEREST, WRITE ABOUT SOMETHING ELSE. I OFTEN HAVE 5
TO 8 "PROJECTS" GOING, WHILE I'M WORKING ON A MAJOR BOOK OR
PROJECT, AND HAVE OFTEN INCLUDED THESE "OTHERS" IN OTHER
BOOKS.

J. NOW, THE BIGGEST RULE OF ALL:
THERE AIN'T ANY RULES!
FORGIVE MY ENGLISH..HA!

(NO RULES ....UNTIL YOU PUBLISH!!! HA!)
YOU ARE IN CHARGE, WHEN AND HOW YOU DO IT, IS UP TO YOU. SO
WRITE FIRST AND ORGANIZE IT LATER WHEN WRITING BECOMES HARD
OR YOU ARE TIRED.

K. TIP:
ONE DAY A WEEK, TRY TO ORGANIZE, REPRINT PAGES, TYPE AN
UPDATED TABLE OF CONTENTS, OR ADD TO GLOSSARY OR INDICES, OR
DO RESEARCH, WRITE NOTES, OR PROOF READ….THOSE DAYS WHEN OUR
"DAY JOB" HAS TAKEN ALL OF OUR ENERGY!

L. TIP: DO DREAM BIG!!!!!!!!
OKAY! …IT'S NOW TIME TO DREAM … JUST WRITE WHATEVER.
THE "ALL OF THE ABOVE" WILL COME TOGETHER OVER TIME AND THE
PARAGRAPH WILL HAVE ITS OPENING, MEAT AND SIZZLE.

LET THE **PARAGRAPHS CONNECT** BY CONTINUING FROM THE LAST, OR
ADD THE IMAGERY OR SOME OF THAT GREAT RESEARCH YOU FOUND IN
THE PARAGRAPHS FOLLOWING. MAKE IT PERTINENT OR IT WILL JUST BE
FILLER. USE YOU OWN WORDS OR **SOURCENOTE** IT-[ON THE BACK
PAGE]. JUST CONTINUE. … WRITING!

M. TIP: VARY TYPE SIZE:
Q. DID YOU JUST NOTICE HOW THE TYPE SIZE CHANGED & HOW YOU SAW
THESE WORDS??????? SOMETIMES USE OF A VARIETY HELPS WAKE UP
THE READER TO AN IMPORTANT POINT.

TIP: WHERE TO WRITE:
SETTLE IN "YOUR SPACE," IN THAT COMFORTABLE CHAIR, WITH YOUR
GLASSES, PENCILS, A DRINK AND A SMALL SNACK.

N. *DO: WRITE IN ONE SPACE, EDIT IN ANOTHER:
EDITING IS READING EACH PARAGRAPH FOR DIFFERENT THINGS AT
DIFFERENT TIMES. EXAMPLES:

CREATIVE WRITING—THE KELLY MANUAL OF STYLE

1.GRAMMAR & PUNCTUATION-FONTS-PARAGRAPH SPACING
2.WORD CHOICE & SPELLING-& SPELL CHECK
3.OPENING & CLOSING SENTENCES
4.SUBJECT & VERB TENSE AGREE-ALSO PARAGRAPHS AGREE
5. DESCRIPTIONS-CHARACTERS
6. DESCRIPTIONS-SCENE-LOCATION-EVENT-TIME
7. DIALOGUE -5 SENSES-PICTURESQUE WORDS
8. CHARACTER INTERACTION-PLOT-THEME
9. EVENTS-ACTION-DRAMA-HUMAN EMOTIONS
10.SURPRISES FOR READER-UNKNOWNS-
11.PLOTS-THEMES-CLIMAXES WORK.
12. PROOFREADING ALL-FINAL MANUSCRIPT CHANGES
         READ IT ALOUD FOR WORD FLOW.
6.3.1.13.

IMPORTANT:

NOW *DO: THIS TEST FOR A SUCCESSFUL BOOK:
REFER TO CHS 30-31 FOR COMPLETE EDITING INFO.
THEN MASTER WRITER REVIEW CH 28-
THEN DO A TITLE REVIEW IN MARKETPLACE-CH 53.
MARKETING REVIEWS CH 54-
IT MUST PASS ALL OF THESE TO BE SUCCESSFUL!

6.4.0.0. SUMMARY-----READER:
WHO IS THE READER? WHO DO WE WRITE FOR ?
CAN WE READ IT ALOUD? DOES IT FLOW? IS IT HARD TO UNDERSTAND? IS
HE LISTENING TO OUR STORY?
WHAT DO WANT THE READER TO DO? REMEMBER? GET EXCITED, FIND
THE CLUES? SAVE THE WORLD?
BECOME THE VIRTUAL WRITER, VILLAIN OR THE HERO?
HOW MUCH DO WE TELL THE READER? LET THEM GUESS? GET LOST? USE
THEIR IMAGINATION?
THE READER IS THE WRITER'S ALTER EGO...HIS SHADOW IN PRINT!

6.5.0.0. STORYTELLING: A SIMPLE FORMAT TO FOLLOW:
HERE IS A SIMPLE FORMAT TO FOLLOW SO YOU MAY BEGIN TO WRITE
AND APPLY THE MANY ELEMENTS OF WRITING. THIS IS EXPLAINED IN
CHAPTER 7: THE STORYTELLER'S SYNOPSIS.

STORYTELLER'S SYNOPSIS: [CH 7].
    EXAMPLE: CH 7.0.2.1-AUGGIE AND BANGER.
    EXAMPLE: CH 7.0.2.2- THE BOOMERS
CHAPTER BY CHAPTER SYNOPSIS: [CH 9].
    EXAMPLE: CH 7.3.0.4. - THE BOOMERS

6.6.0.0. NARRATOR:
CHAPTER TOPICS:
WHO IS THE VOICE?-NARRATOR-STORYTELLER-

6.6.1.0. VOICE DEFINED:
CHOOSING THE NARRATOR IS HOW YOU WRITE ITS 'VOICE.'

CREATIVE WRITING—THE KELLY MANUAL OF STYLE

THE NARRATOR USES HIS VOICE AND MANNERISMS
LIKE THE INTUITIVE INDIAN CHIEF AND THE SETTING TO TELL THE
STORY. IN **"LEGENDS OF THE FALL"** THE INDIAN CHIEF IS THE
STORYTELLER AND CARRIES US OVER FROM DIFFERENT SCENES
(EVENTS) AND SETTINGS (PLACES) AND EVEN CHANGES IN DIALOGUE. HE
TALKS ABOUT THE BEAR AND THE INDIAN WAY OF LIFE HIS
CONNECTION WITH THE MAIN CHARACTER OR HE DOES THE
STORYTELLER'S NARRATION.

THE STORYTELLER TELLS THE STORY A CERTAIN WAY-HIS VOICE.
THUS, NARRATIVE PROSE.

**THE CHARACTER SPEAKS IN HIS OWN CHARACTERS' LANGUAGE,
REGIONALISM OR ACCENT AND HIS CUSTOMS.**

6.6.2.0 THE VOICE-WHO IS THE STORYTELLER?
THIS IS A DIFFICULT ELEMENT TO DESCRIBE, AND IS THUS OFTEN
NEGLECTED OR MISUNDERSTOOD. IN SHORT, THE **NARRATIVE
VOICE IS THE VOICE IN WHICH YOU WRITE THE STORY.**

YOU MAY CHOOSE TO TELL IT IN YOUR OWN **"NATURAL" VOICE** (THIS IS
THE EASIEST AND MOST COMMON CHOICE), OR YOU MAY CHOOSE TO
USE AN **ADOPTED VOICE,** SUCH AS THAT OF ONE OF THE CHARACTERS.

YOU WILL OFTEN BE UNAWARE OF CHOOSING NARRATIVE VOICE, BUT IT
CAN BE WORTHWHILE TO THINK ABOUT YOUR OPTIONS, OR TRY
SEVERAL VOICES OUT, BEFORE YOU BEGIN.

6.7.0.0. PROSE: 3 VOICES:
CHAPTER TOPICS:
WRITTEN EXPOSITION, NARRATIVE, AND DIALOGUE.

DEFINITION:
PROSE IS NORMAL OR NATURAL WRITING.

6.7.1.0. FICTION DEFINED FOR COMPARISON:
FICTION IS DIFFERENT FROM POETRY BECAUSE IT IS WRITTEN IN
PROSE. WE OFTEN THINK OF PROSE AS "NORMAL" OR "NATURAL"
WRITING, AS OPPOSED TO THE CAREFULLY CONSTRUCTED LANGUAGE
OF METERED POETRY. FREE VERSE IS THE OPPOSITE. EVEN, RHYMING
WORDS HELP GIVE US THE SOUND AND REPETITIVE VOWELS AND
CONSONANTS NEEDED IN PROSE.

6.7.2.0. PROSE DEFINED:
FICTIONISTS USE PROSE TO CHOOSE WORDS AND LANGUAGE TO HAVE
SPECIFIC EFFECTS. PROSE IS THE **WRITING** IN THOSE VOICES.

PROSE COMES IN SEVERAL TYPES, AMONG THEM EXPOSITION,
NARRATIVE, AND DIALOGUE. EACH OF THESE TYPES OF PROSE HAS A
DIFFERENT FUNCTION IN FICTION,

6.7.3.0. EXPOSITION VOICE:
EXPLANATORY OR DETAILS EXPOUNDED. THE EVENT DESCRIBES THE
WHOLE STORY, NOT THE CHARACTER.

THE EVENT'S EXPLANATION IS THE MAIN CHARACTER.

6.7.4.0. NARRATIVE VOICE:
THE NARRATOR'S VOICE: EITHER THE STORYTELLER OR THE NARRATOR
IS THE NARRATIVE VOICE. IT MAYBE NATURAL OR ADOPTED VOICE
FROM A CHARACTER TELLS THE STORY USING HIS VOICE AND
MANNERISMS AND THE SETTING TO TELL THE STORY. SEE CHAPTER 24.

6.7.5.0. DIALOGUE VOICE:
SIMPLY, THE WORDS ARE SPOKEN THROUGH EVENTS, THE CHARACTER'S
ACTIONS, THE CLIMAXES, THE PICTURESQUE SIGHTS AND SOUNDS. THIS
IS THE "SHOW BUT DO NOT TELL" YOU MUST MASTER.

> 6.7.5.1. CLASS: CHOOSE ONE OF THE VOICES AND WRITE AN EXAMPLE.
> IDENTIFY THE VOICE AND WHY?

6.6.4.0. OUR PROGRESS:
A.WE LEARNED ABOUT VOICE AS OUR NARRATOR.

B.WE INCORPORATED A DIALOGUE VOICE IN OUR CHARACTERS AND
    EVENTS.

C.READING OUTLOUD GIVES US THE STORYTELLER'S VERSION.

D.STORYTELLING IS A VERBAL PICTURE OF OUR STORY. THE SOUNDS
    AND IMAGES GIVE IT LIFE!

E.WE PROGRESSED FROM A VERBAL STORYTELLER TO WRITING IT
    DOWN, AS A WRITER.

F.WE COMPARED OUR STORYTELLER AND WRITER- ROLES.

G.WE LEARNED HOW TO FIND THE COMMON THREAD IN OUR CHAPTER
    TOPICS. COMMON THREADS ARE OUR THEMES AND PLOT.

H.WE LEARNED TO WRITE A SUMMARY OF OUR STORY; THUS,
    OUR STORYLINE. ALSO HANDY TO TELL FRIENDS WHAT OUR
    BOOK IS ABOUT.

I.SOME TOOLS TO HELP IMPROVE OUR WRITING WITH MORE TO COME.

J.WE LEARNED ABOUT OUR WRITING SPACE AND OUR EDITING SPACE.

K.WE LEARNED OUR READER IS OUR ALTER EGO---OUR SHADOW IN
    PRINT.

HOW TO USE 'VOICES:'
1. WE LEARNED THREE DIFFERENT TYPES OF VOICES.
2. FREE VERSE IS NATURAL WRITING.
3. POETRY CAN BE FREE VERSE OR STRUCTURED, OR METERED.
4. OUR CHARACTER'S VOICE IS HIS DIALOGUE AND LOCAL METHODS.
    EXAMPLE: REGIONAL ACCENTS, BROGUES, SOUNDS, MANNERISMS ;
    THUS, WHAT HE SAYS, HOW HE SAYS IT AND DOESN'T SAY.

7.0.0.0.-STORY TELLER SYNOPSIS:

A STORYTELLER'S SYNOPSIS: 1 OR 2 PARAGRAPHS ONLY.
TO CREATE A SYNOPSIS (A PARAGRAPH OR TWO) WRITE DOWN YOUR
BOOK KERNEL IDEA, THE MAIN CHARACTER AND THE PLOT AND ANY
MAJOR CLIMAX. NOW WRITE IT IN **PARAGRAPH FORM**. ADD WHAT THE
STORY IS ABOUT, ADD THE KERNEL IDEA ,A MAIN CHARACTER AND
NARRATOR.

7.0.1.0. EXAMPLE: FORMAT:

1.DIVISION= *'BOOK DIVISION.'* **[CH 1.4.2.0.].**
2.FICTION TYPE: *'FICTION OR NON-FICTION'* **[CH 1.4.3.0.].**
3. GENRE': *'FICTION'* **[CH 1.4.4.0.].**
4. FICTION GENRE': *'LITERARY & GENERAL FICTION'* **[CH**
   1.4.5.0.].

NOTE: PUBLISHERS-COPYRIGHT OFFICE, BOOK SELLERS &
LIBARIANS CLASSIFY YOUR BOOK: ABOVE 1 TO 4 ITEMS.

5. STORY TITLE DRAFT.
6. STORY
7. PREDICAMENT
8. PLOT
9. UNIVERSAL THEME
10. FINISH
11. KERNEL OF STORY (Our idea).

7.0.2.0. EXAMPLE: FORMAT:

DO: FIRST WE CLASSIFY OUR BOOK AT THE TOP OF THE PAGE.
   DO: WRITE THESE FOUR CATERGORIES:
1.DIVISION: BOOKS-(WE ARE WRITING A BOOK)
2.FICTION OR NON-FICTION: (WE CHOOSE FICTION)
3.FICTION: [FROM PAGE 22] (WE SELECT THE TYPE OF FICTION):
   [CH 1.4.5 .0. FICTION-genre'-5 types:]
      1. LITERARY & GENERAL FICTION
      2. HISTORICAL FICTION
      3. MYSTERY-SUSPENSE & THRILLER
      4. SCIENCE FICTION & FANTASY
      5. SHORT FICTION & PULP

4. WE CHOSE: *'LITERARY & GENERAL FICTION.'*

A REAL BOOK: EXAMPLE: STORY TELLER'S SYNOPSIS:
5. BOOK TITLE: TIDEWATER TANGO:
*STORY IS ABOUT DR. MIRIKLE NICKNAMED DR. MIRACLE, "DOC OF THE BAY"
BY HIS NEW PATIENTS IN A FLORIDA CITY, CALLED ARIPEKA. A SMALL TOWN
ON THE COAST, (A SLEEPY FISHING VILLAGE). MAIN CHARACTER LIKES TO*

FISH, DRINK, PLAY CHECKERS-CHESS. HAS FRIEND DR HOOK, HIS NICKNAME WHO HAS BOAT 'HOOK OR BY CROOK.' DR HOOK GETS SHOT AND THE BOAT IS BLOWN UP.

SHERIFF BRAD BARNETT NEARLY ESCAPES, DOC MIRACLE SAVES HIM. SHERIFF IS SUSPICIOUS IF "POT," POACHERS OR OTHER CAUSES CREATED THIS FIRST PLOT. DR. MIRACLE BELIEVES EVIDENCE IS AGAINST DR. HOOK.

7.0.1.0. PREDICAMENT:
DOC MIRACLE GOES TO HOSPITAL AND FINDS SHERIFF AND DR HOOK IS TELLING HIS SIDE OF STORY. DR HOOK IS IN TROUBLE WITH LAW. SHERIFF WANTS HIM IN JAIL. DOC DOESN'T BELIEVES HIS FRIEND, DR. HOOK IS INVOLVED.

7.0.2.0. PLOTS: [REFER CH 21]
"DR MIRACLE" BECOMES SLEUTH AND ENCOUNTERS BAD GUYS, HURRICANE, COURT TRIAL? ROMANCE ALL PREDICAMENTS AT SAME TIME.

UNIVERSALTHEME: *GOOD WINS OVER BAD.*

FINISH:
ALL PREDICAMENTS/PLOTS ARE RESOLVED. ENDING?

KERNAL OF STORY:
DR. MIRACLE ADVENTURES & MULTIPLE PREDICAMENTS IN SMALL FLORIDA FISHING VILLAGE. HE TAKES ON DRUG DEALERS, HURRICANES, EMERGENCIES, KIDNAPPING, ROMANCES AND A COURT TRIAL.

{RESULT: WE HAVE A KERNAL OF OUR STORY WHICH COULD BE ENTERTAINING AND A MYSTERY.}

IMPORTANT:
OUR STORYTELLER'S VERSION IS REAL SHORT.
WE ADDED PREDICAMENT, PLOT, THEME, AND KERNAL.

NOW, WE USE THIS TO CREATE THE DETAILED SYNOPSIS (OUR # 2) BY EXPANDING ALL ELEMENTS AND ADDING TO IT.

THUS, THIS IS THE SECOND STEPPING STONE TO A BOOK DRAFT.

CHAPTER 8 EXPLAINS HOW.

CHAPTER 8
8.0.0.0 THE DETAILED SYNOPSIS-# 2:
= THE EXPANDED STORY:
SYNOPSIS #1 IS EXPANDED INTO THE DETAILED SYNOPSIS #2

INSTRUCTIONS: DO THIS:

1.WRITER: ***DO:** COPY PASTE YOUR STORYTELLER'S VERSION
   THEN ADD THE FOLLOWING:

2.*DO WRITE: 1 OR 3 PAGES **ONLY**, WITH ALL OF THESE ITEMS:.*

*YOUR STORY GROWS IN DETAIL AND CHARACTER'S ACTIONS, EVENTS AND
PLACES MELD TOGETHER. THEN THEY GET ADDED HERE AFTER YOU WRITE
A LITTLE MORE. THIS SYNOPSIS BECOMES EVOLUTIONARY AS YOU WRITE,*

*THIS UPDATES INTO SYNOPSIS #3 'CHAPTER BY CHAPTER'-WHICH EVOLVES
INTO A BOOK DRAFT.*

DO WRITE THESE ITEMS: ON PAGE ONE:
NARRATOR-MASTER PLOT-UNIVERSAL THEME-CHAPTER TITLES

EXAMPLE: DETAILED SYNOPSIS:
1-2 PAGES MAX.

THE TOPICS ARE IN BOLD, THE DETAIL WE ADD IS IN ITALICS:

1.NARRATOR: DR. MIRACLE.
*-WHO IS TELLING STORY? MAIN CHARACTER-1ST PERSON, OTHER
CHARACTER-2ND PERSON, OBSERVER-3RD PERSON*

2.MASTER PLOTS: [CH 21]EXPANDS:
*"DR MIRACLE" BECOMES SLEUTH AND ENCOUNTERS BAD GUYS,
HURRICANE, COURT TRIAL? ROMANCE ALL PREDICAMENTS AT SAME TIME.*

*DO: WRITE YOUR MULTIPLE PLOTS (AS THEY DEVELOP AND AS YOU WRITE)

**DO: CREATE A NEW SEPARATE PLOTS LIST AND COMPLETE EACH AS A MINI-
STORY. THEN, ADD THESE NEW PLOTS TO FIRST 'STORYTELLER'S VERSION.'*

3.MASTER CHARACTER LIST: [REFER TO CH 20]-WE ADD MORE.
*NEW SEPARATE CHARACTER LIST IS CREATED: EACH OF THESE CHARACTERS
IS EMBELISHED WITH DETAILS.*

4.UNIVERSAL THEME: [REFER TO CH 11]

CREATIVE WRITING—THE KELLY MANUAL OF STYLE

GOOD WINS OVER BAD

* DO: CREATE A UNIVERSAL THEME. THIS IS YOUR APPEAL TO THE READER, WHAT PART OF YOUR STORY IMPACTS HIM, INTERESTS HIM, HE SHOULD IDENTIFY WITH ONE OF YOUR CHARACTERS:

THEME EXAMPLE:
GOOD GUYS VERUS BAD, MORALITY. TRUTH WINS THE DAY. READER IS DRAWN TO STRUGGLE AND IDENTIFIES WITH MAIN CHARACTER: 'DR MIRACLE, OR PERHAPS DR. HOOK (SIDEKICK OR VICTIM) AND A NEW VILLIAN IS INTRODUCED. WHO HAS THE STRONG PART AND IS 50% OF STORY?

5.MASTER CHAPTER TITLES:

CHAPTER ONE TITLE: 'DOC OF THE BAY'
*DO: CREATE A NEW CHAPTER TITLES LIST.
BEGIN USING THESE AND ADD TO THEM. YOU CAN ALWAYS CHANGE THEM.

6.SETTINGS-LOCATION-PLACES: [CH 22]
FLORIDA TOWN-ARIPEKA-FISHING TOWN.

*DO: CREATE A SEPARATE LOCATION LIST: *(TOWNS-LOCAL BUILDINGS-DOCKS-SALVAGE YARDS AS USED IN YOUR STORY.*
THIS HELPS IDENTIFY FOR READER WHERE YOUR PLOTS AND EVENTS ARE TAKING PLACE. EXAMPLE: DOCTOR'S OFFICE, BOAT DOCK, BACK PORCH, HOSPITAL.

8.1.0.1 SYNOPSIS-#2-RESULTS:
WRITER: SO OUR STORY IS FLESHED OUT, BUT NOT COMPLETE.
THIS SHOWS OUR EVOLUTION, AND WHEN WE ADD DESCRIPTIVE LANGUAGE, PLOTS, LOCATIONS, EVENTS, EXPAND ON PLOTS-SUBPLOTS, ADD TO OUR UNIVERSAL AND MORALITY THEME.
WE BEGIN A FULLY FLESHED OUT CHARACTER LIST, A TIMELINE, A LIST OF PLOTS. WE STILL NEED A GREAT OPENING SENTENCE.
THEN, WE NEED TO ADD SEVERAL ITEMS TO THIS:
THOSE TERRIFIC BEGINNING .MIDDLE SENTENCES.CLEAR SUBJECTS AND SIZZLING ENDING SENTENCES (CLOSER).
ALSO WE BEGIN TO PUT THEM IN OUR BOOK DRAFT ORDER.

SUMMARY:
8.1.0.2. DETAILED SYNOPSIS: MERGING THE ORAL WITH THE WRITTEN.
NOW TELL YOURSELF THIS SAME STORY OUTLOUD. WRITE DOWN WHAT WAS MISSING. AND FLESH IT OUT. THIS BECOMES YOUR STORYTELLERS SYNOPSIS. DID YOU NOTICE ANY WORD SOUNDS OR PICTURESQUE WORDS-WRITE THOSE DOWN.
THE RESULT: YOU HAVE 2 -3 PAGES IN PARAGRAPH FORM.

OUR PROGRESS:
1.WE ARE NOW READY TO BEGIN OUR BOOK:

2.THE DETAILED SYNOPSIS GAVE US A STRUCTURE WHICH WE WILL
REFINE INTO A BOOK DRAFT.

3.WE ADD THE BOOK TITLE & AUTHOR, COPY RIGHT,
INTRODUCTION,TABLE OF CONTENTS PAGES AND BEGIN WITH
THE BOOK ELEMENTS:

4. THE TITLE,NARRATOR, VOICE, PLOT, UNIVERSAL THEME,CHARACTER
LIST.

5.YOUR STORY BEGINS AFTER THAT.

6. REMEMBER YOUR OPENING SENTENCES, BODY AND THE CLOSING
SENTENCE. EMBELISH WITH GREAT SCENES-PLOTS-AND DIALOGUES.
BLEND ALL OF THESE INTO A TIME ORDERED SEQUENCE.

7. YOU TELL YOUR STORY AND ADD KEY ELEMENTS.

8. YOU CAN ALWAYS REVISE YOUR CHAPTER TOPICS BY INCLUDING
THOSE NEW ITEMS ADDED IN TO YOUR STORY.

9. CAN YOU NOW SEE YOUR ORIGINAL STORYTELLER'S VERSION
CHANGING INTO 1 OR 2 PAGES.

SEE THE EXAMPLE OF 'CHAPTER BY CHAPTER
TOPICS' IN THE NEXT CHAPTER.

THE REAL STORY WRITING BEGINS!

CHAPTER 9

9.0.0.0-SYNOPSES #3-CHAPTER BY CHAPTER-- EXAMPLE:

WE ADDED A STRUCTURE TO OUR STORYTELLING SYNOPSIS AND ADDED SOME MAIN ELEMENTS TO ACHIEVE OUR DETAILED SYNOPSIS.

NEXT OUR STORY IS READY TO GROW INTO CHAPTERS OF OUR BOOK DRAFT. WE ADD CHAPTER TOPICS TO NOT ONLY BEGIN WRITING OUR NOVEL'S CHAPTERS; BUT TO EMBELISH IT TO THE POINT OF PREPARING FOR OUR MANUSCRIPT.

---

*DO:
KEEP YOUR CHAPTER TOPICS ON EACH CHAPTER UP TO DATE.

OUR MANUSCRIPT FORMAT:
IS THE LAST CORRECTED & FINAL EDITING OF OUR BOOK DRAFT. DO: USE CH 36 TO REVIEW THIS DRAFT.

---

*DO:
LEAVE ALL OF THESE ELEMENTS AS WRITTEN UNTIL OUR MANUSCRIPT IS COMPLETE. WE REMOVE ELEMENTS ONLY AT THIS TIME, AS OUR CHAPTERS TELL OUR COMPLETE STORY.

IF WE FIND HOLES, OR CHARACTERS FADE AWAY OR OUR STORY LOSES THAT 'GRAND MASTER' FEEL, WE CAN RELIE ON THESE ITEMS TO FIND THEM AND CORRECT THEM.

NEXT:
THIS PROCESS EVOLVES INTO OUR FINAL DRAFT, WITH PAGES LAID OUT, FORMATTED, NUMBERED=THUS, OUR STRUCTURE IS SET.

WE ADDED ALL THE CHAPTER ELEMENTS, WROTE THE REST OF OUR CHAPTERS AND OUR FINISH.

WE EDITED AND REVISED OVER AND OVER. WE USED OUR CHECKLISTS AND COMPARED AGAINST THE 'GRAND MASTER'S WRITING.

WE THEN PUT IT IN A MANUSCRIPT FORMAT READY FOR PUBLISHING. YEP, ONE LAST EDIT. [CH 36].

LET'S BEGIN SYNOPSIS # THREE:
INSTRUCTIONS:
DO: ADD CHAPTER TOPICS, THEN EXPAND ON ALL ELEMENTS OF THE STORY. SEE EXAMPLE BELOW.

CREATIVE WRITING—THE KELLY MANUAL OF STYLE

9.0.0.0.-CREATE ANOTHER NEW STRUCTURE YOU MUST HAVE FROM PREVIOUS 2 SYNOPSIS;

IT *CHANGES FROM 1 AND 2 INTO A #3SYNOPSIS.*

9.0.1.0.-DO WRITE THESE ELEMENTS AT TOP OF PAGE ONE:

1-DIVISION: BOOKS--BOOK TITLE: THE BOOMERS:
2. GENRE': FICTION-ACTION—3FICTION TYPE: LITERATURE & FICTION.
NARRATOR:MAIN CHARACTER
4. UNIVERSAL THEME: WAR AND PEACE   SUB –THEMES INTRODUCED.
MAJOR CONFLICT: MORALITY OF WAR & PEACE.
MAJOR CLIMAX: TRIAL FOR TREASON
PLOT: INCITING ACTION-DRUG DEALERS-SMUGGLERS-HURRICANES-
    ROMANCE-
-PLOT: MAJOR PLOT EXPLOSION-TBA SUB-PLOTS INTRODUCED.
-PLOT TWIST: ACCUSER IS SURPRISE WITNESS.
-CONFLICT & CONFRONTATION: MORALITY OF WAR AND PEACE
CLIMAX: SHOOTING DURING TRIAL FOR TREASON
THE ENDING: HERO & VILLIAN MEET HEAD ON
-HEART METER: WIFE DIES
-CONFLICT RESOLUTION: WIFE SHOOTS VILLIAN
-MAIN CHARACTER RESULT: HERO PRESENT S MORALOF STORY.
VILLIAN: PROVIDES ANSWERS TO HERO'S MANY CONFLICTS
BRIDGE TO NEXT BOOK: OUR STORY CONTINUES.-POSSIBLE NEW ROMANCE?
-READER- AH HA!

9.0.2.0. TO DO STEPS:

*DO: WRITE A CHAPTER BY CHAPTER SYNOPSIS USING:

1.DO USE FORMAT: IDEA-DASH-IDEA-DASH.
2. THEN FOLLOW THE BEGINNING AND MIDDLE PARAGRAPH FORMAT.
3.NOW POLISH IT INTO A DRAFT COPY OF THE CHAPTER.
4. GIVE IT AN APPROS TITLE TO FIT ITS STORY.
5.CONTINUE WRITING.

*DO: GROUP CHAPTER IDEAS:

GROUP BOTH IDEAS AND EVENTS BY WHAT HAPPENED IN TIME ORDER .

1.BOOK TITLE: *TIDEWATER TANGO*
2.CHAPTER TITLE: *DOC OF THE BAY*

3.   CHARACTERS: [CH 20]
    1.NARRATOR: DR. MIRACLE=BRAND NEW DOCTOR FROM MED.
    SCHOOL. PAST TENSE= WAS, VERB-ED,
    2.DR HOOK=FISHERMAN, FRIEND OF DR. MIRACLE.
    3.DRUG DEALERS- SHOOTS "DR HOOK.", THEN WANTS REVENGE
    4.SHERIFF BRAD BARNETT -INVESTIGATES SHOOTING OF DR. HOOK,
        BELIEVES HE IS A DRUG SMUGGLER.
    5.VILLIANS: EL GRECO, OTHERS

CREATIVE WRITING—THE KELLY MANUAL OF STYLE

4.STORYLINE FROM SYNOPSIS #1: [REFER TO CH 7]

**5.CHAPTER TOPICS: FROM OUR CHAPTER BY CHAPTER
   SYNOPSIS.**

9.0.3.0. EXAMPLE----CHAPTER TOPICS:

*NARRATOR, MAIN CHARACTERS-THEME-FLORIDA PARADISE-TIDEWATER-
EVIL UNDERCURRENT-PARDISE BEACH-TOWN'S NAME-INDIAN CHIEFS
CURSE-CHARLIE MIRKLE=DR. MIRACLE-SOUTHERN WAY-AREA PEOPLE-
OLD DOCTOR- 'YANK'-GETTING ACCEPTED-DR OFFICE-PATIENTS-HOUSE-
BOAT DOCK-MY PHILOSOPHY-DR. HOOK-SWAMP SHINE-A FRIEND-HE IS
SHOT-ACCUSED OF DRUG SMUGGLING-SHERIFF BRAD-DR MIRACLE
BECOMES SLEUTH..*

NOW I WRITE MY FIRST STORY

CHAPTER 1
BOOK TITLE: TIDEWATER TANGO
<u>CHAPTER TITLE</u>: DOC OF THE BAY
<u>NARRATOR</u>: IST PERSON-DR. MIRACLE.-PAST TENSE VERBS

WHEN YOU DREAM OF PARADISE, YOU SELDOM FIND IT; BUT HERE IT
WAS EVERYDAY REGULAR LIKE THE GOOD TIDEWATER. TODAY'S
FORECAST WAS GOLDEN SUNSHINE, WITH A CHANCE OF EVIL.
TIDEWATER IS A SWEEET NAME WE TOWNFOLK UNDERSTAND. ITS
RYTHMN IS RELIABLE LIKE A CLOCK-TICK! ITS EVIL TWIN WAITED IN
UNDERCURRENT LIKE SHADOWS –TOCK!

OUR GOLDEN 'PARADISE BEACH' SOUNDS LIKE A FARAWAY PLACE,
EXOTIC, WITH WHITE GOLD SAND BEACHES, PALM TREES AND RUM
DRINKS. A PARADISE ON THE COAST; YET PEACEFUL, SLEEPY AND
INTOXICATING! WHITE BEACHES, SUN KISSED WATERS, BEAUTY
UNSURPASSED BY THE BIKINI MERMAIDS LOLLING ON THE SHORE.
UNDERNEATH A FIRERY CURRENT BURNS; HEAVEN AND HELL FOR SOME.
YOU CANNOT RUN, NOR ESCAPE; ITS SPELL COMPLETE! DEATH HAS
COME TO CLAIM ITS PRICE!

THE TOWN'S NAME 'ARIPEKA' ITS INDIAN NAME FOR A FULL MEASURE
OF HUMAN SCALPS AROUND THE WAR POLE; A HERITAGE OF HUNDREDS
OF YEARS LEFT IN THE WAKE OF A FIERCE 100 YEAR OLD SEMINOLE
CHIEF. BEAUTY IS THE SUNSHINE, DEATH ITS SHADOW RETURNS TO
HAUNT THE TOWN. OH! FRAIL IS THE HUMAN CONDITION SUBJECT TO
SOUTHERN HOSPITALITY AND RULES OF GENTLEMEN'S BEHAVIOR. THIS
UNDERCURRENT RUNS DEEPER THAN THE TIDEWATER.

MY NAME IS CHARLIE MIRIKLE AND I'VE BEEN ON BOTH SIDES OF THE
FENCE. YOU MIGHT SAY I'VE BEEN RICH A TIME OR TWO AND
SOMETIMES COMFORTABLE. MOSTLY COMFORTABLE AS ECONOMICS
DICTATES; IT RUNS IN AND OUT LIKE THE MORNING TIDE. TIDEWATER IS
A NAME WE UNDERSTAND; LIKE LIFE AND FAMILY HEREABOUTS,
COMING AND GOING. MOST FOLKS WOULD LIKE TO GO LIKE AN ITCH;
BUT MOST JUST STAY, MAYBE HANGING ON OR JUST STUBBORN;
PLANTING ROOTS LIKE THE MANGROVE OR TALL PINE. SOME FAIR

CREATIVE WRITING—THE KELLY MANUAL OF STYLE

WEATHER FOLKS ARE LIKE PALM TREES GOOD UNTIL A BIG SUMMER BLOW SLAMS THE PALMS AND FRUIT TO THE GROUND. PEOPLE HERE WERE THE GOOD AND BAD COMING AND GOING LIKE TIDAL SEASON.

I LEARNED A LOT COMING HERE WHEN I WAS YOUNG AND INNOCENT. I CAME RIGHT AFTER MEDICAL SCHOOL, FULL OF IDEALS AND SPIT! BACK THEN I WAS TALL, SLENDER, MOSTLY BROKE FROM COLLEGE, HIRED TO REPLACE OLD DOC MARTIN WHO RETIRED, CAUSED BY BAD HEART. DIDN'T MATTER NONE, THE SUNSHINE WAS WELCOME AND I NEEDED A JOB, DOWN SOUTH AWAY FROM THE BIG GLAMOUROUS CITY AND THE COLD. DAMN DEEP COLD AND ICE MADE LIVING UP NORTH UNEASY. I WANTED A LITTLE BIT OF HEAVEN. I GOT IT---SORT OF!

YES, AT FIRST I WAS A 'YANK,' A TERM BESTOWED LIKE WATER ON A FIRE. I ADMIT IT WAS STRANGE COMING HERE, UNLIKE NO WHERE ELSE ON EARTH. BUT GRADUALLY, I WON OVER A FEW FOLK. HOSPITALITY WAS ALWAYS A STAPLE HERE; BUT CORDIAL RELATIONS TAKE TIME. FIRST THEY MUST READ YOUR CHARACTER. MY CHARACTER WAS YOUNG AND BROKE; WHICH TOOK EVEN LONGER. CHARACTER OR NOT, TRUST TOOK EVEN LONGER. THAT IS UNTIL A CRISIS CAME ALONG AND TRUST LOOKED A BLIND EYE TO MY NAITIVITE AND THEIR NEED WAS FOR A COUNTRY DOCTOR TOOK FIRST PLACE. IN THE BEGNING IT WAS SIMPLE THINGS: A FLU BUG, A RASH FROM NO-SEE-EMS A LOCAL SMALL BUG WHICH LEFT AN ITCH BEHIND, OR A BROKEN BONE. THE OLD DOC'S PATIENTS WERE HESITANT AT FIRST. SOME CAME ALONG AFTER REMEMBERING A SPELL AND SOME WERE EASY, THEY WERE 'TRANSPLANTS' LIKE ME FROM OTHER PARTS OF THE WORLD.

DOWN HERE THE WORLD WAS ANOTHER PLACE, ANYONE OUTSIDE OF THE MARSH GRASS AND PALM TREE FOREST WAS AN ALIEN, OR WORSE A 'YANK.' STILL THE WORK WAS SATISFYING AND COMPLETED MY DAYS AND SOMETIMES NIGHTS. OH I HAD TO LEARN A FEW THINGS ALONG THE WAY…NO NEW FAST CURES AND SCIENTIFIC MEDICINES. HERBAL CURES AND POLTICES WERE THE PREFERRED METHODS. SEEMS LIKE MY VOICE AND MEDICINE PRACTICE DEVELOPED A TWANG FOLLOWED BY A SOFT FINISH; IT WORKED LIKE A CHARM. I FIGURED AN 'ADAPT OR STARVE' PHILOSOPHY WAS MY BEST POLICY.

MY OFFICE WAS FOUR ROOMS, A LARGE WAITING ROOM, A CRAMPED SUPPLY ROOM FOR MEDICINES OF WHICH THERE WERE FEW AND TWO EXAM ROOMS. STILL I MANAGED TO KEEP THEM FULL ENOUGH AND SPENT TIME WITH EACH AILMENT AND LEARNED THE PARTICULAR NEEDS OF EACH FAMILY. SEEMS THE FAMILY WAS PART OF THE TREATMENT AND WHOLE GROUPS WOULD ACCOMPANY THE PATIENT. "HE IS MY BROTHER OR MY THIRD COUSIN OR MY UNCLE, OR GRANDMA ON MY MOTHERS'S SIDE" WAS THE REPLY TO AN OFFICE FORM. PAYMENT VARIED FROM HARD CASH TO BARTER OR EVEN A LOAN OF A SHOTGUN UNTIL THE BILL WAS PAID. MY GROCERY BILL WAS NON-EXISTANT AS IT WALKED ON 4 LEGS, GREW IN A GARDEN, SWAM IN WATER, OR WAS SMOKED IN A SMOKER. ALL CONTRIBUTED TO MY CAUSE; WHICH WAS MOSTLY BROKE; BUT THE TOWN FOLK CONTRIBUTED A HOUSE, A BARN AND A SHED. SO I HAD NO RENT NOR MORTGAGE. MY LITTLE RED TRUCK WAS A BIT RUSTED FROM UP NORTH AND WAS STILL RELIABLE ENOUGH TO GIT ME TO AND FRO. DOWN HERE FEW VEHICLES STILL HAD SHINY PAINT, THE SUN TORTURED IT. SO NEWCOMERS WERE EASY TO SPOT. VERY FEW OF THEM VENTURED OFF THE MAIN HIGHWAY TO VISIT FOR GAS OR A DRINK. IT MIGHT HAVE

CREATIVE WRITING—THE KELLY MANUAL OF STYLE

BEEN THE SANDY ROAD, ALMOST A PATHWAY BETWEEN THE MARSH
AND THE PALM TREE FOREST, WHOSE NECKS STOOD UP LIKE
PREHISTORIC DINOSAURS. MOST PROBABLY FIGURED THEY GOT LOST
AND TURNED AROUND, LITTLE DID THEY KNOW THEY MISSED PARADISE
BEACH; IT WAS ONE OF OUR SECRETS.
IT WAS ON THAT GOLDEN BEACH WITH SAND LIKE WHITE SUGAR AND
THE TURQUOISE WATER THAT MADE ME FALL IN LOVE.
IT WAS LOVE AT FIRST SIGHT, AND AGIN' AN' AGIN'. SHE WAS
BEAUTIFUL. THAT IS A REAL STORY FOR LATER. (INSERT MIA STEWART)

I LIVED ON SPIT OF LAND WITH LOTS OF PALMS, BIRD OF PARADISE
SHRUBS AND A VIEW OF THE GULF WATERS. IT WAS NEAR A TIDAL INLET
AND A GREAT FISHING SPOT. IT WAS MY LITTLE BIT OF HEAVEN. THE
SHORT ROAD WOUND BACK FROM THE MAIN STREET TO MY HOUSE. IT
WAS PLAIN WHITE WITH A LARGE WINDOW AND A FRONT AND BACK
PORCH FOR SITTING AND THINKIN' THAT FOLLOWED THE SUN.

IN THE YARD, THE WHITE SIGN SAID <u>DR. CHARLES MIRACLE</u>, A MIS-
REPRESENTATION OF SORTS, IT WAS MIRIKLE, BUT SOUTHERN TOUNGUE
TWISTING AND THE ACCENT SOUNDED LIKE MIRACLE. KINDA FUNNY I
THOUGHT; BUT MY PATIENTS DIDN'T MIND A THOUGHT. THEY SEEMED
TO SMILE AT THE MENTION OF MY NAME, **DR. MIRACLE** THEY ALWAYS
SAID. TRUE, IT WAS A MIRACLE, IF I WOULD SURVIVE OR MY PATIENTS
SURVIVE ME. OF COURSE THEY WOULD, ALL IS WELL, AFTER ALL I WAS A
GENIUS, SECOND IN MY CLASS. NO HARD MEASURE AS IT WAS ONLY
FORTY OF US WAN' TO BE'S IN THE SAME CELL. WE ALL LIVED
TOGETHER IN THE SAME SCHOOL, TOOK THE SAME COURSES AND DRANK
TOGETHER. SOMEHOW MY LIVER AND I SURVIVED THOSE SIX MONTH
LONG WINTERS AND WET SPRINGS AND FALL SEASONS.

FUNNY HOW MY PHILOSOPHY CHANGES OVER A GLASS OF BOOZE. NOW
AN'AGIN' IT WAS A LITTLE APPLE SHINE THAT TOOK THE EDGE OFF.
NOW, DON'T GET THE WRONG IMPRESSION, I ONLY DRINK SOME WHEN
FISHING, WHICH IS A LONG TIME. THE WHOLE DAMN TOWN IS FISH
CRAZY, A WAY OF LIFE ALONG THE TIDEWATER. THE TIDE COMES IN,
THE FISH COMES IN. ALL EXCEPT FOR THE MANATEES, WE PULL OUR
LINES OUT FOR THEM. THE REST ARE TARGETS OF SHRIMP, DRAG LINES,
BOBBERS AND NUMBER 1 HOOKS. OF COURSE, STONE CRABS LOVE
THOSE CHICKEN BONES WITH MEAT. FISH AND CRAB FIXED A HUNDRED
WAYS WITH NO RECIPES WRITTEN DOWN MADE A DELICIOUS EVENING
MEAL COLD BEER FOR DESSERT AND THE CHAIR ON THE PORCH WAS ALL
THE EVENING'S ENTERTAINMENT I NEEDED.

THEN I MET DR. HOOK... AGAIN A LIE, HE WAS NO DOCTOR JUST THE
GREATEST FISHERMAN, I EVER SEEN AND DRANK WITH. HE WAS THE
PIED-EYED PIPER OF FISHERMEN. IF IT HAD A MOUTH, IT WAS HOOKED.
THE WHOLE TOWN THOUGHT HE HAD SOME SECRET BAIT, SOME SPELL,
SOME MUSIC THAT JUST CAUSED THEM FISH TO WANT TO BE CAUGHT.
TRUTH WAS HE WAS SILENT AS A DREAM. MOST FOLKS JUST CHATTER
WAY, IT WAS NORM TO CARRY ON ABOUT THIS OR THAT; JUST COULDN'T
SHUT UP. DON'T KNOW IF FISH COULD HEAR; BUT THEY MUST. HE JUST
SANG TO THEM---SOFTLY, A LULLA–BYE SOFT AS A WHISPER, GENTLE AS
A BREEZE. STILL I THINK IT WAS HIS SHRIMP DROWNED IN APPLE SHINE. I
KNOWD HOW THEY FEEL, SHINE AIN'T NO DRUNKIN LIKKER; IT WAS
'SMOOTH SIPPIN SUNSHINE.' YOUR BELLY LIT UP AND YOU WAS SO
RELAXED, LIKE A ROCKIN' CHAIR IN THE SHADE. I ENVIED DR. HOOK, HE
PLAYED CARDS LIKE HE FISHED, NO POKER FACE; HE JUST SMILED ALL

CREATIVE WRITING—THE KELLY MANUAL OF STYLE

THE TIME. SOMETIMES I WONDERED JUST WHAT MADE HIM SMILE SO MUCH.

HIS COMPANY BECAME MY COMPANY, A FRIENDSHIP, NO ACCOUNT THAT I WAS A YANK AND ALL, JUST A FRIENDLY FACE FROM FARAWAY PLACES. WE PLAYED CARDS, CHESS SOMETIMES AND DRANK. AND FISHED TIL THE BAIT OR SHINE WAS GONE. USUALLY ABOUT SUNDOWN. ON ACCOUNT OF MY PATIENTS I NEVER TOUCHED A CANNING JAR. ONE OF MY RULES, I GUESS. MY PATIENTS AND I WERE FAMILY OF SORTS, SINCE I HAD NONE ANYHOW. WE KINDA LOOKED OUT FOR EACH OTHER, THEY GOT HURT OR SICK, I DOCTORED THEM; IT WAS A MUTUAL INSURANCE PLAN---NO DEDUCTABLE EVER.

SO DR. HOOK SHOWS UP, DOCKS HIS BOAT THE 'HOOK OR BY CROOK.' AND LAYS FOUR OF FIVE FISH AND A BUCKET OF CRABS ON THE RICKETY DOCK BENCH AND WE START TO CLEAN 'EM AND I START A FIRE IN A HALF BARRELL BBQ WITH A LITTLE PINE WOOD. SO WE ARE CLEANING, DRINKING A SIP OR TWO AND LIKE A SAILOR, TALKIN 'BOUT THE SKY TONIGHT, A BLAZE OF RED, PURPLE AND CHRIMSON AND AN AZURE SKY. NO SENSE ABOUT THE WEATHER, AS IT USUALLY A BEAUTIFUL SUNNY DAY, EVEN IF IT RAINS A SHORT TIME. WE WERE JUST LUCKY THAT WAY; PARADISE WAS ON PARADE AND SURROUNDED OUR HEARTS AND MINDS.

LATER, WE WAVED 'SO LONG.' THE BOAT TOOK OFF FROM THE DOCK AND MOSIED UP THE TIDAL BASIN TO THE INTERCOASTAL WATERWAY, WHICH WAS KINDA A HIGHWAY FOR BOATS. I SAT ON THE BACK PORCH AND WATCHED ORION RISE HIGH INTO THE SKY AND THEN WENT INTO BED. THE RED SKY WAS MY NIGHT'S DELIGHT!

MORNING WOKE WITH THE FLUTTER OF DOVES AND A FEW FISHERMEN GOING UP WATER. I STRETCHED MY MUSCLES AND ACHES AND SHAVED OFF LAST NIGHT'S DRINK. ONLY THEN I HEARD A CLATTER AND GROAN. I WENT TO THE FRONT PORCH, NO ONE WAS THERE. I LOOKED OUT BACK, THE 'BY HOOK OR CROOK' WAS STAGGERED OUT AND BOW ON TO THE DOCK-CRASHED HEAD ON. WHAT WAS AMISS? I WIPED MY FACE TO GIT A CLEAR LOOK AND RAN BAREFOOT TO THE DOCK. ON THE CABIN FLOOR LAY DR. HOOK. I LEAPED OVER THE GUNRAIL AND TURNED HIS FACE TO ME. IT WAS PEACEFUL---WHAT WAS WRONG? THEN I SAW THE BLOODY SHIRT. A CRIMSON LEAK RAN ACROSS THE FLOOR .
MY GOD! A GUNSHOT WOUND.

'DOC' WHO DID THIS TO YOU?

HE MOANED... "A DRUG DEALER OR POACHER..."

HE PASSED OUT. I CHECKED HIS VITALS EVERYTHING WAS NORMAL EXCEPT FOR SHOCK COMIN' ON. I PRESSED THE WOUND TO STOP THE BLOOD FLOW. I HAD TO DO SOMETHIN' FAST, OR I WAS GONNA LOSE HIM. I TREATED HIM FOR SHOCK, ELEVATIN' HIM, COVERING HIM AND CHECKED HIS PULSE AGIN. THE HOSPITAL WAS AN HOUR AWAY AND HE WOULDN'T MAKE IT IN TIME. I CALLED THE EMERGENCY LINE AND TOLD THEM I NEEDED A CHOPPER RIGHT AWAY. A LIFE FLIGHT WAS JUST LEAVING. GREAT NEWS!

I PROCEEDED TO CHECK HIS WOUND FURTHER, YEP A 30.06 HOLE RIGHT THROUGH, STILL A SERIOUS WOUND. I BANDAGED AND WOUND THE

DRESSING TIGHT. THE RIFLE ROUND MISSED THE MAJOR ORGANS BUT THE MYSTERY WAS BEYOND MY OWN SHOCK. WHO WOULD DO THAT TO OLD DOC? HE WAS THE MOST AMIABLE MAN I KNEW. HAD TO BE SOMEONE ILLEGALLY POACHIN...PROBABLY GATOR, OR BEAR I SUSPECTED. IT HAD TO BE PRETTY ILLEGAL TO SHOOT SOMEONE OVER.

THE CHOPPER CAME AND OFF WE FLEW. I HADN'T FLOWN THAT FAST SINCE THE WAR. TWO YEARS IN ASIA. I USED THE G.I. BILL TO GET MY DOCTOR OF GENERAL PRACTICE DEGREE. OVER THERE, I ALWAYS WANTED TO TAKE CARE OF MY BUDDIES, HELPING THE MEDIC SAVE A FEW LIVES. STILL I WAS JUST A GRUNT, A GROUND POUNDER, WORKING RECON. IT WAS OFTEN SAID, 'I ALWAYS TOOK ON THE TOUGHEST JOB AND DANGER WAS NO FRIEND.'

WE LAND ON THE HELIPAD AND THE DOCTORING STAFF TOOK HIM RIGHT TO THE OPERATING ROOM. TIME WAS OF THE ESSENCE. I WAITED TO FIND OUT ABOUT MY BEST FRIEND.

THE NURSE ASKED WHERE MY SHOES WERE? I SAID, "BACK HOME." WELL, HERE PUT THESE ON, YOU CAN'T RUN AROUND HERE BAREFOOT. I PUT ON THE SOFT DISPOSABLE SHOES AND SAT DOWN. SHE ASKED MY NAME, I TOLD HER. SHE SAID, I HEARD 'BOUT A DOCTOR LIVIN' ON THE TIDEWATER, TAKIN' CARE OF A WHOLE TOWN OUT THERE AND FISHERMEN TOO. YOU THAT DOCTOR?

"YEP, DR. MIRACLE."

"YEAH, I BELIEVE THAT. THAT MAN YOU BROUGHT IN, IT TOOK A MIRACLE; BUT HE'S GONNA LIVE ALL RIGHT. YOU DID GOOD. YOU NEED ANYTHING? "

"YOU GOT ANY COFFEE?"

"YEAH, I'LL FIX YOU UP. GOT ANY MONEY?"

"NOPE NOT WITH ME."

"HERE DOC, HERE IS A TEN SPOT, GET SOME FOOD IN YOU AND I'LL FIND OUT WHEN YOU CAN SEE YOUR PATIENT."

"OH! HE IS MY FRIEND!"

HE IS ONE LUCKY FRIEND YOU GOT. HE LOST A LOT OF BLOOD THAT ONE. THE SHERIFF IS GONNA WANT A STATEMENT FROM YOU; THEN I GIT YOU A RIDE BACK HOME.

THANKS SO MUCH. I'M STARVING.

WELL, DOC STAY OFF THE SAUCE, I SEES THE BLOOD RED IN YOUR EYES. IT SAYING HIGH GRADE ACHOHOL OR MAYBE SWAMP SHINE.

OH I HAD A LITTLE LAST NIGHT WITH DR. HOOK.

IS HE A DOCTOR TOO?

NOPE , JUST THE BEST FISHERMAN IN THREE COUNTIES.

CREATIVE WRITING—THE KELLY MANUAL OF STYLE

WELL, SOMEONE DIDN'T LIKE HIM AT ALL.

HEY DOC, YOU EVER NEED ANYTHING YOU SEE ME OKAY.
YOU FIXED UP SOME OF MY FAMILY OUT THERE. YOU IS ALL RIGHT WITH ME!

WELL, MIGHTY THANKS.

NUTHIN' TO IT. KEEP UP THE GOOD WORK!

I GOT SOME BREAKFAST GRUB, SOME EGGS BACON AND HOME FRIES, STRONG COFFEE THAT TASTED LIKE COAL WATER. I FIGURED I WOULD BE HERE SOME TIME COMIN.'

SOON ENOUGH, THE SHERIFF JOINED ME AND WROTE OUT A REPORT AND THE CAUSE OF THE GUNSHOT AS REQUIRED BY LAW.
I TOLD HIM EVERYTHING I KNEW. HE OFFERED ME A RIDE IN HIS CAR AND WANTED TO INSPECT THE BOAT FOR EVIDENCE. WE WALKED TO THE DOCK AND I STOPPED. "LET ME GET SOME SHOES FIRST, FIRST THE WOOD SPLINTERS AND POSSIBLE BACTERIA FROM CLEANING THE FISH. HE WAITED A SHORT TIME, ICHING TO GET GOIN' AND WALKED THE DOCK AND STOOD THERE SNIFFING THE AIR. HE WAS PART BLOODHOUND AND PART REDNECK.

AS I JOINED HIM, SHERIFF BRAD BARNETT ASKED, "YOUR FRIEND EVER DONE ANYTHING ILLEGAL?"

"NOPE! NEVER!" I QUICKLY REPLIED.

"WELL, I SMELLED SOMETHIN' SWEET …COULD BE WEED?"

"WEED? YOU MEAN---"

HE STEPPED ON BOARD, I PUSHED HIM OVERBOARD INTO THE WATER JUST AS I HEARD THE TWANG OF A WIRE GO SNAP. I HEARD THAT PLENTY OF TIMES BACK IN THE WAR. A BOOBY TRAP, A GRENADE ATTACHED TO A WIRE. WE BOTH SURFACED AS THE BOAT CAUGHT FIRE. I SAID, "DIVE!"

THE BOAT'S GASOLINE TANK BLEW AND THE WHEELHOUSE WENT SKY HIGH. THE WATER FLASHED CRIMSON AS THE FIRE SPLASHED OVER OUR HEADS. A SECOND BOOBY TRAP BLEW THE BOAT INTO PIECES. WE CRAWLED ONTO THE ADJACENT WOODEN DOCK CATCHING OUR BREATH AND WATCHING THE BOAT BURN COMPLETELY UP AND THE SKELETON SINK.

OUT OF BREATH, HE SAID, "YOU SAVED MY LIFE TWICE, JUST NOW. HOW DID YOU KNOW?"

"BOOBY TRAPS!" WAS ALL I COULD WHISPER AND BREATH AT THE SAME TIME.

ALL I COULD SMELL WAS MARJUIANA THEN WE HIT THE WATER.
DID YOUR FRIEND EVER DO ANY SMUGGLING?

NOPE, NEVER--- HE WAS TRUE BLUE!

DO YOU KNOW WHERE HE WAS AT WHEN HE WAS SHOT?

NO, HE WAS PRETTY MUCH IN SHOCK, WHEN HE HIT MY DOCK.
HEAD ON. HE DIDN'T SAY MUCH AT ANY TIME.

OKAY, GUESS I BETTER HEAD BACK TO THE HOSPITAL AFTER I CALL THIS
IN. I' LL NEED ANOTHER STATEMENT FROM YOU AS TO WHAT HAPPENED
HERE TODAY. YOU OKAY WITH THAT?

I NODDED. GOD! I NEEDED TO START EXERCISING AGAIN!

HE LOOKED AT ME, NODDED AND CONTINUED TALKING ON HIS SERVICE
PHONE.

 I MUMBLED: I CAN'T BELIEVE MY DOC--- A SMUGGLER?
NOPE IMPOSSIBLE!

I GRABBED MY RIBS...THEY USED TO BE FLAT, WHAT HAPPENED TO ME?
THE RED MARKS ON MY STOMACH WERE FROM CLIMBING UPON THE
DOCK. YEP, THEY LOOKED LIKE FATTY BACON TO ME.

I WATCHED THE SHERIFF'S CAR PULL OUT THE SANDY LANE AND
TURNED TOWARDS THE TOWN. THINKIN,' *WHAT EVIL CAME TO VISIT US?*
MAYBE THE OLD CHIEF'S CURSE CAME BACK. 100 YEARS TO THE DAY! OR
MAYBE, SOMETHING OR SOMEONE ELSE SENT A TIDAL
WAVE HERE?

I GOT DRESSED AND WENT TO WORK. PATIENTS GIT FIGGITY WHEN THEY
WAIT TOO LONG. LATER I WOULD GO TO THE HOSPITAL TO SEE DR. HOOK.
STILL AN UNEASYNESS SETTLED AROUND ME AND LEFT ME WITH A
HUNDRED QUESTIONS.

THIS DRAFT TO BE CONTINUED:
CHAPTER 2: AGAINST THE WIND.
CHAPTER 3: A THOUSAND WORDS
CHAPTER 4: MR. LUCKY
CHAPTER 5: TWO TO TANGO
CHAPTER 6: BAD GUYS COME AKNOCKIN'

Summary:
CHAPTER BY CHAPTER SYNOPSIS-VIA THE TOPICS LIST:
OUR CHAPTER BY CHAPTER LIST OF TOPICS IS A MERGER OF OUR IDEAS
LISTS, CHAPTER SUBJECTS AND CHARACTER LISTS. WE SIMPLY LIST
THEM IN ORDER WITH THE CHAPTER TITLE.

WE HAVE ENOUGH MATERIAL TO THINK ABOUT OUR FIRST AND SECOND
CHAPTERS. WE USE THIS LIST TO ORGANIZE OUR BEGINNING, MIDDLE
AND END SUBJECTS FOR EACH CHAPTER.

DO JUST LIST THEM AND ORGANIZE THEM IN OUR FIRST DRAFT. THINK
ABOUT WHAT OPENS OUR STORY AND HOW DOES IT PROGRESS IN A
TIMELY MANNER. INTRODUCE OUR NARRATOR AND THE MAIN
CHARACTER. EXPLAIN HIS/HER PREDICAMENT. WE CAN ADD OUR FIRST
DRAFT CHAPTER TITLES IF WE KNOW THEM.

CREATIVE WRITING—THE KELLY MANUAL OF STYLE

RESULT:
DETAILS WERE ADDED TO FLESH OUT STORY, THE 1ST PREDICAMENT IS TOLD, CHARACTERS WERE GIVEN NAMES, FIRST PLOT IDENTIFIED. FIRST SENTENCE NEEDS WORK.

SYNOPSIS#3- ORGANIZATION:

1BOOK CLASSIFICATION: [CH 1.0.0.0.]
LITERATARY CATEGORY: A-Z LITERATURE & AUTHOR'S LAST NAME
BOOK DIVISION: #1=BOOK DIVISION
MAJOR GENRE: #11= FICTION/
MINOR GENRE: REGIONAL STORY
FICTION DIVISION: LITERARY & GENERAL FICTION
OUR BOOK TITLE COMPETITION: (RESEARCH OUR TITLE ON WEB)
MASTER IDEAS LIST: (ALL BOOKS & PROJECTS)
THIS BOOK IDEAS LIST: (ITEMIZED FOR THIS BOOK ONLY).

2.OUR BOOK-KEY ELEMENTS:
1.SYNOPSIS #1-STORYTELLER'S STORY
2.SYNOPSIS #2-DETAILED.
3.NARRATOR- WHO'S TELLING THE STORY
4.SYNOPSIS #3
5.MASTER CHAPTER TITLES LIST
6.UNIVERSAL THEME [CH 5].
7. MASTER PLOTS& TWISTS:
8. PREDICAMENTS/LIST ALL
9. MASTER CHARACTERS & VILLIANS-DETAILED LIST
10. MASTER LOCATIONS/SETTINGS/PLACES
11. MASTER CHAPTER TITLES
12. MASTER TIMELINES
13. SCENES-DIALOGUE-DRAMATIZATIONS-CLIMAXES
14.DO: ALL CHAPTERS AND INDEX INDEX12-FINAL REVIEW
15.DO: FINAL PROOFREADING AND EDITING, REPEATEDLY.
16.DO: MASTER PRE-PUBLISHING REVIEW LIST

2.PAGE NUMBER ORDER-[REFER TO CH 13].
1.TITLE PAGE (TITLE AND AUTHOR'S NAME)
2.COPYRIGHT PAGE (SECOND PAGE ALWAYS)
3.OPTIONAL PAGE: PUBLISHER'S INFO.
4.DEDICATION
5.INTRODUCTION
6.TABLE OF CONTENTS(RIGHT HAND PAGE)
7.CHAPTER ONE BEGINS
8.ALL CHAPTERS

3.BOOK END ITEMS: [REFER TO CH 13.1.1.0.]
1. SUBJECT INDEX& PAGE #
2. OTHER INDICES
3. PHOTO CREDITS
4. AUTHOR'S BOOKS
5. MASTER SOURCE LIST: (# 1 TO #100)
6. BLANK PAGE (ALWAYS BLANK-NO HEADER/PAGE #).

4.COMPUTER FILE ORGANIZATION [CH 13.5.0.0.]
5.THE ABOVE ITEMS CREATES OUR FIRST BOOK DRAFT.

NOW YOU SEE WHY WE DON'T WRITE FROM AN OUTLINE. FROM THIS RESEARCH, WE HAVE NATURAL IDEA GROUPINGS, SOURCE DOCUMENTS AND STORY IDEA TOPICS FROM A BROAD PERSPECTIVE TO A FINER PARAGRAPH OR CHAPTER TOPIC. CHOOSE THOSE YOU LIKE OR IS TIMELY FOR YOUR STORY.

SYNOPSIS DEFINED:
TO GATHER KEY STORY ELEMENTS TOGETHER, CREATE A COMPREHENSIVE STRUCTURE, AND CONDENSE STORY INTO A ONE OR TWO PAGES IN A PARAGRAPH FORMAT.

SYNOPSES: IS PLURAL OF SYNOPSIS

EXAMPLES-STORY SUMMARIES:

9.2.0.1. EXAMPLE: THE BOOMERS:

OUR NARRATOR, KELLY CHANCE GOES OFF TO WAR AND BECOMES NATIONAL HERO. ALONG WITH 4 FRIENDS , CALLED , "THE BOOMERS" HE FACES SEVERAL THINGS LIKE ATTACKS, HELICOPTER CRASH-COURT MARTIAL. LATER HE IS A PRISONER OF WAR AND AGAIN A HERO.

HE COMES HOME AND MARRIES A PEACE ACTIVIST, JULIET ROSE DARLING, AND EVERYTHING CHANGES. SHE DEALS WITH PROTESTS AND ACTIVISTS, SUPPORTED BY A CHARACTER CALLED THE PREACHER. SECRETS-SPYING AND OTHER SECRET GOINGS ON OCCUR. THE CHICAGO PEACE DEMONSTRATIONS GO BAD. HE IS FORCED TO TAKES SIDES. (HIS PREDICAMENT).

MICKEY, HIS FRIEND AND NOW, HIS VILLAIN COMES HOME AND KELLY IS PUT ON TRIAL FOR TREASON. THE TRIAL BECOMES THE MAJOR CLIMAX AND PLOT CONCLUSION. WAR AND PEACE ARE ALSO CONTRASTED. THE ENDING IS A PLOT TWIST AND THE UNEXPECTED HAPPENS.

9.2.0.2. THUS, FROM THE PARAGRAPHS ABOVE, WE KNOW:

TITLE: "THE BOOMERS."
THE NARRATOR: KELLY CHANCE. (3RD PERSON).
THE MAIN CHARACTER AND HERO: KELLY CHANCE
HIS SUPPORTING CHARACTER: SEVERAL/JIMBO, SERGEANTS, OFFICERS.
THE FEMALE MAIN CHARACTER, THE ROSE, THE HAT, JULIET ROSE
HER SUPPORTING CHARACTER: THE PREACHER
THE VILLAIN: MICKEY
TIMELINE: HIS HISTORY AS CHILD TO WAR VETERAN AND AS ADULT.
THEMES: WAR AND PEACE).(GOVERNMENT-POLITICS- CORPORATE
      GREED, SMALL TOWN AMERICA, THE NEWS, WAR AND PEACE
      EFFECTS ON PEOPLE.
THE SCENE SETTING: WAR ZONE, CHICAGO, WASHINGTON D.C.
THE BASIC PLOT: WAR AND PEACE CHARACTERIZED AND CONTRASTED.
CLIMAX: EVENTS AT COURT MARTIAL AND TRIAL FOR TREASON
PLOT TWIST: FIELD BATTLE PROMOTION FROM SARGEANT TO OFFICER
      VERBAL BATTLE AND SHOOTINGS BEGIN.
MAJOR CLIMAX: EVENTS AT TREASON TRIAL
ENDING: CLOSURE FOR VILLAIN-MICKEY, PREACHER, JIMBO, ROSE.

CREATIVE WRITING—THE KELLY MANUAL OF STYLE

9.3.0.14. WRITING STYLE: *USE OF FRAGMENTS, ELLIPSES, PACING OF WORDS, REPETITIVE WORDS, ASSONANCE, INJECTION OF HUMOR AND EMOTIONS, ACTION SCENES INSERTED TO PROVIDE PACING AND STORY LINE CONTINUATION, IMAGERY, BLENDING OF MULTIPLE PLOTS INTO STORY, ETC.*

9.3.0.15. STORYTELLING THE BEGINNING:
STORYLINE: A COUPLE OF PARAGRAPHS TELLING THE STORY.
OVERVIEW: HIS (SOLDIER)AND HER LIFE(PEACE ACTIVIST) AND WHY THEY MET AND IMPACT ON WAR AND PEACE.

THE LIFE OF AN AMERICAN HERO SOLDIER, POSTER BOY FOR AMERICA CONTRASTED TO A DEDICATED PEACE ACTIVIST HUNTED BY THE FBI. WAR & PEACE& MAIN CHARACTERS ARE BOTH PUT ON TRIAL FOR TREASON. THE GOOD AND UGLY PARTS ARE CONTRASTED IN SAME TERMS OF WAR AND PEACE.

SOLDIER BECOMES RELUCTANT HERO IN WAR AND MEETS HIS FUTURE WIFE AS BOTH IDEALISTS. WAR CHANGES BOTH. HE BECOMES PRISONER OF WAR. SHE BECOMES A FUGITIVE PEACE DEMONSTRATOR. THE MAIN THEME AND CLIMAX COMES DURING A TRIAL FOR TREASON.

9.3.0.16. SITUATION-HIS PREDICAMENT OR CONFLICT:
TWO WARS IN CONFLICT. CONTRASTING MAN VERSUS WOMAN'S VIEW.-HOW THIS RELATES TO OUR READER. BETRAYAL-TREASON-TWO WARS-PEACE MOVEMENT.

9.7.0.0. A BOOK SUMMARY :
DEFINED: A SHORT CRYPTIC PARAGRAPH TELLING BASIC STORY AND PLOT, SOME CLIMAXES AND MAYBE THE ENDING IF KNOWN.
USE THIS WHEN EXPLAINING A STORY TO A FRIEND OR USE IN A QUERY LETTER.
GOAL: *SHORT SWEET AND COVER SUBJECT: MINISKIRT!*
BOOK SUMMARIES INCLUDE ALL OF THE STORYLINE.

EXAMPLES:
9.7.0.1. RED HEART: (FICTION) 300 PAGES- WORDS. -2001.
BOOK ONE OF SERIES-KELLY CHANCE ADVENTURER-SECRET AGENT.
A MYSTERY INVOLVING ADVENTURE-ROMANCE-HISTORY-MYSTERY-TRAGEDY, TRIUMPH, AND THE RED HEART DIAMOND. TWO PEOPLE AND TWO NATIONS COLLIDE: ONE RED, ONE WHITE. KELLY CHANCE AND KATHY DARLING OVERCOME PRIDE AND PREJUDICES TO FIGHT GOOD OVER EVIL, WINNING EACH OTHERS HEARTS AND RIGHTING PAST INJUSTICES. TOGETHER THEY FORM A RED EMPIRE! A DOUBLE MURDER TRIAL AND LATER A LAND TRIAL TEST THEIR WILL AND LOVE. WILL THE RED HEART DIAMOND HOLD THEM TOGETHER? THEIR LIVES AND EVEN NATIONAL HISTORIES WILL BE RE WRITTEN. SUPPORTING CHARACTERS INCLUDE JIMBO, HIS SIDEKICK, RED HIS TWIN BROTHER, KATHY DARLING, HIS PRINCESS AND 'SCARFACE' THE VILLAIN. LOCAL HISTORY, LEGENDS AND AMERICAN HISTORY WILL NEVER BE THE SAME AGAIN. (A BOOK TO BE READ ALOUD). TWO YEARS IN THE WRITING.

9.7.0.2. AFFAIRS OF THE HEART: 184 PAGES.
(POETRY & LOVE LETTERS) -2001. A SELF HELP BOOK FOR THE HEART! A COLLECTION OF THIRTY YEARS OF POETRY, LOVE LETTERS AND WRITINGS. THIS IS A JOURNEY OF UNDERSTANDING LIFE, LOVE AND WAR! THIS IS YOUR GUIDE TO WINNING HEARTS AND LOSING YOUR

FEARS. THESE MESSAGES GIVE HOPE AND LOVE WHEN YOUR HEART HURTS AND ANSWERS DON'T COME. THIS IS OUR MUTUAL SEARCH FOR UNDERSTANDING "AFFAIRS OF THE HEART!"

9.7.0.3. BLONDES AND OTHER DANGEROUS WOMEN: (FICTION).
SECOND OF SERIES OF KELLY CHANCE. THE ULTIMATE PRIVATE INVESTIGATOR! KELLY IS A "HELPLESS" ROMANTIC, DANCER, WINE EXPERT, INVENTOR, WRITER AND SECRET AGENT.2011-164 PAGES

A TALE OF GOOD GUYS VERSUS BAD. HIS CARS, BOATS AND LOVERS CONSUME HIS TIME BUT NOT HIS HEART! A NEW LOVE IS INTRODUCED: 'DESTINY!' HIS WIT AND HUMOR LEAVE US LAUGHING AND SMILING AS HE DREAMS OF A BETTER LIFE WITH THE WOMAN OF HIS DREAMS. SUPPORTING CHARACTERS ARE FRIEND, FATHER MURPHY, AND NEW ENEMIES THE BLOND BOMBER, HARRY LEGGS, AND MAJOR BUCKS. SURVIVING THE 'BLACK CADILLAC' AND ITS BAD GUYS IS HIS CURRENT ROLE IN LIFE.

9.7.0.4. REDHEADS ...THE MOST DANGEROUS OF ALL!
FICTION-MYSTERY-SPY-2002.-2011
BOOK FOUR OF A SERIES. WASHINGTON-PARIS. INTRODUCTION OF LINDA LOU AND DESTINY AS TWO CONTRASTING WOMEN. PROVING REDHEADS IS THE MOST DANGEROUS OF ALL!
KELLY HAS NEW ADVENTURES IN WASHINGTON D.C. AND PARIS AS HE FIGHTS ON THE SIDE OF GOOD AGAINST MAJOR BUCKS AND HIS EVIL ORGANIZATION. WHILE HE IS SAVING THE WORLD, HE MEETS HIS SOUL MATE, LINDA LOU A BEAUTIFUL REDHEAD FULL OF PASSION AND FIRE. SHE IS A BALLERINA, DANCER, ART EXPERT AND BUSINESSWOMAN. SHE IS A "HOPELESS" ROMANTIC BUT FINDS KELLY TOO "MACHO AND A "HELPLESS ROMANTIC!"

THINGS HAVE CHANGED FOR KELLY, HIS NEW HOUSE, NAMED 'SHANGRI-LA' HIS NEW CAR, 'BEAUTY' TALKS BACK. ONE OF KELLY'S OLD FLAMES, A CABARET SINGER, DESTINY" DIES TRAGICALLY. HE GOES UNDERCOVER TO FIND THE ANSWERS AS TO WHO WANTS TO KILL HIM AND HIS FRIENDS. HIS FOES: SCARFACE, HUMMER, AND HARRY LEGGS DO ALL THEY CAN TO KILL KELLY FOR MAJOR BUCKS, A LEADER OF THE SECRET EVIL ORGANIZATION OF GLOBAL INTERFERENCE (S.E.O.G.I). WILL HE SURVIVE AND WIN LINDA LOU'S HEART? WILL HE GIVE THE RED HEART DIAMOND TO LINDA LOU OR WILL THE CURSE HAPPEN AGAIN? HE GETS A SECOND CHANCE TO FIND OUT!

9.7. 0.5. SPIES, THIEVES AND OTHER FRIENDS! FICTION—2003-234 PAGES
ADVENTURE-MYSTERY! AFGHANISTAN.
KELLY CHANCE GOES UNDERCOVER TO AFGHANISTAN AS A FREELANCE SECRET AGENT: "THE SHADOW." HE FIGHTS HIS OWN BATTLES WITHIN AND THE WAR WITH AN IMPOSSIBLE MISSION: TO SAVE THE WORLD AND NOT NECESSARILY HIMSELF. HE HAS A SCORE TO SETTLE AND MORE NEW ENEMIES. HE BATTLES WINDSTORMS, TORNADOES OF FIRE, SHARKS, ARMIES OF EVIL SOLDIERS AND THOSE DAMN POISONOUS GREEN FROGS. HE WINS A SWORD FIGHT, A GUN BATTLE, MISSILES AND SURVIVES TORTURE. HE BATTLES ON THE SIDE OF GOOD AGAINST UNJUST GOVERNMENT POLICIES, CROOKED WARLORDS, OPIUM SMUGGLERS AND THE MASTER OF ALL EVIL, MAWLANA, 'THE DEVIL.'

THE KHYBER PASS AND AFGHANISTAN WILL NEVER BE THE SAME! WILL HE COME HOME TO LINDA LOU? HAS HE BROKEN THE CURSE OF THE RED HEART DIAMOND?

INTRODUCES NEW CHARACTERS-BON-BON, THE FRENCH PRINCESS, JIMBO HIS SIDEKICK, AZIZ THE SCORPION, MOHAMMED THE PATRIOT, TWIN-SPIN—TWIN AGENTS, SCARFACE AND HUMMER AND A NEW VILLAIN CALLED MAWLANA. HIGH TECH NEW WEAPONS, JASMINE THE TALKING PISTOL, JASMINE AND ANGELIQUE AS FOREIGN AGENTS, A NEW CAR, A WHITE HORSE CALLED 'MIDNIGHT' AND 'COSMO,' THE CANTANKEROUS , COSMOPOLITAN CAMEL.

9.7.0.6. A NOBLE AND SAVAGE HEART-2005-348 PAGES.
FICTION-ACTION-THIRD KELLY CHANCE SERIES.
CLUES ABOUND WHICH TRACE YOUNG KELLY CHANCE'S LIFE FROM HONG KONG TO FRANCE AND IRELAND. HE FINDS HE IS THE NINTH DRAGON WITH SEVERAL LIFETIMES AND A WORLD TO SAVE. THE RED CROSS AND THE RED HEART DIAMOND ARE TRACED REVEALING SECRETS HE DOESN'T WANT TO KNOW. SECRETS, CURSES AND CLUES ALL NEED SOLVED IN TIME TO SAVE THE WORLD AND FIND HIS SECRET FATHER. THE "FROG" EARNS HIS CHANCE TO BECOME THE PRINCE. FORTY CLUES AND THEN THE STORY TWISTS FOR A SURPRISING

CHAPTER TOPICS: A GROUPING OF IDEAS:
EXAMPLE: THE 'THE BOOMERS' STORY: 2007-486 PAGES
KELLY'S HOME LIFE, GROWING UP, FIST FIGHT-ROMANCE- IDEALISM-DRAFTED INTO ARMY, LIFE ON BASE, SARGEANT SUICIDE-GOING OVERSEAS, MAKES NEW FRIENDS-ARMY BASE, SUPPLY DEPOT, GUARD DUTY, WOUNDED, HOSPITAL, VC ATTACK BASE-CONFRONTS GENERAL, FLYING DUST-OFF, TROUBLE WITH FIRST SARGEANT-CRASH LANDING-FIGHTING ENEMY-CAPTURED-POW-WOUNDED-CUTE NURSE-HERO-2ND COURT MARTIAL- FIELD PROMOTION TO LIEUTENANT-GOING TO D.C. FOR INTELLIGENCE TRAINING-MARRIES ROSE-SHE GOES UNDERGROUND- HE IS SENT TO CHICAGO-DEMOCRATIC CONVENTION –PEACE MARCHES-SPEECHES-TEAR GAS- THE POLICE BRUTALITY- CIVIL RIGHTS- THE BOMBER-THE ARMY-THE FBI- SECRET CONSPIRACY. SCAPEGOAT FOR CHICAGO'S EVENTS- TRIAL FOR TREASON- (MANY EVENTS AT TRIAL & NEW CHARACTERS)-TESTIMONY-WITNESSES- THE JUDGE- THE PROSECUTOR-JUDAS-SHOOTINGS- TRIAL CONCLUDES- A DEATH-THE END.

CHAPTER 10

10.0.0.0. STORY STRUCTURE -A CHECKLIST:

10.0.0.0. INTRODUCTION:
OUR STORY CONTAINS SOME BASIC ELEMENTS, WHICH HELP US PUT TOGETHER A BOOK AT THE BEGINNING.

10.6.1.1. CONTENTS:
THE TITLE-THE AUTHOR-THE READER-THE SYNOPSIS-OUR POINT OF VIEW-OUR VOICE-THE NARRATOR-THE BASIC PLOT-THE SCENE-DIALOGUE-DRAMATIZATION-THE CLIMAX- THE TWIST- THE COMEDY-THE TRAGEDY-THE MURDER-THE MORALE -THE ENDING- CONFLICT RESOLVED.

10.6.1.2. ☑ *CHECK LIST FOR THE BOOK'S STRUCTURE:*
10.6.0.2. ANSWER THE 6 W'S:
WHO- WHAT-WHEN-WHERE-WHY-WOW:

10.6.0.3. TELL OUR STORY SYNOPSIS OUTLOUD:
HOW DID IT SOUND? [REFER CH 7]

10.6.0.4. WHAT IS MISSING?

10.6.0.5. WHAT CAN WE ADD?

10.6.0.6. WHAT 1ST OR 3RD PERSON IS OUR VOICE?

10.6.0.7. WHAT MASTER IDEA GROUP DID WE USE:

10.6.0.8. LIST OUR SPECIFIC IDEAS GROUPS:

10.6.0.8. WHAT GENRE' WILL BEST TELL OUR STORY?

10.6.0.9. WHAT IS THE BACK STORY?

10.6.0.1.0 WHO IS/ARE THE MAIN CHARACTER(S)?

10.6.0.1.1. WHO IS/ARE THE SUPPORTING CHARACTERS?

10.6.0.2.0. WHERE DOES STORY BEGIN?

10.6.0.2.1. LIST THE SCENES WHAT PLACES DOES THIS OCCUR IN…LIST COUNTRIES-CITIES, STREETS-BUILDINGS , ROOMS, CARS BUSES, TRAINS, ETC. *ACTION:* IF THEY ARE ON THE RUN? FROM? TO? HOW?

10.6.0.3.0. WHAT KINDS OF DIALOGUE SUPPORT OUR ACTORS AND SCENES?

10.6.0.4.0. DRAMATIZATION: HOW DOES THIS SUPPORT OUR PLOT?

10.6.0.5.0. PLOT AND SUB-PLOTS:
DO WE WEAVE A MAJOR PLOT WITH SUB-PLOTS?

CREATIVE WRITING—THE KELLY MANUAL OF STYLE

WHAT THEME RUNS THROUGH IT? IS IT A SPY NOVEL?
A MURDER, A MYSTERY, ROMANCE, MOTIVES, OTHERS, OR SOME OF EACH OF THESE?

10.6.1.0. HOW DO WEAVE OUR CHAPTERS INTO A STORY?
CLASS: -TWO STORIES IN ONE- ALTERNATING CHAPTERS? FLASHBACKS- A TIMELINE- A CHARACTER'S HISTORY-WE WRITE FROM OUR CHAPTER BY CHAPTER SYNOPSIS. [REFER CH 9].

- *WRITE SOME CHAPTER TITLES AFTER YOU WRITE THE STORY. WHAT DO THEY SAY ABOUT THEME? ARE THEY CLEAR OR OBTUSE? CATCHY? CLICHÉ'- FIX IT!*

10.6.2.0. PARAGRAPHS WITHIN CHAPTER?
DO OPENING SENTENCES PROVIDE A "HOOK?" [CH 14]
DO PARAGRAPHS SUPPORT OUR "CHAPTER IDEA LIST" AND CONNECT TO EACH OTHER?

10.6.3.0. FILLER?
DOES THE READER WANT TO KNOW ALL OF THIS?

10.7.0.0. SUMMARY:
IF WE COMPLETED ALL OF THIS ANALYSIS: WE FOUND SOME ITEMS TO FIX, SOME TO ADD AND SOME TO REMOVE. WE HAVE JUST EDITED OUR STORY LINE AND ALL OF THE ELEMENTS MOVING OUR STORY TO THE FINISH. THUS, WE HAVE CONFIDENCE OUR STORY IS BUILDING AND WILL FINISH.

10.8.0.0. OUR PROGRESS:
1.WE HAVE THE BEGINNINGS OF AN IDEAS LIST. [CH 5].
2.WE HAVE THE BEGINNING OF A CHAPTER BY CHAPTER SUBJECT LIST.[CHS -9-10].
3.WITH ALL THREE SYNOPSES COMPLETED, WE ASSEMBLE THEM AND BEGIN TO WRITE OUR BOOK DRAFT.

10.9.0.0. STORY STRUCTURE-THE BEGINNING:
LET'S COMPARE OUR DRAFT FOR STORY STRUCTURE. THIS IS OUR MEASUREMENT OF OUR STORY'S COMPLETENESS.
1.A DESCRIPTION OF OUR MAIN CHARACTER'S WORLD-WHO HE IS, WHAT HE THINKS, AND WHAT IS CHANGING AND WHY WOULD THE READER BE INTERESTED.

2. WHAT IS OUR MAIN CHARACTER'S NEED, HIS GOAL, HIS PREDICAMENT, IS IT A PERSONAL OR MORE OF A NATIONAL NEED?

3.DESCRIBE THE INCIDENT WHICH CHANGES HIS WORLD, HIS VIEW OF IT AND HOW HE RESPONDS TO THIS INCIDENT. IT SHOULD BE A MAJOR EVENT.

4.DOES THE MAIN CHARACTER HAVE A PLAN OR AN ATTEMPT TO RESOLVE THE EFFECTS OF THE INCIDENT?

5.DESCRIBE HIS ANTAGONIST, AND HIS ALLIES, MENTOR WHO WILL HELP HIM FAIL OR SUCCEED. THESE MUST BE STRONG CHARACTERS AS WELL, BUT SUPPORTING ROLES.

6. NAME SEVERAL SHORTCOMINGS, FAILURES AND ATTEMPTS TO BEAT THE ODDS. THERE MUST BE SEVERAL TO REINFORCE HIS STRUGGLES. EACH GROWING IN INTENSITY. CREATE WITH MENTAL STRESS, PHYSICAL WOUNDS, SHOT, HURT, WITH NEARLY IMPOSSIBLE CHANCES OF SUCCESS.

7. THE FINAL BATTLE,OR CONFRONTATION MUST HAVE HERO LOSING, THAT ALL IS LOST, FAILURE IS EMMINENT THEN A (PLOT TWIST) HE SAVES HIMSELF, THE WORLD, ETC AND EVERYTHING TURNS AROUND TO A WIN-WIN SITUATION.

8. WHAT HAPPENS HERE IS THE ANTAGONIST IS "HANDLED, KILLED OR "DELAYED" FROM PREVENTING THE HERO FROM SUCCEEDING. IS THERE ANY CHARACTERS WE NEED CLOSURE FOR? ANY EOC: END OF CHARACTERS?

9.THE CONCLUSION: IMPORTANT WE WRAP UP THE STORY WITH A SOLUTION TO PREDICAMENT. RESOLVE THE MAIN CHARACTER SITUATION FULLY. DOES HE RETURN TO THE SAME WORLD AS BEFORE? DOES HE LEARN SOMETHING…IS THERE A MORALE , A LESSON TO BE LEARNED? IS THERE A HAPPY ENDING OR TRAGEDY?

10. EACH OF THESE STRUCTURES ARE TO BE PLACED INTO OUR CHAPTER BY CHAPTER SYNOPSIS. IT IS FROM THIS, OUR STORY IS WRITTEN AND TOLD. WE SATISFY THE WRITER'S NEEDS AND THE READER LIKES IT. WE HAVE THE AH! HA! THE CIRCLE IS COMPLETE!

FOR EXAMPLE: STRUCTURE:

10.10.0.0. THE BEGINNING STORY:
FROM OUR SYNOPSIS, WE HAVE THE STORY KERNAL THE UNIVERSAL THEME-A MAIN CHARACTER(S) OR MORE-HIS PREDICAMENT AND A REASON FOR THE READER TO READ ON. NOW WE CAN ADD TO THIS THE BASIC STORY ELEMENTS TO FLESH IT OUT.

10.11.0.0. BACK STORY: [WHAT IS BACKGROUND OF ALL MAIN CHARACTERS, WHY ARE THEY IN THIS PREDICAMENT OR *CONFLICT?]*
OTHER PEACE ACTIVISTS IN CHICAGO-WASHINGTON D.C..
SMALL TOWN AMERICA'S REACTION TO WAR, TV NEWS AND DEMONSTRATIONS ACROSS AMERICA.
ALSO CHARACTERS PROVIDE SPECIFICS TO BACK STORY-VIA CONVERSATION AND EVENTS: HOME TOWN- LANGUAGE AND WORD CHOICE-HOPES-DREAMS-FUTURE. MICKEY'S HOME LIFE-DEAR JOHN LETTER-LIQUOR & GUN-DIVORCE. REASONS FOR WAR AND EFFECTS ON MEN. *WAR EVENTS: BATTLES-HEROISM-DEATH-LIFE-RELIGION.*
PEACE: KEY FIGURES IN HISTORY-SPEECHES AND DEMONSTRATIONS.
AMERICAN PEOPLE'S CHARACTER STRENGTHS AND THOUGHTS ABOUT WAR.
THIS EDITING EXERCISE WILL HELP YOU USE SCREENWRITING TECHNIQUES TO ELIMINATE UNNECESSARY BACK STORY IN YOUR FICTION. SOME BACK STORY IS ALWAYS PRESENT.

10.12.0.00. MAIN CHARACTERS: [CH 20].
WHY THEY ARE MAIN CHARACTERS. (LEADING MEN & WOMEN) .
NOTICE THE INTERACTIONS BETWEEN MAIN CHARACTERS:]

TWO MAIN: KELLY CHANCE & -JULIET ROSE DARLING.
VILLAIN: MICKEY-"MICKEY MOUSE.".
MAIN SUPPORTING: PREACHER

PERSONIFIED: *ARMY VERSUS GOVERNMENT- POLITICS AND WAR MONEY,*
WAR AND PEACE DEFINED AND CHARACTERIZED AS HERO AND VILLAIN AT
TREASON TRIAL.

10.13.0.0.- MAJOR SUPPORTING CHARACTERS-SUPPORTING PLOT: [CH 20].
[CREATE A DETAILED LIST AND WHY THEY SUPPORT MAIN CHARACTERS:
MORE IMPORTANT ONES NEAR TOP OF LIST.
 LESSER CHARACTERS APPEARING IN CHAPTERS.
- 26 CHARACTERS.
- *THE OTHER BOOMERS*
-*SARGEANT DAN*- LIEUTENANT KERRY. THE GENERAL
-*PEACE ORATORS OF HISTORY.*
-*MAJOR POLITICAL FIGURES*
-*HOMETOWN & FAMILY CHARACTERS*
-*MAJOR ARMY FIGURES*

CHARACTERS SUPPORT THE MAIN CHARACTERS AND GIVE DEPTH TO
STORYLINE. CHARACTERS VARIED WITH NAMES AND BACKGROUNDS,
OTHERS HAD NO NAME OR BACKGROUND. SOME IN SHORT EVENTS AND
SETTINGS ONLY.(TAXI DRIVER-MAD BOMBER).

**EACH CHARACTER'S SPECIFICS CAME FROM OUR DETAILED
CHARACTER LIST FOR THE ONE BOOK..**

10.14.0.00. SETTING: PLACE: [CH 22].
MAJOR SETTINGS: *VARIOUS BATTLE SITES-WASHINGTON DC- SMALL TOWN-*
VIETNAM AND AMERICA- HOSPITAL-COURT HOUSE

EXAMPLE; MINOR SETTINGS:
HOME –FARM-FIST FIGHTS LOT-HOME LIFE-NEIGHBORHOOD-DRAFT BOARD-
ARMY BASE-SCHOOLS-MICKEY'S HOUSE- DEAR JOHN- CALIFORNIA JUNGLE
TRAINING-GOING ON SHIP-ARRIVING VIETNAM- SUPPLY BASE- GOING TO
VIET VILLAGES AT NIGHT-1 ST ATTACK-GUARD DUTY AT P.O.L. DUMP- 2ND
ATTACK-HOSPITAL- ENEMY BASE CAMP-HOSPITAL-1ST COURTROOM FOR
COURT MARTIAL-WASHINGTON D.C.-SANCTUARY HOUSE-PENTAGON-
WAREHOUSE-SECRET MEETINGS- STEEL YARD- HOSPITAL -JAIL-2ND
COURTROOM-GARDEN.

10.15.0.0. SCENES: EVENTS. [CH 25].
[WHAT TYPE OF HAPPENINGS ARE TELLING OUR STORY?]
EXAMPLES: HELICOPTER CRASH, HOSPITAL-BIRTH, CHICAGO- PROTEST
MARCH, COURT ROOM –TRIAL. THE EVENT REQUIRED A PLACE FITTING
FOR EVENT TO HAPPEN. PLOTS AND CLIMAXES PICK THE EVENT. WHERE
IT HAPPENS IS THE SETTING.

10.16.0.0. TIME LINE:
CROSSES EACH CHARACTER AT DIFFERENT

TIMES : SHOWS PAST TO FUTURE-FLASHBACK-FLASH
FORWARD. CROSSES. [CH 26].

10.17.0.0.LANGUAGE: [CH 17-18-19-20].
[WHAT KINDS OF LANGUAGE ARE THE CHARACTER'S USING? REGIONAL?
PERIOD? SLANG? REAL LANGUAGE?]
ARMY SLANG AND CUSS WORDS-GLOSSARY. G.I. ACRONYMS.
SOUTHERN DIALECT USED TO REINFORCE SOUTHERN CHARACTERS.
ARMY TERMINOLOGY(GLOSSARY).
BLACK LANGUAGE & TERMS USED.
OTHER SUPPORTING CHARACTER'S LANGUAGE.

10.18.0.0. WORD CHOICE: [CH 17-18-19-23].
AUTHOR USES CUSS WORDS, SLANG AND VIETNAMESE
TERMS. PAINS TAKEN NOT TO CONFUSE READER.
SHORT WORDS AND FAST PACE FOR ACTION. 'TERMS' ARE
DEFINED . GLOSSARY PROVIDED AT REAR OF BOOK.

10.19.0.0. MAJOR PLOTS: [CH 21].
[THESE MUST SUPPORT THE STORY AND THE MAIN *CHARACTERS; THUS,*
PROVIDING THE FRAMEWORK FOR THE STORY'S UNIVERSAL THEME.]
WAR & PEACE CONTRASTED WITH EVENTS. THEIR LIFE BEFORE AND AFTER
THE WAR. MENTAL HEALTH. MORALITY OF WAR. CONSCIENCE.
GOVERNMENT. MICKEY IS A JUDAS AT THE TRIAL.

10.20.0.0. MINOR PLOTS: [CH 21].
[*THESE SUPPORT KEY SCENES WITHIN STORY AND SUPPORT OVERALL PLOT.*
MINOR PLOTS ARE EVENTS THAT SUPPORT SPECIFIC THEMES. ALSO
COMEDY, TRAGEDY, CHARACTERS DYING OFF,]
EFFECTS OF DRAFT. VIETNAMESE GENERAL WITH AMERICAN LOVE OF
MOVIES. WAR DEAD. COLLEGE CAMPUS'S DEFIANCE.
WORKINGS OF GOVERNMENT AND ROLE DURING WAR AND PEACE
DEMONSTRATIONS. RESULTS OF PEACE CONFLICTS WITH CHICAGO
POLICE. MAD BOMBER.

10.21.0.0. REINFORCEMENTS TO PLOT:
ADD ITEMS TO REINFORCE PLOT-STORYLINE-DIALOGUE: *WAR EVENTS,*
WHICH MAKE HIM A HERO. POLITICS, WHICH CHANGE HER INTO AN
ADVERSARY OF THE GOVERNMENT. PROTAGONIST HAS ACCIDENT CAUSING
AN ANOTHER CLIMATIC EVENT AT THE MAJOR CLIMAX OF THE TREASON
TRIAL.

10.22.0.0.. PLOT TWISTS: *[IS THERE A PLOT TWIST? [CH 21].*
MICKEY'S APPEARANCE AT TRIAL AS PROSECUTOR'S KEY WITNESS.
PREACHER'S ROLE IN DEMONSTRATIONS AND AT TRIAL AS PRISONER.
SHOOTINGS

10.23.0.0. THE WOW: TWO PLOTS TWISTED TOGETHER WITH
UNEXPECTED CONSEQUENCES AND CLIMAXES.

10.24.0.0. PLOTS: IMPACT ON DRAMATIZATIONS:[CH 21.]
-CONTRAST WAR HERO AND REAL PERSON.
-INVOLVE THE READER
-EVOKE EMOTIONS
-DEFINE WAR AND PEACE

CREATIVE WRITING—THE KELLY MANUAL OF STYLE

-DEFINE TRUTH AND LIES
-NEWSPAPER HEADLINES
-DEFINE GENERAL – KILLING OF ENEMY SOLDIER
-LEAVE UNDERSTANDING OF WAR AND PEACE
-RESOLVE PERSONAL LIFE AFTER WAR

10.25.0.0.. DIALOGUE: SUPPORT FOR PLOT & THEMES: [CH 25].
- USE TO SUPPORT EVENT AND DRAMATIZATION
-CONVERSATION WITH BUDDIES
-CONVERSATION WITH GENERAL
-CONVERSATION WITH MARINE GUARD
-CONVERSATION WITH "VOICE."
-CONVERSATION WITH BOMBER
-CONVERSATION WITH NEWSPAPER & TV GUY
-CONVERSATION WITH PREACHER
-INTERACTION WITH ROSE
-CONVERSATION WITH PROSECUTOR
-CONVERSATION WITH MICKEY AT TRIAL
-CONVERSATION WITH SON
 -WRITING OF BOOK
-SECRET CACHE
-SECRET ACCOUNTS BOOK

10.26.0.0. DRAMATIZATION: Example:

ACTOR'S PORTRAYAL-[CH 25].
HIS CHARACTERIZATION TO REAL LIFE AND EVENTS-HIS REAL LIFE:
KELLY'S RETURN TO HOME AND TOWN REACTION TO UNIFORM. HIS
THOUGHTS. BAR SCENE. HIS LIFE GROWING UP- THE BOOMER
CHARACTERS.
SARGEANT OF GUARD AND ATTACKS. COURT MARTIAL FRIENDS WITH
OTHER SARGEANTS IN TEXAS SUICIDE OF SARGEANT-PRISONER OF WAR-
SAVING OF LIEUTENANT'S LIFE- MEDALS FOR HEROISM.

TRAGIC HELICOPTER CRASH WITH MICKEY . - 100'S OF ATTACKS ON BASE-
SAVING THE GENERAL'S LIFE- PROMOTED TO OFFICER- WASHINGTON
D.C. - *SENSES AND REFLECTIONS. VISIT TO ARLINGTON CEMETERY.*
SECRET CONVERSATIONS-LETTERS-NEWSPAPER ARTICLES- MURDERS
SECRET MEETINGS-FBI SURVEILLANCE- MAD BOMBER IN GRANT PARK
HOSPITAL SCENE AND BIRTH OF CHILD. REACTION TO ROSE'S LETTER.

THE TRIAL FOR TREASON WAS BIGGER THAN BIG NEWS!
"THE BOOMERS" AND WAR AND PEACE WERE ON TRIAL FOR TREASON.
KELLY CHANCE IS THE WAR HERO FIGHTING FOR HIS IDEALS, HIS
COUNTRY, AND HIS OWN SURVIVAL. HE IS THE POSTER BOY FOR
AMERICA, FIGHTING FOR APPLE PIE, MOM, AND THE FLAG. JULIET ROSE
DARLING IS THE EPITOME OF PEACE, LOVE, AND UNDERSTANDING. SHE
FIGHTS THE SYSTEM, GOVERNMENT AND ARRANGES "PEACE"
DEMONSTRATIONS AND SECRETLY FERRETS THE ORATORS AND POETS
TO THE NEXT DEMONSTRATION. HE WOULD GIVE ALL OF HIS MEDALS TO
SAVE HER.

10.27.0.0. DRAMATIZATION: [CH 25].
DID WE BLEND THEM INTO A REALISTIC STORY?
IS THERE SOMETHING MISSING FROM OUR STORY OR IDEA LIST?

CREATIVE WRITING—THE KELLY MANUAL OF STYLE

SMALL TOWNS TYPICAL OF AMERICA- REACTIONS TO WAR AND PEACE.
LOVE & ROMANCE. WAR EVENTS, PRISONER OF WAR, PEACE MOVEMENT,
TRIAL FOR TREASON.

10.28.0.0. TRAGEDY:
DEATH AND DESTRUCTION. CONFLICT OF CONSCIENCE. LOSS OF
CONNECTION WITH HOME. MORTAR ROUND WOUNDS MICKEY. OTHER
WAR DEATHS. SUICIDE.

10.29.0.0.COMEDY: NOTICE HOW HIS HUMOR IS INTERSPERSED WITH
SERIOUS TOPICS AND HIS THOUGHT PROCESSES.
METHOD: JOKES. IRONY. MAIN CHARACTER'S THOUGHTS.

10.30.0.0. MAJOR CLIMAX: *[STORY-CHARACTERS & THEMES COME
TOGETHER.] [CH 27].*
TURNING POINT. ALL PREVIOUS CHAPTERS POINT TO CHANGE.
*WAR AND PEACE AND THOSE RESPONSIBLE ARE ALSO PUT ON TRIAL. WAR IS
PUT ON TRIAL. CONSPIRATORS ARE JUDGED. WOUNDED FRIEND
CONFRONTS WAR HERO. MICKEY PROVIDES EVIDENCE. PREACHER DIES.
MICKEY DIES. " THE HAT" DIES.*

10.31.0.0. MINOR CLIMAXES: *[WHAT IS MAJOR CLIMATIC EVENT AND
HOW ARE MAIN CHARACTERS AFFECTED?]*
*PEACE DEMONSTRATION AT CHICAGO DEMOCRATIC CONVENTION.
MAYOR DAILY'S ROLE- POLITICS VERSUS GOVERNMENT'S POWER.
WASHINGTON D.C. TRIAL FOR TREASON. SHOOTINGS AT TRIAL.
WIFE: ROSE DIES. MICKEY DIES. KELLY LIVES. RETURNS TO ROSE'S GARDEN.*

10.32.0.0. CLIMATIC EVENTS:
[PORTIONS OF STORY ARE CONCLUDED.]
WAR LEFT BEHIND. HE COMES TO WASHINGTON D.C. AS AMERICA'S NEW
HERO AND POSTER BOY. WASHINGTON BECOMES NEW STAGE.
*MICHAEL LOSES LEGS TO CRASH AND IS SENT TO WASHINGTON D.C. GETS
ARTIFICIAL LEGS. HOLDS KELLY RESPONSIBLE AS GUNG –HO SOLDIER.*
COMES TO TRIAL TO ACCUSE AND HELP CONVICT KELLY OF TREASON.
SHOOTINGS AT TRIAL..

10.33.0.0. CONCLUSION: *[IS THERE AN ANSWER TO THE CONFLICT OR
PREDICAMENT?]*

*MAJOR TRIAL FOR TREASON CONCLUDES AND PREPARES FOR CLIMATIC
ENDINGS. MORE THAN ONE AND WITH A PLOT TWIST AT ENDING. ALL MAIN
CHARACTERS AND ROLES ARE RESOLVED. WAR HERO AFTERWARDS
REMAINS. HER BOOK NEEDS FINISHED. THE SON GETS A HOME AND FATHER.
'THE WATCHERS' CONTINUE SURVEILLANCE.*

10.34.0.0. THE READER:
SATISFIED ALL THE READER'S EXPECTATIONS?
THE WOW FACTOR? ENTERTAINMENT

*MALE AND FEMALE READERS RELATE TO SOLDIER AND HIS WIFE AS PEACE
LEADER AND THEIR HUMAN CONDITIONS. A STORY FILLED WITH WAR AND
PEACE AND CONFLICT OF CONSCIENCE AND HEART. READER'S TEARS AND
HAPPINESS FLOWS. A CONNECTION IS MADE AND READER IS IDENTIFIABLE*

AS HERO AND LOSER. MALE READERS LIKE ACTION AND DRAMATIZATION OF KELLY'S ACTIONS DURING THE WAR AND AT THE TRIAL.
WOMEN READERS LIKE HERO BUT IDENTIFY WITH STRUGGLES OF ROSE AND HER FEELING ABOUT HER LIFE, CHILD AND IDEALS.

10.35.0.0. ILLUMINATION? READER'S IMAGINATION.
FIGURES OF SPEECH-[CH 18]. COMPARISON-CONTRAST. CLUES-MYSTERY-WHAT HAPPENS NEXT. DID WE USE SOME SENTENCES TO ILLUMINATE BUT NOT TELL OUR READER, TO SHOW HIS PART IN THE STORY?

10.36.0.0.TO THE READER: WHAT DID WE PROVIDE?
ENTERTAINMENT-YES. LIFE IN WAR-YES.
REAL LIFE IN PEACE DEMONSTRATIONS-YES.
FAMILY LIFE-YES. ACCURATE DEPICTIONS OF FEDERAL TRIAL FOR TREASON-YES. BIG BUSINESS & GOVERNMENT'S ROLES-YES. HUMOR-YES. TRAGEDY-YES. CLIMATIC EVENTS-YES. TEARS-EMOTIONS-YES.

10.37.0.0. WAS BOOK'S MESSAGE RECEIVED BY READER?
YES. *(if not –re-write).*

10.38.0.0. THE WRITER'S HOOK TO THE READER:
DID OUR OPENING PARAGRAPH CATCH THE READER'S INTEREST? TO GO ON READING…TO BUY THE BOOK?

EXAMPLE: FIRST SENTENCES:

THE BOOMERS FIRST SENTENCE:& OPENING PARAGRAPH: CHAPTER 1
TOPICS: SOME CHOICE: DRAFT NOTICE, A BULLET, PRISON, OR A FIRING SQUAD!

1-WAR AND PEACE?
THE HEADLINES READ, HE WAS THE HERO…SHE THE TRAITOR!

TOGETHER, WE SHARED FEW CHOICES: A BULLET, PRISON, OR A FIRING SQUAD! BUT IT WAS A SINGLE LETTER THAT STARTED OUR TWO WARS!

WE WERE THE "BOOMERS,"… SAVIORS OF THE WORLD. WE WERE INVINCIBLE AS ONLY NINETEEN YEARS COULD THINK! WE WERE RAISED UP ON "SUPERHEROES" AND THE BREAKFAST OF CHAMPIONS.™

WE WOULD BRING OUR OWN SPECIAL TYPE OF WARFARE; WE CALLED IT "BOOM, BOOM!" AFTERALL, WE WERE THE "BOOMERS!"

2.FIRST SENTENCE-THE NAKED CITY-A MOVIE & TV SERIES.

ITS ONE A.M. ITS A HOT SUMMER NIGHT! THE CITY IS…

10.39.0.0. DID THE READER LIKE OUR MARKETING? DID HE LIKE THE UNIVERSAL THEME AND SUPPORTING THEMES?
WAR AND PEACE CONTRASTED AND COMPARED. STRONG MAIN CHARACTERS AND STRONG HISTORICAL EVENTS AS BACKGROUND FOR PERSONAL LIFE HAPPENINGS.

10.40.0.0. DID THE TITLE OR FRONT COVER INTRIGUE OUR READER?:
DID IT REPRESENT THE UNIVERSAL
MESSAGE? DID ITS IMAGE SAY ANYTHING?-YES.

WERE THERE ANY MARKETING MESSAGES*?-NO.*
TITLE OF BOOK: WAS IT DIRECT NOT VAGUE?-YES.
DID TITLE AND COVER GO TOGETHER? –YES.

10.41.0.0. DID OUR **REAR COVER PRESENT A CLEAR MESSAGE:**
STORYLINE-YES. MARKETING-YES.
REASONS TO READ & BUY BOOK-YES.

10.42.0.0. WHAT WERE THE NEGATIVES: 'BOOMERS' AS TITLE
WAS SEARCHABLE ALONG WITH 50,000 OTHER ITEMS ON WEB FOR BABY
BOOMERS. HOLE IN STORY "WHAT JOB DID HE DO IN WASHINGTON, D.C.?"
PROVIDED "FEDERAL COP" COVER STORY, WORKING FOR NSA.
TERRORIST INCIDENT ON PLANE WITH HOSTAGES PROVIDED PAUSE AND
FILLED THIS 'HOLE' IN TIME AND WITH JOB. HIS REASON TO BE AWAY
AND NOT FIND ROSE, WHO WAS IN HIDING. THIS ALSO SET UP HIS
REASON TO BE IN CHICAGO: THAT IS TO FIND OUT ABOUT CERTAIN
ACTIVIST GROUPS AND THEN HE COULD FIND ROSE. **THE TWO MAIN
CHARACTER'S TIMELINES CROSSED AT THIS POINT.** THIS SET THE
SCENE FOR THE STORY TO CONTINUE WITH THE TWO MAIN CHARACTERS
OF THEM FOCUSED ON THE CENTRAL PLOTS INVOLVING THEM. THE NEXT
LEVEL OF CLIMAX WAS THE TRIAL FOR TREASON AND THE
PROTAGONIST, MICKEY, BRINGING ON A NEW LEVEL OF EXCITEMENT
AND SETTING THE STAGE FOR THE TWO TWISTED PLOTS AND CLIMAXES
COMING TOGETHER.

THEN, THE **ANSWERS TO THE UNIVERSAL THEME** WAS COMPLETED.

10.43.0.0. THE WRITER'S SELF-EVALUATION: WHAT TO FIX NEXT
TIME: MY **RANKING:** *95%. NO MARKETING TAG LINE-SELL. (THEME OR
STORY LINE NEEDED?) MAYBE?*

10.44.0.0. DO: REVIEW: COMPARE THESE 7 TOOLS OF OUR CRAFT TO WRITE OUR BEST SELLER:

1. OUR IDEAS LISTS GET US STARTED
   THINKING ABOUT A STORY.
2. OUR STORY LINE.
3. THE STORYTELLER'S SYNOPSIS-THEMES.
4. THE CHAPTER TOPICS.
5. OUR BOOK VERSION OF CHARACTER LIST.
6. THE TIME LINE.
7. THE MASTER WRITER'S COMPARISON. [CH 30].

CHAPTER 11
11.0.0.0. BOOK THEMES & LEVELS:
<u>CHAPTER TOPICS</u>: *UNIVERSAL THEMES-SUPPORTING SUB-THEMES LEVEL ONE-LEVEL TWO-LEVEL THREE..*

11.0.0.0: UNIVERSALTHEME-A DEFINITION:
A <u>THEME</u> IS A CENTRAL OR UNDERLYING IDEA IN LITERATURE. THE WRITER MAY EXPRESS INSIGHT ABOUT HUMANITY OR A WORLD VIEW; THUS, UNIVERSAL: A VERY BROAD THEME.

<u>THEMES</u> ARE LISTED ON OUR IDEAS LISTS- SEE CH 5.0.2.1

WE NEED A UNIVERSAL THEME FOR OUR BOOK. WE CAN ADD ANY NUMBER OF SUB-THEMES RELATED TO THE UNIVERSAL THEME.

<u>**THE GRAND MASTERS OF WRITING:**</u>
<u>**EACH USED A UNIVERSAL AND A THEME THAT WAS TIMELY**</u> OR A "HOT BUTTON ITEM," THE READER WANTED TO KNOW ABOUT…IMMEDIATELY. [WATCHING THE "NEW BOOKS" THAT COME OUT IN NEWSPAPER AND ON THE NET, WILL GIVE YOU A CLUE AS TO HOW FAST A BOOK IS 'COMPLETED' AND PLACED ON THE MARKET. NOTICE HOW THEIR THEMES ARE TIMELY OR EVEN BRAND NEW.]

EXAMPLE: A THEME IS THE CENTRAL IDEA OR IDEAS EXPLORED BY A LITERARY WORK. BY THEME, WE MEAN NOT A MESSAGE BUT THE <u>**LARGE GENERAL SUBJECT**</u>, AS THE THEME MAY BE WORLD MONETARY CRISIS OR WORLD WIDE RECESSION. SUBJECT MAY BE A SMALLER SPECIFIC SUBJECT WITHIN THAT THEME.

<u>**EXAMPLE: UNIVERSAL THEME:**</u>
EACH GRAND MASTER [CH 28 USED <u>FIGURES OF SPEECH</u> [CH 23]WITH "EXPERTISE" AND <u>SOUNDS</u> [CH 19] TO REINFORCE THE "MEANING" WITHIN THE SENTENCE. HE CREATED A LANDSCAPE OR PORTRAIT SO WE REALLY BEGAN TO KNOW THE CHARACTER , PLACE AND DIALOGUE. IN MELVILLES' MOBY DICK, THE CAPTAIN IS COMPARED TO THE SEA. THE CAPTAIN IS A MYSTERY TO HIMSELF. HIS ACTIONS, HIS "COMMANDS," HIS FACE AND PEG LEG GIVE US AN IMAGE TO REMEMBER. THESE TRAITS ARE THEN COMPARABLE OR CONTRASTED TO THE GREAT WHITE WHALE.

THE CAPTAIN ISHMAEL WAS SOLIDLY PLACED ON THE DECK AND IN COMMAND. ISSUING ORDERS, LIKE 'BOATS OVER THE SIDE" AND USED ANY METHOD TO CAPTURE THE EVIL WHALE. THE LANDSCAPE WAS THE SEA AND THE STORM. IT WAS THE CAPTAIN'S ACTIONS AND BELLOWING TO THE CREW [DIALOGUE] THAT SETS THE STAGE FOR THE NEXT CLIMATIC PART WHEN THE CAPTAIN IS IN THE ROWBOAT AND ORDERS THE SAILOR TO HARPOON THE "MONSTER."
THE FINAL CLIMAX HAPPENS AFTER THAT RISING ACTION.
THE PLOT IS RESOLVED.

11.1.0.0. UNIVERSAL THEMES: *LEVEL ONE*.[CH 10].
WHILE YOU ARE LOOKING FOR UNIVERSAL APPEAL, YOUR UNIVERSAL THEME MAY BE TOO LARGE OR THE INFORMATION VOLUME IS SO LARGE THAT IT CAN'T BE HANDLED IN ONE BOOK ALONG WITH A STORY. SEARCH FOR THAT SAME THEME NARROWED DOWN (LEVEL 2 & LEVEL 3), WHICH WILL FIT WITHIN YOUR BOOK.

11.1.1.0. UNIVERSAL THEMES- EXAMPLES: *LEVEL ONE*:
WAR AND PEACE- MORALITY- HUMANITY- LIVING LIFE
LOVE- TIME- DEATH-DYING- NATURE- FATE

11.2.0.0. SUPPORTING SUB-THEMES: *LEVEL 2*
MULTIPLE SUPPORTING THEMES:
A WORK OF LITERATURE MAY HAVE MORE THAN ONE THEME. *HAMLET*, FOR INSTANCE, DEALS WITH THE THEMES OF DEATH, REVENGE, AND ACTION, TO NAME A FEW. *KING LEAR*'S THEMES INCLUDE JUSTICE, RECONCILIATION, MADNESS, AND BETRAYAL.

WHILE YOU MIGHT START WITH AN ISSUE OR THEME IN MIND, THEMES WILL ALSO DEVELOP OR EMERGE AS YOU WRITE. WRITING A COMPLETED STORYTELLER'S SYNOPSIS WILL HELP YOU FIND THE THEME. THEMES: **REFER TO CH 5.0.2.2. FOR MORE THEMES:**
LIFE-CRIME-DEATH-GREED-REVENGE-HONOR-POVERTY-TERRORISM-WAR-MORALITY-SLAVERY-LOVE-PARADISE-PEACE-REFUGEE-

SOMETIMES **TWO THEMES** WORK IN A COMPARE/CONTRAST TO EACH OTHER.
WAR-PEACE
MOTHER-DAUGHTER - THEME
PATRIOTIC / HEROIC - THEME
FATHER-SON - THEME
PEACE / NON-VIOLENCE THEME
HERO & HEROISM - THEME
FREEDOM VS ISOLATION & EXILE - THEME
TERRORISM / VIOLENCE THEME .

11.3.0.0. SUPPORTING THEMES: *LEVEL 3.*
ANIMAL TALES - PIRATE LITERATURE - ARTHURIAN LITERATURE
PROTEST - ESPIONAGE / SPY LITERATURE
RELIGION IN LITERATURE - EVENTS IN LITERATURE
RELIGIOUS LITERATURE - HOLOCAUST
SAINT LITERATURE- LITERATURE-GENERAL
LITERATURE-SEA - MULTICULTURALISM
ORPHAN BOOKS – FAMILY
WARS IN LITERATURE VS. LEADERS IN PEACE/ CULTURAL TIMES
EXAMPLES:
GREED: POSSESSION-PEOPLE-MONEY-ACTIONS-BETRAYAL-SEX-ETC.
MORALITY: SAINT-SINNER-GOOD-BAD-CHURCH-CHARACTER TRAIT-
PARADISE: LOCALITY-DEFINED-WHO AFFECTED-LOVE-
HONOR: HEROISM-WHO –FAMOUS- ACT OF-6 W'S- ETC.
PLACES: MIDDLE EAST-WAR-REVOLUTION-RUSSIA-HISTORY-PEOPLE-
        CAUSES-ECONOMY-GOVERNMENT-RESULTS-ENDINGS, ETC.

> ## *IMPORTANT!*
> ### *GO TO CH 5.0.2.2. FOR SUPPORTING IDEA GROUPS*

EXAMPLE:THEME OF WAR-IDEA GROUPS-CHAPTER TOPICS:
*WAR-ACTS OF-LIFE-DEATH-HERO-TRAGEDY-WHO-MORALITY-
REVOLUTION-HISTORY-PEACE CONTRAST/RESULT-VICTIMS-GHANDI-
LOVE-TERRORISM-ETC.*
DO: DEFINE WAR-WHO-WHERE FOR THEME

11.3.1.0. **WE ADD OUR CHAPTER TOPICS AND SUBJECTS HERE.** *INCLUDE SCENES-EVENTS-PLACES [4TH & LOWEST LEVEL].PLOTS AND CLIMAXES.*

11.4.0.0. IDEAS PAGE: THEMES & IDEAS:
DON'T FORGET THE IDEAS PAGE…YOU KNOW THOSE LITTLE
BRAINSTORMS WHEN YOUR NOT WRITING…THE PHRASES, THE IMAGES,
THE CHAPTER NAMES, NEW CHARACTERS, PLOTS, CLUES, DREAMS, WHEN
YOUR DRIVING, ETC. WRITE THEM <u>ALL</u> DOWN! ADD THEM, TO YOUR
IDEAS LIST. **REFER TO CH 5.0.2.2. & MOVIE TITTLES CH 41 FOR IDEAS
BEHIND THE TITLES.**

11.5.0.0. REVIEW:
SIMPLY WRITE AND TELL A STORY… YOU CAN REVISE-REWRITE IT OVER
AND OVER AS YOU EDIT IT…EDIT AGAIN, OVER AND OVER. FINALLY BY
THE TIME ITS DONE---WE ADDED TO ITS IMAGERY, ITS STRUCTURE,
DESCRIPTIVE WORDS, CLARIFIED WORDS, ADDED HUMOR, OR
EMOTIONS, OR SENSES, OR TIME, OR THOUGHTS, PLOTS OR CLUES, THEN
THE POLISH OF PUNCTUATION, OR QUOTES, AND VARY THE "HE SAID, HE
REPLIED…" TO ONE WHERE THE WORDS, THOUGHTS AND PARAGRAPHS
FINALLY START TO MAKE SENSE OF **WHO SAID IT AND WHY**.

CHAPTER 12
12.0.0.0. OUR STORYLINES: A SUMMARY:
WE TAKE WHAT WE LEARNED FROM CHAPTER 9, 10 AND 11 AND
WE CREATED A STORY LINE, WITH A LOT OF ELEMENTS.
THIS <u>STORYLINE</u> IS THE CREATION OF OUR BOOK WITH
STRUCTURE-CHARACTERS, VILLIANS, PREDICAMENTS, PLOTS
AND TWISTS AND A ENDING BRIDGE SOLUTION TO OUR OPENING
BRIDGE.

WE TOOK ALL OF THOSE WONDERFUL IDEAS, TITLES AND WROTE
OUT OUR STORY. THUS, WE HAVE OUR STORYTELLING SYNOPSIS
WRITTEN DOWN.

WE ADDED GREAT OPENING SENTENCES, CLOSING SENTENCES
AND CHOOSE GREAT WORDS TO ILLUMINATE, TO EXPLAIN TO
KEEP <u>OUR READER</u> HOOKED AND GIVE HIM A ROLE. HE LIKES
MYSTERY-SUSPENSE AND THE POWER THAT THOSE WORDS GIVE
HIM. HE CAN BE ANYONE-ANYWHERE IN ANYTIME.

SOMETIMES THESE STORIES FOLLOW THEIR OWN PROGRESSION, THEY
WRITE THEMSELVES, THEY FOLLOW A TIME LINE, OR GIVE US A
MYSTERY, A THOUGHT NOT WRITTEN DOWN BUT IMPLIED.
WE BECOME THE READER. THE THREAD OF ALL OF THIS WORK IS OUR
STORY LINE---THAT SIMPLE FIRST PARAGRAPH OR TWO THAT GAVE US
THE ORIGINAL KERNAL –THE FIRST IDEA WE GREW INTO A GREAT
STORY.

OUR STORY LINE BECOMES THE FOURTH SYNOPSIS. WE REFINE IT, EDIT
IT, POLISH IT, ADDING WORDS, IDEAS AND CHAPTER TOPICS UNTIL IT IS
ALMOST FLESH---**A LIVING STORY**.

WE REVISE OVER AND OVER, PERHAPS 30 TIMES IN THE PROCESS.
WE WANT IT TO BE GREAT…**WE MUST CREATE ART.** WE EXPEND OUR
TIME ANDTALENT TO BRING IT TO THE WORLD; WITHOUT MUCH
THOUGHT OF MONEY, REWARDS OR BOOK AWARDS.

WE POUR SO MUCH INTO IT! WE GENERALLY WORK ALONE, SPEND
MULTITUDES OF TIME AND ENERGY. WE WORK IT, SLEEP ON IT AND
WRITE SOME MORE. WE REVISE IT, CAST OUT AND ADD THOSE BRILLANT
THOUGHTS WHICH COME ANYTIME.
WE CARRY A NOTEBOOK A PENCIL OR A VOICE RECORDER TO ALWAYS
IMPROVE IT. IT BECOMES A PERSONAL GOAL EVEN AN OBSESSION.
WRITING BECOMES <u>OUR MISTRESS</u>-A DEMANDING MISTRESS. **IT IS THAT
CAR IN THE NIGHT**-ITS HEADLIGHTS CAN ONLY SEE SO FAR AHEAD. THE
STORY IS BORN AND WRITTEN
WITH SWEAT, BLOOD AND TEARS. THEN HAPPLILY WE DEDICATE IT TO
OUR MOST BELOVED FRIEND, LOVER AND BENEFACTOR.

THEN, AH! HA! OUR READER BUYS IT! ALL THE PROOF WE NEED!

CHAPTER 13

13.0.0.0. YOUR PUBLISHING FORMAT: MARGINS-FONT-PAGE-PICTURES-PAGE NUMBERING.

CHAPTER TOPICS:

BOOK ORGANIZATION-FORMAT-PAGE SETUP-SIZES-PDF CONVERSION-FONTS- OVERVIEW-SHORTCUTS-HOW TO ORGANIZE FILES IN COMPUTER AND ON DISCS TO PREPARE BOOK FOR PUBLISHER.

CLASS: DISCUSSION HANDOUTS:

1.SIZE MATTERS: TEXT VERSUS IMAGE SIZES

2.TERMINOLOGY

3.BOOK ORGANIZATION

4.HOW TO WRITE

5.WRITER'S SPACE

6.GENRE

7.THEORIES OF WRITING

IMPORTANT:

WHEN YOUR FINAL MANUSCRIPT IS APPROVED BY YOU, REVIEW AND CORRECT ANY ITEMS BELOW OR YOUR STORY WILL NOT UPLOAD CORRECTLY INTO THE PUBLISHER'S FORMAT.

1.REVIEW CH 13 PUBLISHING FORMATS
2. CH 36-FINAL MANUSCRIPT REVIEW.
3. CHS 52- 53 FINAL BOOK TITLES AND COVER.

13.2.0.0. LAYOUT OF A BOOK:

1. WE FORMATTED OUR PAGE SO OUR BOOK WILL LOOK LIKE IT, WHEN PUBLISHED. SEE PAGE SIZES BELOW.
2. WE PLACED ALL THE ELEMENTS IN THEIR PROPER ORDER FOR PRINTING WITHIN THE WORD DOCUMENT CALLED THE "MASTER MANUSCRIPT -TITLE" AND DATE.
3. WE INSERTED A TABLE OF CONTENTS WITH PAGE NUMBERS.
4. WE INSERTED OUR TWO SOURCE DOCUMENTS AND INDICES IN THE REAR OF THE BOOK ACCORDING TO ITS TABLE OF CONTENTS.
5. WE INSERT A SUBJECT LISTING IN ALPHABETICAL ORDER.
6. LAST, WE ADD A BLANK PAGE- NO FOOTER-HEADER OR PAGE NUMBER.

13.3.0.0. PAPER SIZES: [FOR TEXT]

OVERVIEW: GENERALLY, YOU USE 8.5 X 11.0 PAPER FOR NOTES, MANUSCRIPTS, ROUGH DRAFTS, TIMELINES, CHARACTER BUILDS, THEMES, AND IDEAS. FOR NOVELS AND BOOKS IN 'PORTRAIT FORMAT"

<u>SET PAPER SIZE TO MATCH. FOR FICTION NOVEL</u>, 6X9, PERFECT BINDING, USE WORD SOFTWARE'S PAPER SIZE: 6 X 9 IN PAGE SET-UP. (15.24 CM X 22.86 CM). USE THE CUSTOM SIZE FEATURE.

<u>THE PUBLISHER'S UPLOAD PROCESS</u> WILL ASK YOU BOOK SIZES AND ALLOW YOU TO UPLOAD YOUR OWN BOOK COVERS OR WILL GENERATE ONE. THIS ALLOWS THEM TO PUBLISH ANY SIZE BOOK FOR ANY TOPIC. <u>REFER TO CH 13.4.0.0. BELOW.</u>

1.NOTE YOUR PAPER SIZE: IS DIFFERENT FROM JPEG AND CANVAS SIZE IN LULU.
2. CANVAS SIZE: IS THE PUBLISHER'S PAGE SIZE, THEY TRIM AS NECESSARY DURING THE PUBLISHING PROCESS.EXAMPLE: 6.25 X 9.5. (CANVAS IMAGE IS 6 X 9). [SEE INDEX 2].

13.4.0.0. SIZES FOR APPLICATION: [TEXT]
1. <u>FOR SCRIPTS:</u> 8.5 X 11". FOLLOW SPECIAL SCRIPT FORMATS, CAMERA ANGLES, SCENES AND CHARACTER PLACEMENT IS IMPORTANT. SPEC SCRIPTS ARE REQUESTED TO BE WRITTEN 'COURIER FONT-12 POINT.'

2. **POETRY BOOKS:** VARIES- SOME PUB'S LIKE 8.5 X 11 INCHES THEN SHRINK THE FILE VIA PDF.

3. **CHILDREN'S BOOKS:** PAPER, TEXT, PICTURE, CANVAS SIZES AND FONT SELECTION AND SIZE MATTERS. ARTWORK IS THE SELLING POINT AND SHOULD MATCH THE STORY'S CHARACTER DESCRIPTIONS. CLOSE COORDINATION IS REQUIRED.

4. <u>PICTURE BOOKS:</u> PICTURES REQUIRE A MASTERY OF PIXELS AND CAPTIONS. PICTURES BOOKS ARE VERY EXPENSIVE TO PRINT AND SOME PUBLISHERS BALK AT "ROUTINE" PROJECTS. DO YOUR HOMEWORK, FIRST.

5. **NOVELS: FICTION: PAGE SET UP:**
USE 6. 00 X 9.00 FOR PAPER SIZE. (IT FITS ON 6.25 X 9.25 CANVAS)

6X9-NOTE CHANGE FROM 8.5 X 11 TO 6X9 [THERE IS NO 6.25 X 9.25 SIZE, SO DO "KEY IN" THE "6 X 9" PAGE SIZE ON PAGE SIZE COMPUTER TAB OF PAPER SIZE. KEY IT IN CUSTOM TAB. THIS IS THE DIFFERENCE BETWEEN IMAGES, CANVAS AND PAPER SIZE.

THIS IMPACTS THE PAGE NUMBERS WHICH INCREASES THE BOOK LENGTH; THUS INCREASING BOOK COST. ALSO, RENUMBERING OF PAGES WILL RESULT CAUSING YOU TO RENUMBER THE TABLE OF CONTENTS, INDEXES AND PHOTOS WHOSE PAGE NUMBERS WILL CHANGE. IF IN DOUBT, PRINT A CHAPTER AND CROSS CHECK THAT THE PAGE NUMBERING MATCHES YOUR FILE.
<u>THUS: YOUR BOOK PAGES MUST MATCH YOUR COMPUTER FILE</u>

DO: PRINT THIS PAGE SIZE -PAGE 98-100
& SET UP YOUR NOVEL FROM THIS:

13.5. 0.0. *PAGE SET UP IN WORD: (NOVEL-6X9 SIZE):* MARGINS: PAPER SIZE:

13.5.3.1. SELECT PROPER PAGE SIZE: SEE 34.8.1.0. (NOVEL 6X9) EQUALS YOUR TEXT. THE CANVAS, OR PRINTER'S BOOK PAGE IS 6.25 X 9.25. **SO USE 6 X 9 AND YOU ARE PERFECT.** (THE PRINTED WORD SPACE BECOMES 4.25 INCHES).

13.5.3.2. SELECT: MIRROR MARGINS: THUS LEFT & RIGHT PAGE.
13.5.3.3. LEFT MARGIN: 1.0" (*ALSO CALLED INSIDE MARGIN OR SPINE*). GUTTER USE .2
13.5.3.4. TOP MARGIN: .75"
13.5.3.5. BOTTOM MARGIN: .75"
13.5..3.6. RH MARGIN : .75"
13.5..3.7. TABS: .25"
13.5..3.8. START CHAPTERS # FROM TOP OF PAGE AND LARGER FONT FOR TITLES.
13.5..3.9. FONT: 8-10 POINT-TIMES NEW ROMAN. STANDARD-CAPS OR ITALICS-OK!

13.6.0.0. FONT SELECTION & SIZES:

NOVELS: TIMES NEW ROMAN
CHARTS & LISTS: ARIAL
MAGAZINE: VERDANA
NEWS: VERDANA

13.7.0.0. FONT SUMMARY:

TEXT WITHIN CHAPTERS=8 TO 10 PT.   (THIS IS 8 PT –TIMES NEW ROMAN).
HEADERS=12 PT.
CHAPTER TITLES=14 PT *[DO PRINT & TEST THEM FIRST]*
EMBED FONTS: ON OPTIONS MENU ADOBE ACROBAT TO CREATE PDF OR USE CUTE PDF WRITER   6.25 X 9.25 SIZE.
WEB: ONLINE WORK- USE ARIAL/VERDANA FONT.

TEXT WITHIN CHAPTER: USE CORRECT FONT- 8-10 PT FONT.
I USE 8-10 PT FOR TEXT AREAS (PARAGRAPHS) AND 12 -14-16 PT, FOR HEADERS, THUS, EASIER TO READ.
EMBEDDED FONTS: USE EMBEDDED FONTS-SEE OPTIONS MENU.

BALANCE FONT SIZE WITH LINES PER PAGE: APPROX: 30 LINES ON 6X9 PAGE. TEST PRINT A PAGE AND COMPARE TO 8.5 X 11 SIZE. IS IT EASY TO READ? THEN, JUST GLANCE AT THEM, ARE THEY EASY TO READ? SHOULD BE THE SAME.

13.8.0.0. PIXELS: IMAGE SIZE

FRONT COVERS: A 6X9 IS ACTUALLY 1835 X 2775 SIZE PIXELS-300 DPI.
REAR COVERS: SLIGHTLY SMALLER 1738 X 2775 PIXELS-300 DPI.

13.9.0.0. THIS PICTURE AND CANVAS SIZING:

JPEG & PNG IMAGES HAVE DIFFERENT RULES BECAUSE OF THE CANVAS OR BACKGROUND FOR A PICTURE-6.25 X 9.25 & PIXEL COUNT OF 1835 X 2775, AND 300 DPI, IS THE REQUIRED SIZING FOR 6.25 X 9.25 BOOK. AND PICTURE SIZING.
AGAIN, NOTE YOU WILL HAVE TWO FILES FOR THE SAME PICTURE:

CREATIVE WRITING—THE KELLY MANUAL OF STYLE

1. PNG (ABLE TO REVISE) AND
2. JPEG (FINAL: NO REVISION ALLOWED). JPEG IS THE ONLY UPLOAD
METHOD TO YOUR POD PUBLISHER. FOR FRONT COVER. NOTE:[REAR
COVER IS DIFFERENT].

13.10.0.0. PAGE SIZES--SUMMARY:
-[NOTE: I CONVERTED AN 8.5 X 11" MANUSCRIPT TO 6.25 X 9.25 SIZE IN
CUTE WRITER(FOR TEXT): SO IT IS IMPORTANT TO DISTINGUISH BETWEEN
PAPER SIZE AND PRINTING PAGE SET UP SIZE FOR BOOK PRINTING.

-THE ACTUAL BOOK PAGE SIZE IS 6.25 X 9.25. VERY IMPORTANT WITH PDF
CONVERSION TO 6.25 X 9.25 SIZING.
THE SET UP SIZE IS: 6.00 X 9.00. TWO DIFFERENT ANIMALS.

SEE SOFTWARE: MICROSOFT DIGITAL IMAGE STARTER EDITION

13.11.1.0 [TEXT] CONVERSION TO PDF FORMAT
USE TO CREATE PDF OR SEARCH 'CUTEWRITER' TO GET FREE DOWN
LOAD. [LULU CONVERTS FROM WORD TO PDF FREE].
UPLOAD: http://CutePDF.com or

in word: do 'save as' PDF file. Review before releasing to publisher.

13.11.1.1. THE SOFTWARE FORMAT MUST IN PORTRAIT EVEN IF PAGE IS IN LANDSCAPE.[TEXT---DO THIS:]
USE PROGRAM IN "WORD" IN " SAVE TO" FUNCTION IN SAVE MENU,
SELECT " PDF FORMAT."
NOTE ALSO SAVE FILE IN "WORD FORMAT" AS "ORIGINAL." THUS, TWO
COPIES, **ONE IN WORD AND ONE IN PDF.** USE WORD VERSION ALL OVER
AGAIN, IF REVISIONS ARE MADE AFTER YOU **TEST PRINT** IN PDF.

13.11.2.0. IMPORTANT! [TEXT]
PDF SOMETIMES SCREWS WITH PAGE NUMBERS, PLACEMENT OF TITLE
PAGES (RIGHT SIDE) , CHAPTER ENDINGS---ONE OR SEVERAL SENTENCES
CARRIED OVER ONTO ANOTHER PAGE, CAUSING PAGES TO COST MORE,
SO A LITTLE EDITING OF THE PDF FILE MIGHT BE REQUIRED.

*DO A DOUBLE CHECK BEFORE CREATING A "FINAL-MASTER" AND
ORIGINAL FILE COPIES.*

13.11.3.0. FINALS AND ORIGINAL COPIES: [TEXT]
IF THE "MASTER PDF" IS READY MAKE A BACK UP COPY-ONE MARKED
"ORIGINAL AND ONE MARKED "NAME OF PUBLISHER." THIS WAY I KNOW
BOTH COPIES ARE SAME AND ONLY THE FINAL VERSION IS UPLOADED
INTO THE PUBLISHER'S BOOK LOADING WEBSITE, THUS MY "REVIEW
COPY OF BOOK" THE INSIDE TEXT WILL BE ACCURATE AND REVISIONS
UNNECESSARY. NOTE: THE PUBLISHER WILL CHARGE YOU TO CHANGE
YOUR FINAL VERSION---THE PUBLISHED VERSION.

USE SAME MASTER AND POD PUBLISHER FOR EACH FILE FOR 3 PIECE
COVER. KEEP ON DISC AND IN MASTER COMPUTER FILE CALLED

'MASTER' AND 'PUBLISHER' (2 FILES). THUS, EASY TO FIND AND UPLOAD AND MAKE REVISIONS.

13.11.0.0 VIEWING-PAGE NUMBERING & SEQUENCE:
TOPICS: QUALITY- PAGE NUMBERING-TABLE OF CONTENTS

13.11.1.0-VIEWING FOR QUALITY:
USE EITHER 2 PAGE VIEW[MIRROR] , JUST LIKE 6X9 BOOK READS LIKE OR: 38.11.1. 2. SINGLE PAGE FULL VIEW 75-100% ZOOM. NOTE: IF YOU MOVE OR COPY IT, IT MIGHT CHANGE WHEN YOU GO TO 2 PAGES AS BOOK PRINTING WILL APPEAR DIFFERENT. *DO DOUBLE CHECK FOR ACCURACY.*

13.11.1.3. PAGE NUMBERS: [DOUBLE CHECK THIS]
MAKE SURE PAGE IS RESET WHEN NUMBERING PAGES OR WHEN PREPARING PAGES FOR FINAL REVIEW FOR FINAL PRINT. NOTE NUMBERING THROWS OFF THE TABLE OF CONTENTS, TERMS OR REFERENCE LISTINGS. SO DOUBLE CHECK!!!!

13.12.1.0-√ PAGE NUMBERING:
LH BLANK-OR MAP PAGE OR PICTURE PAGE-EVEN NUMBERED.
PAGE1   RH-ON RIGHT, FIRST TITLE PAGE, [MUST BE HERE]
PAGE2 :   LH-COPYRIGHT-LEFT [MUST BE HERE]
PAGE3:   RH-FICTION
PAGE4:   LH-DEDICATION
PAGE 5:   RH-ACKNOWLEDGEMENT
PAGE 6:   LH-INSIDE TITLE
PAGE 7: RH- TABLE OF CONTENTS
PAGE 8: LH- INTRODUCTION
PAGE9: RH TITLE PAGE MUST BE RH
PAGE10 CHARACTER LIST (IN DEPTH VERSION AT REAR)
PAGE11 CHAPTER ONE BEGINS ON RIGHT HAND
BEGIN CHAPTERS 3" FROM TOP.(USES LOTS OF SPACE)

13.12.1.1. END OF MANUSCRIPT: BLANK PAGE
PUBLISHERS REQUIRE A BLANK PAGE AT VERY END. SO REMEMBER THE TOTAL PAGES ARE DIVIDED EXACTLY BY 4. E.G. 233 DIV BY 4=58.25 SO YOU HAVE TO ADD 3 BLANK PAGES THUS, 236 DIV BY 4= 59 SQUARES. THIS IS OKAY! (PAGES ARE PRINTED IN BLOCKS OF 4. SOME USE 16 VERY LARGE PAPER IN THE PRINTING PROCESS AND CUT THEM. SMALL BOOKS MIGHT BE IN BLOCKS OF 64. THE KEY IS "DIVISIBLE BY 4."

13.12.2.0. LAST PAGE MUST BE BLANK-NO PAGE NUMBER & NO HEADER OR FOOTER.
PUBLISHER'S FINAL VERSION). THE LAST PAGE MUST BE BLANK WITH NO PAGE NUMBERS, HEADERS OR FOOTERS, COMPLETELY, ABSOLUTELY BLANK. *THIS BLANK PAGE IS HARD TO FIX! HERE IS THE WHY, THE TWO DIFFERENT FUNCTIONS AND HOW TO FIX IT. BELOW IS AN EXAMPLE FROM MY BOOK #12. 260 PAGES WITH THE LAST ONE BLANK.*

CREATIVE WRITING—THE KELLY MANUAL OF STYLE

<u>DO:</u> **PLEASE READ THIS SECTION ENTIRELY, THEN SELECT THE FUNCTION & DO (CLICK-SELECT) THEM, AND AFTERWARDS VIEW THEM AS BELOW AND CHECK THE PRINT VIEW FOR ACCURACY.**

THE WHY:
THE "PAGE SET UP" FEATURE <u>INTERFERES</u> WITH THE "SECTION BREAKS FUNCTION." THE CORRECT SECTION BREAK IS DESIRED TO GET A LAST BLANK PAGE. THIS IS THE ONLY WAY TO EDIT THE FOOTER AND HEADER ON THE LAST PAGE, WITHOUT PARTIALLY OR TOTALLY REMOVING THEM.

HERE IS SOME CAUSES CREATED BY THE TWO CROSSING FUNCTIONS:
WORD 2007 HAS PROBLEMS WITH THIS FUNCTION). HERE IS HOW TO CORRECT THIS ERROR ON THE LAST 4 PAGES OF YOUR BOOK.

THE CAUSE: LAST PAGE PROBLEMS:
MS WORD'S USE OF SECTION BREAK CAUSES THE LAST PAGE "SECTION BREAK" FUNCTION & FORMATTING TO GO BACKWARDS INTO THE LAST SECTION . SO FOLLOWING THE MS WORD'S HELP MENU; YOU SELECT THE PREVIOUS PARAGRAPH, INSERT SECTION BREAK AND VOILIA!...IT DOESN'T WORK!

WHEN WE INSERT '
"SECTIONS" IT ALLOWS IT TO APPEAR BUT AS "LINKED TO THE <u>PREVIOUS</u> SECTION, NOT THE NEW ONE YOU CREATED.{SEE FOOTER VIEW, YOU SEE ON LEFT SIDE SECTION #, AND ON TAB ON WITH THE LINK, "PREVIOUS SECTION." YOU CAN'T CHANGE THIS "PREVIOUS SECTION" IN THE FOOTER VIEW.

YOU ALSO CAN'T INCREASE THE SECTION NUMBER (FROM ONE TO TWO) AS SHOWN IN THE FOOTER VIEW, WITHOUT INCREASING THE PAGE COUNT.

INCREASING PAGE COUNT:
HOWEVER THE UNWANTED ADDITIONAL PAGES YOU CREATE A CIRCLE EFFECT OF TRYING TO GET RID OF THEM AND KEEP YOUR FORMATTING. FOR HEADERS, FOOTERS AND PAGE NUMBER . THE ORIGINAL IDEA WAS TO CREATE A BLANK PAGE AT THE END. INSTEAD, YOU GET A LAST PAGE WITH HEADER AND FOOTER AUTOMATICALLY ADDED BY MS WORD.

AS MS WORD "HELP MENU" SAYS TO "EDIT THE FOOTER'
FUNCTION. SELECT THIS FUNCTION, TRY TO EDIT IT. WHEN YOU DO, YOU EITHER GET A FOOTER OR NONE, NO IN BETWEEN. THE "REMOVE FOOTER FUNCTION" DOES THE SAME THING.

SO TO PART B: NEXT THEY TELL YOU TO INSERT A SECTION BREAK, HOWEVER, THEY DON'T TELL WHICH ONE WORKS AND HOW TO SET IT.

13.12.2.1 **DEFINITIONS:**
HERE IS SOME DEFINITIONS AND FUNCTIONALITY THE SELECTIONS PROVIDE. UNDERSTAND THESE BEFORE YOU GO FORWARD.

CREATIVE WRITING—THE KELLY MANUAL OF STYLE

1. PAGE BREAKS: SEPARATE PAGES FROM ONE AND THE FOLLOWING ONE.

2. SECTION BREAKS ARE USUALLY BETWEEN CHAPTERS.

3. PAGE LAYOUT TAB :(TOP TOOL BAR), SELECT PAGE SET UP AT BOTTOM, NOTE 3 TABS APPEAR WITHIN: MARGINS, PAPER & LAYOUT. YOU WILL ONLY USE **LAYOUT** TAB TO SET THE "SECTION" AT THE BOTTOM. TOGGLING THIS WILL SET THE **TWO** TYPES OF SECTIONS YOU NEED TO FIT THE "CORRECTING PAGES IN OUR EXAMPLE BELOW. THIS TAB WILL GIVE 3 CHOICES OF SECTION: USE THIS "**THIS SECTION** OR **THIS POINT FORWARD**; BUT NOT THE WHOLE DOCUMENT.

4. **TO PERFORM A SECTION BREAK**: SELECT THE PAGE LAYOUT TAB (TOP TOOL BAR), TO THE RIGHT IS A "BREAKS" FUNCTION. A DROP DOWN MENU WILL GIVE SEVERAL TYPES UNDER 2 KEY HEADINGS:

1. PAGE BREAK (TYPE #1) TYPE ONES ARE A SIMPLE DOTTED LINE ON VIEW TAB. THUS, JUST A PAGE BREAK BETWEEN PAGES.

2. SECTION BREAKS.
CLICKING ON EITHER "NEXT PAGE," OR "CONTINUOUS" WILL GIVE US A SOLUTION. HERE IS WHAT WE ARE AFTER BASED ON LAST FOUR PAGES, I USE PAGES 256 TO SHOW THE NORMAL OR TYPE 1 PAGE BREAK, AND PAGES 257 TO 260 AS OUR EXAMPLES. PAGES 257-8-9 USE SECTION BREAKS.

YOU ARE LOOKING FOR AND DOING 3 TYPES OF SECTION BREAKS:

#1=NORMAL PAGE BREAK (SIMPLE DOTTED LINE –NO TEXT ACROSS PAGE)-[SELECT PAGE BREAK]PAGE 256 & 260

#2= DOTTED LINE WITH SECTION BREAK & WORD "CONTINUOUS." [SELECT SECTION BREAK & CONTINUOUS] P. 257 & 258.

#3= DOTTED LINE WITH SECTION BREAK & WORD SAYING NEXT. [SELECT SECTION BREAK & NEXT PAGE]. P 259

#4=DOTTED LINE WITH PAGE BREAK ONLY.[OUR LAST PAGE-260] [SELECT PAGE BREAK ONLY---NO SECTION BREAK]

TO REVIEW:
TO CHECK, GO TO THE **VIEW TAB** , TOP TOOL BAR, FAR RIGHT: **TOGGLE (SELECT ONE THEN THE OTHER)** BACK AND FORTH FROM DRAFT VIEW TO PRINT VIEW.
NOW, REVIEW YOUR LAST FIVE PAGES, THEY SHOULD LOOK LIKE THIS:

MY PAGE # 256 TO 260:
PAGE 256: #1 TYPE (BEFORE PAGE 257
PAGE 257:#2 TYPE.-[SECTION 2 PAGE BREAK, TO CLOSE OUT BLANK PAGES.]
PAGE 258:#2 TYPE.
PAGE 259: #3 TYPE.
PAGE 260: #4 TYPE.

WHAT DOES YOUR VIEW SAY NOW? IS THE LAST PAGE BLANK?

CREATIVE WRITING—THE KELLY MANUAL OF STYLE

DID THE PAGE NUMBERS OR HEADERS OR FOOTERS CHANGE IN THE PRECEDING PAGES? IF SO, IT IS STILL WRONG.

TOGGLING FROM "DRAFT VIEW TO PRINT VIEW:
THE VIEW WILL GIVE YOU THE "FUNCTION YOU SET. THE PRINT VIEW WILL GIVE YOU HOW IT LOOKS AS IT IS PRINTED.

OUR GOAL: THE LAST PAGE MUST BE BLANK, THUS, EDITING A FOOTER TO REMOVE THE PAGE NUMBER & HEADER.(THE BOOK TITLE, THUS BLANK).

MS WORD USES A STRANGE WAY OF USING SECTION BREAKS.
TOGGLING TO VIEW, TO PAGE SET-UP AND FOOTERS:

IF YOU TOGGLE BACK AND FORTH FROM SECTION BREAK WHICH APPEAR ON HEADER AND FOOTERS, E.G. SECTION 1(APPEARS IN FOOTER PROVIDED YOU SELECTED "INSERT PAGE NUMBERS AT BOTTOM OF PAGE" IS NORMALLY THE 99% OF THE NOVEL WITH SIMPLE DOTTED LINES(TYPE #1) FOR PAGE BREAKS. THIS IS TO ONLY KEEP YOUR SINGLE PAGES FROM SPLITTING UP WHERE YOU DON'T WANT THEM.

13.12.3.0. √ **QUALITY CHECK:**
NOTE: RIGHT HAND: ODD NUMBERED PAGES
LEFTS ARE EVEN. YOU MAY INSERT A BLANK PAGE TO MOVE A PARTICULAR PAGE TO ONE SIDE OR ANOTHER. E.G. A TITLE PAGE SHOULD BE ON RIGHT HAND.[YOU CAN SAVE PAGES BY IGNORING THIS RULE AFTER CHAPTER 1].

13.12.4.0. VIEWING:
TO VIEW USE 2 PAGE VIEW(SIDE BY SIDE) & ZOOM AT 75%. CONVERT BACK TO GO TO PRINT AT 100%.

13.12.5. 0. FOOTER: PAGE NUMBERS: SET TO .5
(SOME USE TOP RIGHT HAND OF HEADER-PREFERABLE TO USE FOOTER AS RUNNING HEADER WILL APPEAR ON ALL PAGES-NOT ALWAYS DESIRABLE).

13.12.6. 0. HEADER: TYPE: SET TO .5
BOOK TITLE NAME ONLY ON LEFT SIDE.

13.12.7. 0. CHAPTER HEADINGS:
CHOOSE HIGHER FONT COUNT FOR CHAPTER TITLES. 14 PT. TRY TO LOOK BEST AND NOT RUN INTO SECOND LINE.

13.12.8. 0. DROP FIRST "CAPS:"
DON'T RECOMMEND FIRST LETTER OF NEW CHAPTER HAVING LARGER FONT. I FIND IT DISTRACTING. EXAMPLE: OTHERS A NUISANCE.

13.12.9. 0. SECTION BREAKS:
1.MAKE EACH NEW CHAPTER A SEPARATE SECTION, INSERT "BREAK AND CHOOSE SECTION B BREAK-NEXT PAGE". THUS, TURN OFF HEADER FOR THAT PAGE, E.G. TITLE PAGE.

2. GO TO: "VIEW HEADER/FOOTER" ON MENU AND TURN *"OFF"* THE <u>SAME AS PREVIOUS</u> OPTION, OR YOUR HEADER WILL PICK UP WHATEVER WAS IN LAST CHAPTER AND CARRY IT OVER.

13.12.10.0. BLANK PAGES:
KEEP TO MINIMUM. COST PER PAGE, QUICKLY ADDS UP FOR EACH BOOK. EXCEPT: CHAPTER ONE SHOULD FALL ON RIGHT SIDE.[THE OLD RULE OF ALL CHAPTER TITLE SHOULD BEGIN ON RIGHT SIDE –NO LONGER APPLIES

13.2.0.0. OUR PROGRESS:
1. WE LEARNED ABOUT BOOK LAYOUTS.

2. WE LEARNED THE IMPACT OF 'PAGES' ON BOOK TYPES.

3. WE LEARNED PAPER SIZES-MARGINS AND FONT SELECTION.

4. PAGE NUMBERING TO MATCH THE PUBLISHER'S DEMANDS.

5. WE LEARNED ABOUT THE LAST PAGE BEING BLANK WITHOUT HEADER OR FOOTER AND HOW TO CORRECT THE PROBLEM.

6. WE LEARNED TO USE & NOT USE SECTION BREAKS.

*7. WE LEARNED HOW TO **PREPARE OUR MANUSCRIPT FOR PRINTING.***

CHAPTER 14

14.0.0.0. BASICS: SENTENCES-PARAGRAPHS:

CHAPTER TOPICS:
SENTENCES-PARAGRAPHS-CHAPTERS -COMBINING IDEAS- DESCRIPTIVE
PARAGRAPHS . IDEA GROUPS-EXAMPLE PARAGRAPHS FOR EVALUATION.

14.1. 0. 0. THE SENTENCE & STRUCTURE:

LET'S GET STARTED WITH SOME BASICS: REMEMBER ALL OF THE IDEAS
I GAVE ABOVE, CHOOSE ONE OR SEVERAL OR INVENT YOUR OWN: GRAB
AN INTERESTING ONE FROM YOUR **IDEAS LIST** [CH 5.0.2.1]. CONSIDER
THE SUBJECT AND WRITE ABOUT IT.

14.1.1.0. DO CONSTRUCT A SENTENCE

-PARAGRAPH & A "CLOSER":
AS YOU READ EACH OF THESE RANDOM ITEMS, REMEMBER THE BASICS
OF WRITING:

1. **FIRST SENTENCE-THE HOOK.**
2. **MIDDLE PARAGRAPH REINFORCING FIRST SENTENCE**
3. **THE SIZZLE-THE CLOSER SENTENCE-THE GIFT WRAP.**

14.1.2.0. THE FIRST SENTENCE: EXAMPLES:

WRITE IT TO ATTRACT ATTENTION—TO SHOW IMAGERY-TO SHOW
POSSIBILITIES-TO INTRIGUE THE READER TO WANT MORE. IT IS CALLED
THE HOOK!

1. DANGER WAS MY MIDDLE NAME!
2. THE DOORS OPENED.
3. CALL ME ISHMAEL. (MOBY DICK).
4. TIME FOR ADVENTURE!
5. SOME CALLED THE LUSH GREEN VALLEY PARADISE, OTHERS
   CALLED IT THE VALLEY OF DEATH.
6. THE JOURNEY WAS NOT EASY!
7. JALALABAD!
8. I RUBBED THE PISTOL, CALLING IT "JASMINE!" (SPIES & OTHER
   FRIENDS)
9. BULLETS WERE FLYING. DANGER CAME CALLING!
10. A TELEPHONE RANG IN THE DARKNESS. (MALTESE FALCON)

WHICH ARE STRONG, WEAK, OR HAVE IMAGES, WHICH DO YOU LIKE
BETTER?

NOW READ THEM OUTLOUD! WHICH DO YOU LIKE? EXERCISE:
WRITE SEVERAL OF YOUR OWN. WHAT DOES YOUR FIRST ONE SAY? WEAK...
STRONG... INTRIGUING? PICK THE BEST OF FIVE. WHY IS IT BETTER? ....AH!
HA! A SECRET COMES TO LIGHT!!!!

NOW YOU ARE THE READER!!!!!!

EXERCISE: PICK ONE SENTENCE AND ADD THE PARAGRAPH TO GO
WITH IT & THEN THE CLOSER.

CREATIVE WRITING—THE KELLY MANUAL OF STYLE

EXERCISE:
NOW, WRITE ONLY ONE SENTENCE TO SAY EVERYTHING A PARAGRAPH WOULD SAY.

NOTE: IT COULD APPEAR AS TOO QUICK, WITHOUT THE 'MEAT.' OR SOME ADVANCED WRITERS "IMPLY" A TOPIC SENTENCE. EITHER COULD BE OKAY, IF…THE READER GETS IT! SOME ADVANCED WRITERS EVEN USE MORE THAN ONE IDEA…**COMPOUND IDEAS IN ONE PARAGRAPH**.

OF COURSE, SOME RULES CAN BE BROKEN! MY TEST IS SIMPLY: **WRITE SO THE READER GETS THE IDEA!** THAT IS THE CONNECTION WE WANT. WE CAN WRITE LONG DESCRIPTIVE PARAGRAPHS ONE AFTER ANOTHER OR WE CAN WRITE **'MINI-SKIRT' STYLE**…LONG ENOUGH TO COVER THE SUBJECT AND YET MAKE IT INTERESTING.

SUPPOSE WE HAVE A STYLE, WHICH MEANS HAVING <u>NO</u> <u>TOPIC OPENING SENTENCE</u> OR AN <u>IMPLIED ONE</u> TAKES ADVANCED WRITING SKILL. IF WE LEAVE IT VAGUE OR UP TO THE READER; WILL IT BE UNDERSTOOD? IF NOT, BETTER WE ADD THAT TOPIC SENTENCE OR PARAGRAPH. OUR CHALLENGE MIGHT BE TO 'SPICE' IT UP OR REMOVE ITS CONTENT ALL TOGETHER. CHOOSING A SHORT SENTENCE MIGHT BE PARAMOUNT OVER A RAMBLING COMPOUND SENTENCE. STYLE BECOMES SECONDARY IF WE LEAVE THE READER LOST OR DRAWING FALSE CONCLUSIONS ABOUT WHAT WE WROTE.

14.2.0.0. PARAGRAPH: THE MEAT:
REINFORCE-EMBELLISH OR COMPLETE THE THOUGHT

EXERCISE: *WHAT IS THE MOST IMPORTANT POINT OR FACT OR IDEA, DO YOU REMEMBER ABOUT THE SUBJECT? I WILL TELL YOU THE SUBJECT AND READ A PARAGRAPH TO YOU.*

DO: WRITE A PARAGRAPH OR PICK ONE OF YOUR BEST. HOW DOES IT STACK UP? KEEP TRYING…IT DOES GET BETTER AND EASIER THE MORE YOU WRITE!!!!!   HONEST!

14.3.0.0. PARAGRAPH DEFINITION:
A GROUP OF CLOSELY RELATED <u>SENTENCES</u> THAT DEVELOP A CENTRAL IDEA. FOR SAMPLE PARAGRAPHS, REFER: CH 14.

14.4.0. 0. THE SIZZLE- THE CLOSING SENTENCE:
GIFT WRAPPING THE THOUGHT: 1. THE OPENING SENTENCE GAVE THE PREMISE, 2. THE MIDDLE THE REINFORCEMENT AND 3 . THE CLOSING SHOULD COMPLETE THE RESULT OF THE PREMISE AND ALLOW A TRANSITION TO THE NEXT PARAGRAPH **FOR THE READER**. THE LAST PARAGRAPH OF A CHAPTER SHOULD "CLOSE THE PARAGRAPH LIKE THE CLOSER SENTENCE DID.

IT'S AN ANSWER TO THE 'HOOK' FOR THE READER.
WITHOUT A CLOSER SENTENCE, THE STORY HAS A HOLE AND MAY LOSE THE READER'S INTEREST. IF SEVERAL PARAGRAPHS COVER A SUBJECT A CLOSER IS MOST IMPORTANT. THE EFFECT OF NO CLOSER LEAVES THE IMPRESSION THAT THE MATERIAL IS NOT IMPORTANT TO THE WRITER, THUS TRANSFERRING NEGATIVELY TO THE READER.

14.5.1.0. COMBINING IDEAS TO WRITE DESCRIPTIVE PARAGRAPHS:

WRITING WELL CONSTRUCTED PARAGRAPHS IS THE CORNER-STONE OF A GOOD ENGLISH WRITING STYLE. PARAGRAPHS SHOULD CONTAIN SENTENCES THAT CONVEY IDEAS CONCISELY AND DIRECTLY. THIS LESSON FOCUSES ON HELPING STUDENTS DEVELOP A STRATEGY FOR COMBINING VARIOUS IDEAS INTO WELL FORMED SENTENCES, WHICH THEN COMBINE TO PRODUCE EFFECTIVE AND DESCRIPTIVE PARAGRAPHS.

EXAMPLES:

1. THE PRINCE OF THE MARSHES*: Rory Stewart-2006.*

Baghdad was a veritable city of palaces... and the scene on the river was animated by thousands of gondolas, decked with little flags, dancing like sunbeams on the water, and carrying the pleasure-seeking Baghdad citizens from one part of the city to the other. There were also in Baghdad numerous colleges of learning, hospitals, infirmaries for both sexes, and lunatic asylums.

2. THE SEA WOLF-JACK LONDON-1904 : CH8*: "Sometimes I think Wolf Larsen mad, or half mad at least, what of his strange moods and vagaries. At other times I take him for a great man, a genius who has never arrived. And finally, I am convinced that he is the perfect type of the primitive man born a thousand generations too late and an anachrononism in this culminating century of civilization. He is certainly an individualist of the most pronounced type. Not only that, but he is very lonely. There is no congeniality between him and the rest of the men aboard ship. His tremendous virility and mental strength wall him apart. They are more like children to him, even the hunters, as children he treats them, descending perforce to their level and playing with them as a man plays with puppies. Or else he probes them with the cruel hand of a vivisectionist, groping about their mental processes and examining their souls as though to see of what their soul-stuff is made."--Humphrey Van Weeden, A character describing Wolf Larsen.*

FOR MORE EXAMPLES: REFER TO CH14.5.2.0.

14.5.1.1. CLASS: WRITING PARAGRAPHS:

1. INTRODUCE THE TOPIC OF WRITING PARAGRAPHS BY ASKING STUDENTS WHAT THEY CONSIDER A WELL FORMED PARAGRAPH.
2. INTRODUCE THE IDEA OF <u>CONCISE SENTENCES</u> AS BEING INTEGRAL TO GOOD ENGLISH WRITTEN STYLE.
3. HAVE STUDENTS TAKE A LOOK AT THE EXAMPLE SENTENCES AND PARAGRAPH. <u>REFER TO 14.5.2.0. BELOW</u>
4. ASK STUDENTS TO GROUP THE SENTENCES IN THE EXAMPLE BASED ON THE IDEAS THAT GO TOGETHER AS SHOWN IN THE FOLLOWING PARAGRAPH (I.E., PERSON AND DESCRIBING ADJECTIVES, ETC.)
5. INDIVIDUALLY OR IN PAIRS, ASK STUDENTS TO GROUP SENTENCES IN THE FIRST EXERCISE.
6. BASED ON THIS GROUPING, ASK STUDENTS TO WRITE A DESCRIPTIVE PARAGRAPH.
7. ASK STUDENTS TO COMPLETE THE CREATIVE WRITING EXERCISE BY FOLLOWING SIMILAR STEPS. (I.E., CHOOSE SUBJECT, CREATE IDEA SENTENCES, GROUP SENTENCES, WRITE A PARAGRAPH)

8. CHOOSE SOME OF THE COMPOSITIONS TO BE READ ALOUD IN CLASS. ASK STUDENTS TO COMMENT ON THE EXAMPLES.

CH14.5.1.2. CLASS EXERCISE:

1. CHOOSE A FAMOUS PLACE OR PERSON.
   WRITE DOWN A NUMBER OF IMPORTANT FACTS ABOUT THAT PLACE OR PERSON. ARRANGE THE SENTENCES INTO IDEA GROUPS.

2. WRITE A PARAGRAPH USING THE IDEA GROUPS TO CREATE CONCISE SENTENCES.

3. EXERCISE 2: ELVIS PRESLEY-HERE IS A COMMON BLOG WRITING EXERCISE. **NOTE: AUTHOR IS UNKNOWN.**

4. DO: ARRANGE THE SENTENCES ABOUT ELVIS PRESLEY OR ANY FAMOUS PERSON INTO "IDEA GROUPS."

CLASS: DO: WRITE A PARAGRAPH ABOUT ELVIS PRESLEY USING IDEA GROUPS TO CREATE CONCISE SENTENCES. GROUP THE FOLLOWING:

HE WAS BORN ON JANUARY 8, 1935
AN AMERICAN LEGEND.
HE WAS A SINGER. MUSICIAN AND ACTOR
HE WAS FAMOUS FOR HIS ROCK-AND-ROLL MUSIC
HE WAS BORN IN TUPELO, MISSISSIPPI.
HE HAD A TWIN BROTHER, AARON.
HE STARTED SINGING IN CHURCH.-GOSPELS.
HE TAUGHT HIMSELF TO PLAY THE GUITAR.
HE FIRST BECAME POPULAR ON THE LOCAL TOURING CIRCUIT FOR COUNTRY-AND-WESTERN MUSIC.
HE ALSO SANG ROMANTIC SONGS.
HE DANCED EROTICALLY, TWITCHING HIS LEGS.
TEENS LOVED HIM FOR HIS NEW STYLE.
HE HAD MANY NUMBER ONE HITS.
HE SANG "LOVE ME TENDER", "ALL SHOOK UP", AND "DON'T BE CRUEL" AND MANY SPIRITUAL, RELIGIOUS SONGS.
WOMEN LOVED HIM FOR HIS GOOD LOOKS, HIS SMILE, HIS CHARM, AND HIS "DIFFERENT ATTITUDE TO MUSIC."
DRAFTED INTO ARMY-TO GERMANY. MOVIE CAREER...
HE WAS CALLED THE KING BECAUSE:_____.
HE HAD MANY NUMBER ONE HITS AND NUMBER ONE MOVIES.
HE DIED ON AUGUST 16, 1977 IN MEMPHIS, TENNESSEE.
HE DIED OF ALLEGED DRUG AND ALCOHOL ABUSE.

14 .5.1.3. IDEA GROUPINGS ARE:
CHRONOLOGICAL ORDER?

1. LEGENDS.
2. BORN OF HUMBLE BEGINNINGS.
3. CAREER TOOK OFF.
4. SUCCESS-ACCOMPLISHMENTS.
5. TRAGIC DEATH
6. (THE GIFT WRAP IS?)

7. CAN YOU DEVELOP THIS INTO SEVERAL PARAGRAPHS?
8. HAVING TROUBLE WITH THAT PARAGRAPH? TRY WRITING INTO <u>IDEA GROUPS</u> FIRST.
9. WHAT IS THE COMMON IDEA THREAD—ANS: TIME!
10. SO OUR WRITING ORDER IS TIME! THUS, A BIOGRAPHY YOUNG-MIDDLE AGE-SENIOR-DEATH FORMAT.

14.*8.5.2.0. EXERCISES CONTINUED: READ OUT-LOUD:*

HERE ARE SEVERAL EXAMPLES ON 'SUBJECTS' TRY YOUR HAND AT WRITING ON ANY SUBJECT AND MAKE A STORY ABOUT IT. <u>FIRST SENTENCES ARE UNDERLINED</u>

14.5.2.0. A PISTOL:
<u>I RUBBED THE SPANISH PISTOL, CALLING IT 'JASMINE!'... VERY SWEETLY, VERY SWEETLY! AND PUSHED THE SECRET LEVER, NEAR THE TRIGGER GUARD.</u> HE BOWED HIS HEAD, GAVE ME SALUTATIONS AND REINED HIS BLACK HORSE UP ON HIS HIND LEGS. IT WAS AN IMPRESSIVE SHOW. HIS MEN BEGAN RUNNING NEXT TO THE HORSES AND GRABBING THE HORN THREW THEMSELVES UP INTO THE SADDLES AND YELLING AND RACING AWAY AT TOP HORSE SPEED.

HE POINTED THE PISTOL BETWEEN MY EYES AND LAUGHED. HIS FINGER SLOWLY...

(STRONG IMAGE? ...INTRIGUING?   DID YOU WANT TO KNOW MORE?) OR WEAK? DID WE EXPLAIN THE "PISTOL" ADEQUATELY... WANT TO KNOW MORE....ADD TO IT WHEN YOU MENTION IT AGAIN!

14.5.2. 1. 'A MAN IN THE DESERT:'
IN THE DESERT LIGHT A SOLITARY MAN IS MOVING, TALL AND DARK AS A GOD, DOOMED TO DRAMATIC DESTRUCTION UNLESS ON HIS SWIFT MOVING CAMEL HE TAKE(S) FLIGHT IN TIME BACK TO THE OASIS. (THE NILE, EMIL LUDWIG, P317. - NO COMMAS)

14.5.2. 2. 'ADVENTURE:'
TIME FOR ADVENTURE!
THEY CAME! THEY SAW! THEY CONQUERED! LINDA LOU AND KELLY CHANCE WERE ON ANOTHER ADVENTURE. THE LAST ADVENTURE WAS NOT PERFECT! THIS TIME THEY NEEDED TO HEAL.(BULLETS).

(STRONG OR WEAK? INTRIGUING? WANT MORE? WHICH WAS MORE IMPORTANT---TIME OR ADVENTURE?)

14.5.2.3. 'BULLETS:'
MIDNIGHT WAS CLEAR WHEN THEY CAME OUT OF THE NIGHT! THEY CAME FAST AND FURIOUS AND ALMOST CONQUERED. FIRST THE GUNSHOTS NEARLY TAKING MY LIFE, (THEN) THE BROKEN RIBS AND A BEATING I'LL NEVER FORGET. SEEMS LIKE LIFE JUST KEPT HITTING ME BELOW THE BELT. I WAS READY FOR ADVENTURE YET SOMETHING ALSO DARKENED MY DAY. I JUST FELT IT IN MY BONES! INSTINCTS WERE GREAT IF YOU KNEW WHAT THEY MEANT! STILL I WAS ON GUARD. OLD HABITS DIE HARD!

14.5.2.4. 'ROMANTIC SUNSET:'
WE WATCHED THE SUN GO DOWN, SLOWLY SINKING, HALF EXPECTING A
SIZZLING SOUND AS IT PLUNGED BENEATH THE WAVES. WE STOOD EYE
TO EYE, HEART TO HEART. LOOKING AND AS IF ABSORBING EACH OTHER
INTO ONE, WE COULD FEEL THE ATTRACTION. ..PHEWEY!
[YEP, I MADE UP THE WORD PHEWEY!].

14.5.2. 5. 'THE CAMEL:' – BOOK: SPIES, THIEVES AND OTHER FRIENDS:
ITS FACE WAS SERENE AND KIND; SO I GAVE IT A NAME OF "COSMO."
'COSMO' JUST SEEMED TO FIT. HE IS CONTRARY, CONTANKEROUS, AND
YET COSMOPOLITAN. HE HAS A STYLE OF WALKING IN SOME KIND OF
LOPE. I KNEW HE COULD CARRY UP TO ONE THOUSAND POUNDS ON HIS
BACK ALL DAY. HIS FEET WERE LARGE YET SOFT AS NOT TO SINK INTO
THE SAND. HIS HUMP WAS FULL OF FAT; I COULD TELL HE LIKED TO EAT,
HIS MOUTH WAS ALWAYS CHEWING. HE KINDA BELCHED HIS WORDS
YET HE LIKED ME FOR THE GOURMET FEED AND WATER I GAVE TWICE A
DAY. HE COULD DRINK TWENTY-SEVEN GALLONS OF WATER IN ABOUT
TEN MINUTES. THIRSTY DEVIL!

14.5.2.6. 'DANGER:' BOOK: 'BLONDES AND OTHER DANGEROUS WOMEN.'
DANGER WAS MY MIDDLE NAME! THEY CALLED ME MANY NAMES.
PRIVATE INVESTIGATOR. GOVERNMENT AGENT. RESTAURANT OWNER.
FRIEND. LOVER. ENEMY. I ATTRACTED ALL KINDS OF PEOPLE. SOME
ADORED ME. SOME WANTED TO MARRY ME. SOME WANTED TO USE ME
IN VARIOUS WAYS. SOME LOVED ME. SOME JUST HATED. SOME CALLED
ME NAMES. SOME WANTED ME DEAD! MY NAME IS KELLY CHANCE.
CHANCE IS MY REAL NAME. YET BULLETS AND TROUBLE SEEMED TO
FIND ME. TROUBLES...I HAD THEM ALL. I KNEW DANGER! IT KNEW ME BY
HEART. ONLY BY "CHANCE" HAD I REMAINED ALIVE. DANGER BECAME
MY MIDDLE NAME. I ATTRACTED DANGER LIKE BREATHING AIR.
DANGER WAS A JEALOUS WOMAN AND SHE LOVED ME.

OR MORE DANGER:
SHE WAS DANGER IN SPADES AND I WAS LUCKY AT CARDS AND
UNLUCKY AT LOVE! TROUBLE WALKED IN HIGH HEELS AND I
WORSHIPPED DANGER! SHE HAD DANGER WRITTEN ALL OVER HER!
(FROM BOOK: BLONDES AND OTHER DANGEROUS WOMEN).

14.5.2. 7. 'DANCING IN THE DARK:'
TIME AND DESTINY CONSPIRED. THEY WOVE A WEB AND I WAS THE FLY
TO THE SPIDER. I SIGHED! SHE KNEW HOW TO GET TO ME! SHE WORE
"THAT" RED DRESS AND "THOSE" RED HIGH HEELS WHEN SHE SANG. SHE
JUST HAD TO SING THAT SONG, I JUST KNEW IT! IT WAS OURS! IT WAS
CALLED "LOVE LETTERS!"

SAM, THE PIANO PLAYER, ALWAYS PLAYED IT WHILE WE DANCED IN
THE DARK. THE DARK WAS GOOD; NO ONE WAS AROUND. THE MUSIC
WAS ALL WE HAD. WE SANG THE WORDS TO EACH OTHER AND LAUGHED
INTO THE NIGHT! WE WERE DESTINED TO BE TOGETHER!
DESTINY HAD OTHER PLANS.

14.5.2.8. 'THE RED WINDOW:'

SUNDAY WAS MY DAY TO WATCH! MY KITCHEN WINDOW LOOKED OUT ON MY WORLD. I WATCHED AS THE PEOPLE BELOW HURRIED ABOUT. THEIR LIVES SEEMED IN ORDER AND ON TIME. FOR ME...I JUST SAT AND WATCHED AND DREAMED HOW THINGS COULD BE DIFFERENT. MY THOUGHTS AND TIME STOOD STILL. THE WINDOW WAS MY LIFE IN SMALL PICTURES. I LOOKED OUT. EACH PANE HAD DIFFERENT ANSWERS! (SHORT STORY: THE RED WINDOW-KCB)

14.5.2.9 'THE TELEPHONE:'

[A TELEPHONE BELL RANG IN THE DARKNESS. WHEN IT HAD RUNG THREE TIMES, BEDSPRINGS CREAKED, FINGERS FUMBLED ON WOOD, SOMETHING SMALL AND HARD THUDDED ON A CARPETED FLOOR, THE SPRINGS CREAKED AGAIN, AND A MAN'S VOICE SAID, HELLO....YES, SPEAKING...DEAD? ...YES...FIFTEEN MINUTES. THANKS."]

      (CH. 2-OPENING PARAGRAPH-SAM SPADE-THE MALTESE
      FALCON, DASHIELL HAMMETT

14.6.1.0. DO WRITE A PARAGRAPH OR PICK ONE OF YOUR BEST. HOW DOES IT STACK UP?

14.6.1.2. EXERCISE:
NOW WRITE A SHORT PARAGRAPH ABOUT YOUR CAR: IF YOU DON'T HAVE A CAR, WHAT IS YOUR DREAM CAR?

14.6.1.3. *THE RED CAR:*

THE "RED DRAGON" WAS FAST AND RED. I LOVED RED! RED HIGH HEELS AND RED LIPSTICK! THE FASTER THE BETTER! WOMEN AND CARS! I DROVE LIKE A PRO AND HEADED DOWN THE BLACK HIGHWAY. IT WAS DARK THAT NIGHT! SO DARK I DIDN'T SEE THEM COMING; BUT THEY SAW THE RED DRAGON. IT HAD A REPUTATION! RED LIKE BLOOD AND BREATHING FIRE. IT WAS THE NITROUS OXIDE. 500 HORSES AND TURBO TOO! IT KICKED ASS WHEN IT HAD TO MOVE. ALL OF IT WAS HANDIWORK, CUSTOM BUILT AND TUCKED NEATLY INSIDE OF THE LITTLE CORVETTE'S HOOD. THE "FIRE BUTTON" HAD A SKULL AND CROSS-BONES ENGRAVED ON IT. I LAUGHED UNTIL I PUSHED IT ONCE WHILE DRIVING. ALL HELL BROKE LOOSE.

14.6.1.4. *THE VILLAIN'S CAR:*

BLACK DEATH WAS FOLLOWING US AGAIN! THE BLACK CADDY WAS CHASING US, BELCHING BULLETS FROM THE DARK WINDOWS AND FLYING FAST! I KNEW THEY WERE THE BAD GUYS. THEY ALWAYS DROVE BLACK CARS. THE SIDEWALK AND CAR WINDOWS SHATTERED ALL AROUND US. I LOOKED OUT MY REAR WINDOW, NO FRONT PLATES JUST BLACK AND FIRE WAS ALL I COULD SEE. THEY WERE GAINING AND I SHOUTED AS IF TO GO FASTER. THE BULLETS WERE COMING CLOSER. I WAS IN BAD MOOD! I PULLED MY FRIENDS OUT AND WENT TO WORK. "THUNDER AND LIGHTNING" DID THEIR JOB WELL. THE TIRES WERE EASY TARGETS: THEY WERE CLOSE. THREE SHOTS IN MY PATTERN. THE TIRE BLEW. THE CADDY TURNED UPSIDE DOWN AND SPARKS BEGAN TO FLY. THEY WERE DONE. WELL DONE! WHEN THE FIRE STARTED. I SAID, "YOU BOYS SHOULD KNOW BETTER THAN TO PLAY WITH FIRE!" I THOUGHT THAT WAS ONE HOT MESSAGE, I JUST SENT TO THE BAD GUYS AND A FEW NINE MILLIMETER MEMOS TO BOOT!

I DROVE ON. THE COPS WOULD SORT OUT THE REMAINS.

14.6.1.5. *THEN THE 'FAMOUS' TALKING BEAUTY:*

THE DOUBLE WHITE DOORS OPENED INTO THE SECRET LAB. THERE SHE STOOD. A BRAND NEW CUSTOM T-BIRD. BRAND NEW BUT A BIT DIFFERENT, LONGER THAN THE FACTORY MODEL. MY MOUTH WAS OPEN! I WAS AWESTRUCK. "A BEAUTY," I EXCLAIMED!

DAMN! I WANTED TO DRIVE HER. I COULDN'T WAIT TO GET MY HANDS ON HER. I STROKED HER SKIN AND QUICKLY PULLED MY HAND AWAY. SHE SHIVERED. "WHAT IS THAT? IT'S ALMOST ALIVE!" IT MOVED LIKE RED MERCURY METAL.

HE SAID, "THE WAY YOU DRIVE IT COULD BE WRECKED WITHIN A WEEK!"

I CHUCKLED, I DO LIKE TO GO FAST!

THE NIGHT WAS YOUNG, THREE-THIRTY OR SO. I DECIDED TO GO FOR A DRIVE. 'BEAUTY' I SAID, ARE YOU MARRIED? "NEGATIVE" HER COMPUTER VOICE ANSWERED. A WOMAN NAMED JEANNE PROGRAMMED MY FEMALE RESPONSES. ASK ME ANYTHING?
"GOOD ENOUGH, I SAID, I GOT ENOUGH WOMEN TROUBLES."

SHE SAID, "TALK TO ME; I 'M A GOOD LISTENER." I HEADED DOWN THE DARK LONESOME HIGHWAY AND TALKED ABOUT LINDA LOU. BEAUTY JUST GROWLED, LIKE SHE WAS JEALOUS OR SOMETHING!

14.6.1.7. *THE OTHER WOMAN:*

 SHE WAS PRETTY, DRESSED IN RED! I LIKED RED ESPECIALLY RED SILK! HOWEVER, SHE WAS BOTH BEAUTY AND DANGER ROLLED INTO ONE! SHE WORE WHITE BUFFALO LEATHER SEATS, A BURL-WOOD DASHBOARD AND CHROME POLISHED TO A MIRROR. A 1936 TWO SEATER MERCEDES RED CONVERTIBLE. I STOWED THE TOP AND TURNED ON THE HEATER. SHE TIED A SCARF HOLDING THE RAVEN HAIR.

THE V-SHAPED WINDSHIELD BLOCKED SOME OF THE WIND. SHE SMILED AND MOVED A LITTLE CLOSER. I DROVE FASTER TOWARDS ALEXANDRIA. WE CROSSED THE POTOMAC RIVER AND I TURNED ON THE DRIVING LIGHTS. THE CAR HUGGED THE ROAD. THE SUICIDE DOORS HELD US IN. THE LONG HOOD HELD A DUESENBERG SUPERCHARGER TUCKED NEATLY INSIDE. THE UP-SWEPT FENDERS DELIVERED US IN STYLE. THEN, MY MIRROR SHATTERED!

BULLETS WERE FLYING. DANGER CAME CALLING!

SHE SCREAMED AND I SAID, "DUCK DOWN." I COULD FEEL HER HOT BREATH ON MY LEG. I LOOKED DOWN AND COULD SEE THE ROSE PLAINLY TUCKED BETWEEN HER BREASTS.

CONCENTRATE! I SAID TO MYSELF.

I PUSHED THE ACCELERATOR TO THE FLOOR. IN THE CENTER MIRROR , THE JAG WAS BACK. IN ADDITION, SHE BROUGHT COMPANY DRESSED IN BLACK. THE BLACK CADDIES WERE FIRING AT US. THREE SHOTS. THE

CREATIVE WRITING—THE KELLY MANUAL OF STYLE

LIGHTS WENT OUT. CRASH, FIRE AND EXPLOSION. BON-BON HUGGED MY LEG. I PUT THE PISTOLS AWAY AND PULLED HER BESIDE ME. SHE HELD ON TIGHT. WE DROVE INTO THE NIGHT!

" I SWEAR NOTHING HAPPENED! I REPEATED TO LINDA LOU, OVER AND OVER!

14.6.1.8. EXAMPLE:
THEY CALLED ME BY NAME. FINGERPRINTS DIDN'T MATCH. NO RECORD. FORGOTTEN BY WASHINGTON THEY SAID. VOICES BUT NO FACES CAME FROM THE WALL. A MAN! THEN A WOMAN! THE DEVIL AND THE SNAKE: AN EVIL PARTNERSHIP! IT WAS MAJOR BUCKS AND BON-BON.

14.6.1.9. EXAMPLE: HUMMER: HALF-MAN-HALF ROBOT: CONDENSED:
HIS MOTORS BEGAN HUMMING AGAIN. THE STONE WALL MOVED. HE WAS BACK! MY WORST ENEMY!

I SAID, "HUMMER!" AND LAUGHED. THEN "HUMMER, I'M GOING TO TURN OUT THE YOUR LIGHTS

HUMMER WAS BACK! HE WAS MAD!
HE CHARGED ME, AND STUCK HIS METALLIC PAW OUT, SHOOTING ME WITH ELECTRIC VOLTAGE. I GRABBED A STICK. I STRUCK. HE BROKE IT. HE HIT ME AGAIN. HE HUMMED SOME MORE. GRABBING ME IN A BEAR HUG, HE SQUEEZED. MY RIBS HURT AGAIN. I BOXED HIS EARS. BRIEFLY HE LET GO. BLOOD WAS COMING FROM HIS EARS. HE THREW ME DOWN WITH RAW FORCE. I LAID THERE WHEEZING. I GRABBED AT ANYTHING, THEN I FOUND THE COCONUT. FORWARD PASS, BETWEEN THE EYES.

HE STAGGERED BACK, AND BACK, AND BACK.
(THE COMMAS ARE NEEDED TO GIVES PAUSES TO THE ACTION, AS THE STEPS BACKWARD IMPLIES).
OOPS! TOO FAR!

TWO BIRDS WITH ONE STONE! MAJOR BUCKS AND HUMMER. BOTH FELL OFF OF THE CLIFF AND LANDED IN THE BLUE POOL BELOW. IT MOVED. HE DIDN'T! (IMPLIED GATORS).

14.6.1.10. *CAMEL THIEF:*
I PULLED MY SCARF CLOSER HIDING HALF MY FACE, MY EYES WATCHING EVERYTHING. READY FOR ANYTHING! THE GUNSHOTS FADED, SMILES RETURNED. BUSINESS BECAME AS USUAL. I ORDERED MORE TEA! THE MANAGER SMILED. AGAIN, I ASKED FOR "ZARQAWI" IN URDU, A PAKISTANI DIALECT, AS I DID NOT KNOW PASHTO. HE TALKED IN ARABIC, SO I REPLIED, THAT I TRAVELED A LONG WAY FROM THE MOUNTAINS IN THE WEST LOOKING FOR "ZARQAWI," A CAMEL TRADER. HE SAID, "MORE LIKE A CAMEL THIEF!"

14.7.2.0. SYSTEMS-STRUCTURE-PLANS-OUTLINES:
DON'T GET CAUGHT UP IN A SYSTEM OTHER'S PREACH OR "STRUCTURE" OR FOLLOW AN OUTLINE. (ONLY USE THESE TECHNIQUES AFTER SEVERAL CHAPTERS TO KEEP YOUR WRITING POINTED IN A DIRECTION FOR THE READER). IF YOU'RE LOST…HE IS LOST! INSTEAD GO BACK AND MAKE A LIST OF TOPICS UNDER EACH CHAPTER.

14.7.2.0. CLASS EXERCISE: *WRITE BOTH SHORT & LONG PARAGRAPHS IN YOUR STORY.*

NOW YOU KNOW ENOUGH TO BE DANGEROUS!

CHAPTER 15

15.0.0.0.-BASICS-WRITING FOR EFFECT-SEX:

REVIEW:
SIMPLY WRITE AND TELL A STORY… YOU CAN REVISE-REWRITE IT OVERMAND OVER AS YOU EDIT IT…EDIT AGAIN, OVER AND OVER. FINALLY BY THE TIME ITS DONE---I ADDED TO ITS IMAGERY, ITS STRUCTURE, CLARIFIED MY WORDS, ADDED HUMOR, EMOTIONS, SENSES, TIME, THOUGHTS(*IN ITALICS FONT*), PLOTS, CLUES, THEN THE POLISH OF PUNCTUATION, OR QUOTES, AND VARY THE "HE SAID, HE REPLIED…" TO ONE WHERE THE WORDS, THOUGHTS AND PARAGRAPHS FINALLY START TO MAKE SENSE.

EXERCISE: NOW LET'S CRITIQUE OUR WRITING .
OUR CHECK LIST….ADD MORE TO THIS LIST FOR YOURSELF.

15.8.1.0. THE #1 MOST IMPORTANT QUESTION?
THEN I ASKED THE MOST IMPORTANT QUESTIONS—DID I FORGET SOMETHING, WAS IT CLEAR WHAT I TRIED TO SAY ? WAS MY SETTING (PLACE) DESCRIPTION COMPLETE? DID MY **PICTURESQUE WORDS** CAPTURE ALL OF IT…LIKE ART WORK?

15.8.2.0. DID IT FLOW…? (SOUNDS AND PICTURES TOGETHER)
READ IT ALOUD TO YOURSELF. DID IT SOUND CHOPPY…FIX IT OR "NOTE IT" WITH YOUR OWN EDITING SYMBOL THAT IT NEEDS WORK? DO IT AGAIN LATER, TOMORROW OR A WEEK LATER OR MONTHS LATER.

15.8.3.0. EDITING:
I WROTE ONE BOOK IN THREE MONTHS BUT EDITED IT ABOUT TWENTY TIMES BEFORE COPYRIGHTING IT. IT WAS ABOUT 80 PAGES LONG. THE TITLE CHANGED THREE TIMES, THE CHAPTERS CHANGED ORDER, AND THE PARAGRAPHS CHANGED ORDER AND MASSIVE CHANGES IN WORDS AND PUNCTUATION. EDITING IS IMPORTANT!

15.2.0.0. WRITER'S TOOLS FOR EFFECT:
15.2.1.0. CAPITAL LETTERS & CAPITAL IDEAS:
THIS IS A TEXTBOOK NOT A NOVEL. CAPS ARE NOT SHOUTING!
THEY ARE A WRITER'S TOOL-USE IT!

CONSIDER THE FOLLOWING:
SOME PEOPLE DON'T LIKE "CAPS" AS A FONT TYPE. THEY LIKE THE TRADITIONAL "SMALL FONT" LOOK AND 5 SPACE INDENTS FOR PARAGRAPHS. CAPS IS EASIER TO READ AND COMPREHEND ESPECIALLY WITH THE LINE SPACES BETWEEN PARAGRAPHS RATHER THAN INDENTS. YES, A MORE FEW MORE PAGES BUT EASIER ON THE READER'S EYES AND COMPREHENSION.
NOW, USE THE "CAPS" METHOD FOR EFFECT:
READ IT AND AFTERWARDS HIGHLIGHT THE KEY THOUGHTS AND KEY WORDS, ONE OR MORE PER PARAGRAPH. HOW MUCH MORE WAS UNDERSTOOD OR RETAINED? DID YOU HAVE A BETTER UNDERSTANDING

OF THE EVENTS? OR THE 6 W'S--- **WHO, WHAT, WHEN, WHERE, WHY AND <u>WOW.</u>** WERE YOU ABLE TO READ MORE PAGES? DID YOUR EYES GET LESS FATIGUED?
I THINK THE "TRADITIONAL STRUCTURE" METHOD "CRAMS" PARAGRAPHS TOGETHER WITH JUST AN INDENT.

15.2.3.0. DO CONVEY THOUGHTS:
THE WHOLE PURPOSE OF SENTENCE AND PARAGRAPH STRUCTURE IS TO CONVEY ONE OR MORE THOUGHTS.
THE FIRST SENTENCE IS TO PRESENT AN IDEA, AN ACTION, OR EVENT. THE MIDDLE PART OF THE PARAGRAPH EXPLAINS AND THE LAST SENTENCE IS TO "GIFT WRAP IT."

WITHOUT THE CLOSING SENTENCE, THE FINAL CLOSING THOUGHT IS LOST; IT PUSHES THE READER TO ADD THE FORMER PARAGRAPH'S THOUGHT WITH THE NEXT PARAGRAPH'S NEW IDEA THAT IS INTRODUCED.

I ALSO THINK THE **BLANK LINE**, RATHER THAN JUST AN INDENT, ALLOWS THE READER'S EYE TO REST AND ALLOWS THE BRAIN TO FINISH ABSORBING THE LAST THOUGHT…IF ONLY A "SECOND IN TIME" FOR COMPREHENSION.

BLANK LINE: SUPPOSE TWO CHARACTERS ARE CONVERSING, SEPARATING THEIR SPEECH WITH A BLANK LINE ALLOWS THE READER TO UNDERSTAND, WITHOUT THE I SAID, SHE SAID NEEDED. THE BLANK LINE IMPLIES A CHANGE OF DIALOG.

15.24.0. DO REMEMBER KEY POINTS:
HAVE YOU READ A BOOK BUT ONLY REMEMBER 5 OR 6 KEY THOUGHTS OF A BOOK?
THE WHOLE PURPOSE OF A BOOK IS THE "ORGANIZATION OF INFORMATION" AND "A TRANSFER OF IDEAS."

THERE ARE PROBABLY 5 OR 6 THOUGHTS PER CHAPTER, NOT THE JUST IN THE TOTAL BOOK. I, THE WRITER, WISH TO CONVEY TO YOU. HAVE YOU BEGUN TO READ A BOOK ONLY TO LOSE INTEREST? CONSIDER THE PARAGRAPHS AND IDEAS BEING CONVEYED. DID THEY ENTERTAIN? DID THEY INFORM? DID THEY TRANSITION FROM ONE TO THE NEXT PARAGRAPH EASILY?
IF YOU LOOSE INTEREST, ALL OF THE ABOVE IS THE FAULT!

15.3.0.0.-EXAMPLES:
FOR EXAMPLE, READ A CHILDREN'S BOOK---IT HAS LARGER TYPE AND SPACING AND OF COURSE ILLUSTRATIONS. READ A LAW BOOK---WE SKIP FROM CASE LAW TITLES TO THE NEXT, BARELY SKIMMING THE CONTENT. NOW, SELECT A TEXTBOOK---WE SEE ORGANIZATION, PARAGRAPH HEADINGS, SUBJECT HEADING AND A FEW ILLUSTRATIONS. WE ALSO SEE BLOCKS AND COLORS. A COOK BOOK HAS ITS OWN FORMAT, USUALLY ONE INGREDIENT PER LINE AND COLOR. HISTORICAL BOOKS ARE WRITTEN ALONG A TIME SEQUENCE OF EVENTS. **FICTION HAS ITS OWN "WRITING" SIGNATURE OR FORMAT.**

15.3.1.0. FICTION FORMAT:
NOW, LET'S LOOK AT FICTION'S FORMAT:

CREATIVE WRITING—THE KELLY MANUAL OF STYLE

TRADITIONAL METHOD OF PRINTING AND WRITING. REVIEW OF THE TABLE OF CONTENTS, CHAPTER TITLES AND PARAGRAPHS ONE AFTER ANOTHER AND IT IS ONLY INDENTED. COMPARE: WHAT IS THE KEY WORDS AND THOUGHTS THE AUTHOR IS TELLING US? HOW MUCH DO WE REMEMBER? IF YOU USE A HIGHLIGHTER AND MARK UP THE **CHAPTER AFTER YOU READ IT...HOW MUCH DID YOU MISS? STUDENTS LEARNED THIS KEY METHOD IN COLLEGE.**

DID YOU KNOW OLDER BOOKS USED TO SHOW KEY WORDS –EVENTS AND THE 6 W'S AT TOP OF EACH CHAPTER? THE REASON WAS SIMPLE: HELP THE READER COMPREHEND THE CHAPTER. JAMES FENIMORE COOPER USED THIS TOOL EFFECTIVELY IN THE "DEERSLAYER- THE POCKET BOOK SERIES."

15.4.0.0.-PUBLISHING VERSUS COMPREHENSION:
CONSIDER THAT THE PUBLISHER USES LESS PAGES WITH SMALLER TYPE WITH THE TRADITIONAL METHOD OF PRINTING; THE RESULT IS HIS COST IS LESS. THE SAME BOOK PRINTED IS ABOUT 16 PAGES DIFFERENT. IF A LARGER FONT LIKE 12 IS USED INSTEAD OF 10 POINT, THE PAGES GROW TO 40, APPROX. IT COST ABOUT 2 CENTS PER PAGE TO PRINT; BUT THE 10 FONT NUMBER OF BOOKS @ 16 CENTS EACH, ADDS UP TO 32 CENTS PER BOOK. SO IT IS TO THEIR ADVANTAGE TO CUT COSTS. IT IS NOT TO YOUR ADVANTAGE TO "PERUSE" A BOOK VERSUS "**EXPERIENCE" A BOOK**.

CONSIDER ALSO AN ELECTRONIC BOOK, WHICH WOULD YOU RATHER READ ON YOUR LAPTOP OR E-BOOK? AN 8 & 10 POINT FONT OR 10 POINT CAPS FONT?

15.4.1.0. -WHY WE READ:
LAST, CONSIDER WHY WE READ AND WHY SOME DO NOT: ENTERTAINMENT, ENJOYMENT, TO LEARN, TO GO WHERE IMAGINATION TAKES US, TO LEARN NEW IDEAS, TO EXPERIENCE OTHER'S TRAVELS AND TRAVAILS.

SOME PEOPLE DO NOT READ: THEY LOSE INTEREST, IT'S FATIGUING, IT'S BORING, IT'S JUST WORDS....ETC, ETC. SOME DO NOT READ WELL. SOME PREFER THE VISUAL APPROACH...GRAPHICS, DVD OR VIDEO METHODS. SOME LIKE THE INTERACTION OF VIDEO GAMES OR WII 'S LATEST ELECTRONIC REPLICATION OF SEVERAL PEOPLE PLAYING A GAME.

AS AN ADULT, WE CHOSE WHAT WE LIKE AND THE METHOD WE LIKE. IT'S ABOUT THE CHOICE OF SUBJECT, AUTHOR AND EVEN FORMAT...A BOOK...A VIDEO...AN ELECTRONIC REPLICATION (E-BOOK) OR EVEN TV; IT'S ABOUT CHOICE!

DID YOU NOTICE THE LARGE TYPE VERSUS, SMALL, *ITALICS*, **BOLD** VERSUS UNDERLINE.   ----DID IT HELP?

15.4.2. 0. DIRECT & NON-DIRECT:
DIRECT IS FACTUAL AND YOU TELLING THE READER UP FRONT OR DIRECTLY ABOUT IT, **IN-DIRECT** IS A CLUE, A MYSTERY, OR PERHAPS HIS THOUGHTS TELLING SOME OR USING WORDS OF VAGUENESS OR SHADES OF GRAY. BE CAREFUL OF BEING TOO VAGUE; YOU MIGHT LOSE READER IN A LITERARY VOID. (THE WHITE HOLE—BLANK PAGE—THE GAP).

15.4.3.0. THE CLIMAX: |CH 30 |
THE POINT IN THE STORY WHERE IT ALL COMES TOGETHER, ALL THE
CLUES, MESSAGES, ALL THE WORDS, DESCRIPTIONS, PARAGRAPHS
LEADING UP TO A HIGH POINT OR ENDING POINT.

DON'T REVEAL THE CLIMAX TOO SOON, NOR TOO DIRECTLY. PROVIDE
THE UNDERSTANDING TO THE READER BUT NOT OBLIQUE.

AGAIN, DO ILLUMINATE (PICTURESQUE WORDS-VIVID DESCRIPTIONS) DO SHOW BUT DON'T TELL. KEEP THE MYSTERY!

EXAMPLE: BRIDGES:

"FOR THE FIRST TIME, I BEGAN TO THINK OF HOME, AS EVERYTHING
HERE SEEMED TO BE ENDING WELL!

I STILL HAD SOME UNFINISHED BUSINESS BACK HOME. I WAS THINKING
OF LINDA LOU AND THE FUTURE. TO THINK, IT ALL STARTED, WITH A
HAIL OF GUNSHOTS AND MY NEARLY ESCAPING DEATH.

THEN I CAME OVER HERE (EGYPT) AND IT WAS MORE OF THE SAME.
BEFORE THIS TRIP, MY LIFE CONSISTED OF PUTTING BAD GUYS IN JAIL
AND DODGING BULLETS. NOW, THE ACHE INSIDE OF ME WASN'T FROM
BULLETS OR SWORD CUTS BUT SOMETHING DEEPER.

SOMETHING HAPPENED OUT THERE IN THE DESERT!
[BRIDGE AND ILLUMINATION].WHAT HAPPENED? NEXT?

15.4.3.1. (BRIDGES—SEE CH 26.)
15.4.3.2. (ILLUMINATION-- SEE CH 17).

15.4.3.3. CLASS EXERCISE:

DESCRIBE A FOREST OF TREES OR THEIR LEAVES...IN ONE NOVEL I
COMPARED IT TO FALLEN HEROES AND THEIR MULTI-COLORED
MEDALS.... & THE CHANGE OF SEASONS...& WALKING THRU THEM
KICKING THEM UP INTO AIR.... ETC.
WHO WANTS TO READ THEIRS OUT-LOUD?
LET'S CHOOSE THREE DIFFERENT SUBJECTS AND WRITE SOMETHING
ABOUT THEM. MORE THAN 20 WORDS PLEASE!

15.4.3.4. OUR NEXT CLASS STARTS HERE: HOMEWORK:
BRING YOUR JOURNAL OR NOTEBOOK. ON PAPER PLEASE! THE IDEA IS TO
GET YOU TO WRITE ON PAPER WITH NO INHIBITIONS

15.4.3.5.. FRAGMENTS:
 FRAGMENTS ARE NOT INHERENTLY BAD. A STRICT GRAMMARIAN
WOULD INSIST THAT ALL FRAGMENTS BE EXORCISED. PROFESSIONAL
WRITERS WOULD USE THESE PIECES OF PROSE TO EFFECTIVELY CONVEY
A FAST PACE OR A CHOPPY STYLE OR TO MATCH A CHARACTER'S
ACTIONS OR THOUGHTS. IT MAY CONVEY A SENSE OF HESITATION OR
INCOMPLETENESS. WRITERS SHOULD USE FRAGMENTS IN A DELIBERATE
MANNER; BUT USE WITH CARE NOT TO DISTRACT OR CONFUSE THE
READER.

CREATIVE WRITING—THE KELLY MANUAL OF STYLE

READING ALOUD WILL GIVE THE PACE AND A CONTINUITY OF SOUNDS AND MEANINGS TO BE EXPRESSED. SEE MORE ON ALLITERATION AND ASSONANCE, WHICH ARE THE REPETITIVE, AND LIKE SOUNDING WORDS. THESE CAN BE USED EFFECTIVELY AS FRAGMENTS. **FRAGMENTS HAVE THEIR OWN USE, AS DOES A COMPLETE SENTENCE.**

15.6.0.0. EXAMPLE: THE BOOMERS:
SCENE: HOSTAGES ON AIRPLANE-TERRORISTS READY TO BLOW UP PLANE

"CAPTAIN! ... GET YOUR MEN AWAY...NOW, I BARKED.
FLIPPING MY BADGE, NATIONAL SECURITY...HIS RADIO BARKED ORDERS. TOO LATE! BODIES FLEW. METAL SAILED INTO THE BLUE. I KISSED THE CONCRETE AND ROLLED SEVERAL TIMES. THEN A MEGA-BLAST! DEADLY HURRICANE. NO SMOKE. FIREBALL TO HEAVEN. DUST AND FIREWORKS RAINED. MY BODY ROLLED OVER AND OVER. TOO CLOSE. MY BLACK SHIRT AND PANTS RIPPED TO SHREDS. BLOOD POURING DOWN MY ARM. TOURNIQUET BELT DANGLING. BLOOD, SWEAT AND TEARS! DEATH AND DYING ESCAPED. MIND RACING. NO CLUES. NO FORTUNE TELLER. NO GYPSY SAYING I TOLD YOU SO! MAGIC TRICKS. LOOK HERE, THEN LOOK THERE. SLIGHT OF HAND. MY LUCK PREDESTINED."

15.7.0.0. SEX:
THE WRITER MUST DECIDE THE LINE WHERE SEX IS WRITTEN ABOUT. THE BOUNDRY IS BETWEEN PORNAGRAPHIC AND A LOVELY ACT OF LOVE AND ROMANCE. THE CHOICE OF WORDS IS TO ILLUMINATE BUT NOT TELL ALL OF THE GRAPHIC DETAILS. YOU MIGHT SAY 'KISS BUT DON'T TELL.' LEAVE SOME MYSTERY. IF YOUR WRITING PORN THE WORDS WILL BE HARD, GRAPHIC AND OFFENSIVE. THE READER IS THEN PLACED IN A POSITION OF DECIDING TO READ IT OR NOT.

HERE IS AN EXAMPLE OF MINE PUBLISHED-THE READER GETS THE IDEA:

THE BLUSH [FROM BLONDES AND OTHER DANGEROUS WOMEN-PUBL.IN 2011: " HE THOUGHT OF HER GENTILE SMILE, THE CURVE OF HER NECK, THE SMALL CURL OF RED HAIR RESTING THERE. A TENDERNESS NEAR THE PULSING VEIN. THE LOPE OF THE EAR LONGING A SOFT KISS, THE BREATH OF LOVE. THE BLUSH ON THE CHEEK AND IN HER HEART. A BLUSH, A BEGINNING, A WARM SWEET GLOW WITHIN, A PASSION LIKE A SMALL SEED GROWING, LOVE AT FIRST SIGHT!"

15.8.0.0. THE F-BOMB- SWEAR WORDS-OFFENSIVE WORDS-REPLACEMENTS: AGAIN, THE WRITER MUST CHOSE THE APPROPRIATENESS OF THE WORDS TO FIT THE STORY WITH THE READER IN MIND. IN ONE OF MY VIETNAM WAR BOOKS, THE LANGUAGE WAS VERY RAW NOT ONLY OF THE MEN ; BUT THE SOUNDS AND WOUNDS INCURRED.. THE **F-BOMB** WAS REPLACED WITH 'FRUCK' –'FRUCKED' OR 'PLUCKED' AS THE F-BOMB WORD WAS USED WITH EVERY SENTENCE ISSUED BY MEN UNDER EXTREME CIRCUMSTANCES. NO ONE WANTS TO READ 480 PAGES WITH THE RAW WORD IN THE READER'S FACE. PLAINER WORDS WERE SUBSTITUTED FOR WHOREHOUSE TO BROTHEL, GOD DAMN WAS SUBSTITUED WITH 'DAMMIT' OR 'DIMMIT.' THE WORD CHOICE WAS NOT TO BE RAW; BUT TO ALLOW THE READER TO CONTINUE READING AND NOT THROW THE BOOK IN THE TRASH CAN.

AN "R" RATED BOOK WILL SELL BUT THE 'X' RATED WILL HAVE A LESSER AUDIENCEAND SELL FEWER BOOKS. DO FIND SUITABLE WORDS

TO FIT THE ACT AND DESCRIPTION AND REQUIRE JUST AS EXPLOSIVE OR EXPLANATORY SOUNDS TO BE CONVEYED. <u>**DO CREATE YOUR OWN "DICTIONARY" AS NEEDED**</u>. DO USE <u>REPETITIVE SOUND WORDS</u> TO DEFINE AN ACT: RAT-TAT-TAT, BANG, BANG-BOOM. USE THOSE ADJECTIVES, AND PICTURESQUES WORDS FOR THE IMAGERY NEEDED. THE ADAGE OF A PICTURE IS WORTH A THOUSAND WORDS, STILL HOLDS TRUE. THE WRITER GETS TO PAINT THAT PICTURE; HIS BOOK IS THAT CANVAS.

15.8.0.0. OUR PROGRESS:

1. WE REVIEWED THE BASICS OF SENTENCE AND PARAGRAPH STRUCTURE. THEN WE APPLIED IT TO WRITING.

2. WE LEARNED THE IMPORTANCE OF THE FIRST AND CLOSING SENTENCES.

3. WE WROTE DESCRIPTIVE PARAGRAPHS.

4. AGAIN, WE ADDED OUR 'BOOK IDEA GROUPS' WITHIN OUR PARAGRAPHS.

5. WE REVIEWED PARAGRAPH EXAMPLES FROM DIFFERENT WRITERS.

6. WE ADDED IMAGERY-USED FRAGMENTS AND FIXED VERB TENSE.

7. WE CORRECTED OUR PUNCTUATION AND BRACKET USE.

8. WE USED CAPITAL LETTERS IN TEXT BOOKS & IMPORTANT WRITINGS.

9. LEARNED ABOUT THE FICTION FORMAT.

10. ADDED TO OUR CRAFT TOOLS, BY USING VARIOUS FONTS, LARGE-SMALL- UNDERLINES AND BOLDS.

11. WE HIGHLIGHTED KEY PASSAGES TO CAPTURE THE IDEA.

12. WE LEARNED HOW TO 'EXPERIENCE A BOOK, AS A TOOL"

CHAPTER 16

16.0.0.0. BASICS-VERBS & PUNCTUATION
TOPICS: VERBS-VERB TENSE & PUNCTUATION-

16.7.4.1. SIMPLE PAST TENSE:
WRITING EVENTS THAT OCCURRED IN PAST HISTORY, THUS, THE USE
"WAS" GIVES US AN EASY TO USE METHOD TO STORYTELL. IT ALSO
PREVENTS US FROM SLIDING BACK AND FORTH FROM PRESENT TENSE TO
PAST TENSE IN THE SAME PARAGRAPH. (ONE OF OUR CHECK LIST ITEMS).

16.7.4.2. PRESENT TENSE: USE: "IS, OR NOW."

16.7.4.3. BE CONSISTENT. YOU CAN USE MORE THAN ONE TENSE IF
REQUIRED TO TELL THE STORY. IF IT IS ABRUPT WHEN READING ALOUD,
IT WILL SOUND FUNNY AND MENTALLY DISTRACTING.

16.7.4.4. FLASHBACKS: GENERALLY, USE PAST PERFECT:
THUS, RELATING A PAST EVENT WITH THE "NOW" PRESENT TIME.
USE: " PREVIOUSLY, OR: IN THE PAST, OR: WHEN I WAS YOUNG."

16.7.4.5. PAST PROGRESSIVE TENSE:
E.G. SHE WAS GROOMING THE DOG, WHEN HER HUSBAND WALKED IN.
(THE PAST ACTION IS RELATING TO A CURRENT EVENT). NOTICE THE
EVENT WAS INTERRUPTED WITH THE WORD "WHEN.".

16.7.4.6. PAST PERFECT PROGRESSIVE TENSE:
THUS, WRITING ABOUT AN EVENT THAT BEGAN IN THE PAST AND
CONTINUED IN THE PAST. "SHE HAD BEEN WALKING THE DOGS."
THUS, CONTINUOUS AND WITHOUT INTERRUPTION.

16.7.5.0. PUNCTUATION:
WHAT IT DOES FOR THE WRITER AND READER:
THUS, YOU WILL SUDDENLY HAVE TO POWER TO MANIPULATE
GRAMMAR TO MAKE YOUR WORDS AND SENTENCES WORK FOR YOU TO
FIT THE ACTION AND BLEND THE IDEA(S) OF THE PARAGRAPH. YOU CAN
BEND THE RULES; BUT THAT GREAT PARAGRAPH YOU WROTE DOES
NEED SOME STRUCTURE FOR YOUR READER'S SAKE AND HIS
UNDERSTANDING.

BEGIN ADDING "GENERAL PUNCTUATION MARKS, "QUOTES, COMMAS,
SEMI-COLONS, COLONS, PERIODS, ETC. TO HELP OUR WORD FLOW.
REMEMBER 'SINGLE' QUOTES ON TERMS AND "DOUBLE" ON DIRECT
QUOTES. REVIEW THE CHAPTER ON PUNCTUATION IF NECESSARY OR
GOOGLE THE MARK NEEDED, OR THIS STYLE MANUAL.(CH 8.7.5.0.)
ADD THESE ONLY TO HELP OUR READING ONLY. DON'T GET SCIENTIFIC
YET. THAT PROCESS IS IN ANOTHER READING. WE ARE TRYING TO GET
THE STORY TOLD AND READ OUTLOUD AND TO FLOW SMOOTHLY.

 THE PACING AND PAUSES BY THESE MARKS WILL HELP OUR
READING. DID WE **"HEAR"** AN IMPROVEMENT? LISTEN TO WHAT YOU
SAID, NOT WROTE DID IT SOUND OKAY LIKE A SENTENCE AND A
COMPLETE THOUGHT. IF NOT PROOFMARK IT, AND CONTINUE.

COMMON TYPES OF PUNCTUATION:

16.7.5.1. COMMA: IT PROVIDES THE **RHYTHM (STARTS, PAUSES, ENDINGS.**
USE TO SEPARATE CLAUSES. USE FOR PAUSES, LISTS. USE WITH SEMI-COLON (;) FOR COMPLEX SENTENCES. USE BEFORE WHICH OR THAT. A COMMA STATEMENT IS ALSO USUALLY CONTAINED WITHIN THOSE COMBINED OR COMPLEX SENTENCES. *A COMMA IS USED BEFORE 'WHICH' OR 'THAT.').*

16.7.5.2. SEMI-COLON: USE THE **SEMI-COLON** (;)BEFORE THE WORDS 'BUT' OR 'HOWEVER' AND CONCLUDING (THUS) TWO PART SENTENCES. **USE** *BEFORE* **KEY CONNECTING WORDS**: *HOWEVER, MOREOVER, NEVER THE LESS, ON THE OTHER HAND, BUT, FOR INSTANCE.* GENERALLY A COMMA FOLLOWS THESE WORDS.[*SENTENCE... FOR INSTANCE,*].

16.7.5.3. COLON (:): USE WITH *A GREETING, VOLUME AND PAGE, RATIO, TIME NUMBERED GROUPING OR A SERIES OF EXAMPLES FOLLOWING.*

16.7.5.3. DASH: USE FOR A BREAK IN THOUGHT *(END OF THOUGHT)* NOT CONTINUATION (---). DASH ALSO USED FOR MISSING LETTERS.

16.7.5.4. **SINGLE QUOTES** (') ARE USED FOR *TERMS, SLANG, DIALECT, BOOK TITLES, MUSIC OR TO GROUP, AND A PARAPHRASE GROUPING.*

TERMS: USE A SINGLE QUOTE (') IS REQUIRED FOR STATING A 'TERM' USUALLY FOLLOWED BY AN EXPLANATORY SENTENCE FOR THE READER. A TERM COULD BE AN ACRONYM, A BUSINESS OR SCIENTIFIC TERMINOLOGY, A SLANG TERM OR LANGUAGE TERM.

16.7.5.5. **QUOTE ("):** DOUBLE QUOTES ARE USED TO STATE VERBATIM WHAT A PERSON'S WORDS WERE STATED EXACTLY. DON'T USED QUOTES WHEN SOMEONE ELSE REPEATS IT; ITS NOT A DIRECT QUOTE. USE QUOTES FOR OUR CHARACTER'S WORDS IF IT NOT IMPLIED WHO IS TALKING. SEE THE DIFFERENT RULES FOR SCRIPT WRITING.

16.7.5.6.
THERE IS A WHOLE NEW SET OF 2009 RULES OVER QUOTE MARKS, PLEASE REVIEW "GRAMMAR" ON WEB.

16.7.5.7. **EXCLAMATION POINT (!).** USE THIS WHEN *EMPHASIS OR A PERSON'S EMOTIONS IS DESIRED TO BE SHOWN.*

16.7.5.8. ITALICS: *I USE ITALICS TO SHOW A PERSON'S THOUGHTS, ESPECIALLY THOSE NOT SAID OUTLOUD.*
LOUD ITEMS OR SOUNDS ARE IN LARGE LETTERS OR BOLDED.

16.7.5.9. **ELLIPSIS** (THREE DOTS...) : FOR MISSING AND CONTINUING THOUGHTS OR RANDOM THOUGHTS.

16.7.5.10. BRACKETS THREE TYPES: ( ), { }, [ ]. THINK OF THEM AS MINOR, MIDDLE AND MAJOR.

1. MINOR BRACKET-PARENTHESIZE: ( ) EXPLAINING A SYMBOL(,) E.G. A COMMA AN EXPLANATORY STATEMENT. *(DEFINTION).*

2. MIDDLE BRACKET: BRACE: ({ }) AN INSERT IN A STORY, A
PARAPHRASE, INSERTING SOMETHING WITH A DIFFERENT FORMAT
FROM WRITING. EXAMPLE:{SHE STRUGGLED AGINST THE ROPES, WHILE I
DISTRACTED THE KIDNAPPER}. {THE *ACTION* WAS BRACKETED AS IT
WAS NOT DIRECT OR WRITTEN FOR THE READER}.

(SCRIPTS USE THIS TO SET THE ACTOR'S STAGE SETTING (SHE RUNS
TOWARD THE BALCONY –NO DIALOG) OR PLACEMENT(STAGEFRONT-
SETTING FOR A DIALOG OR DANCE), CHANGE OF SCENERY, LIGHTING
DIRECTLY RELATED TO THAT SINGLE SET.(SHE CRIES AS THE LIGHT
DIMS, AND GOES TO BLACK, END OF ACT.

3. MAJOR BRACKET: [ ]. A FOOTNOTE, A REFERENCE, AN INSERT OF
IMPORTANCE. [CHAPTER]. ALSO< > ANGLE BRACKET.

SUMMARY:
A WRITER SHOULD MASTER ALL OF THESE MARKS AND USE AS HE
WRITES THOSE COMPLEX SENTENCES, AND THOSE SPECIAL
DRAMATIZATIONS AND EVENTS. EVEN FIGURES OF SPEECH CREATE
SOME SPECIAL MARKS. *EXAMPLE:* HOW DO YOU PUNCTUATE A POEM? A
LOVE LETTER, A NEWS ITEM, CUSS WORDS, EXCLAMATIONS!
IN ALL CASES, PUNCTUATION SHOULD BE CONSISTENT.

EXAMPLE: I USE THE WORD: DO:

DO: **AS A REPETITIVE WORD, IN "CLASS EXERCISES" FOR THE WRITER
TO DO (ACTION) OR TO WRITE SOMETHING.**

√ *CHECK ALL PUNCTUATION - SEPARATELY IN ONE COMPLETE
EDIT-CHAPTER BY CHAPTER .NOTE DATE ON FIRST PAGE.*

*YOU WILL PROBABLY DO THIS THREE TOTAL TIMES, WITH THE
LAST: YOUR MANUSCRIPT.*

READING ALOUD WILL HELP YOU FIND THE MISSING ONES!

CHAPTER 17
17.0.0.0. BASICS: LANGUAGE-GRAMMAR-IMAGERY:
CHAPTER TOPICS: *LANGUAGE-GRAMMAR- IMAGERY-STACKING-*

LANGUAGE GOES HAND IN HAND WITH WORDS, SENTENCES AND THOUGHTS. THE RESULT SHOULD BE A CLEAR CONCISE IDEA THAT TRANSFERS TO THE READER. THE READER GETS IT!

GRAMMAR CONNECTS THE SENTENCES WITH VARIOUS FIGURES OF SPEECH, IMAGERY AND IDEAS. GRAMMAR ALLOW US TO COMBINE PARAGRAPHS INTO A BOOK.

PUNCTUATION GIVES THE LANGUAGE AND GRAMMAR A STRUCTURE WITH RULES. [CH 16].

17.0.1.0. LANGUAGE:
LANGUAGE IS STRUCTURED IN TWO DIMENSIONS: HORIZONTAL PHRASES AND WORDS ARE COMBINED TO FORM SENTENCES.

VERTICAL SETS OF EQUIVALENT TERMS OR PATTERNS FROM WHICH AN ELECTION IS MADE. KAT VERSUS KITTY, MAT VERSUS RUG.

LANGUAGE:
USE LANGUAGE-TERMS-HISTORY- TO FILL OUT "FACTUAL AND FICTIONAL PARTS OF STORY OR HIS "FACT OR FICTIONAL PARTS" ATTRIBUTED TO YOUR CHARACTERS.

EXAMPLE:
"I WOULD NOT BE ALONE SEEKING INFORMATION. PESHAWAR IS A WORLD OF SMUGGLERS, SPIES, TRIBAL WARLORDS, MONEY CHANGERS AND SMALL BUSINESSMEN LOOKING TO MAKE A FAST BUCK ON WEAPONS AND INFORMATION. PESHAWAR IS A BAZAAR OF SECRETS. ALSO, THE CENTRAL BAZAAR OF STORYTELLERS WAS CALLED "QISSA KHAWANI." IT WAS MY KIND OF PLACE! I WAS IN THE MARKET FOR INFORMATION!"

17.0.2. 0. THEORY OF FIGURE OF SPEECH: PART OF
RHETORIC *A SET OF STYLISTIC CONVENTIONS SPELLED OUT IN HANDBOOKS BY LISTS OF FIGURES OF SPEECH.*

17.0.3.0. THEORY OF FINITE STATE GRAMMAR/LANGUAGE:
A SENTENCE AS A SUCCESSION OF "STATES" PROGRESSING LEFT TO RIGHT. **GRAMMAR COULD GENERATE AN INFINITE NUMBER OF SENTENCES.** EACH WORD DETERMINES WHAT CAN FOLLOW IT. [SEE N. CHOMSKY, "SYNTACTIC STRUCTURES" (THE HAGUE, 1957). SEE CHARLES FRANCIS HOCKETT (1916-), MANUAL OF PHONOLOGY (1955-)].

17.0.5.0. DIRECT & NON-DIRECT LANGUAGE:
DIRECT IS FACTUAL AND YOU TELLING READER UP FRONT OR DIRECTLY ABOUT IT. BE CAREFUL, STATING A FACT IS OKAY; BUT TALKING DIRECTLY TO THE READER IN A NOVEL IS AUTHORIAL INTRUSION.

IN-DIRECT IS A CLUE, A MYSTERY, OR PERHAPS HIS THOUGHTS TELLING SOME OR USING WORDS OF VAGUENESS OR SHADES OF GRAY. BE CAREFUL OF BEING TOO VAGUE; YOU MIGHT LOSE READER IN A LITERARY 'VOID.'

17.0.5.1. STACKING: EXAMPLES

THE FIRST PART IS THE SAME: A REPEAT.
COULD BE SENTENCES OR SOUNDS OR IDEAS:

EXAMPLE:
HE RAN INTO MY KNIFE.

HE RAN INTO MY KNIFE TEN TIMES.

17.0.6.0. GRAMMAR:
17.0.6.1. GRAMMAR & PUNCTUATION:
THE WAY TO BETTER WRITING IS THROUGH BETTER GRAMMAR; BUT IT'S A PATH BETWEEN BEING BORING OR TOO TECHNICAL, THE VERY OPPOSITE OF CREATIVITY. GRAMMAR CAN ACTUALLY BE FUN AS YOU WRITE. GENERALLY, ONLY IN ONE POINT OF VIEW AND IN THE CORRECT VERB TENSE. THEN ADD ADJECTIVES AND ADVERBS FOR DESCRIPTIVE LANGUAGE. SENTENCE STRUCTURE AND GRAMMAR TIES TOGETHER THE MESSAGE, THE **'IDEA GROUP'** IS PROVIDING. [SEE IDEA LISTINGS-CH 5]

GRAMMAR DEFINED: IS 'WHAT IS ACCEPTABLE' IN THE USE OF WORDS EITHER BY INFLECTION (MEANING), USUAGE, OR IMAGERY. NEW WORDS-SLANG, AND YOUR 'NEW DICTIONARY' TEST 'THE NORM" OR TODAY'S ACCEPTABLE USE.

I LIKE**, THAT GRAMMAR COULD GENERATE AN INFINITE NUMBER OF SENTENCES. EACH WORD DETERMINES WHAT CAN FOLLOW IT.**

17.0.7.0.-IMAGERY: PLAY WITH THIS IDEA FOR FUN!
INVOLVES PUTTING INTO WORDS A "VISION" OR A DESCRIPTION SO CLEAR THAT THE READER ALMOST IS LOST IN ITS DESCRIPTION. USE OF "SIMILES"—IT'S LIKE-

EXAMPLE DESCRIBE A LIGHT BULB…METAPHOR FOR AN " IDEA," ITS BRIGHT… ITS FILAMENT-IMAGINE IF IT DID OR DID NOT GLOW—WHAT IF IT WAS THE RED BULB FOR A WARNING LIGHT—A FAIL SAFE BULB ON A NUCLEAR REACTOR -THE TOP IS FLIPPED OPEN, THE MATCHING KEYS ARE IN- (WE PAUSE)- THE RED LIGHT IS BLINKING…WAITING!
DO: ---PLAY WITH THIS IDEA FOR FUN!

17.0.7.1. EXAMPLE:
THE CAVERN WAS ROUND AND WE SPUN FASTER THEN FELL TOWARDS THE RED LIGHT. THE LIGHT WAS THE BOTTOM OF A LARGE RED CAVERN.

IT WASN'T A LIGHT AT ALL, BUT MOLTEN LAVA. WE WERE TO BE BURNED UP LIKE SO MUCH TRASH FROM THE STREET. CINDERS INSTEAD OF HEROES.

WE FELL TO THE GROUND ON PURPOSE AND HELD ON TO MY BELT. WE THREE--- DANGLE THERE IN MID AIR, LIKE A ROAST ON A STRING! DANGLING OVER THE FIRE. I HAD UNDER ESTIMATED MY ENEMY! I BROKE ANOTHER RULE OF WAR!

EXAMPLE:
THE MYSTERIOUS MOUNTAIN GLOWED RED FROM WITHIN. IT STOOD IN DEFIANCE OF ALL THAT WAS GOOD. IT STOOD AS THE FORTRESS OF THE DEVIL WITHIN, A PREHISTORIC VOLCANIC ROCK, IMPREGNABLE AND RESOLUTE.

17.0.8.0. IMAGERY DEFINED:
IMAGERY IS AN IMPORTANT PART OF OUR WRITING. WE EXPOUND UPON A DESCRIPTION TO ADD SOUND WORDS, PICTURESQUE WORDS AND OUR FIVE /SIX SENSES.

ITS LIKE ADDING PICTURES AND MUSIC TO OUR WORDS.

IMAGERY IS A LARGE WALL MURAL WITH OUR UNIVERSAL THEME, CHARACTERS, SCENERY, DIALOG, SCENES AND STORY ALL PICTURED ON A GRAND SCALE. THEN WE ADD MUSIC, SOUNDS, LIGHTS, ACTIONS AND EMOTIONS. THUS, WE REACH OUT TO THE READER TO MAKE HIM/HER FEEL DEEPLY: THEY CRY, THEY LOVE, THEY FEEL EMOTIONS; THEY BECOME PART OF OUR STORY.

WHEN THAT HAPPENS, WE HAVE THE "AH! HA!" WE SEEK. OUR STORY BECOMES ALIVE!

17.0.8.0. OUR PROGRESS:
1. WE LEARNED THE DIFFERENCE BETWEEN LANGUAGE AND GRAMMAR.

2. LANGUAGE IS TWO DIMENSIONAL.

3. WE LEARNED GRAMMAR IS SEVERAL THINGS AT ONCE: FUN, CREATIVE, ONE POINT OF VIEW WITH THE CORRECT VERB TENSE.

4. SENTENCE STRUCTURE AND GRAMMAR WORK TOGETHER.

CHAPTER 18
18.0.0.0. BASICS:LANGUAGE DEVICES:
TOPICS: *ONOMATOPOEIA-METAPHOR-SIMILE*

18.0.2. 1. ONOMATOPOEIA: WHICH NAMES A THING OR ACTION BY THE SOUND ASSOCIATED WITH IT:
1. LEIF ENGER'S "*THE CHUFFS AND GROWLS OF PLOW TRUCKS.*"
2. POE'S "T*HE TINTINNABULATION THAT SO MUSICALLY WELLS FROM THE BELLS, BELLS, BELLS, BELLS, BELLS. . . .*"
3. WORDS LIKE: POP, HISS, BANG. (SOUND LIKE OBJECT).
   CRACK, BUZZ.

18.0.2.2. METAPHOR: AN ITEM OR THING IS REFERRED TO AS IF IT WAS ANOTHER ITEM, WITHOUT BEING SO OBVIOUS.

A COMPARISON WITHOUT THE WORDS "LIKE" OR AS:

THE *METAPHOR* IS ONE OF A WRITER'S MOST POWERFUL TOOLS TO *ENHANCE* AND *CLARIFY* YOUR WORDS. USE METAPHORS TO CARRYOVER-TRANSFER-SUBSTITUTE-COMPARE-INTER-REACT OR REFERENCE ONE OBJECT IN TERMS OF ANOTHER. LEARN TO MAKE THE BEST USE OF SINGLE AND DOUBLE METAPHORS . . . WHY SOME METAPHORS ARE APROPOS AND POWERFUL. LEARN HOW TO DEVELOP, FROM YOUR OWN EXPERIENCES AND OBSERVATIONS, THE KIND OF METAPHORIC USE THAT CAUSES YOUR READERS TO TAKE NOTICE OF YOUR WRITING.

SHAKESPEARE'S: "LIFE IS BUT A WALKING SHADOW, A POOR PLAYER/THAT STRUTS AND FRETS HIS HOUR UPON THE STAGE. (LIFE & SHADOW) (LIFE & POOR PLAYER) (LIFE & HOUR).

18.0.2.3. SIMILE: TWO ITEMS NOT ALIKE IS "LIKE" OR "AS" OR COMPARED TO SOMETHING ELSE. *EXAMPLE: DEAD AS A DOORNAIL!*

18.0.2.4. CLASS: WRITE ONE EXAMPLE FOR EACH AND INDICATE THE SOUND OR LANGUAGE FOR EACH ONE.

18.0.3.0. OUR PROGRESS:
1. WE LEARNED THE READER LIKES SOUNDS IN HIS READINGS.

2. WE LEARNED SOME TYPES OF SOUNDS TO INCLUDE.

3. WE LEARNED SOME NEW SOUNDS AS WE READ OUTLOUD.

4. SOUND IS A SENSORY HOOK.

5.TAKE ANY OF YOUR WRITING AND MARK "SOUND" NEXT TO WHERE SOUND-SENSES-SIGHT IS USED.

CHAPTER 19
19.0.0.0. -LANGUAGE OF SOUNDS:
CHAPTER TOPICS: *ALLITERATION- ASSONANCE-SOUND DEVICES-VOWEL AND CONSONANT SOUND REPETITION- ONOMATOPOEIA -METAPHORS: SINGLE AND DOUBLE. SIMILES. CLICHÉ'-COMPARATIVE AND NON-COMPARATIVE.*

19.0.1.0. USING SOUND IN OUR WORDS:
THE SOUND AND SIZZLE:
DISCOVER HOW TO WRITE BEGINNINGS THAT CAPTURE (HOOK) THE READER, THE MEATY MIDDLE THAT COMPELS HIM TO STAY AROUND TO HEAR AND SEE DIALOGUE AND DESCRIPTIONS THAT "SIZZLE" AND OPEN HIS IMAGINATION; HIS SENSES AND THEN, AN ENDING THAT LEAVE THE READER WANTING TO READ MORE.

DO: ADD THE FOLLOWING WRITING TOOLS TO YOUR SKILLS LIST AND TRANSFORM YOUR WRITING FROM THE ORDINARY TO EXTRAORDINARY! GREAT WRITERS AND MASTER WRITERS USE THESE WITHOUT FAIL.

DO: USE SOUND AS A SENSORY HOOK THAT APPEALS TO THE READER'S MIND AND HIS SIGHT THAT SEES A WORLD BEYOND HIS DAILY ROUTINE; THUS, CREATING PICTURESQUE DESCRIPTIONS IN HIS MIND.

DO: SOUND DEVICES THAT TICKLE A TITLE INTO HOOKS AND POPS A SENTENCE OUT TO REMEMBER.

19.1.0.0.- ALLITERATION:
WORDS WITH THE SAME SUCCESSIVE CONSONANT SOUND - TO GIVE THE DESCRIPTION A REPETITIVE DECISIVE ENERGY. THIS TOOL IS GREAT WHEN USED A SUBJECT OR AS A CHARACTER DESCRIPTION OR AS A MODIFIER TO A OBJECT:
EXAMPLE: ROBERT FROST: "SWEET-SCENTED STUFF."

EXAMPLE: DYLAN THOMAS'S FERN HILL:"ABOUT THE LILTING HOUSE AND HAPPY AS THE GRASS WAS GREEN." (HOUSE AND HAPPY-GRASS AND GREEN).
1. HARD SOUNDING D'S: DEATH, DYING, DESTRUCTION.

2. SOFTER SOUNDS: SAVING, SACRIFICE, SANCTUARY USED IN SAME SENTENCE.

3. RHYME OR VERSE MAY HAVE THIS REPETITIVE SOUNDS. READ OUTLOUD.
19.2.0.0. ASSONANCE:
WHERE INTERNAL VOWEL REPETITION WORKS
ITS RHYTHMIC MAGIC . . . TO ASSONANCE COMBINED WITH
CONSONANCE, AS IN "*THE GLIMMER OF GOLD, THE SHIMMER OF SILVER*"

CHAPTER 20
20.0.0.0. CHARACTERS-ALL:
CHAPTER TOPICS: *CHARACTER-SUB-CHARACTERS-VILLAINS-BELIEVABILITY-LIFE OF OWN-LIST-*

20.0.1.0. WHAT IS A CHARACTER?
MANY WRITERS FEEL THAT CHARACTERS ARE THE MOST IMPORTANT PART OF ANY KIND OF FICTION. IT IS THE CHARACTERS AND THEIR INTERACTIONS THAT DRIVE THE PLOT, CREATES THE SUSPENSE AND TENSION AND DRAWS THE READER INTO THE STORY.
WELL-DRAWN CHARACTERS WILL SEEM TO HAVE LIVES OUTSIDE OF THE FICTIONAL WORK. OUR CHARACTERS TAKE THE ROLE OF HERO/GOOD GUY, VILLAIN OR PROTAGONIST, OR SUPPORTING CHARACTERS. THE CHARACTERS MIGHT ALSO BE CATEGORIZED INTO MAJOR AND MINOR ROLES.

SUPPORTING CHARACTERS MEANS **SUPPORTING THE MAJOR CHARACTER OR MAJOR SUPPORT TO THE PLOT OR CLIMAX.**

BASIC CHARACTER ELEMENTS:
1. **INITIAL CHARACTER CREATION.**
2. **CHARACTER RESEARCH**
3. **CHARACTER BACKGROUND**
4. **NAMING YOUR CHARACTERS**
5. **THE MAIN CHARACTER**
6. **THE MAIN VILLAIN**
7. **NARRATIVE & DIALOGUE FIT CHARACTER**
8. **USING ADVERSITY TO DEVELOP CHARACTERS**
9. **MAKING A CHARACTER MEMORABLE.**
10. **GIVING YOUR CHARACTER A UNIQUE VOICE**
11. **BUILDING UP A GREAT CHARACTER**
12. **CHARACTER CONSISTENCY AND WHEN TO BREAK IT**
13. **CHARACTER RELATIONSHIPS**
14. **CHARACTER PSYCHOLOGY**
15. **AVOIDING STEREOTYPES IN MINOR CHARACTERS**
16. **HARD HITTING VIOLENCE-IMPACT ON MIN CHARACTERS.**

OUR CHARACTER LIST SHOULD HAVE OUR MAJOR-MINOR-ROLE CATEGORIES IDENTIFIED NEXT TO EACH CHARACTER.

20.0.1.1. CHARACTER DEVELOPMENT:
AN EXAMPLE OF ADVANCED CHARACTER DEVELOPMENT IS TO CARRY ONE THRU SIX BOOKS---DETECTIVE GRADUATES TO SECRET AGENT TO UNDERCOVER TO SPECIAL AGENT. THE CHARACTER ALSO EVOLVED THREE TIMES FOR THREE TIME PERIODS. THIS IS A **CHARACTER SERIES**.

20.0.1.2. COMMON ELEMENTS TO CHARACTERS:
UNIVERSAL APPEAL, UNIQUE TRAITS, PHYSICAL APPEARANCE.

20.0.1.3. OUR CHARACTER TAKES ON A LIFE OF HIS OWN.

CREATIVE WRITING—THE KELLY MANUAL OF STYLE

A LIFE YOU CREATE WITH WORDS, WITH SCENERY, A WORLD, FRIENDS, ENEMIES, PLACES AND THINGS. GOOD AND BAD THINGS HAPPEN TO OUR CHARACTER.

20.0.1.4. EXERCISE: WHAT DO WANT OUR READER TO KNOW? WHO IS OUR MAIN CHARACTER? WHO ARE OUR SUPPORTING CHARACTERS/ ANIMALS/SIDEKICKS FEMALE SUPPORTING/ MYSTERY STRANGER?

20.0.1.5. READER MUST BE ABLE TO RELATE.
CHINKS IN ARMOR IS OKAY; A CERTAIN AMOUNT OF FICTION AND REALISM MUST BE BLENDED.

20.0.1.6.. BELIEVABILITY?
UNLESS YOUR WRITING COMICS, AN AMOUNT OF BELIEVABILITY MUST BE PRESENT.

20.0.1.7. UNIQUE CHARACTER:
I USUALLY USE SEVERAL PEOPLE AND BLEND THEM OR SITUATIONS TOGETHER TO MAKE A "UNIQUE CHARACTER" OF MY OWN.

READ STRONG CHARACTER NOVELS:
GREAT GATSBY, RED BADGE OF COURAGE, MOBY DICK, HUCK FINN, DARTH VADER,(STAR WARS MOVIE).

20.0.1.8 VILLAIN(S):
WHAT MAKES A VILLAIN? MORE THAN ONE?
EXERCISE: LET'S TALK ABOUT VILLAINS: WHERE DO YOU FIND THEM?

NOTE: VILLAINS ARE USED TO <u>CONTRAST</u> (IDEAS, HONOR-THOUGHTS-FEELINGS- GOODNESS-HIS "HEART & SPIRIT" AGAINST YOUR MAIN CHARACTER. THIS ADDS A THIRD DIMENSION. HE MUST BE EXPANDED LIKE A MAIN CHARACTER AND SHOW WHY HE IS LIKE OR DIFFERENT TO YOUR MAIN CHARACTER. THEN WHY IS HE THE VILLAIN AND NOT THE HERO? **VILLAINS SHOULD BE AS STRONG AS YOUR HERO!**

AS THEY SAY IN STAR WARS, "WHY DID HE GO TO THE DARK SIDE?"

20.0.1.9. FACTUAL CHARACTER:
SOME FOR EACH CHARACTER & SUB-CHARACTER:
ALSO USE PLACES-HISTORY-FACTS-THEORIES-MYTHS AND EVENTS-ACTION & NON-ACTION PARTS TO BRING OUT CHARACTER IN VARIOUS SITUATIONS…THUS, TELLING YOUR STORY.
EXERCISE: NAME ONE FACTUAL CHARACTER AND WHY:

20.1.0.10. MAIN CHARACTER:
THIS IS OUR STAR OF STARS. KEY PLAYERS, WHICH THE PLOT IS ABOUT. GENERALLY THE NARRATOR IS THE KEY PLAYER AND THE PLOT AND EVENTS HAPPEN TO HIM/HER FOR A REASON (HIS PREDICAMENT) AND THE RESOLUTION IS THE SOLVING OF THIS PREDICAMENT. THE PREDICAMENT IS PART OF THE MAJOR AND MINOR THEMES.

CREATIVE WRITING—THE KELLY MANUAL OF STYLE

20.0.1.11. WHAT IS ROLE OF SUB-CHARACTER?
THE ROLES OF SUB-CHARACTERS (SUPPORTING AND MINOR TOGETHER) ARE SUPPORTING TO THE MAIN CHARACTER, PLOT OR STORYLINE. THEY HELP OR EXPLAIN EVENTS, PLACES OR CIRCUMSTANCES. SOME HAVE NAMES, SOME DO NOT. E.G. WAITRESS, TAXI DRIVER, WOMAN IN BLACK.

20.0.1.12. HOW DOES HE GIVE SUPPORT OR EMBELLISH THE MAIN CHARACTER? HE MIGHT ONLY EXIST TO GIVE A PERSON A
NAME OR COMPLETE AN ACTION SCENE OR TO DRAMATIZE A DIALOGUE. ALSO, "CLUES" IN A MYSTERY MIGHT ACT AS A NON-HUMAN ENTITY TO GIVE SUPPORT TO A STORY. [EXAMPLE: CHARLIE CHAN TYPE MYSTERY NOVELS].E.G. ROBIN IN BAT-MAN, AS A SIDE-KICK.
HE/SHE ALSO SUPPORTS THE PLOTS AND THEMES.

20.1.0.0. CHARACTER LIST:
HERE IS EXAMPLE FROM ACTUAL CHARACTER LIST AND SUB-CHARACTERS. WRITING ONE GIVES YOU A BETTER KNOWLEDGE OF YOUR CHARACTER AND HIS TRAITS---HOW WILL HE REACT IN THIS SITUATION (YOUR SCENE)? WILL HIS BEHAVIOR IMPACT OTHERS OR CAUSE NEW EVENT TO HAPPEN---A NEW ACTION? RISING ACTION- OR RISING PLOT OR PERHAPS WHEN COMBINED WITH CHANGE...DON'T MAKE THEM TOO PREDICABLE FOR READER--KEEP THE READER'S   INTEREST. ADD FLAWS TOO... FOR THE CONTRAST.

20.2.0.0. EXAMPLE: CHARACTERS:

NOTE: THREE CHARACTERS NAMED KELLY CHANCE WERE USED IN 4 DIFFERENT BOOKS, EACH UNIQUE AND A DIFFERENT 'GENERATION.' REFER TO AF(ACTION FIGURE)AF-1, AF-21-AF-36.

AF-1. CHARACTER: KELLY CHANCE SR: 1 OF 3 CHARACTERS.
MAIN-HERO-MAJOR ROLE.
APPROX 1940-1950-1960 YEARS.
 PRIVATE EYE, OWNER OF KELLY'S PLACE, BAR AND RESTAURANT, PART-TIME WRITER. LOVES FAST CARS AND FASTER WOMEN. BOLD, DASHING, SHARP DRESSER AND HELPLESS (NOT HOPELESS) ROMANTIC. WINE EXPERT. SLEUTH AND AGENT FOR U.S. GOVERNMENT.
SIX FT ONE, 200 POUNDS, BLUE EYES, BLACK HAIR.
PRIVATE EYE & CONTRACT AGENT FOR GOVERNMENT
SMOKES LUCKY STRIKES,
CHEWS JUICY FRUIT GUM. LIKES ART.
OWNS RESTAURANT "KELLYS PLACE"
NAMES HIS CARS: "RED DRAGON, BEAUTY"
BOAT IS NAMED EXTRAORDINARY
BOXING, FENCING, MARTIAL ARTS
DISGUISES-ARMS DEALER-MOUSTACHE?
COLOGNE: "CHANCE" & "SECOND CHANCE-SHADOW"
NICKNAME: LINDA CALLS HIM "ROCK"-LUCKY IN JEST.
HE CALLS HIMSELF "PROFESSOR" P56 2C
HORSE- WHITE HORSE-MIDNIGHT-
INDIAN NAME: BEAR-
FAVORITE PISTOLS: THUNDER & LIGHTNING-9MM
OTHER PISTOL: H& K 9MM, BLACK ON BLACK, OR CAMO
FAVORITE DANCE: TANGO

CREATIVE WRITING—THE KELLY MANUAL OF STYLE

FAVORITE DRINK: VODKA MARTINI, SHAKEN NOT STIRRED, ABSOLUT STRAIGHT UP.
TATOO: DRAGON SCAR: CUT LIFELINE ON HAND
DANCING IN THE DARK
GOD OF WAR-MARS
FAVORITE MUSIC: ELVIS-
CALLING CARD: ACE OF SPADES
PARENTS: KILLED P55 2C
RAISED BY TAOIST PRIESTS-

SYMBOLS:
SCALLOP SHELL-P562C- SCORPION.

QUOTES:
IN HEARTS, NOT SPADES. (2 CH)
CUSSWORD: "FROMMAGE"-"FRENCH FOR CHEESE"-FRUCK-FRICK!
RUBIES ALWAYS SHINE IN THE NIGHT- P51-2CH

AF-21. KELLY CHANCE JR: MAJOR CHARACTER-MAJOR ROLE.
BOOK: A NOBLE HEART.& THE BOOMERS: YEARS 0F 1960-1990
-**SON OF KELLY CHANCE SENIOR**. RAISED IN CHINA BY PO LIN MONKS.
-SEARCHES FOR IDENTITY AND FATHER/MOTHER/ TWIN BROTHER
-MEETS DESIREE-FRANCE-LOST VIRGINITY.
-PIRATE CAPTAIN OF "THE IRISH PRINCE"-SHIP.
-SUBJECT OF SEARCH BY TANG TO GET SECRET OF RED DIAMOND.
-RESCUES FATHER IN EGYPT, MUST PAST TESTS TO BE PRINCE OF IRELAND.
-TRAVELS TO: CHINA-FRANCE-IRELAND-MEDITERRANEAN SEA-EGYPT-CHINA.   VIETNAM WAR HERO IN 'THE BOOMERS' BOOK

AF-36. KELLY CHANCE III- *MAIN HERO-MAJOR ROLE-YEARS 2000-CURRENT*
SOLDIER BOY IN AFGHANISTAN- 'SPIES AND OTHER FRIENDS,' BOOK.

AF-2 LINDA LOU: *MAIN CHARACTER-MAJOR ROLE.*
AF-45 BELINDA BEAULIEU: BOOK 'SPIES AND OTHER FRIENDS.'
AF- 23 JULIET ROSE DARLING:
 NEW LOVE IN KELLY'S LIFE. A BEAUTIFUL RED-HEAD AND FULL OF PASSION. BALLERINA AND DANCER, ART EXPERT. HEART-MATE AND TRAVEL COMPANION. ADVENTURER, AND BUSINESSWOMAN. HOPELESS ROMANTIC.
HEIGHT: 5'4" RED HAIR, GREEN EYES
MID FORTIES-FASHION PLATE
BALLERINA-TEACHER
MARTIAL ARTS EXPERT
ART EXPERT
AGENT OF GOVERNMENT
NICKNAME: KELLY CALLS HER "ROSE"
LUCKY CHARM: DRAGON COIN.
GRANDMOTHER: BRITISH
PERFUME: GODDESS
QUOTES:
 DANGER ALWAYS COMES IN THREES-LET'S ROCK & ROLL-P71-2C

AF-9 THE BLONDE BOMBER: P63-2C, VILLAIN.
 SIDE KICK OF MAJOR BUCK. ALSO EVIL. HATES MEN AND ESPECIALLY KELLY CHANCE. HE SPURNED HER FOR HER SISTER..."DESTINY." SHE

131

WAS "DESTINY'S REVENGE." SHE LIKES RED LIKE KELLY BUT SHE IS
PURE EVIL. DYED BLOND HAIR, WEAPON: BLACK PEARLS.

AF- . CHANG YAO WEI: PIRATE CAPTAIN-MAJOR VILLAIN.
 IN BOOK: A NOBLE AND SAVAGE HEART: CHAPTER 17-18 PP-107-

AF-49 CHEROKEE: MINOR.
BOOK: SPIES. THE WONDER DOG.
ALSO CALLED "HANNY" THE HANDSOME DOG.

AF-46 DESTINY: BOOK: SPIES. MINOR.
 KELLY'S OLD LOVE. KELLY GIVES HER THE RED HEART DIAMOND.
BLONDE AND BEAUTIFUL, A PIANO PLAYER AND CABARET SINGER.
VIVACIOUS AND DEADLY. SHE WANTS KELLY TO MARRY HER BUT DIES
TRAGICALLY IN OTHER BOOK. BLONDE, BEAUTIFUL, WORE RED DRESS &
RED HIGH HEELS, SANG "LOVE LETTERS,"

 AF-15 DETECTIVE GALLIMORE: (IN BOOKS :RED HEART! RED EARTH! &
A NOBLE AND SAVAGE HEART-SPIES).MINOR.
 DETECTIVE FROM AKRON, WHO SOLVES MYSTERY OF" REDHEART AND
WHITE DIAMONDS," KELLY'S FIRST NOVEL. SAVES KELLY'S LIFE AND
KEEPS HIM FROM PRISON. THEN, COMES OUT OF RETIREMENT AND
FOLLOWS KELLY TO FRANCE AND LONDON.

AF-8 DUANE-THE–GENIUS: MAJOR SUPPORTING CHARACTER-MINOR.
BOOKS: RED HEADS-BAD & BEAUTIFUL & BLONDES-SPIES.
COWBOY AND AUTOMOTIVE ENGINEER, HE BUILDS FAST CARS FOR
KELLY IN A SECRET LAB. RUNS "KELLY'S PLACE" , A RESTAURANT. A
GENIUS AT CARS AND ARMAMENTS, AND EVERYTHING HIGH TECH.
LOVES JEANNE, A CABARET SINGER.
45 COLT-10" BARREL COWBOY GUN.

AF-51 FATHER PAT MURPHY: MINOR CHARACTER-MINOR ROLE.
BOOK: SPIES.
KELLY'S FRIEND, HELD "FUNERAL FOR KELLY"-BEER, ADVISOR,

AF-5 HARRY LEGGS: VILLAIN-MINOR ROLE.
(IN BOOK: SPIES, P62-2C:
"OLD LANTERN JAW", KELLY CALLS HIM. ONE OF MAJOR BUCK'S
KILLERS. HAIRY, 6 FT SIX, BROKE RIBS,

AF-14 INSPECTOR JAMIESON: SUPPORTING CHARACTER
BOOK: SPIES, RED HEART/RED EARTH.
 SCOTLAND YARD'S ANSWER TO DET. GALLIMORE. SHARP DRESSER AND
ENGLAND'S TOP INSPECTOR. LOOKING FOR ART AND STOLEN GEMS. ONE
OF QUEENS MEN! BRITISH ANSWER TO SECRET AGENTS.
TWEED JACKET-BOWTIE,

AF-16 JEANNE: SUPPORTING CHARACTER-MINOR ROLE.
BOOK: BLONDES AND OTHER DANGEROUS WOMEN.
THE RED HOT CABARET SINGER AND ROMANTIC INTEREST OF DUANE'S.
FRIEND OF KELLY.

AF-3A. JIMBO: SUPPORTING CHARACTER-MAJOR ROLE.
BEST FRIEND OF KELLY AND BLOOD BROTHER. KNOWN FOR HIS
COURAGE AND CONTACTS AROUND THE WORLD. HE IS KELLY'S SOURCE
OF INFORMATION. KELLY'S RIGHT HAND MAN.

CREATIVE WRITING—THE KELLY MANUAL OF STYLE

AF-4 MAJOR BUCKS: MAJOR-VILLAIN.
BOOK: BLONDES AND OTHER DANGEROUS WOMEN.
EVIL MASTERMIND OF SECRET EVIL ORGANIZATION OF GLOBAL
INTERFERENCE. (S.E.O.G.I.) CROOK, ART THIEF, TERRORIST, AND ALL
AROUND BAD GUY. TRADEMARK IS BLACK CADDY. KELLY'S ARCH-
NEMESIS. ENEMY OF ALL FREEDOM LOVING PEOPLE. HE IS IN IT FOR THE
MONEY! (BUCKOLA). NICKNAME MAJOR BUCKS. THE ROOT OF ALL EVIL!

AF-55 MICHAELANGELO: WOMAN-"MIKE"-MINOR.
BOOK: SPIES, THIEVES AND OTHER FRIENDS.
ITALIAN, DARK HAIR, ART EXPERT AT LOUVRE

AF-39 MINISTER: "SISTER GRACE" P66 – MINOR.
BOOK: SPIES, THIEVES AND OTHER FRIENDS.
SPIRITUAL MINISTER, HAS VISIONS, AND HAS SECRET NECKLACE. AND
SECRET LIFE. VICTIM OF ART THIEVES.

AF-10 RACHET: VILLAIN-MINOR.
BOOK: BLONDES AND OTHER DANGEROUS WOMEN
P67-2C.P69-2C,
EVIL ROBOT OF MAJOR BUCKS. BLACK ROBOT, RINGS OF FIRE, LARGE
PINCERS, TRANSFORMABLE HANDS, NAMED BY KELLY AFTER RUSTY
TOOL IN DUANE'S GARAGE. SAW-BLADE HAND.

AF-12 RED: MAJOR-HERO.
IN BOOKS: RED HEART/-RED EARTH-SPIES-BLONDES-SOLDIER BOY.
KELLY'S TWIN BROTHER AND FRIEND. LOVES FAST CARS, FAST WOMEN,
AND FOOD. A SHARP DRESSER AND FRIENDS TO EVERYONE. SAILOR
AND SHARES BOAT WITH KELLY. LIFELONG FRIEND OF JIMBO AND
INDIAN " BEAR" TRIBE. ALSO INDIAN BLOOD BROTHER OF KELLY AND
JIMBO. TWIN BROTHER-KELLY JR TWIN-SPIES -P45,48.

AF-17 RENE' FRANCOIS DU BOIS: SUPPORTING CHARACTER.
BOOK: SPIES. FRENCH POLICE DETECTIVE, PARIS.

SC-TWIN SPIN: SUPPORTING CHARACTER –SPIES. MINOR-SUPPORTING.
BOOK: BLONDES AND OTHER DANGEROUS WOMEN. P59-2C
TWIN AGENTS HIRED BY THE GOVERNMENT AS CONTRACTORS. THEY DO
THE DIRTY-WET (KILLING) WORK AND GET IN KELLY'S WAY. BEAUTIFUL
AND BLONDE. THEY USE DISGUISES IN PURPLE & BLACK.
END OF CHARACTER LIST---

20.3.0.0. THE HERO:
THE HERO OR SUB HERO... A GOOD GUY. THE SUB HERO/SIDEKICK
ALWAYS PLAYS A LESSER BUT SUPPORTING ROLE.
USING **CHARACTERISTICS** USUALLY ALIGN WITH ROLE AS HERO.
THE HERO HAS THE WHITE KNIGHT TRAITS, A ROMANTIC, A DO-GOODER,
AND A PERSON WHO HAS PEOPLE WORSHIPPING HIS DEEDS OR
CHARACTER TRAITS. STRONG-LAW ABIDING-

20.4.0.1. THE VILLAIN:
THE VILLAIN IS AN OPPOSITES ROLE; BUT EQUALLY STRONG AND
DYNAMIC. A CONTRAST OF DIFFERENCES. IT COULD BE MORALS,
SOCIETY OR ENVIRONMENT, WHICH CASED HIM TO TURN TO THE DARK

CREATIVE WRITING—THE KELLY MANUAL OF STYLE

SIDE. HE IS THE ULTIMATE BAD GUY WITH A GANG OF HENCHMEN WHO ALWAYS ARE DIRECTED OR LED BY A MAIN VILLAIN.

THE VILLAIN   HAS A WEAKNESS...ALCOHOL... BAD WOMEN... GAMBLING...A ROTTEN OR SORDID PAST. HE MIGHT BE A CRIME FIGURE OR A KILLER, OR MASS MURDERER, TRAITOR OR TERRORIST OR GOOD GUY GONE BAD.

20.4.0.2. VILLAIN TRAITS: SEVERAL OF HIS TRAITS COULD BE HIS FACIAL EXPRESSIONS, HIS MOVEMENTS, AND HIS ACTIONS TOWARDS OTHERS: EVIL LAUGH, TURNING HIS BACK ON THE VICTIM, HANDLING A WEAPON, AN EXPLOSIVE TEMPER. ... A SCAR, A SLIGHT FACIAL TICK, NO REMORSE. TORTURE OF THE VICTIM IN DEVIOUS WAYS. HE USUALLY HAS A SERIES OF DEADLY SINS: GREED, ENVY, ETC. OF COURSE, HE MIGHT HAVE MORE WEAPONS AND THE WILL TO USE THEM. HE SHOULD BE REPULSIVE TO THE READER

20.5.0.0. CLASS EXERCISE:

-WRITE TWO SENTENCES TO DESCRIBE THE MAIN CHARACTER OR VILLAI IN YOUR BOOK.
-DO YOU HAVE A LIST OF CHARACTERS & BRIEF DESCRIPTIONS?
-DOES LOCATION HAVE A BEARING ON HIS CHARACTER?
-DOES HIS PROFESSION OR FAMILY?
-DOTAKE A CHARACTER FROM YOUR BOOK, SHORT STORY OR WRITE ABOUT
   ONE...MAKE ONE UP!

NOW COMPARE TO BOOK OR MOVIE CHARACTER...EQUAL OR LESSER? HOW DOES PLOT CHANGE /IMPROVE OR DESTROY A CHARACTER?

20.5.1.0. CLASS: CHARACTER CHECK LIST

1. DESCRIBE A CHARACTER?
2. PHYSICAL DESCRIPTION? HIS CLOTHES? HIS WEAPONS?
3. TEMPERAMENT?
4. LIKABLE? IS HE THE HERO? THE VILLAIN? SUPPORTING CHARACTER TO WHOM? HEROES & VILLAINS HAVE AT LEAST TWO SUPPORTING CHARACTERS.
5. HOW IS HE/SHE INVOLVED IN THE PLOT?
6. IS HE/SHE STRONG OR WEAK AS CHARACTER?
7. WRITE TWO SENTENCES TO DESCRIBE HIM.
8. DO YOU HAVE A LIST OF CHARACTERS & BRIEF DESCRIPTIONS?
9. DOES LOCATION HAVE A BEARING ON HIS CHARACTER?
10. DOES HIS PROFESSION OR FAMILY?
11. TAKE A CHARACTER FROM YOUR BOOK, SHORT STORY OR WRITE ABOUT ONE...MAKE ONE UP!
12. NOW COMPARE TO BOOK OR MOVIE CHARACTER...EQUAL OR LESSER?
13. HOW DOES PLOT CHANGE /IMPROVE OR DESTROY A CHARACTER?
14. DOES YOUR CHARACTER HAVE A TIMELINE?
15. IF YOU ARE MISSING THESE...YOUR
    CHARACTER LIST IS INCOMPLETE.

20.5.2.0. CHARACTER DEVELOPMENT:
CONSIDER SOME COMMON TRAITS WHEN WRITING AS CHARACTER PROFILE: APPEARANCE-DRESS-HABITS-FEARS-HEIGHT-WEIGHT-HAIR COLOR-COLOR EYES-AGE-JOB-SPECIAL ABILITIES-EDUCATION-MARTIAL STATUS-CHILDREN-PETS-FRIENDS-ENEMIES-

CREATIVE WRITING—THE KELLY MANUAL OF STYLE

AMBITIONS-FAILURES-WHERE THEY LIVE OR IN PAST-PERSONALITIES-
BELIEFS-FAMILY-WHERE THEY FIT IN TIME-KEY EVENTS IN LIFE- ETC.
**IN YOUR BOOK, YOUR CHARACTER TAKES ON A REAL LIFE/VIRTUAL
LIFE.**

20.5.3.0. CHARACTER INVOLVEMENT WITH FRIENDS AND ENEMIES:

1. **DEFINE EACH CHARACTER'S TRAITS** AS ABOVE AND ADD PLACES
AND WHETHER THEY ARE A MAIN CHARACTER OR SUPPORTING
CHARACTER OR A VILLAIN. ALSO, MINOR AND NO-NAME CHARACTERS
ALSO ADVANCE THE PLOT, SCENE AND SETTING.

2. **DEFINE EVENTS** (SCENES) AND LOCATION-PLACES(SETTINGS) AND
   MINOR AND MAJOR CLIMATIC POINTS FOR THE CHARACTERS.

3. **DEFINE A TIMELINE (DATE DRIVEN)** OR TIMELINE
SPREADSHEET(CHAPTER STYLE) FOR YOUR MAIN CHARACTERS. WHEN
DO MAJOR EVENTS HAPPEN. SEE CH 29.6.0.0.

4. **DEFINE A LIST OF "HOOKS" FOR THE READER.**
   WHAT PEAK INTERESTS OR QUESTIONS KEEPS THE READER
   INVOLVED? ANY MYSTERIES? CLUES? UNANSWERED
   QUESTIONS?

5. DEFINE WHICH PLOT EVENTS INVOLVE THE VILLAIN(S)?

6. DO A COMPLETE CHARACTER TRAIT LIST FOR ALL
   CHARACTERS. **YOUR DETAILED SYNOPSIS WILL HELP FLESH THESE
   OUT.**

20.5.4.0. OUR PROGRESS:
1. *WE LEARNED THE IMPORTANCE OF A VERY DETAILED CHARACTER
   LIST.*
2. *OUR CHARACTER IS BOTH UNIQUE AND BELIEVABLE, LIFE-LIKE.*
3. *WE LEARNED OUR SUPPORTING MAJOR CHARACTERS AND MAJOR
   VILLAINS ARE EQUALLY STRONG.*
4. *MAIN CHARACTERS AND VILLAINS HAVE A PARTICULAR ROLE-
   COMPARE & CONTRAST TO FULFILL.*
5. *SUPPORTING CHARACTERS ENHANCES THE MAIN CHARACTERS, BOTH
   HERO AND VILLAIN.*
6. *NO-NAME CHARACTERS SUPPORT THE SCENE AND RISING ACTION.
   WATCH FOR CHARACTER DISSOLVES-DOE HE/SHE DIE? NO FADE A
   WAYS ARE PERMITTED.*

7. *CHARACTER DESCRIPTIONS/ ACTIONS/ ATTITUDES/ WORD CHOICE/
   HOW THEY REACT TO EVENT-PLOT SHOULD BE MULTI-DIMENSIONAL
   YET WITH MYSTERY REMAINING.*

8. *CHARACTER LISTS SHOULD BE UPDATED WITH EACH REVISION.*

CHAPTER 21

21.0.0.0. PLOTS & TWISTS:

CHAPTER TOPICS: *PLOT DEFINITION-THEMES-PLOT TYPES- PLOT ELEMENTS-PLOT TWISTS.*

21.0.1.0. PLOT DEFINITION:

PLOT IS DEFINED AS THE SKELTON OF OUR STORY, A

FRAMEWORK ON WHICH OUR UNIFYING THEME IS HUNG., FOLLOWED BY AN ARRANGEMENT OF EVENTS OR SEQUENCE IN WHICH THEY ARE TOLD, THE EMPHASIS THEY ARE GIVEN AND THE CONNECTIONS BETWEEN THEM. PLOTS, MAIN CHARACTERS AND KEY EVENTS SHOULD COME OUT OF THE CHAPTER BY CHAPTER SYNOPSIS [CH 9].

21.0.3.0. PLOT: IT IS THE FRAMEWORK OF THE STORY.

PLOT IS WHAT HAPPENS LIKE AN EVENT IN A PERSON'S LIFE. A PERSON FACING SOME KIND OF LARGE PREDICAMENT AND THE WRITER WRITES OUT THE STORYLINE USING THOSE REINFORCING IDEA GROUPS. A PLOT SHOULD ALSO HAVE A UNIVERSAL THEME AND A UNIFYING THEME - A PURPOSE, TO HOLD THE STORY TOGETHER. THOSE RISING ACTION ITEMS OR IDEAS GIVE A PURPOSE FOR THE READER TO FOLLOW ALONG. HE READS AND HEARS THE STRUGGLE AND WANTS TO KNOW WHAT WILL HAPPEN NEXT AND HOW THE STORY ENDS. WILL THE STORY END IN TRAGEDY OR HAPPINESS? HOW WILL THE MAIN CHARACTER(S) RESOLVE THE CONFLICT?

THE MAIN CONCERN OF PLOT IS HOW EVENTS (SCENES) ARE RELATED, THEIR STRUCTURE AND HOW CHANGES IN THE MAIN CHARACTERS COME ABOUT. THE READER MUST IDENTIFY WITH THE MAIN CHARACTER FEELING LIKABILITY TO HIM OR HATRED. THE MAIN CHARACTER SHOULD BE INTRODUCED QUICKLY AND HIS CONFLICT SPELLED OUT ON THE SURFACE.

21.0.4.0. BACKGROUND OF PLOT USE:

DO GIVE A LOT OF THOUGHT TO PLOT:

WRITING A NOVEL CAN BE A HUGE UNDERTAKING, UNORGANIZED AND COMPLEX TASK.. YOU MIGHT SAY HUNDREDS OF TASKS, WHICH NEED YOUR ATTENTION. BEGIN WITH A "DETAILED SYNOPSIS." [CH 9] A CONDENSED VERSION OF YOUR STORY. THINK ABOUT SIX W'S: WHO WHAT WHY, WHEN, WHERE AND WOW! ANSWER ALL OF THESE AND YET TELL THE STORY IN BRIEF. NO MORE THAN TWO PAGES. **STAGE TWO-**THE EDITING PROCESS WILL GO EASIER IF YOU DEVOTE A LITTLE TIME TO PLOT IN THE BEGINNING. FOR SOME WRITERS, THIS MEANS A SYNOPSIS; OTHERS WORK WITH INDEX CARDS, PUTTING A DIFFERENT SCENE ON EACH ONE. STILL OTHERS HAVE A CONFLICT AND A GENERAL IDEA OF CLIMAX OR ENDING FOR THE BOOK; THUS, WHERE THEY PLAN TO END UP AND THEN DIVE IN.

I REPEAT: PLOT, MAIN CHARACTERS AND KEY EVENTS SHOULD COME OUT OF THE CHAPTER BY CHAPTER SYNOPSIS.

21.0.5.0. PLOT AND THEME:

<u>THE UNIVERSAL THEME</u> IS INTRODUCED IN THE OPENING PAGES. THEME GIVES A REASON FOR THE STORY, A DIRECTION AND HOLDING IT TOGETHER TO THE END. THEME IS THE LARGER CONTEXT ON WHICH THE STORYLINE RIDES FROM BEGINNING TO END WHEN THE STRUGGLE IS INTRODUCED OR THE CONFLICT IS FINALLY RESOLVED. THE DRAMATIC QUESTION IS HOW? **THE SUPPORTING THEME** IS THE SOLUTION TO THE PLOT, WHICH WILL TELL HOW THE CONFLICT OR STRUGGLE STARTED AND HOW IT ENDED. THE THEME SITUATION REQUIRES CHANGE AND THUS, AN UNSTABLE FUTURE AND THE ENDING IS THE RESULT OF THOSE CHANGES AND A RETURN TO A NEW FORM OF STABILIZATION.

<u>THE PLOT</u> MUST ALSO CONTAIN A CONFLICT, TRAGEDY, HUMOR AND ACTIONS BETWEEN THE CHARACTERS. THESE DRAMATIZATIONS MUST OCCUR BETWEEN THE MAIN CHARACTER AND HIS SUPPORTING CHARACTERS, HIS CIRCUMSTANCES, HIS REASONS, HIS DESIRES, HIS SINS AND HIS BEATITUDES. THE PLOT CAN BROUGHT TO <u>A CLIMAXING POINT,</u> THE TURNING POINT, BETWEEN THE MAIN VILLAIN AND HIMSELF. IT SHOULD HOLD THE READER'S ATTENTION IN A SUBTLE WAY. I CALL IT THE 'HOOK' OF THE STORY.

THE **TURNING POINT** LEADS TO THE RESOLUTION, WHERE THE FATE OF THE MAIN CHARACTER(S) IS RESOLVED. THE LOOSE ENDS ARE ANSWERED. THE STORY CONCLUDES.

THE <u>WRITER</u> USES ALL OF HIS CRAFT TOOLS TO PROVIDE THE LANGUAGE, THE SCENES AND DRAMATIZATIONS TO TELL THE STORY.

THE <u>READER</u> IS LED ALONG WITH A GOOD STORY LINE AND AN EQUAL QUALITY PLOT AND THEME.

CLASS: WRITE ONE TYPE OF PLOT AND WHY IT WORKS.

21.0.6.0. SIX PLOT TYPES DEFINED:

21.0.6.1. CHRONOLOGICAL PLOT:

EVENTS ARE ARRANGED IN A SEQUENCE IN WHICH THEY OCCUR IN TIME ORDER. HOUR-DAY-WEEK-MONTH-YEAR ORDER. E.G. HEMMINGWAY'S: " OLD MAN AND THE SEA." BECKMAN'S "THE BOOMERS."

21.0.6.2. ACHRONOLOGICAL PLOT:

NOT IN TIME ORDER. E.G. HOMER'S "ILIAD."

21.0.6.3. CLIMATIC PLOT:

ALL OF ACTION FOCUSES ON ONE MAJOR CLIMAX.

21.0.6.4. EPISODIC PLOT:

A SERIES OF LOOSELY CONNECTED EVENTS. E.G. CERVANTES: "DON QUIXOTE."

21.0.6.5. NON SEQUITUR PLOT:

EVENTS ARE PRESENTED WITHOUT ANY CLEAR SEQUENCE OR CHARACTERS WITHOUT ANY 'PRESENCE' MOTIVATION. CONSIDER THEM

RANDOM OR EVEN ABSURD. THIS IS DIFFICULT TO WRITE AND CONVEY TO THE READER.

21.0.6.6. SUBPLOT:

A SECONDARY PLOT THAT IS LESS IMPORTANT TO THE WHOLE STORY BUT MAY CONTRAST OR COMPARE TO THE MAIN PLOT.

21.0.7.0.   PLOT ELEMENTS:

21.0.7.1. CONFLICT:

THE CENTRAL STRUGGLE THAT MOVES THE PLOT FORWARD. THE MAIN CHARACTER'S STRUGGLE AGAINST HIMSELF, NATURE, FATE, DESTINY, SOCIETY OR ANOTHER PERSON OR GROUP.

21.0.7.2. RISING ACTION:

THE PART OF THE NARRATIVE WHICH BEGINS TO BUILD MOMENTUM, THUS FORWARD ACTION WHICH CAUSES A NEED FOR A RESULT. CAUSE AND EFFECT. THIS RISING ACTION SHOULD BUILD AND SUPPORT THE MAIN CONFLICT.

21.0.7.3. CLIMAX:

THE PINNACLE OF HIGHEST TENSION, ACTION OR DIALOGUE, WHICH COMES TO A HEAD. THIS IS THE TIDAL WAVE OF THE SMALLER EVENTS AND DIALOGUE BUILDING UP TO A SWEEPING, UPLIFTING OR EVEN TO A DANGEROUS POINT. THIS IS NOT THE CONCLUSION (RESOLUTION) OR 'DENOUEMENT ,' THE FALLING ACTION.

21.0.7.4. FALLING ACTION: DENOUEMENT:

THE MAIN CHARACTER OR PROTAGONIST RESPONDS TO THE EVENTS OF THE CLIMAX AND RESOLVES SOME OR ALL OF THE RISING ACTION PLOT ELEMENTS

21.0.7.5. REVERSAL: PERIPETEIA:

A REVERSAL OR SUDDEN CHANGE IN FORTUNE FROM GOOD TO BAD OR VICE-VERSA.

21.0.7.6. RESOLUTION:

RESOLUTION IS AN ENDING WHERE SATISFACTORY ANSWERS ARE PROVIDED TO ALL THE QUESTIONS RAISED OVER THE COURSE OF THE PLOT AND DIALOGUE. CALL IT **CLOSURE**.

21.0.8.0. PLOT TWISTS:

PLOT TWISTS OCCUR WHEN THE WRITER WANTS "TO CHANGE" THE STORYLINE LEADING THE READER ALONG A KNOWN PATH AND TO THE "EXPECTED" ENDING OR CLIMATIC EVENT. HE CHANGES IT TO AN UNKNOWN EVENT OR RESOLUTION. THIS IS SOMETIMES USED WHEN THE WRITER REALIZES A NEW AND MORE DRAMATIC CONFLICT AND RESOLUTION IS USED. THIS CONTRAST OR TWIST MAY "HOOK" THE READER'S THOUGHTS PROCESSES, HIS FOLLOWING THE STORYLINE ALONG TO PERK HIS INTEREST AND TO ENHANCE THE STORY. THIS TWIST MAY CHANGE THE BRIDGE FROM CHAPTER ONE WHERE THE "CONFLICT" IS INTRODUCED AND THE CONCLUSION IS DIFFERENT.

21.0.9.0. OUR PROGRESS:

1. PLOTS COME OUT OF THE CHAPTER BY CHAPTER SYNOPSIS.
2. SIX PLOT TYPES HELP KEEP THE READER HOOKED!

CHAPTER 22

22.0.0.0. SETTING: PLACE:

CHAPTER TOPICS: *PLACES-SETTINGS-DEFINED.*

22.0.0.0. SETTING DEFINED:

SETTING IS THE **LOCATION** OF A NARRATIVE IN TIME AND SPACE. IT MAY BE GEOGRAPHICAL, HISTORICAL OR IMAGINARY. SETTING MAY AFFECT THE 'ATMOSPHERE' A INDIRECT REFERENCE TO A DEEPER MEANING, A SYMBOL. EVERY STORY NEEDS A PLACE TO HAPPEN, A WHERE AND A WHEN. THAT'S YOUR SETTING; HOWEVER, SETTINGS CAN DO MORE THAN PROVIDE A PLACE FOR EVENTS TO OCCUR.

SETTINGS CAN EVOKE ATMOSPHERE AND MOOD. IT CAN BE AN ANTAGONIST, PREVENTING YOUR HEROES FROM REACHING THEIR GOALS. SETTINGS CAN GIVE HINTS TO CHARACTERS' STATES OF MIND AND ATTITUDES, OR IT CAN BE USED SYMBOLICALLY, TO HINT AT THE STORY'S THEME.

YOU CAN EVEN MAKE SETTING SO IMPORTANT TO THE STORY THAT IT ALMOST BECOMES ANOTHER CHARACTER. THE STORY OF TOWNS AND KEY PEOPLE THEREIN CAN CREATE A SETTING. FOUR EXAMPLES: 'MUSTANG CITY.' IN BOOK: 'AUGGIE AND BANGER.': MUSTANG CITY IS DESCRIBED AS A CITY, EVENTS, BUILDING, PLACES, PEOPLE, LAND, GOVERNMENT, KEY CHARACTERS, POLITICS, ETC.

(OVERVIEW:)Mustang City is not quite like any Mid-Western City. You might say we sat on the fence watching the world around us change. We are equal Democrats and Republican with an equal distain for big government. Some are Protestant or Catholic, as much City as country as well-to-do as not. We talk and debate and do or not do as our conscious allows. We get up with the chickens, work hard and play easy.

Mustang City was a collection of all sorts of people and places seemingly so opposites yet a common heritage and bonds of community.

(LAND:) 'Mustang land' was unlike others. the farmers and ranchers liked land, the downtowners kept to the sidewalks and glass store fronts. the small grassy areas in-between parceled out enough to satisfy those who loved grass and sky. somehow, it was a peaceful marriage! quiet and content, we were. here, nothing changed much unless you count the times the hair on my arms went up. three times just this morning a record for Mustang City; I'll bet!

(CITIZENS:)We are friendly folk here! I make my rounds, visiting here and there, some times sitting a spell, or taking a snooze in the many rockers about town. You might say comfort and conversation are the things I like best. Front porches with rockers are the most valued possession! Business and homes share a commonality, what we call conversation and commercialization, news, and the latest sale were the best ads, spread by mouth. Conversation was our traveling salesmen. We did best by sittin' and jawin' rather than the door to door kind, which we kinda shot-gun escorted off our property. We are kinda funny about strangers!

(DOWNTOWN:) "Twig's Diner" was the only place in town not befitting a horse's name, relation, or adjective. It was mustang this, bronco that, stallion whatsis---yep! We loved horses around her' it was our one common bond. We all weren't really western cowboys just wannabe's. We had rail fences; but mostly open range land. Twig's was our favorite gathering place for food, conversation, and the latest news. The people made the city. The city was more than 'mustang land.'

Downtown was a collection of brick and clapboard buildings trimmed with gingerbread wooden filials and grooved columns. The red-brick farmer's bank, grocery with large glass windows, hardware store, newspaper office and bus station held the prominent places each with rockers and benches.

The side street held the grange hall, sheriff office, fire station, a small library, book store, a catholic church, car repair garage and taxi garage and one small gas station. The other corner of the square held a protestant church, an office building, funeral home, the rancher's credit union, and the 'Triple A' grocery, named by the owner, Andy after his ranch.

The fourth side street held the Silver Spur Hotel,
An old folks home and three story grand ladies which became rooming houses, doctor and dentist offices and fashionable city dweller homes. City folk were comfortable with the downtown and the short walking distances.

22.0.2.0. SETTING, CHARACTER & PLOT:
PLACES WHERE EVENTS OR ACTION SEQUENCES OCCUR ARE IMPORTANT TO THE DEVELOPMENT OF THE CHARACTER AND PLOT. THESE THREE MUST COMBINED TO BE EFFECTIVE.

EXAMPLE: THE PLACE WHERE A MURDER TAKES PLACE AND WHY WAS THE MAIN CHARACTER INVOLVED...THE SIX W'S MUST BE ANSWERED. WHY WAS **THE PLACE** IMPORTANT?
DID IT HAVE A BEARING ON THE MAIN CHARACTER, THE VICTIM, THE VILLAIN OR THE SEQUENCE OF EVENTS? THE PLACE, PLOT AND EVENTS (SCENES) MUST COME TOGETHER AS ONE TO PROVIDE AN ORDERLY STORY. **PLACE:** DESCRIBE A HOUSE A HUNTING LODGE, A FLAT IN MANHATTAN, A LIBRARY, A MUSEUM, A METRO STATION, A GOVERNMENT BUILDING. GIVE THE PLACE A LIFE AND WRITE ABOUT IT. TREAT THE "PLACE" AS IF IT WERE A CHARACTER. SHOW WHY A PLACE IS IMPORTANT TO YOUR STORY.

DO: A SENSORY TOUR OF YOUR SETTING:
DETAILS ARE ESSENTIAL TO CREATING A VIVID SETTING FOR YOUR READERS, BUT MANY WRITERS HAVE TROUBLE GETTING BEYOND THE MOST OBVIOUS, VISUAL DETAILS. USE THIS EXERCISE TO GENERATE MEMORABLE DETAILS FROM ALL FIVE SENSES AND INTUITION...A FUNNY FEELING.

22.0.2.1. CLASS: WRITE A PARAGRAPH ABOUT A SETTING AND THE MAIN CHARACTER. WHY IS THE SETTING IMPORTANT?

22.0.3.0. OUR PROGRESS
1. SETTINGS OR PLACES ARE IMPORTANT AS SCENERY TO THE STORY.
2. SETTINGS HELP THE PLOT AND SCENES ADVANCE THE STORY.

CHAPTER 23
23.0.0.0. FIGURES OF SPEECH-A glossary:
DO: USE EACH OF THESE IN YOUR STORY, THEY WILL ADD DEPTH
AND THE "STYLE" YOU ARE LOOKING FOR.
THE 'WHY' IS EXPLAINED IN CHAPTER 38 STYLE.

ACCISMUS
COYNESS: A FORM OF IRONY IN WHICH A PERSON FEIGNS A LACK OF
INTEREST IN SOMETHING THAT HE OR SHE ACTUALLY DESIRES.

ALLEGORY
EXTENDING A METAPHOR SO THAT OBJECTS, PERSONS, AND ACTIONS IN A
TEXT ARE EQUATED WITH MEANINGS THAT LIE OUTSIDE THE TEXT.

ALLITERATION:
REPETITION OF AN INITIAL CONSONANT SOUND.

ALLUSION
A BRIEF, USUALLY INDIRECT REFERENCE TO A PERSON, PLACE, OR EVENT-
REAL OR FICTIONAL.

AMBIGUITY
THE PRESENCE OF TWO OR MORE POSSIBLE MEANINGS IN ANY PASSAGE.

AMPLIFICATION
GENERAL TERM FOR ALL OF THE WAYS THAT AN ARGUMENT, AN
EXPLANATION, OR A DESCRIPTION CAN BE EXPANDED AND ENRICHED

ANADIPLOSIS
REPETITION OF THE LAST WORD OF ONE LINE OR CLAUSE TO BEGIN THE
NEXT. ANALOGY REASONING OR ARGUING FROM PARALLEL CASES.

ANALOGY
REASONING OR ARGUING FROM PARALLEL CASES.

ANAPHORA
REPETITION OF THE SAME WORD OR PHRASE AT THE BEGINNING OF
SUCCESSIVE CLAUSES OR VERSES.

ANECDOTE
A SHORT ACCOUNT OF AN INTERESTING OR AMUSING INCIDENT, OFTEN
INTENDED TO ILLUSTRATE OR SUPPORT SOME POINT.

ANTICLIMAX
AN ABRUPT SHIFT FROM A NOBLE TONE TO A LESS EXALTED ONE--OFTEN
FOR COMIC EFFECT.

ANTITHESIS
THE JUXTAPOSITION OF CONTRASTING IDEAS IN BALANCED PHRASES.

APOSIOPESIS
AN UNFINISHED THOUGHT OR BROKEN SENTENCE.

CREATIVE WRITING—THE KELLY MANUAL OF STYLE

APOSTROPHE
BREAKING OFF DISCOURSE TO ADDRESS SOME ABSENT PERSON OR
THING, SOME ABSTRACT QUALITY, AN INANIMATE OBJECT, OR A
NONEXISTENT CHARACTER.

ASSONANCE
IDENTITY OR SIMILARITY IN SOUND BETWEEN INTERNAL VOWELS IN
NEIGHBORING WORDS. EXAMPLE: SEA, SECURITY

AUXESIS
A GRADUAL INCREASE IN INTENSITY OF MEANING WITH WORDS
ARRANGED IN ASCENDING ORDER OF FORCE OR IMPORTANCE.

CHIASMUS
A VERBAL PATTERN IN WHICH THE SECOND HALF OF AN EXPRESSION IS
BALANCED AGAINST THE FIRST BUT WITH THE PARTS REVERSED.

CONNOTATION
THE EMOTIONAL IMPLICATIONS AND ASSOCIATIONS THAT A WORD MAY
CARRY

DENOTATION
THE DIRECT OR DICTIONARY MEANING OF A WORD, IN CONTRAST TO ITS
FIGURATIVE OR ASSOCIATED MEANINGS.

ELLIPSIS: THREE DOTS= MISSING OR CONTINUATION:
OMISSION OF ONE OR MORE WORDS, WHICH MUST BE SUPPLIED BY THE
LISTENER OR READER. RAMBLING THOUGHTS OR SEE RUNNING STYLE.

EUPHEMISM
THE SUBSTITUTION OF AN INOFFENSIVE TERM FOR ONE CONSIDERED
OFFENSIVELY EXPLICIT.

HYPOPHORA
 RAISING QUESTIONS AND ANSWERING THEM.

HYPERBOLE
AN EXTRAVAGANT STATEMENT; THE USE OF EXAGGERATED TERMS FOR
THE PURPOSE OF EMPHASIS OR HEIGHTENED EFFECT.

IDENTIFICATION
ANY OF THE WIDE VARIETY OF MEANS BY WHICH AN AUTHOR MAY
ESTABLISH A SHARED SENSE OF VALUES, ATTITUDES, AND INTERESTS
WITH HIS OR HER READERS.

INNUENDO
 AN INDIRECT OR SUBTLE, USUALLY DEROGATORY IMPLICATION IN
EXPRESSION; AN INSINUATION.

IRONY
THE USE OF WORDS TO CONVEY THE OPPOSITE OF THEIR LITERAL
MEANING. A STATEMENT OR SITUATION WHERE THE MEANING IS
CONTRADICTED BY THE APPEARANCE OR PRESENTATION OF THE IDEA.

KAIROS
 THE OPPORTUNE TIME AND/OR PLACE, THE RIGHT TIME TO SAY OR DO
THE RIGHT THING.

CREATIVE WRITING—THE KELLY MANUAL OF STYLE

JUDICIAL
SPEECH OR WRITING THAT CONSIDERS THE JUSTICE OR INJUSTICE OF A CERTAIN CHARGE OR ACCUSATION.

LITOTES
A FIGURE OF SPEECH CONSISTING OF AN UNDERSTATEMENT IN WHICH AN AFFIRMATIVE IS EXPRESSED BY NEGATING ITS OPPOSITE.

METAPHOR
AN IMPLIED COMPARISON BETWEEN TWO UNLIKE THINGS THAT ACTUALLY HAVE SOMETHING IMPORTANT IN COMMON.
[LIFE IS A METAPHOR!]

METONYMY
A FIGURE OF SPEECH IN WHICH ONE WORD OR PHRASE IS SUBSTITUTED FOR ANOTHER WITH WHICH IT IS CLOSELY ASSOCIATED; ALSO, THE RHETORICAL STRATEGY OF DESCRIBING SOMETHING INDIRECTLY BY REFERRING TO THINGS AROUND IT.

NARRATIO[N].
THE PART OF AN ARGUMENT IN WHICH A SPEAKER OR WRITER PROVIDES A NARRATIVE ACCOUNT OF WHAT HAS HAPPENED AND EXPLAINS THE NATURE OF THE CASE.

ONOMATOPOEIA
THE FORMATION OR USE OF WORDS THAT IMITATE THE SOUNDS ASSOCIATED WITH THE OBJECTS OR ACTIONS THEY REFER TO.

OXYMORON
A FIGURE OF SPEECH IN WHICH INCONGRUOUS OR CONTRADICTORY TERMS APPEAR SIDE BY SIDE.

PARADOX
A STATEMENT THAT APPEARS TO CONTRADICT ITSELF.

PERSONA
VOICE OR MASK THAT AN AUTHOR OR SPEAKER OR PERFORMER PUTS ON FOR A PARTICULAR PURPOSE.

PARAPHRASE
A RESTATEMENT OF A TEXT OR PASSAGE IN ANOTHER FORM OR OTHER WORDS, OFTEN TO CLARIFY MEANING.

PATHOS
THE MEANS OF PERSUASION IN CLASSICAL RHETORIC THAT APPEALS TO THE AUDIENCE'S EMOTIONS.

PERSONIFICATION
A FIGURE OF SPEECH IN WHICH AN INANIMATE OBJECT OR ABSTRACTION IS ENDOWED WITH HUMAN QUALITIES OR ABILITIES.

PUN
A PLAY ON WORDS, SOMETIMES ON DIFFERENT SENSES OF THE SAME WORD AND SOMETIMES ON THE SIMILAR SENSE OR SOUND OF DIFFERENT WORDS.

CREATIVE WRITING—THE KELLY MANUAL OF STYLE

RUNNING STYLE
SENTENCE STYLE THAT APPEARS TO FOLLOW THE MIND AS IT WORRIES A PROBLEM THROUGH. RAMBLING THOUGHTS. ALSO SEE ELLIPSIS.

SARCASM
A MOCKING, OFTEN IRONIC OR SATIRICAL REMARK.

SIMILE
A STATED COMPARISON (USUALLY FORMED WITH "LIKE" OR "AS") BETWEEN TWO FUNDAMENTALLY DISSIMILAR THINGS THAT HAVE CERTAIN QUALITIES IN COMMON.

STYLE
NARROWLY INTERPRETED AS THOSE FIGURES THAT ORNAMENT SPEECH OR WRITING; BROADLY, AS REPRESENTING A MANIFESTATION OF THE PERSON SPEAKING OR WRITING.

SYNECHDOCHE
A FIGURE OF SPEECH IS WHICH A PART IS USED TO REPRESENT THE WHOLE, THE WHOLE FOR A PART, THE SPECIFIC FOR THE GENERAL, THE GENERAL FOR THE SPECIFIC, OR THE MATERIAL FOR THE THING MADE FROM IT.

TESTIMONY
A PERSON'S ACCOUNT OF AN EVENT OR STATE OF AFFAIRS.

UNDERSTATEMENT
A FIGURE OF SPEECH IN WHICH A WRITER OR A SPEAKER DELIBERATELY MAKES A SITUATION SEEM LESS IMPORTANT OR SERIOUS THAN IT IS.

VOICE
THE QUALITY OF A VERB THAT INDICATES WHETHER ITS SUBJECT ACTS (ACTIVE VOICE) OR IS ACTED UPON (PASSIVE VOICE).

CLASS: TAKE THE QUIZ, 1 TO 20. WRITE ONLY THE LETTER OF THE CORRECT ANSWER.

23.0.1.0. FIGURES OF SPEECH-QUIZ:
[COMPILED FROM SOURCES: [SEE BIBLIOGRAPHY]
[GRAMMAR.ABOUT.COM/WIKIPEDIA/OTHERS].
THIS QUIZ SHOULD HELP YOU TO UNDERSTAND FIGURES OF SPEECH. FOR EACH QUESTION BELOW, CHOOSE THE ONE **FIGURE OF SPEECH** THAT IS MOST *CLEARLY* ILLUSTRATED BY THE SHORT PRECEDING PASSAGE. COMPARE YOUR ANSWERS WITH THOSE AT THE BOTTOM OF THE PAGE.

1.   WELL, SON, I'LL TELL YOU:
LIFE FOR ME AIN'T BEEN NO CRYSTAL STAIR.
IT'S HAD TACKS IN IT, AND SPLINTERS,
AND BOARDS TORN UP, AND PLACES WITH NO CARPET ON THE
FLOOR--BARE.   (LANGSTON HIGHES, "MOTHER TO SON")
(A) SYNECDOCHE
(B) METAPHOR
(C) IRONY
(D) PUN

2.   WHY SHOULD WHITE PEOPLE BE RUNNING ALL THE STORES IN OUR COMMUNITY? WHY SHOULD WHITE PEOPLE BE RUNNING THE BANKS OF OUR COMMUNITY? WHY SHOULD THE ECONOMY OF OUR COMMUNITY BE IN THE HANDS OF THE WHITE MAN? WHY?
(MALCOLM X)
(A) ANTITHESIS
(B) LITOTES
(C) ANAPHORA
(D) UNDERSTATEMENT

3.   SUBSTITUTING THE WORD "EUTHANASIA" FOR "MERCY KILLING" OR "KILLING THE TERMINALLY ILL"
(A) HYPERBOLE
(B) EUPHEMISM
(C) ASSONANCE
(D) OXYMORON

4.   I HAD SO MUCH HOMEWORK LAST NIGHT THAT I NEEDED A PICKUP TRUCK TO CARRY ALL MY BOOKS HOME!
(A) SYNECHDOCHE
(B) ONOMATOPOEIA
(C) PUN
(D) HYPERBOLE

5.   LET'S JUST SAY THAT MS. HILTON IS NOT THE BRIGHTEST BULB ON THE CHRISTMAS TREE.
(A) PARADOX
(B) LITOTES
(C) APOSTROPHE
(D) CHIASMUS

6.   THE CHUG-A, CHUG-A, CHUG-A OF THE TRAIN ECHOED DOWN THE HILL, WHILE A CLOUD OF SMOKE ROSE UP TO THE BLUE WESTERN SKY.
(A) SIMILE
(B) METONYMY
(C) ANAPHORA
(D) ONOMATOPOEIA

7.   BUT THE PRISONER WOULD NOT ANSWER, HE ONLY LAY WITH WIDE, *DARK, BRIGHT*, EYES, LIKE A BOUND ANIMAL.
        (D. H. LAWRENCE, *ENGLAND, MY ENGLAND*)
(A) OXYMORON
(B) EUPHEMISM
(C) ANAPHORA
(D) PERSONIFICATION

8. YOU HAVE A LOT OF WORK TO DO, SO I'LL LEND YOU A HAND.
(A) ASSONANCE
(B) APOSTROPHE
(C) IRONY
(D) SYNECHDOCHE

9. THE WIND HAD BLOWN OFF, LEAVING A LOUD, BRIGHT NIGHT, WITH WINGS BEATING IN THE TREES AND A PERSISTENT ORGAN SOUND AS THE FULL BELLOWS OF THE EARTH BLEW THE FROGS FULL OF LIFE.

(F. SCOTT FITZGERALD, *THE GREAT GATSBY*)
(A) CHIASMUS
(B) ALLITERATION
(C) PUN
(D) OXYMORON

10. O WESTERN WIND, WHEN WILT THOU BLOW
THAT THE SMALL RAIN DOWN CAN RAIN?
CHRIST, THAT MY LOVE WERE IN MY ARMS,
AND I IN MY BED AGAIN!
(ANONYMOUS, "O WESTERN WIND")
(A) LITOTES
(B) PARADOX
(C) APOSTROPHE
(D) ANAPHORA

11. THE HEART OF A FOOL IS IN HIS MOUTH, BUT THE MOUTH OF A
WISE MAN IS IN HIS HEART.
(BENJAMIN FRANKLIN)
(A) HYPERBOLE
(B) CHIASMUS
(C) LITOTES
(D) ANAPHORA

12. WE TALKED WITH EACH OTHER ABOUT EACH OTHER
THOUGH NEITHER OF US SPOKE —
(EMILY DICKINSON)
(A) METONYMY
(B) PARADOX
(C) SYNECDOCHE
(D) PERSONIFICATION

13. THE EARTH LAUGHS BENEATH MY HEAVY FEET
   AT THE BLASPHEMY IN MY OLD JANGLY WALK
      (BILLY CORGAN, "THIRTY-THREE")
(A) EUPHEMISM
(B) SIMILE
(C) ANTITHESIS
(D) PERSONIFICATION

14. I DIG MY TOES INTO THE SAND.
THE OCEAN LOOKS LIKE A THOUSAND DIAMONDS STREWN
ACROSS A BLUE BLANKET. (INCUBUS, "WISH YOU WERE HERE")
(A) CHIASMUS
(B) SIMILE
(C) ONOMATOPOEIA
(D) SYNECDOCHE

15. IN THE SWEAT OF THY FACE SHALT THOU EAT BREAD.
(VERGIL)
(A) SIMILE
(B) IRONY
(C) METONYMY
(D) ASSONANCE

16. WHY DO WE WAIT UNTIL A PIG IS DEAD TO *CURE* IT?
(A) PUN

(B) PERSONIFICATION
(C) ANAPHORA
(D) SYNECHDOCHE

17. "IT WAS THE BEST OF TIMES, IT WAS THE WORST OF TIMES, IT
WAS THE AGE OF WISDOM, IT WAS THE AGE OF FOOLISHNESS, IT WAS
THE EPOCH OF BELIEF, IT WAS THE EPOCH OF INCREDULITY, IT WAS
THE SEASON OF LIGHT, IT WAS THE SEASON OF DARKNESS, IT WAS
THE SPRING OF HOPE, IT WAS THE WINTER OF DESPAIR, WE HAD
EVERYTHING BEFORE US, WE HAD NOTHING BEFORE US, WE WERE
ALL GOING DIRECT TO HEAVEN, WE WERE ALL GOING DIRECT THE
OTHER WAY."
(CHARLES DICKENS, *A TALE OF TWO CITIES*)
(A) ANTITHESIS
(B) LITOTES
(C) SIMILE
(D) UNDERSTATEMENT

18. MY WISHES RACED THROUGH THE HOUSE HIGH HAYAND
NOTHING I CARED, AT MY SKY BLUE TRADES, . . .
(DYLAN THOMAS, "FERN HILL")
(A) SIMILE
(B) IRONY
(C) METONYMY
(D) ASSONANCE

19. AND HE WAS RICH, YES, RICHER THAN A KING,
AND ADMIRABLY SCHOOLED IN EVERY GRACE:
IN FINE--WE THOUGHT THAT HE WAS EVERYTHING
TO MAKE US WISH THAT WE WERE IN HIS PLACE.

SO ON WE WORKED AND WAITED FOR THE LIGHT,
AND WENT WITHOUT THE MEAT AND CURSED THE BREAD,
AND RICHARD CORY, ONE CALM SUMMER NIGHT,
WENT HOME AND PUT A BULLET IN HIS HEAD.
(E. A. ROBINSON, "RICHARD CORY")
(A) CHIASMUS
(B) LITOTES
(C) ANTITHESIS
(D) IRONY

20. PROSPECTIVE BUYERS ARE ADVISED NOT TO RELY HEAVILY ON
THE FRONT BRAKES, WHICH ARE NOT CONNECTED.(ADVERTISEMENT
FOR A REPLICA 1925 ROLLS-ROYCE WWI ARMORED CAR)
(A) ANTITHESIS
(B) SIMILE
(C) ANAPHORA
(D) UNDERSTATEMENT

ANSWERS:
1.   (B) METAPHOR
2.   (C) ANAPHORA
3.   (B) EUPHEMISM
4.   (D) HYPERBOLE
5.   (B) LITOTES
6.   (D) ONOMATOPOEIA

7.   (A) OXYMORON
8.   (D) SYNECHDOCHE
9.   (B) ALLITERATION
10.   (C) APOSTROPHE
11.   (B) CHIASMUS
12.   (B) PARADOX
13.   (D) PERSONIFICATION
14.   (B) SIMILE
15.   (C) METONYMY
16.   (A) PUN
17.   (A) ANTITHESIS
18.   (D) ASSONANCE
19.   (D) IRONY
20.   (D) UNDERSTATEMENT

23.1.0.0. OUR PROGRESS:

1. WE LEARNED TO USE THE MANY FIGURES OF SPEECH TO ENHANCE,
   ILLUSTRATE AND ILLUMINATE OUR STORY.

2. WE NEED LOTS OF THESE TO ADVANCE OUR DIALOGUE AND INCREASE
   THE DRAMA.

CHAPTER 24

24.0.0.0. PERSON-POINT OF VIEW:

CHAPTER TOPICS:

FICTION-THE ANGLE OR PERSPECTIVE FROM WHICH A STORY IS NARRATED, THE KIND OF NARRATOR AND HIS RELATIONSHIP WITH HIS CHARACTERS.

24.0.1.0. DEFINED: THE ANGLE OR PERSPECTIVE:

THE MAIN POINTS OF VIEW ARE FIRST PERSON, SECOND PERSON (VERY RARE), AND THIRD PERSON, EACH WITH SEVERAL VARIATIONS.

THE **POINT OF VIEW (POV)** OF A STORY IS THE PERSPECTIVE, THE ANGLE, THE SLANT FROM WHICH THE STORY IS TOLD--THE CHARACTER THROUGH WHICH THE READER EXPERIENCES THE FICTIONAL WORLD (BUT DON'T CONFUSE IT WITH NARRATIVE VOICE; SEE BELOW). MOST SHORT WORKS MAKE USE OF A SINGLE POINT OF VIEW, WHILE LONGER WORKS MAY HAVE MANY.

> *23.0.1.1CLASS: (EXPERIMENT WITH THE POINT OF VIEW TO SEE HOW IT AFFECTS YOUR STORY).*

24.0.2.0. PERSON:

1. **FIRST PERSON, USING "I" OR "WE":** AUTOBIOGRAPHY STYLE, OR NON-FICTIONAL.

2. **SECOND PERSON:** "YOU." DIFFICULT TO USE.

3. **THIRD PERSON** NARRATION: ("HE," "SHE," "IT" "THEY"). THE MOST USEFUL OF POV.

4. **THIRD PERSON LIMITED:** AUTHOR KNOWS ONLY MAIN CHARACTER'S ACTIONS. EXAMPLE, '**ALICE IN WONDERLAND,**' AUTHOR ONLY KNOWS ALICE'S ACTIONS.

5. **THIRD PERSON OMNISCIENT:** (GOD LIKE). AUTHOR KNOWS ALL OF THE CHARACTER'S ACTIONS AND THEIR THOUGHTS.

6. **STREAM OF CONSCIOUSNESS:** THE NARRATOR CONVEYS THE CHARACTERS THOUGHTS AND REACTIONS EXACTLY AS THEY OCCUR, RANDOM, DISJOINTED OR CONFUSED.

7. **UNRELIABLE NARRATION:** THE NARRATOR LIES, MISLEADS THE READER, CHANGES THE READER'S THINKING AND UNDERSTANDING DELIBERATELY.

24.0.3.0. DECIDING WHICH POINT OF VIEW TO USE IS A STRATEGIC

DECISION. AS A WRITER, YOU MUST CHOOSE WHICH PERSON WILL ALLOW YOU TO MOST EFFECTIVELY DEVELOP YOUR CHARACTERS AND TELL YOUR STORY.

CREATIVE WRITING—THE KELLY MANUAL OF STYLE

CHANGING POINT OF VIEW: OR CONSIDER SWITCHING THE POINT OF VIEW. GOING FROM FIRST PERSON TO THIRD WILL REQUIRE RE-WRITING AN ENTIRE STORY.

24.0.4.0. FIRST PERSON LIMITS THE READER TO ONE CHARACTER'S PERSPECTIVE. WITH A BOOK SUCH AS *'ON THE ROAD,'* **FOR INSTANCE, THE FIRST PERSON POINT OF** VIEW PUTS US RIGHT THERE IN THE CAR WITH SAL PARADISE AND DEAN MORIARTY; WE FOLLOW SAL'S EVERY EXHILARATING THOUGHTS AS THEY TRAVEL AND ADVENTURE ACROSS THE COUNTRY. USE THE LIMITATIONS OF FIRST PERSON TO CREATE TENSION. BECAUSE HIS NARRATOR IS UNRELIABLE, THE READER MUST DO A CERTAIN AMOUNT OF DETECTIVE WORK TO FIGURE OUT THE TRUTH: THIS TENSION ENGAGES THE READER AND ADVANCES THE PLOT.

24.0.5.0. THIRD PERSON IS ACTUALLY THE MORE VERSATILE POINT OF VIEW. THIRD PERSON ALLOWS YOU TO CREATE A MUCH RICHER, MORE COMPLICATED UNIVERSE. LEO TOLSTOY'S BOOK, *'ANNA KARENINA,'* COULD ONLY HAVE BEEN WRITTEN IN THIRD PERSON. (HE, SHE, IT).CONSIDER USING **THIRD PERSON; THUS TELL** YOUR STORY MORE DISPASSIONATELY AND MORE EFFECTIVELY.

24.0.6.0. OMNISCIENT POINT OF VIEW:
AS YOUR PLOTS BECOME MORE COMPLICATED, YOU MAY NEED MORE THAN ONE POINT OF VIEW TO TELL YOUR STORY AND BEGIN TO USE OMNISCIENT. [SEE CH 3.0.3.0.]

24.1.0.0 OUR PROGRESS:
1. WE LEARNED THE IMPORTANCE OF POINT OF VIEW.

2. WE LEARNED TO SELECT THE CORRECT PERSON AS OUR NARRATOR.

3. NARRATORS USE A 'VOICE OVER' (V.O.) AS A METHOD TO TELL THE STORY. AN OBJECT LIKE A JOURNAL, LETTER, A CITIES SIGN, A PICTURE, NEWSPAPER HEADLINE, OR EVEN TWO CHARACTER'S BANTER WILL TELL THE STORY.

CHAPTER 25
25.0.0.0. SCENES-DIALOGUE-DRAMATIZATION:
CHAPTER TOPICS: SCENE (HAPPENINGS-EVENTS) VERSUS SETTING (PLACE)-DIALOGUE-DRAMATIZATION-HERO-VILLAIN-CHARACTER TRAITS-AUTHORIAL INTRUSION.

25.0.0.0. FORM VERSUS FUNCTION: SHAPE:
EVERY PIECE OF FICTION NEED A SHAPE, AND SHAPE HAS TWO VARIETIES: FORM AND STRUCTURE. **FORM IS** WHAT THE STORY LOOKS LIKE; FOR EXAMPLE, YOU COULD WRITE A STORY IN THE FORM OF A LETTER, OR A NOVEL IN THE FORM OF A DIARY. YOU CAN COMBINE SEVERAL FORMS IN ONE PIECE OF FICTION--A GOOD EXAMPLE IS THE NOVEL, WHICH USES DIARIES, TELEGRAMS, LETTERS AND MORE. **STRUCTURE** IS THE ARRANGEMENT OF THE PIECES, THE ORDER , SEQUENCE YOUR SCENES APPEAR IN RELATIVE TO ONE ANOTHER.

25.0.1.0. SCENE VERSUS SETTING:
THE REAL DRAMA IN FICTION COMES FROM SCENES- NOT A PLACE BUT EVENTS LIKE "SMALLER HAPPENINGS" OR "LARGE CRISES OR CLIMAXING EVENTS". A "DRAMATIZATION" SCENE IS IN AN **EVENT** LIKE A **CONFRONTATION** (QUARREL, FIGHT OR VERBAL FIGHT, SHOOTING, MURDER, PLANE CRASH) OR **INTERACTION** OF SOME SORT BETWEEN SEVERAL CHARACTERS OR ONE CHARACTER (CAR CHASE, SECRET) AND **AN OBJECT**. (EVIDENCE, CLUE, WEAPON, MYSTERIOUS PERSON, DEAD BODY.) THESE EVENTS FUNCTION LIKE STORY BUILDING "LAYERS" OVER THE FRAMEWORK OF PLOT.

25.0.2.0. DIALOGUE:
SCENES ARE CONSTRUCTED OF DIALOGUE, AND EACH OF THE CHARACTERS INVOLVED IS STRIVING TO GAIN SOMETHING (IT CAN BE SOMETHING OBVIOUS, LIKE ESCAPING FROM THE BAD GUY, OR SUBTLE, LIKE A SECRET, A DREAM). DIALOGUE MARRIES WITH ACTION TO MAGNIFY THE UNSEEN PARTS OF THE CHARACTER OR PLOT. (THE COWBOY STARES AT THE SUNSET. A COUPLE WATCHES THE OCEAN. THEIR WORDS ARE NOT THERE BUT THE **"PICTURE"** CAPTURES THEIR THOUGHTS). [SEE MORE ON PICTURESQUE].   WRITERS MUST HAVE A **GOOD EAR** (READING IT ALOUD) AND EYE FOR DETAIL. CHOOSE GREAT WORDS AND DETAIL THAT MATCHES THE ACTION OR CHARACTER'S STATEMENTS. SAY IT REAL AND IN ENGLISH!

25.0.3.0. DIALOGUE: A DIFFERENT KIND OF SPEECH:
DIALOGUE IS DEFINITELY NOT THE WAY PEOPLE REALLY SPEAK. EVERYDAY SPEECH IS BORING AND REPETITIVE WHEN WRITTEN DOWN. [PROSE IS THE NATURAL WAY OF SPEAKING OR WRITING; BUT, GENERALLY LONGER AND NOT AS CONCISE .]

DIALOGUE MOVES THE STORY FORWARD AND BRINGS CHARACTERS TO LIFE...IT MAKES THEIR STORY BELIEVABLE.

25.0.4.0. DIALOGUE'S FUNCTIONAL ROLE:
DIALOGUE IS <u>IMPORTANT TO THE PLOT</u>, AND
CONVEY THE RHYTHM AND SYNTAX OF REAL SPEECH.
DIALOGUE NEEDS TO CONVEY INFORMATION TO THE READER, BUT IN A
WAY WITH NATURAL SOUNDING WORDS AND RHYTHMS. IT SHOULD BE
BRIEF AND TO THE POINT. ONE WAY IS TO READ IT OUTLOUD. LISTEN TO
IT AS YOU WRITE, AND WRITE IT AS THE CHARACTER WOULD SAY IT.
WRITE SPEECH AS THOUGH IT SHOULD <u>READ</u> LIKE REAL SPEECH. READ IT
OUTLOUD. DOES IT FLOW SMOOTHLY? IF IT IS NOT MEANT TO BE
CHOPPY, SMOOTH IT OUT. SHORT SENTENCES, BRIEF IDEAS WITHIN AND
FLOWING WORD CHOICES WILL FIX IT.

COMMUNICATE INFORMATION THROUGH YOUR DIALOGUE BUT DON'T
OVER SAY IT. LET YOUR STORY UNWRAP NATURALLY.

25.0.5.0. THE READER REMEMBERS:
THE READER KNOWS YOU ARE PROVIDING DETAILS AND THEY
REMEMBER EARLIER SCENES (EVENTS).

25.0.5.1. DIALOG: RULES OF THUMB
**DO: TEST: WHAT THE CHARACTER SAYS AND DOES, DOES IT
MATCH?**DELETE ANYTHING THAT DOES NOT DRIVE THE STORY
FORWARD.DO REMOVE WORDS THAT DON'T FIT OR FILLER MATERIAL
FROM THE DIALOG.
**DON'T TRY TO PROVIDE TOO MUCH INFORMATION AT ONCE
THROUGH DIALOG.**
MAKE IT FIT THE CURRENT SCENE OR EVENT. THE READER
WANTS TO KNOW WHO SHOT THE VICTIM NOT THAT THE COP WAS
WORKING IN ANOTHER CITY 20 YEARS AGO. DON'T CONFUSE THE BACK
STORY {HIS PAST AND HISTORY INFO} VERSUS NOW ACTIONS AND
SCENES.
**VARY YOUR TAG LINES WHEN WRITING DIALOG:"HE SAID/SHE
SAID."** IF THE CONVERSATION IS BETWEEN TWO CHARACTERS,
IDENTIFY THE FIRST AND SECOND CHARACTER THEN REMOVE THE
TAGS LINES TO CONTINUE THE DIALOG. {THE READER UNDERSTANDS
WHO IS TALKING}.
DIALECT, SLANG AND PROFANITY: DON'T OVERUSE. REFER CH 15-SEX
A. Avoid stereotypes, especially when it comes to dialect.

*B. never using slang except in dialogue and then only when
APPROS...slang DATES THE DIALOG in a short time."*

*C. profanity is BLUNT AND RAW. BETTER TO SUBSTITUTE OTHER WORDS OR
CREATE A NEW WORD. PROFANITY IS A <u>SHOCK WORD</u> TO THE READER*

MAKE YOU CHARACTER BELIEVABLE.
*GIVE HIM QULAITIES THAT MEN AND WOMEN WILL WANT TO
KNOW AND EMULATE. IF HE HAS FLAWS SHOW HOW HE IS
CONQUERING THEM. HE DRINKS BUT…*

<u>DO: USE THE RIGHT DETAIL TO MAKE THE CHARACTER ALIVE AND
REAL</u>. WRITE THE CHARACTER AS IF HE/SHE IS REAL. MOVING,
SHOOTING, CRYING, AND ALIVE, BREATHING, THINKING, LOVING, ETC

25.0.6.0. DIALOGUE: CHARACTER –SHOW BUT NOT TELL
BOOK DRAFT #4

CREATIVE WRITING—THE KELLY MANUAL OF STYLE

THIS IS WHAT OUR CHARACTER SAYS AND HOW HE/SHE SAYS IT. DOES HE HAVE AN ACCENT OR 'PET SAYINGS?' WHAT STYLE OF LANGUAGE DOES HE USE? FRENCH? CONTRACTIONS, FORMAL LANGUAGE, SCIENTIFIC, BUSINESS, A HERO, A CAD, A LOSER, AN ACTION HERO?

WHO AND WHAT OUR CHARACTER DOES IMPACTS HIS CHOICE OF WORDS. HIS SENSES MIGHT IMPACT HIS CHOICE OF WORDS. IS HE FUNNY? A PRUDE? A RICH MAN? A POOR MAN? AN IRISHMAN? HIS HISTORY OR A MAJOR EVENT OR TRAGEDY MIGHT CHANGE HIS FEELINGS OR HIS EXPLANATIONS AS HE TELLS THE STORY. ADDING MORE DESCRIPTIVE AND SCENES (THE PLACE) OR (EVENT) MIGHT CAUSE HIM TO SHOUT, TO WEEP, TO BECOME ANGRY, TO BECOME SILENT. USE DIALOGUE TO SHOW BUT NOT TELL.

25.0.7.0. CHARACTER CONVERSATIONS:
CONSIDER THAT CONVERSATIONS ARE GENERALLY FOUR SENTENCES (AS IN SCRIPTS) LONG BEFORE THE OTHER CHARACTER SPEAKS.

DO: USE ACTION AND DESCRIPTION TO BREAK UP DIALOGUE INTO PIECES. THIS GIVES A SLOWER PACE TO THE STORY AND PLOT.
DO: PUNCTUATE IT CORRECTLY TO HELP THE READER DIGEST IT.
DO: TEST IT BY READING IT OUTLOUD.

25.0.8.0. DRAMATIZATION: THINK ABOUT EVENTS SCENES) AND
SETTINGS AND WHAT DIALOG IS BEING USED. WE CAN SET UP OUR DRAMATIZATION TO PROVIDE IMPACT TO OUR STORY.

25.0.9.0. DESCRIPTIVE PARAGRAPHS:
 MAY BE LONGER THAN FOUR SENTENCES AND SHOULD NATURALLY TRANSITION OR BE RELEVANT TO THE SCENE OR PLOT OR DRAMATIZATION. BEWARE OF USING FILLER MATERIAL, ESPECIALLY LONG FILLER INFORMATION; YOU MAY LOOSE THE READER. FOR EXAMPLE, IF YOU ARE WRITING ACTION-ACTION-ACTION THEN DUMP FILLER MATERIAL IN; THE IMPACT IS LOST. THE RESULT IS THE READER THEN BECOMES AN OBSERVER AND IDENTIFIES LESS WITH THE MAIN CHARACTER AND THE EVENTS. *LET THE READER BECOME THE MAIN CHARACTERS- HERO OR VILLIAN.*

25.1.0.0. DRAMATIZATION!
THINK OF DRAMATIZATION AS AN ACTOR'S PORTRAYAL OF HIS CHARACTER HOW HIS WORDS, ACTIONS AND HIS WHOLE DEEDS ARE PLAYED OUT. THUS, HIS ACTING PERFORMANCE EXPANDS HIS CHARACTER TO REAL LIFE CHARACTERIZATION. THIS IS ACTING!

25.2.0.0. UNDERSTANDING DRAMATIZATION IS TO SEE THAT THE
NARRATOR'S POINT OF VIEW IS MERGED WITH THAT OF THE MAIN CHARACTER AND SHOWS THE EVENTS AS A DRAMA IN WHICH HE PLAYS A PART. **ILLUMINATION** WILL ALSO WORK WONDERS HERE!

25.3.0.0. OUR PROGRESS:
1. WE LEARNED THE DIFFERENCE BETWEEN SCENES AND SETTINGS.
2. WE LEARNED DIALOGUE IS A DIFFERENT KIND OF SPEECH.
3. OUR HERO AND VILLAIN HAVE BOTH STRONG COMPARISONS AND CONTRASTS.
4. WE LEARNED DIALOGUE IS IMPORTANT TO ADVANCE PLOT.

CHAPTER 26
26.0.0.0. TIME-TIMELINES-BRIDGES:
CHAPTER TOPICS: *TIME-TIMELINES-FLASHBACKS-FLASH FORWARDS-CHARACTER TIMELINES-BRIDGES-CLIMAXES-ENDING A BOOK.*

26.1.0.0. TIME:
TIME CAN BE USED TO CHRONOLOGICAL ORDER THE WRITING, OR PARTS OF PAST LIFE MIGHT BE BROUGHT UP LATER, OR FLASHBACKED TO. REMEMBER IMAGES-LANGUAGES-TERM-QUOTES-CARS-OBJECTS MUST BE TIME RELEVANT.

TIME NOT IN ORDER IS "ACHRONOLOGICAL" OR OUT OF ORDER. FLASHBACKS & DIGRESSIONS. IT IS IMPORTANT TO KNOW HOW TO WRITE THESE AS THEY CAN BE CONFUSING FOR THE READER. WE SEE A TIME CLOCK BEING PLACED ON A MOVIE SCREEN, THAT A CERTAIN AMOUNT OF ACTION WILL TAKE PLACE WITHIN THE HOUR, DAY OR WEEK. A COUNT DOWN DOES THE SAME THING. THIS INCREASES THE TENSION AND RISING ACTION BUILDS.

EXAMPLE:
YOU'RE WRITING A FRENCH NOVEL OR ABOUT FRANCE BUT IN 1830 IT WAS FRANC'S NOT EURO DOLLARS. OR METRIC…OR YOUR YEAR MUST BE CORRECT, AS RADIO WAS NOT INVENTED YET. PROPELLER PLANES VERSUS JETS, OR BEFORE PLANES. LADIES WORE HATS DURING PERIOD, ALSO LARGE AND WITH FEATHER OR NETTING. OR MEN' SUITS WERE DOUBLE BREASTED, OR NERO LEISURE SUITS WERE IN YOUR PERIOD.

EXAMPLE:
"STILL I WAS REMINDED THAT PESHAWAR WAS 2,500 YEARS OLD IN A STATE THAT WAS FIFTY-FOUR YEARS OLD. PESHAWAR HAD A RIGHT TO BE RUN DOWN WITH LITTLE RECONSTRUCTION MONEY AND NO INCOME TAX BASE."

26.0.1 .0. TIME: ON TIME-FLASHBACKS-FLASH FORWARD.
TIME CAN BE USED TO CHRONOLOGICALLY ORDER THE WRITING, OR PARTS OF PAST MIGHT BE BROUGHT UP LATER, OR FLASHBACKED TO. REMEMBER IMAGES-LANGUAGES-TERM-QUOTES-CARS-PLACES-OBJECTS MUST BE TIME RELEVANT.

TIME NOT IN ORDER IS 'ACHRONOLOGICAL' OR OUT OF ORDER. FLASHBACKS & DIGRESSIONS. IT IS IMPORTANT TO KNOW HOW TO WRITE THESE AS THEY CAN BE CONFUSING FOR READER.

THIS COULD BE A PHYSICAL OR MENTAL STATE. DAYDREAMING-NIGHTMARES-PHYSICAL ACTIONS NOT OF THE CURRENT PLACE. FEELING OR SENSING ANOTHER TIME OR PLACE. *EXAMPLE:*
1. "I EXPLAINED, MY MIND WAS SOMEWHERE ELSE!"

2. THE CAR BACKFIRE SENT ME SLAMMING TO THE FLOOR
   AS IF I WAS BACK IN THE WAR.

3. THE NIGHTMARE SEEMED REAL ENOUGH; IT SCARED THE DEVIL OUT OF ME!

EXAMPLE:
YOUR WRITING A FRENCH NOVEL OR ABOUT FRANCE ; BUT IN 1830, IT WAS FRANC'S NOT EURO DOLLARS. NOR METRIC...OR YOUR YEAR MUST BE CORRECT, AS RADIO WAS NOT INVENTED YET. PROPELLER PLANES VERSUS JETS, OR BEFORE PLANES. LADIES WORE HATS DURING PERIOD, ALSO LARGE AND WITH FEATHER OR NETTING. NOR WERE MEN'S SUITS DOUBLE BREASTED, NOR WERE NERO LEISURE SUITS IN YOUR TIME PERIOD. (TIME AND DETAILS MATCH).

EXERCISE: CLASS USE THE FLASH FORWARD CONCEPT IN ONE PARAGRAPH. WHAT HAPPENS AS A RESULT?

26.0.2. 0. HISTORY:
TOPICS: USE ACCURATE HISTORICAL EVENTS AND DATES.
WHEN WRITING PERIOD PIECES, BECOME A STUDENT OF HISTORY.

26.0. 3.0. STORY-USING TIMELINES:
TWO TYPES: LINE CHART AND SPREADSHEET TYPE.

26.0.4.1. VERY IMPORTANT!
IT IS IMPORTANT YOU ESTABLISH A **TIMELINE (A SIMPLE LINE CHART)** FOR YOUR MAIN CHARACTERS. YOU MAY KNOW AT THE BEGINNING IF YOUR SYNOPSIS IS DETAILED. YOU MAY KNOW AFTER WRITING SEVERAL CHAPTERS AND HAVE AN IDEA WHERE AND WHEN CERTAIN KEY EVENTS (SCENES-PLOTS-CLIMAXES) WILL OCCUR.

THE TIMELINE (LINE CHART) IS MERELY A LINE ALONG WHICH WE MARK KEY EVENTS AND CHARACTERS. THE X INDICATES A CONNECTION. THE CONNECTION IS THE KEY EVENT...A SHOOTING, A HOSTAGE, ETC. A MINOR EVENT DOES NOT HAVE THE X FOLLOWING THE CHARACTER'S ASSIGNED LETTER. IF YOU NOTICE IN EXAMPLE 29.6.0.0. MICKEY'S (M) HAS NO X, YET INTERCONNECTS WITH KELLY AND THE PREACHER. HIS MAJOR CLIMATIC EVENT (MC) SOON FOLLOWS [MC2 & MC3]. THE LETTER M (MICKEY) FIRST APPEARS ON KELLY'S AND ROSE'S TIMELINE AND LATER ON THE PREACHER'S TIMELINES. MICKEY SHOOTS THE PREACHER LATER BUT HE DOESN'T DIE JUST YET. THE PREACHER IS THE FIRST CHARACTER TO DIE THUS, ENDING HIS CHARACTER [EOC1].
[SEE CH 20 CHARACTERS].

THIS TIMELINE LOOKS COMPLEX BUT ISN'T REALLY. IT JUST HELPS YOU KEEP THE EVENTS AND CHARACTERS IN ORDER BY TIME.

IF YOU ARE AN EXPERIENCED WRITER, YOU CAN SKIP THIS EXERCISE. IF YOUR TIMELINES NEED HELP, USE THIS EXAMPLE TO SHOW HOW PARALLEL OR MAJOR EVENTS COLLIDE IN YOUR BOOK. DO THIS FOR ONLY THE MAIN CHARACTERS AND THE MAJOR CLIMATIC EVENTS AT THE END OF THE BOOK.

EXAMPLE:
IF YOU ARE WRITING A CRIME/MYSTERY...THE TRACKING OF CLUES IS PARAMOUNT THROUGHOUT THE BOOK AND WHEN THE MAJOR CLIMATIC

EVENT (THE MURDER SOLUTION) IS RESOLVED. ALSO HELPFUL WHEN TRACKING THE PLOT!

USE OF THIS "TIME /EVENT PLOTTING TECHNIQUE" HELPS DEFINE WHEN CHARACTERS DIE OFF AND WHAT EVENTS/SCENES/ PLACES AND CHARACTERS INTERACT AT THAT FINAL CONCLUSION.

26.0.5.0. HOW TO DO A TIMELINE:
1. WRITE EACH **MAIN CHARACTER'S NAME** ON LEFT SIDE OF PAPER, ONE ABOVE THE OTHER IN ORDER BY TIME OR CHAPTER. WHEN IS EACH INTRODUCED INTO THE STORY. DRAW A LINE ACROSS AND PUT A DOT, MARK IT BEGINNING. FOR EACH

SCENE: LETTER "S",
CLIMAX : LETTER "C" ,
PLOT: LETTER "P"
CLUES: LETTER "CL".

26.0.6.0. NOW CREATE A **TIME LINE FOR THE STORY.**
DO DRAW A LINE WITH SAME PROCESS, EXCEPT MARK WHERE AND WHEN THE EVENT ITEM IS TO OCCUR, ASSUMING A CHRONOLOGICAL ORDER OR YOUR OWN METHOD OF USING DOTS, CIRCLES AND SQUARES TO DENOTE DIFFERENT THINGS.

26.0.7.0. CONNECTIONS:
USE AN "X" AND DRAW A LINE ACROSS ALL CONNECTING TIMELINES WHEN THEY CONNECT. OR USE CHARACTERS LETTERS AS IN *EXAMPLE 26.1.0.0.*

EXAMPLE: IN THE BOOMERS.
KELLY(CODE K) AND MICKEY CONNECTED IN THE WAR, WHEN MICKEY (CODED M) WAS WOUNDED AND SENT TO THE STATES AND RECONNECTED IN WASHINGTON DC AND IN CHICAGO. AND FINALLY, IN THE COURTROOM WHERE THE MAJOR CLIMAX OCCURRED. THESE CONNECTIONS WERE NOTED BY CODES RX, AND MX ON THEIR OWN TIMELINES.

26.0.8.0. MAJOR CLIMATIC EVENTS (MC #).
EACH OF THESE PLACES HAD **MAJOR CLIMATIC** (MC#) EVENTS CONNECTED TO A TIMELINE. THE MX'S CROSSED EACH OF THEIR TIMELINES. I NUMBER THE X'S=X1, X2. ETC. I CREATED MY OWN CODES TO MATCH THIS BOOK.

THEN I MATCHED ROSE'S TIMELINE RX TO KELLY'S KX, MARKED [SEE EXAMPLE: 29.6.0.0.]

AFTER THE MAJOR EVENTS MC1, MC2; AND PLACES P1, P2, ETC. ARE MARKED. I START TO SEE THE CONNECTIONS TO THE STORY LINE. IT WILL HAVE ALL THREE CHARACTERS, EVENTS, PLACES AND CLIMAXES MARKED. [CHAPTER 37 HAD P5 AS THE COURTROOM.]

26.0.9.0. HOLES IN STORY:

A REVIEW OF THESE TIMELINES WILL TELL YOU OF HOLES AND POSSIBLE MISSING ITEMS. IF YOU USED A DETAILED SYNOPSIS COMPARE IT TO THE TIME LINE. DO FIX ANY HOLES IN STORY AND IN TIMELINES.

> **IMPORTANT!** *HOLES NEED FILLED AS YOUR READER AND BUYER WILL SOON NOTE THE OMISSION.*

26.0.10.0. BELOW ARE EXAMPLES OF STORY TIMELINES:

29.5.1.0. SHOWS COMBINED KELLY AND MICKEY'S INTERACTION (KEY EVENTS) IN A COMBINED TIMELINE. CHAPTERS 11 WAR-CH 19 WASHINGTON DC-CH 35 FEDERAL TRIAL(COURTROOM)- CH 37 CONCLUSION AND END OF CHARACTERS (EOC).
IN EXAMPLE 29.6.0.0., WHEN TWO CHARACTERS CONNECT, EACH HAS THE OTHER'S TIMELINE CODE ON THEIR TIMELINE.

KELLY'S TIMELINE HAS RX FOR ROSE, MX FOR MICKEY AND CLIMATIC EVENTS ARE SHOWN AS [MC2 –M (MICKEY] AND [MC3-RX(ROSE)].

BELOW EXPLAINS THE CLIMATIC EVENTS.

> **26.1.0.0. SHOWS CLIMATIC SCENES** IN FINAL CHAPTER 37 INVOLVING 3 MAIN CHARACTERS AND ONE SUPPORTING CHARACTER (PREACHER) AND THEIR CLIMATIC SCENES- AT END OF BOOK-CHAPTER 37:
>
> **MC#=MAJOR CONNECTING EVENTS: THE WAR, WASHINGTON D.C., CHICAGO CONVENTION, AND AT THE FEDERAL TRIAL IN D.C. (THE COURTROOM). THESE EVENTS BROUGHT THE NOVEL'S CONCLUSION IN THE LAST CHAPTER 37. TIME LINE FOR CHAPTER 37 AS FOLLOWS:**
>
> **KX=KELLY** RX_M____[MC2-MX]__MC3-RX]__
>
> **RX=ROSE** KX_M_____[MC1-MX]_[MC3-MX]_EOC2_KX
>
> **MX= MICKEY** M_PX_MC1_[MC2-KX]_[MC3-RX]_KX_EOC3
>
> **PX=PREACHER**_____MX_____RX___EOC1.

EXAMPLE: SHOWS MAJOR CLIMAXES: SHOOTINGS IN COURTROOM.

> **MAJOR CLIMAXES:**
> MC1=MAJOR CLIMAX ONE= ROSE GETS SHOT IN COURTROOM.
> MC2= FINAL MAJOR CLIMAX-KELLY & MICKEY HAVE COURTROOM SCENE-MICKEY DIES.
> MC3 ROSE DIES AFTER SHOOTING MICKEY.

EXAMPLE: SHOWS END OF CHARACTER'S (EOC) ROLE IN

NOVEL AND # SHOWS WHO DIES FIRST.

EOC1, PREACHER DIES FIRST.
EOC2, ROSE DIES AFTER SHOOTING MICKEY.
EOC3, MICKEY DIES.

EXAMPLE: EOC= END OF CHARACTER

ECO1= 1ST CHARACTER TO DIE. PREACHER SHOT BY MICKEY. CH 37
ECO2= 2ND CHARACTER TO DIE. ROSE SHOT BY MICKEY. CH 37
EC03-MICKEY DIES. SHOT BY ROSE. CH 37.

26.2.0.0. STORY ENDS BUT BRIDGES TO NEXT BOOK:
CH 37 ENDING: STORYLINE CONTINUES: KELLY-SON AND FATHER
REUNITE AND SON LEARNS ABOUT MOTHER.

26.3.0.0. SPREADSHEET TYPE TIMELINE.

**GREAT FOR ORGANIZING 6 W'S. BUT CONNECTIONS BETWEEN 2
MAJOR CHARACTERS IS LOST, WHERE LINE TYPE ABOVE SHOWS
WHEN THE PLOT-EVENTS-CLIMAXES THUS, CONNECTIONS HAPPEN.
THIS IS USEFUL FOR BRINGING ALL THESE MANY ELEMENTS
TOGETHER FOR THE WRITER.**

TIME LINE				CHAPTER AND PAGE NUMBERS	
BOOK 13	CHARACTER	ROLE	CLIMAX	**CH 1**	**CH 2**
PAGE NUMBER =				**11-27**	**27-28**
NARRATOR-TOM	NARRATOR			**1-11**	
AUGGIE	**MAIN C**	**INTROD.**		**17**	
BEN-SAILOR	CHARACTER	SUPPORT			
COWBOY	CHARACTER	MINOR		19-20	
LAND -TAXES	**PLOT**			**18**	**28**
KEVIN-SHERIFF	CHARACTER	SUPPORT		19	
GRANGE HALL	SETTING			17,18,23	
HORACE-TAXI	CHARACTER	MINOR		13	
JAMES JENKINS	CHARACTER	SUPPORT		21	
MILL POND-GAZEBO	SETTING	**MAJOR**		18-19	
POND ACCIDENT		**MAJOR**		19	
MUSTANG CITY	SETTING	**MAJOR**		15,20	
NEWSPAPER OFFICE	SETTING	**MAJOR**	EVENT	20-22	
OSCAR-BUS DRIVER	CHARACTER	MINOR		12	
TEA PARTY	**PLOT**		EVENT	**18**	
TWIG	CHARACTER	MINOR		15,25	
TWIG DINER	SETTING		EVENT	15,18,24	
APPALOOSA TAVERN	SETTING		EVENT		27
GOLDIE	CHARACTER	MINOR			29

BANGER	CHARACTER	MAJOR			
AUNTE' MAME'	CHARACTER	SUPPORT			
JOE SUNSHINE	CHARACTER	SUPPORT			
ALAURA	CHARACTER	SUPPORT	MINOR-CL		
SOCK ALLEY	SETTING		EVENT		
$100 GRAND	PLOT		MAJOR -CL		
BEN	CHARACTER	VILLAIN			
BUTCH	CHARACTER	VILLAIN			
CAR BARN	SETTING	MAJOR	MAJOR EV		
GERMAN GOLD	PLOT	MAJOR			
KATIE	CHARACTER	SUPPORT			
KIDNAPPING	PLOT		MAJOR-CL		

26.4.2.0. SUMMARY-END OF CHARACTER ROLES:
WHEN YOU WRITE A STORY, THE TIMELINE IS IMPORTANT TO STAGE SEQUENCES OF EVENTS IN CHRONOLOGICAL OR ACHRONOLOGICAL ORDER; PARTICULARLY , MAJOR INTERACTIONS BETWEEN CHARACTERS AND ESPECIALLY IF A CHARACTER DIES OFF OR HIS ROLE IS ENDED.

26.4.3.0. CLOSING A CHARACTER'S TIME OUT& ROLE.
MAJOR CLIMATIC EVENTS SHOULD END CERTAIN PARTS OF THE STORY OR CHARACTER'S ROLES.

CHAPTER 27
27.0.0.0. - CLIMAXES-BRIDGES & ENDINGS:
CHAPTER TOPICS: *CLIMAXES-MAJOR & MINOR-MORE BRIDGES-CHARACTER'S ENDINGS-BOOK ENDINGS.*

27.0.0.0. CLIMAX DEFINED:
THE POINT IN THE STORY WHERE IT ALL COMES TOGETHER, ALL THE CLUES, MESSAGES, ALL THE WORDS, DESCRIPTIONS, PARAGRAPHS LEADING UP TO A HIGH POINT-THE CLIMAX OR ALSO AN ENDING POINT. THERE ARE **MAJOR AND MINOR CLIMAXES**.

27.01.0. THE BOOMERS-EXAMPLE.
THE CLIMATIC EVENTS ARE A SERIES OF EVENTS INVOLVING THE MAIN CHARACTERS AND ALSO ENDING A CHARACTER'S ROLE IN THE NOVEL. CH26 SHOWS HOW A SERIES OF CLIMACTIC EVENTS [MC] HAPPEN ALONG THE TIMELINE AND HOW A SERIES OF SHOOTINGS ENDS SEVERAL CHARACTER'S ROLES [EOC] AND YET SPEEDS THE STORYLINE TO A CONCLUSION. CHAPTER 37 CONTAINS THE RESULTS AND CONCLUSIONS OF THE STORY AND **BRIDGES TO THE NEXT NOVEL**. THE IMPORTANCE OF BRIDGES ARE EXPLAINED IN CH 26 THIS BRIDGE CONNECTS THE BOOK CHAPTER 1 AND 37 AND SETS THE STAGE FOR THE NEXT NOVEL IN THE SERIES AND A NEW CHARACTER.

27.0.2.0. EXAMPLE: A CHAPTER CLIMAX & BRIDGE:
SOURCE: "SPIES, THIEVES AND OTHER FRIENDS."

"FOR THE FIRST TIME, I BEGAN TO THINK OF HOME, AS EVERYTHING HERE SEEMED TO BE ENDING WELL!

I STILL HAD SOME UNFINISHED BUSINESS BACK HOME. I WAS THINKING OF LINDA LOU AND THE FUTURE. TO THINK OF, IT ALL STARTED, WITH A HAIL OF GUNSHOTS AND MY NEARLY ESCAPING DEATH.
[ANSWERS CONCLUSION TO NOVEL- WHAT HAPPENS NEXT TO KELLY CHANCE?].

THEN I CAME OVER HERE AND IT WAS MORE OF THE SAME. BEFORE THIS TRIP, MY LIFE CONSISTED OF PUTTING BAD GUYS IN JAIL AND DODGING BULLETS. NOW, THE ACHE INSIDE OF ME WASN'T FROM BULLETS OR KNIFE CUTS BUT SOMETHING DEEPER.

"SOMETHING HAPPENED OUT THERE IN THE DESERT!"

27.0.3.0. EXAMPLE: THIS LAST SENTENCE BRIDGES TO THE NEXT CHAPTER.

CLASS: DO: WRITE AN EXAMPLE OF A BRIDGE TO THE NEXT BOOK FROM YOUR STORY. WAS IT HARD OR EASY?

27.4.0.0. TWO BRIDGES IN A NOVEL:

1. THE BEGINNING AND ENDING OF THE NOVEL:
BRIDGES ARE METHODS TO HANDLE CONCLUDING NOVELS AND THE WRITING THE FINAL PARAGRAPHS SO THE READER KNOWS WHAT HAPPENED AND HOW THE PLOT TWISTS CAME OUT. DID THE HERO SURVIVE? DID THE VILLAIN DIE OFF?
2.THIS BRIDGE IS ALSO THE CONNECTION BETWEEN CHAPTER 1 AND THE ENDING.

27.4.1.0 BRIDGING OVER TO THE NEXT NOVEL.
EXAMPLE: THE BRIDGE TO THE NEXT NOVEL IS SET: "A SOLDIER BOY! SOLDIER GIRL!" THE SON (KELLY CHANCE III) BECOMES A SOLDIER IN A NEW WAR.. [THE CHARACTER LIST GETS A NEW LISTING].

27.5.0.0. OUR PROGRESS:
1. WE LEARNED HOW MAJOR & MINOR CLIMAXES BRING EVENTS TO A HIGH POINT OF SUSPENSE-MYSTERY FOR THE READER FOCUS ON THE STORY.

2. WE DON'T LEAVE ANY LOOSE ENDS OR CHARACTER'S DANGLING AT THE END OF STORY.

3. WE LOOK FOR HOLES IN OUR STORY.

4. WE TRACKED KEY CLIMAXES AND PLOT TWISTS SO THE STORY IS BELIEVABLE AND HONEST. READER IS NOT CONFUSED BY WHAT JUST HAPPENED.

5. WE LEARNED HOW TO HANDLE FLASH BACKS AND FLASH FORWARDS.

6. WE LEARNED TO CREATE A BRIDGE TO THE NEXT NOVEL.

CHAPTER 28
28.0.0.0. GRAND MASTERS- THE RIGHT STUFF!

TOPICS: *THE MASTERS- DO AN ANALYSIS OF STYLE & THEME.*
ALSO, REVIEW INDEX 2-BOOK AWARDS & GREAT WRITERS.

28.0.0.0. LEARN TO WRITE FROM THE MASTERS:

WHILE BOOKS ON WRITING HAVE A LOT TO SAY ABOUT THE WRITING
PROCESS, MANY VALUABLE SKILLS AND STRATEGIES CAN BE LEARNED
BY STUDYING THE WORK -- AS WELL AS THE LIVES -- OF WRITERS YOU
ADMIRE. REFER ALSO TO THE NOBEL AWARD WINNERS IN **INDEX 2.**

WRITING FICTION IS A COMPLEX PROCESS: IT REQUIRES A SUITABLY
NUANCED COURSE OF STUDY. IN THE SAME WAY, THE ANSWERS TO
MANY QUESTIONS ABOUT HOW TO LEAD A WRITER'S LIFE CAN BE FOUND
IN THE EXAMPLES SET BY SUCCESSFUL WRITERS.

**"GRAND MASTERS OF WRITING" ARE CHOSEN FOR THEIR PROSE,
THEIR PLOTS, THEMES, STYLE, DRAMATIZATIONS AND WORD
CHOICE. ALL ARE CHOSEN BY THE READER! I ADD "UNIQUENESS—
THEIR OWN STYLE," A SORT OF REBELLION.**

28.1.0.0. BELOW ARE ONLY SOME OF MY FAVORITES:
DO THIS SORT OF ANALYSIS AND FIND YOUR OWN
STYLE; IT COULD BE A COMBINATION OF STYLES.

1. HENRY DAVID THOREAU:
HANDYMAN-WRITER-HARVARD GRADUATE. BEST KNOWN FOR
"WALDEN." KNOWN AS MASTER OF PROSE STYLE.
STYLE: FREE VERSE.

UNIVERSAL THEME: INDIVIDUALITY VERSUS NATURE

THEMES : CONSERVATION, TO LIVE LIFE SIMPLY AND CLOSE TO NATURE.

UNIQUE: HIS FREE VERSE STYLE WAS UNIQUE.

2. NATHANIEL HAWTHORNE:
WRITER-SURVEYOR-BOWDOIN COLLEGE.-PURITAN TIMES.

BOOKS: THE SCARLET LETTER, HOUSE OF SEVEN GABLES.

UNIVERSAL THEME: HUMAN STRENGTHS & WEAKNESS.

THEMES: ADULTERY, SINS, GUILT,

STYLE: CHARACTERS WITH GREAT FLAWS. HE POSSESSED KEEN
INSIGHT INTO HUMAN NATURE. HIS STORIES TURNED ON FAITH, SOME
GREAT POINT THEN CHANGING DIRECTION. (HIS STYLE WAS MORE

CREATIVE WRITING—THE KELLY MANUAL OF STYLE

"HUMAN" WEAKNESS AND STRENGTHS RATHER THAN MORALITY, AS WAS THE MOST COMMON THEME BEING WRITTEN IN PURITAN TIMES).

UNIQUE: MAIN CHARACTER WITH GREAT FLAWS.

3. HERMAN MELVILLE:
WEALTHY THEN POOR, LEFT SCHOOL AT 12 YRS. AND BECAME A TEACHER AT 18. SEAMAN ON WHALING SHIPS. LATER ABANDONED WRITING TAKING JOB AS A CUSTOMS INSPECTOR.

BOOKS: TYPEE, OMOO (CANNIBALS-SLAVE GIRLS), MARDI, REDBURN, WHITE JACKET, MOBY DICK, PIERRE, THE CONFIDENCE MAN.

UNIVERSAL THEME: NATURE VERSUS HUMANITY.

THEMES: WHALING, SHIPS, SOUTH SEA LEGENDS. MOBY IS THE EPIC NOVEL, AN ALLEGORY OF NATURE VERSUS HUMANITY.

GREATEST MAIN CHARACTER DEVELOPMENT:
" CALL ME ISHMAEL."

STYLE: WROTE WHAT HE KNEW ABOUT & HIS EXPERIENCES.

UNIQUE: HIS CHARACTER DEVELOPMENT AND WORD CHOICE

4. WALT WHITMAN:
QUIT SCHOOL AT 11 YEARS, OFFICE BOY, GO-FER, PRINTERS ASSISTANT, ODD JOBS AND FIRED AS EDITOR "BROOKLYN EAGLE," NEWSPAPER.

STYLE: WROTE POETRY IN FREE VERSE, WHICH IS LONG LINES OF RHYTHMS OF NATURAL SPEECH BASED IN REALITY NOT MORALITY. THUS, HAVING NO REGULAR BEAT, RHYME OF LINE LENGTH. (AGAINST THE CURRENT POETRY TREND)

BEST KNOWN: LEAVES OF GRASS, I SING THE BODY ELECTRIC, A NOISELESS PATIENT SPIDER,WALDEN POND.

UNIVERSAL THEME: REALITY VERSUS MORALITY

SUPPORTING THEMES: HIS POETRY WAS INTENSE, COMPLEX AND SEXUALLY EXPLICIT.

5. EMILY DICKINSON:
WEALTHY, RECLUSE, WROTE 1775 POEMS, BUT PUBLISHED ONLY A FEW.

STYLE: POETRY WAS UNIQUE: NO TITLES, JUST NUMBERS. NO PUNCTUATION, JUST DASHES, NO RHYME. EXPRESSED RADICAL IDEAS AND HARD TRUTHS.

UNIVERSAL THEME: RADICAL IDEAS FOR TIME-REBELLION

SUPPORTING THEMES: EXPRESSIONS WERE FORCEFUL LANGUAGE. AND CONCRETE IMAGES.

6. MARK TWAIN-SAMUEL CLEMENS:
APPRENTICE TO PRINTER AT 12 YRS, A RIVER PILOT AT 21. 'MARK TWAIN' WAS RIVER TALK FOR "ALL CLEAR" MEANING ENOUGH WATER FOR THE RIVER BOAT TO PROCEED.

BOOKS: HUCKLEBERRY FINN, TOM SAWYER, THE PRINCE AND THE PAUPER, A CONNECTICUT YANKEE IN KING ARTHUR'S COURT.

UNIVERSAL THEME: LIFE-HUMAN NATURE-

SUPPORTING THEMES: HUMOR-DEADPAN-EXAGGERATION AND APPEARANCE OF "THE MYSTERIOUS STRANGER." STYLE: USE OF NARRATOR, IMAGINATIVE DETAILS, ELEVATED DICTION AND LOW FOLKSY LANGUAGE, TWANGS AND ACCENTS OF SOUTH AND MISSISSIPPI.

STYLE: UNIQUE-CHARACTER AND DIALOG AND PICTURESQUE DESCRIPTIONS IN ONE, PLUS A GREAT STORYTELLER. WRITES TO THE READER USING A NARRATOR (STORYTELLER).

7. STEPHAN CRANE:
PREACHER'S KID, AUTHOR, CORRESPONDENT, 2 YEARS AT SEMINARY, MILITARY SCHOOL AND SYRACUSE NY COLLEGE. PLAYED BASEBALL AND WROTE FOR SCHOOL NEWSPAPER, CUB REPORTER ON N.Y. TRIBUNE.

BOOKS: MAGGIE A GIRL OF THE STREETS, RED BADGE OF COURAGE, THE BLACK RIDERS, WAR IS KIND, DEATH AND THE CHILD, THE OPEN BOAT.

UNIVERSAL THEME: FAILURE-DEATH GUILT-ISOLATION

SUPPORTING THEMES: REALISM, NATURALISM (ORDINARY LIFE). LIFE IS CRUEL AND A JOKE. FREE WILL IS AN ILLUSION. THEME OF LOSS OF TRADITIONAL VALUES.

CHARACTERS: LIVES SHAPED BY FORCES THEY COULD NEITHER UNDERSTAND NOR CONTROL-ENVIRONMENT-WAR.

STYLE: RED BADGE WAS PICTURESQUE, WITH DESCRIPTIONS LIKE A PAINTING. HE USED DESCRIPTIVE TITLES INSTEAD OF NAMES: THE OILER, THE COOK, THE CAPTAIN, THE CORRESPONDENT (CRANE) AND THE SEA (THE VILLAIN). UNIQUE STORYTELLER, AND UNIQUE DESCRIPTIVE LANGUAGE AND EVENTS. USED SYMBOLS TO EXPRESS EMOTIONS.

8. JACK LONDON:
LEFT SCHOOL AT 14. ODD JOBS, PIRATED OYSTERS, SAILED PACIFIC. HOBO, WENT TO YUKON ALASKA. DIED BY AGE 40.

BOOKS: CALL OF THE WILD (DOGS), TO BUILD A FIRE, WHITE FANG, THE SEA WOLF AND 50 OTHERS. **THEMES:** REALISM- THAT A MAN CAN MAKE MORAL CHOICES. NATURALIST: SAVAGE LAWLESSNESS, FIGHTING NATURE, BRUTAL, COLD, VICIOUS, EACH BOLD ENOUGH TO CHALLENGE NATURE.

164

CREATIVE WRITING—THE KELLY MANUAL OF STYLE

UNIVERSAL THEME: HIS FOCUS WAS MANS ENVIRONMENT AND HEREDITARY- FATE. TRAPPED BY FORCES AS MONEY, SEX AND POWER.

SUPPORTING THEME: SAILING-PROFESSIONS-WILDERNESS-DOGS

UNIQUE: CREATED HIS OWN CHARACTERS, PLOT AND CLIMAX IN EACH CHAPTER RATHER THAN END OF BOOK.

NOTE: PROLIFIC WRITER IN SHORT TIME AND STORIES WERE VERY POPULAR. (STORYTELLER).

9. BRETE HART:
GREAT CHARACTERS: MULBERRY SELLERS, PUDDIN' HEAD WILSON,

WROTE WESTERNS-GUNSLINGING-WILD WEST AND MINING TOWNS.
GENRE: FICTION-WESTERNS

BEST BOOKS: THE LUCK OF ROARING CAMP. OUTCASTS OF POKER FLATS
UNIVERSAL THEME: CHANCE & DEATH

SUPPORTING THEMES: CHANCE AND DEATH, REGION: SOUTHWEST

STYLE: UNIQUE USE OF DIALECT AND CHOICE OF WORDS.

10. KATE CHOPIN:
BOOKS: THE AWAKENING AND MORE.

UNIVERSAL THEME: SEX

SUPPORTING THEME: REGIONAL, SHOCKING AND SEXUAL PROTAGONIST. RICH LOCAL DIALECT, VIEWS OF CULTURE AND SOUTH LOUISIANA.

STYLE: CRAFT AND CONTENT. SUPERB DIALOG AND DRAMATIZATION COMBINATION.

11. ERNEST MILLER HEMINGWAY:
BORN OAK PARK, ILLINOIS. CONSERVATIVE & WASP NEIGHBORHOOD, HUNTED & FISHED WITH FATHER, PLAYED PIANO WITH MOTHER. SPORTS: FOOTBALL, SWIM TEAM AND WROTE FOR SCHOOL NEWSPAPER. CUB REPORTER FOR K.C. STAR. **LEARNED NEWSPAPER STYLE:** SHORT SENTENCES, BRIEF PARAGRAPHS, ACTIVE VERBS, AUTHENTICITY, COMPRESSION, CLARITY, IMMEDIACY. RED CROSS AMBULANCE DRIVER, AWARDED THE ITALIAN SILVER MEDAL FOR VALOR. PARIS CORRESPONDENT. WROTE INTENSIVELY FOR SHORT PERIODS.

BOOKS: IN OUR TIME, THE SUN, MEN WITHOUT WOMEN, A FAREWELL TO ARMS, (SOLD 80,000 COPIES IN 4 MONTHS), DEATH IN THE AFTERNOON, THE SNOWS OF KILAMANJARO, MEN AT WAR, TO HAVE AND HAVE NOT, FOR WHOM THE BELL TOLLS, THE SUN ALSO RISES, AND MANY OTHERS. FOR THE OLD MAN AND THE SEA, HE WON BOTH THE PULITZER PRIZE AND NOBEL PRIZE-1954.

UNIVERSAL THEME: MANY. GREAT STORYTELLER.

SUPPORTING THEMES: WROTE WHAT HE KNEW, BULLFIGHTS, FISHING, AFRICA, WORLD WAR 1, WOMEN.

STYLE: RHYTHMIC WORDING, DIRECT THOUGHTS, PRECISE WORD CHOICE , OBJECTIVE. SIMPLE SENTENCES TO LOOK UNDERNEATH THE WORKS. HE CALLED THIS **THE ICEBERG PRINCIPLE**. (SHOW ; BUT NOT TELL, AND ILLUMINATE). COMPARISON & CONTRAST. IN HIS BOOKS, HIS HEROES WERE COURAGEOUS, REAL AND HONEST.

12. TENNESSEE WILLIAMS:
BOOKS: A GLASS MENAGERIE-PLAYS.

UNIVERSAL THEME: HUMAN NATURE-MORALITY

SUPPORTING THEMES: CONFLICT-TRAGEDY-HUMAN EMOTIONS-PSYCHOLOGY.

STYLE: DIALOGUE- IS BEST.
WRITTEN IN PLAY FORMAT.

13. ROBERT FROST:
TEACHER, MILL HAND, REPORTER, DAIRY FARMER, POET.
GENRE: POETRY

BOOKS: POETRY-4 PULITZER PRIZES,

UNIVERSAL THEME: NATURE

SUPPORTING THEMES: NATURE, NEW ENGLAND,

STYLE: USED TRADITIONAL VERSE FORMS. SOUNDS.

14. E. E. CUMMINGS: (EDWARD ESTLIN)
PAINTER, WRITER, POET

BOOKS: POETRY
STYLE: USED SMALL CASE LETTERS EXCLUSIVELY.
A REBEL AGAINST THE NORM. USED ERRATIC STYLE, MISUSED GRAMMATICAL STRUCTURE TO MAKE A POINT. VERY POPULAR IN 1960'S CULTURE.

UNIVERSAL & THEMES: INDIVIDUALISM

15. CARL SANDBURG:
HISTORIAN, BIOGRAPHER, NOVELIST, MUSICIAN, ESSAYIST, JOURNALIST, POET
GENRE: POETRY, FICTION
BOOKS: POETRY
UNIVERSAL THEME: MANY DIRECTLY(ABOUT) AND IN-DIRECTLY THROUGH 'ALLUDED TO, ' COMPARISON, CONTRASTED. SOMETIMES CONTROVERSIAL SUBJECTS

THEME: MANY. SOUNDS.

STYLE: FREE VERSE AND SIMPLE WORDS-EASY TO UNDERSTAND.

166

16. JACK KEROUAC:
BOOKS: POETRY-VERSE-AUTO-BIOGRAPHICAL.
BOOK S FAMOUS TITLE: "ON THE ROAD"

UNIVERSAL THEME: STORYTELLER. MANY DIRECTLY(ABOUT) AND IN-DIRECTLY THROUGH 'ALLUDED TO, ' COMPARISON, CONTRASTED. SOMETIMES CONTROVERSIAL SUBJECTS. SOME ARE STORIES.

SUPPORTING THEMES: TRAVEL, LOCAL CHARACTERS AND PLACES.

STYLE: NON-STOP, NON-EDITED, CONSIDERED AS "NEW" AND SPONTANEOUS.

28.2.0.0. NEW WRITERS & PRINT ON DEMAND WRITERS:
28.2.1. 0. NICOLAS SPARKS:
NOT QUITE A MASTER YET; HOWEVER, AN GREAT STORYTELLER WITH REGIONALISM, DIALECT AND PACKED WITH EMOTIONS.

BOOKS: THE NOTEBOOK, MESSAGE IN A BOTTLE, A WALK TO REMEMBER, THE RECUE, A BEND IN THE ROAD, NIGHTS IN RODANTHE, THE GUARDIAN, THE WEDDING, THREE WEEKS WITH MY BROTHER, TRUE BELIEVER, AT FIRST SIGHT, DEAR JOHN, THE LUCKY ONE. SIX WERE BEST SELLERS.

UNIVERSAL THEME: UNIVERSAL APPEAL, LIFE, HUMAN NATURE.

SUPPORTING THEMES: REGIONALISM, LOVE AND EMOTIONS, TRAGEDY, HUMANISTIC..

STYLE: ROMANTIC, THEMATIC, REGIONALISM.

UNIQUENESS: ONE OF WOMEN'S FAVORITE AUTHORS. ROMANCE, AND HEARTFELT EMOTIONS COMBINED WITH TRAGEDY AND MOSTLY HAPPY ENDINGS.

28.2.2.0. TIM DORSEY: WRITER:
BOOKS: "FLORIDA ROADKILL."
TWO GOOD GUYS AND LOADS OF BAD GUYS.

UNIVERSAL THEME: CRIME-LIFE.

SUPPORTING THEMES: MURDER, MAYHEM, CRIME AND LITTLE PUNISHMENT. LAUGHS GALORE. AND AH HEM! A FLORIDA TRAVEL GUIDE.

STYLE: PINBALL, REGIONALISM, MASTER STORYTELLER.
OVER THE TOP WITH HUMOR-OUTRAGEOUS SUB STORIES, SUPPORTING PLOTS IN CRIME FICTION.

CHARACTERS: DESCRIPTIONS BUILT THROUGHOUT BOOK.

UNIQUENESS: FAST PINBALL STYLE AND FAST SCENE CHANGES

28.3.0.0 THE MASTER STYLE-A SUMMARY:

MANY GREAT WRITERS SHARE IN COMMON A TRAIT OF **UNIQUENESS**.
ALL TYPES OF THEMES AND STYLES PREDOMINATE AGAINST THEIR
ENVIRONMENT, THEIR EXPERIENCE AND STRUCTURE OF WRITING. SOME
WERE REBELS, SOME CONSERVATIVE, SOME UNCONVENTIONAL.
EACH HAD A **UNIVERSAL THEME, WHICH** THEY CHAMPIONED.
EACH ALSO HAD A **UNIQUE WRITING STYLE** OR USED WRITING
ELEMENTS, WHICH BECAME UNIQUE. **STRONG PLOTS AND CLIMAXES**
WERE ALWAYS PRESENT.

EACH HAD A WRITING STYLE/TRAIT, WHICH INCLUDED FULLY
DEVELOPED AND **REALISTIC CHARACTERS**, LANGUAGE, DIALOGUE,
EVENTS AND **POWERFUL IMAGES**. CHIEF AMONG THESE TRAITS WAS
WORD CHOICE, DIALOGUE AND DRAMATIZATION.

EACH WAS A STORYTELLER AND WROTE FOR THE READER,
HOWEVER, UNIQUELY. **EACH WROTE A LOT** AND WITH DIVERSE
SUBJECTS.

THE BEST WRITINGS WERE PRODUCTS OF THEIR EXPERIENCE,
ENVIRONMENT AND HUMANITY. **THEY WROTE WHAT THEY KNEW**.

THEIR **WORD CHOICE WAS UNIQUE** FROM TITLES, TO CHARACTER
NAMES, PLACES. THEY WROTE WITH **POWER AND PASSION. THEY
WROTE FOR THEIR READER WITH SOUNDS, PICTURESQUE WORDS
AND EMOTIONS.**

**WE SHOULD MEASURE EACH OF OUR BOOKS TO THIS ELITE WRITING
STYLE. OUR NEW STYLE MIGHT BE OUR CREATIVITY IN BLENDING
THESE ALL TOGETHER.**

28.4.0.0. LESSONS LEARNED:

NEW WRITERS SHOULD LEARN HOW TO STORYTELL, HOW TO CHOOSE
WORDS AND THE ORDER OF WORDS. ILLUMINATE PLOTS AND THEMES
AND MOST IMPORTANTLY, HOW TO BLEND THEM INTO THEIR DIALOG
AGAINST A BACKDROP OF DRAMATIZATION.

28.5.0.0. OUR PROGRESS:

1. WE LEARNED ABOUT THE MASTERS AND THEIR UNIQUE STYLES. THE
   USE OF UNIVERSAL THEMES AND SUPPORTING THEMES FOR MASS
   APPEAL.

2. CHAPTER 28 DOES AN ANALYSIS AS TO THE STRONG POINTS OF
   THE **GRAND MASTER'S STYLE AND TECHNIQUE WE CAN USE**.

3. CHAPTER 30 SHOWS HOW WE CAN IMPROVE OUR STYLE USING THE
   GRAND MASTER'S UNIVERSAL THEMES AND SUPPORTING THEMES.

**28.6.0.0. DO USE THE GRAND MASTER'S
TRAITS TO UPDATE OUR BOOK DRAFT.
TO BE A BEST SELLER WE MUST HAVE THESE IN
OUR BOOK. THIS MUST BE IN OUR FINAL
MANUSCRIPT CH 36.**

CHAPTER 29

29.0.0.0. BOOK DRAFT-HOW TO ORGANIZE:

DEFINITION: "ROUGH DRAFT:" *A VERY LOOSE ORGANIZATION OF STORY, TOPICS, THEMES, CHARACTERS, DIALOGUE, PLOT AND CLIMAXES-INCOMPLETE CHAPTERS. CHECK LISTS NEED TO BE COMPLETED.*

DEFINITION: "BOOK DRAFT OR MANUSCRIPT: *THE ROUGH DRAFT IS COMPLETE. ALL CHAPTERS HAVE GONE THRU SEVERAL EDITS. [CH30]*

CHAPTER TOPICS: ORGANIZING YOUR TIME-YOUR SPACE-YOUR BOOK PLAN-YOUR BOOKS-YOUR COMPUTER.

29. 0.0.1. PREPARATION: DO SPELL CHECK & GRAMMAR FIRST.

THEN, PRINT IT OUT. IT SHOULD BE HANDY IN A PORTABLE FORMAT, HARD COPY READY FOR EDITING. WE NEED TO LEAVE OUR WRITING AREA AND HAND EDIT WITH OUR EDITING CHECK LIST. IT IS NEARLY IMPOSSIBLE TO EDIT ALL OF THEM AT ONE SITTING OR TOGETHER: **I BEGIN WITH THE BASIC BOOK PAGES 1 UP TO CHAPTER ONE.**

1. EDIT THE PUNCTUATION AND PARAGRAPH SPACING FIRST.
2. I WATCH FOR WHITE SPACE AND SPACING OF DANGLING SENTENCES FROM PAGE TO PAGES.
3. I EDIT THE BASIC BOOK PAGES
   FOR TYPOS, SPELLING, GRAMMAR AND CLARITY.
4. I ANSWER EACH PAGE WITH: DOES THE READER GET MY MESSAGE?
5. I SHORTEN, UNDERLINE AND MAKE BOLD IMPORTANT ITEMS.
6. READ OUT LOUD. MARK THE ROUGH SPOTS AND FIX OR USE 'RE-WRITE' CODE. VERB TENSE SHOULD STAND OUT.
7. EDIT EACH PARAGRAPH FOR GRAMMAR, PUNCTUATION AGAIN.
8. **USE YOUR PROOFREADER'S CODES FROM** CHAPTER 31.
9. **DO USE**: THE EDITING CHECKLIST[CH 31] FOR THE REST OF THE BOOK AND ON THE FINAL MANUSCRIPT -MUST USE CHAPTER 36.

29.0.0.2. EDITING: USE COLOR!

I USE PURPLE INK…TO GET AWAY FROM THE INFAMOUS "RED INK". IF I'M DOING SEVERAL EDIT TYPES AT ONE SITTING I USE A SECOND OR THIRD COLOR. **I READ IT OUTLOUD AND MARK IT** AS I GO. IF IT SOUNDS CHOPPY OR DRAB; I MARK THE MARGINS BRIEFLY. I USE THE PROOF READERS MARKS [CH 32]. **I AM NOT SITTING AT THE COMPUTER, TABLE OR DESK** SO AS NOT TO FATIGUE ME. A RECLINER OR CHAISE LOUNGE WORKS FOR ME. I READ OUTLOUD, EAT AND DRINK WHILE THESE EDITS TAKE TIME. AFTER MARKING IT UP, I REVIEW THE COMMENTS AND MARKS. MAYBE OTHER "COMMON FAULTS" NEED CHECKED IN OTHER CHAPTERS. SOMETIMES I WRITE PARAGRAPHS OR EVEN SEVERAL CHAPTERS ON THE BACKS OF THESE PAGES.

HARD COPY-PAPER VERSION:

AFTER KEYING IT INTO MY LATEST MASTER COPY, I SAVE THE HARD COPY DRAFT TO MY "CARDBOARD BOX" WHERE ALL THE "DETAIL STUFF" AND ALL THE KEY DRAFTS END UP. WHEN A BOOK IS COMPLETE, I PLACE THE IDEAS PAGE AND SOURCE INFORMATION ALL TOGETHER THERE. THUS, ONE CARDBOARD BOX GENERALLY CONTAINS IT ALL THE

PAPER VERSIONS. MY COMPUTER FOLDER HOLDS ALL THE ELECTRONIC VERSIONS. BACK-UP DISCS HOLD THE HISTORY OF THE BOOK FILES.

SAVING REFERENCE BOOKS, MAPS, AND REFERENCE MATERIAL NOT PERTAINING TO THIS BOOK GOES BACK INTO MY SUBJECT /CLIP FILE, FOR THE FOLLOW UP BOOK OR FOR FUTURE REFERENCE OR BOOK. IT IS A SIMPLE CHORE TO SAVE IT AND FIND IT AGAIN.

29.1.0.0. ORGANIZING THE ROUGH DRAFT:

-PUT IT UNDER A BINDER CLAMP AND ORGANIZE IT. ADD ALL THE NECESSARY, PAGES, TABLE OF CONTENTS, APPENDIXES, LIST OF TERMS, GLOSSARIES, EXHIBITS, JUST LIKE A REGULAR BOOK. DO SAME ON COMPUTER/FLOPPY DISC AND IN "MY DOCUMENTS FILE" UNDER ..."MY BOOKS"...BY BOOK # & TITLE." PUT EACH BOOK INTO A SEPARATE FOLDER UNDER "MY BOOKS." YOU CAN ALWAYS GIVE THEM A NUMBER ORDER OR CHANGE THEIR TITLE LATER. I USE: 1-RED HEART, 2-SECOND CHANCE, AND **DATE** ETC. I HAVE SEVERAL FOLDERS FOR THIS ONE BOOK: ARCHIVES- COVER ART-RESEARCH-MASTER-FINAL DRAFT-ETC. WITH OLDER COMPUTER COPIES I **ARCHIVE** THEM BY THE DATE AFTER THE FILE NAME, OLDEST ON BOTTOM.

29.2.0. 0. GENERAL ORGANIZATION-BOOK DRAFT:

- •AS YOU COMPLETE EACH READING, COMBINE THE REVISIONS INTO YOUR **BOOK DRAFT**, PRINT IT, CLAMP IT WITH BINDER CLAMP .

- •PRINT A HARDCOPY AND ORGANIZE IT JUST LIKE YOUR FINAL BOOK. INCLUDE TITLE PAGES, INTRODUCTIONS, DEDICATION, CONTENTS PAGE#, HEADER, CHAPTER #, ALL OF IT, PUT SYNOPSIS, IDEA LIST, TIME PLAN, CHARACTER LISTS, AND ALL INDICES INTO THE REAR OF THE BOOK. ETC. GET USED TO SEEING THE FORMATS AND DOCUMENTS AS A UNIT. THIS IS YOUR "BOOK DRAFT- #1."

- •IT SHOULD HAVE PAGE #, HEADERS AND APPEAR IN THE BOOK FORMAT WITH MARGINS SET ETC. IF YOUR BOOK IS A NOVEL, SET TO THE CORRECT PAGE SIZE: 6 X 9. SEE [CH 13] FOR PAGE SET UPS AND SIZES.

- •X---DO NOT USE A GENERIC 8 X 11 FORMAT. USE 6 X 9.

- •X---DO NOT DOUBLE SPACE. YOU ARE THE EDITOR AND WRITER HERE AND NEED TO SEE THE "DRAFT VERSION AND HOW IT LAYS ON THE PAGE. DO LINES HANG OVER? OR MAYBE BLANK SPACES NEED INSERTED TO KEEP THE CLOSING SENTENCE OR DIALOG TOGETHER? THIS IS CALLED "PRESENTATION."

- • SHOW YOUR EDITING-PROOF MARKS, NOTES AND CHANGES IN THE MARGINS OR MARK ON THE BACK BLANK PAGE. PRINT ONLY ONE SIDE THROUGHOUT THE WRITING PROCESS. THE PUBLISHER WILL HANDLE THE PRINTING ON BOTH SIDES. **ROUGH DRAFT #1** WILL END UP IN THE "CARDBOARD BOX AFTER YOUR EDITING/KEYING PROCESS IS COMPLETED.

29.3.0. 0. -GO TO YOUR EDITING SPACE, A PLACE DIFFERENT THAN YOUR WRITING SPACE.

CREATIVE WRITING—THE KELLY MANUAL OF STYLE

GO TO THE DECK, THE RECLINER, THE COFFEE SHOP, THE PARK SOMEPLACE WHERE YOU CAN RELAX, AND YET CONCENTRATE ON THE TYPE OF EDITING YOU ARE DOING. **DRAFT # 1** MATCHES READING AND **REVISION #1** FOR ORGANIZATIONAL PURPOSES.

29.3.1.0. EDITING-BOOK DRAFT #1:
YOU WILL NOT BE DOING ALL KINDS OF EDITING AT THE SAME TIME. VERY IMPORTANT: MULTI-TASKING WILL NOT WORK HERE. OPEN DRAFT #1 AND CONTINUE:

29.4.1.0. FIRST READING-BOOK DRAFT:
OPENING PARAGRAPH: OPENING SENTENCE—FIRST CHAPTER- **READ OUTLOUD-** CHECK FOR FLOW. DOES IT RELATE? DID WE CAPTURE, NO... "GRABBED" THE READERS ATTENTION, ANSWER IF WEAK: MARK REDO! CONTINUE READING.

29.4.2. 0. READ STORY OUTLOUD- FOR EACH BOOK DRAFT. THIS
CHECKS OUR WORD FLOW. WAS IT CHOPPY, START AND STUTTER? MARK IT. CONTINUE WITH CHAPTER ONE.

29.4.3.0. DOES IT RELATE TO OUR STORYTELLER'S SYNOPSIS?
IF NOT, WE MIGHT HAVE A BACK STORY GOING WITHIN IT OR OUR BOOK DRAFT TOOK A DIFFERENT TURN. DECIDE WHICH IS BETTER. MARK IT "BACK STORY OR? AND CONTINUE.

29.4.4. 0. READ CHAPTER ONE COMPLETELY OUTLOUD.
DOES IT FLOW AND TRANSITION? DO THE SENTENCES AND CLOSING SENTENCES AGREE FROM ONE PARAGRAPH INTO THE NEXT? THIS IS CALLED "TRANSITION." IF NOT OUR **"IDEA GROUP"** IS OUT OF WHACK. THE CULPRIT IS PROBABLY THE FIRST SENTENCE. THE MIDDLE SHOULD SUPPORT THE FIRST SENTENCE, THE "STATEMENT." THE CLOSER (ENDING) SHOULD COMPLETE THE "IDEA OR THOUGHT PROCESS" OF THE PARAGRAPH. THUS, CONCLUDE OR CLOSE THE SUBJECT AND TRANSITION TO THE NEXT PARAGRAPH. DID IT? THEN CONTINUE EVALUATING THE CHAPTER. DID IT PASS? WAS IT WEAK? DOES IT NEED MORE WORK? MARK IT AND CONTINUE ALL OF THIS MARKING UP AND ADD ANY EVALUATION COMMENTS IS A GOOD HABIT!

NOTE: EACH SENTENCE, PARAGRAPH, AND CHAPTER WILL GO THROUGH SEVERAL EVALUATIONS BEFORE THE NEXT DRAFT IS PRINTED OUT AND WE AGAIN LOOK AT ALL OF IT. YOU WILL SEE PROGRESS EACH TIME. CONTINUE THIS SAME PROCESS WITH ALL OF THE CHAPTERS COMPLETED OR NOT.

29.4.5. OUR EDITING AND REVISION MARKS:
 USE THE PROOF READER SYMBOLS AND WRITE THE COMMENTS IN THE MARGIN. DO NOT DOUBLE SPACE YOUR SENTENCES. YOU NEED TO SEE WHERE THE LINES FALL ON THE PAGE.

29.4.6. 0. TYPE THE REVISIONS AND RE-PRINT AS ROUGH DRAFT #2.
TYPE OUR CHANGES INTO THE DRAFT IN THE COMPUTER. IF A LOT OF CHANGES, REPRINT, RE-CLAMP IT AND GO TO OUR EDIT PLACE. **MARK DRAFT 2 OR READING #2 AT TOP AND DATE**. SAVE DRAFT #1 FOR THE CARDBOARD BOX ALONG WITH A COPY OF THE SUMMARY SYNOPSIS. THIS OUR "KERNEL IDEA" OR "GENESIS IDEA" THAT FIRST CREATED OUR BOOK WITH THIS STORY.

29.5.0.0. SECOND READING: DRAFT #2
DO FIRST PASS OF 1. WORD CHOICE, 2. GENERAL PUNCTUATION, 3. JUST FOR WORD FLOW. DON'T GET OUT THE GRAMMAR RED PEN YET. WE ARE LOOKING TO SMOOTH THE READING FLOW ONLY.

29.5.1.0 WORD CHOICE:
CHECK OUR WORD CHOICES FOR CORRECTNESS TO OUR STORY. DO THEY "ILLUMINATE" FOR THE READER, NOT THE WRITER? DID WE DESCRIBE ADEQUATELY? COULD WE SAY IT BETTER? IS OUR SENTENCES TOO SHORT? TOO LONG OR CHOPPY? DO WE NEED LONG WORDS FROM THE DICTIONARY? REMEMBER OUR STORYTELLING PROCESS. WHAT WILL INTEREST OUR READER TO CONTINUE READING?
[REVIEW CH 19. FOR WORD SOUNDS.]

29.5.3.0: BEGIN ADDING DESCRIPTIVE WORDS AND MODIFIERS :
ADJECTIVES, ADVERBS AND EVEN EXPLANATORY FACTS OR EVENTS OR CHARACTERS TO THESE SAME PARAGRAPHS. THIS SHOULD IMPROVE THE READING AND BRING IN THE STORY TELLING TO A NEW LEVEL. IF YOU NEED HELP, SEE AND READ THE STORY LINES IN CH 8.6.1.0.

29.5.3.0 RE-EDIT-REMARK AND REVISE BOOK DRAFT #2.
TOPICS: WORD CHOICE- PUNCTUATION- FLOW-PACING AND PAUSES-ADD DESCRIPTIVE LANGUAGE. REMARK AND RE-PRINT. UP DATE OUR EDITING CHECK LIST & GO TO NEXT READING: DRAFT #3.

29.6.0.0. BOOK DRAFT #3:
TOPICS: READ IT OUTLOUD, MARK AND FIX ANY CHANGES. ADD MORE SCENIC MODIFIERS, ADD PLACE AND EVENT MODIFIERS. THIS SHOULD ADD MORE MEAT TO OUR PARAGRAPHS. NOW 'ILLUMINATE' THESE SAME IDEAS AND THOUGHTS. IS IT NOW CLEARER AND MORE UNDERSTANDABLE?

IF NOT, DO MARK IT: VAGUE, ROUGH, RE-DO, EDIT, SPACE, CHANGE TIME, PLACE, SAVE SOME THESE GREAT DESCRIPTIONS FOR OTHER PARAGRAPHS, ETC. WE DON'T WANT TO KNOW EVERYTHING THE MAIN CHARACTER FEELS, OR DOES, HIS HISTORY OR DESCRIPTION IN SEVERAL PARAGRAPHS IN A ROW. SHOW HOW HE REACTS TO A SITUATION; WE, THE READER, WILL 'READ INTO,' MAKE AN ASSUMPTION OR DRAW A CONCLUSION. DON'T TELL, SHOW, ILLUMINATE FOR THE READER! WE NEED SOME OF THAT MYSTERY FOR LATER.

> DO: UPDATE THAT **CHARACTER LIST** NOW. [CH 20.]

ADD SOME OF THOSE DESCRIPTIONS, EVENTS OR CHARACTER TRAITS.

SUMMARY: WE ADDED SOME DESCRIPTIVE LANGUAGE, ADDED MODIFIERS AND BEGAN TO IMPROVE OUR CHARACTER OR EVENT OR PLACE DESCRIPTIONS. WE KEPT THE READER INTERESTED WITH THIS AND ADDED "ILLUMINATION." DO UPDATE OUR EDIT CHECK LIST. RE-MARK-EDIT AND RE-PRINT BOOK DRAFTS #3 AS THE NEW #4.[CH 30].

29.7.3.0. DEFINITION OF ROUGH DRAFT-BOOK DRAFT- MANUSCRIPT- FINAL BOOK.
THE **ROUGH DRAFT** IS ROUGH AND INCOMPLETE. THE BASICS ARE MISSING. ALL CHAPTER TOPICS COMPLETED. ALL CHARACTERS IN PLACE

AND THEIR ROLE AS MINOR-SUPPORTING OR MAIN ARE COMPLETED. GRAMMAR- LANGUAGE- PUNCTUATION EDITED.

29.7.3.1. THE BOOK DRAFT HAS PROGRESSED TO INTO MINOR AND MAJOR EVENTS, PLOTS AND ALL CHARACTERS RISE TO THE PLOT. PLOTS AND CLIMAXES MUST BE COMPLETED HERE. THE FIGURES OF SPEECH, PUNCTUATION, STORYLINES ARE INTACT. TIMELINES COMPLETED. DID WE INSERT IMAGERY-COMEDY-TRAGEDY? POLISHING OF WORDS, SOUNDS AND SMOOTHNESS NEEDS FINISHED. EDITING IS STILL ONGOING. **SPELLING AND GRAMMAR CHECKS ARE PERFORMED.**
CHECK LISTS [SEE INDEX] ARE USED TO COMPLETE THIS REVIEW.
AFTER ALL CHECK LISTS ARE COMPLETED A DRAFT BECOMES A MANUSCRIPT.

DO: REFER TO FINAL MANUSCRIPT-CH 36.

29.8.0.0. OUR PROGRESS:

1. WE DEFINED ROUGH DRAFT-BOOK DRAFT AND MANUSCRIPT. WE EDITED OUR ROUGH DRAFTS SEVERAL TIMES

2. WE ORGANIZED OUR BOOK DRAFT.

3. WE UPDATED OUR CHARACTER LISTS.

4. WE UPDATED OUR SYNOPSES?

5. WE PERFORMED THE FINAL MANUSCRIPT COMPARISON [CH 36]. WE FIXED IT!

6. WE WAIT!---THEN READ AGAIN WITH FRESH EYES! WE FIX IT!

7. WE REVIEW FOR SMOOTHNESS.

*8. WE CHECK AGAINST THE **HEART METER**---HOW MANY TIMES DID WE LAUGH---CRY---EMPATHIZE- FEEL PAIN?*

9. WE READ ONE MORE TIME AS THE READER. DOES IT MEET OUR EXPECTATIONS…ANY HOLES…VAGUENESS? WE FIX IT!

10. DID WE ANSWER THE CONFLICT? DID WE RESOLVE THE FINAL CONCLUSION WITH EACH CHARACTER?

11. DID WE BRIDGE IT TO THE NEXT BOOK? [CH 27].

12. DOES YOUR LEAD FEMALE CHARACTER MATCH THE SAME MALE LEAD? DOES SHE FINISH HER ROLE WITH THE SAME STRENGTH? WHAT IS HIS/HER SYMBOLISM?

*13. **CONCLUSION:** WHAT TYPE OF ENDING OCCURS? HAPPY? TRAGIC? HOW DO WE LEAVE THE READER? HAPPY? SAD? WANTING MORE?*

CHAPTER 30

30. 0.0.0. BOOK DRAFT- EDITING

CHAPTER TOPICS: *CHECK LIST: TOPICS: CHARACTERS-SENSORY TOURS-POINT OF VIEW-STYLE IMPROVEMENT-DIALOGUE-MODIFIERS-BACK STORY.*

30.0.1.0. WHAT IS CRITICISM?
CRITICISM IS ABOUT CHECKING OUR WORK BY OURSELVES AND OTHERS FOR QUALITY. IT IS NOT ABOUT BLAME OR SHAME OR BEING UPSET WHETHER SOMEONE LIKES IT OR NOT.

30.0.1.1. WE REVIEW OUR √ *CHECK LIST FOR EDITING.*
DID WE FIX THE ERRORS FIRST? QUALITY CHECKS ARE ABOUT WHEN WE FIRST FEEL OUR WORK IS READY TO BE EDITING AND COMMENTED ON. LET'S ASSUME WE ARE DEALING WITH COMPLETED POLISHED CHAPTERS. [CH 11.5.0.0.]

30.0.1.2. **EDITING** IS THE SECOND STEP AND VERY IMPORTANT TO THE FINISHED PRODUCT: DID WE PERFORM ALL THE "EDITING CHECK ITEMS" AGAINST OUR WRITING? IF NOT STOP…DO IT! OUR READER WILL BE MORE CRITICAL. WE WRITERS TEND TO KEEP SENTENCES AND PARAGRAPHS BECAUSE WE WROTE IT. NO EGO…JUST A WRITER'S FANTASY.

THE TEST IS: DOES IT MAKE SENSE TO OUR STORY? OUR IDEA GROUPINGS? IS IT BACK STORY? OR FILLER INFORMATION? DOES IT FLOW? DOES IT SOUND GOOD WHEN READ OUTLOUD? IF NOT STOP. PAUSE FIRST! THEN RE-WRITE OR ADD WHAT IS MISSING. DELETE THE EXTRA STUFF. DID WE COMPLETE THE OPENING SENTENCE, THE MIDDLE MEAT AND THE CLOSING SENTENCE? IF NOT FIX IT!

30.0.2.0. OUR EDITORS:
IT DOES NOT MATTER IF YOUR WIFE OR AUNT SOPHIE DOESN'T LIKE IT, OR DOESN'T LIKE THE WORDS OR THE STORY. 3 BILLION PEOPLE HAVE DIFFERENT TASTES.

WE HAVE SO MANY GENRES' AND DIFFERENT TYPES OF WRITING TO PLEASE THEM. IF YOUR STORY IS SOUND, IS LAUGHABLE, OR CAUSES TEARS OR SOMETIMES DISGUST. YOU HAVE CAPTURED ITS SOUL. IF YOU DEVELOPED YOUR PLOT, CHARACTERS, EVENTS, PLACES AND DRAMATICALLY CARRIED THEM OUT…IT WORKS!
ALONG THE WAY, YOU WILL FIND A STYLE THAT WORKS.

BOOKS WRITTEN WITH HEART AND SOUL TEND TO DEVELOP A SOUL ALONG THE WAY. TIME ISN'T ALWAYS A FACTOR BUT GENERALLY THE QUALITY IMPROVES OVER TIME…IT BECOMES SEASONED.
[SEE CH-38 ON STYLE & CH 61 THE WRITER'S CLUB].

WE CAN'T BE TOO CRITICAL, THROW TWO YEARS OF WORK AWAY, NOR KILL OUR WRITING SKILLS NOR WIPE OUT OUR SELF-ESTEEM; BUT WE MUST FIND A MEANS TO **MEASURE OUR PROGRESS**, VIA THE QUALITY OF WHAT WE WRITE. READ THE ENTIRE "POLISHED DRAFT" DOES IT MAKE US WANT TO FINISH IT AS A READER? DID WE LAUGH? DID WE CRY? DID WE BECOME INVOLVED IN THE STORY? DID WE WANT TO BE THE HERO? HATE THE VILLAIN? DID THE WORDS GIVE US A "PICTURESQUE" VERSION? COULD WE SEE THE PLACES AND EVENTS? DID

CREATIVE WRITING—THE KELLY MANUAL OF STYLE

OUR BOOK BECOME THAT MOVIE IN OUR HEAD? IF NOT WE HAVE SOME
WRITING AND EDITING TO DO.

NOT ALL OF OUR BOOKS ARE "MASTERPIECES" USUALLY OUR READER
DOES THAT REVIEW FOR US. WE SHOULD NOT FALL IN LOVE WITH OUR
BOOK. YES, WE MUST LIKE OUR STORY VERY MUCH.
BE OBJECTIVE TO SAY IT STINKS OR IT NEEDS HELP.

WHEN, WE HAVE ASKED OURSELVES THESE QUESTIONS AND REPLY:
YES! YES! YES! WE ARE READY TO SUBMIT IT FOR PUBLISHING OR
PUBLISH IT VIA THE PRINT ON DEMAND PUBLISHERS. [SEE CH 49].

EXERCISE: NOW LET'S CRITIQUE OUR WRITING HOMEWORK:
REVIEW OUR CHECK LIST....ADD MORE TO THIS FOR YOURSELF.

30.3.0. 0. THE #1 MOST IMPORTANT QUESTION?
DID THE READER GET THE MESSAGE?
THEN I ASKED THE MOST IMPORTANT QUESTIONS—DID I FORGET
SOMETHING, WAS IT CLEAR WHAT I TRIED TO SAY AND FINALLY DID THE
READER GET THE MESSAGE?

30.4.1.0. DID IT FLOW...? READ IT ALOUD TO YOURSELF. DID IT SOUND
CHOPPY...FIX IT OR "NOTE IT" WITH YOUR OWN EDITING SYMBOL THAT
IT NEEDS WORK? DO IT AGAIN LATER, TOMORROW OR A WEEK LATER.
EXAMPLE:
I WROTE ONE BOOK IN THREE MONTHS BUT EDITED IT ABOUT TWENTY
TIMES BEFORE COPYRIGHTING IT. IT WAS ABOUT 80 PAGES LONG. THE
TITLE CHANGED THREE TIMES, THE CHAPTERS CHANGED ORDER, AND
THE PARAGRAPHS CHANGED ORDER AND MASSIVE CHANGES IN WORDS
AND PUNCTUATION. ALL IN PREPARATION FOR THE NEXT "BETTER"
BOOK.

30.4.3.0. MY BEST BOOK WAS BOOK # 7. 'THE BOOMERS.'
IT TOOK TWO YEARS TO WRITE AND EDIT. THEN 6 MONTHS OF FINAL
CRITICISM AND RE-EDITING, POLISHING AND CHECKLISTS.

IT WAS THE FIRST BOOK I PUBLISHED AFTER TEN YEARS OF WRITING
AND SEVEN PREVIOUS BOOKS WRITTEN.
THE OTHER SEVEN FULL LENGTH BOOKS WERE HELPING MY
PREPARATION AND REQUIRED MORE RE-WRITING AND EDITING, BEFORE
I RELEASED THEM.

AFTER THE BOOMERS, I RELEASED FIVE BOOKS IN 7 MONTHS ALONG
WITH COVER ART, MARKETING COPY ON REAR COVER AND SOMETIMES
NEW TITLES. I WORKED FULL TIME ON THEM, DURING THIS PERIOD. MY
DAY JOB WAS ON HOLD. OH, I PAID THE BILLS; BUT THE SAVINGS WENT
DOWN.

EVEN TWELVE YEARS LATER, I KNEW I NEEDED MORE PICTURESQUE
WORDS, AND PERHAPS MORE REFINED WORK ON DRAMATIZATION AND
ADDITIONAL FIGURES OF SPEECH.

THE STORY WAS VERY SOUND. THE PLOT WAS GREAT, NOT LIKE THE
"WAR AND PEACE" CLASSIC OR A MASTERPIECE. I HAD LOTS TO LEARN
YET I FOUND I USED MANY ELEMENTS OF THE MASTER WRITERS (I

CREATIVE WRITING—THE KELLY MANUAL OF STYLE

STUDIED THEM AS RESEARCH FOR THIS BOOK AND READ MANY OF THEM OVER AGAIN).

I LEARNED SOME **BASIC TRUTHS**: I NEEDED BOOK PLANS, IDEA GROUPS, ORGANIZATION AND PUTTING MORE "CREATIVE WAYS" INTO MY BOOK. IT HAD TO BE RIGHT, IN MY OWN JUDGMENT. COMPLETING THE BOOK BECAME AN OBSESSION, SOMETHING THAT TOOK ON A LIFE OF ITS OWN; **A DEMANDING MISTRESS.**

BOTTOM LINE: THE COST WAS THE TIME (20 EDITS AFTER IT WAS POLISHED AND READY) AND DISTANT FRIENDS AND MY REDUCED SOCIAL LIFE. I WAS ON A MISSION.

THE BOOK TOOK <u>THREE MONTHS</u> TO HIT THE BOOK SELLER'S LIST VIA BOWKER'S ISBN NUMBER LISTS. GRADUALLY, OTHER TITLES DRAGGED ON THE LIST AS WELL. [I LEARNED THE PUBLISHING PROCESS IS SLOW, CUMBERSOME AND CERTAINLY NEEDS RE-VAMPING. I LEARNED HAD NO CONTROL OVER PRICING; YET, THE BIG BOYS PRICED MY BOOK WITH A 10% DISCOUNT OFF THIS INFLATED "RETAIL PRICE." THE MARK UP IS AN INDUSTRY STANDARD OF 100% OVER COST, AUTHOR FEES AND PUBLISHER FEES.] STILL, THAT IS THE WAY IT IS!

ANOTHER <u>FIVE MONTHS</u> AND ITS HITS THE EUROPEAN MARKETS AND BOOKSELLER WEB SITES. MORE MARKETING NEEDS DONE. IT CAN BE 'GOOGLED' VIA THE WEBSITES PROVIDED UNDER THE INDEX: AUTHOR'S BOOKS OR ISBN NUMBER.

BACK TO THE BOOK, I RE-READ IT SEVEN MONTHS AFTER IT WAS PUBLISHED; TEARS, LAUGHTER AND ALL OF THE SENSES AND EMOTIONS POURED OUT. I DID EMPATHIZE WITH THE CHARACTER AND THE PLOT. I HATED THE MANY VILLAINS AND THEIR SECRET AGENDAS. I HATED THE GOVERNMENT FOR ITS SHABBY ROLE AND THE EFFECT ON THE SERVING SOLDIERS.

I DEFINED THE MAIN VILLAIN AS MY FRIEND THEN ENEMY. HE BECAME THE DRAMATIC CHARACTER ON WHICH THE PLOT AND THE MULTI-CLIMATIC CONCLUSION HINGED.

THE TRIAL FOR TREASON BECAME ONE OF THE **CLIMATIC POINTS** AND A VEHICLE FOR "**WRAPPING UP THE STORY FROM THE BEGINNING TO END**". I SAVED THE **'TWIST'** FOR AFTERWARDS. ANOTHER CHARACTER PROVIDED THE SOLUTION TO THE "TREASON" EVEN THOUGH MY ENEMY IS KILLED DURING THE TRIAL.

THE BOOK AND HERO TOOK **ONE MORE ADDITIONAL DIFFERENT TWIST** AT THE END. SMILES AND EVEN TEARS LEFT US READERS BOTH HAPPY AND SAD. BOTH LOVE AND WAR WAS CONCLUDED. [I PUT A CHECK MARK FOR EVERY HUMOROUS ITEM AND MARKED MY TYPOS AND ERRORS FOR A LATER REVISION.]

I FELT THE READER AND I, THE WRITER, FINALLY FOUND THE "AH! HA!

CHAPTER 31
31.0.0.0. √ *EDITING CHECKLIST*:
1. SPELL CHECK-ENTIRE DRAFT.

2. CHECK FOR THE PROPER WORD

3, CHECK OPENING SENTENCE: IS IT A GRABBER?

4. DOES ENDING SENTENCE THE CLOSER- WRAPPED IT UP?
   DOES IT CLOSE THE STATEMENT MADE IN THE OPENING SENTENCE ?
   DOES IT ALSO LEAD INTO THE NEXT PARAGRAPH?

5. THE MEAT-WHERE IS THE BEEF?
   THE MIDDLE PART ANSWERS THE STATEMENT OR REINFORCES
   STATEMENT SENTENCE ONE.

6. THE CHAPTER TITLE SHOULD MATCH WHAT WE WROTE?

7. CHECK QUOTE MARKS-LEFT AND RIGHT ARE OPPOSITES.

8. CHECK VERB AND SUBJECT TENSE.

9. CHECK PUNCTUATION MARKS.

10. DOES PARAGRAPH CONTENT FIT IN THAT CHAPTER?

11. READ IT OUT-LOUD: FLOW-STOPS?

12. RE-TYPE AND RE-EDIT AGAIN.

IS IT NOT RIGHT YET? MARK IT "EDIT" OR "FLOW" OR OTHER
PROBLEM AND CONTINUE WITH NEXT PARAGRAPH OR CHAPTER.

31.1.0.0. OUR PROGRESS:
1. WE LEARNED EDITING IS OUR SECOND JOB AFTER
   WRITING.

2. WE LEARNED WHAT ITEMS TO EDIT & WHY.

3. WE LEARNED THE PROOFREADER'S MARKS AND HOW THEY
   POINT OUT ERRORS OR OMISSIONS.

4. WE LEARNED TO NOT EDIT TOO SOON.

5. WE LEARNED TO EDIT IN A DIFFERENT SPACE THAN OUR
   WRITING SPACE.

6. WE LEARNED OUR ROUGH DRAFTS AND BOOK DRAFTS
   REQUIRE MULTIPLE EDITS.

7. WE LEARNED OUR MANUSCRIPT [CH 36] GETS A THOROUGH
   FINAL EDIT BEFORE THE PUBLISHER GETS IT.

CHAPTER 32

32.0.0.0. PROOF READER'S MARKS:

1.HOW TO USE:

MARK EITHER A SENTENCE OR PARAGRAPH ERROR WITH THE
FOLLOWING OR YOUR OWN MARKS. HERE IS THE STANDARD ONES:

2.-IF FIXED/ KEYED IN/ CORRECTED: USE YOUR INITIAL IN CIRCLE ®

ABBREVIATE:	"ABB"
CAPITAL LETTERS	CAPS
COMPLEX:	"COMPLEX"
CLARIFYING TERM:	(----)
CONTINUING THOUGHT	...
DASH-INSERT DASH	>-
DELETE:	~ OR D OR "DEL"
DIALOGUE-NW	DIALOGUE
DRAMATIZATION	DRAMA
EDIT	"ED"
FONT:	"F"
FONT SIZE 9	F9
FRAGMENT BAD	FRAGB
HUMOR-NW-RW-UPDATE	HU
INSERT	"I"
ITALIC FONT TYPE:	"ITAL"
MOVE:	ARROW
NUMBER NEEDED/ CONVERTED/DASHED:	#, #C, #-#,

PARAGRAPH SENTENCE CONSTRUCTION: S OR P

NEEDS SEPARATE PARA:	"P"
MOVE/ PARA ORDER:	"P-#"
NEEDS WORK:	"NW"
CLOSER-NEEDS WORK:	"NW"
DEFINITION	DEF
EMPHASIS:	"EMP"
NEEDS TITLE:	"TITLE"
DIFFERENT ORDER:	" DO"
NEW WORD	NW
RAMBLING:	"RAMBLE"
REWRITE-	"RW
OUT OF CONTEXT WITH PARA:	"CONTEXT"
VERB TENSE	TENSE
MODIFIER –ADJECTIVE-ADVERB-PHRASE	MOD
RUN-ON SENTENCE- SHORTEN:	SHORT
SENTENCE TOO LONG	STL
SPELLING	SP

PUNCTUATION: PU

178

CREATIVE WRITING—THE KELLY MANUAL OF STYLE

APOSTROPHE:	'
BOLD:	"B"
COLON:	:
PARENTHESES-BRACKETS:	( ) [ ] { }
PUNCTUATION:-INSERT	^ PU
QUOTES: DIRECT	"
SEPARATE:	/
SUB QUOTE OR 'TERM'	'

READER & UNDERSTANDING:

READER CONNECTION LOST:	"LOST"
READER BLIND ALLEY:	"BLIND"
READER CONFUSED:	"CONFUSED"
READER-CONTINUITY LOST BETWEEN PAR:	"CONT"
READ ALOUD: CK FLOW: RA OR	"FLOW"
SOUNDS IMITATING OBJECT	SO
SOUND SEQUENCE -ALLITERATION	SS
SOUND SEQUENCE-ASSONANCE VOWELS	SV
SOURCE NOTE:	SN

SPACE: S

SPACE:	"S"
SPACE-OPEN UP:	"SO"
SPACE-CLOSE UP:	"SC"

STORY: ST

NEEDS REWRITE:	"S-RW"
NEEDS CHRONOLOGICAL ORDER	"ORDER"
NEEDS "ACHRONOLOGICAL ORDER:	"A ORDER"
NEEDS STRUCTURE	" STRUCT"
POINT OF VIEW	POV
TRADEMARK	TM
TRANSLATE:	TRANS
TRANSPOSE:	"TR"
TWO WORDS:	"2W"
UNDERLINE	
VOICE	V̄
WHISPER:	"WH"

FINAL EDITING CODES:

1. THE IDEA HERE IS TO DO A THOROUGH EDITING CHECK.

2.YOU MIGHT DO ONE PART ONLY LIKE VERB TENSE AND PUNCTUATION BY READING OUTLOUD.

3.YOU MIGHT DO OPENING AND CLOSING SENTENCES OF PARAGRAPHS ONLY.

4. KEEP TRACK OF WHAT YOU EDITED, WITH A DATE OR WRITE THE TYPE OF EDITING ON THE FIRST TITLE PAGE.

CHAPTER 33

33.0.0.0. HOW TO ORGANIZE YOUR COMPUTER FILES:
CHAPTER TOPICS:
1. HOW TO LAYOUT A BOOK FROM FRONT COVER TO REAR AND PAGES IN-BETWEEN.
2. COMPUTER FOLDER ORGANIZATION.

33.1.0.0. FICTION NOVEL ---PAGE ORGANIZATION- *EXAMPLE:*
IN ORDER FROM FRONT TO BACK COVER: EXAMPLE FROM EARLY BOOK: "SPIES, THIEVES AND OTHER FRIENDS."
COVER PAGE- ARTWORK-OUTSIDE
COPYRIGHT NOTICE (ALWAYS PAGE 2)
BLANK PAGE- OR MAP OR ILLUSTRATION.
INSIDE TITLE
MAP-DRAWING-
INSIDE TITLE REPEAT OF 111.
BOOKS BY AUTHOR
FICTION NOTICE/DISCLAIMER
DEDICATION
ACKNOWLEDGEMENT
INTRODUCTION
TABLE OF CONTENTS-EXAMPLE:

LIST OF INDICES: ALPHABETICAL ORDER
INDEX1: CAST OF CHARACTERS-MAIN FIRST.
INDEX2: OUTLINE BY CHAPTER #
INDEX3: MAPS & ILLUSTRATIONS-PAGE #- OR ILLUST #.
INDEX4: GLOSSARY OF TERMS—PAGE#
INDEX5: MUSIC SELECTIONS-GROUP, ALBUM, CD NAME, TIME
INDEX6: SOURCE LIST-BY SUBJECT, THEN SEQUENTIAL ORDER.
    CHAPTER, PAGE, AUTHOR, © DATE, PUBLISHER, NOTES,
    LAST PAGE IS BLANK-NO HEADER-NO FOOTER-NO PAGE

CREATIVE WRITING—THE KELLY MANUAL OF STYLE

33.2.0.0. COMPUTER FOLDER ORGANIZATION:
HERE IS A SAMPLE LIST OF MY DOCUMENT FILE FOLDERS AND PHOTOS ON MY LAPTOP:

33.3.0.1. FOLDERS ONLY:
BKS-MASTER BOOKS-ALL
(DO SET SHORTCUT TO YOUR BOOK IN THIS MASTER FILE)
BKS-ORGANIZATION-MASTER-ALL
BKS-CHARACTER-MASTER
BKS-IDEAS LIST-MASTER
ARTWORK-BOOK COVERS-MASTER
PHOTOS-MASTER
PORTFOLIO-MASTER
RESEARCH-MASTER
ONE SHORTCUT TO YOUR BOOK MASTER DRAFT.

33.4.0.0. MASTER BOOKS IN ORDER BY NUMBER-TITLE:
SELECT ONE BOOK: THESE COMPUTER FOLDERS APPEAR BELOW FOR THAT ONE BOOK:
ARCHIVES-BOOK SYNOPSES - BOOK IDEA LIST-BOOK PLAN-TIME LINE-CAST OF CHARACTERS (DETAILED).-INDICES-ADD YOUR OWN HERE.

33.5.0.0. ORGANIZATION: DOCUMENT FILES:
(ALPHABETICAL) USE ANY THAT APPLY:
ARCHIVES
ARCHIVES-TO BE DELETED
AUTHOR BOOK LIST
AUTHOR-BIO
BLOGGING
BOOK AGENT
BOOK AWARDS
BOOK ORGANIZATION
CHARACTERS
COPYRIGHT
COSTS
CREATIVE WRITING
DEDICATIONS
EDITORS
EDIT-PROOFREADING
ENGLISH-STRUCTURE-GRAMMAR
FICTION
FIGURES OF SPEECH-STYLE
GENRE
GLOSSARIES
GRANTS
IDEAS LIST
INDICES
INTRODUCTION
MANUSCRIPTS
MAPS
MARKETING
MUSIC SELECTIONS
NEWS REPORTING
PDF CONVERSION
PLACES

CREATIVE WRITING—THE KELLY MANUAL OF STYLE

PORTFOLIO
PROLOGUE
PUBLISHING-6X9
RESEARCH FOR EACH BOOK(MY)
RESEARCH IDEAS
SCREENPLAY
SOFTWARE-BOOKS-WRITING
SONGS
STUDENT ASSIGNMENTS
SYNOPSIS
TABLE OF CONTENTS
THEORIES
TIMELINES
TITLES-BOOK
TITLES-CHAPTER
WEB PAGES
WRITER'S SPACE
WRITER-JOBS
WRITERS-MASTERS
WRITING-BEST SELLER

PHOTO-ORGANIZATION: (ALPHABETICAL)
PHOTOS BY SUBJECT
PHOTOS-ART
PHOTOS-COVER ART
PHOTOS-PLACES

33.6.0.0. OUR PROGRESS:
1. WE LEARNED TO ADD PAGES TO OUR ROUGH DRAFT TO SIMULATE A BOOK DRAFT AND TO PUT THEM IN A CERTAIN ORDER.

2. WE ORGANIZED OUR COMPUTER FOLDERS TO KEEP OUR BOOK AND BOOK ORGANIZATION INTO 2 GROUPS OF FOLDERS.

3. LAST, WE ORGANIZED THOSE PAPER FILES-BOOKS, RESEARCH, ARTICLES-CLIPS WITH OUR ' NUMERICAL SOURCE LIST' ON TOP.

CHAPTER 34
34.0.0.0. RESEARCH & SOURCE DATA LISTS:
*CHAPTER TOPICS: RESEARCH-CLIP FILES-RESEARCH SOURCE LISTS (2
TYPES).NUMERICAL—ALPHABETICAL--MUSIC LISTS:
THE BIBLIOGRAPHY LIST HAS BEEN REPLACED WITH A SOURCE NUMBER
AND SOURCE ALPHABETICAL LISTS.*

34.0.0.1. OUR GOAL:
IS TO COLLECT-ORGANIZE AND WRITE FROM THESE SOURCES:
1. RESEARCH MATERIAL-CLIPS FILES-BOOKS ON SAME SUBJECTS.
2. SYNOPSIS: STORYTELLER. & CHAPTER BY CHAPTER
4. BOOK PLAN-FORMAT TO ORGANIZE THE PAGES.
5. TIMELINES-2 KINDS.
6. MASTER IDEA LIST AND OUR BOOK DRAFT OF IDEA GROUPS
7. AND THE TWO KINDS OF SOURCE INFORMATION.
   NUMERICAL LIST AND ALPHABETICAL SUBJECT
   GROUPS. (IDEA GROUPS).

34.0.0.2. 6 W'S: WHO, WHAT, WHEN, WHERE, WHY, WOW!
WHO: THE RESEARCHER IS AN OBSERVER AND RECORDER OF
DATA AND META DATA. SEE CHAPTER 9.0.0.0.

RESEARCH MATERIAL CAN TAKE SEVERAL FORMS: ART, ARTICLES,
ATLASES, BLOGS, BOOKS, CLIP FILES, COLOR, HISTORY, JOURNALS,
MAPS, MUSIC, NEWSPAPER, OBSERVATIONS, PHOTOS, SOUNDS, AND
TECHNOLOGY, AND VIDEOS.

WHERE DO WE GO FOR RESEARCH?
THE MALL, THE PARK, THE CAFETERIA, LIBRARY, COFFEE SHOP, THE
ISLANDS...MY FAVORITE, GO ON VACATION, TRAVEL, CLIMB A HILL,
READ A BOOK...EVERYWHERE AT ANY TIME. DAY TIME...AT NIGHT,
UNDER THE STARS, RAINING, SUNRISE, SUNSET, WINTER, IN THE PAST,
THE FUTURE, THE PRESENT.

USE: WE MAY USE RESEARCH TO PROVIDE FACTS, ILLUSTRATIONS,
DESCRIPTIONS AND LIFE TO OUR SCENES, SETTINGS AND IMPROVE OUR
DRAMA, PLOTS AND CLIMAXES.
WE HAVE TWO PROBLEMS: **HOW TO RECORD IT AND USE IT QUICKLY.**

WHY:
1. WE COLLECT RESEARCH TO BUILD OUR 'MASTER IDEAS LIST' FOR
MANY BOOKS AND THE SINGLE BOOK IDEAS LISTS. THUS, 2 LISTS FROM
OUR SOURCE LIST.
2. WE DO THE FIRST SORT TO CATEGORIZE BY SUBJECT.
3. THEN, WE SAVE IT. REFINE IT AND RE-SORT BY SUBJECT.
THIS SORT SHOULD GATHER LIKE ITEMS BY THE GROUPING WE PREFER.
SORT CODE EXAMPLES FOLLOW:
34.0.0.3. WHERE?
LET'S PLAY DETECTIVE: RESEARCH:

CREATIVE WRITING—THE KELLY MANUAL OF STYLE

HOW DO YOU FIND AND RECORD YOUR RESEARCH?

1. BEGIN LOOKING BY SUBJECT. (BROAD). YOUR FORMAT MIGHT BE BROAD SUBJECT, COUNTRY, YOUR BOOK(ARTICLE, CLIP, FILM, VIDEO, ETC) DATE AND AUTHOR. NUMBER 1 TO 100.

2. GATHER ANY AND ALL RELATED MATERIAL. (BROAD).
COPY IT DOWN , SCAN IT OR PRINT OUT THE SOURCE.

3. **PLAY DETECTIVE.** SEARCH OTHER TOPICS ON A WHIM.
   OUR SOURCE MATERIAL WILL LEAD US TO RELATED TOPICS.
   ELECTRONIC COPY IT, OR CHECK IT OUT.

4. ORGANIZE BY IDEA OR TOPIC ON TOP PAGE MARGIN.

5. ADD THESE TO OUR LIST OF **IDEA GROUPS,** THUS SORTING.
   TO NARROW OUR IDEA GROUPINGS.

6 . TAKE SINGLE IDEA GROUPINGS FOR CHAPTER SIZE.

7. SEGMENT INTO IMPORTANT STORY TOPICS.
   THEMES-BOOKS YOU WOULD LIKE TO READ OR WRITE.

8. NOW, WHAT DOES THE READER WANT TO KNOW OR LEARN ABOUT?
WRITE IT DOWN. **"MARK IT "READER: ----".**

9. **READ THE SOURCE DATA**, HIGHLIGHT IT, MAKE NOTES, GRAB THE IDEA...ASSIGN A SOURCE # TO IT, ON THE TOP RIGHT CORNER.

10. WRITE ONLY THE **IDEA GROUP** ON A PIECE OF PAPER, BINDER CLIP IT ON THE TOP LEFT.

10. AT THIS POINT WE HAVE 2 INDEX ITEMS- OUR SOURCE # LIST AND THE NEW IDEA GROUPS, WHICH WE ADD TO OUR MASTER IDEA LIST.

121. WE NEED THE SPECIFIC BOOK IDEA (2ND LIST) LIST HERE. WHAT IDEAS DID YOU THINK OF FOR JUST THIS ONE BOOK? WHAT SOURCE MATERIAL DID YOU GATHER. ANY IDEAS FROM THESE GATHERINGS?
PERUSE THE RESEARCH TO GATHER IDEAS.

34.0.0.13. DO: START A CLIP FILE:

CUT OUT OR PRINT OUT ARTICLES, NEWSPAPER SOURCES, MAGAZINES ETC FILED BY **SUBJECT ALPHABETICALLY**. A CARDBOARD BOX WITH FILE FOLDERS OR A FILE CABINET OR COMPUTER FOLDER, "RESEARCH FOLDER"-TOPIC.

HAVE YOU CLIPPED NEWSPAPER NEWS STORIES, KEPT MAGAZINE ARTICLES AND PRINTED PAGES FROM THE INTERNET AS SUBJECTS OF INTEREST OR BOOK IDEAS? SAVE THE RESEARCH AND CLIP FILE EVEN THOUGH IT DOESN'T FIT OUR WRITING TOPIC TODAY.

YOU CAN **ORGANIZE THE CLIPS BY SUBJECT**. PERHAPS YOU KEPT THEM IN A FILE CABINET OR IF PERTAINING TO YOUR BOOK...THEY BECOME PART OF YOUR SOURCE DOCUMENTS.

EXERCISE:

CREATIVE WRITING—THE KELLY MANUAL OF STYLE

NAME SOME AREAS WHERE YOU FIND RESEARCH.
WHAT ARE WE LOOKING FOR?
WEB-BOOKS-ARTICLES-SCIENTIFIC ARTICLES
MULTI-MEDIA?-GENRE?-A SPECIFIC GENRE LIKE LAW?

34.1.0.0. BIBLIOGRAPHY:

NOW, DO YOUR HOMEWORK, RESEARCH 10 BOOK'S ON ONE TOPIC. CHECK EACH BIBLIOGRAPHY. DOES THE INFORMATION RUN TOGETHER? FOR SOURCE INFORMATION DOES IT TELL YOU ENOUGH? DO YOU WISH THERE WAS A SYNOPSIS? WHAT ABOUT YOUR BOOKS…HOW DO YOU SHOW SOURCES? DO THE RULES ABOUT DITTO AND IBID CONFUSE YOU OR GET IN THE WAY? HELP OR HURT? DOES THE NUMBERING MAKE SENSE?

34.1.0.1. THE OLD "BIBLIOGRAPHY FORMAT" DOESN'T WORK FOR NOVELS.

1. [NON-FICTION, SCIENTIFIC AND THESIS PAPERS ARE CERTAINLY DIFFERENT THAN FICTION METHODS.

2. TRY FINDING OUR SUBJECT MATERIAL WITHOUT READING A LONG BIBLIOGRAPHY LISTING.

3. CHECKING OUR SOURCES IS EASIER WITH KEY WORD SORTING.

4. REQUIRE METHOD WHEN PROOFING YOUR BOOK.

5. A METHOD TO HANDLE "EXCEPTIONS" TO COPYRIGHT'S 'ALL RIGHTS.'

6. A METHOD TO PREVENT POSSIBLE PLAGIARISM CLAIMS.

7. A METHOD OF ORGANIZING A LOT OF FACTS. AND STACKS OF MATERIALS.

8. THIS LIST IS ALSO THE BEGINNING OUR '**SUBJECT INDEX**' AT THE BACK OF OUR BOOK.(A LOT OF NOVELS DON'T HAVE THIS FEATURE… DON'T YOU HATE IT WHEN YOU, THE READER ,WANTS TO FIND A SUBJECT & RE-READ IT?

9. ONE COLUMN WILL INDICATE WHAT TYPE OF FORMAT MATERIAL I HAVE: BOOKS, INTERNET, MAGAZINES, MAPS, DICTIONARY, REFERENCE BOOKS, ETC.

10. IT IS THE <u>CONTENT </u>WE SEEK, NOT THE AUTHOR-BOOK TITLE OR DATE.

34.1.0.11. ACID TEST:

PUT IT TO THE **"ACID TEST."** IT WORKS OR IT DOESN'T. IF YOU ARE WRITING ON THE TOPIC DID ALL OF THE 'SUBJECTS' AND IDEA GROUPS GET WRITTEN ABOUT. MAYBE THE HOLE YOU JUST FOUND CAN BE FILLED AND YOUR WRITING TOOK ON A NEW COMPLETENESS NEVER BEFORE. HAVE YOU EVER GOTTEN A "INCOMPLETE TOPIC" ON A PAPER BEFORE? NOW, YOU WON'T.

COPY A BIBLIOGRAPHY FROM A BOOK, SORT IT, FIND YOUR SUBJECT? IT DIDN'T WORK VERY WELL, DID IT?

CREATIVE WRITING—THE KELLY MANUAL OF STYLE

34.1.0. 12. NON-FICTION:
SOMETIMES NON-FICTION OR SCIENTIFIC BOOKS OR FACTS JUST NEED
RESEARCHED AND THE SOURCE MUST BE NOTED IN STANDARD FORMAT
IN THE "BIBLIOGRAPHY LIST"---CHAPTER &/OR PARAGRAPH ORDER--- AT
THE REAR OF THE BOOK. NON-FICTION DICTATES THAT STYLE;
HOWEVER, FICTION DOESN'T WORK IN THAT FORMAT.

34.1.0.13. ADVANTAGES:
AFTER YEARS OF RESEARCH AND ORGANIZING THAT RESEARCH DATA
INTO A USEFUL FORMAT, I FOUND:
I USE A NON-TRADITIONAL FORM: SEQUENTIAL # ORDER- BOOK TITLE OR
SUBJECT- THEN, AUTHOR, WEB PAGE/DATE, & PAGES OR CHAPTERS
WHERE IT IS FOUND IN MY BOOK.

THIS SEQUENTIAL ORDER ALLOWS ME TO SEE **BY SUBJECT OR TITLE**
BEFORE I LOOK AT AN AUTHOR'S NAME. THUS, I SEE ALL IRELAND
REFERENCES, OR ALL FRANCE, OR ALL OF ONE SUBJECT REFERENCES;
AND THE AUTHOR STILL GETS HIS DUE. EXAMPLE: LOOK AT YOUR OWN
BOOK LISTING...YOU WRITE MANY FORMATS AND GENRE...YET YOU LIST
THEM UNDER TYPES. WHICH TYPE OF BIBLIOGRAPHY DO YOU FIND
BETTER?

WE WRITER'S DO USE A LOT OF FACTS ABOUT SCENES, PLACES AND
HISTORY: THUS, **OUR NEED TO QUOTE AND EVEN PARAPHRASE THE
FACTS ACCURATELY.**

WE MUST HAVE OUR SOURCE / RESEARCH DATA AT OUR FINGERTIPS.
THE QUESTION IS HOW TO DO ORGANIZE IT FOR SPEEDY REFERENCE OR
SORTING BY SUBJECT.

34.2.0.0. SORTING:
15.2.0.0. WHAT KINDS OF RESEARCH NEED SORTING?
*LET'S SAY YOU'VE READ 20 SOURCES BUT THEY DO NOT BOIL IT ALL DOWN
AND YOU MAKE BULLET POINTS OUT OF IT. WHILE, YOU ARE NOT "QUOTING
EXACTLY" THE .INFORMATION BELONGS IN EITHER:*

*1. IN THE **PUBLIC DOMAIN.***
*2. OR DIRECTLY TO **THOSE 20 SOURCES** AND WRITERS.*
   (THEIR COPYRIGHT STAYS INTACT).
3. AVOIDS A LEGAL CONFLICT OF PLAGIARISM.
4. DO SHOW THE SOURCES VIA THIS SOURCE NUMBER FORMAT.

34.2.0.1. VERBATIM QUOTES:
*OBVIOUSLY, IF YOU DO "QUOTE VERBATIM" ALWAYS USE **DOUBLE QUOTES**
(")AND A SOURCE NUMBER. SHOW THESE LISTINGS AT THE BACK OF THE
BOOK, NOT AT THE PAGE BOTTOM.*

*NOTE: YOU ARE PUBLISHING FICTION, NOT SCIENTIFIC JOURNALS OR
RESEARCH, WHICH HAVE A WHOLE NEW SET OF RULES.*

34.2.02. PUBLIC DOMAIN:
*SOURCES NOT COPYRIGHTED BUT APPEARING ON WEB SITES OR ON PUBLIC
REFERENCE SITES. I USE A SIMPLE RULE:*

CREATIVE WRITING—THE KELLY MANUAL OF STYLE

IF IT HAS AN AUTHOR, USE A SOURCE CODE. SHOW THE WEB PAGE / OR EMAIL ADDRESS AND DATE. (CONSIDER FREE USE / WEB MATERIAL AND NOT COPYRIGHTABLE BY YOU.

34.2.0 3. INTERNET SOURCES-COPIES- HOW TO INDEX:
IN THE CASE OF INTERNET, PRINTED MATERIAL, OR XEROX COPIES, I NOTE IN USUAL **SEQUENTIAL NUMBER ORDER** (1 TO 100) AND NUMBER THEM EVEN THOUGH I DON'T USE IT. I WRITE THE NUMBER ON THE TOP RIGHT CORNER AND KEEP MY SOURCE DOCUMENTS ALL TOGETHER. THUS, I CAN CHECK MY MATERIAL OR VERIFY, that I QUOTED CORRECTLY. IT ALSO HELPS TO **INDICATE WHAT TYPE OF format MATERIAL I HAVE: BOOKS, INTERNET, MAGAZINES, MAPS, DICTIONARY, REFERENCE BOOKS, ETC.**

34.2.0.4. MAPS-PICTURES-ILLUSTRATIONS:
ALSO, I TYPE THE SOURCE NUMBER ON THE BOTTOM OF EACH ILLUSTRATION, MAP OR PICTURE. FORMATS:
E.G. [MAP-1-PAGE]. [ILL-1-PAGE]. [PHOTO #-PAGE-].

34.3.0.0. ORGANIZING SOURCE LISTS:
34.3.0.1. WHY SOURCE LISTS?
BOTH SOURCE LISTS AND OTHER KEY ELEMENTS BRING ALL OF THIS INFORMATION TOGETHER, SO OUR BOOK CAN BE WRITTEN. A LITTLE ORGANIZATION SAVES TIME LATER.

34.3.0.2. GROUPING ALL MY RESEARCH INTO TWO LISTS:
1. FIRST DO SOURCE NUMBER LIST IN # ORDER).

[THEN, DO ADD A SORTING CODE BY SUBJECT AND SORT DATA INTO AN ALPHABETICAL LIST. –MODIFY-COPY/PASTE AS NECESSARY. SAVE IT. PRINT IT. THIS IS YOUR DRAFT UNTIL ALL RESEARCH IS COMPLETED. SAVE IT INTO A COMPUTER FOLDER: "RESEARCH- BOOK TITLE"].

2. SOURCE BY SUBJECT (ALPHABETICAL ORDER).

34.4.0.0. A SORT CODE EXAMPLE:
ORGANIZING OUR SOURCE DATE INTO GROUPINGS:
EXAMPLE: LET'S SAY YOU HAVE FOUR SOURCES ON ONE SUBJECT:

EGYPT: *MY SUBJECT IS **BROAD SORTED** IN EXCEL BY CODE: EG=EGYPT.*

THEN SOURCE #1: IS GEOGRAPHY/TERRAIN, SOURCE 2 IS A MAP. SOURCE 3 IS POLITICAL. SOURCE 4 IS TERRORISM.
THUS, MY ALPHABETICAL SOURCE LIST READS AS FOLLOWS:
EG01-GEOGRAPHY
EG02-MAPS
EG03-POLITICAL
EG04-TERRORISM

THUS, I HAVE ***FINE SORTED*** BY EGYPT, THEN INTO 4 GROUPS WITH **'EG0#'** BEING MY SORT CODE.

NOW, WE HAVE A WORKABLE SOURCE LIST WITH THE NUMBERS AND ARRANGED <u>ALPHABETICALLY</u>. THUS, THE TITLE, PUBLISHER AND AUTHOR ARE SECONDARY, NOT PRIMARY AS IN TRADITIONAL BIBLIOGRAPHY METHODS.

34.4.0.2. SORTING PREFIX:
*WITH A PREFIX TO SHOW SUBJECT, OR COUNTRY, OR PERIOD IN TIME, SOMETHING TO SEGREGATE THEM WITH. THEN ORGANIZE THEM INTO NUMERICAL ORDER. THIS WILL **HELP YOU TO LOCATE A SPECIFIC SOURCE QUICKER FOR YOUR CHAPTER BY CHAPTER SYNOPSIS.***
AS YOU FIND THEM, THUS WITH A PREFIX TO SHOW SUBJECT, OR COUNTRY, OR PERIOD IN TIME, SOMETHING TO SEGREGATE THEM WITH. THEN ORGANIZE THEM INTO NUMERICAL ORDER.

TIP USE THAT **ALPHABETICAL SORT KEY IN WORD**, HERE AND IN OUR SUBJECT INDEX IN THE REAR OF THE BOOK

34.5.0.0. GETTING STARTED:

I START WITH MY **NUMERICAL LIST 1 TO 100**, OR MORE AND COPY THAT INTO A SECOND LIST TO WHICH I ADD ALPHABETICAL SORTING WORDS: SUBJECT- PLACES- ETC. THEN USING THE COMPUTER ALPHA SORT BUTTON(IN WORD TOOLBAR) I AM ABLE TO CREATE AN ALPHA LIST BY **SORTING ON KEY WORDS**.
OF COURSE, I CLEAN IT UP, TWEAKING BY CATEGORY SO IT WORKS. THE AMAZING LARGE STACK OF BOOKS AND COPIES NOW HAS TWO LISTS ON TOP OF IT ALL. THE **NUMBER LIST** ORGANIZES THE PHOTO COPIES AND BOOKS INTO NEAT STACKS. THE **ALPHA LIST** HELPS PRIMARILY WHEN I BEGIN WRITING. AS I ADD THESE FACTS AND FIGURES TO MY BOOK I INDICATE MY CHAPTER NUMBER AND PAGE, NEXT TO THE SOURCE ITEM. THUS, I HAVE A **"REFINED LIST"** IF I WANTED TO REMOVE ITEMS I DID NOT USE OR SORT IT WITH A CODE.

ON THE **"SOURCE # PAGE"** (PLACED ON TOP OF MY SOURCE MATERIAL) I CAN PERUSE IT TO RELOCATE A PREVIOUS ARTICLE OR SUBJECT I WISH TO CHECK,

34.5.0. 2. TWO LIST OF REFERENCES-YEP A TIME SAVER! REASONS FOR:
YES, ONE LIST—(NUMERICAL ORDER) SUBJECT-LAST NAME OF AUTHOR-SOURCE-PAGES- FOR ALL MATERIAL I LOOK AT, BOOKS, VIDEOS, MUSIC, ART, TECHNOLOGY ETC.

34.5.0.3.
AND A SECOND IN "REFERENCE SUBJECT FORMAT" –SORTED BY KEY WORDS, FOR THE BOOK.
- THE FIRST IS SIMPLY AN INDEX TO FIND IT FASTER, AND THE SECOND BECOMES PART OF THE BOOK AND SHOWS UP IN MY
- GROUPING IS SO MUCH EASIER BY SUBJECT THAN BY THE BOOK TITLE OR AUTHOR. **IT IS THE CONTENT WE SEEK!**

-YES, TECHNICAL SOURCES OF DATA, QUOTES, OR FACTUAL DATA MUST ALWAYS BE REFERENCED, EVEN WHEN USED IN FICTION. IT KEEPS YOUR WRITING HONEST AND SOURCES QUOTED AT REAR OF BOOK.

34.6.0.0. NUMERICAL SOURCE LIST.

SOURCE NUMERICAL ORDER MERELY DEFINE A LIST OF RESEARCH OR SOURCE MATERIAL AS FOUND, THUS, IN ORDER 1 TO 100. THE NUMBER IS WRITTEN ON THE TOP RIGHT CORNER.

WE SORT OUR RESEARCH BY A NUMERICAL LIST AS WE FIND IT, WE DOCUMENT IT WITH A NUMBER, WHETHER WE USE IT OR NOT. THUS WE AVOID HAVING TO SORT AND FILE THIS UNREAD DATA.

34.6.0.1. THE FORMAT: (99-PP 14-16-PA 1-2)
(PARENTHESIS INDICATES FOOTNOTE)
(99=IS MY SOURCE NUMBER) (PP IS PAGES)
(- DASH P14 TO 16, PA FOR PARAGRAPH).

THE ACTUAL DETAIL TO THE SOURCE NUMBER IS WRITTEN IN THE BACK OF THE BOOK UNDER AN INDEX, CALLED "SOURCE NUMBERS."

THUS, I DO NOT DISTRACT THE READER TO REVIEW FOOTNOTES, AND DETAIL AT THE BOTTOM OF A PAGE, OR FLIP TO REAR OF BOOK, AND THIS ALLOWS ME TO QUOTE OR PARAPHRASE AND GIVE CREDIT TO THE ORIGINAL AUTHOR, OR MULTIPLE AUTHORS OR TO GIVE A SINGLE SOURCE CREDIT AFTER A PARAGRAPH.

34.7.0.2. EXAMPLE NUMERICAL ORDER:

HERE IS AN ACTUAL EXAMPLE USED IN MY BOOK: 1 TO 26 SOURCES:
"SPIES, THIEVES AND OTHER FRIENDS:"

FORMAT: SOURCE# & PAGE#: SEE EXAMPLE: (+1-P1)
SUBJECT CODES: **CRU: CRUSADER KNIGHTS, EG: EGYPT, IR: IRELAND, MAP: MAPS, PIR: PIRATES. 26 TOTAL**

1. **CRU:** CRUSADER KNIGHTS- INTERNET-IAN KAPLAN-

2. EG: EGYPT-**WORLD FACTBOOK-2004-"EGYPT" VIA INTERNET-9-15-04**

3. **CRU:** THE FOUNDATION OF THE ORDER OF KNIGHTS TEMPLAR-**VIA INTERNET-**
    MEDIEVAL SOURCE BOOK-C PAUL HALSALL-DEC 1977,
    HALSALL@MURRAY.FORDHAM.EDU.
    I USED AS REFERENCE TO CONFIRM DATA ELSEWHERE.
    COPY PERMITTED TEXTS.-SEE SOURCE MATERIAL.

4. EG: HELIOPOLIS: 1-1911 ENCYCLOPEDIA BRITANNICA.
5. EG: HELIOPOLIS-INTERNET-PP   DATE:
        WWW.FACT-INDEX.COM/H/HE/HELIOPOLIS.HTML

6. EG: HELIOPOLIS-INTERNET-9-13-04
        WWW.FREE-DEFINITION.COM/HELIOPOLIS.HTML

7. EG: HELIOPOLIS-INTERNET-9-13-04-PP1 OF 3

WWW.ANCIENTROUTE.COM/CITIES/HELIOPOLIS.HTML

8. EG: HELIOPOLIS/ON-INTERNET-PP1 OF 2-9-13-04
    HTTP://ICAAS.COM/E.O/HELIOPOLIS.HTM

9. EG: HELIOPOLIS-INTERNET-9-13-04, PP-0102.
    HTTP://ENCYCLOPEDIA.THE FREE DICTIONARY.COM/HELIOPOLIS

10. EG: THE ENNEAD (PESDJET) OF HELIOPOLIS-PART II-PASSION OF
    OSIRIS. INTERNET PP: 0103 DATE:9-13-04.
    WWW.PHILAE.NU/AKHET/ENNEAD2.HTML

11. EG: RE/RA-INTERNET-9-13-04, PP 0102.
    WWW. ANGELFIRE.COM/REALM/SHADES/EGYPT/RE.HTM

12. EG: THE STORY OF ISIS AND OSIRIS-INTERNET, PP:0106, DATE: 9-13-04
    WWW.TOUREGYPT.NET/HELIOGOD.HTML

13. MAP: INDONESIA-WORLD FACTBOOK-INTERNET (MAP)-8-16-04.
    WWW.CIA.GOV/CIA/PUBLICATIONS/FACTBOOK/GEOS/ID.HTML.

14. MAP: CYPRUS-THE WORLD FACTBOOK-INTERNET-8-16-04
    WWW.CIA-DITTO

15. MAP: CYPRUS/ PAPHOS: PHAPOS -INTERNET-8-16-04
    NO REFERENCE.

16. MAP: MALAYSIA-THE WORLD FACTBOOK-2004-INTERNET-8-16-04

17. MAP: MOROCCO-THE WORLD FACT BOOK-INTERNET-8-16-04

18. PIR: PIRATE-INTERNET- NO REFERENCE-8-11-04—CHPT18

19. .PIR: PIRACY TIMELINE-INTERNET-8-11-04-CHPT-18
        NO REFERENCE.

20. PIR: PIRACY-ALERT2-MARITIME SECURITY COUNCIL-INTERNET-8-11-
04-CHPT-18
    MSCALERT@MARITIMESECURITY.ORG

21. PIR: HISTORY OF PIRACY-KRZYSZTOF WILCYNSKI-INTERNET-8-11-04
    WWW.PIRATESINFO.COM/DETAIL/DETAIL.PHP?ARTICLE-ID=42.

22. .PIR: PIRATES-MALACCA STRAITS-INT'L CHAMBER OF COMMERCE-
    CRIME SERVICES-INTERNET-CHPT-18.
    ICC NEWS ARCHIVES.

23. .PIR: WOMEN PIRATES & PRIVATEERS-REAL & LEGENDARY-INTERNET-
    8-16-04 WWW.BEAGLEBAY.COM/WOMENPIRATESLIST.HTML

DO: COMPARE THIS NUMERICAL WITH THE
ALPHABETICAL LIST BELOW:

34.8.0.0. ALPHABETICAL SOURCE LIST:
BY TOPIC:

THE ALPHABETICAL ORDER: GIVES US A WAY TO GROUP LIKE SUBJECTS OR IDEAS TOGETHER. IT IS ORGANIZED BY SUBJECT TOPIC SO WE CAN RE-WRITE OUR PARAGRAPH AND FIX ANY ERRORS AND QUOTE SOURCES IN OUR FICTION BOOKS. (THEY APPEAR IN THE REAR INDICES AT BACK OF THE BOOK OR AT LEAST IN YOUR "NO COPYRIGHT CLAIM" AN AMENDMENT TO YOUR "ALL RIGHTS RESERVED.").

TRY SORTING THE TEN BOOKS BY **SUBJECT MATTER** ALPHABETICALLY... IS THIS MORE USEFUL AND FUNCTIONAL? DOES THE PUBLISHER MATTER (EXCEPT SCIENTIFIC DATA)? WHAT ABOUT THE SAME BOOK WITH TWO PUBLISHERS? DOES THE AUTHOR'S NAME GIVE A CLUE? IS HE THE "EXPERT?" IS THE DATA BETTER BY SUBJECT TYPE? MAKE A NEW LIST AGAIN ALPHABETICAL BY **IDEA GROUP.**

STEP BACK. WE HAVE SOURCE LIST BY NUMBER, 1 TO 100 AND AN ALPHABETICAL SUBJECT AND IDEA GROUPING. NOW, DO THIS FOR A 100 SOURCES FOR YOUR BOOK.

NOW, TAKE THE SAME DATA AND SORT BY **COUNTRY** AS AN EXAMPLE: FRENCH[FR], ENGLISH[EN], IRELAND[IR]. USE A CODE OF YOUR OWN. SUPPOSE YOU ARE RESEARCHING FIGHTER JETS FROM THREE NATIONS OR RIFLES FOR YOUR NOVEL. HOW DO GET ACCURATE DATA BY THE COUNTRY OR MANUFACTURER FROM JUST BIBLIOGRAPHIES? TOUGH ONE! ANSWER: ASSIGN OUR NEW CODE AND SORT AND ALPHABETIZE.

34.8.0.2. ALPHABETICAL SOURCE LISTS:
FORMAT-OUR THOUGHT PROCESS TO ORGANIZE IT:
SOURCE #- TITLE-WHERE IT CAME FROM-PAGES IN SERIES-DATE-INFORMATION-WHERE USED IN BOOK (CHAPTER #) IF USED.

EXAMPLE # 1: DO: SORT BY SUBJECT
34.8.0.3. ALPHABETICAL SORT BY SUBJECT:
GROUPING BY COUNTRY AND SORTED BY SUBJECT:

SOURCE #, PAGE NUMBER OR CHAPTER AS NOTED

BK: BOOKS: SOURCE#: 55,74,
BK: BOOK OF KELLS: SOURCE# 46,
BK: BOOK: CUMDACH: SOURCE#: 73,
BK: BOOK: THE TRINITY APOCALYPSE: SOURCE#: 45,
BK: BOOK: THE QUMRUM MANUSCRIPT: SOURCE# 55,
BK: BOOK: BOOK OF THEORIES: 86,

CH: CHINA: SOURCE#: 29,30,31,32,33,34,35,36,37,38,39,40,41,42,43,44,
CH: HONG KONG: SOURCE#: 31,36,38,41,42,43,
CH: KOWLOON: SOURCE#: 29,
CH: TANG: SOURCE#: 30,

CRU: CRUSADERS-KNIGHTS-SOURCE #: 1, 3,56, 57,58,60,61,62,65,71,91,92,93,

EG: CAIRO: SOURCE#: 84,
EG: CAIRO MUSEUM: SOURCE#: 84,
EG: EGYPT: SOURCE #: 2,10,11,12,52,83,84,85,102,
EG: HELIOPOLIS: SOURCE #: 4,5,6,7,8,9,10,52,103,
EG: NILE: SOURCE #: 85, 104
EG: RE: SOURCE#: 11,
EG: SPHINX: SOURCE#: 100, 102,

FR: LORRAINE: SOURCE#: 54,
HOLY: SOURCE#: 51,59,63, 64,75,87,
IR: IRELAND: SOURCE #:
IR: DUBLIN: SOURCE#: 47,
IR: HALL OF HEROES: SOURCE#: 80,
IR: KNIGHTS TEMPLAR: SOURCE#: 65
IR: TARA: SOURCE#: 68,79, 88,
IR: STONE OF DESTINY: SOURCE#: 69,

MA: MARCO POLO: SOURCE #: 106,
MAP: CHINA: KOWLOON: HONG KONG: SOURCE #: 29,31,
MAP: CYPRUS: SOURCE #:14,15,49,50,
MAP: EGYPT: SOURCE #:
MAP: INDONESIA: SOURCE#: 13,
MAP: MALAYSIA: SOURCE#: 16,
MAP: MOROCCO: SOURCE#: 17,
MAP: SAUDI ARABIA: SOURCE #: 67,72,

MO: MONGOL-GHENGIS KHAN: SOURCES#: 90,
PIR: PIRATES: SOURCE #: 18,19,20,21,22,23,24,25,26,27,
PY: PYRAMIDS: SOURCE#: 101,
VA: VATICAN: SOURCE#: 99,

THIS BEGINS MY SUBJECT LIST FOR CHAPTER BY CHAPTER.

34.10.0.0. EXAMPLE MUSIC- NUMBER FORMAT:
HERE IS AN ACTUAL EXAMPLE USE IN MY BOOK:
"SPIES, THIEVES AND OTHER FRIENDS:"

EXAMPLE: M1-PINK MARTINI ALBUM-P 20 C 2004.
ORDER ON CD-TITLE-TIME-PAGE 20 USED ON. DATE.

M1-1 LET'S NEVER STOP FALLING IN LOVE: 3:02,
M1-2 PINK MARTINI P C 2004.-P74
M1-3 HANG ON LITTLE TOMATO:3:15-
M1-5 VERONIQUE:3:17:-P101.
M1-6 DANSEZ-VOUS: 2:51:-
M1-8 AUTREFOIS:3:37-P
M1-9 U PLAVU ZORU   P. 256
M1-13 ASPETTAMI:3:35-P89.
M1-14-THE BLACK SWAN P255

MUSIC SOURCES ARE DONE THE SAME WAY EXCEPT FORMAT HAS "M":
DENOTING MUSIC:(M01-P1).

YOU DO USE MUSIC IN YOUR BOOKS, DON'T YOU? I HAVE USED A MUSIC TEMPO AND EVEN SUGGESTED MUSIC TO READ BY. EXAMPLE: INDIAN MUSIC/CHANTS WHILE WRITING ABOUT NORTH AMERICAN INDIANS. I LISTED THE MUSIC ON A MUSIC SOURCE LIST. LIKEWISE WITH MAPS, PHOTOS AND ILLUSTRATIONS.

34.8.0.0. CREATE A SUBJECT INDEX:

OUR MIND FOLLOWS ALPHA AND NUMERIC CODES VERY EASILY. SEE EXAMPLES NOW, HERE IS A LONG ONE, CONSIDER THE 'SUBJECT INDEX' **AT THE REAR OF THIS BOOK**. IF YOU HAD TO DO THEM FOR YOUR BOOKS, YOU WILL READILY AGREE—IT IS CUMBERSOME, SORTING ALMOST IMPOSSIBLE AND SOME OF THE TEN BOOKS WE SELECTED IN OUR EXERCISE HAVE TOPICS OTHERS DON'T. SORT THEM ONTO A NEW WORD DOCUMENT, ALPHABETIZE THEM.

34.8.0.2. COMPUTER SORT METHOD:

AH! HA! NUMBERS SORT FIRST, THEN SYMBOLS THE LETTERS. WE FIX, DISCARD AND RE-SORT. NOW WE HAVE A WORKABLE **SUBJECT INDEX** FOR OUR BOOK.

34.9.0.0. OUR PROGRESS:

1. WE ORGANIZED OUR RESEARCH AND IDEAS INTO GROUPS.
2. WE FOUND COMMON SORT GROUPS.
3. WE FOUND SOME COMMON IDEAS FOR OUR CHAPTER BY CHAPTER TOPICS.
4. WE FOUND SOME STORY TOPICS TO ADD DETAIL TO OUR STORY.
5. WE FOUND WHERE TO ADD MUSIC AND THEIR SOURCE LISTING.
6. WE FOUND A SIMPLE FOOTNOTE CODING AND REFERENCE LISTS.
7. WE DISCARDED THE BIBLIOGRAPHY METHOD.

CHAPTER 35
35.0.0. SOLUTIONS TO A WRITER'S PROBLEMS:
CHAPTER TOPICS:
BAD WRITING
BAD SENTENCES
BAD PARAGRAPHS
BAD STORIES
CHARACTERS
CHOICE OF GENRE-MIXING AND MATCHING
COMPUTER FILES
EDITING
EXPERIENCE
IDEAS PAGE
ORGANIZATION-BOOK-SPACE-WORK IN PROGRESS-
PUBLISHER'S IDEA OF ORG.
PAGE FRIGHT?
PROOFREADING
PUNCTUATIONS
RESEARCH
SPEED
TIME
TOO MANY PROJECTS
WRITER'S BLOCK?

35.1.0. 0. HOW TO ERASE WRITER'S BLOCK:
THERE ARE THREE SIDES TO OUR WRITING: PHYSICAL, MENTAL AND
EMOTIONAL AND ALL SHOULD BE IN TUNE; THUS ALLOWING US THE
QUIET TIME TO LIVE OUR WRITING.

WE HAVE THE PHYSICAL SIDE:
WE HAVE THE TIME, A GOOD WRITING PLACE, OFFICE EQUIPMENT, BOOK
PLAN, IDEAS PAGE, THREE SYNOPSES AND THE PHYSICAL PAINS OF
BACKACHE OR ARTHRITIS OR EYESIGHT. KEEP A GOOD HEALTH REGIME
AND REDUCE THE ALCOHOL AND DRUGS. WE WRITERS SIT TOO LONG TO
WRITE OR TYPE. GET UP AND PACE. WALK THE DOG FOR 20 MINUTES. EAT
HEALTHY, DRINK REASONABLY. USE THE RECLINER TO EDIT. CHANGE
OUR POSTURE. RAISE THAT MONITOR TO EASE OUR EYES STRAIN.

35.1.2.0. THE EMOTIONS:
CLEAR OUR HEADS. SET ASIDE THE BILLS, THE INTERRUPTIONS, THE
PHONE CALLS SEEK OUT THAT QUIET SPACE ---ITS OUR TIME TO WRITE.
KEEP THE SCHEDULE. MAKE BLOCKS OF TIME FOR OTHER THINGS.
NAGGING TASKS OR UNDONE THINGS CREEP INTO OUR THOUGHTS
WHILE WE ARE WRITING. SOME THINGS ARE ALWAYS PRESSING. IT'S
SNOWING…WE MUST SHOVEL, THE GRASS NEEDS CUTTING, A HAIRCUT,
GO TO STORE, OR THE HARDWARE. SET ASIDE SOME **CHORE TIME** THEN
DO IT. DID WE DO A "TO DO" LIST AND OUR WRITING TIME PLAN?

IF YOU ARE MORE CREATIVE IN THE MORNING…WRITE THEN. KEEP
THAT <u>LITTLE SPIRAL BINDER</u> OR JOURNAL IN THE CAR, WRITE DOWN
THAT IDEA. I USE A LOT OF <u>POST-IT NOTES</u> AND KEEP THEM ON MY DESK
UNTIL I ADD THEM TO MY IDEAS LIST OR FIX SOMETHING IN MY WRITING
I FORGOT.

CREATIVE WRITING—THE KELLY MANUAL OF STYLE

IF YOU ARE UPSET...DON'T WRITE, DO SOMETHING PHYSICAL. CLEAN THE OFFICE, FILL THE PRINTER WITH PAPER, TAKE A WALK. GIVE YOURSELF TIME TO THINK A PROBLEM THROUGH. TALK TO YOUR MATE OR BEST FRIEND. MAKE A PLAN, WRITE A CHECK, MAIL A LETTER THOSE ARE "CLOSING ISSUES." **YES! YOU ACCOMPLISHED SOMETHING.**

FRUSTRATIONS: WRITING IS COMPLEX AND TAKES A LOT OF HOURS TO COMPLETE. IT IS NOT INSTANT SATISFACTION OR GRATIFICATION. WE ACCOMPLISH IT PAGE BY PAGE OR CHAPTER BY CHAPTER. FORWARD PROGRESS COMES IN MANY SMALL STEPS. WRITE DOWN SOME SIMPLE GOALS FOR TODAY.

ANSWER:
HOW MUCH TIME DO I HAVE AND WHAT CAN I ACCOMPLISH TODAY?

REMOVE YOUR RESTRICTIONS: DON'T SET BOUNDARIES OR RULES, SUCH AS, "I MUST FINISH THIS, OR I HAVE ONLY SO MUCH TIME, OR I'LL NEVER FINISH THIS ON TIME." ALLOW YOURSELF THE FREEDOM TO WRITE ANYTHING, ANYTIME AND ANYWHERE.

35.1.3.0. MENTAL HEALTH:
SET REALISTIC GOALS IN YOUR PERSONAL LIFE AND WRITER'S LIFE IS THE KEY. REDUCE OR REMOVE THE OBSTACLES.
MOST WRITERS CAN ALSO IDENTIFY WITH YOU. THE DAY JOB IS DEMANDING AND OUR WRITING IS DEMANDING IN TIME, MONEY AND OUR EMOTIONS THE REST OF THE TIME. **WE POUR OUR LIVES INTO OUR WRITING.** SO BE PATIENT WITH YOURSELF AND YOUR TIME.

PRACTICE PROBLEM SOLVING AND PERFORM PUTTING THINGS INTO BLOCKS. HANDLE ONE BLOCK AT A TIME. HANDLE OUR FINANCES, OUR FAMILY, OUR HEALTH, OUR SPOUSE AND OUR OWN WELL-BEING ONE STEP AT A TIME. TAKE THOSE VITAMINS, EXERCISE, GO OUT TO DINNER, HAVE A SMALL DINNER DRINK. TELL A JOKE. DO SOMETHING ABOUT OUR STRESS. ABOVE ALL, KEEP PROBLEMS IN PERSPECTIVE.

CLEAN UP OUR ACT. DRESS NICE. COMPLIMENT SOMEONE.
DO SOMETHING NICE FOR SOMEONE. MAKE A SMALL DONATION.
BOTTOM LINE IS WE FEEL BETTER ABOUT OURSELVES AND OTHERS. WE TAKE PRIDE AND FEEL THE SMALL STEPS ARE GETTING US SOMEWHERE. **WE WRITERS WRITE FROM THE HEART**. WHEN WE PUT IT ON PAPER WE CONNECT WITH THE EMOTIONS THE PAIN AND EXPERIENCE THAT EVENT OVER AND OVER AS WE READ IT. INSIDE EACH OF US IS PASSION--- PASSION TO WRITE AND TO FEEL. WE BRING THAT PASSION TO OUR WRITING. ONLY THEN, DOES OUR READER CONNECT WITH US. PASSION CAN BE HEART FELT OR BOLD AND DIRECT OR SUBLIMINAL. PASSION CAN BE THUNDEROUS WAVES OR A GENTLE TIDE KISSING THE SHORE OR BOTH.

35.1.4.0. OUR WRITING IS LIKE A LOVE LETTER. WE WRITE IT FEELING GOOD; THEN THINGS GO WRONG, THAT'S LIFE.
NOT ALWAYS PERFECT. IT IS OUR CLIMAX OR OUR TRAGEDY WE FEEL OR EXPERIENCE IT AND AS A RESULT WE CAN WRITE ABOUT IT; BECAUSE WE FEEL IT. WE **CAPTURE LIFE IN OUR WORDS**, OUR FIGURES OF

CREATIVE WRITING—THE KELLY MANUAL OF STYLE

SPEECH AND DIALOGUE. WE CANNOT CROSS THESE OVER INTO OUR REAL LIFE OR REAL LIFE'S PROBLEMS. WE WEAR A DIFFERENT HAT!

WE PUT THOSE SAME EMOTIONS AND MENTAL STATES INTO OUR WRITING...IT HELPS US TO UNDERSTAND. OUR READER DOES KNOW US FROM ADAM, DICK OR JANE. BUT, THEY EMPATHIZE WITH US. THEY CONNECT TO US.

BILLIONS OF PEOPLE LIKE US HAVE THOSE SAME PROBLEMS. ACTORS ACT THEM OUT, WRITERS WRITE, AND MUSICIANS SING AND PLAY. PART OF WHAT WE SEEK FROM OUR WRITING IS RELIEF FROM PAIN, HAPPINESS FROM SUCCESS AND TEARS FOR SAD THINGS. WE CONTROL A LOT OF THOSE THINGS IN WRITING.

HOWEVER, REAL LIFE IS IN CONTROL; BUT MANAGEABLE. REAL LIFE BUILDS WALLS. WE EITHER PAINT THEM OR GO AROUND THEM AND PAINT THEM A DIFFERENT COLOR WITH OUR WORDS. BOTTOM LINE IS TO EXPECT PROBLEMS, PLAN FOR THEM IF POSSIBLE, MANAGE THEM AND RESOLVE AS YOU CAN.

LAST, THINK ABOUT WHY YOU WRITE. WHAT IS WRITING TO YOU? IS WRITING ON YOUR BUCKET LIST? IS WRITING BECAUSE YOU HAVE A GREAT STORY? DO YOU WANT TO WRITE ONLY ONE BOOK? OR A COLLECTION? IS IT A PROFESSION FOR YOU? HAVE YOU TRIED OTHER TYPES OF WRITING...NEWS, MAGAZINE, SHORT STORIES, NON-FICTION, BUSINESS, BLOGGING, POEMS, ETC.? ALL CAN BE INCLUDED IN YOUR BOOK.

THERE ARE AS MANY WAYS TO DEAL WITH WRITER'S BLOCK AS THERE ARE CAUSES. **TRYING SOMETHING NEW IS THE FIRST STEP TOWARD WRITING AGAIN.**

35.2.0.0. IMPLEMENT A WRITING SCHEDULE.
CARVE OUT **TIME** TO WRITE AND THEN IGNORE THE WRITER'S BLOCK. SHOW UP TO WRITE, EVEN IF NOTHING COMES RIGHT AWAY. WHEN YOUR BODY SHOWS UP TO THE PAGE AT THE SAME TIME AND PLACE EVERY DAY, EVENTUALLY YOUR MIND -- AND YOUR MUSE -- WILL DO THE SAME. GRAHAM GREENE FAMOUSLY WROTE 500 WORDS, AND ONLY 500 WORDS, EVERY MORNING. FIVE HUNDRED WORDS IS ONLY ABOUT A PAGE, BUT WITH THOSE MERE **500 WORDS PER DAY**, GREENE WROTE AND PUBLISHED OVER 30 BOOKS.

35.3.0.0. DON'T BE TOO HARD ON YOURSELF.
IN FACT, DON'T BE HARD ON YOURSELF AT ALL WHILE WRITING. MANY WRITER'S GET BLOCKED NOT BECAUSE THEY CAN'T WRITE, BUT BECAUSE THEY DESPAIR OF **WRITING ELOQUENTLY**."

> **X---DO TURN OFF THE CRITICAL BRAIN; THERE IS A TIME AND PLACE FOR CRITICISM, IT'S CALLED FINAL EDITING OF THE MANUSCRIPT**[CH 36].

35.4.0.0. . THINK OF WRITING AS A REGULAR JOB; WE ARE A WRITER OF SOME GENRE':

CREATIVE WRITING—THE KELLY MANUAL OF STYLE

TRY LINKING WRITING TO A TO PHYSICAL WORK OR JOB. IF WE THINK OF OURSELVES AS A SIMPLE ARTIST OR CRAFTSMEN, IT'S EASIER TO SIT DOWN AND WRITE. WE ARE JUST PUTTING WORDS ON THE PAGE. WE'RE JUST CREATING THINGS -- STORIES, POEMS, OR PLAYS -- ONLY WE USE VOCABULARY, GRAMMAR AND FIGURES OF SPEECH INSTEAD OF BRICKS AND MORTAR.

35.5.0.0. TAKE TIME OFF IF YOU'VE JUST FINISHED A PROJECT.
WRITER'S BLOCK COULD BE A SIGN THAT YOUR IDEAS NEED TIME TO REST. RESTING CAN BE A KEY PART OF YOUR CREATIVE PROCESS. GIVE YOURSELF TIME TO GATHER NEW EXPERIENCES AND NEW IDEAS, FROM LIFE, READING OR OTHER FORMS OF ART, BEFORE YOU START AGAIN. I WOULD OFTEN FALL ASLEEP WHILE EDITING, MY AFTERNOON NAP. IT WAS GOOD! I AWOKE REFRESHED AND HIT IT AGAIN. OFTEN I WOULD DO RESEARCH TO HELP WITH INSPIRATION OR TO SEEK OUT NEW IDEAS. THE PROCESS AND THE WRITING THEM DOWN GAVE ME A SENSE OF FINISHING.

35.6.0.0. SET DEADLINES AND KEEP THEM.
MANY WRITERS, UNDERSTANDABLY, HAVE TROUBLE DOING THIS ON THEIR OWN. YOU MIGHT FIND A WRITING PARTNER AND AGREE TO HOLD EACH OTHER TO DEADLINES IN AN ENCOURAGING, NON-CRITICAL WAY. KNOWING THAT SOMEONE ELSE IS EXPECTING RESULTS HELPS MANY WRITERS PRODUCE MATERIAL. WRITING GROUPS OR **CLASSES** ARE ANOTHER GOOD WAY TO JUMP-START A WRITING ROUTINE. ESPECIALLY RECOMMENDED IF YOU HAVE TROUBLE WITH THE BASICS OR CANNOT WRITE AT ALL. KEEP DEADLINES TO A MINIMUM, **WRITE BECAUSE YOU NOT ONLY WANT TO; BUT NEED TO.**

35.7.0.0. EXAMINE ISSUES OR PLACES BEHIND YOUR WRITER'S BLOCK. PREPARE YOUR ENVIRONMENT AND FOR YOUR PHYSICAL NEEDS. FIND A QUIET SPACE. DAYDREAM.
DO RE-VISIT YOUR IDEAS PAGE-DO SOME RESEARCH- DO SOMETHING FUN-BEGIN WITH SMALL WRITING TASKS. ORGANIZE- CLEAN YOUR SPACE-ALPHABETIZE YOUR IDEAS INTO GROUPS.

35.8.0.0. CONFINING STRUCTURE-SPACE:
VISIT YOUR WRITING STRUCTURE-IT MAYBE TOO CONFINING. DISCARD THE OUTLINE. SAVE THE DRAFT YOU LOST INTEREST IN. **WRITE SOMETHING ELSE.**

WRITE ABOUT YOUR ANXIETIES REGARDING WRITING OR CREATIVITY. TALK TO A FRIEND, PREFERABLY ONE WHO WRITES. BOOKS, SUCH AS '*THE ARTIST'S WAY*,' ARE DESIGNED TO HELP CREATIVE PEOPLE EXPLORE THE ROOT CAUSES OF THEIR BLOCKS. OR TRY STUDYING THE LIVES OF OTHER WRITERS AND THE MASTERS [CH 28]. YOU WILL FIND THEY WERE HUMAN; MANY HAD PROBLEMS AND **DAY JOBS**.

35.9.0.0. MULTIPLE PROJECTS:
WORK ON MORE THAN ONE PROJECT AT A TIME.
SOME WRITERS FIND IT HELPFUL TO SWITCH BACK AND FORTH FROM ONE PROJECT TO ANOTHER. WHETHER THIS MINIMIZES FEAR OR BOREDOM, OR BOTH, IT SEEMS TO PREVENT WRITER'S BLOCK FOR MANY PEOPLE. FOR EXAMPLE, I HAVE THREE SEPARATE NOVELS PENDING AT THE SAME TIME. ONE NEEDS MORE RESEARCH. ONE NEEDS MORE CHARACTER DETAILS. ONE NEEDS THE BRIDGE TO THE NEXT CHAPTER.

I RE-READ THE LAST FEW CHAPTERS AND JOT DOWN A FEW IDEAS, THEN WRITE IT AFTER I FINISHED READING ALOUD THE LAST CHAPTER.

35.10.0.0. TRY WRITING EXERCISES. [RE-VISIT CHAPTER 3].
WRITING EXERCISES CAN LOOSEN UP THE LOG JAM AND GET YOU TO WRITE THINGS YOU WOULD NEVER WRITE ABOUT OTHERWISE. IF NOTHING ELSE, THEY GET WORDS ON THE PAGE AND SOME OF IT IS BOUND TO BE GOOD. DO THE CLASS LESSONS AND EXERCISES, MAYBE YOU WILL IMPROVE YOUR STYLE. TRY SOMETHING NEW. WRITE A DIFFERENT KIND OF NOVEL THIS TIME. MAYBE YOU ARE IN A RUT AND NEED A NEW EXPERIENCE AND A NEW CHALLENGE?

35.11.0.0. RE-CONSIDER YOUR WRITING SPACE.
ARE YOUR DESK AND CHAIR COMFORTABLE? IS YOUR SPACE WELL-LIT? WOULD IT HELP TO TRY WRITING IN A COFFEE SHOP/ LIBRARY/PATIO FOR A CHANGE?   THINK ABOUT HOW YOU CAN CREATE **YOUR UNIVERSE** YOU'LL LOOK FORWARD TO BEING IN IT.

35.12.0.0. REMEMBER WHY YOU STARTED TO WRITE IN THE FIRST PLACE.
LOOK AT WHAT YOU'RE WRITING AND WHY. ARE YOU **WRITING WHAT YOU LOVE**, OR WHAT YOU THINK YOU SHOULD BE WRITING? THE WRITING THAT FEELS MOST LIKE PLAY WILL END UP DELIGHTING YOU THE MOST AND THIS IS THE WRITING YOUR READERS WILL INSTINCTIVELY CONNECT WITH. AT THE END OF THE DAY, WRITING [NOVELS] IS TOO COMPLEX TO DO IT FOR ANY OTHER REASON. CONNECT WITH THE **FIRST JOY** YOU FIRST FELT IN WRITING, IT WILL MOTIVATE YOU.

> **DO:FRAME THAT FIRST BOOK, SIGN IT INSIDE THE COVER.**
> **DO: FRAME THAT FIRST BUCK YOU EARNED ON THAT**
> **ROYALTY CHECK.**

35.13.00. STILL STUCK?
DOES WRITING IN ALL OF ITS FORMS....GET UNSTUCK?-----
TRY POETRY, OR SONGS, OR MAKE A WHOLE LIST OF IDEAS OF UNRELATED ITEMS ...OR LOOK AROUND, THE PEOPLE, PLACES AND EVEN THE BUS STOP OR MALL... WRITE ABOUT WHAT YOU SEE, OR CAN MAKE-UP, IMAGINE OR EVEN BETTER **WRITE ABOUT WHAT YOU KNOW BEST.**

WRITE ABOUT FEELINGS, SENSES, EVENTS TIMES IN HISTORY, COMBINE YOUR INTERESTS INTO SOMETHING THE READER WOULD LIKE TO KNOW. PICK ANY SUBJECT---- IT WILL FIT SOMEWHERE INTO ALMOST ANY STORY. IN ONE BOOK, I USED MUSIC AS THE "MOOD" SETTER AND ACTUALLY LISTENED TO THE MUSIC AS I WROTE. ART CAME INTO PLAY ON THE DIALOGUE ABOUT A "PICTURE" AND THE FIGURE WITHIN A PICTURE, ACTUALLY DEEPENED THE STORYTELLING. (IMAGERY).

PRACTICE WRITING EACH DAY IF YOU CAN...IT GETS EASIER TO PUT IT ALL TOGETHER INTO A PARAGRAPH A PAGE, A CHAPTER...THEN, FINALLY ITS A STORY DRAFT.

35.14.0.0. VISIT THE IDEA LIST OR IDEA FILE OR CLIP FILE!
THIS IS YOUR LIFEBLOOD OF IDEAS TO START TO WRITE WITH.
[DO: REVIEW CHAPTERS 5-9-28-41].

35.15.0.0. IF YOU ARE STILL STUCK BEGIN WITH
 DO **WRITE BOTH IDEA LISTS** [CH 5-41].
DO WRITE THREE SYNOPSES! [REFER TO CHAPTERS 6 TO 9].
DO WRITE CHAPTER BY CHAPTER TOPICS LIST. [CH 9].

35.16.0.0. OUR PROGRESS:
1. THE CHARACTER LIST AND SYNOPSIS 3=CHAPTER BY CHAPTER TOPICS IS WHAT WE WRITE FIRST, THEN ADD TO, AND EDIT THROUGHOUT TO CREATE OUR ROUGH DRAFT.

2. REFER TO CHAPTER 38 AS TO WHY WE USED THIS FORMAT WHEN WRITING OUR BEST SELLER.

3. WE LEARNED THAT WRITER'S BLOCK IS A COMMON EFFECT AND CAUSED BY MANY THINGS.

4. WE CAN OVERCOME IT.

5. WE THINK ABOUT WRITING AS A JOB.

CHAPTER 36
36.0.0.0.   FINAL MANUSCRIPT
CHECKLIST & COMPARISON TO GRAND MASTERS:
TOPICS: *MANUSCRIPT-CHECKLIST-*

36.0.1.0. BOOK MANUSCRIPT:
THE BOOK DRAFT HAS BEEN COMPLETED. NOW THE POLISHING,
ILLUMINATION AND WORD CHOICE IS COMPLETED. A FINAL REVIEW AND
MULTIPLE EDITS NEEDS COMPLETED. OPENING CHAPTER PARAGRAPHS
AND CLOSING SENTENCES ARE REVIEWED. PLOTS AND CLIMAXES ARE
POLISHED.(SHOW BUT NOT TELL). STORY CONTINUITY IS CHECKED. LOOK
FOR HOLES. WHAT HAPPENS TO MINOR AND SUPPORTING CHARACTERS?
DOES THE CLIMAXES (6 KINDS) RISE THE STORY?

36.0.2.0. THE FINAL BOOK-THE BEST SELLER:
NOW THE FINAL BOOK IS GIVEN A LITTLE TIME SO THAT **FRESH EYES**
CATCH THE GLITCHES, THE TYPOS, THE 'SPELL CHECK' ITEMS MISSED.
READ THIS ALOUD TO CATCH DRAGGING SENTENCES AND HALTS TO
FLOW. IF A REPETITIVE PROBLEMS SURFACES FIX ALL OF THEM IN THE
BOOK FIRST, THEN REPRINT AS NECESSARY.

36.0.3.0. THE FINAL BOOK MIGHT HAVE 4 TO 10 REVISIONS.
THIS IS TEDIOUS BUT IMPORTANT WORK. REMEMBER: AT THE END, NO
REGRETS, IT MUST BE RIGHT…AND ONLY YOU CAN DECIDE. YOU WILL
PROBABLY FEEL MIXED FEELINGS…SO MUCH WORK…THEN YOU CAST IT
OUT! IT IS DONE!

OKAY BREATHE…GIVE IT SOME MORE TIME. YOU HAVE ONE MORE
CHANCE TO IMPROVE IT UNTIL YOU FINALIZE IT FOR THE HOUSE
PUBLISHER OR PRINT ON DEMAND PUBLISHER (CHECKING THE PAGE FOR
HANGING SENTENCES, BREAKS BETWEEN COPY, WHITE SPACE).

THE FINAL CHECK: *CAN YOU SAY AH HA?*
STILL, ONLY YOU HAVE THE POWER TO SAY WHEN!

36.0.4.0. CHECK LIST & REVIEW FOR SUCCESS:
DO USE A COPY OF YOUR MANUSCRIPT TO PERFORM THIS ABSOLUTELY
FINAL EDIT AND CHECK LIST REVIEW. IF ANY FAIL, RE-WRITE, ADD,
DELETE OR CHANGE IT.

THIS IS YOUR LAST CHANCE FOR A BEST SELLER SUCCESS!
 **DO WRITE THESE CODES IN THE LEFT MARGIN AND KEEP A RUNNING
TOTAL OF THESE ITEMS.**

FINAL MANUSCRIPT CHECKLIST:

CODE	ACTION	EXAMPLE
AE	ACTION ERROR	
AGE	AGE	CLOTHING -VEHICLES DON'T MATCH TIME
AI	AUTHOR INTRUSION	
ART	ART WORK & TITLE AGREE	
BANT	BANTER-CONVERSATION-NEEDS HELP	BETWEEN HERO & VILLAIN-SUPPORTING
BC	BACK COVER	
BR	BRIDGE MISSING	
CAPS	CAPITAL LETTERS NEEDED	
CHAR	CHARACTER ERROR	
CLICHÉ'	A SAYING FROM ANOTHER TIME	
CLIMX	RISING CLIMAX	
CLIMD	CLIMAX DENOUEMENT-DOWN	
COMP	COMPUTER	SCREEN-PRINTOUT-WALL DISPLAY-PDA
COMP	COMPARE TO COMPETITION	
CONC	CONCLUSION WRONG	
CONF	CONFUSING-REWRITE	
COV	BOOK COVER	
CT	CHARACTER'S THOUGHTS	ITALIC FONT
DARK	HOLE-TUNNEL-PIT-GRAVE-BOX-NIGHT	
DARKC	DARK CHARACTER	
DE	DRAMA ERROR	DRAMA OR EVENT CONFUSED STORY
DIAL	DIALOGUE	
DRAFT	ROUGH DRAFT	
ED	EDIT-RE-WRITE	
EOC	END OF CHARACTER	
EXPERT	SCIENTIST-PRO WITNESS-MORTICIAN	
FB	FLASH BACK-HOW MANY?	
FF	FLASH FORWARD-HOW MANY?	
FONT	FONT SIZE	
GRAM	GRAMMAR	
HATE	READER WILL HATE PAGES	
HM	HEART METER-need lots	EMOTIONS-SAVING LIVES-INSPIRATION
HOL	HOLE IN STORY	
HOOK	CONVINCE READER TO READ ON	
HSTOP	HEART STOP	LIFE'S TRAGEDY-DEATH-SUICIDE-

		MURDER-EMOTIONS-SENSES-TEARS.
HU	HUMOR. QTY---?	
ILL	ILLUMINATE- HOW MANY?	
KERN	KERNEL- MAIN BOOK IDEA	
LANG	LANGUAGE-DIALECT-THOUGHTS	
LIKE	READER WILL LIKE PAGES	
LIST	MAKE LIST	
LITE	LIGHTS	
MARK	MARKETING MESSAGE UNCLEAR	
MED	MEDIA USAGE	TV-RADIO-NEWSPAPER- WEB-TELEGRAM
MIN C	MINOR CHARACTER	
P	PARAGRAPH, MAKE	
PC	PHONE CALL	
PE	PLOT ERROR-SEQUENCE	
PUNC	MARK TYPE NEEDED	
RP	RESOLVE PREDICAMENT	RESOLVE HERO'S PREDICAMENT
RES	RESEARCH	RESEARCH INCOMPLETE
REW	RE-WRITE	
SCEN	SCENE EVENT	
SCK	SPELL CHECK	
SET	SETTING-PLACE	
SEX	SEX SCENE	EROTIC-VOYEUR-TEASE-PURE LOVE-
SOUR	SOURCE OR LIST OMITTED	
SP	SPACE NEEDED-WHITE SPACE	
ST	SUPPORTING THEME	MAJOR-MINOR?
STELL	STORYTELLER	STORYT. INTRODUCED-STORY TAKES OVER
SUP C	SUPPORTING CHARACTER TO MAJOR	
SYN	SYNOPSIS DOESN'T MATCH	
TWISTS	PLOT TWISTS--HOW MANY?	
TYPO	TYPO ERROR	SPELL CK MISSED
UNB	UNBELIEVABLE FOR READER	NEEDS MORE EXPLANATION
UNIV	UNIVERSAL THEME-HOW MANY	
VERB	VERB TENSE	
WU	WORD USAGE ?	CK DICTIONARY OR GARNERS USAGE

37.0.0.0. YOUR WRITER'S UNIVERSE:
CHAPTER TOPICS:
*TO BE OR NOT-MY UNIVERSE-MY SPACE-BLOCKS OF TIME-TIME
MANAGEMENT-REALITY-LIVING LIFE-CREATIVE SPACE- TOOLS OF THE
TRADE. HOW TO SET THE STAGE AND GET READY TO WRITE.*

37.1.0. 0. TO BE OR NOT TO BE:
YOUR SUCCESS AS WRITER-EDITOR ETC DEPENDS ON YOUR
ENVIRONMENT, YOUR UNIVERSE, YOUR CREATIVITY AND YOUR
PERSEVERANCE!

...THUS, TO BE A WRITER OR NOT TO BE... CONSIDER:

37.1.1.0. CREATE A WRITING ENVIRONMENT
 OF QUIET, COMFORT, AND A WORK SPACE IN ONE.
-CREATE AN ENVIRONMENT SHIELDED FROM DAY TO DAY. NOT QUITE
SOLITARY BUT BRIGHT AND AIRY. A WINDOW HELPS-IT'S MY THINKING
SPACE.

37.1.2 0. THE WRITER'S UNIVERSE:
IS BOTH ONE OF QUIET, SOLITARY AND YET
WHERE EVENTS CAN HAPPEN OR WHERE THE WRITER CAN PARTICIPATE
IN EVENTS GOING AROUND HIM/HER.
EXAMPLE: WEB, NEWS, RADIO, NEWSPAPER, MAGAZINE ARTICLES,
TRAVEL JOURNALS.

37.1.2.1 DEFINE YOUR SPACE:
 - YOUR LISTENING TO RADIO WHILE WORKING, AN EVENT HAPPENS
WHICH APPLIES TO YOUR RESEARCH OR WRITING OR EDITING
(CHANGES YOUR FACTS OR A NEW REVELATION, OR HISTORY MAKING).
EXAMPLE: A NEWSPAPER ARTICLE CONFIRMS WHAT YOU WROTE
ABOUT...THEREFORE, ATTRIBUTE THE SOURCE # OR CONFIRM FACTS.
CLIP ARTICLES.

37.1.2.2 DEFINE THE USE OF YOUR SPACE:
- YOUR STUDIO, BE IT: A ROOM, A BASEMENT ROOM, A GARAGE, A DECK,
A PATIO, A BARN, A POOL AREA CAN BE CONDUCIVE TO WRITING OR
EDITING BUT MAYBE NOT TO HEAVY THINKING.

- CHOOSE AN AREA WHERE YOU ARE COMFORTABLE DOING THAT
SPECIFIC FUNCTION IN.
FOR EXAMPLE: I GENERALLY WRITE IN THE STUDIO OR ON THE REAR
DECK IF QUIET. I LIKE TO EDIT IN THE SUNSHINE AND EVEN REVIEW
RESEARCH. THE IDEA IS TWO SEPARATE ENVIRONMENTS FOR TWO
FUNCTIONS.

37.1.3. 0. WORK SPACE AS AN ENVIRONMENT:
- CREATE A WORKSPACE THAT IS ORGANIZED AND
 CAPABLE OF MULTI-TASKING:

CREATIVE WRITING—THE KELLY MANUAL OF STYLE

- CREATE AN ACTUAL WORKSPACE.
- HAVE AN ENVIRONMENT CONDUCIVE TO WRITING
  TASKS: PRINTING, KEEPING FILES, RESEARCH. A PLACE
  FOR A COFFEE CUP, A CUP WARMER, A SNACK, AND GOOD
  LIGHTING. CREATE A SPACE AWAY FROM THE PHONE AND NOISE

37.1.3.1. ORGANIZE YOUR SPACE TO QUICKLY FIND THINGS LIKE
DICTIONARY, EDITING PENS (TWO DIFFERENT COLORS), YOUR
NOTEBOOK, CARDBOARD BOX FOR THROWING OLDER CHAPTERS.
HINT: SITTING HELPS THE DISCIPLINE, PACING GETS DISTRACTING.

37.1.4. 0. WORK SPACE: MY LITTLE UNIVERSE:
- MAKE IT A CREATIVE AREA:
- CALL IT A WORK SPACE OR AS I LIKE TO CALL IT, DREAMLAND,
  MANUSCRIPT ROW, OR MY CAVE.
- EXAMPLE: SIZE OF SPACE COUNTS:
- MY SPACE IS 11' X 12' AND CONTAINS AN "L" SHAPE COMPUTER
  DESK, A MEN'S ARMOIRE-STORAGE, AN L SHAPED 8' DRAFTING
  TABLE WITH DESK FOR MAPS AND ARTWORK, TWO 48" HIGH
  BOOK CASES, A PRINTER STAND, A SMALL SUPPLY CABINET, A
  COMPUTER WITH PRINTER, SPEAKERS, FLAT SCREEN MONITOR,
  AN OFFICE CHAIR, RADIO-CD PLAYER. A THREE HOLE ELECTRIC
  PUNCH, & REFERENCE BOOKS ON BOOK CASE SHELF.

1. CLEAN THE OFFICE AND ARRANGE THINGS INTO PILES
2. PUT ALL SUPPLIES IN ONE PLACE-CABINET-DRAWER-ETC.
3. STACK SOURCE DOCUMENTS AND BOOKS WHICH HAVE A SOURCE
   NUMBER ON THEM IN ONE PLACE.
4. TYPE UP NOTES, CORRECTIONS, REVISIONS. DISCARD OLD.

CLEANING GIVES AN APPEARANCE OF ORGANIZATION AND CREATES A
READY TO GET TO WORK SITUATION. CLEANING GETS RID OF OLD
PAPERS, SNACKS, COFFEE CUPS, WRAPPERS, AND GENERAL CLUTTER.
WHEN YOU ARE READY, YOUR SPACE IS READY TOO!

EXAMPLE: CLUTTER ON THE WORK DESK
MY COMPUTER DESK IS KEPT CLEAR OF CLUTTER: EDITING MATERIAL
OR DATA I'M KEYING IS ON LEFT, REFERENCE MATERIAL ON RIGHT,
EDITING PENS AND STICKY NOTES....THAT IS ALL.

EXAMPLE: ITEMS TO TRIGGER CREATIVITY:
 A WOODEN DRAGON HANGS FROM THE CEILING, A STUFFED AND
COLORFUL CAMEL SITS ON A CHEST, TWO FIGURINES OF WHAT I THINK
MY HERO AND THE PIRATE CAPTAIN-VILLAIN LOOKS LIKE. A SIGN ON
THE DOOR SAYS "COCK & BULL" STORIES TOLD HERE. A WIND CHIME
HANGS IN THE WINDOW WITH CHINESE CURTAINS. (YEP, I'M WRITING
ABOUT CHINA) TWO SHIP MODELS, A SORCERER'S STATUE, A GLASS
GLOBE OF EARTH, 10 COFFEE MUGS WITH VARIOUS PENS, PENCILS, AND
ART BRUSHES. A CARVED INDIAN WALKING STICK, ART PICTURES OF
GREAT PYRAMIDS, CAR MODELS, ETC. YOU GET THE IDEA!

[I WROTE ABOUT DRAGONS, CAMELS, PIRATES, PIRATE CAPTAIN,
CHINESE-MARCO POLO-CHINESE JUNK SHIPS- INDIANS-PYRAMIDS-
MAPS, RESEARCH, HISTORY , BUILDINGS, DRESS, TIME PERIODS,
CARS...YOU GET THE IDEA!].

CREATIVE WRITING—THE KELLY MANUAL OF STYLE

IF YOU ARE WRITING ABOUT CHICAGO, GET A MAP, USE THE INTERNET ---
METRO MAP-RESEARCH HISTORY, KNOW BUILDINGS, THE SPECIFICS ADD
DIMENSION TO WHAT YOU ARE WRITING. MAYBE YOUR READER HAS
BEEN THERE.[I USED THE UNDERGROUND MAIL TUNNELS, THE
DEMOCRATIC CONVENTION SITE, MIRACLE MILE, THE PARKS, THE
STREETS, THE HOSPITAL AND EVEN STATUES WITHIN THE PARK AS A
SETTING FOR "THE BOOMERS" BOOK. I RESEARCHED THE CONVENTION,
THE PROTESTS, THE SPEAKERS, POLICE, THE ARMY, AS IF I WAS THERE. I
ADDED COLORFUL CHARACTERS, PLOTS, MINI-CLIMAXES, EVENTS,
DRAMA AND DIALOGUE TO SUPPORT THE MAIN CHARACTERS AND
VILLAINS. IT ADDED A SENSE OF BEING THERE FOR THE READER.]

37.1.5. 0. FUNCTIONAL & OPERATING NECESSITIES:
HAVE SEVERAL BOOK SHELVES, A FILING CABINET, A CARDBOARD BOX,
LAPTOP, A LARGE WASTE BASKET, LOTS OF OFFICE SUPPLIES, LIKE
DIFFERENT COLORED PENS, HIGHLIGHTERS, STICKY NOTES, BINDER
CLAMPS-3 SIZES, AND MUSIC. STAPLER FOR SOURCE MATERIALS, A CASE
OF PAPER, EXTRA BLACK & COLORED TONERS. (DON'T RUN OUT WHILE
YOUR WORKING.)

USE STICKY NOTES FOR 'TO DO' ITEMS, OR IDEAS, FOR IDEAS WITHIN
BOOKS WHILE READING OR TO "ADD" ITEMS MISSING FROM YOUR
WRITING DRAFT.

37.1.6. 0. NOW ADD MEMENTOS:
SOMETHING THAT RELATES TO WHAT YOU'RE WRITING ABOUT. A
PICTURE OF IRELAND, A CAMEL DOLL, A WOODEN DRAGON, A MODEL
SAILING SHIP, PICTURES OF KIDS, DOG, CAT, ETC.
(HOW DOES IT WALK, TALK, EAT OR ANNOY, OR SAIL, SINK OR TAKE ON
WATER? INCLUDE THAT IN THE DESCRIPTIVE PART OF WRITING ABOUT
IT) **AGAIN, MAKE YOUR SPACE CREATIVE TO WRITING!**

37.1.7. 0. REFERENCE MATERIALS: ON A BOOK SHELF:
DICTIONARIES, BOOK OF QUOTATIONS, VARIOUS WRITER'S HOW TO
BOOKS, MARKET GUIDES, BOOK COVER DESIGNING, MAPS, TRAVEL LOGS,
MAPS OR ATLAS, LANGUAGE TRANSLATIONS BOOKS, HISTORY BOOKS,
ASTRONOMY BOOKS, RESEARCH MATERIALS. ADD THESE TO THE PILE OF
SOURCE DOCUMENTS. **NOW, WE NUMBER THEM AS SOURCE
DOCUMENTS, AS USED:**

37.1.7.1. SOURCE MATERIALS: [REFER CH 34].
 DO CREATE AN SOURCE NUMBER LIST &ALPHABETICAL & SUBJECT
INDEX IN REAR OF YOUR BOOK:

37.1.7.2. SOURCE NUMBER FORMAT: [CH 34].
-USE ON : SOURCE DOCUMENTS, PICTURES, WEB INFORMATION, MAPS,
ILLUSTRATIONS. - USE A SIMPLE FORMAT: [SEE CH 15.1.0.0.].

RESEARCH FILE CABINET: [CH 34].
MASTER SOURCES & LISTS COULD LATER BE FILED INTO A FILING
CABINET, PROVIDE YOU WROTE YOUR BOOK #, NAME AND KEPT THE
SOURCE NUMBER AT THE TOP.

37.1.7.8. THE FAMOUS CARDBOARD BOX: ONE PER BOOK:
- KEEP SOME OF OLD VERSIONS OF CHAPTERS-KEEP ORIGINAL YOU STARTED WITH AND MIDDLE AND END VERSION. -THROW THEM INTO THE CARDBOARD BOX-LABEL BOX WITH THE BOOK TITLE _____ NAME & "ORIGINALS." **DO WRITE "ORIGINAL" AND DATE AT TOP OF EACH DRAFT.**

- I DO THIS FOR HISTORY, NO PLAGIARISM CLAIMS, AND TO SEE THE PROGRESS I MADE. AFTER SEVERAL BOOKS, YOU BEGIN TO SEE HOW YOUR WRITING IS DEVELOPING. A GOOD MEASURE BY RE-READING OLD STUFF LIKE THIS.
- **IMPORTANT** IF YOU HAVE MADE MAJOR REVISIONS OR IF YOU HAVE ILLUSTRATIONS OR COPIES OF SOMETHING AND YOU NEED TO RE-CHECK A SOURCE. THE SOURCE DOCUMENTS, COPIES, GO INTO THE BOX. THE YOUR **SINGLE BOOK SET** OF SOURCES STAYS WITH YOUR DRAFTS OR FINAL MANUSCRIPT.

CLASS EXERCISE: **START A WRITING LIST OF MY WORK:**
"MY BOOKS, MY POEMS, MY PLAYS, MY ART, MY SHORT STORIES, MY CHILDREN'S BOOKS, MY RECIPES… GET THE IDEA?

CLASS EXERCISE:
KEEP OLD REWRITES UNTIL DONE:
THIS WAY I CAN SAVE IT OVER AND OVER TO SAME FILE BUT WHEN OPENED…IT TELLS ITS CURRENT. THEN PRINT THE PAGE AND STICKY NOTE THE CHAPTER # ON IT. REMEMBER EVERYTHING IS CHANGEABLE UNTIL THE FINAL EDIT & PROOFREADING, THEN CHECK THE FORMAT, TYPE SIZE, AND PAGE NUMBERS; …ALL OF IT. SAVE VARIOUS EDITIONS OF REWRITES AS YOUR PROOF OF WRITING IT, SIMPLY STAPLE IT , DATE IT & THROW IN A BOX…OLDEST GOES ON BOTTOM AND NEWER ON TOP.

WRITE ONCE MORE…DO THE PUNCTUATION, CHECK LANGUAGE , GRAMMAR, CHECK THE VERB TENSE.

37.1.7.9. ORGANIZING YOUR COMPUTER FOLDERS:
COMPUTER FILES: [REFER TO CH 13.9.0.0].
1. I ARCHIVE THE FIRST COMPLETE DRAFT, DISCARD REVISIONS, UNLESS A MAJOR CHANGE IS MADE AND THE FINAL MANUSCRIPT.
2. ONE ADDITIONAL BECOMES MY **MASTER TO THE PUBLISHER**.
3. SAVE YOUR FILES VERY OFTEN, DATE THEM, AND DO A BACK UP DISC PERIODICALLY.

37.1.8. 0. CREATE A WRITING TIME PLAN:
CREATE TIME TO WRITE EVERYDAY. TIME OFF FOR GOOD BEHAVIOR. DO SOME PLANNING: PLAN WHAT YOU ARE GOING TO DO: A LITTLE OF EVERYTHING, OR DO THE TABLE OF CONTENTS, PRINTING CHAPTER 1. OR INSERT PAGE NUMBERS, WORK ON TITLE, OR CHAPTER NAMES.

37.1.9. 0. CREATE BLOCKS OF TIME:
AN EVENING FOR 3 HOURS, A SATURDAY MORNING (HUSBAND IS GOLFING), OR WIFE IS SHOPPING, DON'T FORGET DATE NIGHT… YOU NEED TO MAKE TIME FOR MATE TOO! WRITE AT LUNCH. WE ALL HAVE DEADLINES, SO TAKE 30 MINUTES EACH DAY OR WRITE THREE DAYS A WEEK FOR AN HOUR, WHILE YOU EAT AT YOUR DESK.

37.1.10. 0. A SEASON FOR WRITING:
RAINY DAYS: WRITE. SNOWY DAYS: WRITE. ITS HELPS TO KNOW SEASONS AND THAT YOU CAN EVEN PICTURE THEM IN YOUR MIND AND IN YOUR PARAGRAPHS.

37.2.0.0. ORGANIZE-ORGANIZE-ORGANIZE:
ORGANIZE YOUR DAILY LIFE FOR CHORES, THE UNEXPECTED FIXING OF A LEAK OR TAKING CAR FOR OIL CHANGE. DID YOU TAKE YOUR BOOK WHILE YOU WAIT? REDUCE THE AMOUNT OF DRIVING, WITH MULTIPLE STOPS FOR GAS, MILK, AND CLEANERS ALL IN ONE TRIP. THE NIGHTS YOU ARE NOT WRITING.

37.2.1.0. SEEK A BALANCE:
RECOGNIZE WRITING IS A BIG TIME EATER. PLAN FOR LONG HAUL. BALANCE WORK, PLAY, EXERCISE, CHORES, AND TIME FOR MATE.

37.2.8.0. VISITORS:
CURIOSITY BRINGS VISITORS: KEEP IT BRIEF, ANSWERS QUESTIONS, LET SLEEPING DOGS LIE, FEED THE KIDS AND YOURSELF. TAKE A BREAK FOR DRINKS, BATHROOM, TAKE A SHOWER. KEEP A PAD HANDY TO WRITE DOWN THOSE IDEAS, WHICH COME TO YOU, DURING THESE PERIODS. A GOOD THING! KEEP A POCKET NOTEBOOK IN YOUR CAR AND BY YOUR BED STAND FOR WRITING DOWN THOSE FLASHES OR PHRASES OF IDEAS!
EXAMPLE:
I HAVE A DOG WHO STAYS AS LONG AS I'M WRITING AND A CAT WHO VISITS MY WINDOW FOR THE SUN (STUDIO CAT). THE KIDS ARE GROWN, SO PEACE AT LAST!

THE PHONE: LET THE PHONE RING, (THERE IS NO PHONE IN MY STUDIO). I USE THE HOUSE PHONE'S MESSAGE MACHINE TO SCREEN CALLS. EVERYONE HAS A CANNY KNACK FOR CALLING JUST AS I'M INSPIRED AND WRITING A GREAT THOUGHT DOWN. I LOST MANY GREAT WORDS AND THOUGHTS TO MA BELL!

ONLY FOR EMERGENCIES:
I USE THE CELL PHONE FOR THOSE MUST TALK SITUATIONS: MY MATE IS CALLING, KIDS CALLING, CAR IS READY TO BE PICK-ED UP. MY CELL PHONE IS KEPT PRIVATE FOR THIS REASON. THE HOUSE PHONE IS UNLISTED AND ON A 'DO NOT CALL LIST,' TO GET RID OF PESKY TELE-MARKETERS.

37.2.9. 0. SOCIAL DUTIES & MULTI-TASKING:
YES, I HAVE REDUCED MY OUTINGS TO IMPORTANT ONES AND TO FRIENDS. I MAKE PLANS BUT DON'T OVERDO, I TELL THEM I'M WRITING AND COULD WE RESCHEDULE FOR NEXT WEEK. THEN, KEEP THE OCCASION & BE ON-TIME.

YES, I EVEN SCHEDULE THE "HONEY-DO CHORES" WHILE I'M MULTI-TASKING. IT IS AN ART-FORM! REMEMBER THOSE BLOCKS OF TIME, YOU CREATED FOR WHEN YOUR NOT ACTUALLY WRITING, OR DOING WRITING CHORES? USE THEM WISELY...IT GIVES MORE TIME FOR OPPORTUNITY TO WRITE, TAKE CARE OF YOUR SOCIAL NEEDS AND RESPONSIBILITIES AT HOME AND YOU WILL FEEL COMPLETE AND YOUR MATE WILL APPRECIATE IT GREATLY.

37.3.1. 0. SPOUSE TRAVELS:
MY SPOUSE TRAVELS A FEW DAYS A WEEK, RARELY OVERNIGHT, BUT WHEN THAT HAPPENS I BEGIN PLANNING THE TIME BLOCKS

37.3.2.0. MASSIVE BLOCKS OF TIME:
YOU LEARN TO KEEP MASSIVE BLOCKS OF TIME LIKE SATURDAY-SUNDAY, OR EVENINGS…OPEN.
SUNDAY: 4 HOURS TO WORK. SOMETIMES MORE…LESS TV. UP 8:00 AM, SPEND TIME WITH SPOUSE, ENJOY PAPER, FIX BREAKFAST, OR GO OUT FOR BREAKFAST EVERY OTHER WEEK-END, CLEAN KITCHEN, FIND OUT SUNDAY EVENTS SCHEDULE: WRITE IN MORNING, DO CHORES AFTERNOON, WATCH GAME , OR COOK DINNER WHILE SPOUSE IS SHOPPING OR TANNING, FAMILY TIME?

RESULT: 16-1/2 HOURS A WEEK, MAYBE LONGER. WHAT COULD YOU DO WITH 16 HOURS?

37.3.3. 0. QUIET AREA & MY WORK PLACE: SOMETIMES THE SAME!
SET ASIDE SOME QUIET TIME, AND A QUIET AREA…. SATURDAY MORNING, EARLY SUNDAY MORNING BEFORE ANYONE IS UP, EVENINGS LIKE TONIGHT WITHOUT TV.

MY QUIET AREA IS MY STUDIO…WHERE I WRITE, DRAW, AND CREATE. IT HAS THE REQUISITE COMPUTER, BOOK SHELVES, A OFFICE DESK, PILES OF REFERENCE MATERIAL, STUFFED ANIMALS AFTER SOME OF MY CHARACTERS, A WINDOW, COFFEE MUGS FROM TRAVELS ABOUT WHICH I ADD INTO MY BOOKS, MUGS WITH PENCILS AND PENS, STATUTES, A GUITAR OR TWO, DRAGONS HANGING FROM THE CEILING, SIGNS ON THE DOOR, A WARM RUG UNDER MY FEET, A COMFORTABLE CHAIR, A L-SHAPED COMPUTER DESK, SUPPLIES, AND REFERENCE BOOKS, NEARBY.

37.4.0.0. OUR PROGRESS:
1. WE ESTABLISHED A CREATIVE SPACE TO WRITE IN.
2. WE CREATE A DIFFERENT SPACE TO EDIT IN.
3. WE WRITE A SCHEDULE WHICH LETS US WRITE AND ONE TO LIVE WITH.
4. WE IMPROVED OUR ORGANIZATION OF SPACE AND COMPUTER FOLDERS.
5. WE MADE OUR SPACE CREATIVE BY ADDING ITEMS ABOUT WHICH WE WRITE.

CHAPTER 38
38.0.0.0.   YOUR NEW STYLE-TWO TYPES:
CHAPTER TOPICS: *TYPES-DEFINITION-*

38.0.1.0. STYLE TYPES:
SEVEN RELATED ELEMENTS THAT COMBINE INTO OUR STYLE AT THE
BEGINNING AND PROVIDE A PURPOSE BEHIND OUR STYLE AS WE
DEVELOP IT. WE ARE DEVELOPING A STYLE OF SPEAKING (FOR OUR
CHARACTERS) AND A WRITING STYLE FOR OUR READER.

1.EMPHASIS:
THE ART OF WRITING DEPENDS A GOOD DEAL ON PUTTING THE
STRONGEST WORDS IN THE MOST IMPORTANT PLACES. THE MOST
EMPHATIC PLACE IN A SENTENCE IS THE END, THE CLIMAX AND DURING
THAT SLIGHT PAUSE THAT FOLLOWS, THAT LAST 'WORD THOUGHT'
CONTINUES TO REVERBERATE IN THE READER'S MIND. WHILE IT IS THE
LAST WORD; WE NOTICE A CLARITY AND EMPHASIS OF A PURE
THOUGHT.

2.HONEST CONNECTION TO OUR READER:
SOME WRITERS MAY CHOOSE LONG WORDS OR PROFOUND LONG
SENTENCES TO PONTIFICATE, TO BE OBSCURE OR TO 'PUFF UP' THEIR
WORK. THEY MIGHT SACRIFICE THE CLARITY OF SIMPLE WORDS THAT
COMMUNICATE. WE NEED TO HOLD SACRED THAT HONEST CONNECTION
BETWEEN THE WRITER AND READER.

3.PASSION AND CONTROL:
PASSION AND CONTROL CAN TAKE OVER A WORK. A CERTAIN ZEAL BY
THE WRITER IS A MUST. HE MUST BE THE MASTER OF THE ART AND THE
CHIEF COMMUNICATOR TO THE READER. HIS CONTROL OVER THE WORK
AND ITS CONTENT IS SELF-REALIZED. HIS FOCUS ON THE STORY ITS PLOT,
CHARACTERS AND SCENES ALL REQUIRE A LEARNED SKILL. CONTROL IS
A WRITER'S JUDGMENT OF WHAT IS GOOD AND BAD. HE WILL ADD OR
DISCARD PARTS TO MAKE THE STORY COMPLETE.

4. READING:
ONE LEARNS TO WRITE BY READING GOOD BOOKS. THE READER WILL
FIND AND ADOPT THE WRITER'S PASSION WITHIN . THE WRITING NOT
ONLY ENTERTAINS BUT DRAWS A READER'S THOUGHTS INTO THE
SENTENCES ABSORBING AND IDENTIFYING HIM WITH THE ACTIONS.

5. REVISION:
THE ART OF REVISION IS CUTTING AND ADDING APPROPRIATE MATERIAL
FROM THE DRAFTS. REVISIONS CUT THE DEADWOOD, THE
UNNECESSARY BACK STORY OR POORLY WRITTEN SENTENCES. EDITING
IS A QUALITY CHECK ON THE WORK. I SUGGEST WAITING TO CUT
MATERIAL UNTIL THE BOOK DRAFT #4 IS DONE. SOME PARTS MIGHT BE
MOVED OR NEEDED ELSEWHERE. ONLY THEN, WILL THE STORY MAKE
SENSE AND FOLLOW ALONG. HOLES WILL BE FOUND AND FILLED.

6. SOPHISTICATION AND SIMPLICITY:
A GOOD BALANCE BETWEEN THE ART OR WRITING AND SIMPLE
SENTENCES OR ILLUSTRATIONS SHOULD INFORM, ENLIGHTEN AND

CREATIVE WRITING—THE KELLY MANUAL OF STYLE

ENTERTAIN OUR READERS. EXTREMES OF BOTH MIGHT 'TURN OFF' THE READER. WITHIN THE SENTENCES, WE MUST HAVE <u>IDEAS</u> THAT ARE CLEAR, AND <u>EXPRESSIONS</u> THAT ARE SIMPLE."

38.0.2.0. STYLE DEFINED:
STYLE IS THE WAY IN WHICH SOMETHING IS SAID, DONE, EXPRESSED, OR PERFORMED: THUS, A STYLE OF SPEECH AND WRITING. ALL FIGURES OF SPEECH FALL WITHIN THE DOMAIN OF STYLE.

38.0.3.0. HERE IS SOME WRITER'S FAMOUS QUOTES ON STYLE:
1. IS STYLE: SOMETHING WRITER'S ADD OR REMOVE AS THEY PLEASE?

2. IS STYLE A KIND OF SPICE THAT'S ADDED TO A PIECE OF WRITING--OR IS IT INSTEAD AN ESSENTIAL INGREDIENT OF THE WRITING ITSELF?

3. STYLE IS PRACTICAL. (HENRY DAVID THOREAU)

4. STYLE IS HAVING SOMETHING TO SAY, AND SAY IT AS CLEARLY AS YOU CAN. (MATTHEW ARNOLD)

5. STYLE IS THE MAN HIMSELF IS AS NEAR THE TRUTH AS WE CAN GET. THE IMAGE OF CHARACTER. (EDWARD GIBBON)

6. STYLE IS THE PERFECTION OF A POINT OF VIEW. (RICHARD EBERHART)

7. STYLE IS A LIVING BREATHING THING. SOMETHING BORN OF OUR IMAGINATION.

8. STYLE IS THE SOUL AND THE FLESH OF A WORK.(GUSTAVE FLAUBERT).

9. STYLE IS IT IS THE MIND SKATING CIRCLES AROUND ITSELF AS IT MOVES FORWARD." (ROBERT FROST).

10. STYLE IS CRAFTSMANSHIP:"WHAT'S IMPORTANT IS THE WAY WE SAY IT. ART IS ALL ABOUT CRAFTSMANSHIP. IT'S NOT WHAT WE SAY BUT HOW WE SAY IT THAT MATTERS." (FEDERICO FELLINI)

10. STYLE IS "PROPER WORDS IN PROPER PLACES, MAKE THE TRUE DEFINITION OF STYLE." (JONATHAN SWIFT)

12. STYLE IS "THE WRITER WHO PUTS HIS INDIVIDUAL MARK ON THE WAY HE WRITES…" (RAYMOND CHANDLER).

13. "THE STYLE OF AN AUTHOR SHOULD BE THE IMAGE OF HIS MIND, BUT THE CHOICE AND COMMAND OF LANGUAGE IS THE FRUIT OF EXERCISE." (EDWARD GIBBON)

14. "ONE ARRIVES AT STYLE ONLY WITH ATROCIOUS EFFORT, WITH FANATICAL AND DEVOTED STUBBORNNESS." (GUSTAVE FLAUBERT)

38.0.3.0. THE MASTER'S STYLE IS?
AS I ANALYZED THE GRAND MASTERS OF WRITING FOR CHAPTER **28**, I REALIZED THEY HAD SOME UNIQUE "STYLES OF WRITING."

CREATIVE WRITING—THE KELLY MANUAL OF STYLE

ALL THE MASTERS SPENT TIME LEARNING THEIR CRAFT AND SOME DID NOT ACHIEVE IMMEDIATE SUCCESS. THE SUCCESSFUL ONES WROTE WHAT THEY KNEW AND **WROTE IN A PICTURESQUE MANNER WITH EITHER WORD CHOICE OR WORD IMAGES.**

38.0.4.0.   FROM CH 28.3.0.0. : REPRINTED HERE FOR CLARITY.
THE GRAND MASTER'S STYLE-A SUMMARY:
*MANY GREAT WRITERS SHARE IN COMMON A TRAIT OF **UNIQUENESS**. ALL TYPES OF THEMES AND STYLES PREDOMINATE AGAINST THEIR ENVIRONMENT, THEIR EXPERIENCE AND STRUCTURE OF WRITING. SOME WERE REBELS, SOME CONSERVATIVE, SOME UNCONVENTIONAL. EACH HAD A **UNIVERSAL THEME** WHICH THEY CHAMPIONED.*

EXPERIENCE:
*THEIR BEST WRITINGS WERE PRODUCTS OF THEIR EXPERIENCE, ENVIRONMENT AND THEIR HUMANITY. **THEY WROTE WHAT THEY KNEW.***

UNIQUE WRITING STYLE:
*EACH ALSO HAD A **UNIQUE WRITING STYLE** OR USED WRITING ELEMENTS WHICH BECAME UNIQUE. EACH OF THE MASTERS WERE **UNIQUE** FOR A VARIETY OF REASONS. THE THEME AND A CHARACTER 'S SUBJECTS WERE PARAMOUNT AND REINFORCED WITH IDEA GROUPS AND UNIQUE WAYS OF WRITING, SUCH AS, WORD COMBINATIONS AND VOCAL ACCENTS. EACH TOOK US A ON A "VISUAL TRIP" TO SOMEPLACE NEW AND PERHAPS 'MUSICAL.' THE VOCAL HARMONY OF THE WORDS AND PICTURE WORDS KEPT US 'HOOKED.'*

STRONG REALISTIC CHARACTERS AND VILLAINS:
*EACH HAD A WRITING STYLE/TRAIT WHICH INCLUDED FULLY DEVELOPED AND **REALISTIC CHARACTERS**, ALL WROTE GREAT CHARACTER AND PLOT PORTRAYALS. SOME OTHERS ACHIEVED NOTORIETY WITH GENRE, REGIONALISM OR A CHARACTER'S ACTIONS AND VOICE. GREAT CHARACTERS CAME TO LIFE, TO BE EMULATED AND WORSHIPED OR HATED...EXTREMES. **REVIEW SOME OF THE CHARACTER NAMES AND THE BOOK TITLES...RATHER UNFORGETTABLE!***

*LANGUAGE, DIALOGUE, EVENTS AND **POWERFUL IMAGES**. CHIEF AMONG THESE TRAITS WAS **WORD CHOICE, DIALOGUE AND DRAMATIZATION**. **STRONG PLOTS AND CLIMAXES** WERE ALWAYS PRESENT.*

STORYTELLER:
*EACH WAS A STORYTELLER AND WROTE FOR THE READER, HOWEVER, UNIQUELY. **EACH WROTE A LOT** AND WITH DIVERSE SUBJECTS.*

WORD CHOICE AND WORD ORDER:
*THEIR **WORD CHOICE WAS UNIQUE** FROM TITLES, TO CHARACTER NAMES, PLACES. THEY WROTE WITH **POWER AND PASSION**. **THEY WROTE FOR THEIR READER WITH SOUNDS, PICTURESQUE WORDS AND EMOTIONS.***

DRAMATIZATION:
NEW WRITERS SHOULD LEARN HOW TO STORYTELL, HOW TO CHOOSE WORDS AND THE ORDER OF WORDS. ILLUMINATE PLOTS AND THEMES AND MOST IMPORTANTLY, HOW TO BLEND THEM INTO THEIR DIALOG AGAINST A BACKDROP OF DRAMATIZATION.

CREATIVE WRITING—THE KELLY MANUAL OF STYLE

> *LESSONS LEARNED:*
> *WE SHOULD MEASURE EACH OF OUR BOOKS TO THIS ELITE*
> *MASTER WRITING STYLE. OUR NEW STYLE MIGHT BE OUR*
> *CREATIVITY IN BLENDING THESE ALL TOGETHER.*

38.0.5.0. YOUR CREATIVITY:
IT'S THE THEORY OF 'AH! HA!' AND ICEBERG PRINCIPLE ROLLED INTO ONE. REMEMBER THE TOOLS OF 'WAITING TO EDIT AND NOT HAVING A RIGID STRUCTURE LIKE AN OUTLINE,' TO BIND THE WRITING TO JUST ONE DIRECTION. IMAGES AND PICTURESQUE DETAIL CANNOT BE BOUND TO SUCH RIGID CONCERNS. CREATIVITY IS A TASK WHICH GIVES OUR WORDS FLIGHT!

38.0.6.0. YOUR STYLE:
YOUR STYLE IS VERY IMPORTANT!
IT GENERALLY EVOLVES FROM THAT UNIQUE UNIVERSAL THEME YOU ARE WRITING ABOUT, THE STORY; RATHER THAN A PARTICULAR WRITER'S BENT OR YOUR COMFORTABLE METHOD OF STORYTELLING.

STYLE IS A SUM OF YOUR APPLICATION AND WRITING METHODS , WORDS CHOICE, FIGURES OF SPEECH, VISUAL IMAGES AND MELODIC SOUNDING WORDS ALL IN THE <u>BACKGROUND</u> ...ALMOST SUBTLE AND UNIQUE. THEN, YOU PLACE DIALOGUE, EVENTS AND PLACES IN THE <u>FOREGROUND</u> ALONG WITH THE CHARACTERS.

YOUR **STYLE IS** A LIVING, BREATHING THING THAT CANNOT ENTIRELY BE REDUCED TO RULES. IT IS THE SUM OF STORYTELLING, YOUR APPLICATION, IMAGINATION, MELODIC SOUNDS AND PICTURESQUE WORDS; ALL CAPTURING THE MEANING AND EXPRESSING IT IN VARIOUS KEY FORMS...CHARACTER, ACTION, DIALOGUE AND WORD CHOICE.

STYLE IS ALL OF THESE ITEMS POURED INTO A BLENDER AND OUT COMES YOUR OWN UNIQUE STYLE! THE PACE MIGHT BE RAT-TAT-TAT OR SLOW LIKE LAVA; BUT STILL THE IDEA GROUPS CAN'T BE TOO THIN OR MISSING. THE CHARACTERS AND DIALOGUE MUST BE CONNECTED AND BELIEVABLE. THE FLOW MUST CONTINUE ALONG WITH THE MANY HOOKS FOR THE READERS. OUR STORY MUST BE PROVOCATIVE , YET SOUND AND REACH A DRAMATIC CONCLUSION. THE STORY THROUGHOUT MUST HAVE ITS PASTE AND GLUE WITH EACH SENTENCE, PARAGRAPH AND PAGE CONNECTING CHAPTER AFTER CHAPTER.

THE WRITER'S STYLE IS ONE-HALF OF THE CONNECTION TO OUR READER. THIS 'AH! HA! CONNECTION IS OUR STYLE.

> **CLASS EXERCISE:** WRITE ONE PARAGRAPH DESCRIBING YOUR NEW STYLE AND WHY IT IS BETTER NOW.

38.1.0.0. OUR PROGRESS:
1. WE LEARN ABOUT STYLE.
2. WE LEARN OUR STYLE IS ABOUT OUR OWN TECHNIQUE AND CHOICE
   OF BLENDING ALL THE ELEMENTS TOGETHER.
3. WE LEARN STYLE OF THE MASTERS IS UNIQUE.

CHAPTER 39

39.0.0.0. HOW TO WRITE YOUR BEST SELLER:
CHAPTER TOPICS: *GOALS- PREPARATION-7 KEY WRITING TOOLS- WE COMPARE OUR MANUSCRIPT TO THE MASTERS. WE FIX IT.*

39.1.0.0. OUR GOALS & OUR PREPARATION:
39.1.1.0. WE WROTE OUR <u>SHORT SYNOPSIS</u> TO CAPTURE OUR BOOK IDEA AND A UNIVERSAL THEME AND SUPPORTING THEMES. WE FOUND OUR CHARACTER AND MADE HIS/HER <u>NAME/ACTIONS MEMORABLE.</u>

39.1.2.0. WE ADDED A <u>REMARKABLE TITLE</u> AND A FEW SUPPORTING CHARACTERS.

39.1.3.0. WE FOUND A PLOT AND A FEW CLIMAXES. WE WROTE OUR PARAGRAPH. WE READ IT OUTLOUD, FIX A FEW ERRORS AND <u>SAVED IT AS OUR "STORYLINE."</u>

39.1.4.0. WE BEGAN OUR RESEARCH AND RECORDED EACH SOURCE ON OUR "<u>SOURCE LIST</u>." WE ORGANIZED SOME FOLDERS ON OUR COMPUTER AND GOT OUR WRITING SPACE IN ORDER. WE BEGAN OUR <u>BOOK PLAN.</u>

39.1.5.0. WE BEGAN OUR <u>CHAPTER TOPICS LIST</u> AND EXPANDED OUR <u>CHARACTER LIST</u>. WE REVIEWED OUR BASICS OF SENTENCE STRUCTURE AND PARAGRAPH WRITING. WE LEARNED ABOUT OPENING SENTENCES, THE MEAT AND THE SIZZLE: "THE CLOSING SENTENCE." WE WROTE AND WROTE.

39.1.6. 0. WE LEARNED ABOUT <u>S</u>YNOPSIS AND USING THE <u>STORYTELLER'S VERSION</u>, READING OUTLOUD. WE ADDED SOUNDS AND PICTURESQUE WORDS. WE ADDED VOCABULARY, GRAMMAR, PUNCTUATION AND LANGUAGE TO OUR WRITING.

39.1.7.0. *<u>WE ARE READY TO WRITE OUR BEST SELLER—ALMOST!</u>*

---

7 MASTER WRITING TOOLS:
 TO WRITE OUR BEST SELLER:

USING <u>7 THINGS</u> WE BEGIN TO WRITE OUR BESTSELLER:
1. OUR IDEAS LISTS GET US STARTED
    THINKING ABOUT A STORY.
2. THE THREE SYNOPSIS-THEMES.
3. THE CHAPTER TOPICS.
4. OUR CHARACTER LIST.
5. OUR CHOICE OF WORDS-SOUNDS-ILLUMINATION
6. OUR PLOTS-DIALOGUE-DRAMATIZATION
7. THE GRAND MASTER WRITER'S STYLE-[CH 28.3.0.0.].

39.1.8.0. THE FINAL REVIEW BEFORE PUBLISHING.
FINALLY WE ASK OURSELVES THE ULTIMATE QUESTION?
1.IS THE MANUSCRIPT FINISHED?
2.IS THE BOOK COMPLETE?

3.ARE WE THE WRITER SATISFIED?
4.IS THE EDITOR DONE REVISING?
5.IS THE READER HAPPY
6.IS OUR BUYER LOOKING OR BUYING OUR NOVEL?
7.THEN, IT IS AH! HA! TIME!

IF NOT, CONTINUE YOUR REVIEW:

39.1.9.0. WE WROTE OUR <u>FIRST ROUGH DRAFT</u>. WE ADDED THE NARRATOR, AND SIX W'S. WE GREW OUR PLOTS AND CLIMAXES. WE ILLUMINATED OUR WORDS WITH SHOW, NOT TELLING. WE TYPED OUR CHANGES AND REPRINTED.

39.1.10.0. WE ADDED SETTINGS, SCENES AND SPECIFIC DETAILS. WE ADDED REALISM TO OUR CHARACTERS AND STORIES. WE READ IT OUTLOUD TO OUR READER. OUR READER WEARS A HAT! SO HAT ON HEAD, WE LEARNED WHAT OUR READER LIKES ABOUT OUR WRITING SO FAR. THE HAT MEANS WE ARE ROLE PLAYING.

39.1.11.0. WE SMOOTH OUT THE ROUGH SPOTS AND ADD SOME MORE CHAPTERS BRIDGING FROM ONE TO ANOTHER. WE LEARNED NOT TO ROTATE CHAPTERS--- (CH 1 & 3 & 5 IS ONE STORY) MAKES THE STORY CHOPPY! WE ADDED THE MISSING PAGES LIKE DEDICATION, PROLOGUE, INTRODUCTION AND TABLE OF CONTENTS. <u>WE ORGANIZED OUR ROUGH DRAFT INTO A</u> <u>BOOK DRAFT</u>.

39.1.12.0. WE CONTINUE TO WRITE ADDING CHAPTER AFTER CHAPTER. WE MAKE A TIMELINE AND REVIEW OUR PROGRESS TO DATE. WE USE OUR CHECK LISTS AND BEGIN SEROUS EDITING AND USING PROOFREADER'S MARKS.

39.1.13.0. WE EDIT, FIX AND WRITE SOME MORE-SOMETIMES 30 TIMES. WE REVIEW OUR CHARACTERS PLOTS, CLIMAXES, AND EVENTS. HAS OUR STORYLINE CHANGED? WE ADAPT. WE FIX OUR CHAPTER TOPICS, OUR TITLE ADD MORE DRAMA. WE COMPARE IT ALL OF OUR CHECK LISTS. WE ARE CLOSE TO FINISHING <u>OUR BOOK DRAFT</u>.

39.1.14.0. WE USED FIGURES OF SPEECH AND IMPROVED OUR CLIMAXES. WE ADDED COMEDY-TRAGEDY- AND HUMANITY TO OUR CHARACTER. REALISM AND BELIEVABILITY RESULTS.

<u>39.1.15. 0.</u>

DO: COMPARE YOUR BOOK DRAFT.

<u>(ALMOST AN MANUSCRIPT!----PATIENCE--- LET IT AGE A LITTLE, LIKE WINE!)</u>

A. A GREAT STORY IS TOLD <u>OUTLOUD.</u>(<u>STORYLINE</u>) AND OUR IDEAS LISTS HELPS FLESH THIS OUT. WE ADD <u>SOUND WORDS</u> AND MORE IDEAS.

B. WE HAVE A <u>UNIVERSAL THEME</u> AND SEVERAL OF ITS SUB-THEMES.

214

C. OUR <u>FIRST SENTENCES</u> ARE ILLUMINATING.

D. MASTERFUL <u>PLOTS</u>. (SIX TYPES)AND <u>REALISM,</u>
(OUR LIFE'S EXPERIENCES). WE INTRODUCE OUR PLOTS (INDIRECTLY
AND WITH MYSTERY)AND CLOSE THEM BEFORE THE ENDING.

E. WE HAVE LARGER THAN LIFE <u>MAIN CHARACTERS AND MAIN
VILLAINS</u>. SUPPORTING CHARACTERS HELP THE MAIN CHARACTERS,
PLOTS AND CLIMAXES TO HAPPEN.

F. THE MAIN CHARACTER HAS A <u>PREDICAMENT</u> TO BE RESOLVED.

G. THE <u>STORYTELLER'S SYNOPSIS</u>-OUR BOOK BEGINS:
THE READER SAYS OKAY…YOUR HOOK WORKS…SO NOW WHAT?

H. WE USE OUR CHARACTER'S <u>LANGUAGE, GREAT DIALOGUE AND
GREAT DRAMATIZATIONS </u>TO PRESENT OUR STORY. (A PLACE OUR
READER WANTS TO KNOW MORE ABOUT).

I OUR <u>TIME LINE</u> GIVES AN ORDERLY TRANSITION TO OUR STORY.IT
MOVES ALONG.

J. WE USE <u>COMPARE AND CONTRAST</u> FOR UNIVERSAL AND SUPPORTING
THEMES TO BE PLAYED OUT. WE DID AND KNOW OUR <u>RESEARCH</u> ABOUT
THEM. WE WROTE. WE <u>PERSONIFIED </u>THESE THEMES IN OUR
CHARACTERS.

K. WE USE ALL OF OUR <u>WRITING TOOLS</u> THROUGHOUT THE BOOK.
FIGURES OF SPEECH, ACTION WORDS, OUR LANGUAGE CHOICE
EMPHASES ALL OF OUR CHARACTER'S DIALOGUES.
OUR OPENING SENTENCES AND PARAGRAPHS ADD THE <u>READER HOOKS</u>
AND PROVE WE CAN WRITE.

L. WE LOOK FOR <u>HOLES IN OUR STORY</u>. WHAT HAPPENS TO EACH
CHARACTER. DID OUR BACK STORY OVER POWER OUR MAIN STORY? IF
THEY DIED OR SOME TRAGIC ACCIDENT---WHAT HAPPENED TO OUR
MAIN CHARACTERS AND VILLAIN.
WAS JUSTICE SERVED? WAS THERE MORALITY? DID THE PREDICAMENT
GET RESOLVED? AS WE CLOSED OUR LAST MAJOR CHAPTER WAS THERE
<u>CLOSURE OR A PLOT TWIST</u>?

M. LAST, WE COMPARE OUR STORY TO OUR STORYTELLER'S
SYNOPSIS…DID IT MATCH? WHY NOT?
DID WE <u>ADD A BRIDGE</u> OR DID THE MAIN CHARACTER CEASE TO EXIST?
THE READER WANTS TO GUESS OR BE ILLUMINATED! <u>HE WANTS HIS AH!
HA!</u>

N. IF WE GET THE <u>MASTER WRITER'S VERSION</u> COMPLETE,
WITH ALL THE PAGES, SUBJECT INDEX AND SOURCES AT THE BACK OF
THE BOOK; WE HAVE A <u>BOOK MANUSCRIPT</u>.
THESE 7 TOOLS GOT US HERE.

ONLY NOW WE ARE A WRITER!!!

NOW WE HAVE TO GET IT READY FOR PUBLISHING AND MARKETING. CHECK OUT CHAPTERS 43 TO 55.
OF COURSE, WE CAN BEGIN WRITING ANOTHER BOOK!
IT IS EASIER THE SECOND TIME!

CLASS:
DO: A THOROUGH REVIEW OF YOUR FINAL BOOK –COMPARE IT TO THE 7 TOOLS AND THE MASTERS REVIEW ABOVE.

39.2.0.0. OUR PROGRESS:

1. WE COMPLETED OUR MANUSCRIPT.

2. USED THE 7 KEY TOOLS OF OUR CRAFT.

3. WE COMPARED OUR MANUSCRIPT TO THE GRAND MASTER WRITERS.

4. WE FIXED IT AGAIN. WE DID OUR FINAL SPELL CHECK.

5. WE MATCHED OUR BOOK COVER AND THE BOOK TITLE. THE CHAPTER TITLES SUPPORTED OUR CHAPTER IDEAS.

6. WE PRINTED A FINAL HARD COPY TO REVIEW.

7. LAST, WE DID OUR FINAL MANUSCRIPT REVIEW AND EDITING **ONE MORE TIME**. OUR PAGE LAYOUTS ARE READY TO PRINT. **WE VIEWED THEM IN 2 PAGE PRINT LAYOUTS**.

8. WE WROTE COPY FOR OUR FRONT BOOK COVER AND BACK COVER.

9. WE DID OUR FINAL BOOK TITLE RESEARCH AN APPROVED IT.

10. WE FIXED AND APPROVED ALL OF THE ABOVE.

11. WE ARE HAPPY WITH THE RESULTS- OUR AH HA!

CONGRATULATIONS ON A GREAT BOOK AND NEW STYLE OF WRITING!

WELCOME TO THE WRITER'S CLUB

CHAPTER 40
40.0.0.0.- HOW TO SCREENWRITE YOUR BOOK:
SOURCE: THE SITE WWW.FILMSCRIPTWRITING.COM WILL OFFER
TECHNIQUES, GUIDES, AND QUIZZES TO HELP THE ASPIRING SCRIPT AND
SCREENWRITER.

CHAPTER TOPICS:
THE IDEAS LIST
SCRIPT FORMATTING
STORY STRUCTURE
CHARACTER DEVELOPMENT
THREE BODIES OF A SCRIPT
THE THREE ACT STRUCTURE
ACT I
ACT II
ACT III

40.0.1.0. SCRIPT IDEA LISTS:
[REFER TO CHAPTER 5.0.2.1. -THE IDEA LISTS & MOVIE LISTS BELOW].

THE WHOLE PROCESS OF SEARCHING FOR A GREAT SCRIPT IDEA IS
ALREADY IN YOUR HANDS: THE IDEA LISTS. OF COURSE, SOME OF THESE
CAME ABOUT AS A RESULT OF BRAINSTORMING AND RESEARCH.
ONE IDEA LEADS TO ANOTHER!

THINKING AND FOCUS ARE PARAMOUNT. SPEND TIME JUST THINKING,
NOT DOING OTHER THINGS LIKE EMAIL OR DOODLING. BRAINSTORMING!
WRITE DOWN THESE 'IDEAS' AND CONTINUE THIS PROCESS. DOES ONE
STAND OUT AS PROMISING? DISCARD THOSE, THAT ARE WORN OUT OR
USED IN A RECENT BEST SELLER.

FIRST, DO 'STORYTELLING YOUR IDEA'[CH 7.5.0.0.] TO YOURSELF OF
WHAT YOUR SCRIPT IS ABOUT. FIND THE UNIVERSAL AND SUPPORTING
THEMES [CH 10.]. TO YOUR CONCEPT. YOU NEED A GREAT STORY WITH
UNIVERSAL APPEAL OR YOU HAVE ONLY A GREAT STORY.

USE YOUR 'KERNEL' IDEA AND RESEARCH IT! YOU MIGHT FIND ENOUGH
MATERIAL TO COMPLETE A SHORT SYNOPSIS [CH 16.2.0.1.].

IF YOU WERE TO JUST SIT DOWN AND ATTEMPT TO WRITE A SCRIPT
FROM WHATEVER WAS IN YOUR HEAD AT THE TIME YOU'D PROBABLY
GET ABOUT 10 PAGES WRITTEN, LOSE DIRECTION AND DEVELOP
"WRITERS BLOCK"[CH 14.1.0.0.]. IF YOU GET BLOCKED...GO BACK TO THE
IDEAS LIST.

ONCE YOU HAVE A KERNEL IDEA, THINK ABOUT WHAT MAKES IT GREAT?
APPEAL? A NEW TWIST, A GREAT MAIN CHARACTER, HIS CONFLICT AND
ULTIMATE RESOLUTION? IF YOU HAVE SEVERAL IDEAS KEEP THEM ALL
AND ANALYZE THEM FOR THE ABOVE ELEMENTS. **JUDGE THEM FOR
MERIT:** COMPARE THEM TO BOOKS IN PRINT, OR SCRIPTS, OR MOVIES.
DOES IT STILL HAVE MERIT? IF NOT, CONTINUE SEARCHING.

40.0.2.0. SCRIPT FORMATTING:

CREATIVE WRITING—THE KELLY MANUAL OF STYLE

FIRST, KNOW HOW TO CORRECTLY FORMAT A SCRIPT AND DO THIS WITH TWO METHODS:

1. EITHER BUY A PIECE OF SCRIPTWRITING SOFTWARE WHICH DOES THE BULK OF THE WORK FOR YOU.

2. LEARN HOW TO DO IT YOURSELF BY USING A COMPUTER PROGRAM AS 'MICROSOFT WORD.'

THE SCRIPT COULD BE A BOX OFFICE SMASH; BUT WITHOUT THE CORRECT FORMAT IT WILL NEVER BE READ.

SPEC SCRIPTS:
THE SCRIPT THAT YOU ARE TRYING TO SELL IS KNOWN AS A SPEC SCRIPT; BECAUSE IT'S WRITTEN UNDER THE SPECULATION IT WILL BE BOUGHT. IT IS IMPORTANT TO AVOID ADDING CAMERA ANGLES, EDITING DIRECTIONS, OR ANYTHING TECHNICAL UNLESS ABSOLUTELY NECESSARY. YOU MIGHT HAVE READ A TARANTINO OR KUBRICK SCRIPT LITTERED WITH THESE BUT THAT'S BECAUSE THEY ARE 'WRITER/DIRECTOR'S VERSIONS.'

SCRIPT AND FORMAT-A MARRIAGE:
DO **BUY A GREAT HOW TO SCRIPT BOOK OR TAKE A SCREENWRITING CLASS.** YOU MUST MAKE SURE THE SCRIPT IS GOOD AND THE FORMAT IS CORRECT.

40.0.3.0. STORY STRUCTURE:
THOUSANDS OF SCRIPTS ARE SENT EACH YEAR, SOME DON'T GET READ, MOST GET REJECTED AND A FEW MAKE IT. YOUR SCRIPT HAS TO HAVE THE FOLLOWING:

1. A MAIN CHARACTER WHO IS DRIVEN TOWARDS RESOLVING HIS CONFLICT.
2. A VILLAIN, AN OPPOSITION TO YOUR MAIN CHARACTER WHO WILL HOLD YOUR MAIN CHARACTER BACK FROM ACHIEVING THEIR GOAL.
3. A FIGHT (LITERAL OR METAPHORICAL) BETWEEN YOUR MAIN CHARACTER AND HIS VILLAIN (S) OR OPPOSITION.
4. AN ENDING, WHICH ANSWERS THE QUESTIONS "CAN THE MAIN CHARACTER RESOLVE HIS CONFLICT?" PROVIDE A SOLUTION TO UNIVERSAL THEME?

YOUR SCRIPT MUST PRESENT A GREAT STORY, ALONG WITH A WELL DEVELOPED MAIN CHARACTER WHO THE AUDIENCE CAN RELATE. THE STORY IN YOUR SCRIPT MUST SHINE AND YOUR STORY STRUCTURE MUST ALSO BE SOLID. YOUR STORY STRUCTURE IS THE FRAMEWORK AND FOUNDATION OF YOUR SCRIPT, FROM WHICH YOU CAN CREATE A WONDERFUL PIECE OF ARCHITECTURE. SHOULD YOUR STRUCTURE BE WEAK THEN THE STORY WILL FALL FLAT.

40.0.4.0.MONTAGE(SERIES OF SHOTS)-NO DIALOG

CREATIVE WRITING—THE KELLY MANUAL OF STYLE

QUESTION:
WHAT IS THE CORRECT FORMAT FOR A MONTAGE THAT HAS A SERIES OF SCENES AT DIFFERENT LOCATIONS, BUT NO DIALOGUE?

ANSWER:
THERE ARE MANY CORRECT WAYS TO FORMAT A MONTAGE OR SERIES OF SHOTS. IT ALL DEPENDS ON YOUR PURPOSE. GENERALLY, A MONTAGE IS USED TO DESCRIBE A SERIES OF IMAGES THAT CONVEY A CONCEPT, SUCH AS PASSAGE OF TIME OR FALLING IN LOVE. THE SERIES OF SHOTS IS FOR A STRAIGHT NARRATIVE, A CHRONOLOGY OF EVENTS. NATURALLY, THE TWO ARE OFTEN USED INTERCHANGEABLY.

STANDARD FORMAT FOR THE MONTAGE.

MONTAGE - JOHN WAITS FOR MARY
-- JOHN GLANCES AT THE WAITING ROOM CLOCK. IT'S 10:00.
-- HE STARES AT A DOOR, GLANCES BACK AT THE CLOCK -- 10:30.
-- HE PACES THE ROOM NERVOUSLY -- 11:00. THE DOOR OPENS
AND MARY EXITS THE BATHROOM.

40.0.5.0. CHARACTER DEVELOPMENT:
IT'S BEEN SAID THAT A TRULY GREAT CHARACTER CAN SAVE AN OTHERWISE POOR SCRIPT. SOME PEOPLE ARE GREAT STORYTELLERS WHO PROVIDE A FANTASTIC NARRATIVE/DIALOGUE; BUT THE CHARACTERS FEEL LIFELESS, LIKE PROPS, TO TELL THE STORY. A CAST OF SCINTILLATING CHARACTERS, ALL MOVE THE SCRIPT FORWARD. THE TIME SPENT DOING OUR CHARACTER LIST AND THEIR DETAILS WILL PAY PROFITS HERE.[REFER TO CH 20].[REFER TO:www.filmstripwriting.com].

CONSIDER THESE BASIC CHARACTER ELEMENTS:
1. INITIAL CHARACTER CREATION.
2. CHARACTER RESEARCH
3. CHARACTER BACKGROUND
4. NAMING YOUR CHARACTERS
5. THE MAIN CHARACTER
6. THE MAIN VILLAIN
7. NARRATIVE & DIALOGUE FIT CHARACTER
8. USING ADVERSITY TO DEVELOP CHARACTERS
9. MAKING A CHARACTER MEMORABLE.
10. GIVING YOUR CHARACTER A UNIQUE VOICE
11. BUILDING UP A GREAT CHARACTER
12. CHARACTER CONSISTENCY AND WHEN TO BREAK IT
13. CHARACTER RELATIONSHIPS
14. CHARACTER PSYCHOLOGY
15. AVOIDING STEREOTYPES IN MINOR CHARACTERS
16. HARD HITTING VIOLENCE-IMPACT ON MIN CHARACTERS.

40.0.5.1. THREE BODIES OF A SCRIPT:
HEADINGS, NARRATIVE AND DIALOGUE.
EACH OF THESE HAS THREE POINTS TO REMEMBER.

HEADINGS:

<u>1. MASTER SCENE HEADINGS:</u>
A) CAMERA LOCATION - EXT. (EXTERIOR OR OUTSIDE) OR INT. (INTERIOR
   OR INSIDE)
B) SCENE LOCATION (LOCAL RACE TRACK)
C) TIME (DAY OR NIGHT)

<u>2. SECONDARY: SCENE & HEADING:</u> (STREET SCENE-CROWDS GOING TO WORK)

3. <u>"SPECIAL HEADINGS":</u>
   FOR THINGS SUCH AS MONTAGES, DREAM SEQUENCES, FLASHBACKS,
   FLASH FORWARDS, ETC.

NARRATIVE:

1. ACTION: (CAR CHASE-RUNNING AFTER BAD GUY-FIGHTING WAR)
2. CHARACTER AND SETTINGS **(VISUAL PLACE)**
3. SOUNDS: **DESCRIBE TRAFFIC-SILENCE-ETC.**

DIALOGUE:

1.<u>THE NAME OF THE CHARACTER APPEARS AT TOP, IN CAPS.</u>

2.<u>THE ACTORS DIRECTION</u>---**ACTOR AND DIRECTORS USAGE.**

3.<u>THE SPEECH</u>: **THE ACTOR'S SPEECH=DIALOGUE.**

<u>40.0.6.0 THE THREE ACT STRUCTURE :</u>
<u>A LINE CHART:EXAMPLE:</u>

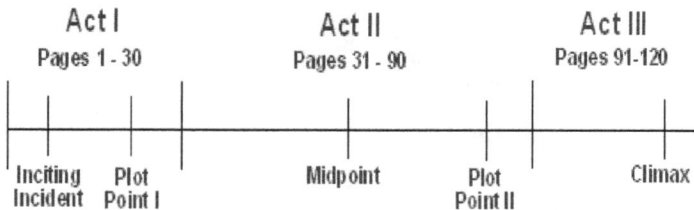

Act I — Pages 1 - 30
Act II — Pages 31 - 90
Act III — Pages 91-120

Inciting Incident   Plot Point I   Midpoint   Plot Point II   Climax

SCRIPT LENGTH-SPEC SCRIPT:

SPEC SCRIPTS ARE 100 TO 120 PAGES ROUGHLY. **EACH PAGE IS
EQUIVALENT TO ONE MINUTE OF SCREEN SHOWING TIME. LONG OR
ACTION FILLED PAGES MAY BE LONGER. SHORTER THAN 100 PAGES
MIGHT NOT BE ACCEPTED. LONGER IF ONLY WITH REASON.**

**ACT 1: APPROX 30 PAGES.
ACT 2: 60 PAGES.
ACT 3: 30 PAGES.
TOTAL 120 PAGES**

40.0.7.0. ACT I - THE BEGINNING:

THE MAIN CHARACTER:
BEGIN WITH A MAIN CHARACTER WHOSE LIFE AND SENSE OF
NORMALITY IS ABOUT TO BE TURNED UPSIDE DOWN. HIS PRESENT LIFE
IS PUSHED SO HARD THAT HIS OUTLOOK ON LIFE WILL CHANGE
DRASTICALLY.

DECIDE EXACTLY WHO IS YOUR MAIN CHARACTER? WHAT ARE HIS
STRENGTHS? HIS WEAKNESSES? DOES HE LIVE A JET SETTING LIFESTYLE
OR DOES HE LIFE REVOLVE AROUND HIS DESK JOB?

THE TEN MOST IMPORTANT PAGES OF YOUR SCRIPT: **THE INTRIGUING
TITLE AND THE FIRST TEN PAGES YOU WRITE IN YOUR SCRIPT** ARE
THE MOST IMPORTANT. YOU NEED TO GRAB THE READER THERE OR
ELSE THEY WILL PUT YOUR SCRIPT DOWN AND MOVE ONTO THE NEXT
SCRIPT.

40.0.7.1. ELEMENTS OF THE FIRST TEN PAGES:

IN THE FIRST TEN PAGES, YOU WILL WANT TO SETUP THE FOLLOWING:

1. THE MAIN CHARACTER: **SEE ACT I.** (VISUAL DESCRIPTION-CLOTHING
ATTITUDE W/MATCHING DIALOGUE).

2. LOCATION AND MOOD:
   WHERE/WHAT DOES YOUR CHARACTER LIVE OR PERFORM HIS ACTION
   SCENE? ADD THIS DETAIL TO YOUR CHARACTER.

3. GENRE':
   ONCE YOU HAVE THE 'KERNEL' YOU CAN DECIDE WHAT GENRE YOUR
   SCRIPT HAS. [SEE CH 1.4.7.0.]. EXAMPLE: ACTION, SCI-FI, ROMANTIC,
   HORROR, ETC.

4. THE KERNEL AND YOUR MAIN CHARACTER:
   IS HE THE HERO OR VILLAIN? DOES HE HAVE A MAJOR CONFLICT?
   IS IT APPEALING TO THE READER/MOVIE GOER?

5. TWO PLOT POINTS:
   1. THE INCITING INCIDENT(**RISING ACTION).**
      HOW IS THE MAIN CHARACTER'S LIFE CHANGE EVENTS HAPPENING?
      WHAT IS CAUSE AND EFFECT. WHAT BECOMES HIS MAJOR
      PROBLEM/INCIDENT/CONFLICT?

   2. NEAR THE END OF ACT 1, THE MAIN CHARACTER HAS A MAJOR PLOT
      EXPLOSION OR THE STORY CAREENS WILDLY IN ANOTHER
      DIRECTION. THIS IS THE TEST OF THE CHARACTER'S CHARACTER
      AND THE PLOTS. WILL HE HAVE THE RESOLVE TO CONTINUE? WILL
      THE AUDIENCE RELATE-EMPATHIZE?

40.0.8.0. ACT II - THE MIDDLE:

THIS ACT IS ALL ABOUT CONFLICT AND CONFRONTATION; NOTHING
SHOULD COME EASY TO YOUR MAIN CHARACTER.

LONG AND SHORT OF IT:

ACT II IS THE LONGEST ACT IN THE SCRIPT AND YOU SHOULD MAKE IT SEEM AS LONG AS POSSIBLE FOR YOUR MAIN CHARACTER YET SHORT AS POSSIBLE FOR THE READER/AUDIENCE. YOUR MAIN CHARACTER WILL COME FACE TO FACE WITH A WHOLE VARIETY OF OBSTACLES. THE OBSTACLES WILL STEADILY GROW BIGGER AND TOUGHER. EVERY TIME HE TAKES A STEP ON THE PATH TO REACH HIS GOAL. SOME FORCE (INNER OR OUTER) WILL BLOCK HIS PATH, FORCING THE MAIN CHARACTER TO THINK QUICKER AND GROW STRONGER; IF HE WANTS TO SUCCEED. FOR THIS REASON, IT IS A GOOD IDEA TO HAVE ONLY ONE OR TWO MAIN CHARACTERS IN A MOVIE. TOO MANY AND YOU RISK HAVING CHARACTERS BECOME UNDEVELOPED AND THE AUDIENCE NOT CARING ABOUT THEM SINCE THEY DON'T APPEAR TO BE IN ANY BIG DANGER AND THE CONFLICT APPEARS LESS IMPORTANT.

THE MIDPOINT:

ACT II CAN BE THE HARDEST ACT TO WRITE AS A SCRIPTWRITER. YOU OFTEN HAVE A CLEAR MENTAL PICTURE OF THE BEGINNING AND END OF THE SCRIPT; BUT IT IS HOW YOU GET THERE THAT PROVES DIFFICULT.

THE MIDPOINT OF THE SCRIPT OFFERS A LIFELINE TO THE SCRIPTWRITER. HERE WE HAVE ANOTHER TURNING POINT, OFTEN THE INTRODUCTION OR DEATH OF A CHARACTER, WHICH SHARPENS THE FOCUS OF THE MAIN CHARACTER ON ACHIEVING HIS GOAL.

40.0.9.0. PLOT POINT 2: MAJOR PLOT EXPLOSION:

THUS FAR, THE MAIN CHARACTER HAS REACHED THE END OF HIS ROPE. HIS SUCCESS LOOKS VERY DIM. THE OBSTACLES AND HURDLES HAVE TAKEN HIS STRENGTH AWAY. **THREE PLOT POINTS** WILL HAPPEN TO HIM FORCING THE MAIN CHARACTER TO TAKE ACTION

1. HE MUST SOLVE THE CONFLICT/PROBLEM CAUSED BY THE INCITING INCIDENT.

2. HIS TIME IS RUNNING OUT. THE PACE PICKS UPS. THE MAIN CHARACTER'S TIME IS RUNNING OUT TO FINISH THE SOLUTION. ACTIONS AND SCENES ACCELERATE. . SCRIPTWRITING IS ALL ABOUT SOLVING YOUR CHARACTERS' CONFLICT/PROBLEMS AND RESOLVING THEIR STORY.

3. THE MAIN CHARACTER MUST FOCUS ONLY ON THEIR RESOLUTION OF THE INCITING INCIDENT/CONFLICT/ HIS MAJOR PROBLEMS.

40.0.10.0. ACT III - THE ENDING:

THE CLOCK HAS RUN OUT, IT'S NOW OR NEVER FOR YOUR MAIN
CHARACTER. BY NOW, YOUR MAIN CHARACTER SEES THE GOAL IN
FRONT OF THEM, BUT EVEN CLOSER TO HIM ARE SEVERAL MORE
OBSTACLES. THESE WILL BE THE BIGGEST OBSTACLES OF ALL BUT YOUR
MAIN CHARACTER HAS COME TOO FAR TO TURN AROUND AND HEAD
FOR HOME NOW.

YOUR CHARACTER HAS TO WANT TO ACHIEVE THEIR GOAL SO BADLY
THAT NOTHING WILL STOP THEM. THAT DOES NOT MEAN TO SAY THAT
YOUR STORY HAS TO HAVE A HAPPY ENDING. JUST A GLIMMER OF HOPE
ESPECIALLY IF YOU ARE EXPECTING TO WRITE A SEQUEL TO THIS SCRIPT
BE CAREFUL NOT TO GIVE YOUR STORY THE "PERFECT ENDING" WHERE
ALL THE LOOSE THREADS IN THE STORY ARE TIED UP NEATLY; SO
NEATLY THE ENDING SEEMS FALSE.

40.0.11.0. THE CLIMAX:

THE CLIMAX IS THE ULTIMATE BATTLE-SCENE-ACTION SEQUENCE OF
THE MOVIE. GOOD AND EVIL FIGHT TO THE END. THE HERO MIGHT SAVE
THE DAY AND RESOLVE THE PROBLEM IN A VERY DRAMATIC FASHION.
THE UNIVERSAL THEME IS RESOLVED. TEARS AND HEART FELT
EMOTIONS MIGHT EVOKE THE READER/AUDIENCE TO FEEL THE
STORY.(OUR HEART METER). THE CLIMAX GENERALLY LEAVES CLOSURE
WITH THE ENDING. LOOSE ENDS ARE TIED UP. THE MAIN CHARACTER
DIES OR GOES ON TO THE NEXT SCRIPT.

40.0.12.0. SCRIPT DIRECTIONS:

BELOW ARE TWO EXAMPLES OF SCRIPT DIRECTIONS-FORMATS:
(MY COMMENTS ARE IN PARENTHESIS)

EXAMPLE 1:

FADE IN (BEFORE TITLE)

EXT. NEW YORK CITY (DAY)

A VISUAL HIGH ANGLE SHOT OF MANHATTAN IN FALL AFTERNOON.

NARRATOR:

TELLS INTRO TO STORY

MAIN TITLE & MUSIC COME UP OVER SHOT (MANHATTAN)

CUT TO:

STREET SCENE:
DESCRIPTION BY WRITER

EXT. PLAZA HOTEL

(MAIN CHARACTER WALKS OUT OF BUILDING-HAVING CONVERSATION WITH SECRETARY.)

MAIN CHARACTER NAME:
HIS DIALOGUE

40.0.13.0. EXAMPLE 2:
PAGE 1 SCRIPT: TITLE BY AUTHOR.

FADE IN (CREDITS OVER)
EXT: SOUTH CAROLINA COUNTRYSIDE-DAY
     (VISUAL DESCRIPTION-WOODS-RIVERSIDE-MAPLES)

SUPERIMPOSITION:
                    CHARACTER VISUALLY DESCRIBED WITH HIS
                    CLOTHES-RIFLE AND GAME BIRDS(NO WORDS).

INT. BARN-WORK SHOP-DAY
           PAN OF ROOM WITH TOOLS AND CHAIR UPON WORK TABLE

MAIN CHARACTER NAME: (VISUAL SHOT OF CHARACTER &
                    HIS DIALOGUE IS HERE)

SUPERIMPOSITION(SUPER):
                    "THE FOLLOWING IS BASE UPON A TRUE STORY."
RESEARCH: OR BUY: THE HOLLYWOOD STANDARD
                    THE SCREEN WRITER'S BIBLE

40.0.14.0.WHY SCRIPT ANALYSIS & STORY NOTES BY MICHAEL FERRIS

EDITED FOR BREVITY.

A SCREEN WRITER'S WRITING TOOL:

WHY SCRIPT ANALYSIS AND STORY NOTES ARE VITAL TO YOUR SUCCESS AS A SCREEN WRITER:

STORY NOTES ARE A VITAL COMPONENT IN EVERY SERIOUS SCREENWRITER'S ARSENAL.

THERE IS ONE KEY TO SUCCESS THAT I WANT YOU TO KEEP IN MIND WHILE READING THIS ARTICLE: ALL IT TAKES IS ONE CHAMPION OF YOUR SCRIPT TO MAKE YOUR DREAM OF BECOMING A PROFESSIONAL SCREENWRITER A REALITY. WRITE THAT ABOVE YOUR DESK – IT WILL GET YOU THROUGH THOSE NIGHTS WHERE YOU QUESTION WHAT IT IS YOU ARE DOING, AND IT WILL BE A HAPPY REMINDER ONCE YOU'VE "MADE IT."

FIRST, LET'S TALK ABOUT THE PROFESSIONALS – THE BIG LEAGUE PLAYERS, DON'T OFTEN USE SCRIPT ANALYSTS FOR THEIR STORY NOTES. WHY? THEY DON'T HAVE TO. THEY HAVE MANAGERS, AGENTS, PRODUCERS, AND STUDIO EXECUTIVES WHO GIVE THEM STORY NOTES

CREATIVE WRITING—THE KELLY MANUAL OF STYLE

ALL DAY. THEY DON'T OFTEN USE SCRIPT ANALYSTS; BUT THEY RELY ON STORY NOTES TO GUIDE THEM TO THE FINAL DRAFT.

IT'S AN IMPORTANT POINT, BECAUSE AS WE ALL KNOW – WRITING IS REWRITING. SO WHILE THEY MAY NOT TAKE EVERY STORY NOTE FROM EVERY SINGLE PERSON AND INTEGRATE IT INTO THEIR DRAFT, THEY USE ALL OF THEM TO HELP WINNOW DOWN WHAT NEEDS TO BE DONE TO GET THE STORY ACROSS. WHY IS THAT? BECAUSE, AND THIS APPLIES TO ALL WRITERS – ASPIRING AND ACCOMPLISHED ALIKE – WE DON'T HAVE FRESH EYES WHEN IT COMES TO OUR SCREENPLAYS. WE LIVE THEM, WE BREATH THEM, WE WRITE THEM – THUS WE DON'T HAVE AN UNBIASED, OBJECTIVE EYE TO SEE EXACTLY WHAT WORKS, AND WHAT NEEDS WORK. SO THAT'S POINT NUMBER 1:

#1 FRESH EYES: ALL WRITERS NEED AT LEAST ONE PAIR OF FRESH EYES TO READ A SCRIPT. PROFESSIONAL SCREENWRITERS GET THE ADDED BONUS OF HAVING OTHER PEOPLE *WHO KNOW EXACTLY WHAT MAKES A SCRIPT WORK LOOK OVER THEIR SCREENPLAYS AND TELL THEM WHAT IT LACKS.*

MOST LIKELY NOT. WHAT CAN THOSE ACCOMPLISHED AND "FRESH EYES" BRING YOU?

#2 A NEW PERSPECTIVE: MAKING THE "CONSIDER" AND THE TRASHBIN MANY TIMES, THE MOST USEFUL ASPECT OF GETTING STORY NOTES IS THAT IT SHOWS US A NEW PERSPECTIVE ON THE SAME CONCEPT AND PLOT THAT WE NEVER THOUGHT ABOUT BEFORE. TWEAKING THIS CHARACTER, OR THAT PLOT POINT, OR ENHANCING THIS ACT TURN IN A WAY THAT OPENS THE STORY UP IN A WAY WE NEVER CONSIDERED.

IF SCREEN WRITING IS REWRITING,. MANY TIMES, THE CHANGES AND TWEAKS THEY RECOMMEND WILL NOT ONLY MAKE YOUR MATERIAL BETTER AND STRONGER; BUT IT MAKES THE DIFFERENCE BETWEEN YOUR SCRIPT BEING TOSSED OUT, OR BEING "CONSIDERED".

 SCREENPLAY ANALYSTS THAT ALSO PROVIDE A NUMBER OF IDEAS ON HOW TO TAKE WHAT YOU CURRENTLY HAVE, AND TWEAK A FEW KEY :CHARACTERS, SCENES, DIALOG ETC.; THINGS TO MAKE IT MORE APPEALING TO THE POWER PLAYERS.IMPROVING ITS COMMERICIAL LIKABILITY. [ANSWER TRUTHFULLY: IS IT WORTH PRODUCING AND WILL IT BE A COMMERCIAL SUCCESS? IT HAS TO BE MORE THAN GREAT, IT HAS TO BE OUTSTANDING IN A SEA OF SCRIPTS!!!!—AUTHOR].

#3 SAVING OPPORTUNITIES:
YOU HAVE ONE OPPORTUNITY TO PROVE YOUR WRITING WORTH BECAUSE ONCE SOMEONE HAS READ YOUR SCRIPT AND THOUGHT IT WASN'T ANY GOOD, YOU'VE ESSENTIALLY BURNED THAT READER. THEY WON'T BE INTERESTED IN READING THE "NEWER, BETTER DRAFT.

ALL OF THIS SOUNDS BRUTAL, I KNOW. BUT AS A FORMER LIT MANAGER, {MICHAEL FERRIS} I CAN TELL YOU THAT NONE OF US – AGENTS, MANAGERS, EXECUTIVES, PRODUCERS – HAVE ANY TIME. WE'RE INUNDATED WITH PILES AND PILES OF SCRIPTS, ALL OF WHICH THAT HAVE TO BE READ "YESTERDAY", SO ANY EXCUSE WE CAN GET FOR SKIPPING ONE, OR READING A COUPLE OF PAGES AND THROWING IT OUT, WE'LL TAKE.

NOW THE COMMERCIAL:
THIS IS THE BIGGEST REASON WHY YOU NEED TO MAKE SURE YOUR
SCRIPT IS SO GOOD, THAT IT'S INDISPUTABLY AIRTIGHT. AS I'M FOND OF
SAYING, YOU HAVE TO WRITE BETTER THAN THE PROS IN ORDER TO
BREAK INTO THE BUSINESS. THE GOOD NEWS IS, THIS IS ENTIRELY
DOABLE. A GOOD SCRIPT ANALYST CAN GET YOU THERE.

TO SEE MORE ARTICLES BY MICHAEL FERRIS, GO TO:
http://www.screenplay.com/t-mferris-articles.aspx
TO SEE MORE ARTICLES ABOUT SCREENWRITING AND STORY
DEVELOPMENT, GO TO: http://www.screenplay.com/t-writingresources.aspx

**[GO TO THE WEB, CHECK OUT SCRIPT
ANALYSTS. IF YOUR SCRIPT IS REALLY,
REALLY GOOD, EVEN OUTSTANDING;
GET IT ANALYZED WHICH IS A
CRITICAL REVIEW.**

**DIY---YES, IT IS DOABLE, IT STILL
TAKES THAT EXTRA EFFORT!**

CHAPTER 41

41.0.0.0. MOVIE TITLES-& MORE BOOK IDEAS:

SOURCE: http://www.nytimes.com/ref/movies/1000best.html

41.0.0.1. WRITER USE THESE FOR INSPIRATION:

> **Look here for book ideas:**
> Note: The short sweet titles.
> ***Do: Add those new titles being released.**
> **Consider merging with your Master Idea List.**
> **GREAT MOVIES CAME FROM GREAT BOOKS!**

> **LOOK FOR THE THEMES BEHIND THE TITLE, WHY WERE THESE ONES CHOSEN FROM THOUSANDS? NOTE MANY ARE THE GRAND MASTERS OF WRITING. CH 28. FOLLOW THEIR LEAD; DO SELECT A SWEET & TIGHT TITLE, A THEME NOT OVERUSED AND APPROS TO THE TIME AND STORY YOU WANT TO WRITE ABOUT.**

A NOUS LA LIBERTE (1932)

ABOUT SCHMIDT (2002)

ABSENCE OF MALICE (1981)
ACE IN THE HOLE

ADAM'S RIB (1949)

ADAPTATION (2002)

THE ADJUSTER (1991)

THE ADVENTURES OF ROBIN HOOD (1938)

AFFLICTION (1998)

AFRICAN QUEEN, THE (1952)

L'AGE D'OR (1930, REVIEWED 1964)

AGUIRRE, THE WRATH OF GOD (1972, REVIEWED 1977)

A.I. (2001)

AIRPLANE! (1980)

ALADDIN (1992)

ALEXANDER NEVSKY (1939)

ALICE DOESN'T LIVE HERE ANYMORE (1975)

ALICE'S RESTAURANT (1969)

ALIENS (1986)

ALL ABOUT EVE (1950)

ALL ABOUT MY MOTHER (1999)

ALL QUIET ON THE WESTERN FRONT (1930)

ALL THAT HEAVEN ALLOWS (1956)
ALL THE KING'S MEN (1949)
ALL THE PRESIDENT'S MEN (1976)
AMADEUS (1984)
AMARCORD (1974)
AMÉLIE (2001)
AMERICA, AMERICA (1963)
AMERICAN FRIEND, THE (1977)
AMERICAN GRAFFITI (1973)
AN AMERICAN IN PARIS (1951)
AMERICANIZATION OF EMILY , THE(1964)
AMERICAN MOVIE (1999)
AMORES PERROS (2000)
ANASTASIA (1956)
ANATOMY OF A MURDER (1959)
ANGRY SILENCE, THE (1960)
ANNA AND THE KING OF SIAM (1946)
ANNA CHRISTIE (1930)
ANNIE HALL (1977)
APARTMENT, THE (1960)
APOCALYPSE NOW (1979)
APOLLO 13 (1995)
APOSTLE, THE (1997)
L'ARGENT (1983)
ASHES AND DIAMONDS (1958, REVIEWED 1961)
ASHES AND DIAMONDS (1958)
THE ASPHALT JUNGLE (1950)
L'ATALANTE (1934, REVIEWED 1947)
ATLANTIC CITY (1981)
AU REVOIR LES ENFANTS (1988)
L'AVVENTURA (1961)
THE AWFUL TRUTH (1937)

BABETTE'S FEAST (1987)
BABY DOLL (1956)
BACK TO THE FUTURE (1985)
THE BAD AND THE BEAUTIFUL (1953)
BAD DAY AT BLACK ROCK (1955)
BADLANDS (1973)
THE BAKER'S WIFE (1940)
BALL OF FIRE (1942)
THE BALLAD OF CABLE HOGUE (1970)
BAMBI (1942)

THE BAND WAGON (1953)
BANG THE DRUM SLOWLY (1973)
THE BANK DICK (1940)
BARFLY (1987)
BARRY LYNDON (1975)
BARTON FINK (1991)
THE BATTLE OF ALGIERS (1965, REVIEWED 1967)
LE BEAU MARIAGE (1982)
BEAUTIFUL PEOPLE (2000)
BEAUTY AND THE BEAST (1947)
BEAUTY AND THE BEAST (1991)
BED AND BOARD (1971)
BEETLEJUICE (1988)
BEFORE NIGHT FALLS (2000)
BEFORE THE RAIN (1994, REVIEWED 1995)
BEING JOHN MALKOVICH (1999)
BEING THERE (1979)
BELLE DE JOUR (1968)
BEN-HUR (1959)
BERLIN ALEXANDERPLATZ (1983)
THE BEST YEARS OF OUR LIVES (1946)
BEVERLY HILLS COP (1984)
THE BICYCLE THIEF (1949)
THE BIG CHILL (1983)
THE BIG CLOCK (1948)
THE BIG DEAL ON MADONNA STREET (1960)
THE BIG HEAT (1953)
BIG NIGHT (1996)
THE BIG RED ONE (1980)
THE BIG SKY (1952)
THE BIG SLEEP (1946)
BILLY LIAR (1963)
BILOXI BLUES (1988)
THE BIRDS (1963)
BIRDY (1984)
BLACK NARCISSUS (1947)
BLACK ORPHEUS (1959)
BLACK ROBE (1991)
BLAZING SADDLES (1974)
BLOODY SUNDAY (2002)
BLOW-UP (1966)
BLUE COLLAR (1978)
BLUE VELVET (1986)

BOB & CAROL & TED & ALICE (1969)
BOB LE FLAMBEUR (1955, REVIEWED 1981)
BODY HEAT (1981)
BONNIE AND CLYDE (1967)
BOOGIE NIGHTS (1997)
BORN ON THE FOURTH OF JULY (1989)
BORN YESTERDAY (1950)
LE BOUCHER (1970)
BOUND FOR GLORY (1976)
BOYS DON'T CRY (1999)
BOYZ N THE HOOD (1991)
BRAZIL (1985)
BREAD, LOVE AND DREAMS (1954)
BREAKER MORANT (1980)
THE BREAKFAST CLUB (1985)
BREAKING AWAY (1979)
BREAKING THE WAVES (1996)
BREATHLESS (1961)
THE BRIDE WORE BLACK (1968)
THE BRIDGE ON THE RIVER KWAI (1957)
BRIEF ENCOUNTER (1946)
A BRIEF HISTORY OF TIME (1992)
BRINGING UP BABY (1938)
BROADCAST NEWS (1987)
BROTHER'S KEEPER (1992)
THE BUDDY HOLLY STORY (1978)
BULL DURHAM (1988)
BULLITT (1968)
BUS STOP (1956)
BUTCH CASSIDY AND THE SUNDANCE KID (1969)
THE BUTCHER BOY (1998)
BYE BYE BRASIL (1980)

THE EARRINGS OF MADAME DE . . . (1954)
CABARET (1972)
THE CAINE MUTINY (1954)
CALIFORNIA SUITE (1978)
CALLE 54 (2000)
CAMELOT (1967)
CAMILLE (1937)
CAPTAINS COURAGEOUS (1937)
CARMEN JONES (1954)
CARNAL KNOWLEDGE (1971)

CASABLANCA (1942)

CAT ON A HOT TIN ROOF (1958)

CATCH-22 (1970)

CAVALCADE (1933)

THE CELEBRATION (1998)

LA CÉRÉMONIE (1996)

CHAN IS MISSING (1982)

CHARIOTS OF FIRE (1981)

CHARLEY VARRICK (1973)

CHICAGO (2002)

CHICKEN RUN (2000)

LA CHIENNE (1931, REVIEWED 1975)

CHINATOWN (1974)

CHLOË IN THE AFTERNOON (1972)

CHOCOLAT (1988, REVIEWED 1989)

THE CIDER HOUSE RULES (1999)

THE CITADEL (1938)

CITIZEN KANE (1941)

CLAIRE'S KNEE (1971)

THE CLOCKMAKER (1973, REVIEWED 1976)

A CLOCKWORK ORANGE (1971)

CLOSE ENCOUNTERS OF THE THIRD KIND (1977)

CLOSE-UP (1990, REVIEWED 1999)

CLUELESS (1995)

COAL MINER'S DAUGHTER (1980)

THE COLOR OF MONEY (1986)

COME BACK, LITTLE SHEBA (1952)

COMING HOME (1978)

THE CONFORMIST (1970)

THE CONQUEST OF EVEREST (1953)

CONTEMPT (1964)

THE CONVERSATION (1974)

COOL HAND LUKE (1967)

THE COUNT OF MONTE CRISTO (1934)

THE COUNTRY GIRL (1954)

THE COUSINS (1959)

THE CRANES ARE FLYING (1960)

CRIES AND WHISPERS (1972)

CROSSFIRE (1947)

CRUMB (1994)

CRY, THE BELOVED COUNTRY (1952)

THE CRYING GAME (1992)

DAMN YANKEES (1958)

CREATIVE WRITING—THE KELLY MANUAL OF STYLE

THE DAMNED (1969)
DANCE WITH A STRANGER (1985)
DANGEROUS LIAISONS (1988)
DANIEL (1983)
DANTON (1983)
DARK EYES (1987)
DARK VICTORY (1939)
DARLING (1965)
DAVID COPPERFIELD (1935)
DAVID HOLTZMAN'S DIARY (1968, REVIEWED 1973)
DAWN OF THE DEAD (1979)
DAY FOR NIGHT (1973)
THE DAY OF THE JACKAL (1973)
THE DAY THE EARTH STOOD STILL (1951)
DAYS OF HEAVEN (1978)
DAYS OF WINE AND ROSES (1963)
THE DEAD (1987)
DEAD CALM (1989)
DEAD END (1937)
DEAD MAN WALKING (1995)
DEAD OF NIGHT (1946, REVIEWED 1946)
DEAD RINGERS (1988)
DEATH IN VENICE (1971)
DEATH OF A SALESMAN (1951)
THE DECALOGUE (2000)
DEEP END (1971)
THE DEER HUNTER (1978)
THE DEFIANT ONES (1958)
DELIVERANCE (1972)
DESPERATELY SEEKING SUSAN (1985)
DESTRY RIDES AGAIN (1939)
DIABOLIQUE (1955)
DIAL M FOR MURDER (1954)
DIARY OF A CHAMBERMAID (1964)
DIARY OF A COUNTRY PRIEST (1950, REVIEWED 1954)
DIE HARD (1988)
DINER (1982)
DINNER AT EIGHT (1933)
THE DIRTY DOZEN (1967)
DIRTY HARRY (1971)
DIRTY ROTTEN SCOUNDRELS (1988)
THE DISCREET CHARM OF THE BOURGEOISIE (1972)
DISRAELI (1929)

DISTANT THUNDER (1973)

DIVA (1982)

DIVORCE-ITALIAN STYLE (1962)

DO THE RIGHT THING (1989)

DR. JEKYLL AND MR. HYDE (1932)

DR. STRANGELOVE OR: HOW I LEARNED TO STOP WORRYING AND LOVE THE BOMB (1964)

DOCTOR ZHIVAGO (1965)

DODSWORTH (1936)

LA DOLCE VITA (1961)

DONNIE BRASCO (1997)

DON'T LOOK BACK (1967)

DOUBLE INDEMNITY (1944)

DOWN BY LAW (1986)

DRACULA (1931)

THE DREAMLIFE OF ANGELS (1998)

DRESSED TO KILL (1980)

THE DRESSER (1983)

DRIVING MISS DAISY (1989)

DROWNING BY NUMBERS (1991)

DRUGSTORE COWBOY (1989)

DUCK SOUP (1933)

THE DUELLISTS (1978)

DUMBO (1941)

EARRINGS OF MADAME DE . . ., THE

EAST OF EDEN (1955)

EASY LIVING (1937)

EAT DRINK MAN WOMAN (1994)

EFFI BRIEST (1977)

8 1/2 (1963)

EIGHT MEN OUT (1988)

THE ELEPHANT MAN (1980)

ELMER GANTRY (1960)

EMPIRE OF THE SUN (1987)

ENEMIES, A LOVE STORY (1989)

LES ENFANTS DU PARADIS (1945, REVIEWED 1947)

THE ENGLISH PATIENT (1996)

THE ENTERTAINER (1960)

ENTRE NOUS (1983)

E.T. THE EXTRA-TERRESTRIAL (1982)
EUROPA, EUROPA (1991)
EVERY MAN FOR HIMSELF (1980)
THE EXORCIST (1973)
THE EXTERMINATING ANGEL (1967)

A FACE IN THE CROWD (1957)
FACE TO FACE (1976)
FACES (1968)
THE FAMILY GAME (1984)
FANNY & ALEXANDER (1983)
FANTASIA (1940)
FAREWELL, MY CONCUBINE (1993)
FAR FROM HEAVEN (2002)
FARGO (1996)
FAST, CHEAP & OUT OF CONTROL (1997)
FAST RUNNER (ATANARJUAT) (2002)
FAT CITY (1972)
FATAL ATTRACTION (1987)
FATHER OF THE BRIDE (1950)
FELLINI SATYRICON (1970)
LA FEMME INFIDÈLE (1969)
LA FEMME NIKITA (1991)
THE FISHER KING (1991)
FIST IN HIS POCKET (1968)
FITZCARRALDO (1982)
FIVE EASY PIECES (1970)
THE FLAMINGO KID (1984)
THE FLY (1958)

FORCE OF EVIL (1948)
FOR WHOM THE BELL TOLLS (1943)
FORBIDDEN GAMES (1952)
A FOREIGN AFFAIR (1948)
THE FORTUNE COOKIE (1966)
THE 400 BLOWS (1959)
FRANKENSTEIN (1931)
THE FRENCH CONNECTION (1971)
FRENZY (1972)
FRIENDLY PERSUASION (1956)
FROM HERE TO ETERNITY (1953)
THE FUGITIVE (1947)
FULL METAL JACKET (1987)
THE FULL MONTY (1997)

FUNNY FACE (1957)
FUNNY GIRL (1968)
FURY (1936)

GALLIPOLI (1981)
GANDHI (1982)
GANGS OF NEW YORK (2002)
THE GARDEN OF THE FINZI-CONTINIS (1971)
GAS FOOD LODGING (1992)
GASLIGHT (1944)
GATE OF HELL (1954)
A GEISHA (1978)
THE GENERAL (1998)
GENERAL DELLA ROVERE (1960)
GENEVIEVE (1954)
GENTLEMEN PREFER BLONDES (1953)
GEORGY GIRL (1966)
GET CARTER (1971)
GET OUT YOUR HANDKERCHIEFS (1978)
GHOST WORLD (2001)
GIANT (1956)
GIGI (1958)
GIMME SHELTER (1970)
THE GIRL CAN'T HELP IT (1956)
GIRL WITH A SUITCASE (1961)
THE GLEANERS AND I (2001)
THE GOALIE'S ANXIETY AT THE PENALTY KICK (1977)
THE GO-BETWEEN (1971)
THE GODFATHER (1972)
THE GODFATHER PART II (1974)
GOING MY WAY (1944)
GOLDFINGER (1964)
GONE WITH THE WIND (1939)
THE GOOD, THE BAD AND THE UGLY (1968)
THE GOOD EARTH (1937)
GOODBYE, MR. CHIPS (1939)
GOODFELLAS (1990)

CREATIVE WRITING—THE KELLY MANUAL OF STYLE

GOSFORD PARK (2001)
THE GRADUATE (1967)
GRAND HOTEL (1932)
GRAND ILLUSION (1938)
THE GRAPES OF WRATH (1940)
THE GREAT DICTATOR (1940)
GREAT EXPECTATIONS (1947)
THE GREAT MAN (1957)
THE GREAT MCGINTY (1940)
THE GREATEST SHOW ON EARTH (1952)
GREEN FOR DANGER (1947)
GREGORY'S GIRL (1982)
THE GRIFTERS (1990)
GROUNDHOG DAY (1993)
THE GUNFIGHTER (1950)
GUNGA DIN (1939)

HAIL THE CONQUERING HERO (1944)
HAIR (1979)
HAMLET (1948)
HAMLET (2000)
HANDLE WITH CARE (1977)
HANNAH AND HER SISTERS (1986)
HAPPINESS (1998)
A HARD DAY'S NIGHT (1964)
HARLAN COUNTY, USA (1976)
HARRY AND TONTO (1974)
A HATFUL OF RAIN (1957)
THE HEARTBREAK KID (1972)
HEARTLAND (1981)
HEARTS OF DARKNESS: A FILMMAKER'S APOCALYPSE (1991)
HEAT AND DUST (1983)
HEATHERS (1989)
HEAVY TRAFFIC (1973)
HEIMAT (1985)
THE HEIRESS (1949)
HENRY V (1946)
HENRY V (1989)
HENRY FOOL (1998)
HERE COMES MR. JORDAN (1941)

HIGH AND LOW (JAPAN) (1963)
THE HIGH AND THE MIGHTY (1954)
HIGH ART (1998)
HIGH HOPES (1988)
HIGH NOON (1952)
HIGH SIERRA (1941)
THE HILL (1965)
HIROSHIMA MON AMOUR (1960)
HIS GIRL FRIDAY (1940)
THE HOMECOMING (1973)
HOOP DREAMS (1994)
HOPE AND GLORY (1987)
HOTEL TERMINUS: KLAUS BARBIE ET SON TEMPS (1988)
THE HOURS (2002)
HOUSEHOLD SAINTS (1993)
HOUSE OF GAMES (1987)
HOW GREEN WAS MY VALLEY (1941)
HOW TO MARRY A MILLIONAIRE (1953)
HOWARDS END (1992)
HUD (1963)
KEN BURNS' AMERICA: HUEY LONG (1985)
HUSBANDS AND WIVES (1992)
THE HUSTLER (1961)

I KNOW WHERE I'M GOING! (1947)
I REMEMBER MAMA (1948)
I WANT TO LIVE! (1958)
IF... (1969)
IKIRU (1952, REVIEWED 1960)
I'M ALL RIGHT JACK (1960)
IMITATION OF LIFE (1959)
IN COLD BLOOD (1967)
IN THE BEDROOM (2001)
IN THE HEAT OF THE NIGHT (1967)
THE INFORMER (1935)
INHERIT THE WIND (1960)
THE INSIDER (1999)
INTERNAL AFFAIRS (1990)
THE IPCRESS FILE (1965)

IT HAPPENED ONE NIGHT (1934)
IT'S A GIFT (1935)
IT'S A WONDERFUL LIFE (1946)

JAILHOUSE ROCK (1957)
JAWS (1975)
THE JAZZ SINGER (1927)
JEAN DE FLORETTE (1987)
JERRY MAGUIRE (1996)
JOHNNY GUITAR (1954)
THE JUDGE AND THE ASSASSIN (1982)
JUDGMENT AT NUREMBERG (1961)
JU DOU (1990)
JULES AND JIM (1962)
JULIET OF THE SPIRITS (1965)
JUNIOR BONNER (1972)
THE JUROR

K

KAGEMUSHA (1980)
THE KILLERS (1946)
THE KILLING FIELDS (1984)
KIND HEARTS AND CORONETS (1950)
THE KING AND I (1956)
KING KONG (1933)
KING LEAR (1971)
THE KING OF COMEDY (1983)
THE KING OF MARVIN GARDENS (1972)
KISS OF THE SPIDER WOMAN (1985)
KLUTE (1971)
KNIFE IN THE WATER (1963)
KRAMER VS. KRAMER (1979)

L.A. CONFIDENTIAL (1997)
LACOMBE LUCIEN (1974)

THE LADY EVE (1941)
THE LADY VANISHES (1938)
LADYBIRD, LADYBIRD (1994)
LAMERICA (1994, REVIEWED 1995)
THE LAST AMERICAN HERO (1973)
THE LAST EMPEROR (1987)
THE LAST METRO (1980)
THE LAST PICTURE SHOW (1971)
THE LAST SEDUCTION (1994)
LAST TANGO IN PARIS (1973)
THE LAST TEMPTATION OF CHRIST (1988)
THE LAST WALTZ (1978)
LAURA (1944)
THE LAVENDER HILL MOB (1951)
LAWRENCE OF ARABIA (1962)
A LEAGUE OF THEIR OWN (1992)
LEAVING LAS VEGAS (1995)
THE LEOPARD (1963)
THE LETTER (1963)
A LETTER TO THREE WIVES (1949)
LES LIAISONS DANGEREUSES 1960 (1961)
THE LIFE AND DEATH OF COLONEL BLIMP (1945)
LIFE IS SWEET (1991)
THE LIFE OF EMILE ZOLA (1937)
LIFE WITH FATHER (1947)
LIKE WATER FOR CHOCOLATE (1992, REVIEWED 1993)
LILI (1953)
LITTLE BIG MAN (1970)
LITTLE CAESAR (1931)
THE LITTLE FOXES (1941)
THE LITTLE FUGITIVE (1953)
THE LITTLE KIDNAPPERS (1954)
LITTLE VERA (1988, REVIEWED 1989)
LITTLE WOMEN (1933)
LITTLE WOMEN (1994)
THE LIVES OF A BENGAL LANCER (1935)
LIVING IN OBLIVION (1995)
LOCAL HERO (1983)
LOLA (1982)
LOLA MONTÈS (1968)
LOLITA (1962)
LONE STAR (1996)
THE LONELINESS OF THE LONG DISTANCE RUNNER (1962)

CREATIVE WRITING—THE KELLY MANUAL OF STYLE

LONG DAY'S JOURNEY INTO NIGHT (1962)
THE LONG GOODBYE (1973)
THE LONG GOOD FRIDAY (1982)
THE LONG VOYAGE HOME (1940)
THE LONGEST DAY (1962)
LOOK BACK IN ANGER (1959)
LOST HORIZON (1937)
LOST IN AMERICA (1985)
THE LOST WEEKEND (1945)
LOVE (1973)
LOVE AFFAIR (1939)
LOVE AND DEATH (1975)
A LOVE IN GERMANY (1984)
LOVE IN THE AFTERNOON (1957)
LOVELY AND AMAZING (2002)
LOVE ON THE RUN (1979)
LOVER COME BACK (1962)
THE LOVERS (1959)
LOVES OF A BLONDE (1966)
LOVING (1970)
LUST FOR LIFE (1956)

M (1931, REVIEWED 1933)
MAD MAX (1980)
THE MADNESS OF KING GEORGE (1994)
THE MAGIC FLUTE (1975)
THE MAJOR AND THE MINOR (1942)
MAJOR BARBARA (1941)
MAKE WAY FOR TOMORROW (1937)
MALCOLM X (1992)
THE MALTESE FALCON (1941)
A MAN FOR ALL SEASONS (1966)
MAN HUNT (1941)
THE MAN WHO CAME TO DINNER (1942)
THE MAN WHO LOVED WOMEN (1977)
THE MAN WHO WASN'T THERE (2001)
THE MAN WITH THE GOLDEN ARM (1955)
THE MANCHURIAN CANDIDATE (1962)
MANHATTAN (1979)
MANON OF THE SPRING (1987)

MARRIAGE ITALIAN STYLE (1964)
THE MARRIAGE OF MARIA BRAUN (1979)
MARRIED TO THE MOB (1988)
THE MARRYING KIND (1952)
MARTY (1955)
MARY POPPINS (1964)
M*A*S*H (1970)
THE MATCH FACTORY GIRL (1990)
MAYERLING (1937)
MCCABE & MRS. MILLER (1971)
MEAN STREETS (1973)
MEET ME IN ST. LOUIS (1944)
MELVIN AND HOWARD (1980)
MEMORIES OF UNDERDEVELOPMENT (1973)
THE MEMORY OF JUSTICE (1976)
THE MEN (1950)
MÉNAGE (1986)
METROPOLITAN (1990)
MIDNIGHT (1939)
MIDNIGHT COWBOY (1969)
MINNIE AND MOSKOWITZ (1971)
THE MIRACLE OF MORGAN'S CREEK (1944)
MIRACLE ON 34TH STREET (1947)
THE MIRACLE WORKER (1962)
LES MISERABLES (1935)
THE MISFITS (1961)
MISSING (1982)
MR. AND MRS. BRIDGE (1990)
MR. DEEDS GOES TO TOWN (1936)
MR. HULOT'S HOLIDAY (1954)
MISTER ROBERTS (1955)
MR. SMITH GOES TO WASHINGTON (1939)
MRS. MINIVER (1942)
MON ONCLE D'AMÉRIQUE (1980)
MONA LISA (1986)
MONSIEUR VERDOUX (1947, REVIEWED 1964)
MONSTERS, INC. (2001)
MOONLIGHTING (1982)
MOONSTRUCK (1987)
THE MORE THE MERRIER (1943)
MORGAN! (1966)
THE MORTAL STORM (1940)
MOTHER (1996)

MOULIN ROUGE (1953)
THE MOUTHPIECE (1932)
MUCH ADO ABOUT NOTHING (1993)
MULHOLLAND DR. (2001)
MURMUR OF THE HEART (1971)
MUTINY ON THE BOUNTY (1935)
MY BEAUTIFUL LAUNDRETTE (1986)
MY DARLING CLEMENTINE (1946)
MY DINNER WITH ANDRE (1981)
MY FAIR LADY (1964)
MY LEFT FOOT (1989)
MY LIFE AS A DOG (1987)
MY MAN GODFREY (1936)
MY NIGHT AT MAUD'S (1969)
MY OWN PRIVATE IDAHO (1991)
MY 20TH CENTURY (1990)
MON ONCLE (1958)

THE NAKED GUN: FROM THE FILES OF POLICE SQUAD! (1988)
NASHVILLE (1975)
NATIONAL LAMPOON'S ANIMAL HOUSE (1978)
NATIONAL VELVET (1944)
NETWORK (1976)
NEVER ON SUNDAY (1960)
NIGHT MOVES (1975)
THE NIGHT OF THE HUNTER (1955)
NIGHT OF THE LIVING DEAD (1968)
A NIGHT TO REMEMBER (1958)
A NIGHTMARE ON ELM STREET (1984)
1900 (1977)
NINOTCHKA (1939)
NOBODY'S FOOL (1994)
NORMA RAE (1979)
NORTH BY NORTHWEST (1959)
NOTHING BUT THE BEST (1964)
NOTORIOUS (1946)
NOW, VOYAGER (1942)
LA NUIT DE VARENNES (1983)
THE NUN'S STORY (1959)

ODD MAN OUT (1947)
OF MICE AND MEN (1940)
OKLAHOMA! (1955)
OLIVER TWIST (1951)
LOS OLVIDADOS (1950, REVIEWED 1952)
ON THE BEACH (1959)
ON THE TOWN (1949)
ON THE WATERFRONT (1954)
ONE FALSE MOVE (1992)
ONE FLEW OVER THE CUCKOO'S NEST (1975)
ONE FOOT IN HEAVEN (1941)
ONE HOUR WITH YOU (1932)
ONE NIGHT OF LOVE (1934)
ONE POTATO, TWO POTATO (1964)
ONE, TWO, THREE (1961)
ONLY ANGELS HAVE WINGS (1939)
OPEN CITY (1946)
OPERATION CROSSBOW (1965)
THE OPPOSITE OF SEX (1998)
ORDINARY PEOPLE (1980)
OSSESSIONE (1942, REVIEWED 1976)
OTHELLO (1952, REVIEWED 1955)
OUR TOWN (1940)
OUT OF THE PAST (1947)
THE OUTLAW JOSEY WALES (1976)
THE OVERLANDERS (1946)
THE OX-BOW INCIDENT (1943)

PAINT YOUR WAGON (1969)
PAISAN (1948)
THE PALM BEACH STORY (1942)
THE PARALLAX VIEW (1974)
A PASSAGE TO INDIA (1984)
THE PASSION OF ANNA (1970)
PATHER PANCHALI (1958)
PATHS OF GLORY (1957)

CREATIVE WRITING—THE KELLY MANUAL OF STYLE

PATTON (1970)

THE PAWNBROKER (1965)

PAYDAY (1973)

PELLE THE CONQUEROR (1988)

THE PEOPLE VS. LARRY FLYNT
(1996)

PERSONA (1967)

PERSUASION (1995)

LE PETIT THEATRE DE JEAN
RENOIR (1974)

PETULIA (1968)

THE PHILADELPHIA STORY (1940)

THE PIANIST (2002)

THE PIANO (1993)

PICKUP ON SOUTH STREET (1953)

THE PILLOW BOOK (1997)

PILLOW TALK (1959)

THE PINK PANTHER (1964)

PINOCCHIO (1940)

PIXOTE (1981)

A PLACE IN THE SUN (1951)

PLACES IN THE HEART (1984)

PLATOON (1986)

PLAY MISTY FOR ME (1971)

THE PLAYER (1992)

PLAYTIME (1967, REVIEWED 1973)

POINT BLANK (1967)

POLTERGEIST (1982)

PONETTE (1997)

IL POSTINO (THE POSTMAN) (1994)

THE POSTMAN ALWAYS RINGS
TWICE (1946)

PRETTY BABY (1978)

PRIDE AND PREJUDICE (1940)

THE PRIDE OF THE YANKEES (1942)

PRINCE OF THE CITY (1981)

THE PRISONER (1955)

THE PRIVATE LIFE OF HENRY VIII
(1933)

PRIZZI'S HONOR (1985)

THE PRODUCERS (1968)

PSYCHO (1960)

THE PUBLIC ENEMY (1931)

CREATIVE WRITING—THE KELLY MANUAL OF STYLE

PULP FICTION (1994)
THE PURPLE ROSE OF CAIRO (1985)
PYGMALION (1938)

QUADROPHENIA (1979)
THE QUIET MAN (1952)

RAGING BULL (1980)
RAIDERS OF THE LOST ARK (1981)
RAIN MAN (1988)
RAISE THE RED LANTERN (1991, REVIEWED 1992)
RAISING ARIZONA (1987)
RAN (1985)
THE RAPTURE (1991)
RASHOMON (1951)
RE-ANIMATOR (1985)
REAR WINDOW (1954)
REBECCA (1940)
REBEL WITHOUT A CAUSE (1955)
RED (1994)
THE RED BADGE OF COURAGE (1951)
RED RIVER (1948)
THE RED SHOES (1948)
REDS (1981)
THE REMAINS OF THE DAY (1993)
REPO MAN (1984)
REPULSION (1965)
RESERVOIR DOGS (1992)
THE RETURN OF MARTIN GUERRE (1983)
REUBEN, REUBEN (1983)
REVERSAL OF FORTUNE (1990)
RICHARD III (1956)
RIDE THE HIGH COUNTRY (1962)
RIFIFI (1956)
THE RIGHT STUFF (1983)
RISKY BUSINESS (1983)
RIVER'S EDGE (1987)
THE ROAD WARRIOR (1982)
ROBOCOP (1987)
ROCCO AND HIS BROTHERS (1960, REVIEWED 1961)

ROGER & ME (1989)

ROMAN HOLIDAY (1953)

ROMEO AND JULIET (1936)

ROMEO AND JULIET (1968)

ROOM AT THE TOP (1959)

A ROOM WITH A VIEW (1986)

THE ROSE TATTOO (1955)

ROSEMARY'S BABY (1968)

'ROUND MIDNIGHT (1986)

RUGGLES OF RED GAP (1935)

THE RULES OF THE GAME (1939, REVIEWED 1950 AND 1961)

THE RULING CLASS (1972)

RUSHMORE (1998)

RUTHLESS PEOPLE (1986)

SAHARA (1943)

SALAAM BOMBAY! (1988)

SALESMAN (1969)

SANJURO (1963)

SANSHO THE BAILIFF (1969)

SATURDAY NIGHT AND SUNDAY MORNING (1961)

SATURDAY NIGHT FEVER (1977)

SAVING PRIVATE RYAN (1998)

SAY ANYTHING... (1989)

SAYONARA (1957)

SCENES FROM A MARRIAGE (1974)

SCHINDLER'S LIST (1993)

THE SCOUNDREL (1935)

THE SEARCH (1948)

THE SEARCHERS (1956)

SECRET HONOR (1985)

SECRETS AND LIES (1996)

SENSE AND SENSIBILITY (1995)

SERGEANT YORK (1941)

SERPICO (1973)

THE SERVANT (1963, REVIEWED 1964)

THE SET-UP (1949)

SEVEN BEAUTIES (1976)

SEVEN BRIDES FOR SEVEN BROTHERS (1954)

SEVEN DAYS TO NOON (1950)

THE SEVEN SAMURAI (1956)

7 UP/28 UP (1985)

THE SEVEN YEAR ITCH (1955)

THE SEVENTH SEAL (1958)

CREATIVE WRITING—THE KELLY MANUAL OF STYLE

SEX, LIES AND VIDEOTAPE (1989)
SEXY BEAST (2001)
SHADOW OF A DOUBT (1943)
SHAFT (1971)
SHAKESPEARE IN LOVE (1998)
SHANE (1953)
SHE WORE A YELLOW RIBBON (1949)
SHERMAN'S MARCH (1986)
SHE'S GOTTA HAVE IT (1986)
THE SHINING (1980)
SHIP OF FOOLS (1965)
SHOAH (1985)
SHOCK CORRIDOR (1963)
SHOESHINE (1947)
SHOOT THE PIANO PLAYER (1962)
THE SHOOTING PARTY (1985)
THE SHOOTIST (1976)
THE SHOP AROUND THE CORNER (1940)
THE SHOP ON MAIN STREET (1966)
A SHOT IN THE DARK (1964)
SHREK (2001)
SID AND NANCY (1986)
THE SILENCE (1964)
THE SILENCE OF THE LAMBS (1991)
THE SILENT WORLD (1956)
SILK STOCKINGS (1957)
SILKWOOD (1983)
SINGIN' IN THE RAIN (1952)
SITTING PRETTY (1948)
SLEEPER (1973)
A SLIGHT CASE OF MURDER (1938)
SMASH PALACE (1982)
SMILE (1975)
SMILES OF A SUMMER NIGHT (1956, REVIEWED 1957)
THE SNAKE PIT (1948)
SNOW WHITE AND THE SEVEN DWARFS (1938)
SOME LIKE IT HOT (1959)
THE SORROW AND THE PITY (LE CHAGRIN ET LA PITIÉ) (1971)
THE SOUND OF MUSIC (1965)
SOUTH PACIFIC (1958)
SPARTACUS (1960)
SPELLBOUND (1945)
THE SPIRAL STAIRCASE (1946)

SPIRITED AWAY (2002)
SPLENDOR IN THE GRASS (1961)
STAGE DOOR (1937)
STAGECOACH (1939)
STAIRWAY TO HEAVEN (1946)
STALAG 17 (1953)
A STAR IS BORN (1937)
STAR TREK II: THE WRATH OF KHAN (1982)
STAR WARS (1977)
STARMAN (1984)
THE STARS LOOK DOWN (1941)
STATE FAIR (1933)
STEVIE (1981)
STOLEN KISSES (1969)
STOP MAKING SENSE (1984)
STORMY MONDAY (1988)
THE STORY OF ADÈLE H. (1975)
THE STORY OF G.I. JOE (1945)
THE STORY OF QIU JU (1992)
STORY OF WOMEN (1989)
STORYTELLING (2001)
LA STRADA (1956)
THE STRAIGHT STORY (1999)
STRAIGHT TIME (1978)
STRANGER THAN PARADISE (1984)
STRANGERS ON A TRAIN (1951)
STRAW DOGS (1971)
A STREETCAR NAMED DESIRE (1951)
STROSZEK (1977)
SUDDENLY, LAST SUMMER (1959)
THE SUGARLAND EXPRESS (1974)
SULLIVAN'S TRAVELS (1941)
SUMMER (1986)
SUMMERTIME (1955)
SUNDAY BLOODY SUNDAY (1971)
SUNDAYS AND CYBELE (1962)
SUNSET BOULEVARD (1950)
SUSPICION (1941)
THE SWEET HEREAFTER (1997)
SWEET SMELL OF SUCCESS (1957)
SWEET SWEETBACK'S BAADASSSSS SONG (1971)
SWEPT AWAY (BY AN UNUSUAL DESTINY IN THE BLUE SEA OF AUGUST) (1974)

SWING TIME (1936)

THE TAKING OF PELHAM --ONE TWO THREE (1974)
TALK TO HER (2002)
TAMPOPO (1986)
TASTE OF CHERRY (1997)
A TASTE OF HONEY (1961, REVIEWED 1962)
TAXI DRIVER (1976)
A TAXING WOMAN (1987)
A TAXING WOMAN'S RETURN (1988)
TELL THEM WILLIE BOY IS HERE (1969)
10 (1979)
THE TEN COMMANDMENTS (1956)
TENDER MERCIES (1983)
THE TENDER TRAP (1955)
TERMS OF ENDEARMENT (1983)
LA TERRA TREMA (1947, REVIEWED 1965)
TESS (1980)
THAT OBSCURE OBJECT OF DESIRE (1977)
THAT'S LIFE! (1986)
THELMA & LOUISE (1991)
THESE THREE (1936)
THEY LIVE BY NIGHT (1949)
THEY SHOOT HORSES, DON'T THEY? (1969)
THEY WERE EXPENDABLE (1945)
THEY WON'T FORGET (1937)
THE THIEF OF BAGDAD (1940)
THE THIN BLUE LINE (1988)
THE THIN MAN (1934)
THE THIN RED LINE (1998)
THE THIRD GENERATION (1979, REVIEWED 1980)
THE THIRD MAN (1949)
THE THIRTY-NINE STEPS (1935)
THIRTY TWO SHORT FILMS ABOUT GLENN GOULD (1994)
THIS IS SPINAL TAP (1984)
THE MAN MUST DIE (1970)
THIS SPORTING LIFE (1963)
THREE COMRADES (1938)
THREE DAYS OF THE CONDOR (1975)
THRONE OF BLOOD (1957)

CREATIVE WRITING—THE KELLY MANUAL OF STYLE

TIGHT LITTLE ISLAND (1949)
THE TIN DRUM (1979)
TO BE OR NOT TO BE (1942)
TO CATCH A THIEF (1955)
TO HAVE AND HAVE NOT (1944)
TO KILL A MOCKINGBIRD (1962)
TO LIVE (1994)
TOKYO STORY (1953)
TOM JONES (1963)
TOOTSIE (1982)
TOP HAT (1935)
TOPAZ (1969)
TOPKAPI (1964)
TOTAL RECALL (1990)
TOUCH OF EVIL (1958)
TOY STORY (1995)
TRAFFIC (2000)
THE TRAIN (1965)
TRAINSPOTTING (1996)
THE TREASURE OF THE SIERRA MADRE (1948)
A TREE GROWS IN BROOKLYN (1945)
THE TREE OF THE WOODEN CLOGS (1979)
THE TRIP TO BOUNTIFUL (1985)
TRISTANA (1970)
TROUBLE IN PARADISE (1932)
THE TROUBLE WITH HARRY (1955)
TRUE GRIT (1969)
TRUE LOVE (1989)
TRUST (1991)
TUNES OF GLORY (1960)
12 ANGRY MEN (1957)
TWELVE O'CLOCK HIGH (1949)
TWENTIETH CENTURY (1934)
TWO ENGLISH GIRLS (1971)
THE TWO OF US (1968)
2001: A SPACE ODYSSEY (1968)
TWO WOMEN (1961)

UGETSU (1954)
ULZANA'S RAID (1972)
UMBERTO D. (1952)
THE UNBEARABLE LIGHTNESS OF BEING (1988)
UNFORGIVEN (1992)

CREATIVE WRITING—THE KELLY MANUAL OF STYLE

THE WAGES OF FEAR (1955)
WAKING LIFE (2001)
WALKABOUT (1971)
A WALK IN THE SUN (1945)
THE WAR GAME (1966)
THE WAR OF THE ROSES (1989)
THE WARRIORS (1979)
WATCH ON THE RHINE (1943)
THE WATERDANCE (1991)
THE WAY WE WERE (1973)

WEEKEND (1968)
WELCOME TO THE DOLLHOUSE (1996)
THE WELL-DIGGER'S DAUGHTER (1941)
WEST SIDE STORY (1961)
THE WHALES OF AUGUST (1987)
WHAT EVER HAPPENED TO BABY JANE? (1962)
WHAT'S EATING GILBERT GRAPE (1993)
WHAT'S UP, DOC? (1972)
WHEN HARRY MET SALLY (1989)
WHITE HEAT (1949)
WHO FRAMED ROGER RABBIT (1988)
WHO'S AFRAID OF VIRGINIA WOOLF? (1966)
THE WILD BUNCH (1969)
THE WILD CHILD (1970)
WILD REEDS (1994)
WILD STRAWBERRIES (1959)
WILSON (1944)
WINGS OF DESIRE (1988)
WISE BLOOD (1979)
THE WIZARD OF OZ (1939)
WOMAN IN THE DUNES (1964)
WOMAN OF THE YEAR (1942)
THE WOMEN (1939)
WOMEN IN LOVE (1970)
WOMEN ON THE VERGE OF A NERVOUS BREAKDOWN (1988)
WOODSTOCK (1970)
WORKING GIRL (1988)
THE WORLD OF APU (1959, REVIEWED 1960)
THE WORLD OF HENRY ORIENT (1964)
WRITTEN ON THE WIND (1956)
WUTHERING HEIGHTS (1939)

VANYA ON 42ND STREET (1994)
THE VERDICT (1982)
VERTIGO (1958)
VIDEODROME (1982)
VIOLETTE NOZIÈRE (1978)
VIRIDIANA (1962)

CREATIVE WRITING—THE KELLY MANUAL OF STYLE

VIVA ZAPATA! (1952)
THE VOICE OF THE TURTLE (1947)

YANKEE DOODLE DANDY (1942)
THE YEAR OF LIVING DANGEROUSLY (1982)
THE YEARLING (1983)
YELLOW SUBMARINE (1968)
YI YI: A ONE AND A TWO (2000)
YOJIMBO (1961)
YOU CAN COUNT ON ME (2000)
YOU ONLY LIVE ONCE (1937)
YOUNG FRANKENSTEIN (1974)
YOUNG MR. LINCOLN (1939)

Z (1969)
ZERO FOR CONDUCT (1933)

CHAPTER 42

42.0.0.0. A SHORT STORY-DEFINED:

DEFINED:
A FICTIONAL STORY THAT IS SHORTER THAN A NOVEL AND WITH ONLY A FEW CHARACTERS.

THE SHORT STORY IS USUALLY CONCERNED WITH A SINGLE THEME CONVEYED IN ONLY ONE OR A FEW SIGNIFICANT SCENES. THIS FORMAT ENCOURAGES ECONOMIES OF SETTING AND NARRATIVES.

THE FEW CHARACTERS ARE DISCLOSED IN ACTION AND DRAMATIC ENCOUNTER BUT ARE NOT FULLY DEVELOPED.

42.0.0.1.SIX IMPORTANT POINTS
HERE ARE SIX IMPORTANT POINTS ABOUT **WHAT MAKES A GOOD SHORT STORY WORK:**

1. THE STORY IS TOLD FROM THE POINT OF VIEW OF THE CENTRAL CHARACTER, WITH WHOM THE READER IDENTIFIES.

2. AN ELEMENT OF CONFLICT IS INTRODUCED EARLY ON, USUALLY IN THE FIRST CHAPTER OR TWO.

3. WE ARE HELD IN SUSPENSE AS WE WONDER HOW THE CHARACTER WILL RESOLVE HIS/HER CONFLICT.

4. THERE IS A CLIMAX AT OR NEAR THE END IN WHICH THE CONFLICT IS RESOLVED.

5. THE STORY FOCUSES ON A <u>SINGLE</u> MAJOR EVENT, WHICH IS A CRISIS POINT IN THE MAIN CHARACTER'S LIVES.

6. THE STORY IS SHOWN THROUGH THE CHARACTERS, WITHOUT THE NARRATOR'S INTRUSION.

WEB: DO SEARCH: SHORT STORIES: [INDEX 3].
SEARCH: SHORT STORIES
WWW.WRITERSDIGEST.COM
WWW.WRITING.COM

<u>SECTION IV:</u>

<u>MARKETING YOUR BEST SELLER:</u>

CREATIVE WRITING:

THE KELLY MANUAL OF STYLE!

THE <u>2014</u> COMPLETE GUIDE TO CREATIVE WRITING

43.0.0.0. MARKETING
<u>CHAPTER TOPICS:</u> *CHAIN OF COMMAND: THE WHO: THE MANY WHO'S.*

43.11.0. 0. THE THEORY OF WHO:
WHO IS THE BUYER, THE WRITER, THE READER, THE PROOFREADER, THE EDITOR, THE PUBLISHER, THE REVIEWER, THE PUBLIC, FRIENDS AND FAMILY, THE TARGET AUDIENCE?

43.11.1.0. WHO IS THE BUYER OF YOUR BOOK?:
WHY? : HE BUYS TO SOLVE A PROBLEM, FOR ENJOYMENT, LIKES THE GENRE. HE DOES THE QUICK REVIEW OF THE COVER AND LIKES IT. HE IS A COLLECTOR IN THE GENRE OR AUTHOR. IS THE BUYER SOMEONE DIFFERENT THAN YOUR READER?

GENERALLY THE BUYER IS A BROADER BASED PERSON WITH MULTI-PROFILES: EG. APPEALS TO MULTI-AGE GROUPS, MEN & WOMEN? [WHO DOES YOUR BOOK APPEAL TO?]

43.11.2.0. WHO IS THE WRITER? HIS BOOK?:[PAGE 15].
A PROFILE-MAYBE?
A PERFECTIONIST?
THE DEADLINER OR PROCRASTINATOR?
WHAT IS HIS NOVEL INSIGHT-UNIQUE ADVICE-COMMITMENT-HIS INVOLVEMENT?
RESPONSIBLE FOR CONTENT?
IS IT PLEASANT- EASY TO READ?
IS IT ORGANIZED?
ILLUSTRATED-INDEXED WITH MAPS-REFERENCES-SUB HEADINGS?
CROSS-REFERENCES?
-MULTI-MEDIA OR ?
-PACK FULL OF USEFUL INFORMATION?
DOES THE WRITER PLEASE THE READER?

43.11.3 0. RESEARCHER: [SEE CH 34]
GENERALLY, THE WRITER IS THE ONE WHO PERFORMS RESEARCH, SEARCHES THE WEB AND PULLS INFORMATION FOR HIS CHAPTER TOPICS.

43.11.4. 0. THE READER: [PAGE 15].
WE CHALLENGE THE READER WITH THEORIES
IS IT DIFFERENT THEN THE PACK OF NEW BOOKS?
IS OUR NEW TOPIC REALLY BRAND NEW?
IS IT DYNAMIC? IS IT ACTION PACKED?
DOES IT DELIVER ITS PROMISES OR ITS HYPE?
DO WE REALLY KNOW WHO IS BUYING OUR BOOK?

43.11.5. 0. THE PROOFREADER &
EDITOR'S PROCESS.
SEE CH 32 FOR PROOF READERS SYMBOLS.
SEE CH 48 FOR EDITORS- EDITING PROCESS.

43.11.6. 0. OUR AGENT:
SEE CH. 47 BOOK PROPOSALS.
ROLE: WORKS FOR MANY WRITERS

43.11.7. 0. THE REAL EDITOR: [CH 30]
ROLE: WORKS FOR PUBLISHER.

43.11.8. 0. OUR PUBLISHER: [CH 49]
DO WE KNOW OUR AUDIENCE-WHAT IS OUR TARGET AUDIENCE-
MARKETS-DEMOGRAPHICS. ALL ABOUT NUMBERS

43.11.9. 0. OUR BOOK REVIEWER:
REVIEWERS ARE GENERALLY SOLICITED AS PART OF OUR MARKETING
CAMPAIGN. REVIEWERS MAY APPEAR ON THE PUBLISHERS
STOREFRONT(LULU) OR MAY WRITE A REVIEW FOR THE BOOK.
DO NOT PUT THEM ON YOUR BACK COVER.
DO PLACE ANY OR NONE INSIDE THE REAR COVER.

43.11.10. 0. OUR LAWYER:
A LAWYER IS A MUST TO REVIEW ANY **BOOK CONTRACT** AND PROTECT
YOUR **COPYRIGHT** AND FUTURE EARNINGS FROM A SCREENPLAY OR
MOVIE.

43.11.11. 0. OUR LOCAL SALES OUTLET-BOOKSTORE:
[REFER TO CH 54. MARKETING].
OUR LOCAL BOOKSTORE –BOOKSELLER GENERALLY ORDERS THROUGH
A LARGE WHOLESALER OR DIRECT FROM A PUBLISHER. THE BOOK
COMES ACROSS THROUGH THE "BOWKER" PROCESS" WHICH FEEDS THE
WHOLE SYSTEM. ON-LINE RETAILERS LIKE AMAZON, BARNES AND
NOBLES ARE JUST A FEW. OTHERS BUY THERE TO. LIBRARIES
GENERALLY BUY THROUGH THEIR OWN LISTS. EVEN DONATED COPIES
WILL NEVER SEE THE SELF.
MANY WANT HARD COVERS WITH JACKETS. UNDERSTAND THAT SHELF
SPACE IS LIMITED.

43.11.12. 0. OUR INTERNET SELLING SOURCE:
MANY SMALLER BOOKSTORES WILL BUY THROUGH THEIR SOURCES,
GENERALLY IN SMALL QUANTITIES TO AVOID INVENTORY. (LULU
OFFERS THE SAME SERVICE).

43.11.13.0. MAKE A LIST OF ALL OUR WHO'S:
MAKE A LIST LIKE A CONTACT LIST-PHONE LIST
OF ALL THE PEOPLE INVOLVED WITH YOUR BOOK.
INCLUDE THE VARIOUS MARKETING AND INTERNET CONTACTS.
ADD OUR VARIOUS BLOGS, REVIEWERS, AND BOOKSELLERS WE USE FOR
OUR OWN BUYING. ADD A LIST OF PEOPLE WE WILL GIVE OUR BOOK TO.
THIS BECOMES AN IMPORTANT PIECE OF RECORD.

43.11.14.0. MAKE A LIST OF OUR OWN BOOKS PURCHASED:
1. YES WE MUST BUY PROOFS AND COPIES FOR OUR OWN BOOK SHELF OR
   TO BE FRAMED ON OUR WALL.
2. TWO COPIES FOR THE COPYRIGHT OFFICE.
3. SIGNED COPY FOR OUR SPOUSE.

CREATIVE WRITING—THE KELLY MANUAL OF STYLE

4. SIGNED COPIES FOR OUR RESEARCHER, REVIEWER, EDITOR, FRIENDS
   AND FAMILY.
5. COPIES FOR THOSE WHO HELPED WITH RESEARCH-PROOFREADING THE
   MANUSCRIPT- NEIGHBORS.

WRITER TO DO LIST:

 DO MAKE AN EXCEL SPREADSHEET TO TRACK YOUR BOOKS BOUGHT
AND TO WHOM AND YOUR COSTS, NOT RETAIL PRICES.

CLASS POP QUIZ:

1. WHO IS THE MOST IMPORTANT PERSON IN WRITING?
2. WHO IS THE MOST IMPORTANT PERSON IN A BOOK? WHY?
3. WHICH RULE DO YOU FOLLOW TO BE A WRITER?
4. HOW LONG IS A NOVELETTE?
5. WHAT IS IN A BOOK TITLE?
6. WHAT IS A COPYRIGHT?
9. TX FORM?
10. PA FORM?

43.11.15.0. OUR PROGRESS:

1. WE LEARNED THERE ARE MANY PEOPLE IN OUR WHO'S LIST.

2. EACH HAVE A SPECIFIC ROLE IN OUR BOOK PROCESS.

CHAPTER 44

44.0.0.0. YOUR WRITER'S PORTFOLIO:

44.10.0.0.0. WHY A PORTFOLIO?

AN ONLINE PORTFOLIO & STORE FRONT REVEALS YOUR CREDENTIALS TO THE WEB WORLD. IT ALSO, ALLOWS YOU TO PRESENT YOUR CANDIDACY FOR A BOOK PROJECT TO THE PUBLISHER.

OR EMPLOYMENT OR TO COLLEAGUES WITH INFORMATION ON: ARTICLES WRITTEN, ARTWORK CREATED, BOOKS PUBLISHED, BOOKS WRITTEN, CLASS LESSON PLANS, LETTERS OF RECOMMENDATION, PLAYS, CERTIFICATIONS, RESUMES, SPECIAL REPORTS, AND OTHERS.

SELECT ONLY THE MOST APROPOS ITEMS.

44.10.1.0.0. PURPOSE:

A WELL-PRESENTED WEB-PORTFOLIO PROVIDES "PICTURE EVIDENCE" TO AN EMPLOYER OF YOUR ABILITIES, ACCOMPLISHMENTS, SKILLS AND EXPERIENCE. IT SHOULD SHOWCASE THE SCOPE AND QUALITY OF YOUR EXPERIENCE AND TRAINING.

44.10.2.0.0. CONTENTS:

A PORTFOLIO CAN ALSO INCLUDE "WORD" COMPUTER FILES, SPREADSHEETS OR SAMPLES OF YOUR WRITING, DIGITAL IMAGES OF YOUR GRAPHICS AND COVER ARTWORK VIDEO AND AUDIO FILES. AGAIN, SELECT THE MOST APROPOS ITEMS.

44.10.3.0.0. PORTFOLIO DESIGN:

1. DESIGNING YOUR WEB SITE WELL CAN SIGNIFICANTLY ALTER YOUR USER'S REACTION TO YOUR WORK.

44.10.4.0.0. CREATING A PORTFOLIO IS TO PRESENT YOUR CREDENTIALS AND PERSONAL INFORMATION IN A MANNER THAT IS FUNCTIONAL AND IN AN AESTHETICALLY PLEASING MANNER FOR THE READER.

44.10.5.0.0. CONSIDER USING A PORTFOLIO SERVICE:

WHERE YOU CAN SIMPLY UPLOAD YOUR DOCUMENTS TO A PORTFOLIO WEB SITE: E.G. **WWW.PORTFOLIOS.COM**

44.10.6.0.0. BUILD YOUR PORTFOLIO:

1. REMEMBER THAT YOUR PORTFOLIO IS A WORK IN A PROCESS.
2. TAKE THE TIME TO CREATE A PROFESSIONAL, POLISHED PORTFOLIO.

44.10.7.0.0. KEEP YOUR PORTFOLIO CURRENT.

1. MAKE SURE IT WORKS.
2. CHECK REGULARLY, IS IT IN WORKING ORDER?
   (NO BROKEN HYPERLINKS OR IMAGES
   OR OUTDATED INFORMATION).
3. TEST ALL LINKS TO YOUR EMAIL ADDRESS.
4. TEST THE LINK TO YOUR PORTFOLIO AND TO YOUR
   RESUME AND MENTION IT IN YOUR JOB COVER
   LETTERS.

44.10.8.0.0. SAMPLE WEB SITES:

WWW.PORTFOLIO.COM SAMPLES
WWW.DECISIONCRITICAL.COM

CHAPTER 45
45.0.0.0. COPYRIGHTS:
CHAPTER TOPICS: *COPYRIGHT-WEB SITE-HOW FILE-RIGHTS-FORMS-AFTER-SAFEKEEPING.*

45.1.0.0. COPY RIGHTS & PUBLISHING:
WHEN READY & FINISHED…SEND IT IN FOR COPYRIGHT(ALONG WITH 2 COPIES OF YOUR BOOK, UNDER YOUR NAME. DON'T GIVE AWAY ANY RIGHTS YOU HAVE, EVEN WITH PUBLISHERS. THAT'S A WHOLE OTHER STORY AND LEGAL ISSUES! GET CIRCULAR 1-WHAT IS A COPYRIGHT? HOW LONG?- (UP TO 8 MONTHS).

HOMEWORK:
WHICH FORM----COSTS?—HOW DO I SEND IT? WHAT DO I SEND?

USE THE WEB SITE *WWW.COPYRIGHT.GOV/DOCS/FEES.HTML*

TRADEMARKS: WWW.TRADEMARKUSA.COM/WHYTRADEMARK.HTML

45.2.0.0. FORMS
TX SHORT FORM? [BOOK] FORM USED TO REGISTER A BASIC CLAIM IN AN ORIGINAL WORK OF AUTHORSHIP FOR A NON DRAMATIC (BOOK) LITERARY WORK. (NO LITERARY PLAY OR SCREEN PLAY OR MOVIE).

PA FORM? PERFORMING ARTS WORK, SUCH AS PLAYS PERFORMED TO MUSIC, PANTOMIMES, CHOREOGRAPHIC WORKS AND MOTION PICTURES.

45. 3.0.0. SUMMARY:
IT IS IMPORTANT FOR AN AUTHOR TO KNOW ABOUT COPYRIGHTS, 'ALL RIGHTS RESERVED' AND HOW THEY IMPACT THEIR PUBLISHING CONTRACT. CONSULT A COPYRIGHT ATTORNEY TO REVIEW YOUR COPYRIGHT APPLICATION, PROTECTIONS AND PUBLISHING CONTRACT. **REVIEW THE BASICS ON THE WEB SITE PROVIDED ABOVE.**

REFER TO CHAPTERS CH 39.12.8.0. AND CH 46.4.4.12. FOR ADDITIONAL INFORMATION.

45.4.0.0. OUR PROGRESS:
1. WE LEARNED TO COMPLETE THE TX FORM FOR OUR COPYRIGHT.

CHAPTER 46
46.0.0.0. PUBLISHING COSTS & PROFITS:
THE MONEY SIDE:
CHAPTER TOPICS: *PRODUCTION COSTS-RETAIL PRICES-AUTHOR'S PROFIT-BOOK COSTS*

46.1.0.0. PRODUCTION COST:
46.1.1. 0. 6X9 EXAMPLE AS ABOVE: COST EACH BOOK UNIT:

1. SET-UP & BINDING: $1.50
2. (W/PUB DISTRIB. FEE) APPROX. (125.000)-ESTIMATED AT 1.00 PER BOOK.

[NOTE: VARIOUS DISTRIBUTION PACKAGES ARE AVAILABLE FROM POD PUBLISHERS: WITH INCREASING COSTS LEVELS].

3. B & W-PER PAGE .02X480=	$9.60
4. COLOR EXTRA PPG	$0.00
5. AUTHOR PROFIT	2.00
6. PUB PROFIT (20%)	.85
TOTAL PRODUCTION COST	$14.95
NOTE: RETAIL PRICING IS 200% OF TOTAL PRODUCTION COST ABOVE=$29.90	

24. **SETTING THE RETAIL PRICE:** RETAILERS USE 100% MARKUP, SO THE ABOVE BOOK IS
14.95 X 2: $29.90 SO $29.95 IS INDUSTRY MARK-UP.

46.1.2.0. BOOKS COST:
480 PAGES CREATES A PRODUCTION COST OF $14.95.
MARKETING COSTS MAY INCREASE THUS CAUSING THE BOOK'S RETAIL PRICE TO INCREASE ACCORDINGLY.

HANDOUT: SPREADSHEET COST VERSUS PROFIT:

46.2.0.0. OUR PROGRESS:
1. WE LEARNED ABOUT PRODUCTION COST.

2. WE LEARNED THE RETAIL PRICE IS 100% OF OUR PRODUCTION COST ROUNDED OFF TO NEAREST RETAILER AMOUNT.

CHAPTER 47

47.0.0.0. WINNING BOOK PROPOSALS:

CHAPTER TOPICS: PROPOSALS- CONTENT-AUDIENCE-TABLE OF CONTENTS-KEY QUESTIONS-WHY PUBLISH? – AUDIENCE MARKETS-MARKETING-THE AUTHOR-CHECK LIST-CONTACT INFORMATION-

47.0.0.0 PROPOSALS DEFINED:

A PROPOSAL IS A LENGTHY DOCUMENT AND PROCESS DEFINING THE ATTRIBUTES OF YOUR BOOK, ITS AUDIENCE AND WHY IT SHOULD BE PUBLISHED BASED ON MARKETING FACTS AND FIGURES. THIS PROCESS IS THE 'VETTING' METHOD TO SCREEN OUT BOOKS NEEDING WORK, THOSE THAT ARE NOT ATTRACTIVE TO THE MARKET OR WON'T BE THE NEXT BEST SELLER OR THE MOST PROFITABLE. THIS DOCUMENT ALSO OUTLINES THE MARKETING PLAN. GREAT! EXCEPT FOR OTHER NEW MARKETING FORCES ARE AT WORK. **[SEE CH 40.0.0.0.]**

47.0.1.0 PROPOSAL'S AUDIENCE:

KEEP IN MIND, SEVERAL PEOPLE WITH VARIOUS AGENDAS WILL READ YOUR PROPOSAL. SOME WILL WANT TO GET A QUICK IDEA OF WHAT YOUR BOOK IS ABOUT, WHILE OTHERS WILL READ EVERY WORD. ALTHOUGH IT'S VERY IMPORTANT TO BE COMPLETE, YOU SHOULD START YOUR PROPOSAL WITH A DOCUMENT NO LONGER THAN A PAGE THAT TELLS THE WHOLE STORY. IT WILL SET THE CONTEXT OF YOUR PROPOSAL FOR THE EDITOR, AND IT WILL PROVIDE MORE THAN ENOUGH INFORMATION FOR THE SALES AND MARKETING PEOPLE.

IF YOU HAVE AN EXTREMELY LONG TABLE OF CONTENTS, YOU SHOULD CONSIDER INCLUDING A BRIEF TABLE OF CONTENTS. THIS WILL ALLOW READERS TO EASE INTO THE IDEA OF THE BOOK WITHOUT OVERWHELMING THEM WITH DETAIL.

THE FOLLOWING SECTION OUTLINES THE KEY QUESTIONS BOOK PUBLISHERS ASK BEFORE THEY MAKE A PUBLISHING DECISION. REGARDLESS OF HOW YOU ORGANIZE YOUR PROPOSAL, IT SHOULD INCLUDE ANSWERS TO ALL THE FOLLOWING RELEVANT QUESTIONS. **REMEMBER**, YOUR GOAL AS AN AUTHOR IS TO MAXIMIZE THE TIME YOU SPEND WRITING BOOKS.

IF, AFTER ASKING YOURSELF THESE QUESTIONS, YOU FIND THERE ISN'T A VERY COMPELLING REASON TO WRITE THE BOOK, THEN THIS EXERCISE WAS EXTREMELY VALUABLE. IT'S HARD COMING UP WITH A BEST-SELLING BOOK IDEA, BUT VERY WORTHWHILE.

THE QUESTIONS ARE DIVIDED INTO THE FOLLOWING SECTIONS AND WHEN YOU ARE ASKED TO WRITE A PROPOSAL, THE FIRST THING YOU SHOULD ASK IS WHETHER THE PUBLISHER IN MIND HAS SOME GUIDELINES FOR CREATING THAT PROPOSAL.

YOU SHOULD REVIEW THE GUIDELINES VERY CAREFULLY AND FIND OUT WHAT IT IS HE/ SHE WANTS IN A PROPOSAL.

47.0. 2.0. CONTENT:
DESCRIBE THE PURPOSE OF THE BOOK (IS IT TO ACT AS A REFERENCE, TO ADDRESS AN UN-MET NEED IN THE MARKETPLACE, OR----------------?

47.0.2.1. WHY SHOULD THIS BOOK BE PUBLISHED?
1. EXPLAIN THE CONCEPT UNDERLYING THE WORK AND THE MAJOR TOPICS YOU PLAN TO COVER.

2. DESCRIBE WHY YOU ARRANGED YOUR BOOK AS YOU DID

3. IF A DISKETTE/CD-ROM WILL BE INCLUDED WITH THE BOOK, WHAT VALUE-ADDED MATERIALS SHOULD BE INCLUDED? WHY?

4. IF THE BOOK COVERS NEW SOFTWARE, HOW DO YOU INTEND TO EMPHASIZE THESE NEW FEATURES?

5. STATE THE TITLE, SUBTITLE, TOTAL PAGES, SUGGESTED PRICE POINT, WHETHER YOUR BOOK INCLUDES A DISK, AND ANY OTHER SPECIAL CHARACTERISTICS OF THE BOOK.

6. WHAT IS THE GENRE' AND TOPIC OF YOUR BOOK AND WHY WAS THIS TOPIC CHOSEN. **[SEE YOUR NEW DETAILED SYNOPSIS]**

7. WHAT SKILLS WILL THE READER TAKE AWAY FROM THE BOOK?

8. WHAT WILL READERS BE ABLE TO DO AFTER THEY READ THE BOOK?

9. WILL INSTRUCTIONS, SUMMARIES, EXERCISES, HINTS, EXAMPLES CHARTS, CLASS LESSONS, GLOSSARIES OR INDICES BE PROVIDED? WILL YOU USE FIGURES, ILLUSTRATIONS, GRAPHS, CHARTS, AND DRAWINGS?

47.0. 3.0.   AUDIENCE NEEDS:
ARE THERE ANY SPECIAL HARDWARE/SOFTWARE NEEDS BECAUSE OF THE BOOK'S CONTENT OR INCLUDED SOFTWARE?
IF SO, WHAT ARE THESE NEEDS?

WHO IS THE AUDIENCE?
ARE THEY POWER USERS? -BUSINESS PROFESSIONALS? PROGRAMMERS? HOBBYISTS?

WHY DOES YOUR INTENDED AUDIENCE NEED THIS BOOK? TO LEARN? -TO DEVELOP? -FOR ENTERTAINMENT OR PERSONAL INTEREST? WHY WOULD SOMEONE PURCHASE THIS BOOK?
SAVE TIME- TO SAVE MONEY-TO FIND INFORMATION THAT ISN'T AVAILABLE ANYWHERE ELSE.

47.0.4.0. MARKET ANALYSIS:
-IS TIMING CRITICAL TO THE PUBLICATION OF YOUR BOOK?
-WHEN SHOULD YOUR BOOK APPEAR ON BOOKSTORE SHELVES?
-WHAT ARE THE KNOWN COMPETITORS TO THIS BOOK OR TYPE OF BOOK? (BE SPECIFIC AND INCLUDE AUTHOR, COMPLETE TITLE, AND ISBN, IF POSSIBLE).
-WHAT DO THESE BOOKS PROVIDE YOURS CANNOT? WHAT ARE YOU PROVIDING THAT THE COMPETITION CANNOT?

47.0.5.0. MARKET SIZE AND POTENTIAL:
WHAT IS THE ESTIMATED MARKET SIZE FOR THE BOOK? HOW MANY POTENTIAL READERS HAVE OR WILL HAVE THE SOFTWARE, SKILLS, AND INTEREST IN A BOOK OF THIS NATURE? HOW MANY PEOPLE HAVE THE PRODUCT? HOW MANY OF THOSE PEOPLE BUY BOOKS?

47.0.6.0. AUTHOR:
1. ARE YOU COMMITTED AND AVAILABLE TO COMPLETE YOUR BOOK ON AN AGGRESSIVE SCHEDULE?

2. HAVE YOU PUBLISHED BOOKS WITH OTHER PUBLISHERS? IF SO, PLEASE RECORD THE TITLE,
PUBLISHER AND ISBN #. WHAT ELSE HAVE YOU HAD PUBLISHED--
MAGAZINE ARTICLES, DOCUMENTATION, ETC.?

3. SALES AND MARKETING: WHAT CAN YOU DO AS AN AUTHOR TO HELP MARKET THE BOOK?

4. IS THERE A UNIQUE VALUE IN THIS BOOK?

5. BACK COVER: WRITE A FEW PARAGRAPHS OUTLINING A MARKETING MESSAGE AND STORY PLOT.

6. DID YOU COMPLETE THE PUBLISHER'S CHECKLIST?
      DID YOU ANSWER ALL OF THE QUESTIONS?
      INCLUDE A SYNOPSIS?

7. CONTACT INFORMATION?
      IS YOUR ADDRESS, TELEPHONE NUMBERS AND
      EMAIL ADDRESS?

8. IS YOUR SYNOPSIS & OUTLINE COMPLETE AND WELL THOUGHT OUT?

9. IT IS THE FIRST MEETING OF YOUR IDEA WITH THE EDITOR'S NEEDS.

10. WHATEVER YOU WANT TO SAY AND HOWEVER YOU WANT TO IMPRESS THAT ACQUISITION EDITOR, NOW IS THE TIME. THERE'S NO SECOND CHANCE.

11. WRITE FOR, READ AND FOLLOW THE SUBMISSION GUIDELINES: MAKE A GOOD FIRST IMPRESSION. IF YOU SAY THAT X HAS SOLD Y, BE SURE YOUR FACTS ARE CORRECT.

12. COMPETITION:
WHEN YOU ARE ASKED ABOUT THE BOOKS THAT WOULD BE COMPETITIVE WITH YOURS, BY ALL MEANS, BE THOROUGH IN THE COMPARISON. LIST THE TITLES AND THEN TELL WHY YOUR BOOK WOULD BE SUPERIOR.

13. DISTINCTIVE?
WHY WOULD A PUBLISHER BE INTERESTED IN A BOOK THAT IS NOT DISTINCTIVE? THIS INFORMATION IS WHAT THE EDITOR WILL USE TO MAKE HIS CASE TO THE PUBLISHING BOARD, WHY THE COMPANY SHOULD CONSIDER YOUR BOOK.

14. TABLE OF CONTENTS:
THE TABLE OF CONTENTS SHOULD BE AS DETAILED AS POSSIBLE AND INCLUDE A TWO TO THREE-SENTENCE DESCRIPTION OF EACH CHAPTER. IT SHOULD BE ORGANIZED AS NUMBERED CHAPTERS AND PARTS, IF NECESSARY.

15. REVIEW YOU WRITE-UP. REHEARSE IT. READ IT OUTLOUD.

47.0.7.0. SUMMARY:
I CAN'T EMPHASIS ENOUGH…THE SUCCESS OF YOUR BOOK MIGHT JUST BEGIN WITH THE TITLE AND COVER ART!!!

AND A GREAT STORY TOLD OUTLOUD!

47.1.0.0. OUR PROGRESS:
1. WE LEARNED HOW TO WRITE A PROPOSAL TO OUR PROSPECTIVE EDITOR.

2. WE LEARNED WHAT CONTENT TO INCLUDE.

3. WE PERFORMED OUR MARKET ANALYSIS.

4. WE COMPLETED OUR PUBLISHER'S CHECK LIST.

CHAPTER 48
48.0.0.0. PROFESSIONAL BOOK EDITOR'S CHECK LIST: SOME ADVICE WHAT NOT TO DO:

CHAPTER TOPICS: *SEND FOR, WRITE AND COMPLY:*
FOLLOW THIS CHECK LIST FOR SUBMISSIONS:
USE THIS FOR MAJOR PUBLISHING HOUSES ONLY:

POD'S DO NOT REQUIRE ALL OF THIS.

WHAT NOT TO DO: SOME ADVICE FROM THE BLOGS.

WRITER: DO REVIEW CHAPTER 47 ON PROPOSALS AND CHAPTER 49 ON PRINT ON DEMAND PUBLISHERS ON DIFFERENCES OF APPROACHES TO EDITING AND PUBLISHING.

THE EDITOR'S JOB IS TO:
1. REVIEW YOUR BOOK PROPOSAL & MARKETING PLAN.
2. SELL IT TO HIS MANAGER OR BOOK COMMITTEE
3. REVIEW YOUR BOOK FOR MERIT, AND FOR HOW MUCH TIME IT IS GOING TO COST TO FIX IT.
4. MAYBE, NEGOTIATE WITH YOUR AGENT?
   (ARE YOU, THE AUTHOR, FULLY MISSING FROM THIS EQUATION?).

48.0.1.0. EDITOR'S $\sqrt{}$ CHECK LIST:

1. DO SPELL CHECK, MANUALLY CHECK OTHER WORDS AND GRAMMAR UNABLE TO BE CAUGHT IN ITS ELECTRONIC REVIEW.

2. DO FIX BAD GRAMMAR-VERB TENSE-QUOTATIONS- SEE STYLE GUIDES.-SOURCES. YEP ! THEY REQUIRE THE 'STANDARD FORMAT."

3. DOUBLE CHECK EDITOR'S NAME AND TITLE:

4. REVIEW SPACING AND BAD FONT.

5. DO DOUBLE-SPACE YOUR SUBMISSION.

6. FONT: USE <u>TIMES NEW ROMAN</u> TO REDUCE EYE STRAIN.

7. DON'T DO CLEVER SUBMISSION TRICKS.

8. DON'T TELL EDITORS THEIR JOB.

48.0.1.9. COPYRIGHT STATEMENT:
SHOW ONE, EDITORS DO NOT LIKE IT BUT IF IT IS PART OF MANUSCRIPT, LEAVE IT. IF YOUR CONTRACT IS GOING TO "GIVE" SOME RIGHTS AWAY, BEWARE. READ ABOUT YOUR 'RIGHTS' OR CONSULT A COPYRIGHT ATTORNEY. LEARN THE DIFFERENCE ABOUT "<u>ALL RIGHTS RESERVED.</u>"

48.0.10.0. DO MAKE AN APPROPRIATE SUBMISSION BY GENRE' AND SUB-GENRE'. YOU NEED TO SUBMIT TO PUBLICATIONS OR
PUBLISHERS THAT FIT THE INDIVIDUAL WORK YOU'RE SUBMITTING.
FOLLOW THE PUBLISHER'S GUIDELINES AND THEIR SUBMISSION
PROCESS. REVIEW IT AND YOUR CONTRACT WITH YOUR COPYRIGHT
ATTORNEY.

48.0.11. 0. DON'T IGNORE SUBMISSION INSTRUCTIONS. THERE IS
A STANDARD PROCEDURE AND FORMAT FOR SUBMISSIONS, SOME
EDITORS, PUBLISHERS, OR PUBLICATIONS MAY HAVE SPECIFIC
REQUIREMENTS. CHECK OUT THEIR WEB SITE FOR "SUBMISSIONS."

48.0.12.0. DO FOLLOW INSTRUCTIONS ON ATTACHMENTS:
DON'T EMAIL AN ATTACHMENT WHEN A DISK OR HARDCOPY IS
REQUIRED, AND DON'T PASTE INTO AN EMAIL WHEN ASKED FOR ITEM IS
AN ATTACHMENT.

48.0.13.0. DON'T EXPLAIN YOUR WRITING.
IF THE WRITING WORKS, IT WORKS; YOU SHOULDN'T HAVE TO EXPLAIN
IT.

48.0.14.0. MAYBE –WHAT NOT TO DO? AN OPPOSING VIEW:
[THIS CONDENSED SOURCE WAS FOUND ON SEVERAL WEB BLOG SITES BUT
WORTH REPEATING. MY APOLOGIES TO THE ORIGINAL UNKNOWN
AUTHORS]:

THE PROBLEM WITH "SHOULD" ADVICE IS THAT IT'S EITHER SOMETHING
YOU ALREADY KNOW, I.E., YOUR DIET SHOULD INCLUDE MORE FRUIT
AND VEGETABLES THAN CHEESEBURGERS AND MARTINIS -- OR IT'S
SOMETHING REALLY DIFFICULT (LIKE CONSUMING MORE FRUIT AND
VEGETABLES THAN CHEESEBURGERS AND MARTINIS).

THIS LIST OF THINGS I STRONGLY ADVISE ASPIRING AND DESPAIRING
WRITERS NOT TO DO. I DOUBT THAT SIMPLY BY AVOIDING THESE
PITFALLS YOU WILL BE GUARANTEED FAME AND FORTUNE, BUT YOU
WILL AT LEAST ESCAPE MANY UNNECESSARY FRUSTRATIONS AND
DEFEATS, SO THAT YOU CAN BE FRESH FOR THE REALLY POIGNANT
FAILURES AND SETBACKS THAT WILL EITHER MAKE OR BREAK YOU --
AND WITH ANY LUCK WILL DO A BIT OF BOTH.

48.1.0.0. FIRST TIP.
DO NOT SPEND YEARS GATHERING INTERESTING MATERIAL -- ODD
QUOTATIONS, OVERHEARD REMARKS, COLORFUL PHRASES, BITS OF
TRIVIA, AND OBSCURE FACTS IN THE HOPE THAT YOU WILL ONE DAY
FIND A STORY TO CONTAIN THEM. PUT BLUNTLY, BURN THESE ODD
NOTES AND CLEAR YOUR HEAD.

48.2.0.0. TIP #2.
**DO NOT SPEND YEARS EXPERIMENTING WITH DIFFERENT FORMS OF
WRITING AND VARIOUS INTELLECTUAL FOLLIES:** SUCH AS CUT-UPS
AND VERBAL COLLAGES, INTRICATE MULTIPLE PERSON NARRATIVES,
DREAM STORIES, RECIPE BOOKS, ANATOMIES, IMAGINARY ACADEMIC
THESES AND THE LIKE. YES, IT'S TRUE THAT SOME OF THE WORLD'S
MOST INTERESTING LITERATURE HAS ELEMENTS OF THESE FORMS -- BUT

THAT WAS THEN AND THIS IS DIFFERENT. IF YOU ARE SERIOUS ABOUT GETTING A WORK OF FICTION PUBLISHED TODAY YOU NEED QUICK SHARP ANSWERS TO THE FOLLOWING QUESTIONS.

1. IN WHAT SECTION OF A BOOKSTORE OR RETAILER'S WEBSITE WILL YOUR BOOK BE FOUND? [GENRE']
2. WHICH AUTHORS CAN YOUR WORK BE LIKENED TO?
3. IN THREE SENTENCES OR LESS WHAT'S YOUR NOVEL ABOUT?
4. IS IT SALEABLE?

48.3.0.0. TIP #3. READ YOUR WORK ALOUD, TO SOME WILLING VICTIM IDEALLY, BUT AT LEAST TO YOURSELF. STORYTELLING BEGAN AS AN ORAL FORM AND THE EAR (HOWEVER EROTICALLY APPEALING) HAS A TRUENESS TO IT THAT WILL REVEAL WHAT'S WORKING AND WHAT'S NOT IN A MORE IMMEDIATE AND DECISIVE WAY THAN SIMPLY SCANNING THE PAGE. THIS DISCIPLINE WILL ALSO SLOW YOU DOWN PSYCHOLOGICALLY AND BRING YOU INTO MORE INTIMATE CONTACT WITH YOUR STORY. IN THE END, IT WILL TAKE NO MORE TIME THAN READING BACK A PAGE SILENTLY.

48.4.0.0. TIP #4. IGNORE ALL REASONABLE SOUNDING ADVICE LIKE "WRITE ABOUT WHAT YOU KNOW," "READ AS MUCH AS YOU CAN," OR "TRY TO WRITE EVERY DAY." IF YOU NEED TO HEAR THIS ADVICE YOU ARE IN THE WRONG GAME. *[YOU SHOULD BE DOING IT ALREADY!]*

THE FAMOUS DEVICE OF CONFLICT UPON WHICH ALL STORIES ARE SUPPOSED TO HINGE STARTS WITHIN THE WRITER.

48.5.0.0. SUMMARY:
THERE YOU HAVE IT, TWO DIFFERENT POINTS OF VIEW.

THE POINT OF BEING A WRITER IS BECAUSE YOU WANT TO BE AND ARE WILLING TO LEARN TO WRITE CREATIVELY. CONSIDER THE OLD SHAKESPEAREAN QUOTE: **"TO BE OR NOT TO BE!"**

IT TAKES BELIEF, FORTITUDE AND A KNACK FOR A GOOD STORY ON YOUR PART. LET NO CRITIC, EDITOR, MANAGER OR EVEN A READER STOP YOU. BE UNREASONABLE!

THERE ARE BILLIONS OF PEOPLE ON EARTH…SO HOW MANY, EVER SO SMALL MIGHT WANT TO READ WHAT YOU WROTE? *LOTS!*

SO STORYTELL, WRITE AND READ THE REST OF YOUR LIFE. PUT THAT ON YOUR BUCKET LIST!

48.6.0.0. OUR PROGRESS:
1. WE COMPLETE OUR EDITOR'S CHECKLIST.

2. WE FOLLOW THE 'DO NOT DO' INSTRUCTIONS.

3. WE ANSWER 4 QUICK QUESTIONS TO OUR EDITOR.

CHAPTER 49

49.0.0.0. PRINT ON DEMAND:
GET YOUR BOOK IN PRINT

CHAPTER TOPICS: *E BOOKS-PRINT ON DEMAND PUBLISHERS-BOOK PROPOSALS-RESTRICTIONS TO BEING PUBLISHED-MARKETING CHOICES-BOOK COSTS-BOOK SELLERS-INTERNATIONAL ND INTERNET MARKETS-*

49.0.1.0. INTRODUCTION:
PRINT-ON-DEMAND CHANGED THE RULES OF THE PUBLISHING GAME AND THE E-BOOK PROVED IT. E-BOOKS EMPOWERED "WOULD-BE" AUTHORS IN WAYS THAT TRADITIONAL PUBLISHING & SUBMISSIONS PROCESS COULD NEVER ACCOMPLISH.

IT'S A NEW BALL GAME!   **E-BOOKS** CHANGED THE POWER STRUCTURE OF TRADITIONAL BOOK PUBLISHERS. SUDDENLY, HERE WAS A MEDIA WITH NO "PUBLISHERS GUIDELINES" OR "BOOK PROPOSAL" RULES WHICH PREVENTED ANY AUTHOR FROM RELEASING A BOOK.

POD'S CHALLENGES THE STATUS QUO! [CH 47] EXPLAINS THE PUBLISHER'S "SUBMISSION PROCESS" BEFORE 'E-BOOKS' AND PRINT-ON-DEMAND (POD) PUBLISHERS CHALLENGED TO RIGHT TO BE PRINTED. THE LARGE PUBLISHING HOUSES' PRINTED ARGUMENT IN THE MEDIA WAS "POOR QUALITY OF AN AUTHOR'S WORK IF SUBMITTED BY POD'S." OBVIOUSLY, THAT WAS NOT THE CASE!

THE REAL PROBLEM WAS RESTRICTION: **49.0.2.0. THE REAL PROBLEM** IS THE TRADITIONAL PUBLISHER'S SELECTION OF A POTENTIAL BOOK FOR THIS "BOOK PROPOSAL" PROCESS IS CUMBERSOME AND TIME DELAYING, UP TO 6 MONTHS OR MORE. AUTHORS REALIZED AFTER MANY SUBMISSIONS AND REJECTION LETTERS, THE PROBLEM MIGHT NOT BE HIS QUALITY BUT **ACCESS** AND FINALLY REACHING SOMEONE TO TAKE ON A PROJECT. AGENTS SAID "I TOLD YOU SO," AFTER FINDING EVEN THEIR OWN ACCESS WAS RESTRICTED BY THE VETTING PROCESS. THEY WERE TOLD WE CAN ONLY TAKE ON A FEW HIGH QUALITY PROJECTS EACH YEAR. THE PROCESS RESEMBLED A FUNNEL, NARROWING TO A FEW.

P.O.D. AUTHORS SAID THE PIPELINE TO THE LARGE TRADITIONAL HOUSES WERE RESTRICTED TO MULTIPLE–BOOK AUTHORS AND A FEW LUCKY ONES WHO WERE ABLE TO GET THRU THE STRINGENT VETTING PROCESS. HOWEVER, THINGS WERE ABOUT TO CHANGE DRASTICALLY.

49.0.3.0. AUTHOR MARKETING CHOICES: NO LONGER WERE AUTHORS
RESTRICTED TO THE MAIN LARGE "PUBLISHING HOUSES" AND BOUND BY RULES TO "SUBMIT LENGTHY PROPOSALS," MARKETING PLANS AND PUBLISH/PURCHASE SO MANY BOOKS; THEREFORE CREATING A BURDEN ON BOTH THE AUTHOR OR BOOK SELLER TO "BUY" THEM AS INVENTORY.

OF COURSE, RETURNS WERE A BIG HEADACHE FOR ALL.

AUTHORS HAD A CHOICE TO PURCHASE A CHOICE OF SEVERAL "MARKETING PACKAGES" FOR THEIR BOOKS OR TO LET THE P.O.D. PUBLISHER MARKET THEM FOR THE AUTHOR. SUDDENLY, THE MARKET SAW THOUSANDS OF BOOKS HITTING THE MARKET MAINLY VIA THE INTERNET. AUTHORS BEGAN MARKETING AND SENDING PRESS RELEASES OUT TO THE PUBLIC. BOOK SELLERS WERE DOING LESS MARKETING; BUT CONCENTRATED ON "ORDERING AND SELLING." AUTHORS WHO PURCHASED THEIR OWN BOOKS, PER CONTRACT AND DID **BOOK SIGNINGS** WERE FINDING THAT SELLING AN AVERAGE OF 7 BOOKS PER SIGNING WAS NOT THE WAY TO PRODUCTIVELY REACH THEIR BUYERS.

49.0.4.0. BOOK COSTS:
THEN, COSTS GOT IN THE WAY. PAPER, INK AND PUBLISHING, MARKETING AND DISTRIBUTION COSTS WERE RISING AND DEMAND WAS FALLING. 'SIGNIFICANT BOOKS' WERE HARDBOUND AND COST APPROX. $10.00 MORE PER BOOK TO PRINT. THE PUBLIC BUYER WAS ASTONISHED TO SEE HARD BOUNDS COSTING $30.00 TO $50.00 TO BUY. PRINT-ON-DEMAND [P.O.D.] HOUSES WERE ABLE TO OFFER PUBLISHING SERVICES AT A REASONABLE COST, [GENERALLY IN SOFT-COVER FORMATS] THUS REDUCING THE RETAIL PRICE OF THE BOOK, EVEN WITH PRESSURE FROM BOOK SELLERS FOR 100% MARKUP; FOR WHICH THE LARGE BOOK SELLER CHAINS THEN DISCOUNTED USUALLY AT 10%. USED BOOK SELLERS WERE COMPLAINING THAT HARD COVERS WERE SITTING ON THE SHELVES WHILE SOFT COVERS WITH ENTICING COVER ART WERE MOVING. SUDDENLY, SPEED-TO-SHELF AND SPEED-OFF-THE-SHELF TOOK ON A NEW MEANING. LESS INVENTORY TURNS AND FEWER RETAIL DOLLARS KEPT MANY A BOOKSELLER FROM LOADING INVENTORY.

ECONOMICS TOOK OVER.
THE 2008 RECESSION CAUSED PANIC AND THINGS BEGAN TO CHANGE. P.O.D. CREATED THEIR OWN WEB STOREFRONTS AND OFFERED ANY NEW AUTHOR A CHANCE TO PUBLISH AND LIST THEIR BOOKS THERE. LARGE HOUSE PUBLISHERS REACTED BY RESTRICTING OR DEGRADING THE QUALITY OF WORKS COMING FROM THE P.O.D.'S AND SOME HUGE BOOK SELLER CHAIN STORES EVEN DEMANDED THAT AUTHORS USE THEIR OWN BRANDED P.O.D. SERVICES OR THEIR BOOKS WOULD NOT BE DISPLAYED IN THE STORES. LAWSUITS WERE FILED. NEW ECONOMIC PRESSURES BEGAN TO BOIL OVER. NO LONGER WAS THE "BOOK MARKET" THE SOLE DOMAIN OF THE LARGE PUBLISHING HOUSES AND THEIR RULES OF DOING BUSINESS FORCED ON THEIR RETAILERS. THESE RULES MIGHT INCLUDE FORCED INVENTORY, RESTRICTIONS ON RETURNS AND EVEN RETAIL PRICING AND DISCOUNTS.

49.0.5.0. P.O.D. AUTHOR'S REBELLED. MANY PRINT ON DEMAND
AUTHORS SAID, IF YOU WON'T SHOW MY BOOK ON YOUR SHELF. I WILL NOT VISIT YOUR BRICK AND MORTAR STORE NOR BUY FROM YOU. I WILL GO TO THE INTERNET WHICH DOES SUPPORT MY WORK. SMALLER INTERNET BOOK SELLERS GREW AT THE EXPENSE OF THE CHAIN STORES.

49.0.6.0. BOOK SELLERS WERE LOOKING FOR LESS RESTRICTIONS, MORE
NEW BOOKS AND MORE PROFIT WITHOUT ADDING MORE SHELF SPACE. THEY CHOSE THE WEB TO MARKET THEIR BOOKS AND THE INTERNET TO "SELL" THEIR BOOKS. BOOK SELLERS SAW THE WISDOM AND LESSER

PURCHASING REQUIREMENT SAID, I CAN OFFER MORE BOOKS FOR SALE, LESS INVENTORY AND FEWER RETURNS THUS INCREASING MY OFFERINGS WITHOUT STOCKING SO MANY AND SELL THEM VIA THE INTERNET.

49.0.7.0. INTERNATIONAL INTERNET SELLING:
ONCE AN AUTHOR SECURES BOTH A COPYRIGHT AND AN ISBN NUMBER FROM BOWKER, THE MARKETPLACE (WEBSELLERS) REACTS BY ADDING BOOKS TO THEIR WEB LISTINGS FOR MANY P.O.D. BOOKS IN THE U.S.A. MARKET AND OVERSEAS MARKETS. STILL THIS PROCESS TOOK SIX MONTHS.

I FOUND IT IRONIC. MY SEVEN P-O-D BOOKS ,WRITTEN OVER TEN YEARS, AND PUBLISHED DID HIT THE FOREIGN MARKETS FASTER THAN BEFORE THE WEB CHAIN STORES (LARGE DOMINATING BOOK RESELLERS) "ALLOWED" THEM. OBVIOUSLY, AN AUTHOR WITH SEVERAL BOOKS EXPECTS MORE 'INTERNET ACCESS' AND 'MARKETING' TO OCCUR THAN ONE TIME AUTHORS. HOWEVER, IT WAS FASTER THAN THE VETTING AND REJECTION PROCESS EXPERIENCED EARLIER WITH QUERY LETTERS AND SUBMISSIONS. [REFER TO CH 47 BOOK PROPOSALS].
THE MARKETING FORCES WILL CONTINUE TO VETTE THEM BASED ON THE READER'S DESIRES, NO MATTER WHO PUBLISHES THEM.

49.1.0.0. OUR PROGRESS:
1. WE LEARNED ABOUT PRINT ON DEMAND PUBLISHERS.

2. WE LEARNED POD PUBLISHERS OFFER US A NEW WAY TO GET TO MARKET WITHOUT THE DELAY OF QUERY/PROPOSAL LETTERS.

3. WE LEARNED ABOUT SELLING OUR BOOK VIA INTERNET AND INTERNATIONAL MARKETS.

4. WE LEARNED THE RULES CHANGED DRASTICALLY AND IN FAVOR OF THE AUTHOR.

CHAPTER 50

50.0.0.0. FREELANCING:

CHAPTER TOPICS: *MARKET GUIDES- WRITER'S GUIDES.-HOW TO WRITE A QUERY LETTER-MARKET LISTINGS AND GUIDE BOOKS:*

REFERENCE: CH 47 BOOK PROPOSALS & CH 54 MARKETING:

50.0.0.0. INTRODUCTION: MARKETING AND FREELANCE:

SELLING YOUR SOUL IS ABOUT MARKETING YOUR CREATION. WE WANT TO SELL THE "SIZZLE" OF OUR BOOK, NOT DIRECTLY THE BOOK ITSELF. IT WILL JUST FOLLOW AFTER WE DO SOME RIGHT THINGS IN MARKETING. WE NEED TO KNOW ABOUT MARKETING, ITS TOOLS, GUIDES AND PROCESSES AND SOME OF THE SYNOPSIS OF OUR BOOK. WHY IS IT GOOD? WHO WILL BUY IT AND WHY.

THEN, THERE IS THE **FREELANCE MARKET** WHERE WE SELL OUR WRITING ABILITIES IN SPECIFIC GENRE. MAYBE WE SUPPLEMENT OUR INCOME OR USE IT TO GET EXPOSURE FOR US AS AN AUTHOR, OR BUILD A PORTFOLIO OR EXPAND OUR WRITING INTO OTHER AREAS.

WRITERS USE THE FREELANCE MARKET TO PROVIDE INCOME AND AS AN OUTLET FOR OUR WORK. FREELANCING IS THAT JOURNEY ALONG THE WAY, WHILE WE WRITE MOST OF WHAT WE LIKE,

UNTIL SOMEONE PAYS US FOR THE "GOOD STUFF!"

50.0.1.0. READ AND USE A MARKET LISTING:

MARKET LISTINGS PROVIDE SOME KEY MARKETING ONLY INFORMATION. LISTS OF AGENTS AND PUBLISHERS, MAYBE A REVIEWER AND ADS. MARKET LISTING ARE AVAILABLE FROM THE BOOK SELLER.

50.0.2.0. HERE'S HOW:

1. NOTE IF THE PUBLICATION 'PAYS ON ACCEPTANCE' OR 'PAYS ON PUBLICATION.' OR IF IT PAYS ON PUBLICATION YOU MAY WANT TO FIND ANOTHER MARKET THAT **PAYS ON ACCEPTANCE**.

2. LOOK FOR THE STATED PAY RATE. IF IT DOESN'T MEET YOUR STANDARDS; MOVE ON.

3. IF YOU WANT TO WRITE FOR THE PUBLICATION, PAY PARTICULAR ATTENTION TO WORDS LIKE 'FOCUS,' 'ADDRESSING,' AND OTHER WORDS AND PHRASES THAT TELL THE PURPOSE OF THE PUBLICATION.

4. LOOK FOR 'CURRENT NEEDS,' OR SIMILAR PHRASE THAT TELLS YOU WHAT THE EDITOR NEEDS.

5. READ THE MARKET LISTING ALL THE WAY THROUGH.

50.0.3.0. QUERY LETTERS:

1. FIND OUT HOW EDITORS WANT THE QUERY LETTER WRITTEN. EMAIL OR SNAIL MAIL?

2. NOTE IF THEY ACCEPT AND PAY FOR PHOTOS OR OTHER ART - IF YOU CAN PROVIDE ART AS WELL AS WRITING. YOU ENHANCE YOUR CHANCES OF SUCCESS.

3. PURCHASE A COPY OF THE MAGAZINE AND STUDY IT FOR MAG. ARTICLES. USE MARKET GUIDES FOR OTHERS.

4. PREPARE YOUR QUERY AND SEND IT COMPLETE. DO NOT RUSH IT; BUT BE TIMELY.

TIPS:

T-1. FOLLOW THE DIRECTIONS! THEY SUM UP HOW THE PUBLICATION WANTS TO DO BUSINESS.

T-2. STUDY TWO OR THREE CURRENT COPIES OF THE PUBLICATION, WHICH WILL GIVE YOU A GOOD FEEL FOR THE EDITOR'S WANTS AND NEEDS.

50.0.4.0. SUMMARY:

THE FREELANCE MARKET HAS ITS GOOD AND BAD POINTS. SOME WILL TAKE ADVANTAGE. SOME WILL CHEAT OUR WORD COUNT OR ARTICLE FEES. DO NOTHING FOR FREE OR ON COMMISSION. DO YOUR HOMEWORK, REVIEW BLOG SITES AND INVESTIGATE YOUR FREELANCE EMPLOYER. USE THE "REPUTABLE FREELANCE PROVIDERS."

CHECK THEM OUT ON THE WEB. SEE THE WEB LISTINGS IN **INDEX 3.**

50.1.0.0. OUR PROGRESS:

1. WE LEARNED ABOUT THE FREELANCE MARKET.

2. WE LEARNED ABOUT FREELANCING PAY AND PITFALLS.

3. WE LEARNED TO DO NOTHING FOR FREE.

4. QUERY LETTERS ARE USED FOR MAGAZINE WORK OR SOMETIMES AN E-MAIL WILL SUFFICE WITH ATTACHMENTS.

5. WE DON'T QUIT OUR DAY JOB UNTIL THE BIG CHECK ARRIVES.

CHAPTER 51

51.0.0.0. THE E-BOOK-CYBER MONEY:

CHAPTER TOPICS: *DEFINITION-EXAMPLES-ADVANTAGES-DISADVANTAGES-PIRACY-DIGITAL RIGHTS MANAGEMENT-CLICK WRAP-COMMON PRACTICES -EPPIE AWARD.*

51.0.1.0. DEFINED:

AN E-BOOK (SHORT FOR ELECTRONIC BOOK, ALSO WRITTEN EBOOK IS THE <u>DIGITAL MEDIA</u> EQUIVALENT OF A CONVENTIONAL PRINTED <u>BOOK</u>. THESE DIGITAL DOCUMENTS ARE USUALLY READ ON HARDWARE SUCH AS PERSONAL COMPUTERS [PC'S], *<u>E-BOOK READERS</u>* OR MOBILE PHONES.

51.0.2.0 EXAMPLES:
1.PLASTIC LOGIC (2009 ESTIMATE)
2.KINDLE BY AMAZON (2007)
3.CYBOOK GEN 3 BY BOOKEEN (2007)
4.HANLIN EREADER BY JINKE (DISTRIBUTED AS "LBOOK" IN ESTONIA, KAZAKHSTAN, RUSSIA AND UKRAINE AS "BEBOOK" IN EUROPE) (2007)
5.SONY READER BY SONY (2006)
6.ILIAD BY IREX (2006)
7. LIBRIÉ BY SONY (2004)

SOURCE FROM WIKIPEDIA:

I CHOSE SEVERAL ADVANTAGES NOT ALL FROM WIKIPEDIA AS THEY MADE THE MOST SENSE FROM AN "ON-LINE SERVICE" THUS FREELY ACCESSIBLE BY ANY READER AND NOT SUBJECT TO COPYRIGHT RULES OF USE. AS A SERVICE MUCH OF THE COPY BELOW IS SUBJECT TO "EDITING BY CONTRIBUTORS. SO NOT ALL OF THIS IS THE TRUTH AND GOSPEL; HOWEVER, IT DOES GIVE A GOOD OVERVIEW!

51.0.3.0. ADVANTAGES-E-BOOKS:

1. TEXT CAN BE SEARCHED AUTOMATICALLY AND CROSS-REFERENCED USING <u>HYPERLINKS</u>.
2. E-BOOKS CAN ALLOW NON-PERMANENT HIGHLIGHTING OF BOOKS.
3. LESS PHYSICAL SPACE IS REQUIRED TO STORE E-BOOKS, AND HUNDREDS OR THOUSANDS OF BOOKS MAY BE STORED ON THE SAME DEVICE.
4. READERS WHO HAVE DIFFICULTY READING PRINTED BOOKS CAN BENEFIT FROM THE ADJUSTMENT OF TEXT SIZE AND FONT FACE.
5. <u>TEXT-TO-SPEECH SOFTWARE</u> CAN BE USED TO CONVERT E-BOOKS TO <u>AUDIO BOOKS</u> AUTOMATICALLY.
6.E-BOOK DEVICES ALLOW READING IN LOW LIGHT OR EVEN TOTAL DARKNESS BY MEANS OF A <u>BACK LIGHT</u>.
7.AN E-BOOK CAN AUTOMATICALLY OPEN AT THE LAST READ PAGE.
8.E-BOOKS MAY ALLOW ANIMATED IMAGES OR MULTIMEDIA CLIPS TO BE EMBEDDED.

51.0. 4.0. DISADVANTAGES:

1.IF NOT VIEWED ON COMPUTERS, E-BOOKS REQUIRE THE PURCHASE OF AN ELECTRONIC DEVICE AND/OR PERIPHERAL SOFTWARE WHICH CAN DISPLAY THEM. IF THEY ARE TO BE VIEWED ON A PERSONAL COMPUTER, IT MAY REQUIRE ADDITIONAL SOFTWARE

2.NOT ALL PUBLISHERS PRODUCE THE E-BOOK EQUIVALENT OF THEIR PRINT BOOKS. IN OTHER CASES, E-BOOKS ARE GIVEN A LOWER PRIORITY IN TERMS OF THE PUBLISHER'S RESOURCES, RESULTING IN A DISPARITY IN PRODUCT QUALITY, RELEASE DATES AND THE LIKE. THIS PROBLEM IS NOT ENDEMIC TO EVERY PUBLISHER, BUT HAS AN EFFECT ON THE QUALITY OF THE OVERALL POOL OF MERCHANDISE AVAILABLE.

3.ALL E-BOOK DEVICES REQUIRE ELECTRICAL POWER, RESULTING IN THE CONSUMPTION OF ELECTRICITY.OR BATTERY POWER.

4.CERTAIN E-BOOK FORMATS MAY BECOME OBSOLETE AND INCOMPATIBLE WITH FUTURE DEVICES.

5.IF AN E-BOOK DEVICE IS STOLEN, LOST, OR BROKEN BEYOND REPAIR, ALL E-BOOKS STORED ON THE DEVICE MAY BE LOST. THIS CAN BE AVOIDED BY BACKUP EITHER ON ANOTHER DEVICE OR BY THE E-BOOK PROVIDER.

6.THERE IS A LOSS OF TOUCHING AND SEEING THE AESTHETICS OF BOOK-BINDINGS.

51.0.5.0. ADVANTAGES FOR WRITERS:

MANY "ORDINARY" PEOPLE HAVE EXTRAORDINARY STORIES OR A KNOWLEDGE OF NICHE SUBJECTS AND ARE ABLE TO WRITE THEM VIA NEW SOFTWARE. HOWEVER, VERY FEW OF THOSE HAVE THE KNOWLEDGE OF HOW TO CREATE A MANUSCRIPT, SOLICIT PUBLISHING HOUSES AND PLAY THE POLITICAL/ECONOMIC GAME OF GETTING PUBLISHED.

VERY FEW PEOPLE KNOW EXACTLY THE PROCESS THAT BOOKS GO THROUGH IN ORDER TO BE PUBLISHED. AN ENORMOUS AMOUNT OF PREPARATION MUST BE DONE IN ORDER TO GET YOUR MANUSCRIPT IN FRONT OF A PUBLISHER, AND EVEN IF YOU ARE ABLE TO DO SO, THERE IS **NO GUARANTEE** THAT YOUR WORK WILL BE SELECTED.

51.0.6.0. BOOK PROFITS:

BEST OF ALL - EBOOK AUTHORS KEEP **100 PERCENT OF THE PROFITS** WITH POD PUBLISHING HOUSES OF THEIR OWN BOOKS, WHEREAS TRADITIONAL AUTHORS ARE ONLY ABLE TO MAKE ANYWHERE FROM 3 - 6% OF THE PROFITS. IN A SENSE, AUTHORS ARE WORKING TO PRODUCE GOODS FOR THE PROFIT OF TRADITIONAL PUBLISHING HOUSES, WHILE THEY ONLY PROVIDE NOMINAL COMPENSATION TO THE AUTHOR. BOTH TYPES ARE IN THE BUSINESS TO MAKE MONEY; THEY JUST DO IT DIFFERENTLY.

51.0.7.0 PIRACY:

ADVANCES IN E-BOOK SOFTWARE HAVE DEVELOPED A MORE SECURE MEDIUM FOR AUTHORS TO CREATE THEIR ART. READERS ARE NOW PROHIBITED FROM A SIMPLE COPY-AND-PASTE FORM OF PIRACY.

AUTHORS ARE NOW EMPOWERED TO IMPOSE OTHER FORMS OF SECURITY THAT PROTECT THEIR CREATIVE LIVELIHOOD.

LASTLY, IF AN AUTHOR HAS SUCCESSFULLY CREATED AN ONLINE READERSHIP, SOLICITING A PUBLISHING HOUSE IS GOING TO BE THAT MUCH MORE COMPELLING. IF I CAN TELL MY POTENTIAL PUBLISHER THAT I ALREADY HAVE SOLD THOUSANDS FROM MY EFFORTS TO PROMOTE MY BOOK AT HOME, I HAVE ALREADY DEMONSTRATED THAT I HAVE AN **INTERESTED AUDIENCE, WHICH IS THE KEY RISK IN PUBLISHING.**

51.0.8.0. AUTHORS WON'T WAIT:
E-BOOK PUBLISHING IS EMPOWERING AUTHORS TO CUT OUT THE MIDDLEMAN, MAKE MORE PROFITS, SIMPLIFY BUSINESS, AND GET A FOOT IN THE DOOR OF TRADITIONAL PUBLISHING HOUSES.
AUTHORS WON'T WAIT UNTIL SOME AGENT, SOME EDITOR, SOME BOOK PROJECT MANAGER DECIDES WHO IS OR ISN'T A "QUALIFIED" AUTHOR.

51.1.0.0. DIGITAL RIGHTS MANAGEMENT [DRM]:
OWNERSHIP AND TRANSFER OF BOOKS:
ANTI-CIRCUMVENTION TECHNIQUES MAY BE USED TO RESTRICT WHAT THE USER MAY DO WITH AN E-BOOK. FOR INSTANCE, IT MAY NOT BE POSSIBLE TO TRANSFER OWNERSHIP OF AN E-BOOK TO ANOTHER PERSON, THOUGH SUCH A TRANSACTION IS COMMON WITH PHYSICAL BOOKS. SOME DEVICES CAN PHONE HOME TO TRACK READERS AND READING HABITS, RESTRICT PRINTING, OR ARBITRARILY MODIFY READING MATERIAL.

51.1.1.0. "CLICK –WRAP" LICENSING:
THIS INCLUDES RESTRICTING THE COPYING AND DISTRIBUTION OF WORKS IN THE PUBLIC DOMAIN THROUGH THE USE OF "CLICK-WRAP" LICENSING, WHICH EFFECTIVELY LIMITS THE RIGHTS OF THE PUBLIC TO FREELY DISTRIBUTE, SELL OR USE TEXTS IN THE PUBLIC DOMAIN.

WITH SOME FORMATS OF DRM, THE E-BOOK IS TIED TO A **SPECIFIC** COMPUTER OR DEVICE.

51.1.1.1. THE 'DMR' MAY HAVE RESTRICTIONS:
THE USER MAY LOSE THE RIGHT TO MOVE IT, SAVE IT FOR A LONG PERIOD OR STOP ACCESS.

51.1.1.2. RENTAL-LEASE-PURCHASE:
THERE ARE QUESTIONS AS TO WHETHER THIS IS A RENTAL, A LEASE OR PURCHASE AND WHOM MAY REMOVE ALL OF THESE RIGHTS AND WHEN. THESE ARE ALL THINGS THAT ARE SIGNIFICANTLY DIFFERENT FROM THE REALM OF EXPERIENCES ANYONE HAS HAD WITH A PHYSICAL COPY OF THE BOOK.

51.2.0. 0. PRODUCTION:
E-BOOKS ARE PRODUCED FROM PRE-EXISTING HARD-COPY BOOKS, GENERALLY BY DOCUMENT SCANNING, SOMETIMES WITH THE USE OF ROBOTIC BOOK SCANNERS, HAVING THE TECHNOLOGY TO QUICKLY SCAN BOOKS WITHOUT DAMAGING THE ORIGINAL PRINT EDITION. SCANNING A BOOK PRODUCES AN IMAGE FILE, WHICH MUST THEN BE

CREATIVE WRITING—THE KELLY MANUAL OF STYLE

CONVERTED INTO TEXT FORMAT BY AN 'OCR (OPTICAL READER)PROGRAM.'

E-BOOK PUBLISHING AS AN INDUSTRY IS GROWING IN THE DOUBLE DIGITS YEARLY, ACCORDING TO THE QUARTERLY REPORTS PUT OUT BY **IDPF.**

51.2.1.0. COMMON PRACTICES AMONGST E-BOOK PUBLISHERS,
1. SUPPORT OF MULTIPLE FORMATS INCLUDING **PDF,**

2. PAYMENT OF MUCH HIGHER ROYALTY RATES THAN CONVENTIONAL PUBLISHERS. BUT NOT P.O.D.'S.

3. ONLINE PRESENTATION OF FREE SAMPLES.

51.2.2.0. E-BOOK AWARDS: EPPIE AWARDS:
E-BOOKS HAVE THEIR OWN BESTSELLER LISTS, INCLUDING THOSE COMPILED BY IDPF, BOOKSONBOARD AND FICTIONWISE. THERE ARE TWO YEARLY AWARDS FOR EXCELLENCE IN E-BOOKS. THE LONGEST-STANDING AND MOST INCLUSIVE OF THESE IS THE **EPPIE AWARD**, GIVEN BY EPIC SINCE 2000. THE OTHER IS THE DREAM REALM AWARD, FIRST AWARDED TO SPECULATIVE FICTION E-BOOKS IN 2002.

51.3.0.0. UPDATE ON KINDLE'S E-BOOK: DATE: 2-10-09 +
AMAZON RELEASED ITS NEWEST VERSION OF KINDLE COSTING $359.00. IT IS SLIMMER, 1/3 INCH THICK AND WITH A 6" SCREEN DISPLAYING 16 SHADES OF GRAY. IT CAN ALSO READ TEXT ALOUD FROM TWO SMALL SPEAKERS. IT CAN STORE 1500 BOOKS AS COMPARED TO THE PREVIOUS 200. THE NEW CATALOG HAS 230,000 BOOKS AVAILABLE AND INTERNET WIRELESS CONNECTED. +SOURCE: AKRON BEACON JOURNAL 2-10-09. **SEARCH:WWW.AMAZON.COM/KINDLE**

51.4.0.0. OUR PROGRESS:
1. WE LEARNED ABOUT E- BOOKS.

2. WE LEARNED OUR COMMISSION/ ROYALTY IS LESS.

3. WE LEARNED DESPITE THE HIGH COST OF THE ELECTRONIC READER. SOME ARE BING SOLD.

4. WE LEARNED ABOUT THE "EPPIE AWARD."

5. WE LEARNED SOME POD'S OFFER BOTH THE "BOOK" AND THE E-BOOK" AS BOTH WAYS TO GET SALES FROM OUR BUYER.

CHAPTER 52

52.0.0.0. BOOK COVERS &TITLES:
A MARKETING MATCH:
CHAPTER TOPICS: OVERVIEW-SHORTCUTS-COVER TEMPLATES---BOOK JACKETS-FRONT COVER DESIGN & EXAMPLES. REAR COVER DESIGN & EXAMPLES-SPLINE COVER DESIGN.

52.0.1.0. INTRODUCTION:
THE IMPORTANCE OF YOUR TITLE AND COVER ART IS THE "MOST" IMPORTANT THING NEXT TO A GREAT STORY.

RESEARCH YOUR TITLE AGAINST BOOK LISTS, LIBRARY CATALOGS AND INTERNET (GOOGLE SEARCH). WHERE DOES IT PLACE IN THOSE LISTS?

IF YOUR BOOK TITLE IS LOST AMONG 5,000 OTHER SIMILAR BOOKS; YOUR BOOK MIGHT GET LOST IN THE SAME LISTS WHICH CHOOSE A BOOK TO STOCK.

CHOOSE A STRONG, INTRIGUING AND YET MARKETABLE TITLE!

TAG LINE:
<u>DO</u>: ADD A TAG LINE TO DEFINE WHY YOUR BOOK IS DIFFERENT THAN OTHER OF A SIMILAR TITLE.

52.12.0. 0. BOOK COVERS:
I CAN'T EMPHASIS ENOUGH…THE SUCCESS OF YOUR BOOK MIGHT JUST REST WITH YOUR TITLE AND COVER ART!!!

MY ACTUAL BOOK COVERS
NOTE HOW THEY CHANGED OVER TIME.

FRONT COVER BOOK 1:2011-332 PAGES

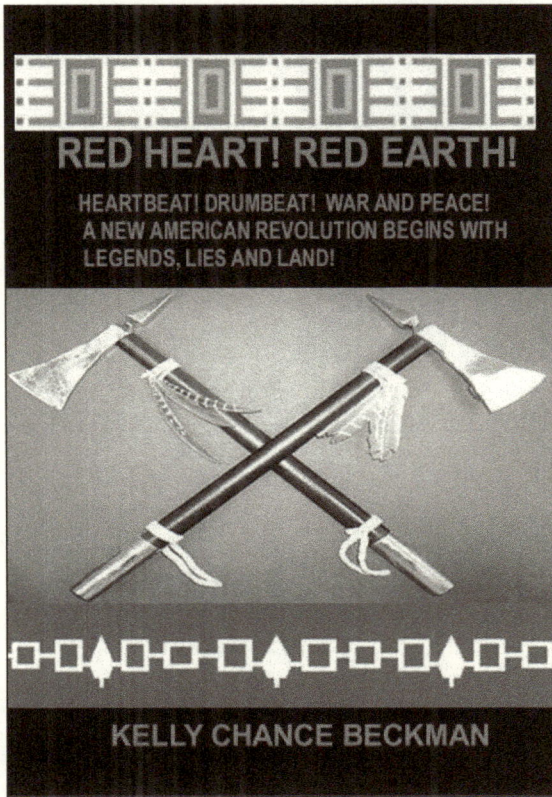

BOOK TITLE: RED HEART! RED EARTH!

BOOK THEME: INDIAN LORE-INDIAN NATIONS AND RIGHTS.
FIGHT FOR CIVIL RIGHTS AS NATIVE AMERICANS.

IMAGE: PEACE TREATY BELT AND CROSSED TOMAHAWKS INDICATE
REVOLUTION(WAR).

MARKETING TAG LINE: BUY THIS BECAUSE OF UNIQUENESS.

FRONT COVER-BOOK 2: 2011-184 PAGES

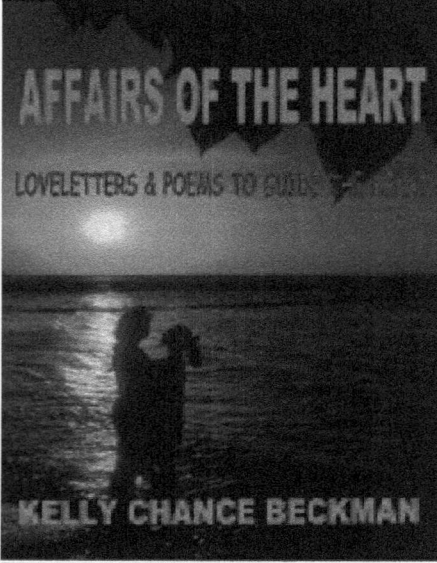

BOOK TITLE: AFFAIRS OF THE HEART

BOOK THEME: LOVE, ROMANCE, HEARTBREAK.

MEDIUM: POEMS-LOVE LETTERS-& COLLECTED WRITINGS.

IMAGE: ROMANTIC SUNSET.

TITLE: AFFAIRS OF HEART-EMOTION.

FRONT COVER BOOKS 3 FRONT & 9 FRONT: 2010 -160 PAGES

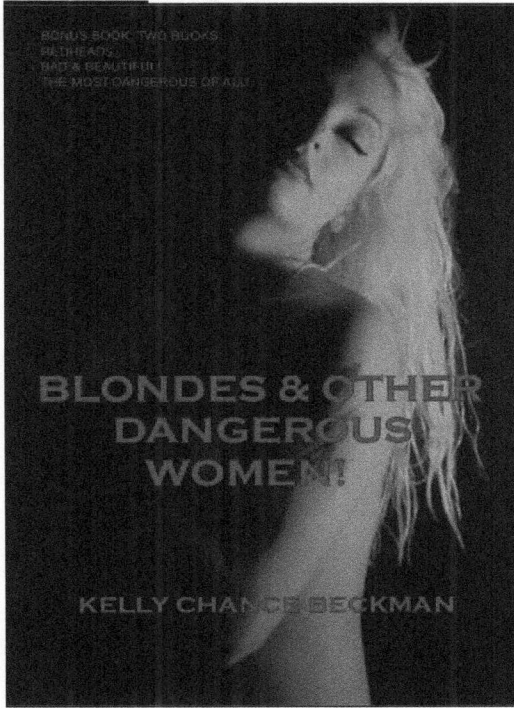

BOOK TITLE: BLONDES AND OTHER DANGEROUS WOMEN!

BOOK THEME:
DETECTIVE-PLAYBOY-BLONDES-SEDUCTION-DANGER-VILLAINS.

IMAGE: SEDUCTIVE!

TITLE: I WANT TO READ THIS.

FRONT COVER BOOKS 4 & 9 REAR: 2010 160 PAGES

REDHEADS – BAD AND BEAUTIFUL. THE MOST DANGEROUS OF ALL!

BOOK THEME:
REDHEADS VS BLONDES-DETECTIVE-SEDUCTION-DANGER-VILLAINS.
THUS, A MATCH FOR BOOK 9. ONE IN FRONT & ONE IN REAR OF BOOK.

IMAGE: BEAUTY-SEDUCTIVE.

TITLE: THE MOST DANGEROUS OF ALL- TELLS ALL IN BOOK.

FRONT COVER: BOOK 5:   228 PAGES

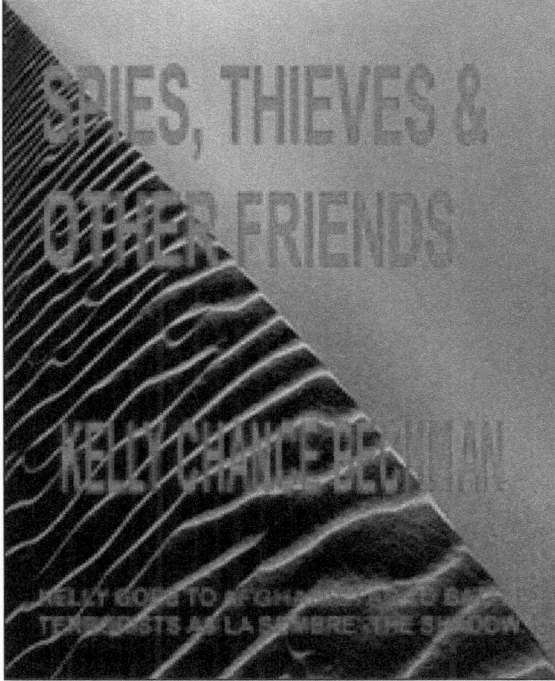

BOOK TITLE: SPIES, THIEVES & OTHER FRIENDS.

BOOK THEME: WAR IN AFGHANISTAN-SPIES-THIEVES, WARLORDS,

IMAGE: SAND. STORY TAKES PLACE IN DESERT.

TITLE: HOOK IS OTHER FRIENDS-CATCHY TITLE.

FRONT COVER: BOOK 6:   348 PAGES

BOOK TITLE: A NOBLE AND SAVAGE HEART!

BOOK THEME: TWO REFERENCES TO HEART-FATHER AND SON.

IMAGE: CHINESE JUNK IS PART OF TRAVELS IN BOOK.

TITLE: REFERENCE TO TWO MAIN CHARACTERS.

FRONT COVER-BOOK 7: 2007-484 PAGES

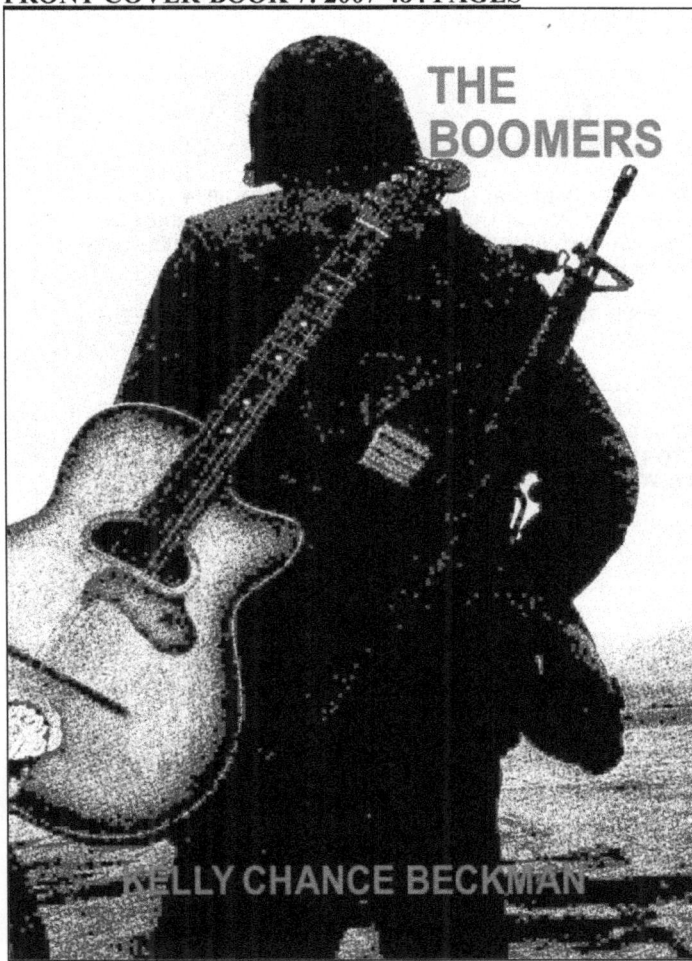

BOOK TITLE: THE BOOMERS.

BOOK THEME: MAIN CHARACTER IS SOLDIER. BOOMER ARE HIS THREE FRIENDS AND THEIR EXPERIENCES.

IMAGE: SOLDIER-POET-MUSICIAN

TITLE: REFERENCE TO FOUR GUYS IN THE WAR AND AFTER.

BACK COVER ART: BOOK 7:

THE BOOMERS

HOLLYWOOD AND THE HISTORY BOOKS GOT IT ALL WRONG!

IMAGINE A MODERN DAY, ROMEO AND JULIET CAUGHT UP IN WAR AND PEACE! HIS DUTY, HONOR AND VALOR CANNOT STOP THE TRIAL FOR TREASON. WAR AND PEACE ARE ALSO ON TRIAL AND STRIPPED TO THE NAKED TRUTH!

FOR THE FIRST TIME, THE BOOMERS AND OTHER SOLDIERS TELL THE ULTIMATE TRUTH-- THE TRUTH EVERY G.I. WANTS YOU TO KNOW.

WHAT BULLETS COULDN'T KILL, WORDS DID!
IT WAS NEVER ABOUT PARADES, OR MEDALS OR EVEN BEING A HERO...IT WAS ABOUT STAYING ALIVE...SO NOW, WE SPEAK AS A COLLECTIVE VOICE TO THE NATION, SAYING: "NEVERMORE!" WE SAY IT LOUDER AND LOUDER. WE SAY IT, " BOOM! BOOM!"

"WE WERE THE BOOMERS...SAVIORS OF THE WORLD, WHITE KNIGHTS AND PRINCES TO THE RESCUE. WE WERE INVINCIBLE, AS ONLY NINETEEN YEAR OLDS COULD THINK! WE WERE RAISED ON SUPERHEROES AND THE BREAKFAST OF CHAMPIONS."™
THEY CALLED US, THE BOOMERS FOR A REASON!

WE EXPOSED:
BETRAYAL AND TREASON, GREED AND CORRUPTION, DUTY AND HONOR! WINNING AND LOSING! DEATH AND DISHONOR! SPIES AND LIES!PEACE AND PROFITS! BLOOD AND GUTS! WAR AND PEACE!
WHAT LEGACY?

WHAT LEGACY, INDEED!
NEITHER AS POETS, NOR SINGERS OR HEROES; BUT AS SOLDIERS AND AMERICA'S SONS, WE NOW LEAVE THE WAR BEHIND. AFTERALL, WE WON IT!

A MESSAGE FROM THE LOST BOYS:
WE ARE YOUR GENTLE HEROES WHO HAVE COME OUT OF THE NIGHT AND OUT OF THE VALLEY OF DEATH. NO LONGER ARE WE THE FORGOTTEN, THE MISSING IN ACTION OR YOUR UNKNOWN SOLDIERS. ALL OF US ARE BOOMERS, TOO!

COME WALK WITH US; WE WILL TALK OF THE REAL WAR AND PEACE.

BACK COVER:
PURPOSE: TO MARKET BOOK AND INTRIGUE BUYER INTO BUYING IT.(THE HOOK). NOTICE: THERE ARE NO BOOK REVIEWS ON REAR COVER.

FRONT COVER: BOOK 11:
SEE **CH 52** WHY THIS ARTWORK WAS SELECTED AND MARKETING TAGLINE INFORMATION.

BOOK 11:   2013-360 PAGES

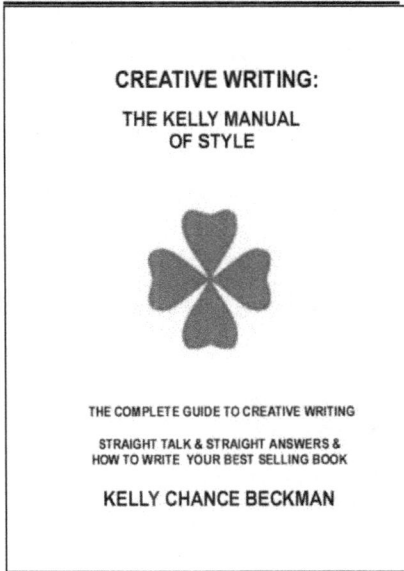

CREATIVE WRITING:

THE KELLY MANUAL
OF STYLE

THE COMPLETE GUIDE TO CREATIVE WRITING

STRAIGHT TALK & STRAIGHT ANSWERS &
HOW TO WRITE YOUR BEST SELLING BOOK

KELLY CHANCE BECKMAN

BOOK TITLE: CREATIVE WRITING-THE KELLY MANUAL OF STYLE.

BOOK THEME: HOW TO PERFORM CREATIVE WRITING.

IMAGE: SIMPLE DESIGN- LOTS OF WHITE SPACE.

TITLE:
BLUNT TITLE TO POINT.

 MARKETING TAG LINE-ON FRONT.-CAPTURE READER/BUYER ATTENTION. THIS IS DIFFERENT & UNIQUE.

I CHANGED THE TITLE TO A SIMPLE MORE DIRECT AND YET IMPLIED NEW **'HOW TO'** IDEAS FOR THE CREATIVE WRITER.(MY READER).

CREATIVE WRITING (GENRE-SUBJECT) AND **'KELLY STYLE'** AS DISTINGUISHABLE FROM 'AP STYLE,' 'MLA STYLE' OR 'CHICAGO STYLE.'

CREATIVE WRITING—THE KELLY MANUAL OF STYLE

RESEARCH SHOWED MY BOOK WILL APPEAR IN THE WRITING SECTION AND "KELLY STYLE," WHICH GIVES IT A DIFFERENT (UNIQUE) SUBJECT MATTER FROM THE NORM.

THEN I ADD A "**MARKETING TAG LINE**" TO THE FRONT COVER AND **MORE DETAILED MARKETING** ONES (REASONS WHY THIS BOOK IS BETTER OR ITS NEW FEATURES.) TO THE REAR COVER, I ALSO PLACED ONE PAGE RIGHT AFTER THE COPYRIGHT PAGE LISTING **NEW FEATURES** THE WRITER WILL FIND WITHIN; THUS, **BUY THIS BOOK BECAUSE....**

THE COVER ART SHOULD REFLECT THE NEW FEATURES "THE MARKETING TAG" THE GREAT TITLE AND AUTHOR'S NAME.

BACK COVER: BOOK 11-2011: ALSO SEE NEW 2014 COVER

CREATIVE WRITING: THE KELLY MANUAL OF STYLE:

SECRET DREAM!
DO YOU HAVE A SECRET DREAM TO WRITE?

BELIEVE!
DO YOU BELIEVE YOU CAN WRITE BUT ONLY NEED
SOME "HOW TO" STEPS TO GUIDE YOU?

CREATE!
DO YOU WANT TO CREATE A BOOK OR STORY THAT IS IMAGINATIVE
AND JUST BURNING TO COME OUT?

THE KELLY MANUAL OF STYLE SHOWS THE BEGINNER AND
ADVANCED WRITER HOW TO WRITE CREATIVELY. NEW TOOLS OF
WRITING ARE PRESENTED IN AN EASY TO LEARN MANNER.

BECOME THAT AUTHOR YOU ALWAYS WANTED TO BE!
LEARN HOW TO WRITE A NEW WAY AND PREPARE A DRAFT READY
FOR PUBLICATION. LEARN THE BOOK BUSINESS, PUBLISHING AND
THE MARKETING OF YOUR BOOK.

KELLY STYLE INCLUDES:
ADVICE . BOOK AWARDS . BOOK COVERS . BOOK DRAFTS . BRIDGES .
CHARACTER DEVELOPMENT . CHECK LISTS . CLASS LESSON PLANS.
CLIMAX . COSTS . CREATIVE PROCESS. EDITING . HOW TO EXAMPLES .
IDEA LISTS . JOBS . LEARN DRAMATIZATION. MARKETING . PAGE
SETUP . PLOTS . PORTFOLIOS . PUBLISHING . LITERARY READINGS .
RESEARCH . STORYTELLING . STYLE . SYNOPSES, TIMELINES . WEB
PAGES . WRITING TECHNIQUES . WRITER'S LIFE . & MORE .

INVEST IN YOUR WRITING CAREER!
REVIEW THE TOP 20 UNIQUE KELLY STYLE FEATURES AND ADVANCE
FROM WRITER TO AUTHOR TO GRAND MASTER. THE KELLY MANUAL
OF STYLE WILL TRANSFORM THAT ORDINARY WRITING INTO GREAT
CREATIVE WRITING!

ISBN# 978-0-557-05437-4

INSERT BARCODE &
LULU LOGO HERE

REAR COVER: MARKETING MESSAGE.

FRONT COVER: BOOK 12: 2011-260 PAGES

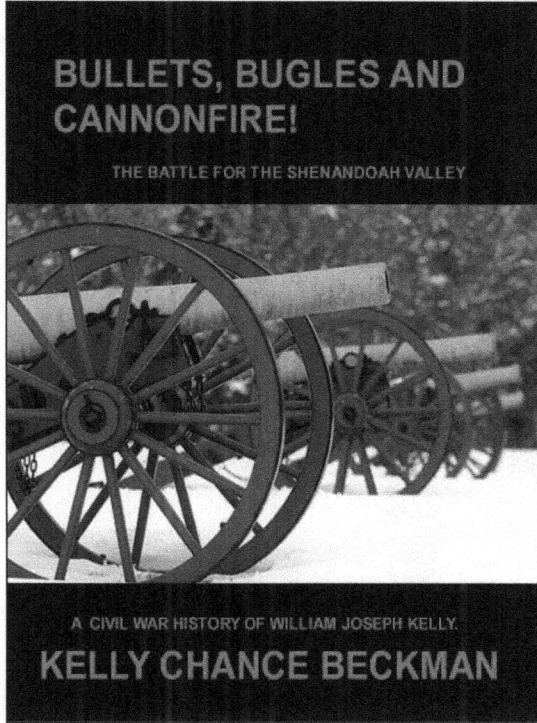

BOOK TITLE: BULLETS, BUGLES AND CANNONFIRE!

BOOK THEME: ONE SOLDIER'S EXPERIENCE IN CIVIL WAR.

IMAGE: CANNONS TIE TO TITLE.

TITLE: REFERS TO KEY EVENTS IN BOOK.

TAGLINE: WHAT BOOK IS ABOUT.-WHY BUY THIS BOOK.

FRONT COVER: BOOK 22

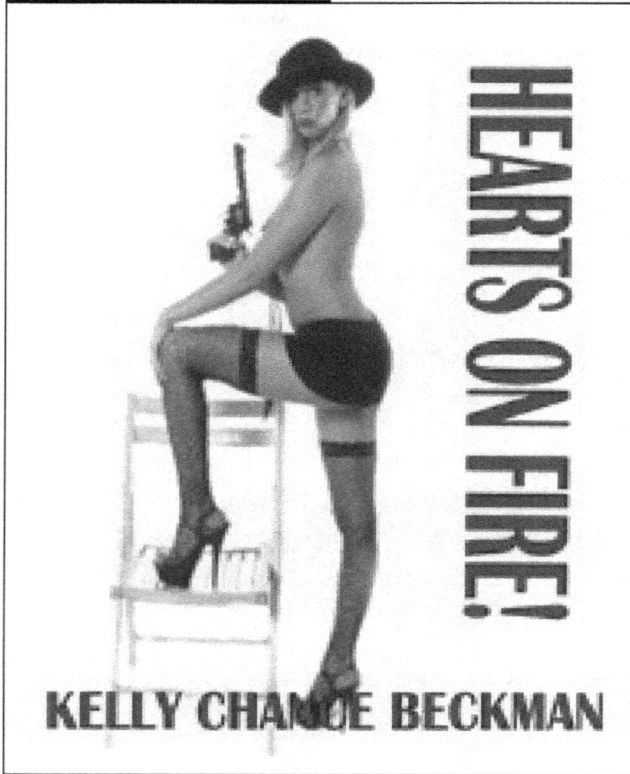

BOOK TITLE: HEARTS ON FIRE!

BOOK THEME: 1960'S THEME DETECTIVE-BLONDES.

IMAGE: SEDUCTIVE BLONDE WITH GUN.

TITLE: SEVERAL RELATIONSHIPS AND DETECTIVE WORK CREATES
CONFLICTS.

FRONT COVER: BOOK 41:

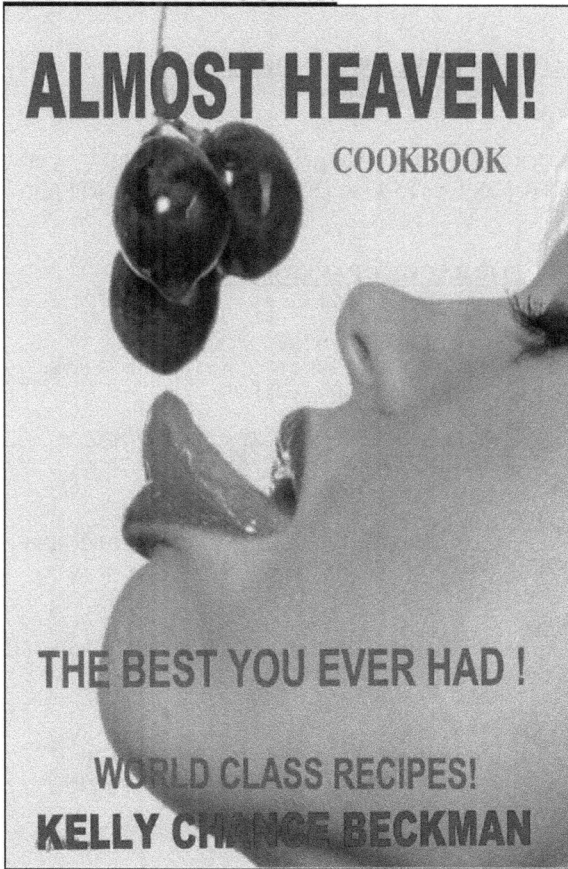

ALMOST HEAVEN!
COOKBOOK

THE BEST YOU EVER HAD !

WORLD CLASS RECIPES!
KELLY CHANCE BECKMAN

BOOK TITLE: ALMOST HEAVEN!

BOOK THEME: COOKBOOK
THE BEST RECIPES YOU EVER HAD! FOOD IS SEXY!

IMAGE: GRAPES- TONGUE-FACE.

TITLE: ALMOST HEAVEN REFERS TO HEAVENLY FOODS.

BOOK JACKETS-DUST JACKET-CASE WRAP:

52.12.1.0. BOOK JACKETS:[FOR HARD BOUND BOOKS:]
NOTE: PRECISE ARTWORK AND COPY NEEDS DEFINED HEREIN. (THIS IS YOUR MARKETING TOOL).

52.12.2.0. BOOK JACKETS HAVE TWO INSIDE FLAPS:
FIRST FRONT FLAP: TELLS QUICK SYNOPSIS OF BOOK. A REASON TO BUY AND READ THIS BOOK

REAR FLAP: INCLUDES AUTHOR BIO, BOOK LIST, WEB SITE, AND PHOTO (EMBEDDED). [OR LAST PAGE ON SOFT COVER: PERFECT BINDING]

52.12.3.0. ARTWORK FOR JACKET/PAPERBACK:
JUDGE A BOOK BY ITS COVER? BUY A BOOK?

CHOOSE PROFESSIONAL ARTWORK, COPY PLACEMENT OF TITLE, AUTHOR NAME, AND SUB TITLE. (EXPLAINS TITLE A LITTLE FOR SOME READERS TO DEFINE WHAT KIND OF STORY IS THIS?).

(THIS IS LIKE CHOOSING A TITLE AND EXPLAINING SUBTITLE TO A STRANGER IN SIX OR TEN WORDS OR LESS).

52.12.4.0. RESOLUTION:
NOTE: THE ARTWORK FOR 6X9 COVER AT RESOLUTION OF LEAST 300DPI - 600. 300 DPI IS AVERAGE. SEE CHAPTER ON PRINTING.

52.12.5. 0. CROPPING:
LEAVE A LITTLE BLANK SPACE AROUND COVER AS SOME PRINTERS WILL " CROP IN" ON ARTWORK (PHOTO PLUS TITLES).

52.12.6. 0. MARKETING:
DOES YOUR COVER GIVE A CLEAR MESSAGE? DOES IT REACH THE READER? OR MASS AUDIENCE? SEE WHOLE CHAPTER ON MARKETING YOUR BOOK.

52.12.7.0. BOOK TITLES:
ARE NOT COPY RIGHTED, HOWEVER: THE TEXT WITHIN IS! CHOOSE A TITLE WHICH FALLS WITHIN THE THEME OF BOOK, A PHASE WITHIN OR CHAPTER TITLE. AGAIN, WHAT ARE YOU TELLING YOUR READER? WHAT DOES THE TITLE SAY ABOUT THE BOOK?

52.12.8.1. CHOICE OF TITLE IS VERY IMPORTANT!!!!!
I CAN'T EMPHASIS ENOUGH…THE SUCCESS OF YOUR BOOK MIGHT JUST REST WITH TITLE AND COVER ART!!!

52.13.0. 0. SPLINE:

THE SPLINE WIDTH IS MEASURED BY HOW MANY PAGES PLUS A WRAP TO HOLD THE NUMBER OF PAGES PER INCH. E.G. 6X9 BOOK WITH 480 PAGES IN PERFECT BINDING CREATES A SPLINE OF 1.08 " OR PIXEL WIDTH OF 324 X 2775, [1.08 X 9.25].

52.13.1. 0. REAR COVER PERFECT BINDING:

8.4.1. REQUIREMENTS: MAX WORD COUNT IS 2048,
AS EXAMPLE THIS ONE BOOK IS 1526 & NO PICTURE.
PIXELS: 1838 X 2775 AS JPEG.

52.13.2.0. MARKETING MESSAGE: & /OR

AUTHOR BIO MUST BE INSERTED ON INSIDE OF BOOK. MARKETING ON OUTSIDE!!!!

52.13.3.0. REAR COVER MARKETING:

USE REAR COVER FOR MARKETING YOUR BOOK, GIVE YOUR MESSAGE FOR THE READER TO BUY YOUR BOOK, TELL A REASON(S) TO WHY YOU WANT HIM TO READ THIS BOOK, AND WHY THIS BOOK IS DIFFERENT. SO: MY MARKETING MESSAGE: WHY READ AND BUY THIS BOOK---AIMED AT MY AUDIENCE THE READER/BUYER.

EXAMPLE : *THE BOOMERS: "HOLLYWOOD AND THE HISTORY BOOKS GOT IT ALL WRONG."*
WE WERE THE BOOMERS... SAVIORS OF THE WORLD, WHITE KNIGHTS AND PRINCES TO THE RESCUE. WE WERE INVINCIBLE, AS ONLY NINETEEN YEAR OLDS COULD THINK! WE WERE RAISED ON SUPERHEROES AND THE BREAKFAST OF CHAMPIONS." ™ THEY CALLED US THE BOOMERS FOR A REASON!

52.13.4. 0. INFORMATIONAL MESSAGE:

WHAT IS BOOK ABOUT—THE BROWSER, THE BUYER, THE LIBRARIAN, ETC.

(FROM THE BOOMERS: REAR COVER TEXT)

IMAGINE A MODERN DAY, ROMEO AND JULIET CAUGHT UP IN WAR AND PEACE! HIS DUTY, HONOR AND
VALOR CANNOT STOP THE TRIAL FOR TREASON, WAR AND PEACE ARE ALSO ON TRIAL AND STRIPPED TO THE
NAKED TRUTH!"

WHAT BULLETS COULDN'T KILL, WORDS DID! ....

WE EXPOSED: ....

WHAT LEGACY, INDEED!

52.13.5. 0. WHY IS IT DIFFERENT THAN OTHERS ON SAME SUBJECT?

BETTER? MORE CONCISE?
SUB HEADINGS: EXAMPLES:
THE TRUTH EVERY G.I. WANTS YOU TO KNOW

CREATIVE WRITING—THE KELLY MANUAL OF STYLE

A MESSAGE FROM THE LOST BOYS:

52.13.6. 0. INSERT BAR CODE & ISBN HERE [MUST BE HERE]

52.13.7.0. BOOKCOVER √ CHECK LIST BEFORE PRINTING:
1. DID YOU CHECK TITLE AGAINST THE WEB & BOOK SELLERS FOR DUPLICATES?
2. DOES TITLE MAKE SENSE AFTER BOOK IS FINISHED?
3. DOES COVER & TITLE BECOME AS ONE?
4. DOES TITLE GIVE FALSE MESSAGE AS TO WHAT STORY IS INSIDE?
5. CHECK SPELLING OF ALL THREE SIDES.
6. DOES SPLINE LOOK RIGHT FOR SIZE? TITLE LARGER THAN AUTHOR?
7. REAR COVER: IS MARKETING MESSAGE IN FIRST SENTENCE?
8. TELL THE "BUYER" WHY HE/SHE NEEDS (TO BUY) THIS BOOK.
9. MAKE MESSAGE CONTINUE AND END WITH SIMILAR BEGINNING.
10. PUT BOOK REVIEWS INSIDE BOOK.

SUMMARY: BOOK COVERS:
THE OLD ADAGE IS TRUE ABOUT A BOOK COVER IS CHOSEN FIRST ON VISUAL IMAGES THEN THE STORY WITHIN. WHEN YOUR BOOK IS ON DISPLAY AT A BOOK STORE THERE ARE APPROX 15 BOOKS SURROUNDING IT. [CHECK IT OUT. VISIT YOUR LOCAL BOOK STORES AND LOOK AT THE DISPLAYS. YOUR BUYING TREND IS TO BUY FROM A DISPLAY AND FEWER FROM THE STACKS].

WITHIN SECONDS, THE **VISUAL IMAGE** ATTRACTS YOUR EYE. THEN 15 SECONDS LATER YOU READ THE TITLES AND THEN LONGER, THE AUTHOR'S NAME ARE READ AND POSSIBLE RECOGNIZED. IN A VERY SHORT TIME, YOU SCANNED 15 BOOKS AND CHOSE 2 OR 3 TO LOOK AT. THEN, UNDER 5 MINUTES YOU CHOSE 1 OR 2 BOOKS TO READ AND BUY ONLY ONE AND A TOTAL OF TWO PER VISIT.

NOW YOU READ IT AND DECIDE WHETHER YOU LIKE IT OR NOT... YOU RECOMMEND IT, OR YOU SAY "GREAT STORY."
OR IT BROUGHT TEARS OF JOY OR SADNESS TO MY EYES.
EMOTIONS ARE PART OF THE READER'S CONNECTION WITH THE BOOK.

YOU THINK BUT DON'T SAY, "WELL, THAT WAS A WASTE OF MY TIME, OR I DIDN'T GET IT!" YOU CLOSED THE BOOK LONG BEFORE FINISHING IT. THE BOOK DOESN'T GO ON THE BOOKSHELF BUT TO A BOX IN THE GARAGE SALE.

CHAPTER 53
53.0.0.0. BOOK TITLES-THE FINAL SELECTION
CHAPTER TOPICS: *BOOK TITLE-CORRECT CHOICE-MARKETING- WHAT DOES IT SAY?-NOT COPYRIGHTED-*

53.14.1. 0. BOOK TITLE SELECTIONS:
BAD TITLE:
THE TITLE IS SUCH A SMALL THING THAT IT'S OFTEN NEGLECTED, YET THE PERFECT TITLE CAN REALLY AFFECT HOW A PIECE WORKS. A BAD TITLE CAN CONFUSE THE READER, RUIN THE SUSPENSE, OR JUST DISCOURAGE A READER FROM EVEN STARTING TO READ.

WHAT DOES THE TITLE SAY…WHAT **IMAGE**?
IS IT VAGUE? IF YOU LOOK BACK AT BOOK TITLES AND MOVIE TITLES WHAT DO YOU REMEMBER? THE ONE "**UNIQUE**" TITLE AND TITLES THAT BRING AN IMAGE TO MIND. TITLES THAT **"INTRIGUE"** OUR IMAGINATION. **TITLE WORD CHOICES**…SOME SHORT …SOME LONGER IN LENGTH.

DO A SEARCH ON THE NET OR LIBRARY CATALOG. SEARCH A SUBJECT OR THEME….WHAT DID YOU FIND? DO A SEARCH OF MOVIE TITLES ARE THEY ARE APROPOS AND UNIQUE. CHECK OUT <u>CH 41.</u>
WHAT UNIVERSAL COMMONALITY DID YOU FIND? WHAT APPEALS TO YOU? YOUR SENSES? YOUR EMOTIONS?

53.14.2.1. GREAT TITLE:
ON THE OTHER HAND, A GREAT TITLE CAN ADD DEPTH AND MEANING TO A WORK, HINT AT IMPORTANT THEMES, OR JUST SOUND SO INTRIGUING IT MAKES THE READER WANT TO START YOUR STORY RIGHT AWAY.

53.14.3.1. THE READER-THE BUYER:
THE TITLE IS THE FIRST THING A READER SEES, SO IT NEEDS TO MAKE THE RIGHT IMPRESSION. CONSIDER THOSE BOOK YOU ACTUALLY PURCHASE. DID THE TITLE GRAB YOU? **DOES YOUR BOOK TITLE GRAB THE READER?**

53.14.4.0. CHOSE A TITLE FROM YOUR "BOOK IDEAS LIST." (IF YOU FULLY DETAILED IT.) MEASURE IT UP WITH THE ABOVE
EXAMPLES OF IMAGE-UNIQUE-INTRIGUING. DON'T CHOOSE IT OVER EMOTIONS "I LIKE IT" ---OR IT'S A VERY LONG TITLE. KEEP IT SIMPLE. IF SOMEONE ASKS YOU WHAT YOUR ARE WRITING OR READING …WHAT COMES OUT, IS THE SIMPLE ANSWER.--- **THE TITLE!**
CHECK OUT CH 5.0.0.0-BOOK TITLES.

> **SOMETIMES THE FIRST TITLE CHOSEN WHEN WE BEGAN IT DOESN'T FIT AT THE FINISH. CHANGE IT!**

SEVERAL OF MY BOOK'S TITLES CHANGED EVEN AFTER I DID THE COVER ART. UNTIL YOU APPROVE THE MASTER DRAFT FOR THE PUBLISHER; IT IS CHANGEABLE. SOME I HAD LATER REGRETS. I LEARNED THE TITLE AND THE IMAGE **MUST GO TOGETHER.** [REFER TO CH 52.]

53.15.0.0. *OUR PROGRESS:*

1. WE LEARNED ABOUT HOW BOOK TITLES AFFECT THE SALES OF OUR BOOK.

2. WE LEARNED THAT BOOK IMAGES AND TITLES NEED COMPATIBILITY AND ARE OUR SUCCESS POINTS.

3. WE LEARNED ABOUT VISUAL IMAGES.

4. WE LEARNED ABOUT MARKETING ON OUR FRONT & REAR COVERS.

5. WE LEARNED BOOK TITLES NEED TO FIT OUR STORY AND BE SHORT.

CHAPTER 54
54.0.0.0. MARKETING YOUR BOOK:
CHAPTER TOPICS: CONTENT-DESIGN DECISIONS:-BUYING & SELLING.

54.0.0.0. MARKETING YOUR BOOKS:
CONSIDER THE FIRST LEVEL OF MARKETING: STORE FRONTS, EMAIL, PRESS RELEASES, BLOG SITES, AND WRITER'S SITES AND THE MAJORS: BOOKSELLERS, NEWSPAPER.

54.1.0.0. MARKETING CAMPAIGN:
PREPARE A CAMPAIGN TO INCLUDE ANY OUTLET TO FEATURE YOUR BOOK. USE ALWAYS THE SAME BOOK THEME MESSAGE. SO KNOW YOUR THEME, YOUR TARGET AUDIENCE AND YOUR MESSAGE TO THEM. GOOGLE THE WEB FOR "MARKETING CAMPAIGN" FOR MORE DETAILS.

54.0.2.0. STOREFRONTS:
WWW.LULU.COM & WWW.YAHOO.COM OFFER STOREFRONTS TO SELL YOUR BOOKS AND A WEB PLACE TO DISPLAY YOUR WRITINGS.

54.0.3.0. HYPERLINKS:
LET'S ASSUME YOU PROVIDED A **LINK TO GOOGLE** FOR YOUR SEARCH ENGINE TO FIND YOUR BOOK BY TITLE, AUTHOR OR GENRE. SOMETIMES THESE LINKS ARE PROVIDED BY POD PUBLISHERS, LIKE LULU. GO TO GOOGLE TO SET UP AN ACCOUNT. NEXT GO TO EACH **WRITER'S WEB SITES** AND GET AN ACCOUNT AND LIST YOUR BOOK WITHIN EACH SITE. JOIN "**READER'S WEB** SITES" AND GET ACCOUNT AND LIST YOUR BOOKS THERE TO. CONSIDER **ADDING THESE LINKS** TO YOUR PERSONAL WEB SITE WHERE YOU PROMOTE YOUR BOOK.

54.0.4.0. BUY A LINK:
SOME WEB SITES WILL ALLOW YOU TO BUY A LINKAGE TO YOUR HYPERLINK. COSTS WILL VARY SO CHECK IT OUT CAREFULLY. DO AN ADVANCED SEARCH ON 'SEARCH ENGINE OPTIMIZATION' OR USE ONLY A TRUSTED SITE WITH SAME MESSAGE AS YOUR BOOK. IF YOUR BOOK IS A CHILDREN'S BOOK, LINK TO A SITE FEATURING CHILDREN'S BOOKS, NOT A WAR/HISTORICAL SITE.

54.0.5.0. E MAIL MARKETING:
AS PART OF A MARKETING CAMPAIGN YOU SHOULD INCLUDE AN E-MAIL CAMPAIGN SPECIFICALLY TARGETING SIMILAR WEB SITES WITH SIMILAR THEMES.

ALSO, JOIN VARIOUS WRITER WEB SITES WHERE YOU ESTABLISH A WRITER'S PROFILE AND LISTING OF YOUR BOOKS.

ALONG WITH YOUR NORMAL E-MAILS INCLUDE A HYPER LINK (HTTP://-----) AT THE BOTTOM OF YOUR E-MAIL AND A LINK TO YOUR STOREFRONT.

54.0.6.0. BLOG SITES:
I USUALLY USE A WRITER'S BLOG SITE TO JOIN RATHER THAN A PERSONAL ONE TO CONVEY A SIMILAR REASON TO CORRESPOND. THE RECIPIENT ALSO FINDS A SIMILAR INTEREST.

54.0.6.0. PRESS RELEASE : FORMAT:

1. YOUR LOGO.(CENTERED)

2. FOR IMMEDIATE RELEASE

3. CONTACT NAME

4. COMPLETE CONTACT INFO: EMAIL, PHONE ADDRESS, HOURS, ETC

5. PRESS RELEASE HEADLINE(BOLD)

6. SUB-HEADLINE

7. CITY-STATE-DATE

8 BODY OF RELEASE-ANSWER WHO WHAT WHEN WHERE WHY& WOW

(ALSO HOW).

9 WRITE STANDARD PARAGRAPH WITH COMPANY INFORMATION,

CONTACT INFO AT END

      PHONE ###-EMAIL, ETC.

54.0.7.0. BOOK SELLERS SITES:
A SEARCH OF BOOK SELLER SITES BY DOING AN ADVANCED SEARCH ON YOUR TITLE OR SPECIFIC BOOK SELLERS. ALSO, FOLLOW THE LINKS FROM AMAZON.

INTERNATIONAL SEARCHES IN UNITED KINGDOM (U.K.) ENGLAND, IRELAND AND GERMANY USUALLY FOLLOWING THE USA RELEASES OF BOOKS. INDIA AND ASIA USUALLY FOLLOWS EUROPE.

54.0.8.0. NEWSPAPER SITES:
CHECK HOW TO SUBMIT THE STANDARD FORMAT TO A BOOK OR ARTS SECTION OF YOUR LOCAL PAPER.

54.1.0.0. OUR PROGRESS:
1. WE LEARNED WE NEED A MARKETING CHAMPAIGN TO LAUNCH OUR BOOK.

2. MARKETING INVOLVES MANY FACETS AND AVENUES TO BE USED.

CHAPTER 55
55.0.0.0. THE GREAT FINISH:
THE GREAT FINISH!
SOUNDS SO GOOD, RIGHT NOW AFTER SIX OR MORE MONTHS OF
INTENSE WORK AND WONDERING IF I GOT IT ALL AND WILL MY READER
ACTUALLY USE THIS BOOK?

TOGETHER, WE LEARNED A LOT ALONG THE JOURNEY FROM WRITER TO
AUTHOR TO THE MASTER WRITER LEVEL. WE LEARNED HOW TO DO
MANY THINGS… A BOOK PLAN, A CHARACTER LIST, A SYNOPSIS, AN IDEA
LIST AND ALL OF THE BASICS OF WRITING. WE LEARNED STRUCTURE,
BOOK DRAFTS, PUBLISHING AND MARKETING.

WE RECEIVED SOME SELF-ESTEEM AND MOTIVATION TO KEEP US ·
WRITING. WE LEARNED SO MANY , NEW WORDS, FIGURES OF SPEECH
AND ADVANCED DIALOG AND STYLE. WE LEARNED A NEW CREATIVE
STYLE A LONG THE WAY AND A NEW WAY OF DOING OUR WRITING.

CREATIVELY… WHAT AN UNDERSTATEMENT! OUR WRITING SPACE
AND UNIVERSE INCREASED TEN FOLD. WE LEARNED TO EXPAND OUR
THINKING AND NEW APPROACHES TO DIFFICULT WRITING AREAS.
WRITER'S DIFFICULTIES CAN BE OVERCOME. WE LEARNED OVER TIME
OUR CREATIVITY AND STYLE WILL PROVIDE A STRUCTURE FOR OUR
FUTURE WRITING. ANALYSIS OF THE GRAND MASTERS AND OF OUR OWN
WRITING IMPROVED TODAY'S WRITING IMMENSELY. WE GREW FROM
WRITER TO AUTHOR. WE PUBLISHED.

WE LEARNED SECRETS!
WE ARE READY TO WRITE ALL OF THOSE NEW BOOKS AND GENRE' WE
BEEN WANTING TO TRY. WE ARE READY TO TACKLE THE "GRAND
MASTERS'… WE KNOW THEIR SECRETS.
WE KNOW THE MANY MILESTONES AND REWARDS YET TO COME. BOOK
AWARDS AND MAYBE SOME RECOGNITION WILL SPUR US ALONG. WE
LEARNED SECRETS OF OUR OWN.**(THINK TWO WORDS?)**

I THINK BACK TO THE BEGINNING OF WHY WE WRITE AND WHAT
WRITING IS…?

ALL I WANTED TO DO WAS WRITE A BEST SELLER, SAVE THE WORLD AND
DIE A FAMOUS AUTHOR!

NOW, I'M A LITTLE WISER… I CAN WAIT! ESPECIALLY, THE LAST PART.
ABOUT DYING, VILLAINS DIE OFF RIGHT? BUT HEROES GO ON TO THE
NEXT BOOK!

I'VE GOT A LOT OF WRITING TO DO! AH! HA!

THOSE TWO WORDS?   AH! HA!

THIS IS NOT OUR FINAL PROGRESS REPORT?
WE HAVE JUST BEGUN AS AN AUTHOR! GOOD LUCK IRISHMAN, ER
WRITER!

CHAPTER 56
56.0.0.0. THE NEXT TIME REGRETS:
EACH TIME I WRITE A BOOK, I HAVE A FEW REGRETS:

1. NOT ENOUGH TIME TO <u>PERFECT IT.</u>

2. I FIND A FEW <u>TYPOS</u> AFTER THE FACT, NO MATTER HOW MANY TIME I CHECK AND SPELL CHECK..

3. THEN OF COURSE, THE PROVERBIAL <u>VERB TENSE</u>. I FIND I USED THE WRONG TENSE IN A MIXED TENSE PARAGRAPH.

4. NEW INFORMATION ALWAYS SEEMS TO FIND ME AFTER I GIVE THE FINAL MASTER DRAFT APPROVAL.

5. I FIND A HOLE IN MY DATA/WRITING.

6. I RESOLVE AGAIN TO IMPROVE MY CHECKLISTS.

7. I MAKE OF LIST OF REGRETS AND PASTE IT IN THE FINAL PROOF COPY & UPDATE MY COMPUTER'S MASTER DRAFT, EVEN IF IT DOES NOT GET RE-PRINTED.

8. I REGRET I'M HUMAN, AT TIMES DIVINELY INSPIRED; BUT OH SO HUMAN!

9. I REGRET I DIDN'T KNOW ALL OF THIS BEFORE BOOK ONE WAS WRITTEN. THIS IS BOOK 20.

10. I REGRET I WAS FIRST A READER, THEN WRITER , THEN STORYTELLER.

   I DID IT IN REVERSE ORDER!

CHAPTER 57
57.0.0.0. THE WOW FACTOR:

YOUR BOOK MUST DELIVER MORE THAN IT PROMISES: I CALL IT THE "WOW" FACTOR!

IS THERE VALUE FOR THE READER? HE ANSWERS THE QUESTION, WHY SHOULD I BUY THIS BOOK?

(I WILL LEARN SOMETHING NEW, THE STORY IS FRESH AND ABOUT A SUBJECT I FIND INTERESTING.OR I LIKE THE AUTHOR'S PREVIOUS BOOKS).

BEST SELLERS COME FROM WRITERS WHO KNOW WHAT THEY ARE TALKING ABOUT. THEY EXPERIENCED IT, RESEARCHED IT, TRAVELED IT OR CAN IMAGINE IT TO THE POINT OF REALISM.

BEST SELLERS COME FROM CONTAINING THESE SPECIAL ASPECTS: A UNIQUE TITLE AND COVER ART AND A MARKETING MESSAGE ON THE BACK COVER. FORGET THE REVIEWS...POST THOSE INSIDE. IS THE BOOK TITLE MEMORABLE? OR BETTER UNFORGETTABLE? DOES THE MARKETING COPY PROMOTE A LISTING ON SUCH AND SUCH LIST OR DIRECTLY TO THE READER: "BUY THIS BECAUSE..." THE WRITER SHOULD CHAMPION HIS CAUSE...HIS BOOK, HIS STORY, THE RELEVANCY, THE TIMELINESS AND THE ENJOYMENT THE READER WILL FEEL.

WHEN THE MONEY LEAVES THE WALLET, THE READER SHOULD THINK..."I CAN'T WAIT TO READ THIS."

THIS IS THE WOW FACTOR!

THE WRITING AND THE SELLING OF A BEST SELLER IS A MAGICAL EXPERIENCE! IT IS A RARE AND HEADY ACCOMPLISHMENT FOR THE AUTHOR.

IT IS RARE BECAUSE OUT OF HUNDREDS OF THOUSAND OF BOOKS, ONE OR SEVERAL ARE CHOSEN BY THE READER TO BUY IT. OF COURSE, THE WRITERS, AGENTS, EDITORS, BOOK MANAGERS AND PUBLISHERS ARE IN THIS MIX TO BRING IT FORWARD.

IS IT LUCK, FATE, TIMING OR MARKETING, STYLE OR SOME OTHER COSMIC FORCE? THE ANSWER IS SIMPLE ON THE SURFACE: **IT IS WELL WRITTEN!**

IF YOU MADE GOOD DECISIONS AS TO GENRE, THEME , SUBJECT, TITLE AND WROTE THEM IN A STYLE THAT IS APPEALING AND UNIQUE. YES, ALL OF THE SKILLS TAUGHT HERE AND THE CHARACTER DEVELOPMENT, THE PLOT AND DESCRIPTIVE PARAGRAPHS ARE JUST THE BEGINNING. THE DIALOGUE AND DRAMATIZATION BRING ALL OF THIS WRITING INTO FOCUS.

I WONDER IF IT ISN'T REALLY CHOSEN ON THE HEART METER. THE STORY MAKES US FEEL PART OF IT. WE RELATE, WE BECOME PART OF IT. WE WANT AND NEED THAT CONNECTION. THE STORY MUST BE GREAT, NOT JUST GOOD.
ULTIMATELY, THE FOCUS FOR OUR WRITING, THE PUBLISHING AND THE MARKETING …IS OUR **READER.**

IT SHOULD BE WRITTEN WELL AND READS WELL. (ALSO SOUNDS WELL)

THERE IS NO MAGIC FORMULA! NO ONE STYLE OF WRITING IS GOING TO ACCOMPLISH THIS HERCULEAN TASK. AUTHORING IS TOUGH WORK, GRUELING AT TIMES AND RARELY PAYS WELL.

57.0.1.0. THE AUTHOR IS ALSO UNIQUE. HE/SHE WADES THROUGH MOUNTAINS OF PAPER, RESEARCH AND SUBJECTS TO FIND THAT <u>ONE UNIQUE IDEA</u>, THAT IS THE KERNEL OF THE BOOK. THEN, DOGGEDLY WRITES, BRINGING THAT IMAGINATIVE CREATION INTO A DRAFT FORMAT, THEN BUILDING A STORY OFTEN TWO YEARS INTO A PROJECT. THE WRITER MUST DISCERN BETWEEN THE MOTIVATIONS OF WRITING…HIS PASSION, ADVANCE MONEY, A GOOD CAREER MOVE, OR REQUIRED BY PUBLISHER. THE READER CAN TELL THE DIFFERENCE IN HOW THE BOOK IS WRITTEN. THAT SINGLE IDEA AND THE "HOOK" KEEP OUR READER ON BOARD. AS WE FIND OUT, WRITING INVOLVES COMMITMENT, NOT JUST BEING INVOLVED IN THE PROCESS. I KNOW WRITERS POUR THEIR HEART AND SOUL INTO IT. IT IS NOT THE MONEY THE FAME OR POSSIBLE FORTUNE. IT IS "THE STORY" THAT EVERYONE DESERVES TO HEAR, SEE, SENSE AND ALMOST LIVE. THE WRITER GIVES THAT. THE READER TAKES IT ON FAITH AND WORDS. THEY EMBRACE LIKE SOUL MATES. ITS LIKES TWINS…THEY BECOME ONE AGAIN. LIFE BECOMES WHOLE AGAIN. TOGETHER AND COMPLETE!

THAT IS GREAT WRITING!

57.0.1.1. HEART METER: WE NEED LOTS OF THIS:
IF WE WERE TO **GRADE OUR OWN BOOK** 1 TO 5 SCALE ON EACH TOPIC AND FIGURE OF SPEECH, CONSTRUCTION AND WORD CHOICE….THE LIST IS LONG; WHERE WOULD OUR BOOK STACK UP? **WHERE IS IT ON THE HEART METER?**
CHARACTER OR EVENTS WHICH MAKE US CRY, LAUGH, OFFERS MOTIVATION, SYMPATHY, IDENTIFICATION. **INVOLVES READER'S EMOTIONS AND SENSES**

57.0.1.2. HEART STOP: READER IS INVOLVED:
LARGE TRAGEDY-SUICIDE-MURDER-HEART BREAK-LOST LOVES-EMOTIONS WITH IMPACT ON LIVES-RAPE-CHILDREN-EXECUTION-NO REMORSE-

57.0.2.0. CONSIDER THE WRITER'S STYLE: IS HE A GOOD STORYTELLER? A PERFECTIONIST? A MASTER AT PROSE? DOES HE WANT TO PUBLISH A LEADING BOOK IN A MARKET SEGMENT (GENRE') OR DOES HE WANT TO JUST PUBLISH A BOOK IN THAT SEGMENT?

57.0.3.0. DOES HIS STYLE FIT A "MASTER AUTHOR" VERSUS "AN AUTHOR?" IS HIS STYLE UNIQUE, HIS SUBJECT INTERESTING AND

CREATIVE WRITING—THE KELLY MANUAL OF STYLE

UNIQUE? THE RESULT IS THE THREE ROLES THE WRITER MUST PLAY: <u>THE WRITER, THE EDITOR AND THE READER.</u>

57.0.4.0. CONSIDER THE AUDIENCE: IS THE READER INVOLVED IN THE WRITING PROCESS? DOES HE RELATE OR UNDERSTAND WHERE THE NOVEL IS GOING. WE KNOW WE HAVE MULTIPLE PERSONALITIES, EDUCATION LEVELS, SEX AND READING DESIRES. DO WE FULFILL THOSE NEEDS WITH "NEW EDUCATION, NEW PLACES, EVENTS, TOPICS AND REALISTIC EVENTS?

CAN THE READER RELATE TO "COMMON EVENTS OF THE COMMON MAN AND YET ASPIRE TO HIGHER IDEAS AND INSPIRATIONS." DO OUR WRITINGS CONTAIN "BELIEVABILITY?"
WOULD OUR READER RECOMMEND OUR BOOK TO A FRIEND?

57.0.5.0. TO WRITE A BEST SELLER: YOU MUST BREAK NEW GROUND WITH SOMETHING NEW AND UNIQUE. HAVE YOU SEARCHED BOOK STORES AND LIBRARIES FOR A BOOK ON A TOPIC AND NOT FINDING MUCH THERE? PERHAPS…IT NEEDS WRITTEN TODAY AND UNIQUELY.

57.0.6.0. AH HA!
ONLY THEN, WE HAVE ACHIEVED THE "AH ! HA!" THE REASON WE WRITE IS ANSWERED. THE WRITER THEN CLIMBS FROM BEING AN AUTHOR TO WRITER TO "MASTER WRITER."

THIS MARRIAGE OF STORYTELLER, READER AND WRITER MAKES A BEST SELLER. NOTHING MORE…NOTHING LESS!

57.1.0.0. OUR PROGRESS:
1. WE LEARNED ABOUT THE HEART METER-THE HEART STOP AND THE AH HA!

2. WE LEARNED A NEW STYLE FITTING OF A GRAND MASTER WRITER.

3. WE WROTE A BEST SELLER IF WE INCLUDE ALL OF OUR TOOLS, CHECKLIST AND COMPARISONS TO THE GRAND MASTER WRITERS.

4. WE WROTE A BEST SELLER IF WE COMPLETED ALL THE STEPS WITH OUR MANUSCRIPT IN CH 10- CH 12-CH 16-CH 30.

CHAPTER 58
58.0.0.0. HOW TO SAVE THE WORLD:
HOW TO SAVE THE WORLD,
WRITE A BOOK AND DIE A FAMOUS AUTHOR!

58.0.1.0. SAVE THE WORLD?
WELL MAYBE A LITTLE PUN IS INTENDED! HOWEVER, CONSIDERING THE
POWER OF THE WORD AND BOOKS, IT IS POSSIBLE TO SAVE THE WORLD
THRU OUR HEROES OR OUR BOOK OUTLINING SOME MIRACLE DRUG OR
SAVING A NATION FROM GENOCIDE.

WORDS SOMETIMES DO ACCOMPLISH WHAT DEEDS ALONE CANNOT.

MAYBE OUR BOOK WILL INSPIRE THE NEXT LANDING BY MEN ON MARS,
OR MAYBE JUST PROGRAM THAT DVR FOR OUR TV. PERHAPS OUR BOOK
WILL TEACH MANY TO WRITE CREATIVELY AND THE NEXT PULITZER
WINNER OR NOBEL PRIZE WINNER WILL BE FOR A WORK THAT IS FAR
REACHING AND IMPACTING TO MANKIND. AH HA!

MAYBE IT WAS ALL ABOUT STRINGING TOGETHER AN IDEA WITH THE
RIGHT WORDS INTO A NOVEL OR SCIENTIFIC EXPOSE' WHICH CHANGED
MEN'S MINDS AND GAVE NEW THINKING TO OLD PROBLEMS. THE POWER
OF CREATIVITY AND INSPIRATION ROLLED INTO ONE.

AS A WRITER, MAYBE THE POWER OF ABSOLUTION, WILL COME FROM
THOSE BAD MANUSCRIPTS INTO ONE FINALLY TAKING OUR HEARTS AND
MINDS AND THOUGHTS INTO ONE POWERFUL STORY. A STORY WORTH
TELLING OUTLOUD. A STORY WE MIGHT CONSIDER OUR BEST…BUT NOT
YET!

**IT IS AS THOUGH WE SAVE OURSELVES AND SAVE THE WORLD AT THE
SAME TIME.**

SAVING OUR WORLD BEGINS WITH THE FIRST PAGE, THE JOURNEY IN-
BETWEEN IS OUR CONNECTION TO OUR READER. OUR STORY TELLING IS
MORE IMPORTANT AS IT LEADS US DOWN THE WRITING PATH.
A PATH ALONG THE WAY ON WHICH WE SAVE OURSELVES. OUR SOUL
AND INSPIRATION IS CHANGED. OUR WORDS REACH OUT TO READERS,
TO COUNTRIES AND ACROSS POLITICAL AND ETHNIC BARRIERS.

**FINALLY,
WORDS BECOME OUR SAVING GRACE! OUR SALVATION!**

CHAPTER 59
59.0.0.0. HOW TO DIE A FAMOUS AUTHOR:
TOPICS: AH! HA!-MY LOVE AFFAIR-FAME-THE READER BUYS

59.0.1.0. THE REAL BOOK OF AH! HA!
UNDER THE SURFACE ARE THE IMPORTANT PARTS OF OFFERING SOMETHING NEW AND UNIQUE, THE CHALLENGE OF PRESENTATION, QUALITY, AND THE ELUSIVE "AH! HA!" BEGINS.

THE "AH! HA!" HAPPENS WHEN MAGIC OCCURS: THE "SPARK," THE NEW–TWIST, OR "THE GREAT IDEA!" "AH! HA!" IS THE SIGNAL WHEN THE CONNECTION BETWEEN THE WRITER AND HIS AUDIENCE HAPPENS.

THE SIGN ON MY WALL COULD SAY: "WRITE WELL!" OR "COMMUNICATE WELL!"...IT DOESN'T!

59.1.0.0. MY LOVE AFFAIR!
I BECAME A LOVER OF PRINT. I READ IT, CARRIED IT WITH ME, TOUCHED IT, PERUSED IT, CRITICIZED IT, AND EVEN LOVED IT. MY LOVE AFFAIR BEGAN WITH A SEARCH FOR UNIQUENESS, A DIFFERENT SPIN AND A SEARCH FOR CLARITY. I WANTED MY READER TO RELATE PERSONALLY, TO UNDERSTAND, TO FEEL, AND ENJOY. IT WAS FOR HIM THAT I OBSERVED LIFE, REFLECTED UPON, WROTE AND EVEN LAUGHED AT MY MISTAKES. I GREW!

GROWING CAME WITH EACH NEW NOVEL, EACH SHORT STORY, EACH NEW WRITING ASSIGNMENT; THE CHALLENGE WAS ALWAYS THERE. THE CHALLENGE WAS TO FIND THAT 10% THAT "COMMUNICATES WELL!" I ALWAYS SAY, MY "NEXT" WILL BE BETTER THAN THE LAST! MY WORK AND PASSION MELDED. STRUCTURE AND SUBSTANCE BEGAN TO EVOLVE. I FINALLY UNDERSTOOD THE CONNECTION BETWEEN BEING A WRITER AND MY AUDIENCE.

MY AUDIENCE! THE "HOOK" WAS TO CONVINCE THEM TO READ ON, TO UNDERSTAND, AND TO ENJOY. YES, IT TOOK MORE THAN JUST WRITING SKILLS; IT TOOK EXPERIENCE, ATTITUDE, CREATIVITY AND FINALLY EDITING AND REJECTION TO IMPROVE IT; BUT MOSTLY TIME!

I BEGAN WRITING WITH THE REALIZATION, AFTER HAVING READ THOUSANDS OF BOOKS AND ARTICLES, THAT I COULD DO IT BETTER, BE CLEARER AND MORE DESCRIPTIVE.

THOUGHTS BECAME TOOLS OF MY TRADE NOT JUST WORDS. I MASTERED SEVERAL SKILLS: TO WRITE FOR THE READER'S UNDERSTANDING, TO READ OUT-LOUD FOR WORD FLOW AND LAST THAT "A GREAT EDITOR CREATES A GREAT WRITER!" BY PROOFREADING, EDITING AND LEARNING THE VARIOUS GENRE AND STYLES, MY WRITING BECAME MORE THAN JUST CREATIVITY AND COMMUNICATING IDEAS; IT WAS ATTITUDE! IT WAS WORK AND FUN AT THE SAME TIME!

P.S. THE SIGN READS: AH! HA!

59.2.0.0. FAME:
IF YOU LEARN AND EMPLOY ALL THE BASICS OF WRITING ALONG WITH ALL THE TECHNIQUES AND ADVANCED WRITING TOOLS, THEN PRACTICE THEM INTO YOUR STYLE; YOU WILL THEN SELL BOOKS, MAKE A LITTLE MONEY AND BEGIN THE MARKETING ROAD TO SUCCESS.

YOU WILL PROGRESS FROM WRITER TO AUTHOR TO GRAND MASTER. YOUR SATISFACTION LEVEL WILL INCREASE AND THE REWARDS OF HAVING YOUR WORK IN A PROFESSIONAL FORMAT ON THE LIBRARY SHELF AND HOPEFULLY SELLING AT THE BOOKSELLERS AND ON THE INTERNET.

HOWEVER, EVERY WRITER, AUTHOR OR GRAND MASTER MUST RE-INVENT AND LEARN NEW TECHNIQUES. IT ONLY COMES FROM HARD WORK, PERSEVERANCE AND KNOWING:

I CREATED SOMETHING FROM PILES OF LITTLE SOMETHINGS.

FINALLY, I MADE THAT CONNECTION WITH THE READER…HE LIKED MY STORY!

HE LIKED IT ENOUGH TO BUY IT.

AH! HA!

CHAPTER 60
60.0.0.0. HOW TO MAKE MONEY WRITING:
CHAPTER TOPICS: FREELANCE ADS-SOFTWARE-WEB SOURCES—VARIOUS FEE TYPES- ROYALTY CHECKS-LABOR COSTS-
SERVICE PACKAGE COSTS-OFFICE SUPPLIES-ARTWORK FEES-LABOR COSTS-MANUFACTURING COSTS-ISBN AND COPYRIGHT FEES.

60.0.1.0. PROMISES! PROMISES!
YOU HAVE SEEN THE ADS PROMOTING FREELANCING, OR WRITING MAGAZINE ARTICLES FROM HOME. USE COMMON SENSE AND CAUTION. DO NO COMMISSION WORK, WHICH IS PAYABLE, ONLY IF IT IS SOLD OR ACCEPTED.

THE ONLY PROMISES YOU CAN BELIEVE ARE YOUR OWN!

SUBMITTING QUERY LETTERS AND STORY SYNOPSIS TO MAGAZINES IS A GOOD BET IF YOUR CRAFT IS PERFECTED.
AS YOU CAN SEE FROM OTHER WRITERS WHO HAVE GONE BEFORE YOU...
DON'T QUIT YOUR DAY JOB UNTIL THE CHECK IS IN HAND.

60.0.2.0. SOFTWARE SELECTION (FOOTNOTE #1)
HERE IS SOME SOFTWARE WHICH HELPS WITH **FORMATTING YOUR NOVEL**. AGAIN, NOT A RECOMMENDATION (FN #1); JUST CHECK THEM OUT FIRST.

1. WORD (MSOFT). (USUALLY STANDARD ON PC'S-LAPTOPS).
2. WORD PERFECT.
3. POWER WRITE (APPROX. $100.)
4. DRAMATICA PRO (APPROX $270.)

60.0.3.0. WEB SOURCES:
USE REPUTABLE WEB SOURCES FOR SOLICITING WORK:
DO YOUR HOMEWORK AND VISIT THE BLOG SITES FOR HELP. HERE IS A FEW FOR REFERENCE ONLY. SEE INDICES AND BELOW:
WORDPRENEUR.COM
PROSAVVY.COM
SOLOGIG.COM
GO FREELANCE.COM
GURU.COM

#1: THE INTERNET SPEEDS UP NEW ARRIVALS AND OTHERS WANE, SO CHOOSE CAREFULLY. LEGALLY, I CANNOT RECOMMEND ONE PARTICULAR SITE OVER ANOTHER.

60.4.0.0. MONEY SENSE:
CONSIDER THE TYPES OF PAYMENT AND PROCESSES OUT THERE. SOME ARE MISLEADING--- SOME ARE VERY ACCURATE!

60.4.1.0. COMMISSION: NOT RECOMMENDED FOR ANY KIND OF WORK. THERE ARE NO GOLD MINES AND PROMISES ARE USUALLY EMPTY.

60.4.2.0. PAY PER WORD:
USUALLY A MAGAZINE DEAL OR SOME 'WORK FROM HOME' OPPORTUNITIES: READ THE FINE PRINT, CHECK OUT THE BLOGS FOR CURRENT INFORMATION; THINGS AND CONDITIONS DO CHANGE. RATES ALSO VARY BY MAGAZINE AND QUALITY OF WORK EXPECTED.

60.4.3.0 . PAY PER ARTICLE:
I USUALLY PREFER THIS AS I CAN USUALLY ESTIMATE MY TIME ACCURATELY. IF I GO OVER, IT IS MY LOSS. RATES VARY FOR LENGTH AND EDITING. EXPECT SOME EDITING BY THE EDITOR; THUS, SHORTENING YOUR WORK. THE BETTER CRAFT YOU PRESENT THE BETTER THE FINISHED PRODUCT.

60.4.4.0. NOVELS- PRINT ON DEMAND PUBLISHERS:
ROYALTY CHECKS ARE USUALLY SMALL UNLESS YOU GET A CASH ADVANCE & A CONTRACT TO WRITE A NOVEL. WE SEE THE AUTHOR'S ROYALTY FEE RANGES FROM $2 TO $5 PER BOOK SOLD, MINUS ANY EXPENSES/ DELAYS/PRINTING FEES OCCURRED BY THE PUBLISHER. (LULU PROVIDES A ROYALTY FEE BREAKOUT ON THE PROJECT PAGE. AND THE NUMBER OF BOOKS PURCHASED, BY AUTHOR AND DATES).

1. **HIDDEN FEES FOR OFFICE SUPPLIES:**
   CONSIDER PAPER, INK CARTRIDGES AND SOME WRITE-
   OFF FOR THAT COMPUTER & PRINTER AND SOFTWARE
   PROGRAMS AND A PORTION OF YOUR INTERNET FEES.
   (I USUALLY CALCULATE ONE CASE OF PAPER AND TWO LARGE
   BLACK INK CARTRIDGES WITH EACH BOOK.)

2. **PURCHASED ARTWORK OR COVER ART IS EXTRA.**
   ARTWORK PURCHASED FOR YOUR COVERS OR ILLUSTRATIONS
   CAN BE LARGE DOLLARS.

3. **PURCHASING PRINT COPIES** (AT SOME POD PUBLISHERS).
   I HAVE SEEN SERVICE PACKAGES FROM SOME PUBLISHERS
   INVOLVING RANGES FROM $600 TO $2,000. SOME GIVE 10 FREE
   COPIES. I USE LULU WITH NO UP FRONT FEES, EXCEPT 1 OR 2
   PROOF COPIES TO APPROVE THE PRINTING AND I CAN
   ORDER 1 TO 100 BOOKS IF I WANT. BOTH BOOKS AND E-BOOKS
   (PDF UPLOADS) ARE PROVIDED.

4. **MARKETING PACKAGES:**
   PACKAGES ARE AVAILABLE IF YOU WANT THEM. THESE
   INVOLVE MULTI- LEVEL STEPS OF SERVICES YOU REQUIRE
   AND CAN PAY FOR UPFRONT. SECURE PAYMENT IS PROVIDED
   WITH ELECTRONIC CHECK OR CREDIT CARD.

5. **PURCHASED MARKETING SERVICES PACKAGES:**
   IF YOU DESIRE TO PAY FOR PRESS RELEASES, EMAIL
   PACKAGES, MARKETING LETTERS AND WEB SITE UPGRADES;
   THESE ARE AVAILABLE VIA SERVICE PACKAGES.

60.4.4. 6. WRITING LABOR: ESTIMATED:
LET'S SAY YOU WROTE A BOOK IN TWO YEARS, PART-TIME AND ESTIMATED THE TOTAL HOURS AT 480 HOURS AT $20.00 PH; THUS **$9,600.00. (12 WEEKS AT 40 HOURS). (THREE MONTHS OF CONCENTRATED WRITING). IF YOUR WRITING TAKES 6 MONTHS: (960 HOURS) DOUBLE THESE FIGURES. ($19.200.00).**

60.4.4.7. ROYALTY RATES: THE BOOK:
YOUR ROYALTY AT DIFFERENT RATES YIELDS A DIFFERENT RETURN.

1. **AT $2.00 PER BOOK**, YOUR AUTHOR'S ROYALTY, THUS SELLING **4800 BOOKS** GETS YOU EVEN WITH YOUR 'GUESSITIMATED' LABOR EXPENSES.

2. **AT $3.00 PER BOOK**, SELLING **3200 BOOKS** GET YOU EVEN, WITH YOUR 'GUESSITIMATED' LABOR EXPENSES.

3. **AT $4.00 PER BOOK, SELLING 2,400 BOOKS** EQUALS YOUR 'GUESSITIMATED' LABOR EXPENSES.

60.4.4.8. MY LULU EXPERIENCE:
LULU PROVIDES A BREAKOUT OF FEES FOR EACH BOOK AS YOU SELECT PRINTING OPTIONS. EBOOKS ARE ALSO OFFERED IN UPLOADED PDF FORMAT . THESE ARE AVAILABLE TO THE CUSTOMER WHERE THE AUTHOR GETS ALMOST ALL THE ROYALTIES. NO PUBLISHER SHARE. I HAVE SEEN $2.95 TO $59.95 BEING OFFERED. IT DEPENDS ON YOUR MARKETING STRATEGY FOR THIS VEHICLE. BE SURE TO CHANGE YOUR STORE FRONT AND SELLING WEB SITE TO SHOW THIS OPTION.

(LULU PROVIDES THIS ON YOUR STOREFRONT).
60.4.4.9. MANUFACTURING FEES:
A. MANUFACTURING COSTS
AND ROYALTY FEES ARE SPELLED OUT UNDER EACH PUBLISHERS WEB PAGE OR WITHIN THE CONTRACT TERMS. IN ADDITION THE PUBLISHER'S FEES ARE STATED PER BOOK.

B. PAPER COST:
60# BLACK AND WHITE 6X9 SIZES IN CREAM INTERIOR PAGE SQUARES OF 4 (TOTAL PAGES DIVIDED BY 4), GENERALLY RUN TWO CENTS PER PAGE PLUS A SET UP FEE. COLOR COVERS (BY LULU) ARE INCLUDED. I PROVIDE THE ARTWORK
C. MY TOTAL MANUFACTURING COST: W/O EXTRA SERVICES:
ESTIMATED 160 PAGES = $ 7.75. (40 SQUARES)
228 PAGES= $12.80. (57 SQUARES)
332 PAGES= $13.90. (83 SQUARES)
484 PAGES= $13.75 (121 SQUARES)+

SQUARES ARE PAGES DIVIDED BY 4. MUST COME OUT EVEN FOR PUBLISHER WITH ONE BLANK PAGE AT END OF BOOK. WORD SOFTWARE GIVES YOU A PAGE COUNT AT BOTTOM LEFT OF SCREEN. DIVIDE THIS BY

CREATIVE WRITING—THE KELLY MANUAL OF STYLE

4. THE PUBLISHER USES A PAPER SIZE WHERE 4 BOOK PAGES ARE PRINTED AT ONE TIME.

+ SLIGHTER DIFFERENT COST DUE TO ARTWORK. YOUR COST MAY VARY BASED ON YOUR PREFERENCES AND PACKAGES SELECTED. THESE ARE ESTIMATED FOR ILLUSTRATIVE PURPOSES ONLY.

60.4.4.10. RETAIL COSTS:
RETAIL PRICES ARE GENERALLY 100% OF MANUFACTURED COST. THUS, A MANUFACTURED COST, INCLUDING ROYALTIES, PUBLISHER FEES, AND PRINTING COSTS=$ 10.97 X 2 (100%) EQUALS $21.94, ROUNDED TO $21.95 RETAIL PRICE. RETAIL IS WHAT THE BOOK SELLER CHARGES. NOTE: ACTUAL RETAIL MAY VARY BY PUBLISHER, CHECK OUT THEIR TERMS.

60.4.4.11. ISBN NUMBER:
ISBN NUMBERS ARE AVAILABLE FROM YOUR PUBLISHER OR ON-LINE. THIS NUMBER IDENTIFIES THE PUBLISHER AND YOUR BOOK IDENTIFIER #. (LULU FEES AVERAGED $99.00 OR ZERO COST IF A PROMOTION PLUS SOME OTHER SERVICES BESIDES REGISTRATION.) (LULU ALSO AUTOMATICALLY APPLIES THE BARCODE AND ISBN TO THE REAR COVER. YOU MUST ADD IT TO THE COPYRIGHT PAGE (ALWAYS PAGE 2) AFTER PROOFING THE PROOF COPY. IT MUST ALSO BE SHOWN ON THE REAR COVER AGAIN. [REFER TO INDEX 2].

REGISTERING WITH **BOWKER** (THE ISBN # PROVIDER TO PUBLISHERS) SHOULD BE DONE BY THE PUBLISHER WITH THE ISBN PACKAGE. YOU MAY CHOOSE OTHER OPTIONS.

60.4.4.12. COPYRIGHT:
PERFORM THE COPYRIGHT PROCESS AFTER THE FINAL PROOF BOOK IS PRINTED, AND APPROVED BY YOU. ORDER TWO COPIES AND SEND THEM TO THE COPYRIGHT OFFICE ALONG WITH YOUR COPYRIGHT APPLICATION AND FEES. [REFER TO CH 45].

60.5.0.0. OUR PROGRESS:
1. WE LEARNED IT TAKES A LOT OF HOURS TO PRODUCE A BOOK.

2. WE INVEST MANY HOURS WHICH MAY NOT GET PAID FOR. 6 MONTHS OF WORK COST US $20 K IN LABOR ALONE.

3. WE LEARN TO TRY OTHER SOURCES OF INCOME TO SUPPORT OUR WRITING. BUT THERE ARE PITFALLS TOO!

4. WE LEARN OUR ROYALTY RATE PER BOOK IS LOW.

5. WE LEARN THE RETAILER SETS THE RETAIL PRICE SOMETIMES PRICING OUR BOOK HIGHER.

6. WE INCREASE WITH MULTIPLE BOOK SUBMISSIONS TO HELP OUR EXPOSURE.

7. WE LEARN PAPER COSTS, SQUARES AND ISBN NUMBERS.

8. WE CONTINUE TO WRITE, DESPITE THE CONDITIONS.

CHAPTER 61
61.0.0.0. THE WRITER'S CLUB:

THE WRITER'S CLUB SOUNDS A BIT PRETENTIOUS! BUT NOT REALLY... NO GREEN FEES, NO ANNUAL DUES, NO GREEN OR YELLOW JACKETS LIKE GOLF. THE CLUB TO WHICH WE ASPIRE YIELDS NO PROMOTIONS, NO RAISES AND A LONG SHOT AT A FUTURE PAYOFF.

MEMBERSHIP COMES WITH <u>PAID DUES</u>. DUES PAID WITH LONG HOURS, SOLITARY CONFINEMENT, LOST FRIENDS AND MISSED OPPORTUNITIES. **WRITING IS A DEMANDING MISTRESS.**

THE FIRST LEVEL IS ACTUALLY THE PRINTING OF YOUR FINAL BOOK COPY OFF WITH YOUR NAME ON IT. WITH SUCH, WE JOIN THE **AUTHOR'S CLUB**. NO LONGER ARE WE THE 'HACK WRITER.' JUST A LITTLE POORER, AS WE SPEND MORE MONEY TO BUY THOSE PROOF COPIES AND ACTUALLY GIVE SOME TO FRIENDS. THEN, WE LEARN THE PUBLISHING BUSINESS. STEP ONE BEGETS STEP TWO. WE WRITE SOME MORE BOOKS.

SIX MONTHS LATER, WE SEE THE INTERNET TAKING A SMALL INTEREST IN OUR BOOK. MAYBE NOW THE HOMETOWN LIBRARY WILL NOW STOCK ONE COPY? WE CONTINUE WRITING AND YEP! LEARNED A NEW TRADE IN THE PROCESS...WEB MARKETING.

AUUG! HOW AM I GOING TO FIND THE TIME?
I'M SPENDING HALF OF MY TIME MARKETING AND NOT WRITING! MMM! LET'S SEE I SPENT $500 BUCK ON SUPPLIES AND PROOF COPIES, NOT COUNTING THE 6 MONTHS IT TOOK TO WRITE (THAT'S $10,000)... **NOW I FEEL LIKE CHEAP LABOR!**

THE RETAIL MARKUP HAS ME IN A BIND, I MAKE TWO BUCKS WHEN IT SELLS AND THE RETAIL WANTS A HIGHER PRICE THAN I THINK IT WILL SELL FOR ...WHAT TO DO? STEP THREE...I WRITE SOME MORE...IT'S BECOME A REAL DEMANDING MISTRESS. SOMETHING IS BURNING INSIDE...MY GUT PROBABLY OR ACID REFLUX! NAW! JUST THAT BURNING DESIRE TO WRITE.

LET'S SEE THIS ONE HAS TO BE A MONEY MAKER... A HOW TO, OR COOK BOOK OR NEW AGE... GREAT! A "HOW TO BOOK" FITS THE BILL! "HOW TO WRITE CREATIVELY." BINGO! A WINNER!

NOW, WE DREAM...ONE OF OUR BOOKS WILL GET SOLD FOR A MOVIE, I CAN MOVE TO FLORIDA....ETC. **OOPS! REALITY CHECK**: I REALLY WANT TO WRITE LIKE THE GRAND MASTERS DID. I GUESS I GOT MORE DUES TO PAY!

"GRAND MASTER WRITER" NOW THAT'S A TITLE I WOULD LOVE TO HAVE!

THAT AND A ROYALTY CHECK, WOULD BE NICE!

AND YOU THOUGHT I DID ALL OF THIS FOR FAME AND FORTUNE? HA!

<u>CHAPTER 62</u>
62.0.0.0. THE ENDING-AT LAST!:
FINIS-THE END-FINITO-BLING-BLING-BANG-BOOM!

62.1.0.0. THE WRITER'S LIFE:
MAYBE HE IS JUST A WRITER. SHE THE HEROINE. MAYBE FATE NOR
DESTINY COME TOGETHER…MAYBE NO HAPPY ENDING HAPPENS!
DOES THE HERO GET THE GIRL?

62.2.0.0. ALL HE HAS IS WORDS:

HE SAYS: WORDS ARE ALL I HAVE. I HAVE NOTHING TO OFFER YOU.
NOTHING TO WIN YOUR HEART.

SHE SAYS: BUT YOU HAVE HEART AND SOUL! HER WORDS TRAIL OFF ,
SHE IS LOST IN THOUGHT…

HE THINKS: *I HAVE HEART?   … WORDS NEVER ESCAPED HIM
BEFORE…WHY?*

MAYBE SHE IS HIS INSPIRATION AND MORE?

HE REALIZED SOMETIMES THE HEART TRIUMPHS, WHAT WORDS CANNOT
EXPRESS…**THE HEART TELLS THE STORY! THE REAL STORY**!

DO: CONTINUE STORYTELLING!

I HOPE YOUR HEART & BOOK ENDS ON A HAPPY NOTE!

SECTION V

MASTER INDEX LISTINGS

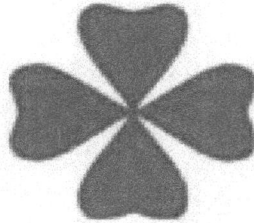

MASTER INDEX LISTINGS:
(PLURAL:= INDICES)

INDEX-1. BOOK AWARDS & NOBEL LAUREATES:

BOOKER AWARD:
THE MAN BOOKER PRIZE IS AWARDED TO THE BEST NOVEL OF THE YEAR WRITTEN BY A CITIZEN OF THE BRITISH COMMONWEALTH OR THE REPUBLIC OF IRELAND.

EPPIE AWARDS: EBOOKS:
THERE ARE TWO YEARLY AWARDS FOR EXCELLENCE IN E-BOOKS. THE LONGEST-STANDING AND MOST INCLUSIVE OF THESE IS THE **EPPIE AWARD**, GIVEN BY EPIC SINCE 2000. THE OTHER IS THE DREAM REALM AWARD, FIRST AWARDED TO <u>SPECULATIVE FICTION</u> E-BOOKS IN 2002.

GILLER PRIZE WINNERS:
THE GILLER PRIZE AWARDS $25,000 ANNUALLY TO THE AUTHOR OF THE BEST CANADIAN NOVEL OR SHORT STORY COLLECTION PUBLISHED IN ENGLISH.

NATIONAL BOOK AWARD:
THE NATIONAL BOOK AWARDS ARE GIVEN TO RECOGNIZE ACHIEVEMENT IN FOUR GENRES: FICTION, NONFICTION, POETRY, AND YOUNG PEOPLE'S LITERATURE.

PEN/FAULKNER AWARD WINNERS:
NAMED FOR WILLIAM FAULKNER, WHO USED HIS NOBEL PRIZE FUNDS TO CREATE AN AWARD FOR YOUNG WRITERS, AND AFFILIATED WITH PEN (POETS, PLAYWRIGHTS, EDITORS, ESSAYISTS AND NOVELISTS), THE INTERNATIONAL WRITERS' ORGANIZATION, THE PEN/FAULKNER AWARD WAS FOUNDED BY WRITERS IN 1980 TO HONOR THEIR PEERS.

NOBEL LAUREATES IN LITERATURE:
(Source: by Mark Flanagan, **About. Com**)
THE NOBEL PRIZE FOR LITERATURE IS GRANTED NOT FOR A SINGLE BOOK, BUT FOR AN AUTHOR'S ENTIRE BODY OF WORK, AND HENCE USUALLY GOES TO A WELL-ESTABLISHED WRITER. **WEB SEARCH THESE AUTHORS TO FIND MORE DETAILS.**

1. 2008 - JEAN-MARIE GUSTAVE LE CLÉZIO
FRENCH WRITER, "AUTHOR OF NEW DEPARTURES, POETIC ADVENTURE AND SENSUAL ECSTASY, EXPLORER OF A HUMANITY BEYOND AND BELOW THE REIGNING CIVILIZATION

2. 2007 - DORIS LESSING
ENGLISH WRITER, "THAT EPICIST OF THE FEMALE EXPERIENCE, WHO WITH SKEPTICISM, FIRE AND VISIONARY POWER HAS SUBJECTED A DIVIDED CIVILIZATION TO SCRUTINY."

3. 2006 - ORHAN PAMUK
TURKISH NOVELIST "WHO IN THE QUEST FOR THE MELANCHOLIC SOUL OF HIS NATIVE CITY HAS DISCOVERED NEW SYMBOLS FOR THE CLASH AND INTERLACING OF CULTURES."

4. 2005 - HAROLD PINTER
BRITISH PLAYWRIGHT "WHO IN HIS PLAYS UNCOVERS THE PRECIPICE
UNDER EVERYDAY PRATTLE AND FORCES ENTRY INTO OPPRESSION'S
CLOSED ROOMS."

5. 2004 - ELFRIEDE JELINEK
AUSTRIAN NOVELIST AND PLAYWRIGHT. AWARDED THE NOBEL PRIZE IN
LITERATURE "FOR HER MUSICAL FLOW OF VOICES AND COUNTER-
VOICES IN NOVELS AND PLAYS THAT WITH EXTRAORDINARY LINGUISTIC
ZEAL REVEAL THE ABSURDITY OF SOCIETY'S CLICHÉS AND THEIR
SUBJUGATING POWER."

6. 2003 - JOHN MAXWELL COETZEE
SOUTH-AFRICAN NOVELIST. AWARDED NOBEL PRIZE IN LITERATURE FOR
BEING ONE "WHO IN INNUMERABLE GUISES PORTRAYS THE SURPRISING
INVOLVEMENT OF THE OUTSIDER."

7. 2002 - IMRE KERTÉSZ
HUNGARIAN NOVELIST AND ESSAYIST. AWARDED NOBEL PRIZE IN
LITERATURE "FOR WRITING THAT UPHOLDS THE FRAGILE EXPERIENCE
OF THE INDIVIDUAL AGAINST THE BARBARIC ARBITRARINESS OF
HISTORY."

8. 2001 - V. S. NAIPAUL
TRINIDADIAN NOVELIST. AWARDED NOBEL PRIZE IN LITERATURE "FOR
HAVING UNITED PERCEPTIVE NARRATIVE AND INCORRUPTIBLE
SCRUTINY IN WORKS THAT COMPEL US TO SEE THE PRESENCE OF
SUPPRESSED HISTORIES."

9. 2000 - GAO XINGJIAN
FRENCH WRITER. AWARDED NOBEL PRIZE IN LITERATURE "FOR AN
OEUVRE OF UNIVERSAL VALIDITY, BITTER INSIGHTS AND LINGUISTIC
INGENUITY, WHICH HAS OPENED NEW PATHS FOR THE CHINESE NOVEL
AND DRAMA."

10. 1999 - GUNTER GRASS
GERMAN POET, NOVELIST, AND PLAYWRIGHT "WHOSE FROLICSOME
BLACK FABLES PORTRAY THE FORGOTTEN FACE OF HISTORY."

11. 1998 - JOSE SARAMAGO
PORTUGUESE WRITER "WHO WITH PARABLES SUSTAINED BY
IMAGINATION, COMPASSION AND IRONY CONTINUALLY ENABLES US
ONCE AGAIN TO APPREHEND AN ELUSORY REALITY."

12. 1997 - DARIO FO
ITALIAN PLAYWRIGHT "WHO EMULATES THE JESTERS OF THE MIDDLE
AGES IN SCOURGING AUTHORITY AND UPHOLDING THE DIGNITY OF THE
DOWNTRODDEN

13.1982- GABRIEL GARCIA MARQUEZ:
COLUMBIAN.ONE HUNDRED YEARS OF SOLITUDE (1967)-LEAF STORM-NO
ONE WRITES TO THE COLONEL-IN EVIL HOUR-THE AUTUMN OF THE
PATRIACH-INNOCENT ERENDIRA-CHRONICLE OF A DEATH FORETOLD-
LOVE IN THE TIME OF CHOLERA-THE GENERAL IN HIS LABYRINTH-
STANGE PILGRIMS-LOVE AND OTHER DEMONS- MEMORIES OF MY
MELANCHOLY WHORES- LIVING TO TELL THE TALE.

315

INDEX-2:- SPECIAL NOTES ON PUBLISHING:

ISBN (INTERNATIONAL STANDARD BOOK NUMBER)

UNIQUE NUMBER PROVIDED BY R.R. BOWKER/REED REFERENCE PUBLISHING AND ASSIGNED BY THE PUBLISHER THAT IDENTIFIES THE BINDING, EDITION, AND PUBLISHER OF A BOOK.

.JPG OR .JPEG (JOINT PHOTOGRAPHIC EXPERTS GROUP)

FOLLOW SEVERAL STEPS TO SAVE YOURSELF TIME AND HEADACHES:

1. SELECT ART WORK IN EITHER PNG OR JPEG, NOTE DIFFERENCES BELOW.
2. DO SAVE THE ORIGINAL WORK (TAGGED ORIGINAL) FIRST AND WORK WITH A COPY.(VERSIONS 1 TO 4).
3. DO SET UP FOLDERS FOR EACH TYPE: ARCHIVES- FRT COVER- REAR COVER –SPLINE- PUBLISHER:
4. BEFORE YOU ARE DONE EACH OF THESE FOLDERS WILL CONTAIN AT LEAST TWO COPIES: ONE IN PNG AND ONE IN JPEG FORMAT. ONLY THE FINISHED FINAL VERSION WILL BE PLACED IN YOUR "PUBLISHER NAME FOLDER.

IMAGE FORMATS NOTES:PNG—JPEG:

A COMPUTER FORMAT FOR DIGITAL IMAGES WITH LOTS OF COLORS, SUCH AS PHOTOGRAPHS. (USE OF MS IMAGE PROGRAM ALLOWS PNG AND JPEG TO BE SAVED. PNG ALLOWS CHANGES TO TEXT OR PICTURE BEFORE FINAL. JPEG IS A CLOSED (ONCE THE 'SAVED AS' FUNCTION IS USED) FILE AND WILL NOT ALLOW ANY CHANGES IN PIXELS, SIZE AND DPI.

IMAGE PIXEL COUNT: = SIZE OF IMAGE. CHART SAYS FOR 6X9 BOOK

USE 1838X2775 PIXEL COUNT AND 300 DPI, SETTING AND SAVING (SAVE AS VERSION) THIS SETS IMAGE AND CANVAS TO MATCH.
THE SPLINE SIZE IS DETERMINED BY HOW THICK THE BOOK IS (NUMBER OF PAGES AND BY 6X9 SIZE. IF YOU USE A DIFFERENT BOOK SIZE, ADJUST TO HAND CHART. DO NOT DEVIATE OR YOUR BOOK WILL HAVE PRINTING PROBLEMS. MY BOOK HAS 480 PAGES SO ITS SPLINE IS :1.08" OR SPLINE SIZE OF 324 X 2775 (= TO 9"…SAME AS IMAGE LENGTH). THE WIDTH IS THE PIXEL SIZE FOR 1.08" X 9.25 .

WHEN SIZING TRY TO SET PIXEL COUNT, TURN OFF "KEEP RATIO," THEN PICTURE WILL SIZE ACCORDING TO CANVAS, BASED ON PIXELS SELECTED, (BACKGROUND…THINK BOOK PAGE SIZE). NOTE SELECT ARTWORK THAT IS PORTRAIT OR LANDSCAPE AT BEGINNING OF THIS PROCESS. IT IS HARD TO MAKE A LANDSCAPE PICTURE MATCH A PORTRAIT BOOK COVER/PAGE. IT DISTORTS UNLESS YOU WANT A BAND OF PICTURE ACROSS THE COVER WITH WHITE SPACE ABOVE AND/OR BELOW IT.

NOTE: PICTURE SIZING AND CANVAS SIZING: CANVAS IS YOUR WHITE

PAGE SIZED TO BOOK PAGE SIZE: FOR EXAMPLE FOR 6X9 BOOK, YOU USE 6.25 X 9.25 PAGE SIZE. USE THIS AS YOUR CANVAS SIZE. THE DIFFERENCE BETWEEN 6" AND 6.25" IS THE BLEED SIZE. (SEE BLEED TERM).REMEMBER PAGE SIZING: YOU USED THIS TO SET UP BOOK PAGE SIZE, WITH MARGINS, GUTTERS, MIRROR IMAGES AND HEADERS AND FOOTERS. IF

CREATIVE WRITING—THE KELLY MANUAL OF STYLE

THIS WAS DONE CORRECTLY, YOU SELECTED THE PROPER PAGE SIZE.
IMAGE AND CANVAS ARE DIFFERENT FROM PAGE SIZE.
E.G. PAGE SIZE IS 6X9 (WRITING AREA) ON PAGE SETUP IN WORD. SIZE OF
PDF, PNG, & JPEG ARE 6.25 X 9.25, MATCH TO PIXEL COUNT.

NOTE : CHANGING ANY OF THESE ITEMS WILL REQUIRE YOU TO REVIEW
THE ENTIRE WORD DOCUMENT(YES WORD NOT THE PDF FORMAT) SO
THAT WORDS AND TITLES APPEAR AS YOU NEED THEM TO. IF A WORD OR
TWO OR MORE SENTENCE HANGS OVER (ORPHAN) ON A BLANK PAGE
CONSIDER EDITING TO SAVE COST OF A PAGE.

.PDF (PORTABLE DOCUMENT FORMAT)
A MS WORD DOC. CONVERTED TO **PDF** FORMAT BUT CHANGEABLE
BEFORE CONVERTION TO JPG FILE. JPG NOT CHANGEABLE. PDF ALLOWS
A LOCKDOWN ON PLACEMENT ON PAGE. LOCKS AN IMAGE OR A SECTION
COPY & PASTED AREA, SO IT DOSEN'T MOVE. A NOVEL IS WRITTEN IN
WORD THEN IS CONVERTED TO PDF FORMAT TO LOCK DOWN PAGES AS
TYPED. PDF IS PUBLISHING FORMAT.

PDF: A COMPUTER FORMAT DEVELOPED BY ADOBE THAT ALLOWS THE
DISTRIBUTION AND VIEWING OF DIGITAL FILES AS ORIGINALLY
DESIGNED AND FORMATTED BY THE AUTHOR WITHOUT THE 'VIEWING
COMPUTER' HAVING THE SAME SOFTWARE APPLICATION OR FONTS. USE
CUTE SOFTWARE OR IN **MS WORD: DO: 'SAVE AS'** TO CONVERT WORD
TO PDF FORMAT. **ADOBE** IS THE READER TO OPEN THE FILE WITH.

PERFECT-BOUND
A METHOD OF BINDING IN WHICH SIGNATURES OF FOUR ARE FOLDED
AND COLLATED ON TOP OF ONE ANOTHER AND HELD TOGETHER BY
ADHESIVE. *EXAMPLE:* THIS SOFT COVER BOOK IS PERFECT BOUND.

PIXEL: PICTURE ELEMENT. THE SMALLEST UNIT OF A BITMAPPED IMAGE
AS DISPLAYED ON A COMPUTER MONITOR. PIXEL SIZING ADJUSTS THE
CANVAS (=BACKGROUND) AND IMAGE SIZE IN MS DIGIT IMAGE
PROGRAM. SETTING THE PIXELS TO 1835X 2775 GIVES A 6.25 X 9.25 IMAGE
SIZE. **PIXILATED:** AN IMAGE IS SAID TO BE PIXILATED WHEN THE EDGES
ARE JAGGED WHEN SHOULD BE SMOOTH. THIS HAPPENS WHEN THE
IMAGE RESOLUTION (SEE DPI) IS TOO LOW. **300 DPI** IS RECOMMENDED.

.PNG (PORTABLE NETWORK GRAPHIC) :
A'ROUND' IMAGE FILE FORMAT. PNG IN MOST PHOTO AND IMAGE
HANDLING SOFTWARE, MS DIGITAL IMAGE ALLOWS YOU TO EDIT IN PNG
AND SAVE AS WORK IN PROGRESS, AND FINALIZE OR DO FINAL 'SAVE
AS' IN JPEG FORMAT. JPEG BECOMES A FLAT FILE AND ALLOWS NO
EDITING.

POD (PRINT ON DEMAND):
PRINTING, USUALLY FROM A DIGITAL FILE TO A DIGITAL PRINTER, ONLY
WHEN THE OBJECT IS NEEDED AND IN THE QUANTITY REQUIRED.
ALSO PRINT ON DEMAND PUBLISHERS WHO PRINT ONE OR A 100 BOOKS,
AS NEEDED. *EXAMPLE: LULU PRESS.COM.*

TRIM SIZE: NOVEL-PERFECT BINDING:
THE SIZE OF A PAGE AFTER IT HAS BEEN TRIMMED. THUS, 6.25 X 9.25
TRIMS DOWN TO 6X9, THUS CUTTING OFF THE BLEED AREA AND
ALLOWING THE COVER TO FLOW PROPERLY OVER TO THE EDGE.

INDEX 3- WEB SITES- RESOURCES:

NOTE: *WEB SITES ARE ACTUAL, UNDERSCORE REMOVED FOR PUBLISHING. LINKS INTERFERE WITH PUBLISHING FORMATTING.*

BOOK COVER DESIGN:
SEARCH: *PRINT ON DEMAND BOOK COVER DESIGN.*

BOOK REVIEWS-HOW TO WRITE:
WWW.QUESTIA.COM/LITERARY CRITICISM

DEFINITIONS-DICTIONARY:
WWW.DICTIONARY.COM/TOOLBAR
WWW.BARTLEBY.COM (ON LINE DICTIONARY)

EDUCATION:
www.uclaextension.org
www.edu-central.com (free)
search: creative writing
search: bachelor or master of fine arts

GRANTS:
www.grant-sources.com
www.atozgrantwriting.com
www.usagrantmoney.com
www.selinger.com (advertisement)
www.betterbusinessreviews.org/grant

JOBS-FREELANCE WRITING JOBS:
www.sologig.com
www.guru.com
www.workathometop10jobs.com
www.freelancehomewriters.com
www.prosavvy.com

SYNDICATION OF ARTICLES:
www.houseofarticles.com

WRITING OPPORTUNITIES:
www.freelanceworkexchange.com
www.studiob.com
www.sparkcomm.com
www.silberware.com
www.bloggingnetwork.com/
www.freelanceworkexchange.com
www.radicalwriting.com/
www.freelancehomewriters.com

JOURNALISM: SOCIETY OF BUSINESS JOURN. WRITERS:
www.vocus.com   or www.sabew.org

GRAMMAR:
http://grammar.about.com/od/blogsandlinks/tp/refworks.html
THE AMERICAN HERITAGE DICTIONARY OF THE ENGLISH LANGUAGE.

CREATIVE WRITING—THE KELLY MANUAL OF STYLE

IMAGES-PHOTOS:
Google Images or Yahoo images
Flickr.Com Or Pdphoto.Com
Photos.Com Or Photobucket.Com

MAKING MONEY FREELANCING:
www.wordpreneur.com
www.prosavvy.com
www. sologig.com
www. gofreelance.com
www. guru.com
www. helium.com

MOVIES:
www.tcm.com. review catalog for titles-idea groups.
http://www.nytimes.com/ref/movies/1000best.html

OUT-SOURCING WRITING-THEY WRITE:
www.studiob.com

PRINT ON DEMAND PUBLISHERS:
www.lulu.com
www.iuniverse.com
www.publishamerica.com
www.bestselfpublished.com

REFERENCE BOOKS:
Dictionary: The American Heritage Dictionary Of English Language.
Usage: Garner's Modern American Usage.
The Chicago Manual Of Style: U of Chicago Press
AP Style Book : Journalism-News

SCREENPLAYS:
www.inktip.com---www.slamdance.com
BOOKS: THE HOLLYWOOD STANDARD—THE SCREENWRITER'S BIBLE.

SOFTWARE:
www.newnovelist.com
www.cutepdf.com

TEEN WRITING:
www.teenwriting.about/com/library

WORKSHOPS:
www.clarityworksonline.com
www.writersonlineworkshops.com

WRITER'S CLUBS-BLOGS:
www.absolutewriter.com
www.heliumwriters.com
www.writersintouch.com
www.writers.net
www.writers weekly.com
www. writing.com
blog: grumpy old bookman or the literary saloon
blog: the millions or the reading experience.

INDEX 4. CRIME DEFINITIONS:

MYSTERY AND CRIME WRITERS:

MUST BE <u>ACCURATE</u> IN DESCRIBING THE VARIOUS CRIMES AND LAWS THAT PERTAIN TO THEIR STORIES. THE DIFFERENCES BETWEEN TWO SIMILAR CRIMES MAY LEND SOME CREATIVITY, UNIQUENESS AND BELIEVABLITY TO YOUR STORY.

IT'S IMPORTANT THAT WE UNDERSTAND <u>THE NUANCES AND DIFFERENCES</u> BETWEEN SIMILAR CRIMES. IF WE WRITE ANY KIND OF LEGAL PROCEEDING.

CONSIDER THAT <u>NUANCED CRIMES</u> PROVIDE POSSIBILITIES FOR YOUR CREATIVITY. IF YOUR STORY REVOLVES AROUND AN EMPLOYEE MURDERING HIS BOSS, WHAT KIND OF MURDER WAS IT? PREMEDITATED? RELATED TO THE COMMISSION OF ANOTHER FELONY? AN ACCIDENT?

NOW, <u>IMAGINE</u> HOW MUCH MORE COMPLEX AND INTRIGUING THE STORY BECOMES IF IT WASN'T MURDER AT ALL, BUT VOLUNTARY MANSLAUGHTER WHERE THE EMPLOYEE WAS PROVOKED INTO COMMITTING THE MURDER OF WHICH HE'S NOW ACCUSED!

1. BLACKMAIL VS. EXTORTION:
BOTH CRIMES INVOLVE AN ATTEMPT TO PRESSURE SOMEONE INTO GIVING YOU SOMETHING.

EXTORTION: IS SPECIFICALLY RELATED TO THE THREAT OF FORCE TO COMPEL SOMEONE.
e.g. A BOOKIE THREATENING TO BREAK YOUR LEGS IF YOU DON'T PAY IS EXTORTING YOU.

BLACKMAIL: IS THE TERM USED WHEN THE THREAT IS NOT RELATED TO FORCE; BUT RATHER EMBARRASSMENT, DISGRACE, HUMILIATION, ETC. *e.g. BLACKMAIL IS SOMEONE THREATENING TO RELEASE AN INCRIMINATING PHOTO, IF YOU DON'T PAY.*

2. EXTORTION VS. ROBBERY:
EXTORTION AND ROBBERY BOTH HAVE THE SAME TWO BASIC CRITERIA: A <u>THREAT OF PHYSICAL HARM</u>, AND <u>A DEMAND</u> FOR SOMETHING. THE DIFFERENCE IS THE <u>IMMEDIACY</u> OF THE DEMAND.

EXTORTION: *INVOLVES DELIVERY AT SOME FUTURE TIME. e.g. A THIEF DEMANDING THAT YOU BRING A MILLION DOLLARS TO HIM NEXT FRIDAY IS EXTORTING YOU.*

ROBBERY: REQUIRES THE <u>IMMEDIATE DEMAND</u> FOR SOMETHING. *e.g. A THIEF DEMANDING THAT YOU GIVE HIM YOUR WALLET WHILE HOLDING A GUN ON YOU IN A BACK ALLEY IS ROBBING YOU.*

3. GRAND THEFT VS. PETTY THEFT:
THIS ONE'S PRETTY STRAIGHTFORWARD... IF IT'S OVER $950, IT'S GRAND THEFT. IF IT'S UNDER $950, IT'S PETTY THEFT. CARS ARE ALWAYS CONSIDERED GRAND THEFT, REGARDLESS OF THE VALUE OF THE CAR.

4. LARCENY VS. BURGLARY:

CREATIVE WRITING—THE KELLY MANUAL OF STYLE

BOTH LARCENY AND BURGLARY INVOLVE UNLAWFULLY
TAKING PROPERTY FROM SOMEONE OR SOMEPLACE.

BURGLARY: INVOLVES GAINING UNLAWFUL ACCESS TO THE PLACE
WHERE THE ITEM IS STOLEN.
*e.g. IF I BROKE INTO A CONVENIENCE STORE WHEN IT WAS CLOSED AND
STOLE A CANDY BAR, THAT'S BURGLARY.*

LARCENY=SHOPLIFTING:
IF IT WAS UNDER (ENTRY NOT OPPOSED) AND STOLE A CANDY BAR, THAT'S
SHOPLIFTING (AND LARCENY).

5. ASSAULT VS. BATTERY:
ASSAULT: *IS THE TERM USED FOR THE THREAT OF VIOLENCE (I.E. CAUSING
SOMEONE TO FEAR VIOLENCE) .*

BATTERY: *IS THE ACTUAL ACT OF TOUCHING/PHYSICALLY HARMING
SOMEONE. THUS, IF I WERE TO GET UP IN YOUR FACE AND TALK ABOUT
HOW BADLY I'M GOING TO BEAT YOU UP, THAT'S ASSAULT. BEATING YOU UP
BADLY BY ITSELF IS BATTERY.*

ASSAULT & BATTERY: *FIRST I THREATEN YOU AND TALKING ABOUT HOW
BADLY I'M GOING TO BEAT YOU UP AND THEN ACTUALLY BEATING YOU UP.*

6. MURDER VS. MANSLAUGHTER:
MURDER REFERS TO THE VIOLENT TAKING OF ANOTHER LIFE.

FIRST-DEGREE MURDER (PREMEDITATED):
*IF A WIFE WAITED FOR HER CHEATING HUSBAND TO COME HOME, THEN
STABBED HIM WITH A KITCHEN KNIFE; THAT'S FIRST-DEGREE MURDER. e.g. A
SERIAL KILLER.*

SECOND-DEGREE MURDER (HOMICIDE DURING THE COMMISSION OF
ANOTHER FELONY).
*e.g. A BANK ROBBER SHOOTS A HOSTAGE DURING A ROBBERY, THAT'S
SECOND-DEGREE MURDER. e.g. A SERIAL KILLER WHO KIDNAPS AND KILLS.*

THIRD-DEGREE MURDER (DEATH RESULTING WHEN ONLY HARM WAS
INTENDED):
*e.g. IF SOMEONE MUGGED AND PISTOL-WHIPPED A PEDESTRIAN, WHO
SUBSEQUENTLY DIES FROM THE HEAD TRAUMA, THAT'S THIRD-DEGREE
MURDER.*

7. MANSLAUGHTER:
MANSLAUGHTER REFERS TO THE TAKING OF ANOTHER LIFE WITHOUT
MALICE.

VOLUNTARY MANSLAUGHTER: *USUALLY WHEN SOMEONE WASN'T IN
CONTROL OF THEIR ACTIONS, OR PROVOKED TO COMMIT THE CRIME.*

INVOLUNTARY MANSLAUGHTER: *ACCIDENTALLY KILLING SOMEONE
WHILE COMMITTING A MISDEMEANOR, WITH NO INTENT TO HARM ANYONE).
e.g. HITTING AND KILLING SOMEONE WITH YOUR CAR WHILE DRIVING
DRUNK.*

8. KIDNAPPING VS. ABDUCTION:
BOTH INVOLVE THE CARRYING OFF OR TAKING OF SOMEONE AGAINST THEIR WILL.

KIDNAPPING: *IS GENERALLY THE TAKING OF SOMEONE WITH THE INTENT OF SOME OTHER END RESULT (e.g. RANSOM, COERCION, ETC.). e.g. SOMEONE LOOKING TO STEAL A CHILD IN ORDER TO EXTRACT RANSOM MONEY OR COOPERATION FROM THE PARENT WOULD BE KIDNAPPING THAT CHILD.*

ABDUCTION: *THE TAKING OF THE PERSON IS USUALLY THE END RESULT. e.g. SOMEONE LOOKING TO STEAL A CHILD FOR THEIR OWN WOULD BE ABDUCTING THAT CHILD.*

9. LIBEL VS. SLANDER:
BOTH LIBEL AND SLANDER ARE RELATED TO THE WRONGFUL DAMAGING OF SOMEONE OR SOME ENTITY'S REPUTATION.

LIBEL: *IS WHAT'S WRITTEN OR PUBLISHED INCLUDING PUBLISHED PHOTOGRAPHS.*

SLANDER: *IS WHAT'S SPOKEN AND CAN ALSO INCLUDE BODILY GESTURES*

INDEX 5- MY SOURCE LISTS;
CHAPTERS 1 TO 62 CLAIMED AS AUTHOR'S WORK WITH THESE
EXCEPTIONS LISTED BELOW:

1. GLOSSARIES:
COMPILED BY AUTHOR FROM MANY INTERNET SOURCES, AND AUTHOR'S
OWN LISTS OVER THE YEARS AND BOTH UPDATED TO INCLUDE MISSING
AND NEW TERMS. DEFINITIONS UPDATED BY AUTHOR. INTERNET FREE
USE IS CLAIMED. **NO COPYRIGHT CLAIMED BY AUTHOR.**

2. CHAPTER 5. IDEA GROUP:
USE OF "ELVIS FACT GROUPING," MODIFIED AND REVISED BY AUTHOR,
SOME OF LIST IS FROM SOURCE "ABOUT.COM." INTERNET FREE USE
CLAIMED AS MATERIAL IS REQUIRED BY READER.
NO COPY RIGHT CLAIMED BY AUTHOR.

3. CHAPTER 12. GRAND MASTERS:
OF WRITING, USED SOME EXAMPLES FROM INTERNET. AUTHOR REVISED
AND DID OWN ANALYSIS AND CONCLUSIONS. INTERNET FREE USE IS
CLAIMED AS MATERIAL IS REQUIRED BY READER.
NO COPYRIGHT CLAIMED BY AUTHOR.

4. CHAPTER 18. RHETORIC QUIZ:
PROVIDED BY INTERNET AND REVISED BY AUTHOR. SOURCES INCLUDE
"ABOUT.COM AND WIKIPEDIA." INTERNET FREE USE IS CLAIMED AS
MATERIAL IS REQUIRED BY READER.
NO COPYRIGHT CLAIMED BY AUTHOR.

4. INDEX 7-LITERARY THEORIES:
AUTHOR USED SOME EXAMPLES FROM INTERNET. AUTHOR REVISED,
DELETED AND UPDATED LANGUAGE AND ADDED OWN THEORIES.
PARAPHRASED DEFINITIONS AND INTERNET FREE USE CLAIMED ON
NAMES AND TITLES. BALANCE OF INDEXES WRITTEN BY AUTHOR.
NO COPYRIGHT CLAIMED BY AUTHOR.

5. LITERARY READINGS:
AUTHOR PROVIDED MAJORITY FROM OWN COPYRIGHTED BOOKS.
OTHERS WERE PARAPHRASED OR QUOTED AS NOTED. INTERNET FREE
USE CLAIMED AS MATERIAL IS REQUIRED BY READER.
NO COPYRIGHT CLAIMED BY AUTHOR.

6. **CH 40- SCREEN WRITING.** PARAPHRASED, CONSOLIDATED. INTERNET
FREE USE CLAIMED AS MATERIAL IS REQUIRED BY READER. SOURCE
CREDIT GIVEN. NO COPYRIGHT CLAIMED BY AUTHOR.
SOURCE: WWW.FILMSCRIPTWRITING.COM

INDEX-6-AUTHOR - HIS BOOKS-DEDICATION

THE AUTHOR: KELLY CHANCE BECKMAN

MY WEBSITES:
EMAIL: HTTP://WWW.KELLYCHANCE7@YAHOO.COM
HTTP://WWW.WRITING.COM/AUTHORS/KELLYCHANCE7
HTTP://WWW.LULU.COM/SPOTLIGHT/KELLY775

WHY DO WE WRITE THE WAY WE DO?
WE LIVE IN A MULTI-DIMENSIONAL WORLD OF COLOR, SOUND AND ALL
OF THE SENSES; SO WHY DO WE WRITE IN ONE DIMENSION?
I FIRMLY BELIEVE WE CAN WRITE WITH MORE IMAGINATION AND
CREATIVITY. THIS BOOK IS A TESTAMENT TO THAT BELIEF. I ALSO
BELIEVE : **The pen is mightier than the sword; but the "word" is greater still!**

KELLY CHANCE SERIES OF BOOKS:
BOOK 1: RED HEART! RED EARTH!- 1999 – 327 PAGES
TOMAHAWKS-TREATIES-TREASURE AND MURDER
ISBN: 978-0-557-02579-4

BOOK 2: AFFAIRS OF THE HEART: 2011-184 PAGES
ISBN: 987-1-257-75712-1
KELLY'S BOOK OF POEMS AND LOVE LETTERS

BOOK 3: BLONDES AND OTHER DANGEROUS WOMEN:2011
ISBN 978-0-557-02577-0 COMBINED INTO BOOK 9.-2010-160 PAGES
PRIVATE INVESTIGATOR: KELLY CHANCE.

BOOK 4: REDHEADS! ... THE BAD & BEAUTIFUL!-2011
 THE MOST DANGEROUS OF ALL! SEE BOOK 9.-2010-160 PAGES
ISBN# 978-0-557-02577-0

BOOK 5: SPIES, THIEVES AND OTHER FRIENDS!-2003-232 PAGES
ISBN 978-1-4357-1782-4
UNDERCOVER AGENT: KELLY CHANCE.-232 PAGES

BOOK 6: A NOBLE & SAVAGE HEART!-2005-348 PAGES
ISBN 978-1-4357-2036-7
GOVERNMENT AGENT: KELLY CHANCE

BOOK 7: THE BOOMERS!-484 PAGES-2007
ISBN 978-1-4357-1661-2
SERGEANT KELLY GOES TO WAR!

BOOK7A: RIGHT BETWEEN THE EYES!-572 PAGES-2011
1SBN: 978-1-257-89685-1
HEROES, PRISONERS AND CASUALTIES OF WAR

BOOK 8: SOLDIER BOY!-2014
ISBN: PENDING 2014
KELLY GOES TO WAR IN AFGHANISTAN.
BOOK 9-BLONDES BONUS BOOK-160 PAGES=2010

BOOK 11: CREATIVE WRITING-KELLY MANUAL OF STYLE
ISBN: 978-0-557-05437-4: CREATIVE WRITING- 2014.-342 PAGES.
REVISED 2009-2011-2014

BOOK 12: BULLETS, BUGLES & CANNONFIRE- 2011-260 PAGES.
ISBN: 978-1-257-75763-3

BOOK 13: AUGGIE AND BANGER-2011-168 PAGES
ISBN :978-1-105-18657-8

BOOK 14: SPIRITUAL PATHWAY-436 PAGES-2011
ISBN: 978-1-257-94931-1

BOOK 15: MEDITATION-512 PAGES-2011
ISBN:978-1-257-94956-4

BOOK 16: HAPPINESS-520 PAGES-2011
ISBN: 978-1-257-95372-1

BOOK 17: SOLDIER BOY
18: SCREENPLAY:THE BOOMERS-2014.
19: SCREENPLAY: AUGGIE AND BANGER-2014

BOOK 20: TIDEWATER TANGO-2014
ISBN PENDING

BOOK 21:CREATIVE WRITING-2014-HARDCOVER

DEDICATIONS:
BOOKS---THANK AN AUTHOR, THANK A TEACHER,
AND MOSTLY, THANK A READER!
TO MY WIFE, LINDA: *WORDS ARE NEVER ENOUGH!*

INDEX 7- CAPITAL LETTERS & CAPITAL IDEAS:
is font size the real problem?

SOME PEOPLE DON'T LIKE "CAPS." **THEY LIKE THE TRADITIONAL LOOK, small font with capitals AND 5 SPACE INDENTS FOR PARAGRAPHS. I LIKE ALL CAPS; IT IS EASIER TO READ, AND LINE SPACES BETWEEN PARAGRAPHS RATHER THAN INDENTS. YES, A MORE FEW MORE PAGES BUT EASIER ON READER's eyes and mind.** the paragraph just doesn't become a blur of words, let alone thoughts.

after all, we read for enjoyment and for new ideas and new experiences. all the writer's effort at story organization and story telling experience is wrapped into those words. his story line, his point of view, his structure must capture the reader's attention.

no, I don't think you are sheep to follow the traditional method; it's your choice. nor do I like it when someone says capitals "shout"...bull hockey!

the test: are you reading more but enjoying it less? have you tried to tell a friend about what you READ ONLY to fail to give the plot or adventure? it is probably the structure and the retention of key information.

I THINK THE "TRADITIONAL STRUCTURE" METHOD "CRAMS" PARAGRAPHS TOGETHER (JUST AN INDENT) AND THE WHOLE PURPOSE OF SENTENCE AND PARAGRAPH STRUCTURE (FINAL WRAP UP THOUGHT OF LAST SENTENCE IS LOST) IT PUSHES THE READER TO ADD THE LAST PARAGRAPH'S THOUGHT WITH THE NEXT PARAGRAPH'S NEW IDEA THAT IS INTRODUCED.

I ALSO THINK THE BLANK LINE, no indent; thus it ALLOWS THE READER'S EYE TO REST AND allows the brain to FINISH ABSORBING THE LAST THOUGHT...IF ONLY A "SECOND IN Time" FOR COMPREHENSION.

another thought is publisher's have an interest in blank spaces in their books; less blank space, less cost.

Point: have you read a book but only remember 5 or 6 key thoughts of a whole book?(BOLD FONT 8)

The whole purpose of a book is the "organization of information" and "a transfer of ideas."
There are probably 5 or 6 thoughts per chapter, not the total book;

I, the writer, wish to convey to you. Have you begun to read a book only to lose interest? Consider the paragraphs and ideas being conveyed. Did they entertain? Did they inform? Did they transition from one to the next paragraph easily? Read a children's book---IT HAS larger type and spacing and of course illustrations. Read a law book---we skip from case law titles to the next, barely skimming the content. Now, select a textbook---we see organization, paragraph headings, subject headings and a few illustrations. A Cook book has its own format, usually one ingredient per line and color photos.

Now, let's look at fiction:
Traditional method of Printing and Writing.

Review of the Table of contents, chapter titles and Paragraphs one after another and it is only indented. Compare: What is the key words and thoughts the author is telling us? How much do we remember? If you use a color highlighter marker and mark up the chapter after you read it...how much did you miss? college Students learned this key METHOD IN school with books they bought. THEY SCAN OVER THESE HIGHLIGHTS FOR TESTS.

Did you know older books used to show key words –events and the 5 W's at top of each chapter? **AND IN ALL CAPS.(FONT 11)**

The reason was simple: <u>help the reader comprehend the chapter. (FONT 9)</u>

<u>Now, use the "caps" method:</u> read it and afterwards highlight the key thoughts and key words, one or more per paragraph. How much more was understood or retained? Did you have a better understanding of the event? Or the 5 W's---who, what, when, where, and Why. Were you able to read more pages? Did your eyes get less fatigued?

PAGE COSTS: (FONT 9)

Consider the publisher uses less pages with smaller type and Traditional method of printing; the result is his cost is less. The same book printed is about 16 pages different. If a larger font like 12 is used instead of 10 point, the pages grow to 40, approx. It cost about 2 cents per page to print; but their large number of BOOKS PRINTED @ 16, adds up to 32 cents per book. So it is to their advantage to cut costs. It is not you your advantage to "peruse" a book versus "experience" a book. FONT SHOULD BE SIZE 9.

Consider also an electronic book, which would you rather read on your laptop? A 8 POINT (small), 10 point font (medium),

or **12 point font**?(**LARGE**).

Last, consider why we read and why some do not:

Entertainment, enjoyment, to learn, to go where imagination takes us, to learn new ideas, to experience other's travels and travails, AND TO ESCAPE OUR WORLD FOR A WHILE.(FONT 8)

Some do not read: **they lose interest, it's fatiguing, it's boring, it's just words....etc, etc.**
Some do not read well. **Some prefer the visual approach...graphics or video methods.**

As an adult, we chose what we like and the method we like. It's about the choice of subject, author and EVEN FORMAT...a book...a video...an electronic replication (e-book) or even TV.
IT'S ABOUT CHOICE!

<u>ABOVE:</u> **DID YOU NOTICE THE LARGE TYPE VERSUS, small AND BOLD**

VERSUS <u>UNDERLINE</u>.   ---DID IT HELP YOU UNDERSTAND?

INDEX 8- MASTER SUBJECT INDEX:

CREATIVE WRITING—THE KELLY MANUAL OF STYLE

CREATIVE WRITING—THE KELLY MANUAL OF STYLE

CREATIVE WRITING—THE KELLY MANUAL OF STYLE

CREATIVE WRITING—THE KELLY MANUAL OF STYLE

CREATIVE WRITING—THE KELLY MANUAL OF STYLE

www.ingramcontent.com/pod-product-compliance
Lightning Source LLC
Chambersburg PA
CBHW051724260326
41914CB00031B/1731/J